PARALLEL DEVELOPMENTS

A Comparative History of Ideas

PARALLEL DEVELOPMENTS

A Comparative History of Ideas

HAJIME NAKAMURA

Edited by Ronald Burr

With a Preface by Charles Morris

KODANSHA LTD.

TOKYO NEW YORK

Distributed in U.S.A. by Kodansha International U.S.A., Ltd.
through Harper & Row Publishers, Inc.

Published 1975 by Kodansha Ltd., Japan

Printed in Japan by General Printing Co., Ltd., Yokohama
LCC 75-24947
ISBN 0-87011-272-4
3010-256711-2253 (0) (術B)

First edition 1975

PREFACE

Parallel Developments—A Comparative History of Ideas is a remarkable book by a remarkable man, Hajime Nakamura. It is the most interesting and most worthwhile book I have read in many years. It indeed sets a new standard for dealing with the history of thought across many cultures, especially India, China, Japan, and the European West.

These cultures are not treated separately, one after another, as is usually done in histories of thought. Rather the emphasis is upon such problems as the concept of God, the question of immortality, the controversy over universals, the nature of orthodoxy and heterodoxy, the problem of moral values, and many others. The thought of the various cultures is then collected around such problems.

The discussions are carried on with amazing erudition. There are thousands of quotations and references. And yet the work is not ponderous or directed solely to the specialist. The style is simple and lucid, and the tone is never dogmatic. The result is a book that anyone interested in world-wide thought will treasure and find rewarding.

Professor Nakamura believes that all the intellectual problems which a given culture faces are problems found in all great cultures, and that the order they are dealt with is about the same in all cultures and reflects the general order of human social development. But in stressing the similarities Nakamura is equally aware of the subtle differences found in the various cultures.

Hajime Nakamura is indeed a world-citizen. While he has spent much of his life on Indian and Buddhist thought, he is not concerned with showing the superiority of the thought of any specific culture. He has lived long in Europe and the United States even though his homeland is Japan.

This is a time in which many persons are showing a concern for the whole of mankind. Nakamura's book meets in an eminent way this interest. As a remarkable book by a remarkable man it deserves a wide and varied circle of readers.

Charles Morris

Graduate Research Professor
in Philosophy, Emeritus,
University of Florida

EDITOR'S PREFACE

Professor Nakamura's book represents an effort to discuss the history of ideas primarily from the perspective of Asian thought, though perhaps sometimes with an Indian emphasis. As a result, it presents problems in intellectual history from quite a different perspective than most European and American historians of ideas, who view the history of philosophy using European thought as a norm or criterion. This is part of the genius of the work; but it must not be overly stressed because it is based on the *differences* in traditions. For it becomes clear as one works through Professor Nakamura's book that the old East-West dichotomy in many respects is simply inadequate. Certain common intellectual problems have surfaced wherever man has appeared; and methods must be found for getting beyond the East-West preoccupation if significant intellectual progress is to be made with respect to understanding the history of ideas. At the same time, however—and this is the paradox of Professor Nakamura's book—it becomes clear in the end that many of the problems of what is called "modern thought" (by Western philosophers) did not manifest themselves in India, China, and Japan before the period of "Westernization" except in scattered and tentative ways. In place of the Western scientific orientation, however, very human ethical considerations were often emphasized.

The reader will find Professor Nakamura's work to be a source book in at least two important ways. In the first place, he stands in a tradition of scholars who have held the chair of philosophy at Tokyo University, and who are of astonishingly high caliber in the amount and quality of the scholarship they have produced. Going back only two generations from Professor Nakamura is Junjiro Takakusa who, among other things, oversaw the publication in his own lifetime of the Taisho edition of the Buddhist Tripitaka. Succeeding him was Professor Nakamura's famous teacher Dr. Hakuju Ui, who, in addition to an immensely helpful Buddhist dictionary and other important works, published what stands as *the* authoritative work on Chinese Zen, his three-volume *Zenshū Shi Kenkyū*. In that work, Professor Ui offered long quotations and commentaries from works that would be very difficult for the average (and sometimes not so average) reader to find. In a somewhat similar way, the reader will find Professor Nakamura's scholarship to be authoritative and documented in the extreme, and that in place of hiding his sources behind paraphrases he often offers quotations from the widest range of texts and commentators imaginable so that the reader may constantly appreciate the original touch of great figures in the ongoing history of ideas.

This work also serves as a source book in that scholars of the history of ideas (especially those in comparative philosophy and comparative religion) will find it to be especially rich in ideas. Many of the comparisons mentioned by Professor Nakamura have been elaborated on under this cover. In some instances, however, eager to explore other areas, he has moved on, leaving behind a challenge for succeeding authors to do further research on what has been brought to light. Many times Professor Nakamura has suggested specific points that deserve further scrutiny. If he had elaborated all of the comparative points of interest himself, this book would have been larger by at least another volume.

As to the editing of the work, it was done, so to speak, in two "shifts." Dr. Gerald Larson began work on the task early in the summer of 1971 in Honolulu. After readying for publication Chapter I and a large portion of Chapter II (parts I and II) his previous commitments necessitated his return to "the mainland." At that time Professor Nakamura was preparing to return to Tokyo for resumption of his duties as chairman of the department of Indian and Buddhist philosophy at the University of Tokyo. So it became necessary to engage a second editor to complete the work. It was then decided that Ronald Burr would go to Tokyo in August of 1971 for this purpose. Beginning with Part III of Chapter II, he completed preparation of the manuscript in Tokyo in March, 1972. Then it was sent to Santa Barbara, California, where Dr. Larson gave the entire manuscript a final reading.

Of the people without whom this editing task could not have been accomplished, the highest inspiration came from Professor Nakamura himself. Simply by working with him many a colleague has been prompted to persevere in the mentor's fashion (see for instance Professor Inada's foreword to his new translation of Nāgārjuna's *Mūlamadhyamaka-kārikās*, Hokuseido, 1970). Professor Nakamura unconsciously gets the best from those who come into contact with him. He is jolly, kind and willing to give complete concentration at a moment's notice to the problems that arise in each of the myriad projects in which he is constantly involved.

As to the people without whom the editing in Tokyo could not have taken place (at least as smoothly and happily as it did) thanks must go first to Dr. Dorothy Roberts at the East-West Center in Honolulu, who got us all together when it was learned that the editing must be completed in Japan. Secondly, without the friendship, companionship, and myriad assistances of Yoshihiro Matsunami, who manages the affairs of

Professor Nakamura's Eastern Institute in Tokyo, the task would have been much more lengthy and difficult as well as much less enjoyable. Mrs. Miriam Gould of the East-West Center offered many suggestions on proof reading the finished copy. Finally, the Tokyo editing could not have been done without the day-to-day typing and doctoring of Mrs. Nancy Burr, whose uncanny feel for good idiomatic English has made it possible to present a book which is, hopefully, as easy to read as it is important.

RONALD BURR

University of California
at Santa Barbara

ACKNOWLEDGMENTS

A number of people who have been kind enough to read this work in manuscript have expressed some concern at its form, or more precisely at its striking limitations. The point, I realized, that they were puzzled about was whether or not this was intentional. Perhaps I had set a precedent by writing in a very different style in my *Ways of Thinking of Eastern Peoples* (WTEP). There I set forth a number of propositions, theories if you will, and set about providing the requisite examples that would make my theses more plausible. In the present work I have attempted to describe and assess certain key problems in the history of ideas, both East and West. It seemed to me, at a very early stage of this work, that I would be forced to choose one of two mutually exclusive procedures: either I was painfully to extirpate nine-tenths of all my examples and to turn the remaining one-tenth into a theoretical structure around which the rejected material might be imagined by the lively reader; or I was to avoid elaborate theorizing and allow the data to speak for themselves. As a glance at the following pages will show, I have chosen the latter method. Some theoretical considerations are, of course, unavoidable, but whatever theories emerge in this work do not wander far from the problems that emerge from the data of intellectual history.

Mere clerical work, one honest friend told me, but then it is the kind of clerical work that has taken years to complete, involving, it is true, less creativity than mere speculative theorizing would have done, but providing, I hope, much of the material for those more adventurous theories. The material has been patiently collected; it was there, and it seemed a pity not to put it into some kind of order and present it to a public, that might, after all, find something of value hidden within these pages.

This work does not necessarily cover all important religions and philosophical systems. It covers only those features or problems of thought which are common to East and West through the end of the nineteenth century. Synchoronical considerations are chiefly presented in the main text, while diachronical similarities between thinkers of different ages are mentioned mostly in the footnotes.

This work was originally based upon a series of four public lectures delivered at Harvard University in 1963. For my lectures there I should also like to thank especially: Professor Robert H. L. Slater, former Director of the Center for the Study of World Religions, Harvard University; Professor Daniel H. H. Ingalls of Harvard; Mr. J. Masson, a student at Harvard. The suggestions and arrangements by Professor Charles W. Morris and Professor Delton L. Scudder of the University of Florida were helpful to me in my studies.

Since then I have been engaged in revising and developing the theme. In summer, 1969, I joined the Fifth East-West Philosophers' Conference held at the East-West Center, University of Hawaii, and remained in Honolulu after the close of the Conference to complete the manuscript. I am most grateful to Dr. Minoru Shinoda, Professor of History, University of Hawaii, and formerly Director of the Institute of Cultural Learning, East-West Center, who kindly assisted me in my work during my stay then. Without his kind arrangements this book would not have been brought to existence. Mr. Clifford Miyashiro kindly went over the manuscript up to the end of the second chapter, spending a great deal of his time to check various points and to improve the style.

I came again to Honolulu in summer, 1971, at the invitation of the East-West Center under the thoughtful arrangements by Dr. Everett Kleinjans, Chancellor of the Center, and Professor Eliot Deutsch, Editor of *Philosophy East and West* to revise the manuscript in its finalized form. Also, I am much indebted to Professor Winfield E. Nagley of the University of Hawaii for his kind friendship for many years.

The merit of completion of the manuscript should be ascribed especially to Professor Gerald Larson of the University of California at Santa Barbara, who kindly consented to come to the Center solely for the purpose of revising the manuscript. He and I worked together every day from 8 o'clock A.M. to noon, and worked in the afternoon also. I learnt quite a lot from conversation with him. Without his kind collaboration this book would not have been brought to this state of completion.

After Professor Larson left for California, Mr. Ronald Burr of the East-West Center came to Tokyo for the purpose of completing the work and editing the manuscript. During his stay in Tokyo in August of 1971 through December he kindly devoted most of his time to editing. I am greatly thankful for his enthusiasm in collaboration.

For publication of this work in its final form I was especially honored and encouraged by Professor Charles Morris who kindly read the whole work through, and whose preface, I hope, will harbinger a new way of approach in philosophy and the history of ideas. I am very grateful to him for a long chain of friendship extending for many years, almost a quarter of a century.

I feel greatly honored by the kind help of all these scholars.

Although I know full well that this work has many passages which need much revision and further enlargement, I decided to bring it to the public as a stepping stone for further studies.

Publication of this book was effectuated by the thoughtful consideration of Mr. Teikichi Tarusawa and Mr. Yasuo Yamamoto of Kodansha Ltd. Mr. Hiromitsu Fukuda spent much of his time in putting the manuscript in due order for printing. I am very thankful to them.

Hajime Nakamura

Professor Emeritus, University of Tokyo
Director, The Eastern Institute, Inc.

CONTENTS

Chapter V. COMMON FEATURES OF MODERN THOUGHT

N.B. Bibliographical details of a work cited in this manuscript are mentioned when it is cited for the first time.

PARALLEL DEVELOPMENTS

A Comparative History of Ideas

INTRODUCTORY REMARKS

1. The Aim of the Work

THIS work represents an attempt to isolate, describe and analyze certain key philosophical problems that have appeared historically in almost parallel development within different cultural areas, East and West. The terms "religion" and "philosophy" will be used in this work in the broadest possible sense. In the West the two terms have been fairly sharply distinguished from each other, while in Eastern traditions the dividing line is often difficult to discern.[1] If we insist on being too strict in our definitions, we fail to catch many common problems. It is possible that an idea or attitude held by a Western philosopher finds its counterpart not in an Eastern philosopher but in an Eastern religious thinker and vice versa. For example, the virtue of tolerance was stressed in the West more by enlightened philosophers than traditional religionists, whereas in Japan and China it was emphasized more by traditional religionists than by modern philosophers. Thus, if we limit our scope to only one of the two, either religion or philosophy, we are apt to miss some interesting common features. Although this work is chiefly focused on "philosophical thought," we shall occasionally deal with symbols and practices which are inseparable from it.

By "parallel developments" I refer to the fact that in different areas of the world similar problems, even if not similar concepts, emerged at certain stages of cultural development. In other words, it appears that certain intellectual problems are characteristic of certain stages in the history of culture. I do not mean, of course, that similar problems occurred at precisely the same time, but hopefully the following discussions will

1. We encounter a very outspoken assertion. "I seriously suggest that terms such as Christianity, Buddhism, and the like must be dropped, as clearly untenable once challenged. The word 'religion' has had many meanings; it too would be better dropped. This is partly because of its distracting ambiguity, partly because most of its traditional meanings are, on scrutiny, illegitimate. The only effective significance that can reasonably be attributed to the term is that of 'religiousness'." (Wilfred Cantwell Smith, *The Meaning and End of Religion. A new approach to the religious traditions of mankind*. New York, Macmillan, 1962, p. 178)

show that the history of ideas in each cultural area has undergone a similar development with respect to intellectual problems.

By "cultural area" I mean the area in which a culturally advanced people has established its own cultural tradition in its own way. For example, India, China, Japan, Israel, Greece, etc.; or Medieval Europe; or, the modern European nation-states can be called cultural areas. By using the notion of "cultural area," I wish to avoid the old dichotomy of East and West. The East is not a cultural unit; it consists of various cultural areas. For example, although we cannot deny some points of similarity, Japanese culture is radically different from Indian culture. When a clear and specific statement is intended, this dichotomy will not be used. On occasion, of course, the conventional appellation will be used for convenience of exposition; and on such occasions, by "West" I mean the tradition of Graeco-Judaic-Christian thought, and by "East" I mean chiefly the traditions of India, China, Japan, etc. One of the main purposes of this work, however, is to show the conceptual inadequacy of this dichotomy, and generally I shall focus on specific areas such as Greece, India, Japan, etc.

When discussing common problems that emerge at various stages of cultural development, my aim throughout is to let the facts and texts speak for themselves. I would rather not specify how many stages one ought to admit, though I firmly believe that there have indeed been *some* stages. I must add that my division into different stages or periods is only tentative; my main point is to indicate some common ideas or problems noticed in various cultural areas.

In recent scholarship there has been a tendency to avoid comparative studies. This reaction is expressed in the truism: "Apparent similarities are really disguised dissimilarities." Similarity always involves differences. It is urged that there is a need to consider the meaning of each particular term in the light of its own particular historical and systematic context. One result of this view has been that the whole attempt at any comparative analysis has come to be suspect. Especially in Japan, scholars have recently engaged in minute and highly specialized studies. I also have followed this tendency. For example, when I wrote an article on Early Vedanta for the *Harvard Journal of Asiatic Studies*, I focused on problems of a purely textual nature. I placed all my attention on the identification of Tibetan citations with the Sanskrit original. Gradually, however, I have come to believe that this tendency to avoid comparative study has gone too far. Each study by a specialist should, at some point, be placed in a comprehensive framework to make clear the significance of the total subject matter. I think that there is a need now to reconsider some of the problems of the history of thought from a comparative perspective, and although no one has the massive competence to treat all cultural traditions in comparable depth, perhaps something of importance can emerge from modest efforts in a comparative direction.

Methodologically, the present work follows a "problem approach."[2] Many works on comparative religion are available but they usually are arranged according to what might be called an "-isms approach" (Hinduism, Buddhism, etc.) and are seldom arranged problematically. Books on the history of philosophy are not less in number, but their descriptions are mostly based upon the differences of schools or individual philosophers, and not on problems as such. Differing from this usual method, I would like to discuss the history of ideas focusing on certain core problems in each stage of cultural development. When one discusses or evaluates an idea *qua* idea, a broad scope is necessary. Similar ideas or problems in different traditions must be examined. By means of this method an idea can be evaluated more adequately. When the concept of 'law' (dharma) in Indian or Buddhist philosophy is examined, for example, the "problem approach" proves illuminating. If we pay attention to concepts of similar purport in different cultural areas, the problem of law is clarified. The idea will be located, analyzed and reviewed in a wider scope, and the unique feature of the idea or concept will be made clear. It must be recognized, of course, that similar assertions or similar wording may play different or even contrary roles in different historical contexts. For example, respect for Confucius played a progressive role in the age of Enlightenment in the West whereas it played a conservative role in Japan after the Meiji Restoration.

In this work I wish to avoid comparing any religion as a whole with any other religion as a whole. Scholars of comparative religion have already made such studies with varying degrees of success, and there is no need to repeat their findings. Since such studies are also beyond my capacity, I will limit myself to pointing to some common problems of various religious or philosophical systems.

I have painfully learned that what has interested me in the deep seas of my study of eastern philosophy is, from the standpoint of time, too deep down to reach within the short time allowed for exploration. To my regret I have been obliged all too often to skim the surface. In this volume I do not discuss every important problem in each tradition; that would be a task far beyond the scope of the present work. I have stressed, rather, only those key problems which appear at certain stages in a variety of cultural areas.

2. This approach was used in western philosophical studies, e.g., by Wilhelm Windelband, *Lehrbuch der Geschichte der Philosophie*, Neunte und zehnte, durchgesehene Auflage, besorgt von Erich Rothacker, Tuebingen, Verlag von J. C. B. Mohr (Paul Siebeck), 1921. E. Tr., *History of Philosophy with Special Reference to the Formation and Development of its Problems and Conceptions*. Authorized translation by James H. Tufts. New York, 1921.

The divisions of periods or stages of development are only tentative. Only after we have located common problems or common concepts in the history of ideas within different traditions are we able safely to pass judgments about divisions of periods or stages. This, of course, must be based on sound and reliable facts. Otherwise, a preoccupation with any given theory must surely lead to distortion. Some concepts or ideas which I shall discuss cannot be categorized into one period. For example, the subjects discussed in the chapter on the ancient period are not necessarily limited to the ancient period; many of them linger to remain even in the modern period. But when those ideas seem to be peculiarly characteristic of the ancient period, I discuss them in that chapter.

Some Eastern thinkers hold that Eastern thought in the most ancient period has a uniqueness and significance which cannot be found in Western philosophy. In order to counteract that view, I have cited many parallel problems and concepts from classical works of the West. On the other hand, "medieval thought" is an amorphous category within Eastern traditions. Scholars differ about periodizations of medieval thought in Eastern countries, whereas the medieval period in the West is relatively fixed. Hence, in the chapter on Medieval Thought I have concentrated not so much on elaborating examples from the West, but on citing Eastern parallels.

Many intellectual historians have suggested that modern thought did not exist in Eastern countries prior to the introduction of European civilization. Differing from the usual approach, I wanted to locate modern thought in its incipient stages, concentrating chiefly on citing instances from Eastern countries. In sum, the method of locating problems and ideas is the same throughout the work, but the emphases in citing instances vary. This reflects nothing but the present state of research and the general climate of opinion held by those interested in the field.

As a student of Indian and Buddhist philosophy, I cannot help viewing problems from my own perspective. Important problems in other religious and philosophical traditions may have eluded my attention. But I hope that this series of discussions will help create an arena for discussion of problems common to various traditions, and provide a larger framework for understanding the significance of each tradition.

In my research I have consulted relevant passages from translations by experts in their respective fields. For Western texts, I have relied completely upon translations or studies by specialists; but in citing passages from Eastern texts (chiefly Japanese, Chinese and Indian), I frequently have revised existing translations by collating them with the original texts. Where I cite verbatim, I have mentioned the sources in footnotes. Moreover, I have translated many passages of Eastern, especially Japanese, works from the originals. These are also mentioned in the footnotes.

As the aim of this work is to give a synopsis of parallel developments in intellectual history,[3] I cannot discuss any item in full detail. Even one item would require a book of explanations. Where possible, I have mentioned relevant works to consult for each item.

2. Some References to Comparative Attempts in the Classical Period

THE fact that certain religio-philosophical ideas were common to East and West was noticed by some of the ancient Greeks. Megasthenes (c. 300 B.C.), a Greek who was sent by Seleucus, the monarch of Syria, to India as ambassador pointed out similarities: "On many points their opinions (i.e. the opinions of Indian Brahmins) coincide with those of the Greeks." He continues: "Concerning generation, and the nature of the soul, and many other subjects, they express views like those maintained *by the Greeks*."[1] Clement of Alexandria also asserted that philosophy is universal, and can be found among various culturally advanced peoples of East and West. "Philosophy, then, with all its blessed advantage to man, flourished long ages ago among the barbarians, diffusing its light among the Gentiles, and eventually penetrated into Greece. Its hierophants were the prophets among the Egyptians, the Chaldeans among the Assyrians, the Druids among the Gauls, the Sarmanaeans who were the philosophers of the Baktrians and the Kelts, the Magi among the Persians, who, as you know, announced beforehand the birth of the Saviour, being led by a star till they arrived in the land of Judaea, and among the Indians the Gymnosophists, and other philosophers of barbarous nations."[2] Some common features in Greek and Indian thought were also

3. A work which is especially important is Walter Ruben (Indische und Griechische Metaphysik, *Zeitschrift der Indologie und Iranistik*, Deutsche Morgenländische Gesellschaft, Band 8, 1931, S. 147–227). As I wrote this work during my stay at several American universities, I could not incorporate all important results of studies by German scholars mentioned in this article.

1. Megasthenes, *Indika*, fr. XLI, pp. 100–101. For a new study on Megasthenes, cf. Allan Dahlquist. *Megasthenes and Indian Religion. A Study in Motives and Types*, Stockholm, Gutenborg and Uppsala, Almquist and Wiskell, 1962.

2. Megasthenes, *Ind.* fr. XLIII, p. 104. According to Clement of Alexandria, Megasthenes asserted that Greek philosophy was not essentially different from Indian and Jewish philosophy. "That the Jewish race is by far the oldest of all these, and that their philosophy, which has been committed to writing, preceded the philosophy of the Greeks, Philo the Pythagorean shows by many arguments, as does also Aristoboulos, the Peripathetic, and many others whose names I need not waste time in enumerating. Megasthenes, the author of a work on India, who lived with Seleukos Nikator, writes most clearly on this point, and his words are these: —"All that has been said regarding nature by the ancients is asserted also by philosophers out of Greece, on the one part in India by the Brachmanes, and on the other in Syria by the people called the Jews." (Megasthenes, *Ind.* fr. XLII, f. p. 103)

admitted by Aristoboulos the Peripatetic.[3] Nor did the similarity of ideas escape the attention of medieval Arabians. On the subject of "created things, both intelligibilia and sensibilia," Alberuni, the Muslim scholar of Arabia (c. 1030 A.D.), states: "The ancient Greeks held nearly the same views as the Hindus."[4]

In contrast, Chinese thought came to be noticed much later by Western thinkers such as Leibniz,[5] Wolff, Voltaire, etc. The history of ideas in Japan seems not to have been given its due attention by scholars of comparative studies. Where relevant, I hope to be allowed to cite examples from Japanese culture. Attention should also be drawn to the fact that in the East comparative study also was a topic of great interest in the classical period. Hindu philosophers engaged in sophisticated comparative descriptions of various philosophical systems, and left wonderful masterpieces such as the *Sarvadarśana-saṃgraha* by Mādhave (c. 1350). In China, after the introduction of Buddhism, comparison of various religious and philosophical systems created heated debate; such voluminous works as the *Hung-ming Chi* by Seng-yu (445–518) and the *Kuang Hung-ming Chi* by Tao-hsuan (596–667) were the results. In Japan Master Kūkai,[6] the founder of Japanese Vajrayāna Buddhism (Mikkyō), showed great interest in comparative analysis. Tominaga Nakamoto left ingenious works[7] in comparative studies on Buddhism, Shintoism, Confucianism and Taoism. Years ago I translated some of Tominaga's work into contemporary Japanese, wrote a book on him, and was greatly impressed by his pristine scholarly spirit. The motivation for undertaking this volume is found, therefore, not only in Western scholarship[8] but also in the cultural areas of Asia.

3. Megasthenes, *Ind.* fr. XLII C, p. 104.
4. *Alberuni's India. An account of the religion, philosophy, literature, geography, chronology, astrology, astronomy, customs, laws, and astrology of India about A.D. 1030*. An English edition, with notes and indices, by Edward C. Sachau, vol. I. London, Trübner and Co., 1888, p. 33.
5. Leibniz' view on Chinese thought was discussed by Philip P. Wiener in *Philosophy East and West*, vol. XII, No. 3, Oct. 1962, pp. 195–202.
6. His works in the field of comparative studies are: *Sangō Shiiki*, *Jūjū-shin-ron*, and *Hizōhōyaku.*
7. *Shutsujō Kōgo* and *Okina-no Fumi.*
8. Recently various books on the world history of philosophy appeared:

   Encyclopédie de la Pléiade, Histoire de la Philosophie, I. *Orient-Antiquité Moyen Âge*, volume publié sous la direction de Brice Parain, Éditions Gallimard, 1969, 1728 pp.

   Hans Joachim Störig, *Kleine Weltgeschichte der Philosophie*, Stuttgart: W. Kohlhammer Verlag. Zehnte, überarbeitete Auflage, 1968.

   Kurt Schilling, *Weltgeschichte der Philosophie*, Berlin: Duncker und Humbolt, 1964.

CHAPTER ONE

Myths, Gods, and Sacrifice: Thought in Early Agricultural Communities

I. SOCIAL BACKGROUND

1. Introductory Remarks

The periodization beginning with this and subsequent chapters is the following: (1) thought in early agricultural communities; (2) the rise of philosophy and the development of heterodoxies; (3) early universal religions and the ideology of the universal state; (4) medieval thought; and (5) modern thought. In each chapter, the cultural area of India will serve as a point of departure for developing a set of characteristic problems of a particular stage and for providing a context in which broader comparative analyses can be discussed. I choose India as a starting-point or norm for exposition for the following reasons: (1) Indian culture provides an extensive body of data ranging from the Vedic period to the present thus furnishing rich documentation diachronically for all of the above-mentioned stages; (2) Indian culture, both ancient and modern, preserves in any given period a great diversity in its religious and philosophical traditions thus furnishing synchronically a wide range of problems characteristic of a particular stage; and (3) the religions and philosophies of India have been the primary focus of my own research over several decades and thus serve as a natural starting point in all of my own reflections regarding problems in the history of ideas. The latter reason clearly indicates a bias but one of which I am fully conscious and for which I make no apology. So long as one is fully aware of one's own presuppositions and perspective, one minimizes the risk of distortion.

An important corollary to the above comments should also be mentioned at this point. By discussing common problems in the history of ideas using Indian thought as a norm for exposition, differences in intellectual history also become apparent and, hopefully, from a somewhat new perspective. In the period of the rise of philosophy and the development of heterodoxies (Chapter II), for example, no systematic treatment of the thought of Plato and Aristotle is presented because thinkers of this level of sophistication are quite unique to Greece. In other words, they have no counterparts outside of the Greek context in this ancient period. Only in later medieval times do India, China or Japan produce thinkers of similar sophistication. Or again, no effort is made in this work to discuss systematically the Hindu and Buddhist tantra cross-culturally because these movements are clearly unique to medieval Indian thought (Chapter IV). Likewise in the discussion of early modern thought (Chapter V), many problems in contemporary European philosophy—e.g., problems relating to physics, mathematics, philosophy of history, etc.—are not emphasized because they have no counterparts in the cultural areas of India, China, Japan, etc. Thus, although the present work focuses on similar problems in the development of intellectual history in various cultural areas; nevertheless, at every stage important differences also become manifest.

2. Sedentary Life

A crucial stage in the development of culture emerged when people came to live a sedentary social life, a life in which, having forsaken a nomadic life of wandering, they engaged in cattle-raising and agriculture. This does not mean that there had been no thought until the 'agricultural' stage was reached. On the contrary, many remarkable studies in anthropology and the history of religions indicate the importance of ideas or thought which occurred prior to the agricultural stage. This discussion, however, takes up the great traditions at the point where they are traceable in documents or records.

Vedic culture is often said to resemble that of the Homeric Greeks and Celtic Irish at the beginning of the Christian era or that of the later pre-Christian Teutons and Slavs. The social life which can be inferred from the Ṛg-veda has many points of similarity with that of the primitive Greeks or of the primitive Germans as depicted by Caesar. The people lived in simple villages (*pur* in Sanskrit, *polis* in Greek; later *grāma* in Sanskrit). During the Vedic age" . . . the tribe, in fact, was the political unit, organized much in the same way as the Afghans are at the present day, or the Germans were in the time of Tacitus. The tribe (*jana*) consisted of a number of settlements (*viś*), which again were formed of an aggregate of villages (*grāma*). The fighting organization of the tribe appears to have been based on these divisions. The houses forming the village seem to have been built entirely of wood, as they still were in the time of Megasthenes. In the midst of each house the domestic fire burned. For protection against foes or inundations, fortified enclosures (called *pur*) were made on high places. They consisted of earthworks strengthened with a stockade or occasionally with stone. There is nothing to show that they were inhabited, much less that *pur* ever meant a town or city, as it did in later times."[1] In Indian texts the term for "village" is *grāma* from the Ṛg-veda onwards. The Vedic Indians seem to have dwelt in villages which were scattered over the country, some close together, some far apart, and which were connected by roads. The village is contrasted with the forest (*araṇya*), and its animals and plants with those that lived or grew wild in the woods.[2] The villages sheltered cattle, horses, and other domestic animals, as well as men. Grains were also stored in them. In the evening the cattle regularly returned from the forest. The villages were probably open, though perhaps a fort might on occasion be built within it. Presumably they consisted of detached houses with enclosures, but no details are to be found in Vedic literature.

The relationships among villagers is difficult to ascertain with precision. In several passages the word *grāma* occurs in what appears to be the derivative sense of 'body of men.' This presumably began with the use of the word to denote the 'village folk.' The *grāma* may be regarded as an aggregate of several families, not necessarily forming a clan, but only part of a clan (*viś*). Vedic literature tells us little about the social economy of the village. There is nothing to show that the community as such held land. What little evidence there is indicates that individual tenure of land was known; but this, in effect though not in law, presumably meant tenure by a family rather than by an individual person.

The village does not appear to have been a unit for legal purposes and it can hardly be said to have been a political unit. It no doubt included, other than owner-cultivators, various menials, and also Brāhmaṇas and Kṣatriyas who might by royal grant hold an interest in a village without actually cultivating the land. The menials were chariot-makers (*rathakāra*), carpenters (*takṣan*), smiths (*karmāra*), and others, but apparently, they did not, in any sense, participate as members of the formal village group. All people in the village were politically subject to a "governor" rather than to a popularly elected officer. That post, however, may have been hereditary or filled by a kind of election. There is no clear evidence of the existence of towns. "The basis of Vedic society being the patriarchal family, the government of the tribe was often hereditary. . . . The governor's power was by no means absolute, being limited by the will of people expressed in the tribal assembly (*samiti*)."[3] *Sabhās* and *Samitis* (popular assemblies) formed checks on the power of the governor. (The word *sabhā* is associated with the German word *Sippe*.[4])

1. A. A. Macdonell, *A History of Sanskrit Literature*, New York, D. Appleton and Co., p. 157 f.
2. Arthur Anthony Macdonell and Arthur Berriedale Keith, *Vedic Index of Names and Subjects*, London, J. Murray, 1912, vol. I, pp. 224–247.
3. *Ibid.*, p. 158.
4. Adolf Kaegi, *The Ṛg-Veda: The Oldest Literature of the Indians*, translated by R. Arrowsmith, Boston, Ginn and Co., 1886, p. 114, n. 59.

Earliest agricultural life in the great river-valley civilizations of the Ancient New East indicate a similar social context, although, as is well known, at a much earlier time than in Aryan India, the system of villages was transformed into an "urban" framework among other reasons because of agricultural problems arising out of local conditions of the river—i.e., the Tigris, Euphrates, Nile, etc.

A comparison of Vedic life with that of the Greek *polis* produces an interesting contrast. In Greece the city was the unit of organization. The Greek city had a common hall which contained a Holy Hearth upon which a perpetual flame often was maintained. Such a religious nexus, essential to the city, is not found in India. Although there existed the city hall (*santhāgāra*), at least in the age of the rise of Buddhism, it had no direct connection with any specific religion.[5]

Another contrast of some interest appears when one compares the Vedic village with the situation in ancient Japan. The social structure of prehistoric Japan is not clear, but the huge tombs[6] in prehistoric Japan, as well as in Korea, indicate an aristocratic society. The men buried in the tombs must have had a large number of workers at their command. The later Japanese attitude of esteeming the emperor and the political and military rulers is perhaps thus foreshadowed, an attitude not markedly conspicuous in the history of pre-Muslim India. This difference was decisive in forming the respective characters of both societies. In addition in Japan numerous clans and tribes were united in early times under the rule of one powerful family, which evolved later to become the Imperial Family. The Japanese had already reached the stage of settled agricultural communities and engaged in rice-cultivation before the introduction of Chinese culture from the mainland of Asia.

The Chinese reached the stage of sedentary life at a very early period. Although the structure and nature of agricultural communities in early China are difficult to ascertain, sedentary life in China seems to have been very similar to that of India. The ideal was to enjoy life in this world. The fulfillment of life was sung:

> Things they have in plenty
> Only because their ways are blessed.

5. *DN.* vol. I, p. 91. The term *santhāgāra* was never applied to a conference at a royal court. Cf. Edward James Rapson, *The Cambridge History of India*, Cambridge University Press, 1922, vol. 1, p. 156; *Journal of the Pali Text Society*, 1909, p. 65.
6. History of the Kingdom of Wei (*Wei Chih*) says about ancient Japan: "When Pimiko (a great queen of Japan) passed away, a great mound was raised, more than a hundred paces in diameter. Over a hundred male and female attendants followed her to the grave." *Sources of Japanese Tradition.* Compiled by Ryūsaku Tsunoda, William Theodore de Bary, and Donald Keene. Columbia University Press, New York, 1958, p. 8.

Things they have that are good,
Only because they are at peace with one another.
Things they have enough and to spare,
Only because their ways are lovely.[7]

They were grateful to Heaven: "Heaven indulged them and cherished and protected them."[8]

3. Establishment of an Hierarchical Order

FROM about 1000 B.C. the Aryans moved farther to the southeast to settle in the districts along the upper part of the Ganges. They formed many small village communities and engaged chiefly in agriculture. The social system and the cultural complex formed here profoundly influenced the India of later periods. Although the tribal governments of the Ṛg-Veda probably grew in size by expansion or amalgamation, there were no great kingdoms even in this later period; nor was city life much developed.

The Gṛhyasūtras seem to hint at the existence of petty principalities, kingdoms or rulerships. Land was regarded as being under the jurisdiction of the "king." The king's[1] share in a village is referred to as early as in the *Atharvaveda*. The expression "desirous of a village" (grāmakāma), frequent in the later *Saṃhitās*, points to the practice of the king's granting to his favorites royal prerogatives over villages so far as fiscal matters were concerned. Later the idea developed that the king was owner of all the land, and parallel thereto the view that the holders of such grants were subordinate landlords. But of either idea there is no trace in Vedic literature beyond the word *grāmakāma*, which much more probably refers to a grant of regalia than to the grant of land, as Teutonic parallels show. Such grants probably tended to depress the position of the actual cultivators and to convert them into tenants.[2] It has been shown that villages of the fourth century B.C., were marked out by natural boundaries, such as forests, thickets, rivulets, hills, jungle and plains (prastara).[3]

7. *The Book of Songs*, tr. from the Chinese by Arthur Waley (New York: Grove Press, 1960), no. 168.
8. From *Shu ching* (*Sources of Chinese Tradition*, compiled by W. T. de Bary, Wing-tsit Chan and B. Watson, Columbia University Press, 1960, p. 13)
1. V. M. Apte, *Social and Religious Life in the Gṛhyasūtras*. With brief surveys of social conditions in Vedic literature (from the Ṛg-veda to the sranta-sūtras) and in early Avestan literature. (Ahmedabad, published by the author, 1939), p. 52.
2. Macdonell and Keith, *Vedic Index*, *op. cit.*, p. 246.
3. Vasudera Sharana Agrawala, *India as Known to Pāṇini*, a study of the cultural material in the Ashtadhyayi. Lucknow, University of Lucknow, 1953, pp. 141–143.

The village proper consisted of houses, mostly peasant cottages, covered with roofing of reed and straw. A separate house sheltering one family formed the unit of village-life. The entire settlement was called *vasati* and a multitude of villages by the name *grāmatā*. A village depended for its water-supply on wells, to which were attached water-troughs (*nipāna*). Wells were cleaned by specially trained laborers who acted as dredgers called *udagāha* or *udakagāha*. The area surrounding the village settlement consisted of arable land, pasture, plantations of bamboo thickets, reeds, fruit-bearing trees, reserves of herbs and plants, forests of timber, and waste saline tracts. Cultivated land was divided into a number of holdings (*kṣetra*) which were specially defined as plots where crops were grown.

A systematic survey of agricultural land appears to have been undertaken by special officers called "field-makers" (*kṣetrakāra*), who measured each field. The estimated area of individual fields was further expressed in terms of the quantity of seeds required. The division of arable land into separate holdings (*kṣetra*) shows that they were held under individual ownership. Consolidated fields also existed. Pastures seem to have been held in common by the village for cattle-grazing. The village held cattle ranches (*goṣṭha* or *vraja*) and settlements of cowherds were known (*ghoṣa*). The site of ranches shifted, owing to exigencies of fodder. The village land was entirely marked out, as today, for habitation, agriculture, grazing, and dumping of manure. The village land was distinct from the forest. The forests were used, however, for domestic animals. When a particular range was denuded of its fodder supply, the herdsmen moved the ranch to a different area.

The Aryan invaders of the Indus Valley were divided by differences of culture and racial ancestry from the peoples they conquered. At the time of the invasions the Indo-Aryans brought with them a "tripartite" system of social and religious ideology. Dumézil in his many books and articles has brilliantly demonstrated the correlation between the tripartite social order and the Indo-European mythological system—i.e., the correlation between *brāhmaṇa*, *kṣatriya*, and *vaiśya*, on the one hand, and Varuna-Mitra, Indra, and the Aśvins, on the other.[4] As the Vedic religion developed its increasingly elaborate ceremonialism, those versed in ritual—namely, the priests or *brāhmaṇas*—became ever more important. They were regarded as an intellectual aristocracy charged with the moulding of the higher life of the people. The warriors or princes (*kṣatriyas*) functioned as rulers of the common people. The word *kṣatriya* is derived from *kṣatra* ("rule dominion"). (It has the same meaning in the Vedas, the Avesta, and the Persian inscriptions). This class ranked below that of the Brahmins.[5] A third class was composed of the people, or the Vaiśyas. They

4. Works of George Dumézil on Indo-Europeans.

5. "The king is the principal among men" (*Suttanipāta*, v. 568); *Vinaya*, VI, 35, 8;

engaged in agriculture, cattle-raising, trade and crafts. It apparently is the case that the conquered population of dark aborigines was treated as menials and came to make up the fourth class, the Sūdras.[6]

The division of these classes was originally functional, but gradually became hereditary. Members of different castes were not allowed to marry and to take meals together. The right of connubium and commensality was limited to the members of the same class.[7] With the lapse of years these four castes divided into sub-branches and new castes arose from them. Present-day India, it has been estimated, has nearly three thousand distinct castes, although the caste system is officially not admitted.

Some features of the caste system can be found in other cultural areas. An approximation of the Indian caste system is found in the cultures of the Pacific, especially in the Fiji Islands.[8] Something similar to the caste system also existed in ancient Persia, a fact mentioned by Alberuni: "All this is well illustrated by the history of the ancient Chosroes (Khusrau), for they had created great institutions of this kind, which could not be broken through by the special merits of any individual nor by bribery. When Ardashir ben Babak restored the Persian empire, he also restored the classes or castes of the population in the following way:

The first class were the knights and princes.
The second class the monks, the fire-priests, and the lawyers.
The third class the physicians, astronomers, and other men of science.
The fourth class the husbandmen and artisans.

And within these classes there were subdivisions, distinct from each other, like the species within a genus. All institutions of this kind are like

---

Saṃyutta-Nikāya, vol. 1, p. 6 gāthā.; p. 153; Dīgha-Nikāya (*DN*), vol. 1, p. 99; III, p. 97; *Majjihima-Nikāya* (*MN*), vol. I, p. 358; II, p. 284; *Aṅguttara-Nikāya* (*AN*), vol. V, pp. 327; 328 gāthā; seṭṭhasaṃmata, *AN*, vol. II, p. 76. (These are all cited from the editions of the Pali Text Society, London). In Sanskrit texts of early Buddhism kings come first, and then brāhmaṇas (e.g., Ernst Waldschmidt, *Das Mahāparinirvāṇasūtra*. Akademie Verlag Berlin. Teil II, 1951, S. 300–301). However, in Chinese versions of the scriptures of Early Buddhism, Brahmins came first, and next kings. One explanation is that when the original Sanskrit texts of early Buddhism (equivalent to Pali scriptures) were compiled, the influence of Brahmins had increased and the order was changed. Alternatively, Chinese translators may change the order.

6. The strongest protest against the caste was made in the *Vajrasūcī* by Aśvaghoṣa. Its Chinese version ascribes its authorship to Dharmakīrti. This work is closely related to the *Vajrasūcyupaniṣad*, which, interesting enough, attacks the caste system, *from the standpoint of orthodox Brahmanism*.
7. In the Brāhamanas the restriction on commensality was not strong, but in later days, it became strict.
8. Daniel H. H. Ingalls in *Journal of the American Oriental Society* (*JAOS*), vol. 77, 1957, p. 222 b.

a pedigree, as long as their origin is remembered; but when once their origin has been forgotten, they become, as it were, the stable property of the whole nation."[9]

As for China, Hughes[10] states: "The data is very scanty for the Western Chou period (1122–771 B.C.) but by solid inference we can visualize an aristocratic society welded together by ritual practices of equally religious and political significance. The Royal Fane, where the Chou ancestors were worshipped in regularly recurrent occasions, was a center of meeting until ancestral temples in the various fiefs assumed more and more importance."

The ascendancy of the Brahmin class is somewhat similar to that of the Ju in ancient China of approximately the same period. "The divining experts and experts in temple ritual, being the masters of writing and recording, took over the new work of administering. These Ju were probably of Shang descent, and therefore not members of the ruling military caste, nor of the serf class below. They acted as a sort of 'domestic chaplain' in the great houses, and came also to act as tutors to the young lordlings. They were, therefore, both repositories of traditional culture and exponents of new methods of efficiency." The function of the Ju especially reminds us of that of the *purohitas* at the royal courts of ancient India. The purohitas were chosen from among the Brahmins, whereas the status or qualification of the Brahmin had nothing to do with acknowledgement by the royal court. It was independent of political influence.

The observance of the duties of each caste was strictly prescribed in the law-books of Brahmanism (*dharmasūtras* and *dharmaśāstras*). It is well known that Confucianism also taught obedience to the hierarchical order of society.[11] Even Lao-tzu admitted the validity of the existent hierarchical order: "He who would assist a lord of men in harmony with the Tâo will not assert his mastery in the kingdom by force of arms."[12] In Taoism and Confucianism, however, class duties were not prescribed in such detail as in the Indian law-books. In China, moreover, tradition was the sovereign principle, and the Confucian system of education facilitated cultural stability. In spite of the fact that China has been for thousands of years the arena of incessant strife and turmoil, the continuity of tradition has not

9. *Alberni's India. An account of the religion, philosophy, literature, geography, chronology, astrology, astronomy, customs, laws, and astrology of India about A.D. 1030.* An English edition, with notes and indices, by Edward C. Sachau, vol. I. London, Trübner and Co., 1888, p. 100. See work of Dumézil and Duchesne Guillemin.
10. Ernest Richard Hughes, *Chinese Philosophy*, London, (in classical times, edited and translated by E. R. Hughes. London: J. M. Dent & Sons, Ltd.; New York: E. P. Dutton & Co., Inc., 1942.) (Everyman's Library), Introd. pp. XXV-VI.
11. Cf. Analects of Confucius (*Lun-yu*), XVII, 24, 25.
12. *Tao-teh-ching*, 30 (*The Tao Teh King*, translated by James Legge, in SBE, vol. XXXIX, Oxford, the Clarendon Press, 1891, p. 72)

been interrupted. There exists the traditional dictum: "Follow the laws of the ancient kings."[13] In India, however, a similar principle, "Follow the rules established by former kings," seems to have been meant for kings alone, not for the people in general.

The hierarchical structure of the Japanese was striking even to the eyes of the Chinese. A Chinese historical chronicle describes the situation in ancient Japan as follows: "When the lowly meet men of importance on the road, they stop and withdraw to the roadside. In conveying messages to them or addressing them, they either squat or kneel, with both hands on the ground. This is the way they show respect."[14] This attitude continued until the last days of the pre-modern period in Japan. It was a secular respect, however, and not really similar to the type of respect received by the Brahmins.

In Greece, on the other hand, the authority of an hereditary priesthood was very weak. "In the East the priests had generally held the keys of knowledge. But in Greece from the earliest times the sacerdotal influence was slight. Priests of course existed, but they never became a corporation, much less a caste."[15] This undoubtedly proved favorable for the advancement of free thinking and early scientific reflection. A way of justifying the hierarchical social system, however, was not lacking in ancient Greece. Aristotle thought that justice involves, not equality, but proportion, which is only sometimes equality.[16] According to him, "the slave is a living tool." "Qua slave then, one cannot be friends with him. But qua man one can, for there seems to be some justice between any man and any other who can share in a system of law or be a party to an agreement."[17]

Israel also knew a hierarchical order of society. The Old Testament speaks of Abraham's arming his "trained men, born in his house, three hundred and eighteen."[18] These "trained men" were most probably hereditary slaves. That such slaves were, even in this early epoch, something more than the chattels of ancient Greece and Rome is evidenced in Genesis,[19] where "all that were born in his [Abraham's] house, and all that

13. *Mencius*, IV. 1, 1.
14. History of the Kingdom of Wei (*Wei Chih*), c. A. D. 297, cited in De Bary etc., *Japanese Tradition, op. cit.*, p. 7.
15. Arthur Anthony Macdonell, *Lectures on Comparative Religion*. University of Calcutta, 1925, p. 93. In the field of comparative religion there are many good works which can serve as general outlines. As Macdonell published his work *Comparative Religion* from the standpoint of Indian studies, his comments have been very helpful to me.
16. *Nicomachean Ethics*, 1131 a–b.
17. *Ibid.*, 1161 b. (*The Works of Aristotle*, translated by W. D. Ross, vol. IX, Oxford, Clarendon Press, 1925)
18. Genesis, 14, 14.
19. Genesis, 17, 23.

were bought with his money" underwent the rite of circumcision. This is a clear indication that in Israel the master owed some sort of familial obligation to the slave.[20] But in India śūdras and outcastes (*caṇḍālas*, etc.) were excluded from the rites of Brahmanism.[21]

Hence, hierarchical order in itself is not peculiar to India. Yet in India the highest functionaries—i.e., the "social elite"—were neither warriors nor literati, but the sacerdotals, who were held in special respect. They claimed divinity for themselves. A passage runs as follows: "Verily there are two kinds of gods; for the gods themselves assuredly are gods, and then the priests who have studied and teach Vedic lore are the human gods."[22] The highly stylized nature of the sacrificial ceremonies necessitated special training for the priestly office. The specialized knowledge made priesthood a respectable profession and an hereditary one; sacrifices and literacy were monopolized by the Brahmins. "The state of society in the valley of the Ganges at the time of the rise of Buddhism, was not so different from the state of society in other races at similar stages of their history. The hereditary priesthood, the exclusive privileges of the Brahmans, were, no doubt, as incontestable as the hereditary priesthood and exclusive privileges of the corresponding classes in Judaea in the time of Christ. Superstitions regarding purity and impurity, which play so great a part elsewhere in the establishment of early religious and social customs, were held as strongly as among the Jews and Persians."[23] But the supremacy of the clergy not only in religious, but also social and political affairs was manifest to an extraordinary degree in India. The clergy as a social stratum wielded great influence upon the daily life of ancient Indians.

Max Weber[24] explained this social phenomenon by the term "Charismatic authority" ("*charismatische Autorität*"). "Charisma," as a special quality transcending ordinary human character, could be given not only to individual persons but also to a class, or *gens*. In the case of the Brahmins this character is obvious. Such a quality Weber called "Gentilcharisma." But development of a stratum of magicians to the gentilcharismatic status is not a social phenomenon particular to India. For example, in Miletus in ancient Greece the guild of holy dancers formed the ruling class. Such a phenomenon can also be found in ancient Japan. Before the introduc-

20. *Encyclopaedia of Religion and Ethics*, edited by James Hastings (Edinburgh, T. and T. Clark, 1908 f. Abbr: *ERE*), vol. XI, p. 619.
21. As terrible examples, *Gautama-dharma-sūtra*, XII, 4–6; *Manu* V, 104; VIII, 417.
22. *Śatapatha-brāhmaṇa*, II, 2, 2, 6; II, 4, 3, 14.
23. T. W. Rhys Davids, *Lectures on the Origin and Growth of Religion as Illustrated by Some Points in the History of Indian Buddhism*, second edition, London, Williams and Norgate, 1891, p. 4.
24. Max Weber, *Religionssoziologische Schriften*, I, S. 268; *Gesammelte Aufsätze zur Religionssoziologie*, Bd. II: *Hinduismus und Buddhismus*, Tübingen, 1921, S. 129.

tion of continental civilizations three kinds of persons performed religious rites:[25] (1) the heads of families or clans, considered priests *de facto*; (2) shamans, men and women with occult powers who performed divination, sorcery and lustration; and (3) hereditary lines of priests and shamans, known to have existed in at least some clans. Supposed divine lineage was a fundamental pre-requisite for sorceresses. A family whose members were qualified as sorcerers was respected as belonging to a special higher class. In Japan the priests of local shrines are called *Kannushi*, that is, *kaminushi* or 'God-master.' Their duties are to recite the usual prayers and to attend to the repairs of the shrine. Although they marry and their position is hereditary the *kannushi* do not constitute a caste. They wear distinctive dress only when engaged in worship. This custom is somewhat similar to that in India where Brahmins make it a rule to dress themselves in religious costumes only on ceremonial occasions. During the ceremonies however, the Brahmins put on robes with expressly religious significance, whereas in Japan the dress worn by the *Kannushi* is not a sacerdotal costume but only an old official garb of the Imperial court indicative of the close connection of Shintoism with the imperial state. This situation was quite different from India where Brahmins were strictly distinguished from the warrior class, i.e., the military ruling class.

In ancient Indian society there was no universal sovereign and no national unity. Brahmin or Hindu thinkers confined the scope of their political thinking to a localized area. They did not propose a unified state; their ideal, "universal monarch" (*cakravartin*), could be plural, not necessarily a single person.

A similar situation existed in ancient Greece. Since each city was autonomous, the Greeks failed to develop a loyalty towards a union of the whole Greek world. They could not organize and act together, and their lives were spent in violent conflicts. Plato, it is true, dreamed of an ideal society, but it was conceived as a city-state, not a common-wealth of mankind.[26]

Although there was no national unity, Indians, especially Brahmins, prided themselves on being civilized people. They despised outsiders as "barbarians" (*mleccha*). On this point there is some similarity with the people of Israel who conceived themselves to be "a holy people," a "chosen people," and did not feel at least initially a mission to convert other people.[27] The Greeks had a very strong feeling of superiority to the bar-

25. There exist many conflicting theories about this problem in Japan. For convenience sake I cite the explanation by Joseph M. Kitagawa under the heading "Shinto" in *Encyclopedia Britannica*, University of Chicago, 1961.

26. S. Radhakrishnan, *Eastern Religions and Western Thought*, New York, Oxford University Press, 1959, (A Galaxy Book), pp. 6–7.

27. Deuteronomy, 2, 2.

barians; Aristotle expresses the general view that the northern races are spirited, the southern races civilized, but the Greeks alone are both spirited and civilized. The national pride of the Chinese was even more assertive. The ancient Chinese regarded their country as the only civilized country. All outsiders were classified as various kinds of barbarians.[28]

4. The Compilation of the Holy Scriptures of Each Tradition

The Vedas were compiled by Brahmins. Hindus today regard them, at least nominally, as their national or traditional religious scriptures. There are four Vedas: Ṛg-Veda, Sāma-Veda, Yajur-Veda, and Atharva-Veda. The first three agree not only in their form and language, but also in content. Of the four scriptures, the Ṛg-Veda, a collection of hymns, is considered to be the oldest and most important. The Ṛg-Veda was composed in the latter half of the second millenium B.C. and its language shows indisputably that it is the oldest Indian literature which we possess. The collection is not a single work written by one author but, as in the case of the Psalms, songs composed at widely separated periods of time and later ascribed to famous personages. There probably exists no more important literary source for investigation of the mythology and religion of the Indo-European peoples than the songs of the Ṛg-Veda.

Each Veda contains Saṃhitās, Brāhmaṇas, and Upaniṣads. The Saṃhitās are collections of hymns and incantations. The Brāhmaṇas include precepts and reflections about the meaning of the hymns. The Upaniṣads deal with philosophical problems. The Āraṇyakas are inserted between the Brāhmaṇas and the Upaniṣads and, as their name implies, are intended to serve as objects of meditation for those who live in forests (*araṇya*).

Most of the scriptures of Brahmanism seem to have been compiled before the rise of Buddhism in the 6th or 5th century B.C. In China the date of the compilation of traditional scriptures seems to belong to a somewhat later period. The five books of Moses (Pentateuch, Torah), included in the Old Testament, were in existence by the 4th century B.C. It is a striking coincidence that the important holy scriptures of the great religious traditions, excepting universal religions, were compiled at nearly the same period.

Unlike the Vedic religion, the religion of the Greeks[1] was not handed down in the form of sacred books, but almost entirely through secular

28. I once noticed that in a Chinese restaurant in China Town of San Francisco western wine was designated as "brabarian wine" in Chinese characters.

1. Macdonell, *Comparative Religion, op. cit.*, pp. 93–94.

literature. Greek secular literature, however, is deeply infused with religion and religious myth. There is thus an abundance of material for the study of the history of Greek religion. It begins with the Epic poetry of Homer in the 10th or 9th century B.C., followed in the 8th and 7th by the poems of Hesiod and the so-called Homeric hymns. In fact, all the great fields of Greek literature contribute information on the subject of religion. Among later writers, Plutarch and Pausanias (180 A.D.) left valuable works, although their opinions are somewhat biased. The Early Christian Fathers also furnished us with a good deal of information. Another and important source for the history of Greek religion are the monuments of art; the high art of Greece was mainly religious, and the greatest artists worked in the service of the state. We find a similar situation in other cultural areas such as China and Japan where sacerdotalism was not strong.

The Vedic scriptures were transmitted by oral tradition alone in ancient times. This was an almost unbelievable fact to Fa-hien the Chinese pilgrim to India, who exclaimed, "Brahmins recite a hundred thousand verses from memory!"[2] Even today, although important texts are accessible in inexpensive printed editions, these scriptures are taught orally. The written text can at most be used as an aid to memory, but it has no authority. When Western scholars first wanted to publish critical editions of the Vedas, they consulted living manuscripts, whose memory was much more accurate than written manuscripts. Writing and copying were more liable to error. It was regarded as a great sin for an Indian Pandit to make even a tiny mistake in memorizing the scriptures. In ancient times we find a similar attitude as far west as Gaul, where according to Julius Caesar[3] the Druids "did not think it proper to commit their utterances on philosophy to writing. They seemed to have adopted the practice for two reasons. . . they do not wish the rule (discipline) to become common property, nor those who learn the rule to rely on writing and so neglect the cultivation of the memory; and, in fact, it does usually happen that the assistance of writing tends to relax the diligence of the student and the action of the memory."[4] The latter reason was also stressed by Plato: "This discovery of yours will create forgetfulness in the learners' souls, because they will not use their memories; they will trust to the external

2. "They convey the Vinayas from teacher to disciple by oral tradition, and they do not write them down in letters." "In Northern India there was no manuscript to be copied by me." *Biography of Fa-hien.* (*Taisho Tripiṭaka*, vol. 51, p. 864 h)
3. *De Bello Gall.* VI, 14.
4. A. C. Bouquet (ed.), in *Radhakrishnan; comparative studies in philosophy presented in honour of his sixtieth birthday.* Editorial board: W. R. Inge, A. C. Bouquet and others. London, George Allen and Unwin, 1951, p. 155.

written characters and not remember of themselves."[5] He probably meant that to put one's trust in written characters is a hindrance to that recollection that is in and of the Self.

In ancient Japan, also, orthodox history was conveyed to later generations by means of memory. The myths and rituals of Shinto were transmitted by oral tradition only, chiefly by the Nakatomi and Imbe, hereditary priestly corporations attached to the Imperial court. There were 'reciters' (kataribe) who pronounced the 'ancient words' at the coronation ceremony and on other occasions. Some myths are incorporated in the *Kojiki* ("Records of Ancient Matters"), compiled by Imperial order in 712 A.D. and the *Nihongi* or *Nihon-shoki* ("Chronicles of Japan"), completed in 720 A.D. The former is said to have been collected from oral traditions. Both are legendary histories which contain stories of the gods and their descendents down to the historical period. "The aim of these compilations was primarily to preserve the memories of ancestral times, but another motive, perhaps more important than the former, was to demonstrate the divine origin of the ruling family and other aristocrats, and also the remote antiquity of the foundation of the State."[6] Although Shinto has no concept of scripture comparable to the Bible of Christianity or the Koran of Islam, these records are an important storehouse of early Japanese myths, and they are often considered as quasi-sacred scriptures of Shinto. The prayers and rituals of Shinto were not committed to writing until the beginning of the 10th century. However, the practice of memorizing chronicles and holy texts was later discontinued in Japan, except for some short texts for recitation at ceremonies.

In India, on the other hand, the oral tradition is still alive. This fact reflects the Indian belief in the sanctity of scriptures. Radhakrishnan[7] says: "The religion of nature of the hymns, the religion of law of the Brāhmaṇas and the religion of spirit of the Upaniṣads, correspond in a very close way to the three great divisions in the Hegelian conception of the development of religion. Though at a later stage the three have existed side by side, there is no doubt that they were originally developed in successive periods. The Upaniṣads while in one sense a continuation of the Vedic worship, are in another a protest against the religion of the Brāhmaṇas." The Vedas, the chief sacred scriptures of the Hindus, register

5. *Phaedrus*, 275 a. (*The Dialogues of Plato*. Translated into English with analyses and introductions by B. Jowett, vol. 1, 3rd edition, Oxford, Clarendon Press, 1892, p. 484)
6. Masaharu Anesaki, *History of Japanese Religion with Special Reference to the Social and Moral Life of the Nation* (London: Kegan Paul, Trench, Trübner and Co., 1930), p. 87. In many passages of these two texts, Chinese influence can be discerned both in ideas and expressions.
7. S. Radhakrishnan, *Indian Philosophy* (London, George Allen and Unwin, Ltd.; New York, The Macmillan Company) vol. I, 1923, pp. 65–66.

the intuitions of perfected souls.[8] According to the Hindus the Vedas themselves are perennial. They were not composed by mortals; they are more eternal than the universe. In a similar way, a fundamental doctrine in Islam is that the Koran is "uncreated."

8. *Taittirīya-Āraṇyaka*, I, 2.

II. GODS AND MAN

1. The Gods in Ancient Mythology

In the last several decades there has been a revival in the study of comparative mythology from a variety of perspectives and disciplines. Extensive work has been done on Ancient Near Eastern, Indo-European, East Asian and archaic or pre-literate mythology by linguists, anthropologists, area specialists and historians of religion. One thinks, for example, of the work of Eliade, Lévi-Strauss, Dumézil, Wikander, Duchesne-Guillemin, etc., to name only a few. For purposes of this work it is impossible to probe into the technical problems being debated as a result of this new research. What I want to do, rather, is to characterize briefly the kind of religious experience that one finds in ancient cultural areas before the rise of philosophical reflection. I shall confine myself mainly to the mythologies of ancient India and Japan with only occasional references to other contexts.

The mythologies reflected in the Ṛg-veda and the Avesta of Iran have many points of contact—e.g., in the names of gods and other terms—indicating that both mythological systems had a common source in ancient times. "We should find the affinity in the domain of mythology much greater between the Veda and the Avesta, had not the religious reform of Zarathustra, which of course took place after the separation of the Persian and Indian branches, brought about a very considerable displacement and transformation of mythological conceptions in the Iranian religion. If we possessed Avestan literature dating from before the reform, the approximation would thus evidently have been much greater."[1] Both mythologies had a god associated with the sun (Vedic *Mitra*=Avestic *Mithra*), a deity called the 'son of waters' (Vedic *apām napāt*=Avestic *apām napāt*), and a divine being connected with *soma* (Vedic *Gandharva*=Avestic *Grandareva*). From the earliest Indian and Iranian texts it is clear that the united Indo-Iranian peoples recognized two classes of deity, the Vedic *asuras* or Avestic *ahuras*, on the one hand, and the Vedic *devas* and Avestic *daevas*

1. A. A. Macdonell, *Comparative Religion, op. cit.*, p. 60.

on the other.[2] The former were conceived initially as mighty kings, drawn through the air on their war chariots by swift steeds, benevolent in character, and almost entirely free from guile and immoral traits.[3]

The texts indicate that Vedic man's religious experience was focussed on this world. There was a correlation between the world of nature, the cosmos, and man's own communal life. People made sacrifices to the gods, and natural phenomena themselves were either deified or at almost every point closely allied with the sense of the holy or sacred. The Vedic seers delighted in sights of nature and were lost in the wonders of the phenomena of nature; to them, the wind, the rain, the sun, the stars were living realities and were inextricably a part of the spiritual life. Many of the hymns are not addressed to a sun-god, nor a moon-god, nor a fire-god, etc.; but the shining sun itself, the gleaming moon in the nocturnal sky, the fire blazing on the hearth or on the altar, or even the lightning shooting forth from the cloud were all manifestations of the holy or numinous. This spiritual interpenetration of the phenomena of nature and man's corporate life can be regarded as the earliest form of Vedic religion.

Such an attitude also characterizes early Shinto. The religion of early Japan emphasized gratitude to the beneficient forces of nature, while also to some degree appeasing the malevolent forces. These forces were indiscriminately called 'kami' which is usually translated as "gods" or "deities."

Subsequent to this stage there occurred various speculations regarding the meaning of the religious life. Vedic poets sought to penetrate the essence of natural phenomena. Poets projected their own experiences into divine images and sought to explain phenomena by causes analogous to their own experience. Natural phenomena were gradually sharpened, transformed into mythological figures, into gods and goddesses.

The worship of a god of the sun, for example, is one clear example.[4]

2. *The Concise Encyclopedia of Living Faiths*. Edited by R. C. Zaehner. New York, Hawthorn Books, Inc. 1959, p. 210.
3. A. A. Macdonell, *Comparative Religion, op. cit.*, p. 60.
4. In Egyptian mythology, "it is said in the Turin Papyrus that the Sun-God is Khepera in the morning, Ra at noon, and Atum at evening, but the distinction was never carried out consistently; an ancient text, for example, represents the rising sun as Ra and the setting sun as Khepera." James George Frazer, *The Worship of Nature*, vol. I (London: Macmillan and Co., Ltd., 1926), vol. 1, p. 559.
"The Sun-God Tum or Atum was originally the local god of Heliopolis, and in the dynastic period at all events he was held to be a form of the great Sun-God Ra and to personify the setting sun in contradiction to Khepera, the morning sun." (*Ibid.*, p. 570)
In Japan the sun god as a male deity also was conceived; Hiruko or Hiko, but the concept of the sun god as a male deity did not develop. In Ryukyu the sun was called "Tedako" as a male deity. Genchi Katō, *Shintō no Shūkyō Hattatsushi teki Kenkyū*, Tokyo, Chūbunkan, 1935, p. 38. "In Babylonia the Sun-God Shamash is always masculine, but in South Arabia his namesake Shams is feminine." (Frazer, *op. cit.*, vol. 1, p. 529) The Angami Nagas personify the sun that they regard him as female, the wife of the moon, whom they look on as a male (Frazer, *ibid.*, p. 635)

In India the sun was deified as *sūrya* (cf. Phoebus-Apollo, Sol).[5] In later Hinduism sun-worship became an important religious rite. In the Puranas, mention is made of royal families who claimed to be the descendents of the sun. The Buddha himself was said to have belonged to a family descended from the sun (ādicca-bandhu). In Japan the sun was deified as the Goddess Amaterasu-Ō-mikami (lit. the Heaven-Shining-Great-August Deity), who was worshipped as the ancestor of the Imperial Family. It was thought that the sun at midday was deified. The myth of the solar ancestry of the imperial clan was widely accepted among the various clans resident in Japan, including many clans of Chinese and Korean descent. This tendency was not lacking in India. The Sun-Goddess of Japan, however, was regarded by most Shinto believers as a real or actual historical personage, whereas the sun god of India was not. Of the Greeks it is said: "Every Greek philosopher, whatever he may have come to think in adult life, had been taught in childhood to regard the sun and moon as gods; Anaxagoras was prosecuted for impiety because he thought that they were not alive."[6]

The dawn likewise came to be extolled in the Vedas as Uṣas, a beautiful and shy maiden. In the West we have Eos, and Aurora, and we find a Japanese counterpart in the goddess Waka-hirume-no-mikoto, the deification of the rising sun. In the Vedas the moon was worshipped as Soma; in Japan moon-worship was not strongly evident, but the divine figure Tsuki-yomi-no-mikoto is pertinent.[7] The wind was worshipped in the Vedas as Vāyu or Vāta, and the storm as the Maruts. We find counterparts also in China and Japan.[8] The Vedas deified the waters as Apas. In Japan it is likely that waters themselves were not deified, but it was supported that a deity lived in them. In India the goddess of the lake, Sarasvatī, appeared at an early stage. Worship to her was adopted by Vajrayāna Buddhism,[9] and she was ultimately introduced into Japan to be adopted as a folk deity under the name of "Benten." Worship to her is still prevalent among the Japanese populace.

The names of these deities in both India and Japan, and also in many

5. Heinrich Robert Zimmer, *Philosophies of India* (New York, Pantheon Books, 1951), p. 10.
6. B. Russell, *A History of Western Philosophy,* fifth printing, (New York: Simon and Schuster, 1945), p. 204.
7. In Japanese classics the moon god was regarded as a male deity with the name of Tsukiyomi-no-otoko. (*Manyōshū*, vols. 4; 6. Genchi Kato, *Shinto no Shūkyō Hattatsushi teki Kenkyū,* Tokyo, Chūbunkan, 1935, p. 38 f.)
8. The wind also was deified in Japan, and was called Hayachi. In China he was conspicuously personified in terms of appelations as "Wind-Master" or "Flying Screen." Katō, *Shintō*, p. 26 f.
9. Even in non-Vajrayāna Buddhist literature Sarasvatī is an important figure. Cf. *Suvarṇaprabhāsa-sūtra.*

other countries[10] still indicate their origins. Many prominent figures of Ṛg-vedic mythology have proceeded from personifications of the more striking natural phenomena.[11]

There are also other figures in Vedic mythology more closely linked with the life of the community. They are honored as mighty beings, distinguished through miraculous deeds. To this group belong Indra, Varuṇa, Mitra, Viṣṇu, Pūṣan, the two Aśvins (literally horsemen, comparable to Greek diokouroi) and Rudra. The god Aditi (the Boundless), corresponding to Greek apeiron, is said to be space and air, mother, father and son. She is all comprehending.

Heaven was personified and deified as the Vedic Dyaus, and the counterpart in Greek religion was phonetically equivalent the Zeus (=Dyaus). The latter, however, was a much more complex figure, more like a human being than the Vedic Dyaus. The Ṛg-vedic poets addressed the Heavenly Father with the vocative form 'Dyauṣ pitaḥ'[12] (O Father Heaven!), which is equivalent to the Greek Zeus 'pater' and Latin 'Jupiter' (Jovis Pater=fatherly Jove). In ancient China, Heaven was the chief Deity. The Chou king called himself "Son of Heaven," and the Chou justified their conquest of the Shang dynasty on the grounds that they had received the "Mandate of Heaven" (*T'ien-ming*). They were thus mediaters between man and nature.[13] In Japanese mythology heaven was not a god but the region where the gods reside, quite different from Dyaus or Varuṇa of India or Zeus of Greece. It has an essential place in Japanese mythology however. Compared with other traditions, the worship of heaven did not develop fully in India.

The earth is called a mother in the Ṛg-veda. This was the case also in Greek religion,[14] but not in ancient Japan.[15] Heaven and Earth were

10. We can mention more parallels. For example, the Vedic god of rain, parjanya, is etymologically identical with the Lithuanian god of thunder called Perkunas. Cf. Friedrich Max Müller: *India. What can it teach us?* A Course of lectures delivered before the University of Cambridge, London, Longmans, 1910 Lecture VI, pp. 189–192. Other instances of this kind are mentioned in this work.
11. H. and H. A. Frankfort, John A. Wilson, Th. Jacobson, *Before Philosophy; the intellectual adventure of ancient man. As essay on speculative thought in the Ancient Near East.* Middlesex, 1951, (A Pelican Book), pp. 12–13.
12. *Ṛg-Veda*, VI, 51, 5, etc.
13. Edwin O. Reischauer and John K. Fairbank, *East Asia. The Great Tradition*, Boston, Houghton Mifflin Company, 1958, p. 50. Fully discussed by T'ang Chün-i (The T'ien ming [Heavenly Ordinance] in Pre-Ch'in China, *Philosophy East and West*, vol. XI, No. 4, Jan. 1962, pp. 195–218). Homer H. Dubs tries to find Theism in pre-Han China (Theism and Naturalism in Ancient Chinese Philosophy, *Philosophy East and West*, vol. IX, Nos. 3 and 4, Oct. 1959–Jan. 1960, pp. 145–162)
14. "The true Greek Goddess of the *Earth* was Gaia or Ge, whose name means nothing but the actual material earth, and is constantly used in the sense by Greek writers

often invoked together in the hymns of the Ṛg-veda in the dual as Dyāvā-pṛthivī. In Thessaly, Zeus was worshipped along with his female counterpart, Dione, but Dione was later forgotten.[16] The idea of Heaven and Earth being universal parents probably goes back to remote antiquity, for it is common to the mythology of China and of New Zealand, and can be inferred in Egyptian mythology.[17]

The fire-god,[18] Agni (cf. Latin: ignis. cf. English: Ignition) is pre-eminently the god of sacrifices in India. Fire carries the offerings from earth to the heavenly gods. It is a well-known fact that fire was esteemed in the religion of Iran, and among the Parsis. In Japan the fire-god was worshipped under the name of Kagu-tsuchi[19] (radiant father) or Ho-musubi (fire-growth). The idea of fire as all-pervading was common to both ancient India and Japan.[20] But it is difficult to identify the special feature of the fire god of the ancient Indians. Although fire was essential to the sacrifices of the Indo-European races, the god Agni, so popular in the religion of the Ṛg-veda, gradually lost his pre-eminence. A conception of fire as the fundamental principle of the universe, such as held by Heraclitus, did not occur among Hindu philosophers who sought rather a quiet and calm mental condition.

Among the many gods of the Vedic Indians, Indra was the most popular. Armed with a thunderbolt, he was believed to have killed a demon called Vṛtra. His chief and specific epithet is *Vṛtrahan*, "slayer of Vṛtra." *Indra Vṛtrahan*, the demon-slaying god Indra, appears in the

---

from the earliest to the latest times." (Frazer, *Worship of Nature, op. cit.*, vol. 1, p. 318)

15. In Japan the earth was not deified, quite different from Pṛthivi-mata of India and Gaia or Demeter of Greece which were deifications of the earth. The earth was rather regarded as the entrance to Hades (Yomi-no-kuni; i.e., the realm of darkness), a sinister place. (Katō, *Shinto, op. cit.*, p. 43 f.)
16. George Aaron Barton, *The Religions of the World*, 3rd ed. Chicago, University of Chicago Press, 1929, p. 247.
17. Izanagi and Izanami in Japanese mythology may have been the deifications of heaven and earth, but there remains no trait which definitely allow such a conjecture.
18. "Fire is an excellent example of a phenomenon worshipped *per se* without implication of a spirit in it. Even the civilized Vedic Aryans regard the actual leaping fire as a living thing swallowing oblations, while acting also as messenger to the heavenly gods. They do not pray to a spirit of fire but to fire itself conceived in priestly fashion but still phenomenal, a divine creature instinct with life and power." (W. Hopkins, *Origin and Revolution of Religion*, New Haven, Yale University Press, 1923, p. 50).
19. The Ho-musubi-no-kami is the same as the Kagutsuchi-no-kami in the *Kojiki*.
20. Fire worship in Japan is noticed in the Hi-shizume-no-matsuri-no-norito in the *Engishiki*, according to which Ho-musubi-no-kami the Fire God ruling various forms of fire, (cf. the Vedic Vaiśvānara Agni) was not clearly distinguished from the physical fire perceivable by senses (cf. the Vedic Agni). (Katō, *Shinto*, p. 24 f.) (*Engishiki*, vol. 8, *Kokushi Taikei*, vol. 13, p. 271). Fire worship also existed among the Ainus. (Katō, *op. cit.*, p. 1002 f.)

Avesta in the altered capacity of the demon Indra and as a god of victory *Vərəthragna* (a change doubtless caused by the mythological dislocation produced by Zarathustra's religious reform). Many scholars think that Indra was originally a god of the thunderstorm, and that the mountains in which the waters are enclosed represent the clouds. Vṛtra—the demon of drought—was thought to keep the waters imprisoned.[21] Many hymns in the Vedas are addressed to Indra. Since the Vedic Aryans were still violently fighting and struggling with the aborigines, Indra is represented as a thoroughly warlike god. His enormous strength and combativeness are described again and again. The Vedic singers were especially fond of relating the battles of Indra with the demons, whom he destroys with his thunderbolt. Heaven and earth tremble when Indra slays Vṛtra. He does not destroy the dragon only once, but repeatedly, and he is asked always to kill Vṛtra in the future to release the waters. He should be regarded as a counterpart of the Teutonic Thunar, who swings the thunder-hammer Mjolnir.

The warlike Indra was, in the earliest times, undoubtedly a king among gods. He corresponds to Zeus[22] of the Greek Olympus, or Jupiter of the Romans concerning his being the lord of gods.[23] The features of Zeus were very similar to those of Indra,[24] and yet he has one feature that was lacking in Indra: Zeus acts as the righteous Judge. This feature is also missing in Japanese mythology. It is said that the gods of Japanese mythology do not judge. It is a feature which has played a large role in the legal thought of East Asian countries. (One exception is Yama, who was the ruler of the dead in Vedic mythology. In the Great Epics he became the judge of the dead. This figure was introduced into Chinese Taoism, and then into Japanese popular belief. He is called "enma,"

21. Recently a new theory has been set forth that *vṛtra* means a dam, the myth representing the historical fact that the dams constructed by the people of the Indus civilization were destroyed by the Aryan invaders. (Damodar Dharmanand Kosambi, *An Introduction to the Study of Indian History*. Bombay, Popular Book Depot, 1956). But to prove this theory the word *vərəthra* in the Avesta also would have to be similarly explained.
22. "Zeus, the mighty lord, holding the reins of a winged chariot, leads the way in heaven, ordering all and taking care of all; and there follows him the array of gods and demi-gods, marshalled in eleven bands." (Plato, *Phaedrus*, 246–247. Jowett's translation, 3rd ed. Oxford University Press, Humphrey Milford, 1892, vol. 1, p. 453) This exactly corresponds to the figure of Indra in the *Ṛg-veda*.
23. Formerly P. Deussen made the following supposition: Generally speaking, the shift of the position of the main god corresponds to the difference of cultural periods: In the period of invasion the god of heaven (Ouranos, Dyaus), in the period of settlement the god of order (Varuṇa, Chronos) and in the period of rule by heroes the god of power (Indra, Zues) are most important. (Paul Deussen, *Allgemeine Geschichte der Philosophie* I, Vierte Auflage, Leipzig, F. A. Brockhaus, 1920, S. 83)
24. Macdonell, *Comparative Religion*, p. 95.

the Japanese translitaration of the Sanskrit word "Yama." But in China and Japan he was regarded as somewhat alien to the common people in general.)

In Japanese mythology some counterparts to Indra can be found, e.g., the god of thunder, 'Narukami,' etc. The storm-god Susano-wo-no-mikoto[25] killed an eight-headed dragon with a miraculous sword, which is said to have been transmitted by the Imperial Family as a symbol of sovereignty. His strong and occasionally outrageous character is quite similar to that of Indra. However, where Indra is completely a god, Susano-wo-no-mikoto is god and man simultaneously, and appears in a *historical setting* as a relative of the ancestor of the Japanese imperial family.

Among the above-mentioned gods of the Vedic religion, the gods of productivity or fertility cannot be clearly discerned. On the other hand, gods of that genre were conspicuous in early Shintoism. The god of growth (Musubi) is a personification of an abstract quality of generation. Taji-kara-no-wo (the male of the hand-strength) is a human quality personified and raised to divine rank.

The Vedic pantheon sometimes was called "all the gods" (Viśve Devāḥ). On one occasion "all the gods" were numbered at 3339, reflecting the three spheres of the world: the earth, the air and the sky.[26] In ancient Japan there was a similar notion of "myriads of gods" (literary 'eight million gods,' Yao-yorozu-no-kami-gami). The number of Shinto deities constantly fluctuates. Some are forgotten and later re-established under new names; or again, wholly new gods are added to the pantheon. The characters of these myriad gods are ill-defined. Analogous to the division between the Olympian gods and the mystery gods in Greek mythology, however, a division was made between the children of the Storm-god and the deities associated with the Sun-goddess (*Ama-terasu-Ō-mi-kami*). In Japanese mythology the "realm of the visible" belongs to the latter and "the domain of the invisible" to the former.

The gods[27] of the Ṛg-veda were invited as guests to feast on oblations. They took food and drank wine; they were invoked, flattered, propitiated,

25. Susano-wo-no-mikoto was a deification of storm like Greek Pallas Athene, Babylonian Rimmon, or Vedic Indra. (Katō, *Shinto*, p. 45 f.) The Japanese classics the rain god is called Kura-okami, Taka-okami or Mizuha-no-me in classics. Okami means 'serpent god.' (Katō, *Shinto*, p. 47 f.) The thunder-god is found in the figure of Narukami (lit. thundering god). (*Mannyōshū*, vol. 8.) (cf. Katō, *Shinto*, p. 30 f.) Later the thunder god was called Takatsu-kami or Kandoki-no-kami (in *Engishiki*, 8 and 3, *Kokushi Taikei* 13, pp. 269; 134; 108). In some Japanese shrines the thunder god was worshipped for ample harvest like the German Thor. (Katō, *Shinto*, p. 47 f.) With the advent of Buddhism the worship of Indra was introduced into Shintoism at Tenman. In Tenmangū shrines, Indra was conjured too.
26. *Ṛg-veda*, III, 9, 9.
27. In other languages, *daeva*, *tivar*, *diewas*, *dia*. (P. Deussen, *Geschichte*, *op. cit.*, I, p. 39)

and pleased. Men had direct communion with gods without any mediation; the gods were looked upon as intimate friends of their worshippers. They were addressed with such phrases as 'Father Heaven,' 'Mother Earth,' 'brother Angi.' There was a very intimate personal relationship between men and gods, and every daily phenomenon was regarded as dependent on the gods. In like manner, Japanese villagers sometimes prayed to individual deities, sometimes to special categories of deities, and sometimes to the gods generally. The prayers comprised petitions for rain, for good harvests, for protection from earthquake and conflagration, for children, for health and long life to the sovereign, and for peace and prosperity in the nation.[28] To some extent the physical aspect of the Ṛg-vedic gods is anthropomorphic just as that of the Greek gods; head, face, eyes, arms, hands, feet, and other portions of the human frame are ascribed to them; yet their forms are often shadowy and their limbs or parts are often simply meant figuratively to describe their activities. Thus the tongue and limbs of the fire-god are merely his flames; the arms of the sun-god are simply his rays, while his eye represents the solar orb.[29] The gods were not always moral in their character. They often shared human weakness and were easily pleased by flattery. They conferred benefit in exchange for oblation offered to them. In one hymn the gods discuss what they should give. "This is what I will do—not that, I will give him a cow or shall it be a horse? I wonder if I have really had Soma wine from him."[30] A simple law of give and take prevails.

In the Homeric religion we find the gods arranged in a hierarchy, organized as a divine family under a supreme god.[31] Like the Vedic gods they are personal, but they are not vague and indefinite beings; they are concrete and individual deities of robust and sharply defined personality.[32] They are not spirits, but immortal beings of superhuman body and soul, conceived as glorified men.[33] Such an elaborate hierarchy of gods with specific personalities is quite different from the Vedic conception of the gods. One might suspect that the Vedic gods represent an earlier phase of the development of mythology, but the individual character of each Vedic or Hindu god was not clear even in later periods. The difference

28. *ERE*, XV, p. 468.
29. Macdonell, *Sanskrit Literature, op. cit.*, pp. 71–72.
30. Hermann Oldenberg, *Ancient India: Its language and religions*. Chicago, London, Open Court Publishing Company, 1896, p. 71.
31. Jane Ellen Harrison, *Themis*. A Study of the social origins of Greek religion. Cleveland and New York, The World Publishing Company. Meridian Books, 1962, p. 134.
32. Sophocles, *Oedipus Coloneus*, mentioned in S. Radhakrishnan, *Eastern Religions and Western Thought* (New York: Oxford University Press, 1959. A Galaxy Book), pp. 4–5.
33. Macdonell, *Comparative Religion, op. cit.*, p. 94.

was not that of stage of development, but rather that of the nature of the respective conceptions of god. The gods in Indian myths had little personality, and ultimately orthodox Hindu thinkers came to deny all individuality to the gods. For example, Indra, who received much respect in the Ṛg-veda, came to be regarded as only a common name—i.e., a godly being who occupies that position is called by the name of 'Indra.' He was not an individual person.[34] In connection with the problem of the individuality of the gods, we may point out that before the rise of Buddhism, Brahmanism had no idols. Indian art can be traced chiefly from the time of the Maurya Dynasty, when Buddhism flourished.

Shintoism, also, had practically no idols, not because the ancient Japanese were especially enlightened, but because they had no high art before sculpture and painting were introduced from China and because they only very feebly assigned an individual character to each god. It was after the introduction of Buddhism that Japanese art flourished.

In Japan, it was consciously asserted in later periods that everything in the natural world is divine. Kitabatake Chikafusa (1293–1354) states: "Our land is the creation of the two deities, male and female. Even its mountains and rivers, trees and plants all have divine names. The mountain deity is Oyama-tsumi, the deity of the waters is Mizahanome, the deity of the sea is Wadatsumi-no-mikoto, the deity of ports is Haya-akitsuhi-no-mikoto, the earth deity is Haniyasu, the fire deity is Kagutsuchi and the wind deity is Shinatobe-no-mikoto. There is not the least particle anywhere that is not divine. How wondrous it is that everything that can be touched, heard or seen partakes of the divine nature. How much more then when we look up to the sky, the sun deity that illuminates the day is Ō-hirume-muchi-no-mikoto, the ancestral sovereign of our Imperial Family, while the moon that brightens the night is Tsuki-yomi-no-mikoto, and Shinatobe-no-mikoto is the wind deity who blows away all impurity. And the precious breath of man which is his breath of life is this deity. Therefore he must not abuse it."[35] Motoori Norinaga, the great early modern Shinto theologian, states: "The term *kami* is applied in the first place to the various deities of Heaven and Earth who are mentioned in the ancient records, as well as to their spirits (*mi-tama*) which reside in the shrines where they are worshipped. Moreover, not only human beings, but birds, beasts, plants and trees, seas and mountains, and all other things whatsoever which deserve to be dreaded and revered for the extraordinary and pre-eminent powers which they possess, are called *kami.* They need not be eminent for surpassing nobleness, godness, or service-

34. Śaṅkara ad *Brahmasūtrabhāṣya* I, 3, 28. (Ānadāśrama Sanskrit Series, No. 21. Poona, Anandasrama Press, 1900) Cf. Richard Garbe, *The Philosophy of Ancient India,* Chicago, The Open Court, 1897, p. 36.

35. *Jinnō-shōtō-ki,* vol. 1. Interpretation by Genchi Katō.

ableness alone. Malignant and uncanny beings are also called *kami*, if only they are the objects of general dread. Among *kami* who are human beings I need hardly mention Mikados. . . . Amongst others there are thunder (in Japanese *Naru kami* or the Sounding God); the dragon, the echo (called in Japanese, *Kodama*, or the Tree-spirit), and the fox, who are *kami* by reason of their uncanny and fanciful natures. The term *kami* is applied in the *Nihongi* and *Manyōshū*, a collection of ancient poetry, to the tiger and wolf. Izanagi gave to the fruit of the peach, and to the jewels round his neck, names which implied that they were *kami*. . . . There are many cases of seas and mountains being called *kami*. It is not their spirits which are meant. The word was applied directly to the seas or mountains themselves, as being very awful things."[36]

Another feature characteristic of Shintoism is the fact that many Japanese gods are regarded as historical and human beings of superior quality. To the ancient Japanese the mythical world and the natural world interpenetrated one another to the extent that human activities were explained and sanctioned in terms of what *kami*, ancestors or heroes, did in primordial time. The whole of human life and the cosmos was accepted as sacred, being permeated as it is by the *kami* nature.

2. Principles and Efficacy of Rituals

It is known that even in the prehistoric period when the Indo-Aryans and the Persians formed a single people, they performed sacrifices (Vedic *yajña*: Avestic *yasna*), and that they already had a sacred drink (Vedic *soma*: Avestic *haoma*), i.e., the intoxicating juice of the Soma plant which was offered as the main oblation. Many rituals can be traced back to the period of the early Indo-Europeans. For example, "elements and even whole complexes of the marriage ritual are found to be identical in ancient India, Rome, Lithuania and among the pre-Christian Germans. The ritual as a whole is among the most persistent and the oldest traditions of the Indo-European speaking peoples, older than any of their recorded myths and far older than Vedic times."[1]

The Vedic religion was an enormous system of rituals, some of which can be traced back to the days of the Proto-Indo-Europeans. The sacrifices were made in the open air or in a shed erected for the purpose near the house of the sacrificer. There was no set altar place nor any temple; an

36. Translated by W. E. Aston, *ERE*, XI, p. 463.
1. Daniel H. H. Ingalls in *Journal of the American Oriental Society*, vol. 77, 1957, p. 22. Cf. M. Winternitz, *A History of Indian Literature*, Calcutta, University of Calcutta Press, vol. 1, 1927, pp. 272–275.

altar was chosen for each rite. In the Ṛg-vedic tradition, the altar was strewn with sacred grass, in order that the gods might come and sit down on it. Upon the altar oblations were laid; and there the sacred fires were prepared. The chief oblations were milk, melted butter, grain, and cakes. The main priest (adhvaryu) shed these offerings on the fire while muttering his formulas. At certain points in the ceremonies the sacrificer priest (hotṛ) recited hymns.

Many of these features also appear in Shintoism, the ancient Japanese religion which existed before the introduction of Buddhism. In the Shinto rites of Japan, offerings such as rice, salt, sake (wine), meats, fish, fruit, vegetables, etc., and also clothing were put on the altar. Priests uttered various prayers (norito).

In the Soma-sacrifices of India the priests gathered the twigs of the soma plant, pressed the juice with two stones, purified it by a sieve, mixed it with milk, and then poured it into basins and set it out on the altar for the gods to drink. Animal sacrifices accompanied both the fire-oblations and the soma-rites. The animals—the goat, the ox, the cow, the ram, or the horse—were killed and cut up according to rule and pieces were laid out on the altar, while certain parts were burned in the fire. The flesh was divided between the sacrificer and the priests.[2]

The Soma-sacrifice reminds us of the rites of Bacchus in Greece and, in fact, we can find much similarity with Homeric religion. The ritual of the altar consisted in offering to the deity an animal victim or a gift of fruits and cereals. The sacrifice might be accompanied with wine or be wineless. The ritual ". . . consists of prayer accompanied by the sprinkling of the grain, followed by animal burnt offerings. Part of the flesh is tasted by the worshippers and then made over, by burning, to the gods. The rest is eaten as a banquet with abundance of wine."[3] The Greeks also had a fire cult, and they placed importance on commensality.[4] Similarly, the Shang people of ancient China made frequent sacrifices to the spirits. Usually animals were used, but sometimes liquor, probably a sort of beer, was poured on the ground in libation. Sacrifices were made to the earth and the wind and to various rather vague nature deities, as well as to the cardinal points.[5]

Despite these similarities we, of course, find differences in the social contexts in which these religions functioned. From about 700 B.C. the

2. John Nicol Farquhar, *An Outline of the Religious Literature of India* (London: Oxford University Press, 1920), p. 14.
3. Martin P. Nilsson, *Greek Folk Religion* (New York, Harper and Brothers, 1961), p. 105.
4. Jane Ellen Harrison, *Themis*. A Study of the social origins of Greek Religion. Cleveland and New York, the World Publishing Company. Meridian Books, 1962, pp. 133–139.
5. Reischauer and Fairbank, *East Asia, the Great Tradition*, p. 46.

oracle of the god Apollo at Delphi became the main nexus and the strongest bond of spiritual unity in the Greek world. But in the Vedic religion there was no special holy place. In Hinduism there existed many holy places (*tīrtha*) visited by pilgrims, but there was no central coordination.

This lack of unity among the Hindus does not mean, however, that there did not exist social control or restriction by religious proscription. In early village communities the secular and the sacred were but little distinguished. In ancient India the dharma-sutras, which prescribed social institutions, was nothing but one branch of the science of rituals (kalpa), which was one of the six subsidiary sciences (Vedāṅga) of the Veda. Social institutions were regarded as part of ritualism. There is a counterpart to this in ancient Japan. The early Japanese word for 'political administration' or 'governing,' *matsurigoto*, literally means "a matter of sacrifice," or "religious rites"; and *miya* means both "palace" and "shrine." Hirata Atsutane, the famous Shintoist theologian, states: "The worship of the gods in the source of Government, nay, it is Government." Sacerdotal knowledge included the lore about society and politics.

In his life-cycle every Hindu had to receive the twelve sacraments (saṃskāra), form the moment he was conceived in the womb until the time of his death. The Hindu sacraments are roughly similar to the sacraments of the Roman Catholic Church. Baptism is the Western counterpart of the Hindu birth-ceremony (*jāta-karman*), the fourth samskara. Corresponding to the giving of a Christian name to the baby, in Hinduism there is the sacrament of Name-giving (*nāma-karaṇa*). The Western rite of confirmation might correspond to carrying out (*niṣkramaṇa*), the sixth sacrament, and also to the Japanese custom of Miyamairi (Paying homage to a shrine). Marriage is a sacrament for both Catholics and Hindus.[6]

In the Brahmana literature enormous importance is sacribed to the sacrifice. A crowd of priests conducted a large and complicated system of ceremonies to which symbolical significance was attached. In the Brāhmaṇas the Brahmins may be seen as being not so much devout priests who served the gods by earnestly petitioning them, but as magicians who compelled and drove the gods by magical power. The Brahmins in India came to think that there was a close relationship between sacrifices and the course of natural events. Sacrifices not only symbolized and imitated various aspects of nature but also were regarded as being able to change the very course of nature. For example, it is stated: "As people perform the fire-sacrifice every morning, therefore, the sun rises effulgent. On the contrary, if they don't perform it, the sun would never rise."[7]

In ancient China a somewhat similar ideology was set forth by orthodox Confucianists which might be called a sort of "cosmophysiology,"

6. Cf. *Manu*, II, 27, f.
7. *ŚBr.*, II, 3, 1, 5.

according to which the microcosm and the macrocosm are established on the same pattern. In India this type of thought can be traced from the Atharva-Veda up to the Tantrism of later periods.[8] According to the Indian sacerdotalists, they could control every phenomenon in the universe by practicing sacrifices correctly. The sacrifice itself was omnipotent; even gods were bound by the miraculous power embodied therein. They thought that if people invoked gods by following the right rules of sacrifices, the gods were compelled to confer grace. The relation of a god and a votary was that of "give and take." "He offers a sacrifice to the gods with the text" 'Do thou give to me and I will give to thee; do thou bestow on me and I will bestow on thee!'[9] The religion of the Brahmanas eventually disappeared in the soulless mechanism of rites and the pedantries of formalism. By practicing sacrifices they sought to achieve specific aims, i.e., abundant harvests, good and healthy children, increase of cattle, recovery from sickness, social fame, etc. The Brahmins became strongly this-worldly.

In Greece we can find a definition of happiness attributed to Solon and approved by Herodotus (484?–425 B.C.): "He is whole of limb, a stranger to disease, free from misfortune, happy in his children and comely to look upon. If in addition to all this he ends his life well, he is of a truth the man of whom thou art in search, the man who may rightly be termed happy."[10] Solon prays to the Muses: "Let me at all times obtain good fortune from the blessed gods and enjoy honorable repute among men." Techomachus in the Economics of Xenophon (c. 434–c. 355 B.C.) reckons among subjects of prayer "health, bodily strength, good repute in the city, kindly relation with friends, safety in war, increase of wealth."

We do not find any one definite view about the future life in the Brahmanas. Rebirth on earth was sometimes looked upon as a blessing and not as an evil which was to be escaped from. But the most dominant view was that the practice of sacrifices promised man immortality in heaven, the abode of the gods, or at least longevity. "He who sacrifices thus obtains perpetual prosperity and renown and conquers for himself a union with the two gods; i.e., the Sun God (Āditya) and the Fire God (Agni) and an abode in the same sphere."[11] However, other passages in

8. J. Przyluski and M. Falk, "Aspects d'une ancienne psycho-physiologies dans l'Inde et en Extreme-Orient," *Bulletin of the School of Oriental Studies*, University of London, 1938, pp. 223–288.

9. *Vājasaneyi-Saṃhitā*, III, 50; cf. *ŚBr.*, II, 5, 3, 19.

10. 1–32, Herodotus, *History*. A new English version, edited with copious notes and appendices, by George Rawlinson assisted by Henry Rawlinson, and J. G. Wilkinson. New ed. London, J. Murray, 1862, p. 142.

11. *ŚBr.*, XI, 6, 2, 5.

the Brahmanas which are relevant to the problem of future life are inconsistent.

Sin was regarded as alienation from the gods.[12] But there were moral sins as well as ritual sins.[13] Consciousness of sin called for propitiatory sacrifices and penances (prāyaścitta) especially to Varuṇa, the god most feared by the Indians of the period of the Brahmanas. Concerning the general characteristic of the religion of the Brahmanas it has been said that "the age was, on the whole, one of Pharisaism, in which people were more anxious about the completion of their sacrifices than the perfection of their souls."[14]

Corresponding to the prāyaścitta, the ceremony of 'Great Purification' (Oharai) was performed in Shintoism twice a year in order to absolve offenses against the gods. The offenses enumerated and incest (within narrow limits or relationship), bestiality, wounding, and certain interferences with agricultural operations. It is apparent that the concept of sin in Japanese Shintoism was quite concrete. A person wanting to be purified, for example, might have a small piece of paper shaped in his image floated down a river to carry his sin away, as a type of scapegoat. The Shinto concept of sin appears to correspond quite closely to that found in the Brāhmaṇas.

3. Man's Destiny

a. After-life

The early Indo-Aryans enjoyed worldly life. Their view of the world was not tainted by a sense of gloom, and they showed no great concern about the future of the soul. They wished for themselves and their posterity a life of a hundred autumns.[1] They had merely vague conceptions about heaven or hell. They were convinced, however, that death was not absolute. They believed that the soul survived after the body, which enclosed it, had passed away. The good and brave and generous were to enjoy a new life of happiness into which the soul of the deceased was transferred after death. It was believed that the soul of the good passed after death into Yama's heaven of light where they lead a blissful life in the company of the Fathers (*pitaraḥ*).[2] The kingdom of the dead is in the heavens and

12. *Ṛg-veda*, VII, 86, 6; cf. VII, 88, 5; 6.
13. *Ṛg-veda*, I, 23, 22; I, 85.
14. S. Radhakrishnan, *Indian Philosophy*, *op. cit.*, vol. 1, p. 136.
1. *Ṛg-veda*, X, 18.
2. *Ṛg-veda*, X, 14, 10.

the dying man is comforted by the belief that after death he will live with King Yama in the highest heaven. A ruler of the dead, the Vedic Yama, son of Vivasvat, corresponds to the Avestic Yima, son of Vivahvant, ruler of Paradise.

Yama and Yamī, his sister, were the first mortals who entered the other world to rule over it. In the abode of Yama, the fathers, i.e., the dead live an immortal life revelling with Yama: the joys of heaven are those of earth perfected and heightened. The Aryans looked for an immortal life of sensual bliss.[3] They believed in the possibility of meeting their ancestors in the kingdom of Yama[4] and in this life they worshipped and showed much concern about the ghosts of departed ancestors.

In Japan, the ancient myths frequently mention a land of Yomi or darkness as the abode of the head. Several of the gods are said to have gone their at death, but there is little to show that the ancient Japanese in general believed in a future state of existence.[5] The Chinese likewise seem to have only a vague conception of retribution of good and evil in the future. There was neither heaven in the sense of a paradise, nor hell in the sense of a paradise, nor hell in the sense of a place of final judgment.

In the Ṛg-veda it seems to be the destiny of the wicked to fall and disappear into the dark depths. Varuṇa was said to thrust the evil-doer down into the dark abyss from which none ever return. The gods appeal to Indra to consign to the lower darkness the man who injures his worshipper.[6] There was as yet no trace to be found of the belief in transmigration, which was so predominant in the philosophical thought of later Indians. Concerning the eschatology of the Ṛg-veda, one scholar states: "In their most essential elements these ideas of the future life were not only Vedic, they were the common inheritance of the "seven" Aryan races; they were retained among the Persians in a form strengthened, no doubt, and altered along the same lines, but very little modified by opposing conceptions. And when we find that the oldest Hebrew books show little trace of that belief in an immortal future life which became very common among the Jews after captivity in Mesopotamia, and that no other Semitic tribe seems to have originated the idea, the question springs spontaneously to one's mind, whether we have not met in these Aryan beliefs with the foundation-stone of a far-spreading edifice, of that all-powerful belief in

3. *Ṛg-veda,* IX, 113, 7–11; *Atharva-veda,* IV, 34, 2–4 and other passages, quoted in J. Muir's *Original Sanskrit Texts* (Reprint Amsterdam: Oriental Press, 1967), vol. V, p. 306 f.
4. *Ṛg-veda,* I, 24, 1; VII, 56, 24.
5. *Kojiki-den,* vol. 2. (*Motoori Norinaga Zenshū,* edited by Hoei Motoori, vol. 1, p. 150) His interpretation was inherited by Hirata Atsutane, his disciple in his work, *Kodō Taii* (*Hirata Atsutane Zenshū,* edited by Mannen Ueda Tokyo: Naigai Shoseki Co., 1932, vol. 7, p. 37)
6. *Ṛg-veda,* X. 132, 4; IV, 5, 5; IX, 73, 8; X, 152, 4.

the immortality of the soul which has played so mighty a part in the influences which have shaped the Europe of today."[7]

b. Ancestor-Worship

WANDERING nomads or cattle-raising people rarely practice ancestor-worship. But where settled habitation occurs and where lands are inherited by descendants, the custom of ancestor-worship is often found and its rituals are usually developed into a detailed and elaborate form.

In India, ancestral spirits (*pitaras*) were worshipped and propitiated. They were addressed by hymns[1] composed in the last stage of the period associated with the Ṛg-Veda. The lord of these ancestral spirits in Yama. He rules in the kingdom of the deceased, high up in the highest heaven. In origin he is identical with Yima who in the Avesta is the first human being, the primeval ancestor of the human race. As the first departed, he became the king in the realm of the dead.

The Pitṛs, the departed ancestors, occupied an important place in the life of the Hindus. Sacrifice to the manes (*pitṛyajna*) was the most important duty of the householder. In the Vedic hymns the Pitṛs were regarded as the companions of the gods and were invoked together with the gods.[2] They live in the highest heaven with the gods. They receive prayers and oblations as their food. Sacrifice is offered in the hope that they will intercede for and protect their votaries. They have the power to injure their descendants for any sin committed against them. They are capable of giving wealth, offspring, and long life to the sons who follow their way. The blessings of the fathers (*pitṛyajna*) are regarded as more important than the way of the gods (*devayāna*).

Sacrifice to the manes figures even more prominently in the Hindu social and religious life of later times. It had to be performed regularly not only in the appointed season of the year but also at the time of important social ceremonies such as investiture with the sacred thread, marriage, etc. Without imploring the favor of the manes, one could not fulfill any of these family duties properly. The importance attached to ancestor-worship (*pitṛyajna*) in ancient times is still maintained in Hindu life today.[3]

As is well known, the manes occupied a large place in early Chinese religion. Next to Heaven, the influence of the manes was considered as

7. T. W. Rhys Davids, *Lectures on the origin and growth of religion as illustrated by some points in the history of Indian Buddhism* (2nd ed., London, Williams and Norgate, 1891), pp. 16–17.

1. *Ṛg-veda*, X, 15, 54.
2. *Ṛg-veda*, X, 15.
3. Based upon Prabodh Chandra Bagchi, *India and China*, a thousand years of cultural relations, 2nd ed. Bombay, Hind Kitabs, 1950, pp. 183–184.

most important in shaping the future. Sacrifices were offered periodically to please the departed ancestors so that their children could expect to attain prosperity, longevity, happiness, peace, etc. The ancestral way was considered as the "straight road" to be followed by their descendants.

Much information about sacrifice to the manes is found in the ancient odes preserved in the Shih-Ching: "Ah, the glorious ancestors. Endless their blessings, boundless their gifts are extended; to you too, their needs must reach. We have brought them clear wine; they will give victory. Here too is soup well seasoned, well prepared, well mixed. . . . The charge put upon us is vast and mighty, from heaven dropped our prosperity, good harvests, great abundance. They come, they accept, they send down blessings numberless."[4]

Thus it was not merely for long life and prosperity that sacrifices had to be offered to the ancestors; good harvest also depended on their kindness. They had to be offered all the best things available; the first fruits, good food and drink, the best animal for sacrifice, etc. Some data concerning the procedures for sacrifices are available in the *Odes*. We are told that one person while sacrificing to his ancestors presented cucumbers, and the hair, the blood and the fat of an ox killed for the occasion. He offered perfumed wine as libation. The hair of the animal was offered to prove that the animal was pure. Its blood was offered to show that the animal had been really killed. The libations of scented wine were given so that its smell could attract the ancestors to the sacrificial place.[5]

In the China of the Shang dynasty one important deity was called *Ti* or *Shang Ti* (Supreme Ti). Probably Shang Ti represents merely a "first ancestor." Traditional Chinese ancestor-worship seems to date back to these early times. Many of the inquiries on the oracle bones concern the aid or harm of an ancestor to his living descendants.[6] In the Chou dynasty the chief ceremonial activities of the state centered around the ancestral temple of the kings. Sacrifices were also made to the supposed founder of the ruling house, Hou Chi, or "Millet Ruler," who was obviously an agricultural deity.[7] The data concerning ancestor-worship of ancient China (before Confucius) however is related mostly to the ruling class; the practice among common people is not clear. It is only in later days that ancestor-worship among people came to be noticed.

In Japan, the worship of ancestors is not clearly discernible in early Shintoism. Only the *uji-gami* cult is something which might be comparable to it. Japanese methology identified many of the deities with progenitors of the *uji* (clan) and in time other mythological or historical figures

4. *Ode*, No. 204, translated by Arthur Waley.
5. P. C. Bagchi, *India and China*, p. 183.
6. Reischauer and Fairbank, *East Asia*, pp. 46–47.
7. *Ibid.*, p. 50.

jointed their rank. Later, ancestor-worship became popular among the populace; it has become well known as a practice characteristic of the Japanese.[8] In ancient times the local chieftainships and the offices of the central government were hereditary in certain families. The result was that the official designation of positions held by families came to be equivalent to family names. These families or clans each had its special deity, called *ujigami*, or "surname-deity," for whose worship family members convened from time to time.

There is insufficient evidence to prove that ancestor-worship existed in Homer's time, but it seems that the custom of worshipping a hero or the mortal ancestor of the state occurred. The earliest evidence we have of this custom dates from about 700 B.C., but there are strong reasons for believing that the cult of hero-ancestors was already a part of the pre-Homeric religion. Elaborate attendance upon the dead is attested of the Mycenaean period by the graves discovered at Tiryns and Mycenae. But Homer seems to ignore deliberately their divine or semidivine character.[9] In the period in which the Hellenic spirit acquired its definite instincts and bias (c. 900–500 B.C.) the custom of worshipping the hero or the mortal ancestor of the state (or, the tribe, clan) was clearly established.

4. Cosmic Law

THE conception of cosmic and ritual order, of natural and moral law had already been formed when the Indo-Aryans and the Iranians formed a single people (Vedic *ṛta*=Avestic *aša*). When the Vedic singer extols a god in song, he does not look up to the god with that shuddering awe and faith with which the Psalmist looks up to Yahweh. The Vedic poets stood on a more familiar footing with the gods whom they honoured in songs; they invoked gods in an almost fawning manner. When they sang a song of

8. ". . . Foremost among the moral sentiments of Shinto is that of loving gratitude to the past, — a sentiment having no real correspondence in our own emotional life. We know our past better than the Japanese know theirs; — we have myriads of books recording or considering its very incident and condition: but we cannot in any sense be said to love it or to feel grateful to it. Critical recognitions of its merits and of its defects; — some rare enthusiasms excited by its beauties; many strong denunciations of its mistakes: these represent the sum of our thoughts and feelings about it. The attitude of our scholarship in reviewing it is necessarily cold; that of our art, often more than generous; that of our religion, condemnatory for the most part." (Lafcadio Hearn, *Some Thoughts about Ancestor-Worship*) To most Japanese the English idiomatic expression: "to do honor to the memory of our ancestors" is very difficult to understand. Ancestors are not mere memory, but they are still alive (!) to most Japanese.

9. *ERE*, VI, 398 b.

praise to a god, they expected him to present them with wealth in hero-sons, cows, food, etc.

One exception, however, is the god Varuṇa. He is conceived as the king of all, both gods and men, the universal monarch. He sends the dawn, makes the sun cross the sky, and causes the rains. He is the upholder of both the physical and the moral orders. He is the great lord of the laws of nature. He established heaven and earth. He dwells in all the worlds. He is the guardian of the whole world and supporter of the earth and the heaven. By Varuṇa's ordinances the moon and the stars move and shine. He regulates the seasons and the months, and also the waters that bring prosperity to the earth. Varuṇa concerns himself more with the moral ways of men than any other god. His anger is roused by sin, the infringement of his ordinances. He punishes sinners severely. He is an ominiscient god and a constant witness of men's truth and falsehood. No creature can do, think, or devise anything without his being noticed, so great and so powerful is Varuṇa.

Varuṇa's order is called cosmic law (*ṛta*).[1] He is the chief guardian of this order. He does not allow anybody, neither god nor man, to infringe upon it. The gods were the upholders of the cosmic law (*ṛta*). They protected the good and punished the wicked. The Indian poets ventured to approach Varuṇa only with trembling and fear, in humble reverence. They approach him contritely and plead for forgiveness of their sins. Varuṇa is the only god who stands nobly elevated above mortals. The following verses addressed to Vuruṇa, can be compared with the poetry of the Psalms:

"Sing forth a hymn sublime and solemn, grateful to glorious Varuṇa, imperial ruler.
Who hath, like one who slays a victim, laid out the earth as a skin to spread in front of the Sun-God (Sūrya).
In the tree tops, he has extended the air, put milk in kine and vigorous speed in horses,
Set intellect in hearts, fire in waters, the Sun-God (Sūrya) in heaven and Soma (plant) on the mountain. . . .
If we, as gamesters cheat at play, have cheated, done wrong unwittingly or sinned of purpose,
Cast all these sins away like loosened fetters, and, O Varuṇa, let us be thine own beloved."[2]

This highly ethical god Varuṇa corresponds to the Avestic Ahura

1. In Egypt the Truth and Righteousness was personified as goddess *Ma at,* the daughter of *Ra* and the wife of *Dhuti,* god of intelligence. This can compared to *ṛta.* (Cf. John B. Noss, *Man's Religions,* New York, Macmillan, 1956, p. 52.)
2. *Ṛg-veda,* V. 85.

Mazda, the 'wise spirit,' who is parallel in character, though not in name. Some characteristics of Varuṇa, however, were such as would not fit in with the frame work of the Iranian religion. In Varuṇa there is a quality predominantly 'nocturnal,' which made possible his assimilation to the demon 'Vṛtra'.[3] Further, Varuṇa was also a god of mercy; he is merciful to the penitent. "There is no hymn addressed to Varuṇa that does not contain a prayer for forgiveness of guilt. The element of divine mercy thus finds a place in the Vedic religion, but was excluded in the Avestic system owing to the juristic character of that religion."[4]

As mentioned above, the cosmic law is called *asa* in the Zend-Avesta, which is of the same etymological origin as *ṛta*. In the qualities of the god Varuṇa we find the Vedic conception of cosmic or moral law (*ṛta*). It is the law which pervades the whole world, which not only men but even gods must obey. It furnishes us with the standard of morality. The ways of life of good men who follow the path of *ṛta* is called *vrata*.[5] To the Ṛg-vedic people the universe was an ordered whole. This notion was shared by the Greeks: "Philosophers tell us that communion and friendship and orderliness and temperance and justice bind together heaven and earth and gods and men, and that this universe is therefore called Cosmos or order, not disorder or misrule."[6]

Ṛta, has sometimes been compared to the Greek *moira*, and to the Chinese *tao*.[7] Like these, *ṛta* was never personified. The meaning of the word "*ṛta*" would seem to have passed through some such evolution as "motion, rhythmic motion, order, cosmic order, moral order, the right." The idea, which was held by the Aryans before their invasion into India, may with reasonable probability be traced back to the second or third millennium B.C. The use of the word died out in India before the time

3. Mircea Eliade, *Images and Symbols*. Studies in Religious Symbolism. Translated by Philip Mairet, New York, Sheed and Ward, 1961, p. 98.
4. Macdonell, *Comparative Religion*, p. 62.
5. *Ṛg-veda*, IX, 121, 1; X, 37, 5.
6. Plato's *Gorgias* 507–508, translated by Jowett (vol. II, p. 400.)
7. "The conception of natural or cosmic laws dominated the thought of common people even in recent times. Professor de Croot saw a boy with a hare-lip, and this was explained to him by the father; who said that the mother of the boy had, during her pregnancy, accidentally made a cut in an old coat of the father's she was mending. Professor de Groot brings this belief under demonology. But is this really correct? There is not a word in the story, as he tells it, about any demon. Surely the only conclusion we are justified in drawing is that the Chinese father believed that given x, y would follow, and it would follow of itself. What is this but recognition of a law, a rule? (*Religion of the Chinese*, New York, 1910, p. 12.) We may not agree with it. The rule may seem to us foolishness. But we must add in simple justice to the Chinese father that similar ideas about experiences of a pregnant mother affecting the child are quite solemnly discussed in Europe at the present day. And the validity of the rule is not here in question. The point is that people believe that the event in question takes place without the intervention of any soul or god.

of the rise of Buddhism,[8] but the conception of cosmic law dominated later Indian thought, being expressed with other words (*karma*, or *dharma*).[9]

In China, also, Confucius based his teaching on cosmic law. His elder rival, Lao-tzu, goes much farther. In the work attributed to Lao-tzu, the *Tao Te Ching*, the pregnant sayings are concerned almost exclusively with the Tao, or cosmic order. It is upon the *Tao* that his ethics, religion, and philosophy are built.

The Chinese concept of *Tao* to a great extent influenced the Japanese of the ancient period. In particular, the ethical and political theory of Confucianism, and the legal and educational institutions of China, all based on the universal principle of *Tao* (*michi* in Japanese), exerted tremendous influence. The idea of a cosmic principle was asserted by Prince Shōtoku, with strongly Confucian insights: "The lord is heaven, the vassal is Earth. Heaven overspreads, Earth upbears. When this is so, the four seasons follow their due course, and the powers of Nature develop their efficacy."[10]

8. T. W. Rhys Davids, Cosmic Law in Ancient Thought; *Proceedings of the British Academy*, 1917–1918, (Rhys Davids, *op. cit.*, pp. 279–289.)
9. Of the pre-Buddhistic Upanisads it occurs only in one, the Taittiriya. In the peroration to that work Ṛta is placed above, before the gods. The word occurs, it is true, in three or four isolated passages of post-Buddhistic works, but these are archaisms. It has not been traced in either the Buddhist or the Jain canonical literature. (Rhys Davids, *op. cit.*)
10. The Seventeen Article Constitution, Article III.

III. THE SEARCH FOR THE ABSOLUTE

1. Introductory Comments

Quite early there arose doubts with respect to the power and even to the existence of the gods. Already in a hymn[1] to Indra, we hear that there were people who did not believe in Indra: "Of him they ask 'where is he?' Of him indeed they also say 'He is not' . . . Believe in him: for he, O men, is Indra."[2] To overcome such scepticism, the god "Faith" (*śraddhā*) was invoked in India to confer faith upon the man who prayed.[3] This god was invoked as a separate god, although Vedic man prayed to other gods as well. Doubt is also expressed in a remarkable hymn[4] where the priests offer a song of praise to Indra, saying, "May say: 'There is no Indra; who has ever seen him? To whom are we to direct the song of praise?' " Whereupon Indra personally appears, in order to give assurance of his existence and his greatness: "There I am, singer, look at me here, in greatness I tower above all beings."

A little later in Greece the Sophists similarly questioned the sense of what religion taught. Protagoras expresses the view of the Sophists: "About the gods, I am not able to know whether they exist or do not exist, nor what they are like in form; for the factors preventing knowledge are many: the obscurity of the subject, and the shortness of human life."[5]

Along with scepticism about the existence of gods, there arose doubts concerning the plurality of gods in general and the merit in sacrificing to any particular god. In a Vedic hymn[6] in which the god Prajāpati is praised as the creator and preserver of the world and as the one god, the following refrain recurs in verse after verse: "Which god shall we honor by means of sacrifice?" Here the poet wants to annul the plurality of the

1. *Ṛg-veda,* II, 12.
2. Cf. also *Ṛg-veda,* X, 86, 1.
3. *Ṛg-veda,* X, 151, 2–3. On the god "Faith," see Muir, *Original Sanskrit Texts,* pp. 346–348.
4. *Ṛg-veda,* VIII, 151, 2–3 f.
5. Protagoras' fragment 4. Kathleen Freeman, *Ancilla to the Pre-Socratic Philosopher* (Oxford, Basil Blackwell, 1948), p. 126.
6. *Ṛg-veda,* X, 121.

gods and to suggest that the one and only god, the Creator Prajāpati, alone deserves worship. In other hymns the sun was regarded as the agent of generation. Thus he is described as "the soul of all that moves and stands."[7] It is said, "Him who is the One Real, sages name variously,"[8] and "The wise (priests and poets) with words make into many the hidden reality which is but one."[9]

Shintoism has no supreme deity. There has been, however, a tendency to exalt some of the gods to a supreme position. The sun-goddess is described as the most exalted of all the gods. In more modern times she has increased in degree of honor as a general providence, her solar quality being left in the background.

Some Indian thinkers eventually formulated the conception of a central principle which was called "being" (*sat*). They were convinced that there was an ultimate of which the many gods were only forms or names. That ultimate was not plural but one, impersonal principle, ruling "over all that is unmoving and that moves, that walks or flies, being differently born."[10] Thinkers came to hold that all gods are nothing but the emanation of the One, and that all plurality is only imaginary. Later in an Upanishad when the philosopher Yājñavalkya was called upon to state the number of gods, he started with the popular number 3306, and ended by reducing them all to one, Brahman. "This indestructible enduring reality is to be looked upon as one only."[11]

In the Greek sources similar views can be found. Plutarch states: "There is One Sun and One Sky over all nations and One Deity under many names."

O! God, most glorious, called by many a name,
Nature's great King, through endless years the same;
Omnipotence, who by thy just decree
Controllest all, hail, Zeus, for unto thee
Behooves thy creatures in all lands to call.
(The Hymn of Cleanthes, c. 300–c.232 B.C.)[12]

7. *Ṛg-veda,* I, 115, 1.
8. *Ṛg-veda,* I, 164, 46. Cf. 170, 71.
9. *Ṛg-veda,* X, 114, 2. This verse is very often cited as representing the idea of unity of all religious and philosophical thought. But the original purport of this verse is not so clear. Geldner's literal translation is as follows: "Die redekundigen Seher teilen den Vogel, der nur einer ist, mit Worten in viele." (*Der Rig-veda,* aus dem Sanskrit ins Deutsche, ubersetzt und mit einem laufenden Kommentare versehen von Karl Friedrich, Geldner. Harvard Oriental Series 35. Cambridge, Mass., Harvard University Press, 1951, S. 337.)
10. *Ṛg-veda,* III, 54, 8.
11. *Bṛhad. Up.* IV, 4, 20.
12. *Philosophic Classics,* vol. 1. Thales to Saint Thomas. Basic Writings of the great Western philosophers. Selected and edited by Walter Kaufmann, N. J. Englewood

In Greece the ancient stage of Aryan religion was represented in the mythology of the Homeric age and was continued in the tragedies of the Athenian theatre. As philosophical criticism developed, however, first among the Ionian Greeks and later by philosophers and sophists from Thales to Socrates, (supported then by the advance of the natural sciences, with "astronomy"—i.e., cosmology based on mathematics—in the lead), myths were no longer accepted as valid interpretations of the processes of nature. The human features and biographies of the gods were rejected, even satirized. The glory and brilliance of the Olympian gods declined with the development of the city-states.

In India, however, the situation was different. There the sceptical attitude was held by intellectuals only, whereas the common people continued to adhere to traditional beliefs and practices. Moreover, even on the intellectual level, in India the older deities were never completely overthrown, but incorporated as manifestations of the absolute. When the notion of emergence from the one and only primordial principle became popular among thinkers and began to infiltrate popular thought, the gods gradually came to be regarded as manifestations of that primordial principle. Nevertheless, the existence of the gods themselves was not denied. Although they were reduced in significance and prestige, they still served some functions even in later periods.

Among the ancient Chinese and Japanese the existence of gods was fully accepted and we find almost no scepticism. Although the Confucian tradition often expresses an agnostic attitude regarding the gods, no attempt is made to deny their existence. In both China and Japan, one finds no self-claimed atheist, insofar as documents remain, in the period prior to the introduction of Buddhism. After the introduction of Buddhism to Japan, however, we find some attempts (called *Honji Suijaku*) to seek for the fundamental principle or principles of the gods.

2. The Tendency towards Monotheism

In the Brahmana period, the Vedic religion moved to some extent towards a chief god—a creator, called Prajāpati. But this tendency never led to monotheism. Rather, the Vedic religion developed the incipient identification of the gods with one another and with nature into the one world-principle of the Upanisads. Similar developments also occurred in Greek thought. Monotheistic thinking in India and Greece stopped in its incipient stages and did not develop. Some Indian scholars assert that mono-

Cliff, Prentice-Hall, Inc., 1963, p. 553. Cf. Epictetus, *Encheiridion*, 53. (Kaufmann, *op. cit.*, p. 569)

theistic thinking developed in the form of devotional Vaiṣṇavism or Śaivism. However, the votaries of these sects admitted the existence of gods other than Viṣṇu or Śiva. In this respect they still remained within the range of the older mythological tradition, however devotional their attitude may have been.

On the other hand, the Iranian god Ahura whose character was once much like that of the Indian Varuṇa was, by the reform of Zoroaster, almost transformed into a monotheistic god. Zoroaster, however, assigned a metaphysical status to the power of Evil in opposition to Ahura, thus establishing a theological dualism quite different from monotheism.

It can also be said that monotheism did not develop in ancient China or Japan. In some respects the notion of T'ien among the ancient Chinese had the character of God, and some medieval Shintoists of Japan advocated the monotheistic conception of God. Yet the character of God as a personality was not conspicuous in ancient Chinese or Japanese thought.

Monotheism in the sense of Faith or belief in one transcendent personal God who creates and maintains the world appears to have developed only in those religious traditions influenced by the ancient faith of Israel —i.e., Judaism, Christianity and Islam.

In most other traditions, the earliest religious reflections centered around various cosmogonies, to which we shall now turn.

3. Cosmogony

a. Introductory Remarks

The endeavour of man to account for the origins of his existence and of the world in which he lives is one of the most important adventures of the human mind. The science of comparative mythology has given it the name of cosmogony (Greek cosmos, 'world-birth'). Some of the earliest "philosophical" speculation appeared in the form of cosmogony in India, Egypt, Babylonia, Greece, etc. Although the philosophical hymns of the *Ṛg-veda* betray much confusion of ideas, these early speculations are of great interest as the sources from which flow various streams of later Indian thought. The fundamental motif of many kinds of cosmogony is that the Primordial One is the source of the Many.[1] Sometimes creation is referred to as an act of natural generation (begetting (*jan*)), and at other times the poems speak of it as a formulation from some original material.

1. "*Ekaṃ vā idaṃ vi babhūva sarvam*" (*ṚV*, VIII, 58, 2) "hen to on kai pan Xenophanen hypotithesthai phesin ho Theophrastos." Simplicius ad *Physica* 6r 22 (Deussen, *Allgemeine Geschichte der Philosophie*, *op. cit.*, I, 1, p. 118)

b. Creation from the Primordial Man

THE development of religious thought in the *Ṛg-veda* led to the conception of a creator distinct from any of the chief deities and superior to all the gods. He is called "primordial Man" (Puruṣa), "All-Creator" (Viśvakarman), "Golden Germ" (Hiraṇyagarbha) or "Lord of Creatures" (Prajāpati), etc., differently in each of the cosmogonic hymns.

In the well-known Hymn of Primordial Man (*Puruṣa-Sūkta*),[1] the material out of which the world is made consists of the body of a primordial giant (*puruṣa*, man). It is thousand-headed and thousand-footed; it extends even beyond the earth, as he covers it. "Puruṣa is all that has been and that will be." He is coextensive with the whole world including the gods. He is the lord of immortal gods; he becomes superior to gods by receiving sacrificial food. The gods are only agents. A fourth of him is all beings; three-fourths of him are what is immortal in heaven. (v. 3) With three quarters Puruṣa rose upward (to the world of immortals); one quarter of him here (in this world) came into being again (from his original form). Thence he spread asunder in all directions to what eats and what does not eat. (From this earthly quarter he developed into animate creatures and inanimate things in all directions.) (v. 4) "When the gods performed a sacrifice with "Puruṣa as an oblation," from that came forth horses, cattle, goats, sheep, and other animals, the four castes of people, the sun, the god of thunder (Indra), the god of fire (Agni), the god of wind (Vāyu), the air, the sky, the earth, the four quarters. The Puruṣa hymn may be regarded as one of the oldest products of cosmogonic speculation in India.

The idea of a primordial man existed in many countries of the world during the ancient period. The fundamental idea of the world being created from the body of a giant is, indeed, very ancient; it is met with in several mythologies. In the Edda mythology of Scandinavia, there is a legend of the dismemberment of a giant called Ymir. This Scandinavian conception of creation bears some resemblance to that of ancient India. "In the beginning yawned the great abyss and naught beside, save that it was flanked on the north by a region of cold and mist, and on the south by a region of fire. The hot air from the sought region beating upon the ice melted it, and the drops of moisture so formed took life and became a giant called Ymir, the progenitor of a race of gigantic beings. He was slain; his body was cast into the abyss, and from his blood were created

1. This hymn (*ṚV.* X, 90) is one of the very latest poems of the Ṛg-vedic age. This conception is the forerunner of atman (*Bṛh.* I, 4, 1; cf. *ŚBr.* VI, 1, 1, 8; XI, 1, 6, 2) The idea of Primordial Man and other principles as the sources of the universe were discussed by W. Ruben (*Indische Metaphysik, op. cit.*, S. 157–158)

the sea and waters, from his flesh the soiled firmament, from his bones the mountains, from his skull the dome of the sky, from his brain the clouds, and from his eyebrows the dwelling of the race of men. Afterwards human beings were born."[2]

In China there exists a legend of the emergence of the universe from the members of the body of a primordial person called "the Ancient One." "When the Ancient One died, his head became the mountains of the four quarters; his eyes became sun and moon; his fat became seas and bays; his hair became plants and trees."[3] In Japan also we find a similar myth. When the god Izanagi killed his son, Kagutsuchi, eight mountain gods came forth, each from one part of his body; i.e., from his head, breast, abdomen, pudenda, left hand, right hand, left leg and right leg.[4]

Perhaps these kinds of cosmogonical speculations reflect the ritual of human sacrifice prevalent among many ancient peoples. Such sacrifices aimed at securing the crops at the time the fields were sowed. In some instances the flesh cut from the victim was used to fertilize the fields. In the rites of some tribes the human victims appear to have been regarded as divine. In others, the victim was regarded as the representative of a god. This view can be confirmed in the pains which seem to be taken to secure a physical correspondence between the victim and the natural object which he embodies or represents.[5]

A sacrificial ritual seems clearly indicated in the following Japanese legend describing how the princess Ogetsu-hime was killed and how various kinds of grain came forth from different parts of her body. "He (the god called His-Swift-Impetuous-Male-Augustness) begged food of the Deity, Princess-of-Great-Food. Then the Princess-of-Great-Food took out all sorts of dainty things from her nose, her mouth, and her fundament, and made them up into all sorts (of dishes) which she offered to him. But His-Swift-Impetuous-Male-Augustness watched her proceedings, considered that she was offering up to him filth, and at once killed the Deity, Princess-of-Great-Food. So the things that were born in the body of the Deity who had been killed were (as follows): in her head were born silkworms, in her two eyes were born rice-seeds, in her two ears was born millet, in her nose were born small beans, in her private parts was born barley, in her fundament were born large beans. So His Augustness the Deity-Producing-Wonderous-Ancestor caused them to be taken and used as seeds."[6] In the Nihon-shoki, another historical chronicle of ancient

2. This explanation is based upon Lewis Spence, *An Introduction to Mythology* (London: George G. Harrap, 1921), p. 170.
3. Jen-fang, *Shu-i-chi*.
4. *Kojiki*.
5. Based upon James George Frazer, *Spirits of the Corn and of the Wild*, I (London, 1912), pp. 236–251.
6. *Ko-ji-ki*, Records of Ancient Matters, trans. by Basil Hall Chamberlain, *Transactions of the Asiatic Society of Japan*, Yokohama, October, 1906, p. 70.

Japan, a similar legend is mentioned in regard to the slaying by Tsuki-yomi-no-mikoto.

Although there is no evidence of human sacrifice for the fertility of the soil in ancient Chinese literature,[7] we cannot positively assert that human sacrifice did not take place. In Greece human sacrifice existed as an immemorial and enduring tradition, and lingered till the end of paganism. The Olympian gods demanded occasional human sacrifice, and this practice was recorded in myth and drama.[8]

Whether or not one agrees with tracing the motif back to actual human sacrifice, it is nevertheless quite clear that in one tradition of Indian cosmogony, the act of creation is treated as a sacrificial rite, and the primordial man is conceived as a victim. The world was created out of the body of Primordial Man as a result of an elaborate sacrificial process.

c. Creation from the Non-existent

ANOTHER Vedic cosmogonic poem philosophically explains the origin of the world as the evolution of the existent (*sat*) from the non-existent (asat) by means of the work of the Creator called the Lord of Prayer (Bṛhaspati).[1] Here the Lord of Prayer lays claim to the supreme rank:

> "Even as a smith, the Lord of Prayer,
> Together forged this universe.
> In earlier ages of the gods,
> From what was not arose what is."[2]

The non-existent ("what was not") was conceived of as something concrete. The term "forging" is a reflection of the work of smiths which came to flourish in those days.

d. Creation from "What is neither existent nor non-existent."

THE philosophical speculations of the ancient Indians culminates in the

7. Idzuishi's article in "*Iwanami's Tōyōshichō*," Tokyo, Iwanami Press, p. 21.
8. B. Russell, *A History of Western Philosophy*, p. 249.

1. *ṚV.* X, 72.
2. Macdonnell, *Sanskrit Literature*, p. 136. Geldner's translation may help here:

Brahmanaspati hat diese wie ein Schmied zusammengeschweisst. In dem fruhesten Zeitalter der Gotter entstand das Seiende aus dem Nichts; nach diesem entstanden die Weltraume: Dieses wurde von der Kauernden (geboren).

Die Erde wurde von der Kauernden geboren, aus der Erde entstanden die Weltraume. Von Aditi wurde Daksa geboren und von Daksa die Aditi.

Denn Aditi wurde geboren als deine Tochter, o Daksa. Nach ihr wurden die Gotter geboren, die guten Unsterblickeitsgenossen. (K. F. Geldner, *Der Rig-Veda*, ad X, 72)

profound poem on creation from a primordial principle which is neither non-existent nor existent.[1] It begins as follows:

> There was not the non-existent nor the existent then;
> There was not the air nor the heaven which is beyond.
> What did it contain? Where? In whose protection?
> Was there water, unfathomable, profound?
> There was not death nor immortality then.
> There was not the beacon of night, nor of day.
> That one breathed, windless, by its own power.
> Other than that there was not anything beyond.[2]

In the beginning there was no existent or non-existent. This conception of neither-existent-nor-non-existent is very important. The existent in its manifest aspect was not then. But we cannot on that account call it the non-existent; for it is the positive being from which all existence derives. The absolute reality which is at the basis of the world cannot be characterized by us as either existent or non-existent, nor by saying that there was no phenomenal entity or action at all.[3] The concept of the One which breathed breathless by its own power reminds us of Aristotle's unmoved mover. In China, Lao-Tzu also explained the primeval origin of everything in a similar way: "It is bottomless; the very progenitor of all things in the world."[4] "There was something formless yet complete, that existed before heaven and earth; without sound, without substance, dependent on nothing, unchanging, all pervading, unfailing. It was from the Nameless that Heaven and Earth sprang."[5]

The hymn then continues: "Darkness was in the beginning hidden by darkness; indistinguishable, this all was water. That which, coming into being, was covered with the void, that One arose through the power of heat."[6] In the Tao Te Ching we find: "We can but call it the Mystery or rather the 'Darker than any Mystery'; the Doorway whence issued all Secret Essences";[7] and in *Genesis* (1:2) "And darkness was on the face of the deep and the spirit of God was moving on the face of the waters."

1. *ṚV.* X, 129. Cf. X, 5, 3, 1.
2. Deussen (*Allgemeine Geschichte der Philosophie*, I, 1, 5. 122) says: "Das Eine war svadhaya durch Selbstbesetzung, durch sich selbst (vgl. Svayambhū, Kath'hauto, causa sui, Ding an sich)."
3. Cf. *ŚBr.* X, 5, 3, 1.
4. Tao-tê-ching, IV. Arthur Waley, *The Way and its Power*. A study of the Tao tê ching and its place in Chinese thought. New York, Grove Press, Inc. 1958, p. 146.
5. *Tao Te Ching*, XXV.
6. *ṚV.* X, 129, v. 3. A hymn (*ṚV.* X, 121, 1; 3) mentions "der Gott, des Schattenbild Unsterblichkeit und Tod sind, — der durch seine Macht der alleinige König uber alles, was atmet und schlummert, uber die Kreatur geworden ist." (Geldner's Translation)
7. *Tao Te Ching*, I.

In the Vedic hymn, then, the power of "heat" (*tapas*) arose. This word "tapas" also means "religious austerity" and reflects the high esteem in which religious austerity was held among the Indian people. "Desire in the beginning came upon that (desire), that was the first seed of mind (*manasaḥ retas*). Sages seeking in their hearts with wisdom found out the bond of the existent in the non-existent." (v. 4) According to the hymn, aroused by the primeval heat, "Desire" (*kāma*) came forth. The word "kāma" in Sanskrit very often means "sexual desire, love"; but here "desire" is regarded as a fundamental principle in evolution.

According to the hymn (*ṚV.* X, 129), out of that principle (That, *tad*) there arose, through *tapas* (self-renunciation, turning of the will to affirmation), Desire (*Kāma*). The Greek counterpart would be Eros, who according to Hesiod and Parmenides[8] is the oldest of the gods. In one passage[9] of Hesiod (8th? B.C.), Chaos was the first to exist, then came Earth (with the abyss, or Tartarus) and Eros. From Chaos were born Erebus (a place of darkness which the shades of the dead pass on their way to Hades) and Night; Earth first brought forth of herself the sky, the mountains, and the sea; then in marriage with the sky she produced the progenitors of the different families of gods. This representation certainly attempts to present some notion of the world's origin, and we may even consider it to be the beginning of cosmology among the Greeks. The poet asks himself what was really the first of all things, and he eventually returns to the Earth as the immovable basis of the Cosmos. Outside the Earth was nothing but gloomy night, for the luminaries of heaven were not as yet in existence. Erebus and Night are therefore as old as the Earth. In order that another should be produced from this first one, the generative impulse, or Eros, must have existed from the beginning. Such then are the causes of all things.[10]

In Greek mythology, therefore, Eros the god of love, corresponding to Kāma, was connected with the creation of the universe. Parmenides sang of genesis: "First of all the gods, she devised Love."[11] Another Greek states: "Thus numerous are the witnesses who acknowledge Love to be the eldest of the gods. And not only is he the eldest, he is also the source of the greatest benefits to us."[12] In a later Indian Epic the God of love, Kama, himself says: "None can destroy me. I am the one immortal and

8. Cf. Paul Deussen, *The Elements of Metaphysics*. Translated from the second German edition with the personal collaboration of the author by C. M. Duff, London and New York, Macmillan and Co. 1894, p. 147.
9. Hesiod, *Theogony*. Cf. Aristotle, *Metaphysics*, p. 984, b.
10. Edward Zeller, *A History of Greek Philosophy from the Earliest Period to the Time of Socrates*. Translated by S. F. Alleyne. 2 vols. London, Longmans, Green and Co. 1881, vol. 1, p. 88.
11. Parmenides' fragment 13. Cf. Aristotle, *Metaphysics* Book I, Chap. 4, p. 984, b 25.
12. Plato's *Symposium* 178. Tr. by Jowett, vol. I, p. 548.

indestructible."[13] He is "most ancient" (*sanātanatamaḥ*) among gods.[14] Plato also said: "He (=Love) is the eldest of the gods, which is an honor to him; and a proof of his claim to this honor, is that of his parents there is no memorial; neither poet nor prose-writer has ever affirmed that he had any."[15] In China Lao-Tzu says: "Because all this is so, to be constantly without desire is the way to have a vision of the mystery (cf. heaven and earth): For constantly to have desire is the means by which their limitations are seen. These two entities although they have different names emerged together; and (emerging) together means 'in the very beginning.' "[16] Here the Chinese word "desire" designates, to be sure, something different from the Sanskrit word "desire" (*kāma*). The former is of a practical, ethical, and social significance, while the latter is of metaphysical significance. "Their cord was extended across: was there below or was there above?"

"There were impregnators, there were powers; there was energy below, there was impulse above. Who knows truly? Who shall here declare whence it has been produced, whence is this creation? By the creation of this (universe) the gods (come) afterwards: who then knows whence it has arisen?" In the Vedic hymn the ultimate creative principle receives no particular name; it is only called "the one." In this hymn the great idea of Universal Unity in the Upanishads is already foreshadowed. Moreover, the final verses of the hymn indicate the growing sense of the irrelevance of the gods.

Although Indian cosmogony is sometimes connected with theogony, the cosmogonical interest was predominant as evidenced in this hymn. The gods played a less important role in India than in Greece. The cosmological or cosmogonical interest comes, not only from the urge to account for the manifoldness of nature, but very often from the desire of the ritual priests to give reasons for the cult, to interpret the cult's relationship to the whole (*sarvam*). The latter interest does not appear in the creation-hymns of the Ṛg-veda, but is quite apparent in the Brahmanas.

e. Creation from Primeval Water and the Cosmic Egg

According to one Indian tradition, creation begins with the primeval water: "In the beginning there existed here nothing but water, a sea of water. These waters desired to propagate their kind. They tortured them-

13. *Mahābhārata* 14, 13, 12f. E. Washburn Hopkins, *Epic Mythology* (Strassburg: Trubner, 1915), p. 164.
14. *Mahābhārata*, XIII, 85, 11. W. Hopkins, *Epic Mythology*, p. 165.
15. *Symposium*, 178. (Tr. by Jowett, vol. I, p. 548)
16. Lao-tzu, translated by Hughes, (*Chinese Philosophy*, *op. cit.*, p. 145)

selves, they mortified themselves. And when they had originated themselves, a golden egg originated in them. The year did not yet exist at that time; but as long as the duration of a year, this golden egg swam about. After a year a man arose out of it; that was Prajāpati. Therefore, a woman or a cow or a mare gives birth within a year, for Prajāpati was born after a year. He broke the golden egg open. But at that time there did not yet exist any standing-place. So this golden egg, which bore him, swam about as long as the duration of a year.

"After a year he tried to speak, and he said: 'bhūḥ,' and this (word) became this earth; (he said:) 'bhuvaḥ' and this became yonder atmosphere, (he said:) 'suvar' and this became the sky yonder. Therefore, a child tries to talk after a year, for after a year Prajāpati spoke. When Prajāpati first spoke, he uttered monosyllabic and bi-syllabic words; therefore a child, when it first speaks, utters monosyllabic and bisyllabic words. Those (three words) from five syllables. Out of these he made the five seasons of the year (spring, summer, rainy season, autumn, and winter).

"Prajāpati rose up above the worlds created in this manner after a year; therefore, after a year, a child tries to stand up, for after a year Prajāpati rose up.

"He was born with the life of a thousand years. As one perceives the other bank of a river from a distance, so he perceived the other bank of his life. And, singing praises and torturing himself, he lived on, as he desired to propagate his species. He placed reproductive energy into himself, and with his mouth he created the gods. . . . Then he saw that there was, as it were, daylight (*divā*) for him, and that is the divinity of the gods (*deva*). Now he created with the breath of life what is below, the demons (*Asuras*). . . . And after they were created, he saw that there was, as it were, darkness."[1]

This cosmogony calls to mind Thales' reflections about water. Thales, however, was regarded as a "philosopher" by Aristotle, and his first principle (*arkhē*) was not the beginning of a cosmogonical evolution, happening only once, but the principle of perpetual becoming. Although water was very often regarded as the beginning of the cosmogonical development in India, we cannot find such a conception regarded as the ultimate principle in the nature-philosophy of India.[2] In one passage of the Upan-

1. *ŚBr*, XI, 1, 6, 1 f.
2. *Kāṭhaka-Saṃhitā*. VIII, 2; *Vāj. Saṃh.* XXXII, 1 = *Tadeva-Up; Tait. Saṃh,* V, 6, 4, 2; *ŚBr*. VI, 8, 2, 3; XI, 1, 6, 1–16; *Tait. Br.* I, i, 3, 5; *Bṛhad. Up.* III, 6; V, 5, 1; *Chānd. Up.* VII, 10, 1–2; *Kauṣ. Up.* I, 7; *Kaṭha-Up.* IV, 6; *Manu* I, 8–11; *MBh.* XII. 183. 2–10. Cf. Hermann Oldenberg; *Vorwissenschaftliche Wissenschaft; die Weltanschauung der Brāhmaṇa-texte*. Göttingen, Vandenhoeck & Ruprecht, 1919, 175; R. Garbe, *Die Sâṃkhya-philosophie, Eine Darstellung des indischen Rationalismus nach den Quellan,* 2nd ed., Leipzig, Haessel Verlag, 1917, pp. 23–24.

ishads[3] it is said that earth, space, heaven (the three worlds), and gods, men, animals, and plants are nothing but water in different forms. In this relatively late text, however, water was not the ultimate principle, but only one of a series of causes.

When the Ionian philosophers asked what the universe was made of, or how "all" matter behaved, they were assuming a general notion, namely that of a fundamental substance, a final, universal matter to which all sorts of accidents or modifications could relate. This notion dictated the terms of their inquiries. In ancient India, however, early speculations did not stray far from a specifically religious context involving the sacrificial ritual, religious austerities, and the established priesthood.[4]

In the myth cited above[5] the "Golden Egg" was regarded as something primordial, which corresponds to the cosmic "Egg" of Epimenides[6] and of the third Orphic theogony.[7] In the fourth theogony a cosmic "Silver God" is mentioned.[8] In India the theory of the "Cosmic Egg" (*aṇḍa*) was retained even in later periods.[9]

3. *Chānd. Up.* VII, 10.
4. *Ait. Br.* V, 32, Cf. Deussen, *Allgemeine Geschichte* I, 183.
5. *ŚBr.* XI, 1, 6.
6. Epimenides admitted two first causes, Air and Night; and proceeding from these a third, Tartarus. From them sprang two other beings, not precisely designated, whose union produced the egg of the universe. From this egg other beings were produced (Eduard Zeller, *Die Philosophie der Griechen, in ihrer geschichtlichen Entwicklung*, I, 1, 6th ed., Leipzig: O. R. Reisland, 1919. p. 97)
7. "A third Orphic cosmogony places at the beginning of cosmical development water and primitive slime, which latter solidifies and forms the earth. From these two a dragon arises, winged, and with the face of a god: on one side he has the head of a lion, and on the other that of a bull. He is called by the mythologists, Heracles and Chronos, the never-aging one; with him is united Necessity, or Adrastea (according to Damascius, in a hermaphrodite form), who is said to be spread abroad incorporeally throughout the universe to its remotest ends. Chronos-Heracles produces a gigantic egg, which, dividing in the midst, forms with its upper half the sky, and with its lower, the earth. There seems to have been further mention of a god who had golden wings on his shoulders, bull's heads on his haunches, and a huge snake appearing among various animal forms on his head; this god, described by Damascius as incorporeal, is called Protogonos or Zeus, and also Pan, as bringing order into all things (Zeller, *A History of Greek Philosophy from the Earliest Period to the Time of Socrates.* Translated by S. F. Alleyne, 2 vols. London: Longmans, Green and Co., 1881, pp. 100–101; cf. Viśvakarman)
8. Here (in the fourth Orphic cosmogony) Chronos is represented as the first of all existences. He brings forth Aether and the dark immeasurable abyss, or Chaos; from these he then forms a silver egg, out of which, illuminating all things, proceeds Phanes, the first-born god, called also Metis, Eros, and Epicapaeus; he contains within himself the germs of all gods. When Zeus attains sovereignty he devours Phanes, and consequently is himself the idealism (Inbegriff) of all things. (Zeller, *History*, I, 104)
9. *Manu* I, 5–16; *Viṣṇu-Purāṇa* I, 2, 58f.

China also possessed a similar creation-myth using the imagery of a cosmic egg: "When the heaven and the earth were not divided, chaos was like an egg of a hen. The Primordial Man was born out of it. After the lapse of eighteen thousand years, heaven and earth (=the universe) developed. The pure and bright portion became the heaven, and the dirty and dark portion became the earth. The Primordial Man was situated between them."[10]

In the first chapter of an ancient Japanese chronicle,[11] the world-creation is depicted as follows: "In the beginning, when the heaven and the earth, Yin and Yang, were not divided, Chaos was like an egg of a hen; it contained the germs of everything in its abyss. Its pure and bright portion went up and became the heaven, and its heavy and dirty portion precipitated and became the earth. . . . Afterwards gods were born between them." This was obviously influenced by the cosmology of the Chinese classics.

According to the original Japanese creation-mythology, however, the creation was related as follows: "Before the heavens and the earth came into existence, all was chaos, unimaginably limitless and without definite shape or form. Aeon followed aeon: then, lo! out of this boundless, shapeless mass something light and transparent rose up and formed the heaven." Then the Three Creating Deities arose. "In the meantime what was heavy and opaque in the void gradually precipitated and became the earth, but it had taken an immeasurably long time before it condensed sufficiently to form solid ground."

"In its earliest stages, for millions and millions of years, the earth may be said to have resembled oil floating, medusa-like, upon the face of the waters. Suddenly, like the sprouting up of a reed, a pair of immortals were born from its bosom. Afterwards many gods were born. But as long as the world remained in a chaotic state, there was nothing for them to do. Whereupon all the heavenly deities summoned the two divine beings, Izanagi and Izanami, and bade them descend to the nebulous place, and by helping each other, to consolidate it into terra firma." They churned the water and created the islands of Japan. This creation-myth of Japan may be compared to the mythology of Viṣṇu and the churning of the ocean in Hinduism. (1) Izanagi and Izanami appear and work only after several prematerial stages of creation. Viṣṇu begins to send down Avataras to take a material body perceptible to man only after an 'original creation.' (*Matsya-purāṇa*, III, 51, 3). (*ādi-sṛṣṭi*) (2) Izanagi and Izanami are commanded by all the heavenly Kami, not only to 'make, consolidate and give birth to this drifting land' (*Kojiki*, I, iii), but also to 'proceed and bring it into order'. (*Nihongi*, I, 8). The purpose of the first Avatāra,

10. Hsü-chêng Josei, *Sango rekiki: San-wu li-chi.*
11. *Kojiki*, vol. 1.

Matsya is to help Manu, who not only 'wished' to bring all creatures into existence and visibly to create all living beings', but whose task 'consisted in creating all beings in appropriate and exact order.' (*Mahābhārata*, Vana-Parvan CLXXXVI). (3) Izanagi and Izanami had to find the ocean before they could carry out their task. The Fish (*matsya*)-avatāra of Viṣṇu had to be taken to the ocean to carry out his task. (*Matsya-Purāṇa* I, 25). (4) Izanagi and Izanami used a lance (*nu-hoko*) as the instrument to seek for land and eventually to make land by stirring the ocean. In the Indian legend the fish could carry out its task with a horn (sringa). (*Agni-purāṇa* 13, *Matsya-purāṇa* I, 12 and 19, 36, 44 ff.; *Śatapatha-brāhmaṇa* I, 8, 1, 5; *Mahābhārata*, Vana-parvan, CCLXXXVI). (5) Izanagi and Izanami erect the Pillar of the Center of the land (Kuni-no-naka-no-mi-hashira). (*Nihongi* I, 5). The second Avatāra, Kūrma, the tortoise, upholds the central pillar of the Earth, Mount Mandara. (*Garuḍa-purāṇa* CXLII). (6) Izanagi and Izanami circumambulate and then turn the pillar before they proceed to actual creation (*Kojiki* I, iv; *Nihongi* I, 8). By rotating Mount Mandara, Kūrma brings out of the ocean the basic principles of the universe. (Bhāgavata-purāṇa VIII, 7f.). (7) After having churned the ocean and circumambulated the pillar, Izanagi and Izanami gave birth to children (*Kojiki* I, iv). Having rotated the pillar and churned the ocean, the Creator, called for this purpose Prajapati, creates an offspring, praja. (*Śatapatha-brāhmaṇa* VII, 5, 1, 5). This process is set forth in the legend of a churning of the ocean (*samudra-mathana*). In spite of these striking similarities of both creation-myths, some differences are also apparent: (a) In Hindu legends the creation of the world is a fall from a higher state to a lower and less satisfactory state, whereas in the Shinto legend creation is regarded as a development for which man should be unqualifiedly grateful. (b) In Hindu legends creation is cyclic, periodical. It takes place repeatedly. On the other hand, the Japanese legend completely ignores the concept of cyclic return. (c) The Japanese creation-myth is set forth to explain the origin of the Imperial Family, whereas the Indian myth is set forth to explain the genesis of the figure of the saviour.[12]

f. Speculation about the Word

In India, speculation about the Word represents yet another tradition of cosmogonical speculation. The word (*vāc*) as the hypostatized creative power or the personified female god was regarded as the cause of all

12. These similarities were pointed out and discussed by Jean Herbert in his work, *Shintō at the Fountain-head of Japan* (London: George Allen and Urwin, 1967), pp. 525–535.

things;[1] here *causa materialis* and *causa efficiens* were not differentiated. Speech (*vāc*) was regarded as the highest principle.[2] In two hymns, which were composed in a later phase of the Ṛg-veda, Speech is said to be the ultimate principle of the universe. Speech, or the Word, is personified. It holds, cherishes, and sustains all the gods;[3] through it alone all partake food.[4] It is regarded as if it were a God in charge of grace and providence. "I make the man I love exceedingly mighty, make him a sage, a seer (ṛṣi), and a Brahmin."[5] Its essence transcends the context of empirical perception. "All living beings do not know it, but yet they dwell beside me."[6] ("Me" refers to "Speech."). Again the poet says: "One man, seeing, does not see Speech; another, hearing, does not hear it."[7]

Similar assertions can be found among other peoples of antiquity. According to Genesis (1:3) the word of God was efficient in the action of creation. "God said, Let there be light and there was light. And God said, Let there be a firmament in the midst of the waters and let it divide the waters from the waters." (I, 6) In the Gospel according to St. John, (1, 1) the Word is the primeval principle: "In the beginning was the Word, and the Word was with God, and the Word was God."[8] Heraclitus designated the eternal World-Law according to which everything occurs by the word, "Logos" (originally, "word" or "speech"). The Stoics picked up this conception from him. Philo again adopted the *logos* doctrine from the Stoics, and the doctrines of Philo subsequently influenced Neo-Platonism. Albrecht Weber[9] suggested some years ago that the Indian conception of the "Word" (*vāc*) might have had some influence upon the idea of the *logos* which appears in Neo-Platonism. Richard Garbe also discusses the possibility.[10]

In China, Lao-tzu said: "When the Tao had no name, that was the starting-point of heaven and earth; then when it had a name, this was the 'mother of all creation'. "[11] Similarly, an Indian scripture states that the Word divided itself into many and produced many beings.[12] It is the basis, matrix of variety and individuality, even of gods. It sprang out of

1. *ṚV.* X, 125.
2. *ṚV.* X, 71; X, 125.
3. *ṚV.* X, 125, 1–2.
4. *Ibid*, 4.
5. *Ibid*, 5.
6. *Ibid*, v. 4.
7. *ṚV.* X, 71, 4.
8. Words (vāc) were regarded as the mother of the Vedas. (Vedānāṃ mātā. *Tait. Br.* II, 8, 8, 5.)
9. "*Vâch* und *logos*" in Albrecht Weber, *Indische Studien*, Leipzig: F. A. Brockhaus, 1865, vol. IX, pp. 473–480.
10. R. Garbe, *The Philosophy of the Ancient India* (Chicago: Open Court, 1899), p. 54.
11. Tao Te Ching, I, translated by Hughes (*Chinese Philosophy*, p. 145)
12. ārabhamāṇa, v. 8.

water and created heaven, just as Prajāpati made intercourse with the Word.[13]

The Word was regarded, ultimately, as the principle of life and of the intelligence of a person; a person eats, lives, and becomes wise by means of it.[14] The Indians from an early period developed a theory of language, and elaborated systems of grammar, which continue to be useful even in modern linguistics. Starting from an essentially magical way of thinking about the names of things (sorcery, curses, secret names), they came to regard the world as "name and form" (*nāma-rūpa*).[15] That is, each thing has its own name; it is an individual thing only through its name. The name (not the empirical proper name) is connected with a person (*puruṣa*) even after his death, when his body, his five organs (*prāṇa*), all that constitute his form, are dissolved into the macrocosmical elements corresponding to each of them.

Speculation about the nature of words was carried on with a kind of mystical awe in the early writings of India, viz. the Ṛg-Veda, the Brāhmanas, and the Upaniṣads;[16] and it wielded great influence upon later Indian Philosophy. Indian philosophers often used grammatical theory and argument as a model for philosophizing.[17] In Greek thought, on the other hand, a mathematical model was most often used.

The ancient Japanese had a concept of "Word-Soul" (*Koto-tama*). They claimed that Japan was "the country supported and favored by 'Word-Soul,' or the country where Word-Soul flourished."[18] However, the metaphysics of the Word-Soul did not develop among the Japanese.

Related to cosmogonical speculations on the Word in the hymns of the Ṛg-Veda and the Brāhmaṇas, is the tendency to reflect on the meaning of the syllable as a creative utterance. The holy syllable *Oṃ* was often regarded as the highest principle. The function of the syllable is comparable to that of *amen* in the sense of "yes," or "So may it be." The syllable was originally used in the ancient sacrificial liturgy by the priests. Later it came to be symbolically used by some Mahayana Buddhists and the Jains. Even today Hindus still chant *Om* at religious ceremonies. The holy syllable gained significance as a symbol of the metaphysical quest to

13. H. Oldenberg, *Vorwissenschaftliche Wissenschaften*, 80; Deussen, *Allgemeine Geschichte* I, 1, 206 f.
14. This was meant literally. The word (*vāc*) eats (*Bṛhad. Up.* II, 2, 4) and smells (*ŚBr.* VIII, 5, 4, 1; X, 5, 2, 15). Besides, we can find here the forerunner of the relation of the subject and object, respectively as the eater and as the food eaten.
15. Otto Strauss, *Die indische Philosophie*, Munchen, Ernst Reinhardt, 1925, S. 35; 95.
16. Cf. R. C. Pandeya, *The Problem of Meaning in Indian Philosophy* (Delhi: Motilal Banarsidass, 1963), pp. 9–10.
17. Daniel H. H. Ingalls, "The Comparison of Indian and Western Philosophy," *Journal of Oriental Research* (Madras), XXII (1954), p. 4.
18. *Mannyōsū* , XIII, 10; V, 31.

attain the One. All words were regarded as joined together by the holy syllable *Om*, which is nothing but the whole world.[19] The holy syllable is held to be the quintessence of all the Vedas.[20] It is the Imperishable (*akṣara*), Immortal, Fearless.[21] (The term *akṣara* literally means "syllable."). It is the Absolute (*brahman*) which man becomes, when he knows it,[22] or into which even gods flee in order to become immortal.[23]

g. Time as the Fundamental Principle

A hymn in the Atharva-Veda praises time (*kāla*) as the first cause of all existence: "Time, the steed, runs with seven reins (rays), thousand-eyed, ageless, rich in seed. The seers, thinking holy thought, mount him, all the beings (words) are his wheels.

"With seven wheels does this Time ride, seven[1] navels has he, immortality is his axle. He carries hither all these beings (worlds). Time, the first god, now hastens onward.

"A full jar has been placed upon Time; verily, we see him existing in many forms. He carries away all these beings (worlds); they call him Time in the highest heaven."[2]

"Time begot yonder heaven, Time also (begot) these earths. That which was, and that which shall be, urged forth by Time, spreads out. Time created the earth, in Time the sun burns. In Time are all beings, in Time the eye looks abroad." Various gods and principles were enumerated as being created by Time: Prajapati, Brahman, Tapas (asceticism), prana (breath of life), etc.[3] There also appeared several cosmogonical myths in which the "year" was regarded as the ultimate principle.[4] Such assertions were later developed by some Indian philosophers into the notion that "time" is the ultimate principle of the universe (*Kālavādin*).[5]

19. *Chānd. Up.* II, 23, 3.
20. *Chānd. Up.* I, 1, 1–2. It is the basis of all gods (*ṚV.* I: 164, 39, according to Sāyaṇa's third interpretation)
21. *Chānd. Up.* I, 4, 5.
22. *Tait. Up.* I, 8, Cf. *Māṇḍ. Up.* 12. *Gauḍapādīya-kārikā*, chapter 1.
23. *Chānd. Up.* I, 4, 5.

1. In the *Atharva-Veda* the number 7 is used as a mystical number. In a hymn extolling the Ox, the poet says, "He who knows the seven inexhaustible milkings of the ox, gains offspring and heaven." (*AV.* IV, 11) The use of the number seven is common in Mediterranean cults also; cf., e.g., Sabbath, the Seven Sacraments.
2. *AV.* XIX, 53. Translated by Bloomfield, *Sacred Books of the East*, XLII, 224.
3. *AV.* XIX, 53 ff.
4. *ŚBr.* XI, 1, 6.
5. Kālaḥ pacati bhūtani kālaḥ saṃharate prajāḥ/kālaḥ supteṣu jāgarti kālo hi duratikramaḥ// This verse is cited in such passages as: *Mahābhārata*, ed. by Sukhtankar,

Such a conception of time corresponds to Chronos of Pherecydes[6] and to the third Orphic theogony. According to the latter, Chronos or Time, 'who grows not old', existed first, and from it sprang ether and the formless chaos. From them was formed the universe, an egg which bursting in due time disclosed Eros (or Phanes), the firstborn, at once male and female and having within himself the seeds of all creatures. Phanes creates the Sun and Moon and Night, and from Night arise Uranos and Gaea, Heaven and Earth. These two give birth to the Titans, among whom is Kronos, who defeats his father Uranos and succeeds to his throne. He is in turn deposed by Zeus, who swallows Phanes and thus becomes the father of gods and men.[7]

The fact that Time was raised to the level of a fundamental principle probably reflects the development of an agricultural economy.[8] Moreover, both in ancient cosmogony and in later Indian philosophy, time as a fundamental principle is understood cyclically, perhaps reflecting agricultural man's sensitivity to the pattern of recurring seasons. A linear, historical sense of time like that found in the *Old Testament* or the *Koran* never developed in India.

h. Food as the Fundamental Principle

In some passages of the Brahmana literature, food (*anna*) is claimed to be the source and substance of all things.[1] Brahman, the divine essense, makes itself known to the priestly seer in the following stanzas: "I am the first-born of the divine essence. Before the gods sprang into existence, I was. I am the navel (the center and the source) of immortality. Whoever bestows me on others—thereby keeps me to himself. I am FOOD. I feed on

XI, 2, 14; also *Garuḍapurāṇa* 11, 2, 14. (Cf. Sternbach in *Journal of the American Oriental Society*, vol. 83, p. 54) *Madhyamakavṛtti*. p. 386, 11.6–7. (cf. Poussin's note, l.c.); Guaḍapāda ad *Sāṃkhyakārikā*, 61; *Ānandajñāna* ad *Bṛhad. Up. Vārttika*, p. 1825 (*ĀnSS*); Bhaṭṭotpala's comm. ad *Bṛhatsaṃhitā* (VizSS. p. 9); cf. *Taisho Tripiṭaka*, XXXII, 158 a.

6. Pherecydes says that there existed before all things, and from eternity, Zeus, Chronos, and Chthon. By Chthon he seems to have understood the earth; by Chronos that part of heaven nearest the earth, and the deity ruling it; by Zeus, the highest god, disposing and forming the whole universe, and himself at the same time the highest heaven. Chronos produces from his seed fire, wind and water; the three primal beings then beget numerous other gods in five families. Zeller, *History*, *op. cit.*, I, p. 90 f.
7. Based upon Legge, *Forerunners and Rivals of Christianity* (1925), I, 125, cited from Radhakrishnan's Eastern Religion etc. *op. cit.*, p. 138; cf. Zeller, *History*, I, p. 101 f.
8. This problem was fully discussed in Mircea Eliade, *Images and Symbols*. Studies in Religious Symbolism. Translated by Philip Mairet. New York, Sheed and Ward, 1961, pp. 57–91.
1. *Tait. Br.* II, 8, 8,

food and on its feeder." In some cases, Soma, the moon was equated with food.[2]

The divine material out of which the living universe and its creatures are composed is proclaimed here as food, which means matter and force combined. This life-sap builds up and constitutes all forms of life. Creatures live by feeding on each other; i.e., by devouring; but the divine substance itself lives on, without interruption, through the ceaseless interruptions of the lives of all living beings. This hymn expresses a relentless vital dynamism.[3] Here we have a philosophy of life-matter and life-force, a philosophy of the struggling life and body rather than of the mind and spirit. The dynamism of actual life is stressed.

i. Reflections on the Structure of the Universe

Mention has already been made of the tripartite structure of the universe in ancient India. The notion of the three spheres, i.e., heaven, earth and the intermediate region, first appeared in the Vedas and became traditional among later Hindus. In Greece, likewise the Pythagoreans, and Ocellus in particular, distinguished heaven, the earth, and the interval between them. Pythagoras and Ocellus people the middle or aerial region with demons, heaven with gods, and earth with men. They agree precisely with the Hindus, who place the gods above, man beneath, and spiritual creatures, flitting unseen, in the intermediate region.[1]

The Indians seem to have thought of the universe as a sphere or hemisphere, or perhaps a disk.[2] "The light which shines higher than this heaven, on the back of all, on the back of everything in the highest worlds, than which there are no higher—verily, that is the same as this light which is here within a person."[3] Sages behold the world 'from above',

2. *Bṛhad Up.* I, 4, 6.
3. For details, cf. H. Zimmer, *Philosophies of India*, *op. cit.*, pp. 345–350. "When he rises up on food," becomes "all this, both what hath been and what shall be" (*ṚV.* X, 90, 2; cf. *ṚV.* I, 25, 10–12; *Śvet.* Up. III, 15). "What Golden Person in the Sun . . . is even He who dwells within the lotus of the heart and eats food" (*Maitri-Up.* VI, 1). "The son of man has come eating and drinking; and you say, Behold a glutton and a drunkard, a friend of tax collectors and sinners!" (*Luke* 7:34)

1. Colebrooke, *Miscellaneous Essays*, 2nd ed. (London: Trübner, 1878), I, p. 24.; Monier Williams, *Brahmanism and Hinduism* (London, John Murray, 1891), p. 28.
2. *ṚV.* III, 55, 20; X, 89, 4. cf. A. A. Macdonell, *Vedic Mythology*, p. 9; A person who produced works of merits was supposed to enjoy happiness on the top of the firmament of heaven (nākasya pṛṣṭhe, *Muṇḍ. Up.* I, 2, 10). *Āpastamba-dharma-sūtra, Adhyātma-paṭala*, 23, 1.; such an expression as "the disc of the world" (*jagad-bimba*) is often used. *Śaṅkara ad Brahma-sūtra*, p. 488, 11; 489, 3; 490, 7.
3. ataḥ paro divo jyotir dīpyate viśvataḥ pṛṣṭheṣu sarvataḥ pṛṭṣheṣu, *Chānd. Up.* III, 13, 7.

i.e., "on the back of the heaven."[4]

A similar conception appears in the *Phaedrus*: "When they (blessed gods) go to banquet and festival, then they move up the steps to the top of the vault of heaven. . . . The immortals, when they are at the end of their course, go forth and stand up on the outside of heaven, and the revolution of the spheres carries them round, and they behold the things beyond. But of the heaven which is above the heavens, what earthly poet ever did or ever will sing worthily?"[5]

In Greek philosophy it was a traditional idea that the universe is a circular and complete globe. This theory perhaps originated in Xenophanes[6] and was advocated explicitly by Parmenides who maintained that existence (*to eon*), as the fundamental principle of the world, is a complete globe.[7] Pythagoras and his followers held that 'What is determinate is more excellent than what is not determinate.'[8] Empedocles taught that the universe was globular in its primordial chaotic condition.[9] It was this idea of the globular universe that was inherited by Plato[10] and Aristotle.[11]

The abode of the gods was supposed to be located on the highest mountain in the center of the world; i.e., Mount Meru[12] in India, and Mount Olympus in Greece. In Buddhist and Jain works, in the Mahabharata, and in later literature, Mount Meru is said to form the central point of the continent (*Jambudvīpa*). All the planets revolve around it; its summit is the residence of Brahma, and a place of meeting for the gods, sages (*ṛṣis*) and other divine beings. In Greece and Rome it was believed that gods sat upon the sunny mountaintop of Olympus. The Parnassus mountain in southern Greece was sacred to Apollo and the Muses. In Japanese mythology Takama-ga-hara, the field in heaven was the gathering place for gods. Mount Fuji, located in the center of Japan, although

4. *nākasya pṛṣthe*, *Muṇḍ. Up.* I, 2, 10. Nearly the same expression was used by Plato also. (epi tōi tou ouranou nōtōi, Plato, *Phaedrus*, p. 247 C.)
5. *Phaedrus* p. 247 C. (Jowett's translation, vol. I, p. 453)
6. E. Zeller, *Die Philosophie der Griechen*, Bd. I, Abt. 1, S. 661; P. Deussen, *Allgemeine Geschichte*, II, 1, S. 74.
7. Zeller, *op. cit.*, I, 1, 2. 695; Deussen, *op. cit.*, II, 1, S. 83.
8. Zeller, *op. cit.*, I, 1, S. 521. S. 458; cf. S.
9. Zeller, *op. cit.*, I, 2, S. 973; Deussen, *op. cit.*, II, 1, s. 117.
10. Zeller, *op. cit.*, II, 1, S. 808; Deussen, *op. cit.*, II, 1, S. 278.
11. Zeller, *op. cit.*, II, 2, S. 448; Deussen, *op. cit.*, II, 1, S. 354.
12. It was believed that in the north there was the country of the Hyperboreans, who live beyond the pole, at the sources of the cold north wind. This corresponds to Uttarakuru, the country of eternal beatitude, which was supposed to be located in the north of India or in the northern direction of Mount Meru. Mount Meru has been compared to the mountain Ḳaf in Arabian mythology. (*Alberuni's India*, p. 249 cf. p. 326)

sacred in the eyes of the Japanese, was not thought to be the gathering place of gods.[13]

13. Comparison of various theories of cosmogony is not a new attempt. In ancient and medieval Japan where philosophical ideas of various countries of Asia were introduced, various theories were discussed in comparison with indigenous ones. Master Kukai, the founder of Japanese Vajrayana Buddhism (Mikkyō), put both the theory of the *I-ching* and the Hindu theory of world creation on the same level of thought (*The Stage of the Mortal Ram*). "(The I-ching teaches:) One becomes Two, and the Two produces another, making up the number of Three, and then come out all phenomena of the world. To say that they are the creation of Īśvara or Brahman is simply revealing the ignorance of the origin of life." He criticized these theories: "Who can speak with authority as to the origin of the dead?" "That which is profound and that which is shallow have been described by stages in the Sutra and in the treatise. They are arranged and described in detail in the sections to follow:" (*Hizō Hōyaku*, Introductory verse). (The translation of these passages are from the dissertation on the Hizō Hōyaku submitted to the University of Tokyo by Professor Minoru Kiyota of the University of Wisconsin.) Differences between creation-myths in various countries was noticed by Kitabatake Chikafusa, (De Bary, etc., *Japanese Tradition*, 277–279) a medieval Japanese thinker. "The creation of heaven and earth must everywhere have been the same, for it occurred within the same universe, but the Indian, Chinese and Japanese traditions are each different. According to the Indian versions, (The Indian myth of cosmogony set forth by Kitabatake Chikafusa is chiefly based upon that in the *Abhidharmakośa* by Vasubandhu, and the Chinese version of the *Dīrghāgama-sūtra*. It represents a more advanced stage of the myth than that of the Veda) the beginning of the world is called the "inception of the kalpas." A heavenly host called "Light Sound" spread golden clouds in the sky which filled the entire Brahmaloka. Then they caused rains to fall, which accumulated on the circle of wind to form the circle of water. It expanded and rose to the sky, where a great wind blew from it foam which it cast into the void; this crystallized into the palace of Brahma. The water gradually receding formed the palaces of the Realm of Desire, Mount Sumeru, the four continents, and the Iron Enclosing Mountain. Thus the countless millions of worlds came into existence at the same time. This was the kalpa of creation. "The heavenly host of Light-Sound came down, were born, and lived. This was the kalpa of settlement. During the kalpa of settlement there were twenty rises and falls. In the initial stage, people's bodies shone with a far-reaching effulgence, and they could fly about at will. Joy was their nourishment. No distinction existed between the sexes. Later, sweet water, tasting like cream and honey, sprang from the earth. (It was also called earth-savor) One sip of it engendered a craving for its taste. Thus were lost the godlike ways, and thus also was the light extinguished, leaving the wide world to darkness. In retribution for the actions of living creatures, black winds blew over the oceans, bearing before them on the waves the sun and the moon, to come to rest half-way up Mount Sumeru, there to shine forth on the four continents under the heavens. From that time on there were the day and night, the months, and the seasons. Indulgence in the sweet waters caused men's faces to grow pale and thin. Then the sweet waters vanished, and vegetable food (also called earth-rind) appeared, which all creatures ate. Then the vegetable food also vanished, and wild rice of multiple tastes was provided them. Cut in the morning, it ripened by evening. The eating of the rice left dregs in the body, and thus the two orifices were created. Male and female came to differ, and this led to sexual desire. They called each other husband and wife, built houses, and lived together. Beings from the Light-

Sound Heaven who were later to be born entered women's wombs, and once born became living creatures. "In China, nothing positive is stated concerning the creation of the world even though China is a country which affords special importance to the keeping of records. In the Confucian books nothing antedates King Fu-hsi. In other works they speak of heaven, earth, and man as having begun in an unformed, undivided state, much as in the accounts of our Age of the Gods (of Japan). There is also the legend of King P'an-ku, whose eyes were said to have turned into the sun and the moon, and whose hair turned into grasses and trees. There were afterwards sovereigns of Heaven, sovereigns of Earth, and sovereigns of Man, and the Five Dragons, followed by many kings over a period of 10,000 years." About the Japanese creation-myth he is very brief: "The beginnings of Japan in some ways resemble the Indian descriptions, telling as it does of the world's creation from the seed of the heavenly gods." As Chikafusa's comparison made clear, the difference bears witness to the fact that Indian creation-myths, although substantially different from each other, were highly elaborate. It betrays the fondness for fanciful imaginations by the ancient Indians. The ancient Chinese and Japanese were not much concerned about the details of creation. As Chikafusa states, the ancient Chinese were highly concerned with keeping records, but not with mythology. The significance of creation-myths in the context of each tradition differed greatly. For Indian Buddhists the above-cited creation-myths were nothing but preambles to explanations of the origin of human society. Chikafusa, having set forth the origin of man according to Indian Buddhist texts, continues his arguments: "Later, the wild rice ceased to grow, to the dismay of all creatures. They divided the land and planted cereals, which they made their food. Then there were those who stole other people's crops, and fighting ensued." Here we are reminded of the Western concept of *bellum omnium contra omnes*. "As there was no one to decide such cases, men got together and established a Judge-King whom they called kshatriya (which means landowner) (The Sanskrit word 'kṣatriya' is explained here as relevant to '*kṣetra*' [land or paddy]; i.e., as a synonym of '*ksetrasya pati*' [lord of land]). The first king bore the title of People's Lord (Minshu)." Here we find an Eastern counterpart of the Western theory of *social contract*. He says that this was the beginning of the lineages of royal families. But this theory could not be accepted by Japanese who were faithful to the Imperial Family. Chikafusa boastfully continues: "Whereas in our country the succession to the throne has followed a single undeviating line since the first divine ancestor, nothing of the kind has existed in India." Even theories of cosmogony cannot be considered without referring to the social context in which they were brought forth.

IV. CONCLUSION

In this chapter we have discussed religious and philosophical thinking of ancient villagers in agricultural communities. We have cited data from various countries, with Indian thinking as the axis for our considerations. The discussion has been limited chiefly to thought before the rise of philosophy, i.e., the stages prior to the Upanishadic philosophers in India, the Ionian philosophers in Greece, and the individual teachers of ethics in China. Although there are many divergencies, numerous parallels are quite apparent. These common features reflect ways of thinking and patterns of behavior which can be noticed in common among agricultural village communities in different cultural area. In terms of religious development of mankind they reflect phases of religious thought of primitive peoples before the rise of philosophical speculation as such.

CHAPTER TWO

The Twilight of The Gods: The Rise of Philosophy and The Development of Heterodoxies

I. INTRODUCTORY REMARKS

Already in the cosmogonical reflections of the later Vedic hymns and the ancient texts of other civilizations (Greece, China, Japan, etc.), thought had reached a level of development which can in some important respects be characterized as "philosophical." Generally speaking, however, such cosmogonical speculations continued to reflect the older mythological interpretation of the world, and it was not until the period of the Ionian thinkers in Greece and the Upaniṣadic thinkers in India that this older world-view began to break up (*ca.* 800–500 B.C.). In this latter period individual thinkers appeared whose thought was characterized (1) by a more or less apparent tendency to move away from the older mythic and ritualistic context; and (2) by a desire to find first-principles either rationally or intuitively with respect to interpreting the meaning of the world and man's existence. It can be said that philosophy as an enterprise distinct from purely religious concerns begins to manifest itself in this period. As mentioned earlier, of course, it is difficult to distinguish the terms "philosophy" and "religion" not only in this ancient period but in more recent periods in the development of culture as well; nevertheless, a new intellectual era did emerge with the Ionian and Upaniṣadic thinkers—a new intellectual era which can be conveniently designated as the period of the rise of philosophy.

This early period of the rise of philosophy was followed by one of the most creative periods in the intellectual history of civilization. From the fifth to the third centuries B.C., an amazing array of creative minds appeared in Greece, India, China, Israel, and ancient Persia: Pythagoras, Empedocles and Plato in Greece; Gotama and Mahavīra in India; Confucius and Lao-tzu in China; Second Isaiah, Jeremiah, Ezekiel in Israel; and Zarathustra in Persia, although the precise date of the latter is open to question. Jaspers has referred to this period as the "axial age" in the history of philosophy. Heidegger has commented with respect to Greek thought in this ancient period that it was perhaps the most creative period in the history of western philosophy. Fairbank and Reischauer comment:

> One cannot but be struck by the parallel in time between this intellectual outburst in China and the heyday of the Greek philosophers,

> the Hebraic prophets, and the historical Buddha and other early religious leaders in India. Throughout the whole civilized world it was a time of prodigious philosophical activity. One reason for this may have been the intellectual stimulation among the great centers of civilization. Mention has already been made of the acceleration of communications at this time. . . . A more fundamental explanation, however, may be the stage of civilization which all these areas had achieved by this time. They had become wealthy enough to support large numbers of thinkers.[1]

This entire period was one of incredible intellectual ferment and social change. In India the stable village life was giving way to a rising urban culture. Merchants were beginning to exert political power; a money economy was emerging; the prestige of the priests was declining while that of the "warrior-class" (*kṣatriyas*) was rising. In China during the later Chou period a transition was taking place from the old tribal "closed society" to a period in which individuals had to deal with political instability and the breakdown of the old system of values. In the Ancient Near East and Persia tremendous power struggles were taking place between peoples causing widespread insecurity and chaos—indeed, in Israel, resulting finally in destruction and exile! Likewise in the Greek context, the period was one of uncertainty and strife.

> . . . the age was one of unrest—political and social, moral, religious and intellectual. Old orders were being overturned, old traditions challenged. Revolutions were in the air. Kingship and aristocracy were being supplanted, amid much disorder, by cycles of oligarchy, democracy and tyranny.[2]

As a result of this rapid cultural and social change occurring throughout the civilized world, a new self-consciousness emerged. Men were no longer satisfied with the values, rituals and intellectual content of the older religious traditions. A need was felt for new principles or criteria by means of which one could relate oneself meaningfully to the new world that was coming into existence. The most creative minds in China, Greece, India and the Ancient Near East began to fashion new images of man and to generate new perspectives with respect to the nature and structure of the world. Some of these new images and perspectives were destined to become permanent visions by means of which generations of men would interpret their world—e.g., the intellectual visions of men

1. Fairbank and Reischauer, *East Asia*, pp. 62–63. Cf. Charles Eliot, *HB*, I, p. xix.
2. B. A. G. Fuller, *A History of Philosophy*. New York: Henry Holt and Co., 3rd edition, 1955, p. 26.

like Plato, Lao Tzu, Second Isaiah, Yājñavalkya, etc. Other images and perspectives were short-lived and were judged in subsequent generations as "heterodox," unproductive or at best "maverick" or non-conformist —e.g., the early Stoic perfectionists, the Greek sophists, many of the "hundred schools" in ancient China, the Carvākas and Ājīvikas in ancient India, etc.

As was our method in the first chapter, taking India as a norm for exposition, this whole period—i.e., the eighth to the third centuries B.C.—can be divided roughly into two phases: (1) the period of the rise of philosophy as seen in the development of speculation in the oldest Upaniṣads; and (2) the period of the development of heterodoxies as seen in the Ājīvikas, Jains, etc. The Buddhist tradition also begins in this latter period, but because the Buddhist faith eventually becomes a universal religion, a detailed discussion of it will be taken up primarily in the next chapter.

II. THE RISE OF PHILOSOPHY

A. The Early Critical Attitude

1. Yearning for the Beyond

THE term "philosophy" derives from the Greek word *philosophos* meaning a "lover of wisdom" and *philosophia* meaning "love of wisdom or knowledge."[1] Two Sanskrit words, *darśana* and *ānvīkṣikī*, represent, roughly speaking, the Indian equivalent. The word *darśana* originally meant "seeing the truth," especially "intuition," but in a wider sense it applies to all views of reality taken by the mind of man.[2] Eventually, it came to mean any "philosophical system." Buddhism is one *darśana* from the standpoint of the Hindus. Śaṅkara's Vedānta philosophy is another *darśana*. *Ānvīkṣikī*[3] means any philosophical system which has been built up by reasoning only.[4] It excludes philosophical systems which admit a higher authority, e.g., the traditional Vedic Scriptures. This term was applied to materialists, Sāṃkhya and Yoga philosophers.[5] In application, *ānvīkṣikī* has a narrower sense than *darśana*. The use of these terms shows clearly that the ancient Indians had a conception of philosophy not unlike that of ancient Greece. In China and Japan, on the other hand, the genetal term "Way" (*tao*, in Chinese, *dō* or *michi*, in Japanese) was used to refer to a religion or philosophy.

The first attempt to develop *darśana* by individual thinkers in the Indian tradition can be traced to the oldest Upaniṣads. The names of

1. Fuller, *op. cit.*, p. 1.
2. As in the case of the *Sarvadarśana-saṃgraha* by Madhava.
3. *Arthaśāstra* of Kauṭilya, ed. by J. Jolly, Lahore, 1923, p. 425. This passage was discussed in full detail by H. Jacobi in his article: Zur Fruhgeschichte der indischen Philosophie, *SPA*. 1911, S. 732 ff.
4. *hetubhir anoīkṣamāna*. . . According to Vātsyāyana, *ānoīkṣikī* means logic (*nyāyavidyā, nyāyaśāstra*). (Bhāṣya ad *Nyāya-sūtra*, I, 1. 1. pp. 4–5; 10, ĀnSS.) Cf. *Nyāyavārttika*, Benares: Chowkhamba Sanskrit Series, 1915, p. 12.
5. Cf. n. 3.

individual thinkers who were active in the older Vedic period were generally not transmitted. In the Upaniṣads, however, the names of many thinkers are mentioned, and particular thinkers are often associated with particular theories. A similar tendency to associate particular interpretations of the world and man with individual thinkers can also be noticed in other cultural areas such as Greece and China—i.e., in the Ionian and later Chou periods respectively.

Although it is difficult and hazardous to characterize the early Upaniṣads as a whole, some preliminary comments may prove helpful before presenting a more detailed analysis of particular problems.

(1) The word *upa-ni-ṣad* literally means "sitting down beside (a teacher)." Substantially, it means any "confidential session." Afterwards it came to signify "secret or esoteric doctrine," because these doctrines were taught to selected pupils (probably towards the end of their apprenticeship) in lectures from which the wider circle was excluded. These works mark the last stage of the Vedic literature—i.e., they fit in the sequence as follows: *saṃhitā*, *brāhmaṇa*, *āraṇyaka* and *upaniṣad*. It is generally accepted that the oldest pre-buddhistic Upaniṣads are *Bṛhadāraṇyaka*, *Chāndogya*, *Taittirīya* and *Aitareya*. Among these various Upaniṣads, *Bṛhadāraṇyaka* is simpler, more beautiful, and more ancient. The *Chāndogya* shows a more complex style and in content reveals a somewhat later period of intellectual development.

(2) The central problem running throughout the oldest Upaniṣads appears to be the effort to find or achieve "knowledge" regarding the ultimate or the absolute. Even in those passages which still reveal the older Vedic religion, a concern for finding ultimate truth tends to be clearly evident. In the *Kāṭhaka Upaniṣad*, for example, an old Vedic tradition concerning life after death is re-interpreted in terms of the new search for "knowledge."

A young Brahmin, Naciketas, visits the realm of the Death-God (Yama), who offers him three boons.[6] For the third one, Naciketas chooses the answer to the question: Does man exist after death? Yama replies, "On this point formerly even the gods have doubted; it is not easy to understand. That subject is subtle. Choose another boon." The youth still insists on that boon. Yama makes efforts to evade the question by offering him earthly goods:

"Choose sons and grandsons who will live a hundred years, herds of cattle, horses, elephants, and gold. Choose the wide abode of the earth, and reap yourself as many harvests as you desire."

"If you can think of any boon equal to that, choose wealth and long

6. At the age of fifty-three Emerson confided to his diary, "A grander legend than Western literature is contained in the story of Nachiketas." (Journals IX, 58. A. Christy, *The Orient in American Transcendentalism*, p. 161)

life. Be (king) of the whole earth. I make you the enjoyer of all desires." "Whatever desires are difficult to attain among mortals, ask for them according to your wish; these fair maidens with their chariots and musical instruments—such are indeed not to be obtained by men—be waited on by them whom I give to you, but do not ask me about dying."

But the youth is not seduced by this proposal. He says, "These things last till tomorrow, O Death, for they wear out the vigor of all the senses. Even the whole of life is short. Keep you your horses, keep dance and song for yourself."

"No man can be made happy by wealth. Shall we possess wealth, when we see you? Shall we live, as long as you rule? Only that boon (which I have chosen) is to be chosen by me."

Yama at last yields to his persistence and reveals the secret. Life and death, he explains, are only different phases of development; true knowledge, which consists in recognizing the identity of the individual self with the universal self, raises its possessor beyond the reach of death.

"When all desires that dwell in the human heart vanish, then the mortal becomes immortal, and obtains the Absolute (*brahman*)."[7] This search for knowledge about the nature of the individual self and the relationship of that self to the ultimate or absolute is a recurring theme throughout the Upaniṣads. We shall be returning to this problem later in the chapter.

(3) The oldest Upaniṣads in tone and flavor are characterized by an emphasis on secrecy and by frequent recourse to allegory and myth as a vehicle for expression. In the Upaniṣads the teacher refuses to impart any instruction to a pupil who approaches him, until by persistence in his endeavor the pupil has proved his worthiness to receive the instruction. The warning not to impart a certain doctrine to unworthy students is often repeated in the Upaniṣads. "The teacher shall not impart (this doctrine) to anyone who is not his immediate pupil (*antevāsin*), who has not already lived for a year in his house, who does not himself intend to be a teacher."[8] "This shall be communicated to no one, except the son or the pupil,[9] or except one's eldest son."[10] A woman or a slave was forbidden to be imparted formulas.[11]

The attempt to maintain secrecy with regard to abstruse and, therefore, easily misunderstood doctrines has numerous parallels in the Greek tradition. Pythagoras required of his pupils mystical silence (*mystike siope*). Plato finds fault with the art of writing: "When they (=speeches) have

7. *Kāṭhaka-Up.* VI, 14.
8. *Ait. Ār.* 3, 2, 6, 9.
9. *Bṛhad. Up.* III, 11, 5; VI, 3, 12. Cf. *Śvet. Up.* VI, 22; *Maitri-Up.* VI, 29.
10. *Chānd. Up.* III, 11, 5. *Muṇḍ. Up.* III, 2, 11. *Rāma-Up.* 84.
11. *Nṛsiṃh. Up.* I, 3.

been once written down they are tumbled about anywhere among those who may or may not understand them, and know not to whom they should reply, or to whom not: and, if they are maltreated or abused, they have no parent to protect them; and they cannot protect or defend themselves.[12]

In addition to secrecy, the Upaniṣadic texts as well as much subsequent Indian metaphysical speculation often assume an allegorical and more or less mythical character. The above-cited story of Naciketas is one example, and it would be possible to list many others. Both Greek and Indian thinkers resorted to allegories and myth. This was noticed explicitly by the ancient Greek, Megasthenes, who said,

> They (i.e., *Brahmins*) express views like those maintained by the Greeks. They wrap up their doctrines about immortality and future judgment, and kindred topics, in allegories, after the manner of Plato.[13]

In the fragments of Parmenides, there is an agreement in style of presentation with that of the Upaniṣads; in both one finds a lofty, forceful, graphical mode of expression and the employment of verse.[14]

(4) Although there is a central problem in the Upaniṣads as mentioned above, nevertheless it must be recognized that there is no one solution to the problem that can be found in the texts. In other words, the Upaniṣads, either individually or as a whole, do not offer a complete, consistent and logically systematized conception of the world. They are, rather, a mixture of half-mythological, half-philosophical dialogues and disputations which deal somewhat hesitantly with metaphysical questions.[15] The speculations of the Upaniṣads were only later reduced to a system by the several schools of Vedānta, Mīmāṃsā, Sāṃkhya, etc. It is true, of course, that later Vedānta philosophers wanted to show that all passages in the Upaniṣads expressed the central dogmas of Advaita Vedānta; but in reality there are many divergent traditions in the texts many of which are wholly incompatible with one another. The Upaniṣadic period was one of great intellectual ferment which produced varying traditions and "schools." In this respect the oldest Upaniṣads remind the reader of the divergent traditions among the pre-Socratics and the period of the "hundred schools" in ancient China.

12. *Phaedrus*, 275 E.
13. Megasthenes' Fragments, No. 41. *Ancient India as Described by Megasthenes and Arrian*, tr. by J. W. McCrindle, London etc., Trubner & Co., 1877. P. 101.
14. R. Garbe, *The Philosophy of Ancient India*, pp. 32–33.
15. Hajime Nakamura, *"Approaches to the Upaniṣads: Swami Nikhilananda's The Upaniṣads,"* *Philosophy East and West*, vol. XI, No. 4, Jan. 1962, pp. 245–254.

2. Re-evaluation of the Gods and the Sacrifice

IN the religion of the *Brāhmaṇas*, the merits gained from performing sacrifices were highly valued. The performance of the rites in accordance with minute rules described in the literature became the primary focus. As speculation developed, however, knowledge of the significance of the sacrifice gradually came to be more and more esteemed. Already in a passage of a later *Brāhmaṇa* it was asserted that those who merely perform rites without knowledge would be born again and repeatedly become the food of death.[1] Some passages also point to the essential futility of works. "The yonder world cannot be obtained by sacrificial gifts or by asceticism by the man who does not know this. That state belongs only to him who has this knowledge."[2]

Euripides said that the small sacrifice of the pious often outweighs a hecatomb (i.e., the public sacrifice of 100 oxen).[3] The purport of his saying sounds similar, but what mattered in Euripides was piety, in the *Brāhmaṇas* knowledge. In India, finally, the knowledge of the Self (*ātman*) came to be considered the most important knowledge: "He who sacrifices to the gods does not gain so great a world as he who sacrifices to the Self (*ātman*)."[4] The Brahmins came to hold that all sacrifices were for the sake of realizing the Self of man. Life itself is a sacrifice. "The true sacrifice is man; his first twenty-four years are his morning libation—in hunger, in thirst, in abstinence from pleasure standeth his consecration. . . . In his eating and drinking and in his pleasures he keeps a holy festival, and in his laughter, feasting, and marrying he sings hymns of praise. Self-discipline, generosity, straightforwardness, non-injury (*ahiṃsā*), and truth in speech, these are his payments, and the bath of purification when the sacrifice is over is death."[5] Here the importance of sacrifices was transferred to the daily activities of man. Although they preserved the term "sacrifice," sacrifices as such were minimized in importance.

We find a similar transition in other contexts. In the Old Testament Isaiah says, "Is not this the fast that I have chosen to loose the bands of wickedness, to undo the heavy burdens, and to let the oppressed go free, and that ye break every yoke? Is it not to deal thy bread to the hungry, and that thou bring the poor that are cast out to thy house? When thou seest the naked, that thou cover him, and that thou hide not thyself from

1. *ŚBr.* X, 4, 3, 10; Cf. X, 1, 4, 14; X, 2, 6, 19; X, 5, 1, 4; XI, 4, 3, 20.
2 *ŚBr.* X, 5, 4, 15.
3. Macdonell, *Comparative Religion, op. cit.*, p. 105.
4. *Ait. Br.* XI, 2, 6.
5. *Chānd. Up.* III, 16.

thine own flesh?"[6] Hosea also states: "They shall not pour libations of wine to the Lord; and they shall not please him with their sacrifices."[7] "I desire steadfast love and not sacrifice, the knowledge of God, rather than burnt offerings."[8] Here, however, the transition away from sacrifice is in the direction of personal piety and ethics rather than mystical knowledge as in the Upaniṣads.

Even though thought in the Upaniṣads is breaking away from the old sacrificial ideology; nevertheless, it is also true that the early Upaniṣadic thinkers are using the sacrificial imagery as a framework for their reflections. In the Vedic literature, every fire is a part of the god of fire; Agni lives in celestial remoteness, but he is present wherever a flame is kindled. Every eye is a manifestation of the sun; the human breath a manifestation of the god of wind. Such correlations came to be more systematized in the *Brāhmaṇas.* Diverse phenomena in widely different spheres of the universe came to be identified. (A) The elements of the microcosm were identified with (B) the faculties, organs, and limbs of the microcosm (man's organism), and both with (C) the details of the inherited and traditional sacrificial ritual. In the *Brāhmaṇa* literature the ritual was the principal instrument through which the forces of the universe were invoked, brought under control, and harnessed to man's needs and desires. The philosophers of the Upaniṣads begin with this older brahmanical thinking, but generally, in the Upaniṣads only (A) and (B) stand in correlation with each other.

In one passage,[9] for example, the three elements, earth, fire and water, correspond to (1) the human breath, (2) sight and (3) skin; and again, (1) atmosphere, (2) heaven, (3) the four quarters. The four intermediate quarters correspond, on the one hand, to wind, sun, moon,[10] and stars, and, on the other, to hearing, mind, speech, and touch. Further, plants, trees, space, and one's body are matched by flesh, muscle, bone and marrow. Many of the identifications were tentative and arbitrary, excessively schematic; they did not prove convincing to posterity. But the practical effect of the movement as a whole was progressively to impersonalize the universe and to undermine the prestige of the earlierVedic gods as well as the sacrificial process itself.[11]

6. Isaiah, LVIII, 6–7.
7. Hosea, 9, 4.
8. Hosea, 6, 6.
9. *Tait. Up.* I, 7.
10. According to the scheme in the Veda, Mind (*manas*) corresponds to the moon. The reason is not clear. "Dass endlich sein *Manas* zum Monde wird, hat vielleicht seinen Grund darin, dass die ruhige Klarheit des Mondlichts (welches ja auch nach Goethe "die Seele lost") als Symbol des Intellektuellen erschien." (Deussen, *Allgemeine Geschichte der Philosophie,* I, 1, S. 156)
11. H. Zimmer, *op. cit.,* pp. 341–342.

As this kind of speculation developed, the dignity and significance of the gods were lessened. To the man who had acquired metaphysical knowledge of the unity of the self and the ultimate, the entire religious system of different gods and of the necessity of sacrificing to the gods was seen to be a stupendous fraud: "When peoples ay, 'Sacrifice to this god!' 'Sacrifice to that god,' each god is but the manifestation of the self (*ātman*), for he is all gods."[12] Here "the self" is to be regarded as the fundamental principle underlying our existence. Another passage runs as follows: "So whoever worships another divinity (than himself), thinking 'He is one and I am another,' he does not know. He is like a sacrificial animal for the gods. Verily, indeed, as many animals would be of service to man, even so each single person is of service to the gods. Even if only one animal is taken away, it is unpleasant. How much more when many are taken? Therefore, it is not pleasing to those gods that men should know this. (i.e., it is unpleasant to the gods that men should know that the gods are only phases of the Self and that an individual man may himself become the absolute by knowing himself to be such.)"[13] Here we find a bold assertion that gods are nothing but a phase of the Self.

In Greece the Olympian pantheon was disintegrated and dissolved by criticism and natural science in the age of the Sophists and the philosophers—Anaxagoras, Democritus, Aristotle, etc. The gods of Homer became laughable[14] and were mocked because of their all-too-human love affairs and excesses of wrath. Such qualities were regarded as incompatible with the later more spiritual and ethical concept of divinity. Moral critics were offended by the philandering of Zeus and the family quarrels of Olympus. However, so far as the speculation by Greek philosophers dealt with the physical origin of things, it did not clash with any orthodox belief held by the average Greek; for the Greek had no fixed religious canon that dictated to him what he should believe about the origin or the constitution of the natural world. The religion of the people was a living faith till late, still untouched by the influence of science and philosophic scepticism.

In Japan, which culturally developed later than India and Greece, the situation was somewhat different. Protest against ritualism was directed not against the native religion, but against the already established universal religion, i.e., Esoteric Buddhism (Vajrayāna, Mikkyō) which was overlaid with a highly developed and complicated ritualism. Those who made such a protest were the thinkers of medieval Shinto (Ise Shintō).

12. *Bṛhad. Up.* I, 4, 6.
13. *Bṛhad. Up.* I, 4, 10.
14. "Homer and Hesiod attributed to the gods all things that are shameful." (Xenophanes, fr. 11, tr. by Freeman, cf. Fr. 12)

Philosophical Shintoists of the medieval period wrote: "What pleases the Deity is not material offerings. The true offerings are virtue and sincerity."[15] Truthfulness, faithfulness, honesty, integrity, purity of heart, not bodily purity, were the ethical standards of philosophical Shintoism. There was a strong emphasis on Shintoism as a religion of complete sincerity and integrity: "The favor of the gods depends on integrity. The sun and moon circumambulate the Four Regions and illumine the Six Cardinal Points, but particularly do they shine on the basis of the upright."[16] "If you serve the god with uprightness and sincerity he has no need of offerings."[17] Purity of mind was especially esteemed. Ichijo Kaneyoshi states: "There are two kinds of purity, the inner purity and the outer purity. And the meaning is that sincere intimacy with the divine is the inner purity. The integrity of the inner purity means a sincere mind."[18]

Such a conspicuous protest reminds us of that of the Hebrew prophets. Dr. Genchi Kato states: "In this respect, Shinto above all, resembles the prophetism of Israel in the 8th and 7th centuries B.C., because both Shinto and Prophetism were national religions, not universal religions, and yet each is a culture religion in full bloom."[19] Whereas justice or righteousness was esteemed in the prophetism of Israel, universal love in Christianity, and loving-kindness or compassion in Buddhism, sincerity or truthfulness held the central place in later philosophical Shintoism. This probably reflects a characteristic way of thinking of the Japanese who traditionally emphasized personal relationships in a human nexus.[20]

3. Brief Summary

The earliest philosophy in India, although taking its point of departure from the older sacrificial context, quickly moved in new directions. Knowledge of the sacrifice gave way to knowledge about man. Knowledge of the gods gave way to knowledge about the world. Thinking moved in the direction of a search for a basic unity underlying the manifoldness

15. *Shintō Gobusho*, passim.
16. *Shintō Gobusho* in the chapter of Yamato-hime-no-mikoto-seiki.
17. *Gochinza-hongi.*
18. *Nihonshoki-sansho.*
19. Genchi Kato, *Shinto in Essence as Illustrated by the Faith in a Glorified Personality* (Tokyo, the Nogi Shrine, 1954, p. 9).
20. Hajime Nakamura, *Ways of Thinking of Eastern Peoples* (Honolulu: East-West Center Press: 1964), pp. 407–530.

of the universe. This search, or inquiry, was conducted along two main lines which eventually were to converge in significance. First, responding to the question, "What is the one and only essence that has become manifest in diversity?", thinkers sought the highest power or principle behind the formations of the outer world. Second, to the question, "What is the essence of our existence?," or, "What is the source from which the forces and organs of my own life have proceeded?", they were directed toward introspective analysis. Such self-analysis thus developed as a parallel discipline, correlative and contributive to the search for the essence of reality itself. In the search for the absolute principle, Indian thinkers sometimes regarded a certain element in the natural world as the highest principle; at other times, they regarded any function or power in human existence as the highest principle.

B. Elements Regarded as the Fundamental Principle

In the attempt to reach a fundamental principle, several early thinkers suggested that some element noticed concretely in the natural world is the fundamental principle. Some of the earliest metaphysical speculations arose out of such reflections.

1. Water

In India water was regarded as such a first principle in an early stage of philosophical speculation. A number of scriptures[1] set forth the idea. Later Vedantic theologians identified the water in these passages with *brahman*, but this is a highly contrived interpretation.[2] Likewise, at an early stage of Greek philosophy Thales asserted that Water was the material cause of the world. Concerning the reason why Thales chose water as the first principle, Aristotle suggests that "he got the notion perhaps from seeing that the nutriment of all things is moist, and that heat itself is generated by the moist and kept alive by it . . . and that the seed of all creatures has a moist nature, and water is the origin of the nature of moist things."[3] Another suggestion is that "water makes life possible. It was part of the plot by which our planet engendered life. Every egg-cell is mostly water, and water is its first habitat. Water is turns to endless purposes."[4] The fact that both Greek and Indian thinkers admitted that "water was the principle employed in the making of the world" was pointed out in antiquity by Megasthenes.[5]

1. *Bṛhad. Up.* V, 5, 1, etc.
2. Water as the world-principle in Greece and India is discussed by W. Ruben (*Indische und Griechische Metaphysik, op. cit.*, S. 158–159).
3. W. K. C. Guthrie, *The Greeks and Their Gods* (London: Methuen, 1950), p. 134.
4. An opinion by Sir Charles Sherrington, cited by Guthrie (*A History of Greek Philosophy*, Cambridge University Press, 1962, p. 71).
5. Megasthenes, *Ind.* p. 101, fr. 41.

2. Ether or Space

ETHER or space (*ākāśa*) was described in a similar way. It was regarded as that from which everything arises,[1] or out of which everything appears and into which everything is dissolved.[2] A man asked Pravahana Jaivali, a philosopher, "What is the origin (*gati*) of the world?" He replied, "Ether, for all these beings rise out of ether and return to ether. Ether is older than these; ether is their foundation (*pratiṣṭhā*)."

Ether was worshipped as the absolute (*brahman*). He urged: "In the ether or space we rejoice (when we are together), and do not rejoice (when we are separated). In the ether everything is born, and towards the ether everything tends when it is born. Meditate on ether. He who meditates on ether as the absolute (*brahman*), obtains the worlds of ether and of light, which are free from pressure and pain, wide and spacious; he is, as it were, lord and master as far as ether reaches."[3]

We see that the word "ether" did not mean a mere empty space or a limited element, but an undifferentiated one; it could, therefore, be called the foundation (*pratihṣṭā*). The appellation "ether" was rather metaphorical, and such an assertion can be seen as an effort to get away from the cosmological thinking of earlier times. On this account it can be compared with Anaximander's conception of "the Non-Limited" (*apeiron*) which is the unlimited and undifferentiated principle and the source of everything. He said: "The Non-Limited is the original material of existing things; further, the source from which existing things derive their existence is also that to which they return at their destruction, according to necessity."[4] "This (essential nature, whatever it is, of the Non-Limited) is everlasting and ageless."[5] "The Non-Limited is immortal and indestructible."[6]

The fact that space or ether was admitted as the fundamental principle by both Greek and Indian thinkers was also pointed out by Megasthenes, who said: "In addition to the four elements there is a fifth agency, from which the heaven and the stars were produced."[7] This calls to mind the following passage: "From this Self (*ātman*), verily, ether arose; from ether air; from air fire; from fire water, from water the earth."[8] Although

1. *Chānd. Up.* VII, 12, 1.
2. *Chānd. Up.* I, 9, 1.
3. *Chānd. Up.* VII, 12, 1–2.
4. Anaximander's fragment, 1.
5. *Ibid*, 2.
6. *Ibid*, 3.
7. Cf. n. i.
8. *Tait. Up.* II, 1.

both the Indians and Greeks regarded ether as the source of everything else, such metaphysical thinking in the Upaniṣads was often set forth in passages giving fanciful explanations related to sacrifices, while in Greece such explanations were conspicuously lacking.[9]

3. Wind or Breath

In India the wind (moving air; later as an element) also was regarded as the material cause by some philosophers (Yājñavalkya, et. al).[1] It was characterized as the "thread" (*sūtra*), which holds together this and other worlds, all beings and the members of the body.[2]

The question was asked: "Do you know that thread by which this world and the other world, and all beings are strung together?" A philosopher, Yājñavalkya, answered: "Air (*vāyu*) is that thread. By air, as by a thread, this world and the other world, and all creatures are strung together. Therefore, people say of a dead person that his limbs have become unstrung; for by air, as by a thread, they were strung together."

In other contexts, the conception of the wind as "collector" or "that which holds together" was widely current in India. It was not a cosmological conception in this case, but was rather regarded as the basis of everything. Raikva, the wandering philosopher, said: "Air (*vāyu*) is indeed the end of all (lit. that which holds together). For when fire goes out, it goes into air. When the sun goes down, it goes into air. When the moon goes down, it goes into air. When water dries up, it goes into air. Air indeed consumes them all. So much with reference to the Deities[3] (*devas*).

"Now with reference to the body. Breath (*prāṇa*) is indeed the end of all. When a man sleeps, speech goes into breath, so do sight, hearing, and mind. Breath indeed consumes them all."

"These are the two ends, air among the deities, breath among the senses."[4]

In several passages of the Upaniṣads, the "breath of life" (*prāṇa*), which also means life itself or the life-principle, was regarded as the highest

9. More references to German studies on this subject are cited by W. Ruben (*Indische und Griechische Metaphysik, op. cit.*, s. 159–160).
1. Cf. *Bṛhad. Up.* I, 5, 12.
2. *Chānd. Up.* IV, 3.
3. The word "Deities" is used on conformity with the contemporary that different deities resided in different celestial bodies and elements.
4. *Chānd. Up.* IV, 3, 1–4.

principle.[5] Indeed, it was almost identified with the intelligent self by later scholars. The psychological fable about the dispute of the vital organs, which is related often in the Upaniṣads, points up the supremacy of the breath of life over other vital organs. (These organs also are denoted by the same Sanskrit word *prāṇa*).[6]

At nearly the same time, one finds conceptions which correspond to these in Greece. Anaximenes (c. 546 B.C.) discovered and demonstrated his fundamental principle; i.e., air, by the analogy of microcosmos and macrocosmos. "As our soul, being air, holds us together, so do breath (*pneuma*) and air (*aer*) surround the whole universe.[7]

The connection of life with breath and so with air is easily understandable. The Latin word for soul, *anima*, means both air and breath. For Anaximenes air is *theos*; it is the primary substance. Anaximenes chose an air in perpetual motion as the *arkhe*. He respected "an age-old and still flourishing popular belief which associated, and in fact identified, breath and life. That the air which we breathe should be the life itself which animates us is a common idea, and the breath-soul a world-wide conception."[8]

Diogenes of Apollonia (fifth century B.C.), a follower of Anaximenes, makes out that air is not only the one original and permanent substance but is also in its purest form the substance of all *psykhe* in the universe. It has special affinities with the soul in animals and human beings.[9] Simplicus quotes from his book, *On Nature*: "Mankind and the other animals live on air, by breathing; and it is to them both soul and mind. The soul of all animals is the same, namely, air, which is warmer than the air outside, in which we live, though much colder than that near the sun. In my opinion that which has intelligence is what men call air, and by it everything is directed and it has power over all things; for it is just this substance which I hold to be God."[10]

The conceptions of wind and ether (together=*avyaktam*)[11] were related by Yājñavalkya to that of the "Indestructible" (*akṣaram*),[12] and both were interpreted as synonyms of *brahman* in the later theology.[13]

5. Cf. *Bṛhad. Up.* I, 5, 12.
6. *Chānd. Up.* V, 1. Cf. *Bṛhad. Up.* VI, 1, 7–14.
7. Anaximenes' fragment, 2. Cf. 4.
8. W. K. C. Guthrie, *A History of Greek Philosophy*, I, 1962, Cambridge University Press, p. 128.
9. S. Radhakrishnan, *The Principal Upanishads*, p. 404.
10. W. K. C. Guthrie, *The Greeks and Their Gods* (London: Methuen, 1950), pp. 135–36.
11. *Bṛhad. Up.* II, 3, 3.
12. *Bṛhad. Up.* III, 8, 8.
13. *Brahma-sūtra*, I, 1, 22 ff.

4. Fire

In the Indian scriptures, especially in the Upaniṣads, the Universal Fire (*Agni Vaiśvānara*) was regarded as the fundamental principle. Already in the Ṛg-Vida, Fire (*Agni*) as a god was addressed as "the king of all worship, the guardian of Ṛta (cosmic law), the shining one,"[1] "never-failing,"[2] He was lauded as the "god who knows all the world."[3] Later, Fire came to be regarded as the fundamental principle of human existence: "This fire which is here within a person is the Universal Fire (*Vaiśvānara*) by means of which the food that is eaten is cooked (digested). It is the sound thereof that one hears by covering the ears thus. When one is about to depart (from this life) one does not hear this sound."[4] The whole universe was identified with the cosmic fire: "This world is fire. The earth itself is its fuel, fire the smoke, night the flame, the moon the coals, the stars the sparks. In this fire the gods offer rain. Out of that offering food arises."[5]

In Greece Heraclitus is said to have asserted that "the cosmos is born out of fire and again resolved into fire in alternate periods for ever."[6] Chrysippus (280–207 B.C.) held that only Zeus, the Supreme Fire, is immortal; the other gods, including the sun and moon, are born and die. Zeus as the Supreme Fire can be compared to Agni Vaiśvānara.

5. Numbers

The starting-point of the Pythagoreans, viz., identification (*homoiomata*) of numbers and micro- or macrocosmical factors, can also be found in the *Brāhmaṇas* and *Upaniṣads*. Such magical associations of numbers were widely prevalent.[1] For example, the first twenty-four years of a person's life were identified with the morning Soma-libation, because the Gayatrī meter has twenty-four syllables and the morning Soma-libation is offered with a Gayatrī hymn. If any sickness should overtake him in this period of life, it was believed that he could be cured of such sickness by reciting a magical formula which has some connection with this ceremony.

1. *ṚV.* I, 1.
2. *ṚV.* I, 143.
3. *Īśā-* Up. 18.
4. *Bṛhad. Up.* V, 9.
5. *Bṛhad. Up.* VI, 2, 11.
6. Diogenes Laertius, IX, 8. W. K. C. Guthrie, *A History of Greek Philosophy*, I, Cambridge University Press, 1962, pp. 454–464.

1. e.g. *Chānd. Up.* III, 16.

In India, however, such arbitrary identifications had only a kind of magical significance in order to show how to attain long life. In contrast to Greece, no mathematics, no theory of music, and no astronomy developed out of such speculation; Indians of the days of the Upaniṣads did not yet realize the speculative implications of the laws of numbers, just as they acknowledged no natural laws as such. (Indian mathematics and astronomy developed in later times.) One therefore cannot say that Indian speculation on numbers explained, as did the Pythagoreans, the principles of mathematics by associating them with the principles[2] of the universe.

6. Summary

In this ancient period both the Greek and Indian philosophers were reacting against the older religious ideas and rituals, and thinkers in both traditions were searching for an ultimate principle by means of which the world could be rendered intelligible. It is clear, however, that whereas the Ionian philosophers were developing a natural philosophy which would eventually become a basis for scientific thinking, the Indian thinkers were moving in a different direction. In Indian thought, not only the gods but the whole outer world was dwindling in importance. Indian philosophy in this ancient period did not create a basis for scientific thinking; rather, the philosophy of India was driving towards a metaphysics of the inner life of man.

A verse from an Upaniṣad shows the introspective character of the philosophy of the Upaniṣads:

> The Creator, the divine Being who is self-existent (*svayambhu*), drilled the apertures of the senses, so that they should go outward in various directions; that is why man perceives the external world and not the Inner Self (*antar-ātman*). The wise man, however, desirous of the state of immortality, turning his eyes inward and backward (*pratyag*, 'into the interior') beholds the Self."[1]

2. Cf. John Burnet, *Early Greek Philosophy*. Third Edition, London, A. & C. Black, Ltd. 1920, pp. 307 f.
1. *Kāṭhaka-Up.* II, 1, 1.

C. The Concept of the Absolute

THE search for a fundamental principle which could be considered as the Ultimate or Absolute was developing in a variety of cultural areas in this ancient period—e.g., Greece, China, India, Persia, Israel, etc.—but in India, as was suggested earlier, the concept of the Absolute was manifesting itself in terms of a metaphysics of the inner life of man. The early Upanisadic philosophers sought to identify the Absolute (*brahman*) with the Self (*ātman*). In order to understand the full significance of this identification, it is necessary in this section to discuss the following: (a) the content of the notions *brahman* and *ātman*; (b) how the notions came to be identified; (c) the various Indian conceptions of being as such and the source of being; (d) the various Indian notions regarding the structures of human existence and the Absolute Subject; and (e) some later Indian ideas regarding the deified Self. Following our usual method, these problems in the Indian context will serve as a basis for a more general comparative analysis.

1. The absolute and the Self

THE etymology of the word *brahman* is uncertain.[1] Some scholars suggest that it is etymologically related to the Greek *phlegma* (flame). The word *brahman* in the *Ṛg-veda* means often little more than the lifting and spiritualising power of prayer, "magical power" or "magic formula" or "magical words in rituals." There is nowhere any clear indication of its later metaphysical significance; it always means mere formulae and verses containing secret magic power, by which men influence divine beings, or obtain and even force something from them. Later it came to mean sacred knowledge or even the Vedic scriptures themselves. As a philosophical conception, it came to mean "the universal holiness" or "divinity," as manifested in prayer, priest and sacrifice in the *Brāhmaṇas*. Finally, in the Upaniṣads it becomes "the holy principle which animates

1. Deussen, *Allgemeine Geschichte der Philosophie*, I, 1, S. 249 f. Macdonell and Keith, *Vedic Index, op. cit.*, S. V. brahman.

the world," "the fundamental cause" or "primordial principle"; it was hypostatized as the highest principle. It is the central force of nature, shaping and supporting everything. In some later philosophical schools it became an Indian appellation for the absolute. The history of this term may be compared with that of the Logos which incurred a similar abstraction and hypostatization.[2]

On the other hand, the place of the more personal Prajāpati in the *Brāhmaṇas* was taken over by the *ātman* as a creative power in the Upaniṣads.[3] The etymology of the word *ātman* is also uncertain. Some have suggested that it is of the same etymology as German *ātman*, *Odem* and Greek *atmos*. In the Ṛg-veda, *ātman* meant no more than "breath"; wind, for instance, was spoken of as the *ātman* of Varuṇa. In the *Brāhmaṇas*, *ātman* was generally a principle or an entity which confers life or divine individuality on a person, always going from the human plane to the sacrificial one, from the sacrificial to the divine.[4] In the *Brāhmaṇas*, occasionally it means "self," and in Sanskrit literature this word is often used as a reflexive pronoun, like French *se* and German *sich* or *selbst*. As a substantive it denotes one's own person or one's own body in contrast to the outside world; sometimes, the trunk in contrast to the limbs; but, most frequently, it denotes the soul, the true self, in contrast to the body. The term *ātman* is occasionally compared, in some respects, to Greek *ontos on* or *auto kath hauto*.[5] The change and development of the word *ātman* is parallel to that of the word *psykhe* in Greek.[6] The *ātman*, however, was always strictly distinguished from mind (*manas*).[7]

2. P. Deussen. *The System of the Vedanta*. Tr. by Charles Johnston. Chicago, the Open Court Publishing Company, 1912, p. 49.
3. Cf. *Ait. Ār.* II, 4, 1.
4. Louis Renou, "*On the Word Ātman,* " *Vāk*, No. 2, (Deccan College, Poona, 1952), p. 156.
5. Plato called the essential reality, *to on, to ontos on*, the *auto* (*atman*) *kath hauto* (*an sich*). (P. Deussen, *The Philosophy of the Upanishads*. Authorized English translation by A. S. Geden. Edinburgh: T. and T. Clark, 1906. New York: Dover Publications, 1966, pp. 41–42) Cf. Deussen, *System*, p. 97; *Allgemeine Geschichte der Philosophie*, II, 3, S. 482–484.
6. Rohde, *Psyche*.
7. There developed the idea that every sensible perception is a work of the mind (manas), which involved the conclusion that the rest of the organs of sense are subordinated to the mind: "My mind was elsewhere, (therefore) I did not see it, my mind was elsewhere, (therefore) I did not hear. It is with the mind, truly, that one sees. It is with the mind that one hears. Desire, determination, doubt, faith, lack of faith, steadfastness, lack of steadfastness, shame, intellection, fear, all this is truly mind. Therefore even if one is touched on his back, he discerns it with his mind." (*Bṛhad. Up.* I, 5, 3)

   Uddālaka, the Upaniṣadic philosopher, said: "When a man is said to be hungry, water is carrying away (i.e., digesting) what has been eaten by him. When a man is said to be thirsty, fire is carrying away what has been drunk by him. Among in-

In the philosophy of the Upaniṣads these two conceptions of *brahman* and *ātman* were treated as almost synonymous with each other. Yet strictly speaking, *Brahman* represents the cosmic principle which pervades the universe, and *Ātman* represents the psychic principle manifested in man; and the latter, as the known, is used to explain the former as the unknown.

Those who reflected about the principles of *ātman* or *brahman* tried to explain why multifarious phenomena came out of the fundamental principle. Some attempted an explanation based upon an analogy of sex. A creation-myth[8] relates that in the beginning of the universe there was the *ātman* alone. It became frightened in its loneliness and felt no pleasure. Desiring a second being, it became man and woman, and from them the human race was produced: "He (*ātman*) caused that self to fall into two parts. From that arose husband and wife. He became united with her. From that human beings were produced."[9] It then proceeded to produce

---

gredients of man what keeps life is breath. Mind is fastened to breath. Just as a bird when tied by a string flies first in every direction, and finding no resting-place anywhere, settles down at last on the very place where it is fastened, exactly in the same manner, that mind after flying in every direction, and finding no resting-place anywhere, settles down in breath." Here the importance of mind is noteworthy.

According to another Upaniṣad, desire, judgment, doubt, belief, unbelief, firmness, weakness, modesty, knowledge, fear—all this is only *manas* (mind). Then when anyone is touched from behind he knows it through the manas. (*Maitr.*, 6, 3). In Greece Epicharmos asserted the same thing. "Mind (nous) sees and Mind hears; everything else is deaf and blind." (fr. 12)

"When the Soul-bird at last escapes from the net of the fowler (Pa. 124. 7) and finds its King then the apparent distinction of immanent from transcendent being dissolves in the light of day, and it hears and speaks with a voice that is at once its own and its King's saying:

'I was the Sin that from Myself rebell'd:
I the remorse that tow'rd Myself compell'd. . . .
Pilgrim, Pilgrimage and Road
Was but Myself toward Myself; and Your
Arrival but Myself at my own door.'

Faridu'd-Din 'Attar, Mantiqu't-Tair, Fitzgerald's version. Cf. Ialalu'd-Din Rumi, Mathnawi, I. 3056–65 and JUB 3. 14. 1–5. Swami Nirbhyananda said:

'I am the bird caught in the net of illusion,
I am he who bows down the head
And the One to whom he bows:
I alone exist, there is neither seeker nor sought,
When at last I realized Unity, then I knew what had been unknown,
That I had always been in union with Thee.'

(H. P. Shastri, *Indian Mystic Verse,* London 1941) (cited from Coormaraswamy; Recollection, Indian and Platonic, Supplement to *Journal of the American Oriental Society*, New Haven, 1944, pp. 36–37)

8. *Bṛhad. Up.* I, 4, 1.
9. *Bṛhad. Up.* I, 4, 3.

male and female animals in a similar way; and finally it created water, fire, the gods, and so forth. In the same way, Plato also sets forth a myth of the androgynous man.[10]

This conception of the creation of the universe is also somewhat similar to that of Yin and Yang held by the Chinese. In ancient Chinese philosophy, the primaeval chaos was supposed to have been broken up by the antagonism of two principles, namely, expansion and contraction. They were called Yin and Yang. The Yang is held to be the male force in all creatures, and the Yin to be the female. Since this conceptualization ascribes all negative characteristics to the female or *Yin*, it undoubtedly reflects a context in which the power and influence of men had become predominant.

In Greece Acusilaos represented Chaos as bringing forth a male and a female being—Erebus and Night; Aether, Eros, Metis, and a number of divinities, being the result of their union.[11] Aristophanes told a myth to the same effect. "Let me treat of the nature of man and what has happened to it; for the original human nature was not like the present, but different. The sexes were not two as they are now, but originally three in number; there was man, woman, and the union of the two, having a name corresponding to this double nature, which had once a real existence, but is now lost." The two halves wandered about longing after one another.[12]

The all-pervasiveness of the *ātman* was emphasized in one Upaniṣad in an exalted strain: "It (the *ātman*) is here all-pervading down to the tips of the nails. One does not see it any more than a razor hidden in its case or fire in its receptacle. For it does not appear as a whole. When it breathes, it is called breath; when it speaks, voice; when it hears, ear; when it thinks, mind. These are merely the name of its activities. He who worships the one or the other of these organs, has not (correct knowledge. . . .) One should worship it as the Self. For in it all these (breath, etc.) become one."[13] This means that senses or organs are not the true self. In the last sentence cited one is reminded of Plato's immanent "Daimon" and "Hegemon," who care for nothing but the truth"and whom God has given to each one of us to dwell along with him and in him."[14]

The distinction between the true self and the false self was also dis-

10. *Symposium* 189c.
11. Zeller, *op. cit.*, ETr. I, pp. 97–98.
12. Plato, *Symposium*, 189 ff.
13. *Bṛhad. Up.* I, 4, 7. A. A. Macdonell, *History of Sanskrit Literature, op. cit.*, pp. 220–221. According to A. K. Coomaraswamy's "*Recollection* etc." p. 40. ātmano' tmā netā mṛtaḥ (*Maitri-Up.* 6, 7; viśvo devasya (savitur) netur marto vurīta sakhyam, *ṚV.* V. 50, 1).
14. Greater *Hippias* 288 D. *Timaeus* 90, A. B.

cussed in other ways. In a famous dialogue[15] we find the following teaching. Once a proud and learned Brahman, Gargya Balaki went to Ajātaśatru, the King of Benares, and pledged himself to explain *brahman* to him. At first he explained the personal spirit (*puruṣa*) in the sun as *brahman*. But Ajātaśatru was not satisfied with that notion. He then explained, one after another, the personal spirit in the moon as *brahman*, and then the personal spirit in the lightning, in the ether, in the wind, in the fire, in the water; then the spirit which appears as a reflected image or shadow, and then the spirit in the echo, in sound, in dreams, in the human body, or in the eye as Brahman. Ajātaśatru, however, was not satisfied with any of these explanations. Finally, the learned Brahman himself asked the king for instruction. The latter then explained to him that the true *brahman* is to be sought only in the intelligent spirit (*puruṣa*) in man; i.e., in the *ātman*, in the self. Moreover, this spirit is identical with the fundamental principle of the universe. King Ajātaśatru used the following metaphor: "Just as the spider comes out of itself by means of its thread, or as tiny sparks come forth out of the fire, so do all senses, all worlds, all gods, all beings come forth from that Self." A conception of the soul similar to the above can also be found in Plato. 'Philosophy . . . admonishing the soul to collect and assemble herself in her Self, and to throw in nothing but, her Self, that she may know her Self itself, the Self of (all) beings.'[16]

In another famous Upaniṣadic passage, the difference between the true and the false *ātman* is taught in a similar way:[17] " 'The Self (*ātman*) which is free from sin, free from old age, from death and grief, from hunger and thirst, whose wishes are true,[18] whose intentions are true, that Self should one investigate, that Self should one endeavor to know: he who has found and known this Self, obtains all worlds and all desires.' " In connection with this, several theories of the Self are mentioned successively: 1) body is the Self; 2) spirit in dreams is the Self; 3) spirit in sleep is the Self; and finally 4) the theory that one who knows is the true self. "This body is mortal and always held by death. It is the abode of that Self which is immortal and without body. While the Self is united with the body (by thinking, this body is I and I am this body) the Self is held by pleasure

15. *Kauṣītaki-Up*, IV; *Bṛhad. Up.* II, 1.

16. *Phaedo* 83 B. Coomaraswamy's Tr. ("*Recollection* etc." p. 14). Coomaraswamy mentions the following materials; Phaedo 83B, C "The Self of (all) beings" (*hauto ton onton*) and "Soul of every man" (psykhe pantōn anthropou. Fowler's version, preferable to Jowett's "every soul of man") corresponds to the "Self of all beings" (sarveṣāṃ bhūtānām ātmā), cf. *Phaedrus*, 246 B, pasa he psykhe pantos and 249 E. Hermes Lib. 10, 7, *tsykhe ton pantos, Phaedo* 77 A we are told, not that 'our souls existed before we were born,' but that 'the soul of us (*tēn te psykhēn hēmōn*) existed before we were born.'

17. *Chānd. Up.* VIII, 7–12.

18. =whose wishes are realized without fail.

and pain. So long as he is united with the body, he cannot be free from pleasure and pain. But when he is free of the body (i.e., when he knows himself to be different from the body), then neither pleasure nor pain touches him. . . . Now when the eye is directed to yonder ether, then there is the spirit (*puruṣa*) in the eye; the eye itself is the instrument of seeing. And it is the *ātman* who knows: This I will smell; the organ of smell serves only for smelling. (It is nothing but the instrument of smelling.) And it is the Self who knows; this will I speak; the voice serves only for speaking. And it is the Self who knows; this will I hear; the organ of hearing serves only for hearing. And it is the Self who knows; this will I think; the organ of thought is his divine eye. Him, indeed, this Self, do the gods worship; therefore, do they possess all worlds, and all their desires are fulfilled. And he obtains all worlds and the fulfillment of all desires, who has found and recognizes this Self." In this legend also the true Self (*ātman*) is explained as the knowing and intelligent spirit in man.

In the *Timaeus*, Plato distinguishes two souls, one immortal and the other mortal. The mortal soul consists of passions and affections. It is the empirical ego which identifies itself with the perishing world of change and death. The immortal soul is the intelligent principle common to man and the world, the divine spark enclosed in the human personality (*Timaeus* and *Phaedo*). We have also the same distinction in Aristotle's *intellectus agens* as opposed to perishing mind and memory.[19]

In one Upaniṣad[20] the nature of the *ātman* is explained in three stages. The soul in the body as reflected in a mirror or water is first identified with *brahman*; then the dreaming soul; and, lastly, the soul in dreamless sleep. In some cases dream and deep sleep were not strictly distinguished, and ancient thinkers extolled the state of sleep.[21] In the state of sleep ones'

19. Radhakrishnan, *Indian Philosophy*, Vol. I, p. 157.
20. *Chānd. Up.* VIII, 7–12.
21. As for dreaming Coomaraswamy (*Recollections*, etc. pp. 3–4 made elaborate comments. In this technical sense 'sleep' and 'dreaming' are not the sleep of fatigue but the act of imagination. And this is quite universal. For example, "I will pour out my spirit upon all flesh . . . your old men shall dream dreams, your young men shall see visions" (Joel 2. 28); "My thought had soared high aloft, while my bodily senses had been put under restraint by sleep—yet not such sleep as that of men weighed down by fullness of food or by bodily weariness—methought there came to me a Being. . . . the Mind of the Sovereignty . . . (who said;) 'Keep in mind all that you desire to learn, and I will teach you.' (Hermes Trismegistos, Lib. I, 1-ib. 28. He refers to the sleep of fatigue as 'irrational sleep')"; "Me bi-fel a ferly . . . I slumberde in slepying gon I meeten a meruelous swenene . . . I beo-heold. . . ." (Piers the Plowman, Prologue). Rumi, Mathnawi 4, 3067 contrasts the sleep of the vulgar with that of the elect; the latter "has nothing in common with the sleep of ignorance (khwab-i-ghaflat) in which most people pass their conscious lives" (Nicholson's note on Mathnawi 2. 31, Cf. 1, 388–393; and BG. 2. 69). Life is an "awakening" from non-existence; "sleep" is an awakening from life. Cf. P. Arunachalam, Luminous Sleep (reprinted from the *Westminster Review*; Colombo 1903). As for deep sleep where man does not dream we shall discuss it later.

mind feels as if it were enjoying more freedom, and displays fully the powers of perception and action. In the waking state, nerves and the brain are held in close unity by the conscious will, but in sleep the conscious will becomes latent and its organs are isolated from each other and act freely. "There, in 'dream' (*svapne*),[22] that divinity (mind) intuits (*anubhavati*) Greatness. Whatever has been seen, he sees again. Whatever has been heard, he hears again. Whatever has been and has not been seen, whatever has been heard and has not been heard, intuitively-known or unknown, good or evil, whatever has been directly-experienced in any land or air, again and again he directly experiences; he sees it all, he sees it all.[23] In China Chuang Tzu expressed a similar thought. "The mind of the sage at rest becomes the mirror of the universe." Such reflections were also prevalent among the ancient Greeks.[24]

Later the four stages of consciousness were systematized; i.e., the waking state, the dreaming state, the deep-sleep state and the fourth state.[25] The waking soul is in this instance called "the Common-to-all-men,"[26] perhaps because all men in their waking hours have a world in common, but in dreams each has his own world. Heraclitus said: "To those who are awake, there is one ordered universe common (to all), whereas in sleep each man turns away (from this world) to one of his own."[27]

In spite of these many similarities between Indian and Greek notions, there is also an important difference. In India the term *ātman* was made a philosophical concept, and the metaphysics of *ātman* was stressed, whereas in Greece the word *seautos* or *autos* in the nominative form never became the subject of philosophical discussion. This difference perhaps reflects the fact that Greek philosophy tended to view things as existing primarily in an objective world, whereas the main trend of Indian philosophy, i.e., the Upaniṣadic and Vedantic philosophy, tended to view things as relevant only to the subject or the Self.

22. About dreams in the Upaniṣads a good and detailed explanation is given in E. Frauwallner, *Geschichte der indischeon Philosophie*, I Band, Salzburg, 1953.
23. *Praśna-Up.* 4, 5.
24. Homer gives sleep the unequaled epithet of "the limb-loosening" (lysimeles). (Deussen, *Elements of Metaphysics, op. cit.*, p. 60)
25. *Māṇḍ. Up.*
26. *Māṇḍ. Up.* 7; *Maitr. Up.* VI, 19; VII, 11.
27. Heraclitus' fragment 89.

2. The Identification of the Self with the Absolute

ALTHOUGH the oldest Upaniṣads reflect a great variety of intellectual traditions; it can be said with some justification that one dominant assertion appears again and again: "The universe is the *brahman*, and the *brahman* is the *ātman*." One can almost say that all the philosophical efforts of the Upaniṣadic philosophers center around these two conceptions and the problem of the relation between them.

This identification was expressed most explicitly by the philosopher Śāṇḍilya.[1] Śāṇḍilya called truth or reality *brahman*, and identified it with everything that we experience. Therefore, according to him, truth or reality does not exist latent behind the phenomenal world, nor does it transcent it, but every phenomenon itself is nothing but reality. He states, "Verily, this whole world is *brahman*. Being tranquil let one meditate upon it as that from which he came forth, as that into which he will be dissolved, as that in which he breathes." Moreover, this *brahman* should be regarded as our proper Self. He identified it with the individual Self. "The person or Soul (*puruṣa*) consists of mind, his body is life (*prāṇa*), his form is light, his thoughts are true (his thoughts are realized without fail), his soul (*ātman*) is space (ether), containing all words, containing all desires, containing all odors, containing all tastes, encompassing this whole world, he never speaks, he is unconcerned. . . ."

His conception of the absolute is very similar to that of Xenophanes who said: "There is one god, among gods and men the greatest, not at all like mortals in body or in mind."[2] "He sees as a whole, thinks as a whole, and hears as a whole."[3] "But without toil he sets everything in motion, by the thought of his mind."[4] "And he always remains in the same place, not moving at all, nor is it fitting for him to change his position at different times."[5] According to Zeno, God runs through the material world as honey runs through the honeycomb.

Yājñavalkya, an Indian thinker, also expressed similar views: "Verily, while he does not there smell, he is verily smelling, though he does not smell (what is [usually] to be smelled); for there is no cessation of the smelling of a smeller, because of his imperishability (as a smeller). It is not, however, a second thing, other than himself and separate, that he may smell."[6] With regard to other organs also the same is repeated.

1. *Chānd. Up.* III, 14.
2. Xenophanes' fragment, 23.
3. *Ibid.*, 24.
4. *Ibid.*, 25.
5. *Ibid.*, 26.
6. *Bṛhad. Up.* IV, 3, 24.

Here the doctrine of the unity of the world with *brahman* and of *brahman* with *ātman* is expressed most clearly. This *ātman*, the soul, is the inner self and yet it comprises all. Royce comments on this: "In such passages, which are very frequent in the Upaniṣads, and immediate sense of the unity of all things runs parallel with an equally strong sense that the unity is wholly in myself who knows the truth—in my heart, just because what for me is, precisely what I know."[7]

Moreover, the *brahman* as the absolute or the Self is the maximum and at the same time the minimum; i.e., it is extremely immense and at the same time extremely minute. Śāṇḍilya says: "This self of mine within the heart is smaller than a grain of rice, or smaller than a barleycorn, or smaller than a mustard-seed, or a grain of millet, or the kernel of a grain of millet; this Self of mine within the heart is millet, or the kernel of a grain of millet; this Self of mine within the heart is greater than the earth, greater than the atmosphere, greater than the sky, greater than all these worlds."

In another Upaniṣad one also finds a saying to the same effect. "That gigantic divine Being is by nature inconceivable. It appears to be more than the subtlest, much farther off than the farthest yet here, quite near—deposited right here, within the cave (the inmost recess of the heart) of those who see."[8]

The character of extreme minuteness of the absolute was noticed by Alberuni, the Muhammedan scholar, who said:[9] "Some Hindu scholars call God *a point*, meaning to say thereby that the qualities of bodies do not apply to him. Now some uneducated man reads this and imagines, God is small as *a point*, and he does not find out what the word *point* in this sentence was really intended to express. He will not even stop with this offensive comparison, but will describe God as much larger, and will say, He is twelve fingers long and ten fingers broad.[10] Praise be to God, who is far above measure and number!"

Śāṇḍilya's assertion reminds us of a somewhat similar conception of the *coincidentia oppositorum* advocated by Nicholas of Cusa. His leading motive was to show that the individual is identical with the most uni-

7. Royce, *The World and the Individual*, vol. I, p. 159.
8. *Muṇḍ. Up.* III, 1, 7. Cf. "He (Christ) calls it (man's soul) 'God's Kingdom,' and finds it in every one. He compares it to little things, to a tiny seed, to a handful of leaven, to a pearl." (Oscar Wilde, *De Profundis*)
9. *Alberuni's India*, p. 32.
10. "The person of the size of a thumb (angusthamatra) resides in the middle of the body." (*Kāṭhaka-Up.* IV, 13). Later Vedantins took this passage as referring to *ātman* or *brahman*. The term 'the size of the thumb' occurs in *Kāṭhaka-Up.* III, 13; *Śvet. Up.* III, 13; V, 8; IV, 12; The Chinese version of the *Abhidharma-mahāvibhāṣā-śāstra*, translated by Hsuan-tsang, vol. 200, (*Taisho*, vol. 27, p. 999 b).

versal, the divine essence. The conception of the identity of God with the world was formulated by him in the assertion that in God the same absolute Being is contained infinitely, which in the world presents itself in finite forms. The infinite is the living and eternal unity of that which in the finite appears as extended plurality. God is the unity of all opposites, the *coincidentia oppositorum*. He is, therefore, the absolute reality in which all possibilities are *eo ipso* realized. God is the greatest (maximum) and at the same time also the smallest (minimum).[11] In Him opposites are not two, but one simple essence; the distinction is 'logical, but not real.' So Nicholas of Cusa speaks of the 'wall of Paradise' that conceals God from our sight as constituted of the 'coincidence of opposites' and of its gate as guarded by 'the highest spirit of reason, who bars the way until he has been overcome.'[12]

But Nicholas established his doctrine by using examples of geometrical figures. His way of thinking grows out of the long tradition of western thought which emphasized mathematical conceptions. This was conspicuously lacking in Śāṇḍilya. He asserted his doctrine of identification of the Self with the absolute by introspective intuition only.

On this issue of introspective intuition, the Chinese tradition is perhaps closer to the Indian. Chung-tzu states: "The six cardinal points, reaching into Infinity, are ever included in Tao; an autumn spikelet, in all its minuteness, must carry Tao within itself."[13] (*Chung-tzu*, XXII, transl. H. A. Giles). Such expressions were beloved by the masters of Ch'an Buddhism (Chinese Zen). The third partriarch of Chinese Zen Buddhism, Seng-ts'an (c. 529–606), asserted:

> "The smallest is the same as the greatest; it transcends objects.
> The greatest is the same as the smallest; its limitation is not seen."[14]

Someone asked a Zen master, Hui-hai:

> "Is the wisdom (*prajñā*) great?" The master replied, "Yes, great."
> "Then, how great is it?" The master replied, "Unlimited."
> "Is the wisdom small?" The master replied, "Yes, small."
> "Then, how small is it?" The master replied, "We want to see it, and yet we cannot see it."[15]

The main difference here is that Śāṇḍilya and other Upaniṣadic thinkers

11. Windelband, *History of Philosophy*, pp. 345–346.
12. *Devis. Dei* 9, 11. Cf. *JUB.* I, 5. Cited by A. K. Coomaraswamy, *Recollections*, etc., p. 26.
13. *Chung-tzu*, XXII, translated by H. A. Giles.
14. *Shinjin-mei.*
15. *Shoho-monjin-sanmon-goroku.*

regarded the absolute as the sole substance, while masters of Zen Buddhism did not want to assume any permanent substance.

The *brahman* is a cosmic and, at the same time, a psychic principle. Śāṇḍilya's fundamental opinion of man was that "man consists of will." He said: "Now, verily, a person consists of will (*kratumaya*). According to the will which a person has in this world, so will he become when he has departed from this life. So let him have this will and belief." Therefore, man should keep his mind pure. Keeping his mind tranquil, he should meditate upon the reality of the universe. That is, *brahman* should be made the object of worship. He taught: "Being tranquil, let one meditate upon *brahman*." Plato expressed a similar thought, "When the soul has communion with divine virtue and becomes divine, she is carried into another and better place, which is perfect in holiness."[16]

Alberuni pointed out some Greek philosophers also emphasized the importance of directing one's desire and exertion to a union with the first cause of the universe. Alberuni comments, "With regard to similar views of the ancient Greeks we can quote Ammonius, who related the following as a sentence of Pythagoras: "Let your desire and exertion in this world be directed towards the union with the *First Cause*, which is the cause of the cause of your existence, that you may endure forever. You will be saved from destruction and from being wiped out; you will go to the world of the true sense, of the true joy, of the true glory, in everlasting joy and pleasures."[17] He then cites parallels from Plato and Proclus. According to his physician Eustochius, the last words of Plotinus were: "I was waiting for you, before the divine principle in me departs to unite itself with the divine in the universe."[18]

Alberuni finds a parallel in Islam also.[19] Abu-Yazid Albistami once being asked how he had attained *his* stage in Sufism, answered: "I cast off my own self as a serpent casts off its skin. Then I considered my own self, and found that *I* was *He*, i.e., God."[20]

In thought such as Śāṇḍilya's, Royce seeks to find the forerunner of mysticism. His comments deserve quoting at some length. He says, "Historically speaking, mysticism first appeared in India. As to the history of mysticism, it began in India, with the Upaniṣads."[21]

16. *Laws*, X, 904.
17. *Alberuni's India*, p. 85. This passage is set forth in connection with the concept of deliverance by the Sāṃkhyas. But the purport of the comment by Alberuni can apply to the thought of some Upaniṣadic thinkers.
18. Cited from S. Radhakrishnan, *The Principal Upaniṣads* (London: George Allen and Unwin, 1953), p. 304.
19. *Alberuni's India*, p. 88.
20. *Ibid.*
21. Josiah Royce, *The World and the Individual*, 1st series (New York and London: Macmillan Co., 1927), I, p. 78.

"What is, is at all events somehow One. This thought came early to the Hindoo religious mind. For the sake of its illustration and defence, the thinkers of the Upaniṣads seize, at first, upon every legend, upon every popular interpretation of nature, which may serve to make the sense of this unity living in the reader's or hearer's mind. For the writers of the greater Upaniṣads, this unity of Being is not so much a matter of argument as it is an object of intuition. You first look out upon the whole circle of the heavens, and upon the multitudes of living forms, and you say of the whole; it is One, because at first you merely feel this to be true."[22]

"A metaphysical realist also can attempt, however inconsistently, to call all Being One. In this case there would result such a doctrine as that of the Eleatic school. But to what obvious objection any Eleatic doctrine is open, we also saw. For if the Real is the Independent Being, existent wholly apart from your idea about it, there is no way of escape from the assertion that our false opinions are themselves real in the same sense in which the One is real. The realist is essentially a dualist. The Hindoo was early aware of this danger threatening every monistic interpretation of the Real. He undertook to escape the danger by a device which in the Upaniṣads appears so constantly, and with such directness of expression as to constitute a sort of axiom, to which the thinker constantly appeals."

"The Hindoo seer of the period of the Upaniṣads is keenly and reflectively self-conscious. (His own thinking process is constantly before him.) He cannot view any reality as merely independent of the idea that knows it, because he has a strong sense that he himself is feeling, beholding, thinking, this reality, which he, therefore, views as an object meant by himself, and so as having no meaning apart from his point of view. The axiom which our European idealists often state in the form: No object without a subject, is therefore always, in one shape or another, upon the Hindoo's lips. He states it less technically, but he holds it all the more intuitively. The world is One—why? Because I feel it as one. What then is its oneness? My own oneness? And who am I? I am *brahman*."

"I myself, in my inmost heart, in my Soul, am the world principle, the all. In this form the Hindoo's Monism becomes at once a subjective Idealism: and this subjective Idealism often appears almost in the epistemological form in which that doctrine has so often been discussed, of late, amongst ourselves. But the further process of the Hindoo's monistic philosophy leads beyond this mere beginning, and results in an elaborate series of reflections upon the mystery of the Self. The final product of these reflections transforms the merely epistemological Idealism, which, if abstractly stated, has with us often led to a rather trivial scepticism,

22. *Ibid.*, pp. 156–157.

into something very different from mere scepticism, namely into a doctrine not merely epistemological, but metaphysical.[23]

3. The Manifestation of the World from Being as Such

As representative of those philosophers in India who raised the ontological question—i.e., the problem of being as such—one can mention Uddālaka. Uddālaka[1] regarded his own philosophy as fundamental, the knowledge of which was the key to the understanding of all of reality: "My dear, just as by one clod of clay all that is made of clay is known, the difference is only a name, grasped by speech, but the reality is just clay—just as by one copper ornament all that is made of copper is known, the difference is only a name, grasped by speech, but the reality is just copper—just as by one nail-scissors all that is made of iron is known, and the difference is only name, grasped by speech, but the reality is just iron. So is that teaching." By knowing the teaching, one could know everything. He thought that phenomena are just names, whereas reality is one.

Yājñavalkya also asserts that if the Self is known, everything will be known: "Verily, the Self is to be seen, to be heard, to be perceived, to be pondered on. When the Self has been seen, heard, perceived, and known, that all this is known."[2] He mentions similes: "The sounds of a drum, when beaten, cannot be seized externally (by themselves). But when the drum or the beater of the drum is seized, the sound is seized." "The sounds of a conch-shell, when blown, cannot be seized externally (by themselves), but when the shell or the blower of the shell is seized, the sound is seized. The sounds of a lute, when played, cannot be seized externally (by themselves), but when the lute or the player of the lute is seized, the sound is seized." As a final consequence of the identification of the microcosm with the macrocosm—i.e., the self (*ātman*) with the absolute (*brahman*)—Yājñavalkya explicitly elucidated the concept of the sole valuable and essential one, through whose knowledge everything is known.

In Plato one also finds a similar thought: "Seeing, then that Soul is immortal and has been born many times, and has beheld all things both in the world and in Hades, she has learnt all things, without exception: so that it is no wonder that she should be able to remember all that she knew before about virtue and other things. And since all Nature is congeneric, there is no reason why we should not, by remembering but one

23. *Ibid.*, pp. 157–158.
1. *Chānd. Up.* VI.
2. *Bṛhad. Up.* II, 4, 5.

single thing discover all the others, if we are brave and faint not in the enquiry; for it seems that to inquire and to learn are wholly a matter of remembering."[3]

Uddālaka wanted to establish "being" and reality on a level beyond "words" and "names." In the same way, Parmenides said that it was men who had put distinguishing names to things. He said: "All things that mortals have established, believing in their truth, are just names. Becoming and Perishing, Being and Not-Being, and change of position, and alteration of bright color."[4] According to him, these are nothing but names. Parmenides says: ". . . Nor let ordinary experience in its variety force you along this way, (namely, that of allowing) the eye, sightless as it is, and the ear, full of sound, and the tongue, to rule."[5] He taught that men erroneously give names to what they think they have grasped. "Thou shalt inquire into everything: both the motionless heart of well-rounded Truth, and also the opinions of mortals in which there is no true reliability. But nevertheless thou shalt learn these things (opinions) also—how one should go through all the things-that-seem, without exception, and test them."[6]

Further, Uddālaka's concepts, i.e., "only a name," "grasping by speech," seem to be somewhat similar to the concept of "opinion" (*doxa*) of Xenophanes.[7] Plato refers to the distinction between the phenomenal world, which he calls "the Becoming and Perishing, but never really Being"[8] and Being-in-itself, to which he denies all change.[9] He expressly excludes from Being-in-itself, Space[10] and Time.[11] Accepting a similar idea, later Upaniṣadic thinkers acknowledged the "lower science" besides the "higher science."[12] In the same way Xenophanes admitted the manifoldness and changeability of the theory of "opinion" besides that of "truth." There are "two minds, pure and impure."[13] Pure, 'by disconnection with desire; impure, by contamination with desire.'[14] One is reminded of Plato's unchangeable Mind 'in which only the Gods and but

3. *Meno* 81 C, D. Cf. 50 A, B.
4. Parmenides' fragment, 19.
5. *Ibid.*, 7.
6. *Ibid.*, 1.
7. Xenophanes' fragment, 34.
8. *Timaeus*, 28 A.
9. *Phaedon*, 78 D.
10. *Timaeus*, 52 B.
11. *Timaeus*, 37 E. (Deussen, *Elements of Metaphysics*, p. 31)
12. *Muṇḍ. Up.* I, 1, 4.
13. *Maitri-Up.* VI, 34, 6.
14. The pure mind is the daivam manas of *Bṛhad. Up.* I, 5, 19, identified with Brahma in *Bṛhad. Up.* IV, 1, 6 (mano vai samrat paramaṃ brahma) and with Prajāpati in *Tait. saṃhitā* 6, 6, 10, 1, *ŚBr.* 9, 4, 1, 12 and passim.

few men participate,' as distinguished from irrational Opinion, subject to persuasion.[15]

Uddālaka sets forth his ontology as follows: "In the beginning this world was just Being (*sat*), one only, without a second; others say, in the beginning this world was just Non-being, one only, without a second. From that Non-being Being was produced. . . . How from Non-being could Being be produced? On the contrary, in the beginning this world was just Being, one only, without a second."[16] He asserts that anything which is has to come from something which is. According to him reality is Being, the One, besides which nothing can exist. Being cannot rise out of non-being[17] (cf. *satkāryavāda*). One finds a similar assertion in Parmenides.[18] He says: "Nor shall I allow you to speak or think of it (Being) as springing from Non-being; for it is neither expressible nor thinkable that What-Is-Not is. Also, what necessity impelled it, if it did spring from Nothing, to be produced later or earlier?" Being was considered, not only by Parmenides, but also by Uddālaka, as something extending in space. Bertrand Russell, speaking of Western philosophy, asserts: "The Greek view, that creation out of nothing is impossible, has recurred at intervals in Christian times, and has led to pantheism. Pantheism holds that God and the world are not distinct, and that everything in the world is part of God. This view is developed most fully in Spinoza, but is one to which almost all mystics are attracted."[19]

Uddālaka continues: This One Being, somehow mysteriously resolved to become many. Immediately there follows an evolution which the various principles appear in an order which at first consideration seems thoroughly realistic. "It (=that Being) thought, may I be many, may I grow forth (=procreate myself). It sent out fire. That fire thought, may I be many, may I grow forth. It sent forth water. Water thought, may I be many, may I grow forth. It sent forth food." Here food was regarded as one of the three elements which are born first. Later Vedantic theologians found it strange and explained it as meaning "earth."

The process of origination and dissolution can be summarized as follows: The One Being somehow mysteriously resolved to become many. This Being sent out fire. This fire sent out water. Water sent forth food.

15. *Timaeus*, 51, D. E.
16. Śaṅkara adopted this view, "(Brahman cannot have sprung) also from non-Being, for this is essenceless (*nirātmaka*)." (ad *Brahma-sūtra*, II: 3, 9. Ānandāśrama Sanskrit Series 21, vol. 2, p. 23, 1, 7)
17. "Nothing, Falsehood, may indeed stand as the great Night or shade, on which as a background the living universe paints itself forth, but no fact is begotten by it; it cannot work, for it is not. It cannot work any good; it cannot work any harm. It is harm inasmuch as it is worse not to be than to be." (Emerson, *Compensation*)
18. Parmenides' fragment, 8.
19. B. Russell, *History of Western Philosophy*, p. 254.

As will be discussed later, these three elements are dissolved into the primordial Being in the reverse order.

In a similar manner, Zeno states: "Originally there was only fire; then the other elements—air, water, earth, in that order—gradually emerged. But sooner or later there will be a cosmic conflagration, and all will again become fire." This, according to most Stoics, is not a final consummation, like the end of the world in Christian eschatology, but only the conclusion of a cycle. The whole process will be repeated endlessly. "Everything that happens has happened before, and will happen again, not once, but countless times."

The primordial Being and the three elements were also regarded as divinities. "That divinity (i.e., Being), (after having produced fire, water and earth), thought: 'Come! Let me now enter those three divinities (fire, water and food) with this living Self (*jīva ātman*), and let me then reveal (develop) names and forms.' " Here "names and forms" mean the individuality of all things. Then that Being said: "Let me make each of these three threefold." Anaxagoras had a similar idea. He said: "In everything there is a portion of everything, but some things contain Mind also."[20] "Other things all contain a part of everything, but Mind is infinite and self-ruling, and is mixed with no Thing, but is alone by itself."[21] For Anaxagoras, however, Mind and elements were different, whereas for Uddālaka they were substantially the same.

In the ontology of Uddālaka, Being thinks in order to develop the world. It is often explained that for Parmenides also, Being and thinking were the same, and thinking and an object of thinking were the same. "To think is the same as the thought that it is; for you will not find thinking without Being, in (regard to) which there is an expression. For nothing else either is or shall be except Being, since Fate has tied it down to be a whole and motionless."[22]

In the philosophy of Uddālaka and others there is no antagonism between 'real' and 'unreal.' In this strictly nondualistic realization, there is no dichotomy; for the transcendent supreme Reality and its mundane manifestations (whether these be perceptible or verbal-conceptual) are

20. Anaxagoras' fragment, 11.
21. *Ibid.*, 12.
22. The Being of Parmenides was regarded as of global form and of thick oneness in itself (synekhes. fr. 8). Such a way of description is based upon the Greek penchant for resorting to physical images (cf. 13). "But since there is a (spatial) Limit, it is complete on every side, like the mass of a well-rounded sphere, equally balanced from its center in every direction; for it is not bound to be at all either greater or less in this direction or that; nor is there Non-Being which could check it from reaching to the same point, nor is it possible for Being to be more in this direction, less in that, than Being, because it is an inviolate whole. For, in all directions equal to itself, it reaches its limits uniformly." (Fr. 8)

in essence one. Hence, according to Uddālaka, that Being then entered into those three elements with this living Self only, and developed into the names and forms of things in the empirical world.

Uddālaka's teaching can be explained as follows: each of the three elements (fire, water, food) is combined with the other two. Thus all bodies in the world are made up of three elements. For example, empirical fire, i.e., fire which is perceived in daily life, is made of fire, water and food, but fire is predominant. The red color of burning fire is the color of fire; the white color of fire is the color of water, the black color of fire is the color of food. Thus what we call fire is dissolved, the phenomenon as a fire is only a name, grasped by speech; what is true (*satya*) are the three colors. In all material bodies beginning with the sun, the moon, and lightning, and red color is the color of fire, the white color is the color of water, the dark color is the color of food (earth). What we call the sun, the moon and the lightning and so on, are only names, grasped by speech; what is true are three colors.

Being was considered, not only by Parmenides, but also by Uddālaka, as something extending in space, and was not Being as an abstract conception. It was the substrate of all. For Parmenides, however, Being does not change, and change is false; while for Uddālaka Being itself changes, although changed phases are inferior in their reality.

Here one could refer to the phlogiston theory in the old chemistry of the West. The human body also consists of three elements, just as material bodies in the outer world. Food, when eaten, becomes divided into three parts. Its grossest portion becomes the feces; its middle portion becomes flesh; its subtlest portion becomes mind. Water, when drunk becomes divided into three parts. Its grossest portion becomes urine; its middle portion becomes blood; its subtlest portion breath. Fire (i.e., in oil, butter, etc.), when eaten, becomes divided into three parts; its grossest portion becomes speech. That which is the subtle portion of curds, when churned, rises upwards, and becomes butter. In the same way the subtle portion of these three, when taken, rise upwards.

Parmenides also held somewhat similar notions.[23] "They (mortals) established (the custom of) naming two forms, one of which ought not to be (mentioned); that is where they have gone astray. They have distinguished them as opposite in form, and have marked them off from another by giving them different signs; on one side the flaming fire in the heavens, mild, very light (in weight), the same as itself in every direction, and not the same as the other. This (other) also is by itself and opposite: dark night, a dense and heavy body." Anaxagoras held that everything

23. Parmenides' fragment 8. (cf. *Muṇḍ. Up.* 6, 34, 3 yac cittas tanmayo bhavati; St. Augustine, Conf. 13. 11 esse, nosse, velle—in his tribus—et una vita et una mens et una essentia.)

is infinitely divisible, and that even the smallest portion of matter contains some of each element.[24] Things appear to be that which they contain most. Thus, for example, everything contains some fire, but we only call it fire if that element dominates.[25]

Royce comments upon Uddālaka's cosmogony as follows: "The instruction begins with a statement of the general monistic view of Being, uses arguments at first partly identical with those of the Eleatic school, illustrates unity by various observations of nature; but then, in the very midst of what at first seems a merely realistic doctrine, suddenly, and with a dramatic swiftness of transformation, identifies the world principle with the inmost soul of the disciple himself, and with him, in so far as he is the knower of the Unity."[26]

"The beginning of the argument, I repeat, appears from one side, realistic. The world, says Uddālaka, is, and is one. The disciple is to note this fact and to bring it home to himself by frequent empirical illustrations taken from the outer nature. Then he is to observe that he, too, in so far as he is at all real, is for this very reason one with the world principle. The teaching seems at this state still a realism, only now a realism that has become reflective, recognizing the observer of the reality as also a real being, and therefore asserting of him, as knower, whatever one also asserts of the Being that he knows."[27] "But suddenly, even as one speaks, one becomes aware that, through this very identification of the essence of the knower and of the object known, the inmost reality of the world has itself become transformed. It is no longer a world independent of knowledge. One never really has observed it as an external world at all. It has no independent Being. It is a world identical with the knower. It is a vision of his soul. Its life is his life. It is in so far as he creates it. Whatever he is as knower, that is his world."[28]

Uddālaka continues: "But even breath, which is so important as a life-principle, in not the true Self of man. The true Self of man is *ātman*, which is nothing but Being (*sat*) as the primordial principle. When one is working in a waking status, he is separated from the true Self. But when he sleeps deeply, he becomes united with the reality; he is his own Self. (*svamapītaḥ*)."[29]

24. Anaxagoras maintained that there were countless elements differing in form, color, and taste. He held that they were present throughout the entire universe in a very finely divided state. Their coming together or compounding constitutes the arising, their separation, the passing away, of individual things. (Windelband, *History*, ETr. p. 41)
25. B. Russell, *op. cit.*, p. 62. (Cf. Anaxagoras' fragment, 6; 11)
26. Royce, *The World and the Individual*, I, pp. 159–160.
27. *Ibid.*, I, p. 160.
28. *Ibid.*, I, p. 160.
29. *Chānd. Up.* VI, 8, 1. In Greece, also, argument by etymology was given. An older

Among three ingredients of the human body, the root of food is water; the root of water is fire; the root of fire is Being. All creatures have Being as their root, have Being as their abode, have Being as their support.[30] Being is the fundamental principle of our human existence. Although we cannot perceive Being as something concrete, it lies latently at the bottom of our existence or personality as something unseen.

As already mentioned, according to Uddālaka's metaphysics the ultimate principle of the universe is "being" as the genuine spiritual principle. From that Being fire springs forth; from fire, water; from water, food. Phenomenal fire, water, and food (or earth), which we perceive daily, have developed through the mixture of these three elements. In the dissolution of the phenomenal world into the ultimate principle, everything returns again into Being in the reverse order. This order of development and dissolution coincides with that of the downward and upward ways of Heraclitus. Heraclitus regarded the fundamental principle of the universe as fire, and asserted that "everything dissolves into it again; everything that becomes is nothing but an interchange of fire" (according to Diogenes' Laertes). The process was described as follows: (1) The way downward, by which fire becomes everything, in which fire first becomes water, and then water becomes earth; and (2) the way upward, by which everything becomes fire, in which earth first becomes water, and then water becomes fire. In order, both philosophers coincide; but Uddālaka clearly distinguished the fire which men experienced daily and that which was the fundamental element, while Heraclitus is not clear on this point. The important difference is that Uddālaka conceived of the being behind fire. Heraclitus regarded fire itself as the ultimate principle.[31]

In the form of a dialogue, Uddālaka elucidates the relationship of the Many to the One by using metaphors. He teaches his son: When we look at water wherein salt is dissolved, we don't perceive salt, but when we sip of it, undoubtedly we feel salt. "You do not perceive the Being here. Verily, indeed, it is here." "That which is the subtle essence, in it all that exists has its Self. That is Reality. That is the Self (*ātman*). Thou are that."[32] Here "thou" means the empirical, individual self, which very often tends to be egoistic, while "that" means the universal Self.[33]

---

cosmological thinker Pherekydes used etymology as an argument, or rather as a kind of joking, associative addition to a myth. (Zeller, *op. cit.*, ERr. I, p. 90, n. 3)

30. *Chānd. Up.* VI, 8, 6.

31. Cf. Hajime Nakamura, The Kinetic Existence of An Individual, (*Philosophy East and West*, I, 2. July, 1951, published by the University of Hawaii Press, p. 37)

32. *Chānd. Up.* VI, 13.

33. Emerson acknowledges the doctrine of "That art Thou." He said: "Blessed is the day when the youth discovers that Within and Above are synonymous." (Emerson, *Journals*, III, 399, cited from A. Christy, *The Orient in American Transcendentalism*, p. 77)

Another simile: When you break a fig and then break the seeds therein, you will find nothing. "That subtle essence which you do not perceive—verily, from that finest essence this great fig tree thus arises." "Believe me, my dear, that which is the subtle essence, in it all that exists has its Self. That is Reality. That is the Self (*ātman*). Thou are that."

Although we cannot perceive anything inside the seeds, yet it is certain that trees come out of the tiny seeds. In the same way, although we cannot perceive the fundamental self directly, yet it is certain that it is hidden at the bottom of our existence.

H. Zimmer[34] comments on the similes: "Uddālaka's instruction by analogy can be summed up as follows: The supreme principle transcends the sphere of empirical phenomena and yet is all-penetrating, like the salt in water. The Reality as the fundamental principle is as subtle as the seed of the fig within the fruit; it is inherent in all beings, as the potentiality of their unfolding life."

Another passage[35] expresses the same doctrine thus: "Whoever knows this, 'I am *brahman*' (*aham brahma asmi*), becomes the All. Even the gods are not able to prevent him from becoming it. For he becomes their Self (*ātman*)." "Thou art That" and "I am *brahman*"—these two sentences have been regarded in India as two "great formulas" (*mahāvākya*) which represent the central purport of the Upaniṣadic thought.

In the case of Uddālaka a difficult problem was left unsolved. Royce commented: "The relations of body and soul to the universal world life have been illustrated, the meaning of growth and decay in nature has been brought into relation to the doctrine of the absolute One; but still the theory has not been made clear in what sense the One can have decreed to itself: 'I will be Many.'"[36] The problem was discussed by later Vedanta philosophers.

According to Uddālaka the Self is immortal. "When life has left it, this body dies. But life does not die." Life is nothing but the Self, the Reality which never dies. (Parmenides[37] said: "How could Being perish? How could it come into being?") "When a man dies, his voice goes into his mind and into his breath, his breath into heat (fire), the heat into the highest divinity which is the Being. Then he loses consciousness."[38]

Here mind and the Self were clearly distinguished. Pythagoras and Hindu philosophers agree generally in distinguishing the sensitive, material organ (*manas*) from the rational and conscious living soul (*jīvātman*):

34. *Philosophies of India*, p. 337.
35. *Bṛhad. Up.* I, 4, 6.
36. Royce, *op. cit.*, p. 162.
37. Parmenides' fragment, 8.
38. *Chānd. Up.* VI, 15; VIII, 6.

the *thymos* and *phren* of Pythagoras; one perishing with the body, the other immortal.[39]

Uddālaka continues: In deep sleep and in death, all creatures reach Being; they are unified; they are not conscious that they have reached Being. It is just as the bees make honey by collecting the juices of different trees, and reduce the juice into one form, and they are not able to discriminate, saying "I am the essence of this tree," "I am the essence of that tree."

In awakening or birth all creatures appear out of Being, but they are not conscious that they have come forth from it. This fact is explained with an interesting simile: All these creatures come forth from Being and return back into it, but they do not know that process. It is just as water circulates. The rivers flow, the eastern (like the Ganges) toward the east, the western (like the Indus) toward the west. Water goes just from the ocean to the ocean, i.e., the clouds lift up the water from the ocean to the Sky, and send it back as rain to the ocean. They become the ocean itself. In the ocean they do not know "I am this river," "I am that river." All these creatures repeat this process. "Whatever these creatures are here, whether a lion, or a wolf, or a boar, or a worm, or a midge, or a gnat, or a mosquito, that they become again and again."[40]

It is clear that the metaphysical tendency of Upaniṣadic thinkers towards oneness is very similar to that of the Eleatics. The "becoming" or "development" which had been put in the center of philosophical thinking since the age of cosmogony came to be regarded as dubious. The ultimate principle was decisively evaluated much more highly than its products,[41] and was looked upon as Reality in a metaphysical sense.

Xenophanes teaches that God and the Universe are one, eternal, and unchangeable. Parmenides holds that reality is due alone to this universal being—neither created nor to be destroyed, and omnipresent—that everything which exists in multiplicity and is subject to mutability is not real; and further, that thinking and being are identical. All these doctrines have common features with the chief contents of the Upaniṣads[42] and some of the later Vedanta systems. This similarity was noticed by Alberuni who stood as an objective reviewer independent of both sides. In describing Hindu thought, the medieval Muslim scholar pointed out that some fea-

39. Richard Garbe, *Philosophy of Ancient India*, Chicago, Open Court. p. 32.
40. *Chānd. Up.* VI, 9.
41. Alexander was once asked, 'Why do you show greater respect and reverence to your instructor than you do to your father?' He answered, 'From my teacher I obtain life eternal; and from my father a perishable existence. Moreover, my father brought me down from heaven to earth but Aristotle has raised me from earth to heaven.' *History of the Early Kings of Persia*, by Mīr Khwānd, E. Tr. by David Shea (1832), p. 423. Cited from S. Radhakrishnan, *The Principal Upaniṣads*, p. 464.
42. *Chānd. Up.* VI, 14.

tures of Hindu (probably Upaniṣadic) thought are also noticed in Greek thought. Like the Indian . . . "the Greek thinks that the existing world is only *one* thing; that the First Cause appears in it under various shapes; that the power of the First Cause is inherent in the parts of the world under different circumstances, which cause a certain difference of the things of the world notwithstanding their original unity."[43]

As mentioned above, there exist many similarities between Uddālaka and the Eleatics, but there are also important differences. Parmenides taught that men should not be cheated by the senses, but should rely upon reason. "(You must) judge by means of Reason (Logos) the much-contested proof which is expounded by me."[44] Contrarily, the Indian thinker urged his disciples to grasp the absolute by intuition.

Royce also comments on this problem: "An Eleatic doctrine would at this point remain fast bound, dimly suggesting perhaps, as Parmenide, did, that Being and thought are somehow one, but not making anything definite of the suggestion, and meaning it, as no doubt Parmenides also did, in the purely realistic sense, as an assertion that thought knows Beings even while Being is independent of thought. But the Hindoo goes further. He, at just this stage, turns from the world directly to the disciple himself. This mystery, he says, this oneness of all Being, in this you too at all events share. In whatever sense the world is real, you are real. Is the world but One Being, then you, so far as you are real, are identical with that One."[45]

"And still the mystery of the nature of the One Being has not been lighted up. But Uddālaka means his teaching to be taken from this point on, in quite another sense. The variety is illusory. But whose illusion is it? The One Being exists. But how? As known Being, and also as One with the knower. The very reflection that knowledge is real—that reflection which Realism finds it so hard and so fatal to make, is now to furnish the solving word."[46]

"The reality cannot be independent. Its life is the Knower's life and his alone. Its multiplicity is his illusion, and his only. The disciple has been taught by nature symbols. They were, in a way, to mediate the higher insight. But still their interpretation was itself intuitive and in so far unmediated, just because only unmediated intuition was from the outset really present. There was and is only the Knower. The disciple was the Knower. It was he who blindly resolved, 'Let me become many.' He shall now, in a final intuition, grasp the immediate fact that he is, and eternally was, but One."[47]

43. *Alberuni's India*, p. 34.
44. Parmenides' fragment, 7.
45. Royce, *op. cit.*, I, p. 163.
46. *Ibid.*, pp. 163–164.
47. *Ibid.*, p. 164.

4. The Source of Beings

In the later Upaniṣads the absolute was given a somewhat different interpretation. One Upaniṣad[1] defines the *brahman* as follows: "That from whence these beings are born, that by which, when born, they live, that into which they enter at their death, try to know that. That is *brahman.*" *Brahman* is the womb whence all living beings proceed, and it seemed very natural to assume that they return at death into *brahman.* Here we see formulated, the doctrine of *brahman* as destroyer of individual creatures. As Anaximander says: "The source from which existing things derive their existence is also that to which they return at their destruction, according to necessity."[2]

Aristotles' definition of the "*stoikheion*"[3] is somewhat similar, and the definition which was advocated by the nature-philosophers is nearly the same as the definition of "brahman" in the *Taittirīya-Upaniṣad*, III. 1. There it is said: "Of the first philosophers, then, most thought the principles which were of the nature of matter were the only principles of all things. That of which all things that are consist, the first from which they come to be, the last into which they are resolved (the substance remaining, but changing in its modifications), this they say is the element and the principle of things and, therefore, they think nothing is either generated or destroyed." The Chinese concept of *tao* also should be considered in this connection.

"Tao is hidden and nameless
Yet Tao alone supports all things and brings them to fulfillment."[4]
"For the Way is a thing impalpable, incommensurable,
Yet latent in it are forms."
It is the "Mother of all things under heaven."[5]

In a later period, from the *Śvetāśvatara-Upaniṣad* and after, the idea of the periodical origination and destruction of the universe by *brahman* developed. Here again there is a Western counterpart. The teaching of Heraclitus that all things come forth from fire (*hodos katō*), and return into it (*hodos anō*), originally signified a twofold process linked together everywhere in the universe in the rise and disappearance of individual creatures. This idea, however, was then generalized, perhaps by Hera-

1. The definition in *Tait. Up.* III, 1, became the basis for the concept of brahman for later Vedāntins.
2. Anaximander's fragment, 1.
3. *Metaphysics*, I, 3; 983 B 8.
4. *Tao Te Ching* XLI.
5. *Ibid.*, XXV.

clitus himself nor perhaps by his successors, the Stoics, into a periodically recurring dissolution of the universe in fire (*ekpyrosis*) and reconstruction out of it (*diakosmesis*). We know very little about the reasons which may have led to this generalization in Greek philosophy. "In India to a great extent it gave support to the doctrine of recompense, in as much as the latter, as already shown, was only capable of being reconciled with the doctrine of a creation, if for the single creation taught in the ancient Upaniṣads there was substituted an eternally recurring process, a re-creation of the universe occurring after each dissolution, and determined by the actions of the souls."[6]

5. The Structures of Human Existence

IN the later Upaniṣads one also finds an attempt to view individual existence in a somewhat more detailed manner. The "Layered" or "sheath-like" (*Kośa*) structure of human existence was investigated. The *Tattirīya-Upaniṣad* (II, 2–5) assumes five *ātmans* (or *puruṣas*) by the division of the intermediate, individual *ātman* into five principles: 1) the self consisting of food, 2) the self consisting of the vital breath, 3) the self consisting of mind, 4) the self consisting of knowledge and 5) the self consisting of bliss. The last is the true self, which can be realized by meditation. "Bliss" here is a translation of the Sanskrit word *ānanda*,[1] which sometimes means "sexual joy." St. Jerome[2] also employed a kind of erotic mysticism in the Christian tradition. Well-known also is the thought of Plotinus in this regard. "Plotinus affirms that in the soul are included the principles of unity, of pure intellect, of vital power, and of matter itself. It touches every grade of value and existence. The human souls that are sunk in the material are ensnared by the sensuous and have allowed themselves to be ruled by desire. In attempting to detach themselves entirely from the true being and strive after independence they fall into an unreal existence."[3]

6. Deussen, *The Philosophy of the Upanishads*, pp. 225–226 3. Richard Garbe, *The Philosophy of Ancient India*, p. 32.

1. Deussen's explanation is as follows: "*Brahman* is not *ānandin*, possessing bliss, but *ānanda*, bliss itself. This identification of *brahman* and *ānanda* is effected through the medium of the view that, on the one hand, the deep, dreamless sleep, by destroying the existing contrast of subject and object, is a temporary union with *brahman*; while on the other hand, since all suffering is then abolished, the same state is described as a bliss admitting of no enhancement." (*The Philosophy of the Upanishads*, p. 141)
2. B. Russell, *History*, etc., p. 342.
3. Radhakrishnan, *Eastern Religions*, etc., p. 211.

A fivefold structure was also proposed by Augustine: "Step by step was I led upwards, from bodies (*anna*) to the soul which perceives by means of the bodily senses (*prāṇa*); and thence to the soul's inward faculty which is the limit of the intelligence of animals (*manas*); and thence again to the reasoning faculty to whose judgment is referred the knowledge received by the bodily senses (*vijñāna*). And when this power also within me found itself changeable it lifted itself up to its own intelligence, and withdrew its thoughts from experience, abstracting itself from the contradictory throng of sense-images that it might find what that light was wherein it was bathed when it cried out that beyond all doubt the unchangeable is to be preferred to the changeable; whence also it knew that unchangeable; and thus with the flash of one trembling glance it arrived at That which is (*ānanda*)."[4] Augustine describes the highest state as one of joy: "The highest spiritual state of the soul in this life consists in the vision and contemplation of truth, wherein are joys, and the full enjoyment of the highest and truest good, and a breath of serenity and eternity."[5]

One also is reminded on this issue of Plato who compares the notion of the soul to a charioteer and two horses (anticipating the division into intellect, conscious and unconscious will). This comparison, with slight differences, also appears in the later Upaniṣads—i.e., *Kāṭhaka-Up.* 3.3.[6]

6. The Absolute Subject

THE cognitive character of the true Self is presented most explicitly by Yājñavalkya in the beautiful conversation[1] with his wife Maitreyī. According to his view, the Self is one with the universe and everything exists only in so far as it is the cognitive Self. When Yājñavalkya wanted to retire to the forests, Maitreyī, his wife, asked a question, "My lord, if this whole earth, full of wealth, belonged to me, tell me, should I be immortal by it, or not?" Yājñavalkya replied: "No, your life will be like the life of rich people. But there is no hope of immortality by wealth." He explains: Everything we experience is nothing but the Self (*ātman*). The *brahmins*, the warriors, the worlds, the gods, the creatures, and anything else are nothing but the Self. The Self is called "the great Being." Everything has been "breathed forth" from this Self, just as clouds of smoke proceed by themselves out of lighted fire kindled with damp fuel.

4. *Confessions* VII, 23. Cited from S. Radhakrishnan, *The Principal Upaniṣads*, pp. 557–558.
5. Dum Cuthbert Butler, *Western Mysticism*, p. 59.
6. Deussen, *Elements*, p. 207, *Phaedrus*, p. 253 C sq.
1. *Bṛhad. Up.* II, 4; IV, 5.

Parallel to this, Heraclitus states: "God is day-night, winter-summer, war-peace, satiety-famine. But he changes like (fire) which, when it mingles with the smoke of incense, is named according to each man's pleasure."[2]

The universal Self or the spirit of the all, which is the *ātman-brahman* advocated by Yājñavalkya and other thinkers and also the God of Xenophanes, could be regarded as the *causa materialis* (*stoikheion*, *upādāna-kāraṇa*) of the empirical world.

Such a doctrine had already been advocated by other Upaniṣadic philosophers before Yājñavalkya, but had not been advanced beyond that stage. Yājñavalkya goes further to make remarkable assertions. He tells his wife: "Verily, a husband is dear, not for love of the husband, but for love of the Self a husband is dear. Verily, a wife is dear, not for love of the wife, but for love of the Self a wife is dear." He continues and states that sons, wealth, cattle, etc., the *brahmins*, the warriors, the worlds, the gods, the Vedas, the creatures and every other thing are dear, not for love of them, but for love of the Self.

This passage is very famous in India, but the true meaning is somewhat obscure and it sounds strange. Many later scholars disputed over the true purport of this passage, but it is certain that here the Self does not mean the ego of man but some basic principle which lies at the foundation of human existence. When the unique inner essence of everything is realized within, the various masks that it assumes become transparent. All mutual understanding, not to say all sympathy and love, is based on the intrinsic identity of the Knower and the Known. Hatred arises only from the illusion of diversity. If such illusion is taken away, love will certainly appear. Mutual love is not of one another as such, but is of the immanent spiritual Self.

What were the Upaniṣadic thinkers indicating when they stressed the importance of knowing the Self? The Self is not an object of cognition in the sense of external objects in general. It is "pure knowledge." It has neither inside nor outside, just as a mass of salt has neither inside nor outside, but is altogether a mass of taste. Therefore, the Self cannot be predicated by any positive concept. But it is not mere nothingness. The Self is the subject of cognition. The Self is that by virtue of which man can cognize everything. "It is imperishable, for it is unattached, for it does not attach himself; unfettered, he does not suffer, he does not fail."[3]

Yājñavalkya goes even further. He holds that our body is made up of elements, and that when it is dismembered, it vanishes, and we lose consciousness. "Having arisen out of these elements, one vanishes again in them. After one has departed, there is no more consciousness." Here,

2. Heraclitus, fragment, 67.
3. P. Deussen, *The Philosophy of the Upanishads*, pp. 225–226.

his position appears to be similar to the Stoics who held that the soul perishes with the body. An exception is Posidonius who held that it continues to live in the air, where, in most cases, it remains unchanged until the next world conflagration.[4]

Upon hearing Yājñavalkya's remark, his wife becomes very much astonished. "Here, Sir, you have caused me to arrive at utter bewilderment. Indeed, I do not understand it." He replied: "O Maitreyī, I say nothing that is bewildering. Verily, that Self is imperishable, and of an indestructible nature."

Yājñavalkya's wife continues: "The doctrine confuses me. How, in fact, should the immortal One be unconscious?" In reply, Yājñavalkya can only give, as *reductio ad absurdum* of every objection, the argument that "all dualism involving the reality of objects outside the Knower is illusory, while all consciousness in daily life implies just such dualism."[5]

Individuality disappears in deliverance.[6] Consciousness loses its meaning "where everything has become just the Self";[7] "actively Itself when it is not intelligizing."[8]

"When there is as it were duality, then one sees the other, one smells the other, one tastes the other, one speaks to the other, one hears the other, one perceives the other, one touches the other, one knows the other; but when the Self only is all this, how should he see another, how should he smell another, how should he taste another, how should he speak to another, how should he hear another, how should he touch another, how should he know another? How should he know him by whom he knows all this?"[9]

He explains that when the duality on which consciousness is based disappears, consciousness must necessarily cease. But the basic principle does not perish. In our daily life there is the dualistic opposition of the subject and the object. The subject of cognition perceives various objects. But when one becomes conscious of the Self and everything becomes his Self, then one does not perceive any object, i.e., everything becomes unified with the Self. This state is that of pure subject without an object (cf. *Noesis noeseos*).

Royce comments on this dialogue: "The sage Yājñavalkya teaches his wife Maitreyī, first that nothing in the universe is real or is desirable except the absolute Self. But then the Self, he goes on to say, is in its immortality unconsciously. For all consciousness involves partially dis-

4. B. Russell, *History of Western Philosophy*, p. 258.
5. Royce, *op. cit.*, I, p. 170.
6. *Bṛhad. Up.* IV, 4.
7. *Bṛhad. Up.* 2, 4, 14.
8. Plotinus, *Enneades*, 4, 4, 2.
9. *Bṛhad. Up.* IV, 5, 15.

satisfied ideas of a Beyond, and includes desires that seek another than what is now wholly present. But in the true Self all is attained, and therefore all is One; there is no Beyond, there is no Other. There are then, in the true Self, no ideas, no desires, because he is the final attainment of all that ideas and desires sought,"[10] ". . . all our relative satisfactions take the form of finite ideas. The Absolute must then be ineffable, indescribable, and yet not outside of the circle within which we at present are conscious."[11] "It is no other than we are; consciousness contains it just in so far as consciousness is knowing. Yet, when we speak of the absolute, all our words must be: 'Neti, Neti,' 'It is not thus; it is not thus.' So the sage Yājñavalkya himself, more than once in these legends, teaches: To us, it is as if the Absolute, in its immediacy, were identical with Nothing. But once more: —Is the Absolute verily a mere nothing?

"The Hindoo's answer to this last question is in a sense precise enough. The Absolute is the very opposite of a mere Nothing. For it is fulfilment, attainment, peace, the goal of life, the object of desire, the end of knowledge. Why then does it stubbornly appear as indistinguishable from mere nothing? The answer is: That is a part of our very illusion itself. The light above the light is, to our deluded vision, darkness. It is our finite realm that is falsity, the mere nothing. The Absolute is all Truth."[12]

"It is by contrast with our finite seeking that the goal which quenches desires and ideas at once appears as all truth and all life. But to attribute to the goal a concrete life and a definite ideal content would be, for this view, to ruin this very contrast. For concreteness means variety and finitude, and consequently ignorance and imperfection. The Absolute home appears empty, just because, wherever definite content is to be found, the Hindoo feels not at home, but finite, striving and deluded into a search for something beyond."[13]

In another dialogue Yājñavalkya calls the Absolute "the Imperishable." He states: "The *brahmins* call this the *akṣara* (the imperishable). It is neither coarse nor fine, neither short nor long, neither red (like fire) nor fluid (like water); it is without shadow, without darkness, without air, without ether, without attachment, without taste, without smell, without eyes, without ears, without speech, without mind, withoug light (vigour), without breath, without a mouth (or door), without measure, having no within and having no without; it consumes no one and is consumed by no one."[14] "Let a wise *brahmin*, after he has discovered him,

10. Royce, *op. cit.*, pp. 169–170.
11. *Ibid.*, p. 170.
12. *Ibid.*, pp. 170–171.
13. *Ibid.*, p. 171.
14. *Bṛhad. Up.* III, 8, 8. Macdonell: SL. p. 219.

practice wisdom. Let him not seek after many words, for that is mere weariness of the tongue."[15]

Here, for the first time in the history of human thought, one finds the Absolute grasped and proclaimed negatively. The negative character of the absolute is stressed by a later poet. Calling the absolute the Person, he says: "His form is not to be seen, no one beholds him with the eye. He is imagined by the heart, by wisdom, by the mind. Those who know this, are immortal."[16] "He (the Self) cannot be reached by speech, by mind, or by the eye. How can it be apprehended except by him who says: He is?"[17]

William James explained that the negation in the form of "not this, not that" (neti neti) is nothing but the affirmation of the absolute standpoint. "Their very denial of every adjective you may propose as applicable to the ultimate truth, —He, the Self, the Ātman, is to be described by "No! no!" only, say the Upaniṣads, —though it seems on the surface to be a no-function, is a denial made on behalf of a deeper yes. Who so calls the Absolute anything in particular, or says that it is this, seems implicitly to shut it off from being that.

"It is as if he lessened it. So we deny the 'this,' negating the negation which it seems to us to imply, in the interests of the higher affirmative attitude by which we are possessed."[18]

The "Not so, not so" (neti) of Yājñavalkya reminds us of the sayings of mystics in other countries. In China, Lao-tzu declared a similar position. "We cannot describe the *Tao*. There is no name for it."[19] "Those who know do not speak; those who speak do not know."[20]

The poet Po Chu-i wrote about Lao Tzu:

"Those who speak know nothing;
Those who know are silent.
These words, as I am told,
Were spoken by Lao Tzu.
If we are to believe that Lao Tzu
Was himself one who knew,
How comes it that he wrote a book
Of five thousand words?"[21]

15. *Bṛhad. Up.* IV, 4, 21.
16. *Kāṭhaka-Up.* II, 6, 9.
17. *Ibid.*, II, 6, 12.
18. William James; *Varieties of Religious Experience*, New York, Longmans, Green, 1928, p. 418.
19. *Tao Te Ching*, XXXVII.
20. *Ibid.*, LVI.
21. Arthur Waley, *A Hundred and Seventy Chinese Poems*, E. T. (London: Constable 1923), p. 166.

In another dialogue Yājñavalkya calls the absolute the Inner Controller (*antaryāmin*).[22] The Inner Controller is he who, dwelling in the worlds and other beings, controls them. Yājñavalkya at first explains it as follows: "He who dwells in the earth, yet is within the earth, whom the earth does not know, whose body the earth is, who controls the earth from within, he is your self, the inner controller, the immortal."[23] Yājñavalkya also states: "He who dwells in the sun, yet is within the sun, whom the sun does not know, whose body the sun is, who controls the sun from within, he is your self, the inner controller, the immortal."[24]

Finally, Yājñavalkya says: "He is unseen, but seeing; unheard, but hearing; unperceived, but perceiving; unknown, but knowing. There is no other seer but he, there is no other hearer but he, there is no other perceiver but he, there is no other but he. This is your Self, the Inner Controller, the Immortal. Everything else is of evil."

According to Yājñavalkya, there is nothing independent of knowledge and there is no diversity within knowledge. The Self is precisely the very knower, not as a thing that first is real and then knows, but as the very act of seeing, hearing, and thinking. In its innermost essence the mediating presence of some other, of some object that is known, seen, heard, and thought, is simply removed, and the very diversity of the acts of knowing, seeing, hearing, and thinking, is also removed. Therefore, the attainment of the Self means getting out of diversity. It was regarded as the beatitude of man, and being apart from it without knowing it was regarded as suffering.

We can compare the above views with the theories of Plato. Plato is the first Western philosopher to have held that the ultimate reality—what he termed the Idea of the Good—could be intuited only by "pure intelligence."[25] He asserts that "the good is not essence, but far exceeds in dignity and power," while on the other hand, it is "not only the source of intelligibility in all objects of knowledge, but also of their being and essence."[26] Thus, he who seeks to know the Good, knows "that place where is the full perfection of being."[27] However, with Plato the subject and the object are clearly distinguished from each other; with Yājñavalkya both are at one.

Yājñavalkya says: "That *brahman*, is unseen, but seeing; unheard, but hearing; unperceived, but perceiving; unknown, but knowing. There is nothing that sees but it, nothing that hears but it, nothing that perceives

22. *Bṛhad. Up.* III, 7.
23. *Bṛhad. Up.* III, 7, 3.
24. *Bṛhad. Up.* III, 7, 9.
25. *Republic*, 532a5–b2.
26. *Ibid.*, 599 6–10.
27. *Ibid.*, 526e3–4. (Gauchwal, *op. cit.*, p. 157)

but it, nothing that knows but it. In the Imperishable (that *Akṣara*), then, the ether (*ākāśa*) is woven, like warp and woof."[28] "Do you know that Thread by which, and that Inner Controller by which and by whom, this world and the other and all beings are strung together and controlled from within, so that they move like a puppet, performing their respective functions?"[29]

The principle is imperishable; it does not change.[30] The personality, which we generally take to be our self, is conscious only by fits and starts. There are large gaps in it, without consciousness. The seer always exists. Even if death comes, the seer cannot die. A man asked him: "When the sun and the moon have both set, the fire has gone out, and speech has stopped, Yājñavalkya, what serves as the light for a man?" He answered: "The self serves as his light (*ātmaivāsya jyotir bhavati*). It is through the light of the self that he sits, goes out, works and returns."[31]

According to Yājñavalkya, this is the eternal principle. It does not change. "This eternal being that can never be proved, is to be perceived in one way only; it is spotless, beyond the ether, the unborn Self, great and eternal." "And he is that great unborn Self, who consists of knowledge, is surrounded by the senses, the ether within the heart. In it there reposes the ruler of all, the lord of all, the king of all. He does not become greater by good works, nor smaller by evil works. He is the lord of all, the king of all things, the protector of all things. He is a bank and a boundary, so that these worlds may not be confounded. *Brahmins* seek to know him by the study of the Vedas, by sacrifice, by gifts, by penance, by fasting, and he who knows becomes a sage (*muni*)."[32]

Yājñavalkya esteemed only the knowledge of the absolute. He says: "Everything else is of evil."[33] He gave up everything and became a hermit. "Wishing for that world (i.e., for *brahman*) only, mendicants leave their homes. Knowing this the people of old did not wish for offspring. What shall we do with offspring, they said, we who have this Self and this world (of *brahman*)."

"And they, having risen above the desire for sons, wealth and new worlds, wander about as mendicants. For desire for sons is desire for wealth, and desire for wealth is desire for worlds. Both of these are indeed desires only."[34] Having taught the doctrine of immortality to his wife, he went away into the forest.

28. *Bṛhad. Up.* III, 8, 11.
29. *Bṛhad. Up.* III, 7, combined with its commentary.
30. Cf. *Bṛhad. Up.* III, 9, 28.
31. *Bṛhad. Up.* IV, 3, 6.
32. *Bṛhad. Up.* IV, 4, 20–22.
33. *Bṛhad. Up.* III, 5, 2.
34. *Bṛhad. Up.* IV, 4, 22.

Here we can find the beginning of the pessimistic and other-worldly tendency of later Indian thought. "By renunciation thou shouldst enjoy."[35] We can enjoy the world if we are not burdened by worldly possessions; we are princes in the world if we do not harbor any thought of convetousness. A call to renunciation in the sense of eliminating the sense of separateness and developing disinterested love was thus put forward by thinkers of those days. In a later Upaniṣad[36] the pessimistic trait of Indian thought appears more explicitly. We shall meet it again and again in later Indian literature.

In Greece pessimistic melancholy was also not lacking.[37] For example, one thinks of the melodious lament of Sophocles:[38] "Not to be born is of all the best; but by far the next best is, if one is born, to return thither whence he came as quickly as possible." Although there is much similarity between the Upaniṣadic doctrines and Western thought, the latter, whether Greek, medieval or modern, is always, or nearly always, entirely uninfluenced by the longing to escape from life. There are passages in Plato which ask us to mistrust our nature, to see in it an incurable taint, and exhort us to live in the world of the unseen;[39] but in them Plato is not voicing the Greek spirit in general. Contemplation, was ragarded to be the highest happiness by Aristotle,[40] but he cannot be called otherworldly. A call to renunciation begins in later periods in the West, and Christianity also was tinged with it. "Thou fool, that which thou sowest is not quickened, except it die."[41] In Christianity the pessimistic view of life is justified only so far as it is a presumption of the doctrine of deliverance: "We know that we are of God, and the whole world (*ho kosmos holos*) lieth in wickedness (*en toiponeroi*)."[42]

It is in ancient China, rather, that we meet with similar ideas at a period even before the rise of Cynism, Stoicism and Christianity:

"Banish wisdom, discard knowledge,
And the people will be benefited a hundredfold.
Banish human kindness, discard morality
And the people will be dutiful and compassionate.
Give them simplicity to look at, the uncarved block to hold,

35. *Īśā-Up.*
36. *Maitri-Up.* I, 2–4.
37. Pessimism as held by Greek thinkers is discussed in detail by Walter Ruben in his article: Indische und griechische Metaphysik, *Zeitschrift für Indologie und Iranistik,* Band 8, 1931 (Leipzing, Deutsche Morgenländische Gesellschaft), S. 152–158.
38. Deussen, *Elements*, p. 274.
39. *Laws*, 918.
40. B. Russell, *History of Western Philosophy*, p. 181.
41. I Corinthians, XV, 36.
42. I John 5, 19.

Give them selflessness and fewness of desires."[43]

Another passage states: "Establish nothing in regard to oneself. Let things be what they are, move like water, rest like mirror, respond like an echo, pass quickly like the non-existent, and be quiet as purity. . . . Become the channel for the world."[44]

One of the features of modern life is a radical this-worldliness. People are distracted by outward objects in their daily lives, by telephones, movies, television, games, etc. It is needless to enumerate them all. Yet, in the midst a busy life of activity, to hearken to the voice of the Self would be valuable for us. Heinrich Zimmer says: "We of the modern Occident are at last prepared to seek and hear the voice that India has heard. But . . . we must hear it not from the teacher but from within ourselves. Just as in the period of the deflation of the revealed gods of the Vedic pantheon, so today revealed Christianity has been devaluated. The Christian, as Nietzsche says, is a man who behaves like everybody else.[45] Our professions of faith have no longer any discernible bearing either on our public conduct or on our private state of hope. The sacraments do not work on many of us their spiritual transformation; we are bereft and at a loss where to turn. Meanwhile, our academic secular philosophies are concerned more with information than with that redemptive transformation which our souls require. And this is the reason why a glance at the face of India may assist us to discover and recover something of ourselves."[46] In this respect the philosophy of the "absolute subject" still has something worth heeding.

7. The Deified Self

The fundamental principle which transcends both subject and object, when thought of as a personality, is God. In the later Upaniṣads the Self was deified, and the notion of grace makes its appearance. The will of the Universal Self is described as follows: "He makes those perform good actions whom he wishes to lead upwards from these worlds; he makes those perform bad actions whom he wishes to lead downwards. He is the protector of the world, he is the sovereign of the world, he is the lord of the world."[1] A thought which reminds one of the theory of predestination was also advocated. "This self cannot be attained by instruction, nor by

43. *Tao Te Ching*, XIX.
44. *Chuang-tzu*, XXXIII.
45. I would like to add that this is also applicable to Buddhists in present-day Japan.
46. *Philosophies of India*, pp. 13–14.
1. *Kauṣ. Up.* III, 8.

intellectual power, nor even through much hearing. He is to be attained only by the one whom the (self) chooses. To such a one the self reveals his own nature."[2] Moreover, the deified Self was looked upon with awe. "Through fear of him, fire burns; through fear of him the sun gives heat; through fear both Indra (the god of thunder) and wind and Death, the fifth, speed on their way."[3]

In the Old Testament we see: "At thy rebuke they fled; at the sound of thy thunder they took to flight."[4] St. Paul also states: "Work out your own salvation with fear and trembling; for God is at work in you, both to will and to work for his good pleasure."[5] It should be noted, however, that these notions concerning the Deified Self were rather exceptional in the Upaniṣads, whereas they constitute the main current in the Hebrew and Christian traditions.

It perhaps may be more accurate to compare the notion of the deified Self with the concept of Zeus among some Greeks. This similarity did not escape the attention of the medieval Muslim, Alberuni: "If you compare Greek theology with that of the Hindus, you will find that *brahman* is described in the same way as Zeus by Aratos." He cites the praise of Zeus with which Aratos begins his book on the *Phainomena*:

"We, mankind, do not leave him, nor can we do without him;
Of him the roads are full,
And the meeting-places of men.
He is mild towards them;
He produces for them what they wish, and incites them to work.
Reminding them of the necessities of life,
He indicates to them the times favorable
For digging and ploughing for a good growth,
Who has raised the signs and stars in heaven.
Therefore, we humiliate ourselves before him first and last."[6]

Finally, in the *Śvetāśvatara-Upaniṣad* the idea of God as a Creator appeared. He is the god (deva)[7] called Rudra,[8] who punishes and condones. But this idea was rather exceptional in the Upaniṣads. Moreover, the Indian God was regarded not necessarily as a separate being different from the Self, but very often the deified self. If we compare this with the monotheistic concept of God in Hebrew thought there is, indeed, a striking contrast.

2. *Kāṭhaka-Up.* II, 23. Radhakrishnan, *The Principal Upaniṣads, op. cit.*, p. 619.
3. *Kāṭhaka-Up.* VI, 3.
4. Psalms, 104, 7.
5. *Philippians*, I, 12–13.
6. *Alberuni's India, op. cit.*, vol. I, p. 97.
7. *Śvet. Up.* II, 16, etc.
8. *Śvet. Up.* III, 2, etc.

D. Problems of Practice

1. Retribution and Deliverance as Hereditary

AMONG many ancient people it was supposed that the deeds of parents or ancestors brought forth retributions on their children or descendants. Varuṇa in Indian mythology releases men not only from the sins they themselves commit, but from those committed by their fathers. In the Upaniṣads one also finds remnants of ritualism associated with the family system of those days. One of these Upaniṣadic rituals is called "Transmission" (*samprasāraṇa*). When a man thinks he is going to die, he says to his son: "You are *brahman* (the Veda, so far as acquired by the father); you are the sacrifice (so far as performed by the father); you are the world." The son answers: "I am *brahman*, I am the sacrifice, I am the world." "When a father who knows this departs this world, then he enters into his son together with his own spirits (with speech, mind and breath). If there is anything done amiss by the father, of all that the son delivers him, and therefore he is called putra (lit. one who saves),[1] son. By help of his son the father stands firm in this world. Then these divine immortal spirits (speech, mind, and breath) enter into him."[2]

In Greece there was a similar view that "a man should leave behind him children's children to be the servants of God in his place forever."[3] A remnant of this view that the deeds of the father carry over to the son is found even in the New Testament.

> "As he (Jesus) passed by, he saw a man blind from his birth. And his disciples asked him, 'Rabbi, who sins, this man or *his parents*, that he was born blind?' Jesus answered, 'It was not that this man sinned, or *his parents*, but that the works of God might be made manifest in him.'"[4]

In India the son was regarded as delivering his father, while in Israel

1. This conception accords with the later etymology of son as 'savior from hell,' *putra*, *Manu* IX, 138. (pratirūpo 'smāj jāyase; *Bṛhad. Up.* II: 1, 8. cf. *Śvet. Up.* II: 16; V: 11)
2. *Bṛhad. Up.* I: 5, 17.
3. Plato, *Laws*, 774.
4. John IX, 1–3.

the son was regarded as afflicted by the sin of his parents. Early Hebrew thought that "sins" of the parents were visited also upon the children; and, secondly, that sin was possible while still in the womb, since the embryo, in its later stages, was possessed of consciousness (cf. Augustine's "*peccatum Originale*"). In ancient China and Japan it was thought that the merits and sins of ancestors were visited upon their posterity. In China it was said: "A family which has done good deeds will certainly incur calamities."[5] In Japan there was a belief that "the deeds of parents will result in the destiny of their children."[6]

But, such ancient concepts of filial responsibility were later rejected. This step occurred early in the religious traditions of Israel. Jeremiah advanced the idea of a valid, personal relationship between Yahweh and the individual. He makes a succinct statement of individual responsibility: "In those days they shall no longer say: 'The fathers have eaten sour grapes, and the children's teeth are set on edge.' But every one shall die for his own sin; each man who eats sour grapes, his teeth shall be set on edge."[7]

Jeremiah brought men as individuals face to face with God and suggested that they were responsible directly to Him for their conduct. Men could no longer say that God dealt with them only through their group relationships.[8] The same change occurred in India, but the Indian interpretation of individual responsibility moved in quite a different direction. To that unique Indian approach, we must now direct our attention!

2. Individual Responsibility

a. Transmigration and Retribution

IN the early Vedic scriptures reference is made to the joys of heaven and to the torments of hell, thus indicating in a general way that good deeds are rewarded and evil deeds punished. There are no references to the doctrine of transmigration. The situation seems to have been the same among the Greeks also. "They (the Greeks) had, it is true, a vague and misty belief that wrongdoers were punished after death, but this was not a doctrine that influenced the conscience of the ordinary man. The sinner was punished not as a moral offender, but as a trespasser against a vindictive power. The general attitude towards the conception of a future life

5. *I-ching.*
6. "Oya-no Ingwa-ga ko-ni mukuiru."
7. Jeremiah, 31, 29–30.
8. Noss, *Man's Religions*, *op. cit.*, p. 503.

was one of contemptuous indifference. Thus Achilles in the Odyssey says: 'rather would I be a serf on some poor man's farm than lord over all the spirits of the dead.' So little did the early Greek (any more than apparently the Vedic Indian) care to extend his vision to the other side of the grave."[1] This feature holds true with the moral ideas in the *Vedasaṃhitās* and the *Brāhmaṇa* literature. Where then is the difference between the Indian and Greek concepts? The Indians systematized the theory of retribution[2] in minute detail with the idea that any action made intentionally entails an effect in this life or another. The notion of transmigration or metempsychosis and that of *karma* appeared for the first time in the Upaniṣads and became overwhelmingly predominant in later Indian thought.

On the level of popular superstition, of course, belief in rebirth in another body in this world can be seen among many ancient peoples. Rhys Davids says: "The belief in the passage of the soul after death, not to another world only, but also into other human bodies in this world, is not uncommon, and has evidently had an independent origin in different times and countries. The various tribes of North-American Indians believed that the soul animating the body of an infant was the soul of some deceased person; enslaved negroes have been known to commit suicide, that they may revive in their native land; and the aborigines of Australia hold white men to be the names or ghosts of their own dead. They are said to express this in the simple formula, 'Black-fellow tumble down, jump up White-fellow'; and a native hanged at Melbourne is represented to have given vent to the hopeful belief that he would 'jump up White-fellow and have lots of sixpences.' The Jews, at different periods of their history, seem to have held a similar doctrine; for though we don't discover a reference to it in the New Testament, it is found distinctly in several parts of the Talmud."[3] Caesar reported of the Druids that "souls do not die, but pass at death from one to another; and that this was a great incentive to virtue, for the fear of death was disregarded."[4] Even in recent years the common people in China held the belief that they can immediately be reborn after death. These cases, however, do not represent the systematized conception of transmigration and retribution as Deussen and others have shown.

> "When it is said occasionally of the fathers that they 'move along, adopting the external form of birds'; or when the soul of the Buddhist mother at death enters into a female jackal in order to warn her son

1. A. A. Macdonell, *Comparative Religion, op. cit.*, p. 112.
2. A detailed description of the theory of *karma* can be seen in the *karmasthana* of Vasubandhu's *Abhidharma-kośa*.
3. Hershon's Telmudic Miscellany, pp. 40, 57, 325–328; Goldstucker's Remains, & c. i, 215, cited from Rhys Davids, *Lectures*, etc., p. 78.
4. *De bello Galico* VI, 14; cf. Diodorus Sic. V, 28.

on his journey of the unhealthy forest; when the dead pass into an insect that buzzes round the last resting-place of the bones; or when the fathers creep into the roots of plants; there are popular representations, which are on a level with the entrance of the Vetala into the corpse, or the yogin's animating of several bodies, but have nothing to do with belief in transmigration. They have as little to do with any such doctrine as the ancient Egyptian idea that the dead can return and assume any form at pleasure (which Herodotus in ii. 123 seems to interpret erroneously of the soul's migration), or the seven women in Goethe's poem, who appear by night as seven were wolves."[5]

"Superstitious ideas like these have existed amongst all peoples and at all times, but do not imply belief in transmigration, nor have they given rise to such teaching, least of all in India. Indeed they have exercised scarcely any influence upon it; since, as we shall show, the theory of transmigration rests on the conviction of due recompense awarded to good and evil works, and this was at first conceived as future. Only later, for reasons which the texts disclose to us, was it transferred from an imaginary future into the present life; if therefore this recompense involves at times existence as an animal or plant, this is merely an incidental consequence on which no stress is laid from first to last; though it is true that this circumstance appeared to the opponents of the doctrine from the very beginning to be its especial characteristic, and has called forth their derision since the times of Xenophanes. (Diog. L. i, 36)"[6]

One might guess that the pre-Aryan occupants of the valley of the Ganges were believers in something like a primitive notion of rebirth and that the Aryans first derived the idea from them.[7] Some notions suggesting the beginnings of the concept of transmigration can be found already in the *Brāhmaṇa* texts. The Aryans in the *Brāhmaṇas* generally thought that there was only one after-life and that its nature was determined by our conduct here. "A man is born into the world which he has made."[8] "Whatever food a man eats in this world by that food he is eaten in the next world."[9] Good and evil deeds find their corresponding rewards and punishments in a future life: "Thus have they done to us in yonder world, and so we do to them again in this world."[10] In some later *Brāhmaṇa* passages, however, one does begin to find references to the problem of

5. H. Oldenberg, *Die Religion des Veda*, 2nd ed. Stuttgart and Berlin: J. G. Cotta'sche Buchhandlung Nachfolger, pp. 563, 581 f.
6. Diog. L. i, 36. Deussen, *The Philosophy of the Upanishads*, p. 316.
7. Rhys Davids, *Lectures*, etc., p. 82.
8. *ŚBr.* VI, 2, 2, 27.
9. *ŚBr.* XII, 9, 11.
10. *ŚBr.* II, 6.

"re-death" (*punar-mṛtyu*) which undoubtedly show a movement towards the later notion of transmigration.

In the Upaniṣads, according to a certain King-philosopher, Pravāhana Jaivali, the destiny of the dead is threefold.[11] There are three paths after death:

(i) "Those who have a secret doctrine and those who have practised the worship of the true being, after their death, go to light, from light to day, from day to the half-month of the waxing moon; from the half-month of the waxing moon to the six months when the sun moves northward; from those six months to the world of the gods; from the world of the gods to the sun, from the sun to the place of lightning. When they have thus reached the place of lightning a spirit comes near them, and leads them to the worlds of the *Brahman.* In these worlds of *Brahman* they dwell exalted for ages. There is no returning for them." This is the path leading to the gods.

(ii) "But they who conquer the worlds (future states) by means of sacrifice, charity, and austerity, go to smoke, (of the-cremation-fire), from smoke to night, from night to the half month of the waning moon; from the half month of the waning moon to the six months when the sun moves southward; from these months to the world of the fathers, from the world of the fathers to the moon. Having reached the moon they become food (of the gods), and then the gods feed on them, just as sacrificers feed on soma-wine, as it increases and decreases."

But when this (the result of their good works on earth) ceases, they return again to that ether, from ether to the air, from the air to rain, from rain to the earth. And when they have reached the earth, they become food, and they are taken into the body of men. Thence they are born out of the body of women. "Thus they rise up into the world, and go the same round as before." This is the path leading to the fathers.

On the curious belief of souls going to the moon, Tylor says:[12] "In old times and new, it has come into men's minds to fix upon the sun and moon as abodes of departed souls. When we have learnt from the rude Natchez of the Mississippi and the Apalaches of Florida that the sun is the bright dwelling of departed chiefs and braves, and have traced like thoughts on into the theologies of Mexico and Peru. . . . And when in South America the Saliva Indians have pointed out the moon as their paradise, where no mosquitoes are, and the Guaycurus have shown it as the home of chiefs and medicine-men deceased, and the Polynesians of Tokelan, in like manner, have claimed it as the abode of departed kings and chiefs, then these pleasant fancies may be compared with that ancient theory mentioned by Plutarch, that hell is in the air and elysium in the

11. *Bṛhad. Up.* VI, 2, 1–16. Cf. *Chānd. Up.* V, 3–10 f. *Kauṣītaki-Up.* I, 2.
12. Tylor, *Primitive Cultures*, II, pp. 69, 70.

moon."[13] Jamblichus informs us that Pythagoras held that the islands of the blessed were the sun and the moon.[14]

The Manicheans had a belief which appears to be similar. Epiphanius (Adv. Haer. 66) gives the following as the views of Tyrbo: "The wisdom of the more than good God, bethinking itself that the soul diffused through everything, being captive of princes and opposite principle and root, was cast into bodies—for its sake . . . placed these lights in the heavens, the Sun, the Moon, and the Stars—having performed this work by what the Greeks say are the twelve elements. And the elements, he (i.e., Tyrbo) maintains, draw the souls of drying men and other animals, they being of the nature of light, bear them to a light boat (because he wishes to call the sun and moon voyages), and the light boat, or ship, is laden up to the fifteenth day, according to the fullness of the moon, and so it (the soul) is sent on and set down from the fifteenth day in the great ship, that is the sun. The sun then carries them on into the world of life and the region of the blessed. And the souls are sent on by the sun and the moon." This is confirmed, though with some difference in detail, by the Disputation of Archelaus, where it is said of the doctrine of Manes.[15]

(iii) Concerning the third path, Pravahana states: "Those, however, who know neither of these two paths, become worms, birds, and creeping things."

Although these three paths probably represent various ideas from an archaic religious context, it is also the case that the second and third paths represent some of the earliest references to transmigration in the Brahmanical context.

The idea of *karma* was likewise new in the Aryan context in the time of the Upaniṣads. When asked about the destiny of the dead Yājñavalkya said: "Take my hand, my dear. We two alone will know of this; let this question of ours not be (discussed) in public." Then these two went out and argued, and what they talked of was *karma* (work, action), what they praised was *karma*, viz., that a man becomes good by good work, and bad by bad work. After that the man held peace.[16]

Elsewhere the Upaniṣads state: "According as one acts, according as one behaves, so does he become. The doer of good becomes good. The doer of evil becomes evil. One becomes virtuous by virtuous action, bad by bad action."[17] In a similar manner, Plato says: "Such as are the trend of our desires and the nature of our souls, just such each of us becomes."[18]

13. Rhys Davids, *Lectures*, etc., p. 247.
14. Vit. Pyth. 82. Cited from Rhys Davids, *Lectures*, etc., p. 247.
15. Rhys Davids, *Lectures*, etc., pp. 247–249.
16. *Bṛhad. Up.* III, 2, 12 f.
17. *Bṛhad. Up.* IV, 4, 5.
18. *Laws* 904, C.

In another passage which is ascribed to Yājñavalkya, the process of the departure of the soul out of the body is related in a detailed and vivid manner.[19] It is stated that when a man has died, his knowledge, his works, and his acquaintance with former things (i.e., instinct) take hold of him. He passes away with these three.[20] "As a grass-leech[21] after having reached the end of a blade of grass, and after having made another approach (to another blade), draws itself together towards it, thus does this Self, after having thrown off this body and dispelled all ignorance and after making another approach (to another body), draw himself together towards it (for making the transition)." "And as a goldmith, taking a piece of gold, turns it into another, newer and more beautiful shape, so does this Self, after having thrown off this body and dispelled all ignorance, make unto himself another, newer and more beautiful shape, whether it be like the fathers, or like the Gandharvas (heavenly beings), or like the gods, or like the Lord of Creatures (Prajāpati) or like Brahman, or like other beings."[22] "As he has acted, as he has lived, so he becomes; he who has done good, is born again as a good one; he who has done evil, is born again as an evil one. He becomes good through good action, bad through bad action. Therefore it is said: 'Man here is made entirely of desire, and according to his desire is his resolve, and according to his resolve, he performs the action, and according to the performance of the action is his destiny.' " "To whatever object a man's own mind is attached, to that he goes strenuously together with his deed; and having obtained the end (the last results) of whatever deed he does here on earth, he returns again from that world (which is the temporary reward of his deed) to this world of action."

Concerning the situation on earth after rebirth, another passage states: "Those whose conduct has been good, will quickly attain some good birth, the birth of a *brāhmaṇa*, or a noble (warrior), or one of common people (vaiśya). But those whose conduct has been evil, will quickly attain an evil birth, the birth of a dog, or a hog, or a *caṇḍāla*."[23] A *caṇḍāla* is an

19. *Bṛhad. Up.* IV, 4, 2 f.
20. "Kālidāsa in his Śakuntalā, Act IV, says that when a being who is (in all other respects) happy becomes conscious of an ardent longing when he sees beautiful objects or hears sweet sounds, then in all probability, without being aware of it, he remembers with his mind the friendships of former lives, firmly rooted in his heart." (S. Radhakrishnan, *The Principal Upaniṣads*, p. 271)
21. B. M. Barua, *Pre-Buddhistic Indian Philosophy*, p. 175. We are only too often reminded of Goethe's grasshopper "that ever flits, and flitting leaps, and still in the grass sings its old song." (P. Deussen, *The Philosophy of the Upanishads*, p. 117)
22. "As a goldsmith takes the material of one piece of work, and out of it hammers another, newer, more beautiful form, so this soul also, after it has shaken off the body and let Ignorance go, shapes itself another, newer, more beautiful form, whether of the Fathers or the Bandharvas or the Gods or Prajapati or the Brahman or other Beings." (Śaṅkara ad *Bṛhad. Up.* IV, 4, 2, or 3. cf. *Bhag. G.* II, 22)
23. *Chānd. Up.* V, 10, 7.

outcast, a man of the lowest and most despised class; he is put in the same category as a dog or a hog.

After the Upaniṣadic period, the ideas of *karma* and transmigration were everywhere accepted by all Indians. The Brahmins, along with heterodox teachers, held the belief. In later centuries Indians generally believed that there is within the body of every man a soul, which at the death of the body, flies away from it like a bird from cage, and enters a new life, either in one of the heavens, in one of the hells, or on this earth.

The only exception is the rare case of a man having in this life acquired a true knowledge of the absolute. In the later theory of the Advaita Vedāntins, such a man's soul is directly absorbed into the Great Self, is lost in it, and no longer has any independent existence. The souls of all other men enter, after the death of the body, into a new existence in one or another of the many different modes of being,—e.g., in heaven, becoming a god, in hell, becoming an afflicted being. All superhuman beings were looked upon as not eternal, but merely temporary creatures. If the soul returns to earth, it enters a new body; and this can be that of a human being, an animal, or a plant. All these are possessed of souls, and there is no essential difference between their sould and the souls of men. The outward condition of the soul is, in each new birth, determined by its action in previous lives. The precise relation between the act (*karman*) and its fruit (*vipāka*) was generally undetermined, so that it was impossible to trace in ordinary cases any exact law or proportion between the cause and the effect. The effect, however, was considered to follow the cause inevitably and naturally, very often without the intervention of any deity to apportion the reward or punishment.

In contrast, the Greeks in general were little concerned with the belief of transmigration. In the Hellenic period, the Greek mind remained positivist and humanistic and was indifferent to the fate of the soul. An ordinary young Athenian, Glaucon, asked the question "Have you not heard that our soul is immortal?", answered, "No, really I have not."[24] There were exceptions, however. The Orphic theology taught transmigration. For them it was the soul, and not the imprisoning body, which was the important part of man. The soul is the real man, and is not the mere shadow-image of the body as it appears in Homer.[25] There were some philosophers who believed in transmigration, although sometimes in a wry manner. Concerning Xenophanes it is said: Once, they say, passing by when a puppy was being beaten, he pitied it, and spoke as follows:

24. Plato's *Republic,* 608.
25. Frederick Copleston, *A History of Philosophy,* Maryland, Westminster. The Newman Bookshop, 1946, vol. I, p. 32.

'Stop! Cease your beating, because this is really the soul of a man who was my friend: I recognized it as I heard it cry aloud.'[26]

The Pythagoreans are said to have held the doctrine of transmigration, and it was ascribed to the founder of the school. It is said that Pythagoras taught ". . . first, that the soul is an immortal thing, and that it is transformed into other kinds of living things; further, that whatever comes into existence is born again in the revolutions of a certain cycle, nothing being absolutely new; and that all things that are born with life in them ought to be treated as kindred."[27] However, the doctrine seems to have had little connection with their philosophy.[28] Empedocles (c. 470–c. 430 B.C.) is reported to have said that he had been "a boy, a girl, a bush, a bird, a fish."[29]

As can be seen from these instances, with early thinkers, i.e., Yājñavalkya, etc., as well as Pythagoras and Empedocles, the doctrine of reincarnation was—as in early Buddhism—not yet closely combined with a theory of an immortal, everlasting soul.

In later periods, however, the immortality or imperishability of the soul came to be explicitly and theoretically set forth.[30] Verses of a later Upaniṣad say:

> "The knowing self is never born; nor does he die at any time.
> He sprang from nothing and nothing sprang from him.
> He is unborn, eternal, abiding and primeval. He is not slain when the body is slain.
> If the slayer thinks that he slays or if the slain think that he is slain, both of them do not understand. He neither slays nor is he slain."[31]

Plato also asserted the immortality of the soul.[32] He states: "The soul of man is immortal, and at one time comes to an end, which is called dying away, and at another is born again, but never perishes . . . and

26. Xenophanes' fragment, 7.
27. B. Russell, *A History of Western Philosophy*, p. 32.
28. E. Zeller, *History* etc., vol. 1, pp. 481–487.
29. Diog. Laert. viii, 12. But this does not seem consistent with his fragment, 9.
30. Coomaraswamy (*Recollections*), pointed out the following parallels.—the Buddha's knowledge (*abhinna*) extends to all 'former abodes.' When at death this Self recollects itself (*Bṛhad. Up.* IV, 4, 3; VI, 1, 13, etc.; *Enneads* 4, 9, 2) then 'we' are no more (*Bṛhad. Up.* II, 4, 12; *Chānd. Up.* VIII, 9, 1, etc.), 'we who in our junction with our bodies are composites and have qualities that shall not exist, but shall be brought into the regeneration by which, becoming joined to immaterial things, and shall become incomposite and without qualities' (Philo, cher. 113 f; cf. Plato, *Phaedo* 78 Cf).
31. *Kāṭhaka-Up.* II, 18–19. Radhakrishnan, *The Principal Upaniṣads, op. cit.*, pp. 616–617. Cf. *Bhag. G.* II, 18 f.
32. *Phaedo*, 69.

having been born many times has acquired the knowledge of all and everything."[33] This is cited as the doctrine of learned priests and priestesses, and is approved by Socrates. In the *Timaeus* it is stated that the Creator made one soul for each star. Souls have sensation, love, fear, and anger. If a man lives well, he goes after death to live happily forever in his star. But if he lives badly, he will in the next life be a woman; if he (or she) persists in evil-doing, he (or she) will become a brute, and go on through transmigrations until at last reason conquers. God put some souls on earth, some on the moon, some on other planets and stars, and left it to the gods to fashion their bodies.[34]

But neither Pythagoras nor Plato held to a view identical with the popular Indian notion of transmigration, either in its Hindu or in its Buddhist form. Their views of the continued existence after death of the human soul in the bodies of other men, or of beasts, are philosophical speculations. They were not universally accepted beliefs among ordinary people. They are most probably modifications of Egyptian or Orphic ideas which are themselves very different from the Indian belief.[35]

The problem as to whether Greek notions of transmigration were influenced by Indian ideas has been subject to much debate. Macdonell observed years ago that the "dependence of Pythagoras on Indian Philosophy and science certainly seems to have a high degree or probability. The doctrine of metempsychosis in the case of Pythagoras appears without any connection or explanatory background, and was regarded by the Greeks as of foreign origin.[36] More recent research has shown, however, that it is possible to explain the conception each cultural context without referring to the possibility of cross-cultural influence.

In certain early Christian traditions, also, it is from the worldly process, the wheel of becoming (*trokhos tes geneseos*, James e, 6 comparable to the Sanskrit *bhavacakra*)[37] that deliverance is sought. Palladius of Caesareia, who suffered martyrdom in 309 A.D., referred to the notion of "transincorporation," that is, the transmutation of souls.[38] Many Gnostic

33. *Meno*, 81 B.C. cf. *Gorgias*, p. 523 E.
34. B. Russell, *A History of Western Philosophy*, p. 145.
35. Cf. Rhys Davids, *Lectures*, etc., p. 75.
36. A. A. Macdonell, *A History of Sanskrit Literature*, p. 422.
37. The authorized version translates it as "the course of nature."
38. In his "Apology for Origen," which, with the exception of a few fragments, only survives in a translation made by Rufinus of Aquileia (died A.D. 410), he thus explains the position taken up by the great Alexandrian upon the subject: "The most recent charge is that of transincorporation, that is, the transmutation of souls. To which, as we have done with regard to other charges, we will reply in his own words." He then quotes Origen as saying, "But these things, so far as we are concerned, are not dogmatic but spoken of for the sake of discussion, and that they may be rejected," (e.g., in Migne, Patrol. Graec. xvii 608 & Routh, Relig. Sacr. IV. 383) and proceeds

sects believed in pre-existence and the rebirth of human souls. They also had a magical theory of the spiritual world. The disembodied soul travels by the dark or bright path and is saved from the perils on the way by certain magical words.[39] This notion can be compared with that of the path of the fathers and that of the gods as previously mentioned.

Even in Islam there were some thinkers who admitted metempsychosis as was pointed out by Alberuni. In connection with the Sāṃkhya conception of metempsychosis, he states that there were some Muslim thinkers who allowed it. "Abu—Ya kub of Sijistan maintains in his book, "*The disclosing of that which is veiled*," that the species are preserved; that metempsychosis always proceeds in one and the same species, never crossing its limits and passing into another species."[40]

b. The Final Goal

THE ideal or final goal, aspired to by early thinkers was sometimes expressed symbolically in terms of becoming similar to the gods (*brahmasamata*,[1] cf. the concept of the path of gods mentioned previously). Such expressions were not limited only to India. Plato asserted: "We ought to fly away from earth to heaven as quickly as we can; and to fly away is to become like God, (*homoi osis toi theoi*) as far as this is possible: and to become like him, is to become holy, just, and wise."[2]

---

to allege four other passages from his writings in proof that he really held them to be false. Some passages will be cited here. "They brought in the dogma of transincorporation, that is, the transmutation of souls, as if Jesus himself were confirming this. But it ought to have been seen that, if this were true, something similar should be found in many writings of the Prophets and the Gospels as well. . . It should be added that, according to what they think, the transmutation of souls takes place because of sins." (C. x. in Migne, u. s. 609)

Again he said: "The assertion that souls are transformed from bodies into other bodies seems to have occurred to some of those also who appear to believe in Christ, in consequence of some passages of sacred Scriptures, they not understanding what is written. For they do not observe how a man may become or made a chicken, or a horse, or a mule, and they thought that the human soul is transmuted into the bodies of cattle, just as they thought that it sometimes assumed the body of a viper." (Migne, u. s. 613) These passages have been cited from Rhys Davids, *Lectures*, pp. 238–243.

39. S. Radhakrishnan, *Eastern Thought*, etc., p. 200.
40. *Alberuni's India*, p. 65. Alberuni, having cited the concept of metempsychosis of some Islamic thinkers, said: "This was also the opinion of the ancient Greeks; for Johannes Grammaticus related as the view of Plato that the rational souls will be clad in the bodies of animals, and that in this regard he followed the fables of Pythagoras." (*Alberuni's India*, p. 65)

1. *ŚBr.* XI, 5, 6, 9.
2. *Theaetetus*, 176 B.

We find in one Upaniṣad that *brahman*, the final goal which the dead attain, is personified and his abode glorified. A departed man goes to the world of Brahmā.[3] There go forth five hundred *apsaras* (heavenly maidens), one hundred with fruits in their hands, one hundred with ointments, one hundred with garlands, one hundred with vestments, and one hundred with powdered aromatics. They adorn him with the adornment of Brahmā. Having crossed many places he shakes off his good deeds and his evil deeds. His dear relatives succeed to the good deeds; those not dear, to the evil deeds. Just as one driving a chariot looks down upon the two chariot-wheels, thus he looks down upon day and night, thus upon good deeds and evil deeds, and upon all the pairs of opposites. Finally he comes to the throne of Brahmā.

In other traditions one finds similar symbolic stories. Enoch himself is proclaimed the Son of Man. "He was taken up on chariots of the Spirit" where he sees "the patriarchs and the righteous, who have dwelt in that place from time immemorial." "Thereafter my spirit was hidden and it ascended into heaven," where he sees angels clothed with the garments of glory. He himself is transformed into an angel. Thereupon "the spirit transported Enoch to the heaven of heavens," where he saw "the Aged One (God Himself)."[4]

Er, the son of Armenius, was slain in battle and on the twelfth day after his death he returned to life. He spoke of the other world. "There those who knew one another embraced and conversed, the souls which came from earth curiously enquiring about the things above, and the souls which came from heaven about the things beneath."[5]

As philosophical thinking developed, however, the realization of the absolute (*brahman*) itself was regarded as the ideal of deliverance and came to be expressed directly. As already described, this is particularly obvious in Yājñavalkya. Such a tendency can be found in varying degree throughout the Upaniṣads. For example, the ultimate situation is described in the following statement: "The knot of the heart is cut, all doubts are dispelled and his deeds terminate when He is seen—the higher and the lower."[6] This is said of a person who has attained the absolute and whose evils have all fallen away.

In the Upaniṣads the highest object to be aimed for is union with the absolute, and this union can be attained only by an intuitive knowledge which enables one to see beyond the changing phenomena of mundane existence. Only those who have forsaken the illusions and infatuations of empirical existence will attain complete union of the self with the absolute,

3. *Kauṣītaki-Up.* I, 3 f.
4. Enoch, LXX, 2 f. (Radhakrishnan, *Eastern Religions* etc., p. 161)
5. *Republic*, X, p. 614.
6. *Muṇḍ. Up.* 11, 2, 9.

and obtain deliverance. Indian sages taught that the root, out of which the varied world of everyday existence emerges, is ignorance (*avidyā*).[7] "Ignorance (*avidyā*) is perishable while knowledge (*vidyā*) is immortal."[8] In the Upaniṣads and later Indian philosophy, knowledge itself is the dominant means for deliverance. Similarly, some Greek philosophers (Parmenides, Plato, etc.) held that ordinary phenomena deceive us. Plato taught that only the eternal is an object of *episteme*, while of the world of phenomena subject to change, only a *doxa* is possible. The Greeks, however, did not teach that the elimination of ignorance brings about union with the absolute. Similarly, early Christianity taught that the moral failure of man arises partly out of a darkening of intellect.[9] The Christian tradition, however, directs man's attention to God, so that "your faith might not rest in the wisdom of men but in the power of God."[10]

The ultimate of final goal of deliverance (*mokṣa*) was always negatively described by Upaniṣadic thinkers. They felt, however, with utmost confidence that, despite the wholly negative expression of the nature of their absolute, they were teaching a truth that is not only indubitable, but positively significant. Similarly, other traditions have used negative expressions for describing the ultimate goal of deliverance or salvation, and have sometimes compared the final condition to sleep or death. Socrates says: "We shall see that there is great reason to hope that death is good. . . . If you suppose that there is no consciousness, but a sleep like the sleep of him who is undisturbed even by dreams, death will be an unspeakable gain." Even the greatest king, he claimed, did not have many days or night which are comparable in happiness with that state.[11] In Taoist doctrine, also, everything is one during sleep: the soul, undisturbed, is absorbed into thc unity; in the waking state, diverted, it distinguishes various beings. (cf. Shakespeare, also,—"And by a sleep to say we end the heartache and the thousand natural shocks that flesh is heir to,—'tis a consummation Devoutly to be wished.'")[12]

Some Indian thinkers declared that the released souls become one with the absolute, even as the rivers losing their name and form become one with the ocean. "As the flowing rivers disappear in the sea, losing their name and their form, thus a sage, freed from name and form, is merged in the divine Person, who is greater than the great."[13] Here the divine Person means the divine and highest spirit. "Greater than the

7. E. G. Radhakrishnan, *The Principal Upaniṣads*, pp. 95–113.
8. *Śvet. Up.* V, 1.
9. Ephesians 4, 13; I Corinthians ii.
10. I Corinthians 2, 5.
11. *Apology*, 40 d.
12. *Hamlet* III, 1.
13. *Muṇḍ. Up.* III, 2, 8.

great" means, according to the commentator, "greater than the conditioned *brahman.*"

Similar imagery is common in Christian mysticism. The following statement is attributed to St. Theresa: "One might speak of the water from the sky, which falls into a river or a fountain, and is so lost in it that we cannot any longer divide or distinguish which is the water of the river and which the drop from the sky. Or better, of a tiny brook which throws itself into the sea, and which it is impossible to separate from thence."[14]

c. *The Basis of Ethics*

THE metaphysical doctrine of *ātman* implies an ethical ideal. According to Yājñavalkya, for *ātman*'s sake we love our fellow-creatures. Since it is the universal Self which we love in each individual, so love for all creatures wells up from the recognition of the fundamental Self. On this issue, Deussen says: "The Gospels quite correctly establish as the highest law of morality, 'Love your neighbour as yourselves.' But why should I do so since by the order of nature I feel pain and pleasure only in myself, not in my neighbour? The answer is not in the Bible . . . but it is in the Veda, in the great formula 'That art Thou,' which gives in three words the combined sum of metaphysics and morals. You shall love your neighbour as yourselves because you are your neighbour."[1] Radhakrishnan says: "Every person round me is myself at a different point of space and time and at a different grade of being. When one realizes that all beings are but the self (*ātmaivābhūt*), one acts not selfishly but for all beings."[2] Edgerton asserts: "The 'Golden Rule,' that one ought to treat others like oneself, is as important in Hindu ethics as in Christianity. It is even carried farther, for it applies to animals (which like men are involved in transmigration under '*karma*'). It is summed up in the doctrine of *ahiṃsā*, 'no injury' to any living being. Now in Christianity this doctrine rests, so far as I can see, simply on its natural appeal to thoughtful men. In Hinduism it has a metaphysical background; it is a logical deduction from the Upaniṣad doctrine mentioned above (which has always been widely accepted in India), that the soul or real self of every man is identical with that of the universe (*tat tvam asi*, 'That art thou'). It follows, since things which are equal to the same thing are equal to each other, that one must identify his own self with all other selves. If he harms others, he harms himself. The Golden Rule is thus proved, in a logically irrefutable way,

14. Interior Castle, Seventh Mansion, chap. II, cited from Radhakrishnan, *Eastern Religion*, etc., p. 132.

1. Paul Deussen: *The Philosophy of the Upanishads, op. cit.*, p. 204.

2. S. Radhakrishnan: *Eastern Religions*, etc., p. 102.

if you accept the premises. That is why the supremely moral man, even while he lives by the ordinary norm 'identifies himself with the self of all beings' (*sarvabhūtātmabhūtātman*,[3] and 'delights in the welfare of all beings' (*sarvabhūtahite ratāḥ*,[4])."[5]

The fundamental idea of the Hindu altruistic principle is set forth in the following statement. "Recognizing himself in all beings and all beings in his own self, he, kindling the sacrifice to Self alone, enters into absolute freedom (*svarājya*[6])."[7] The law of love should be obeyed not because it is known, but because life consists in loving. He who realizes the universal self sees all human beings as belonging to a kingdom of ideals. Human spirits must altimately be in unity with one another. Longing for the *ātman* is innate in all beings, and equally for him who knows himself as the *ātman*: "His (Brahman's) name is 'longing for him' (*tadvanam*), as 'longing for him' ought he to be worshipped. He who knows himself as such, for him assuredly all beings long."[8]

Sacrifices and pious works only lead to new re-births, while knowledge alone leads from this mundane existence of infatuation to the One and Eternally True. Therefore, it is often stated in the Upaniṣads that in order to attain the highest object it is necessary to give up all works, good as well as bad. "As water does not cling to a lotus leaf, so no evil deed clings to one who knows it."[9] Likewise, the highest situation of deliverance was depicted by Yājñavalkya as follows: "Just as a man fully embraced by his beloved wife does not know anything at all, either external or internal, do does this man (*puruṣa*: the individual life-monad), embraced fully by the supremely knowing Spiritual-Self (*prajñātman*), not know anything at all, either external or internal. That is his form devoid of sorrows, in which all desires are fulfilled; in which his only desire is the Self (which he has now attained); in which he is without desire. In that state a father is no father, a mother no mother, the worlds no worlds, the gods no gods . . . a thief no thief, an ascetic no ascetic. Unattended by virtuous works, unattended by evil works, he has crossed to the other shore, beyond the sorrows of the heart."[10]

Royce's comment on this passage is worth quoting in full: "The contrast between the real and the desirable is itself a dualism. It must be cast off, together with the false realism that regards any truth as independ-

3. *Bhag. G.*, V, 7.
4. *Ibid.*, V, 25: XII, 4.
5. F. Edgerton, Dominant Ideas in the Formation of Indian Culture (*Journal of The American Oriental Society*, vol. 62, 1942, p. 155 f).
6. *Manu*, 12, 91.
7. Coomaraswamy, *Recollection*, etc., pp. 40–41.
8. *Kena-Up.* 31 (=IV, 6).
9. *Chānd. Up.* IV, 14, 3; cf. *Kauṣītaki-Up.* I, 4; III, 8.
10. *Bṛhad. Up.* IV, 3, 21–22.

ently real. The finite world is simply the process of striving after self-knowledge. And in this process the seeker pursues only himself. But if he found himself, if all desires were fulfilled, if knowledge were complete—what would remain? Or rather, since this use of *if* and of *would* is itself a mere expression of finite illusion, since in very truth there is only the Self, since finite process of striving after the self is wholly illusory, and the Self in its perfection is alone real, what now remains as the Absolute?"

"Well, in the first place the true Self does not strive. It has no idea of any other. It has no positive will. Object and Subject are in it no longer even different. It has no character. That is the murderer no longer murderer, nor the slave a slave, nor the traitor a traitor."

"Differences are illusory. The Self *merely* is. But now *is* in what sense? Not as the independent Other, not as the object of a thought, not as describable in terms of an idea, not as expressible in any way, and still less as mere nothing. For it is the All, the only Being. There remains to hint that the being of the Self is only what we now call the immediacy of present experience. Only henceforth we must regard the absolute immediacy not as the raw material of meaning, but as the restful goal of all meaning,—as beyond ideas, even because it is simpler than they are."[11]

Then what does it mean to give up all works, good as well as bad? Will such a thought not engender moral corruption? When the individual soul is liberated from egoism and attains spiritual freedom, it is spontaneously unified with the universal will. It acts in an impersonal way without effort or expectation. It has become a passive instrument of the Divine, itself without any selfish initiative.

Only in this sense do the Upaniṣads declare: "The immortal man overcomes both the thoughts 'I did evil' and 'I did good.' Good and evil, done or not done, cause him to pain."[12] A sage said: "Give up good and evil, truth as well as untruth. Having given up truth and untruth, give up the consciousness that you have given them up."[13]

Concerning this problem, Radhakrishnan explains: "Even self-consciousness is an obstacle. The liberated individual is lifted beyond the ethical distinctions of good and evil. When the Upaniṣad says that 'sin does not cling to a wise man any more than water clings to a lotus leaf' it does not mean that the sage may sin and yet be free, but rather that any one who is free from worldly attachments is also free from all temptation to sin."[14]

11. Royce, *The World and The Individual,* vol. I, pp. 166–167.
12. *Bṛhad. Up.* IV, 4, 22.
13. tyaja dharmam adharmaṃ ca
    ubhe satyānṛte tyaja
    ubhe satyānṛte tyaktvā
    yena tyajasi tat tyaja (*Mahābhārata* XII: 337, 40)
14. Radhakrishnan, *Eastern Religions*, pp. 102–103.

In another context, Radhakrishnan says further: "When the individual spirit realizes its divine nature and acts from it, he transcends the distinctions of good and evil. Not that he can do evil and yet be free from sin, but that it is impossible for him to do wrong, for he is no more the agent or the enjoyer. Good and evil presuppose the basis of egoism. Good acts are those which aim at the well-being of oneself and others, and evil ones are those which interfere with the well-being of oneself and others." "Ethics presuppose the separatist view of life. When we transcend it, we get beyond ethical laws."[15]

Regarding the issue of ethics, therefore, early Upaniṣadic thought ends in a paradox. The metaphysical doctrine of the *ātman*, though providing a profound rationalization for an altruistic principle, leads man ultimately to transcend or to go beyond good and evil. Yet it is precisely when man has gone beyond good and evil that he comes to see the Self (*ātman*) which allows him *to be* truly Good!

15. *Ibid.*

III. THE DEVELOPMENT OF HETERODOXIES

A. Materialism

1. Materialism (—Elements—)

EVEN in the earliest *Upaniṣads* there were some who doubted the efficacy of established orthodoxy. The *Chāndogya-Upaniṣad*[1] likens the orthodox clergy to a procession of dogs, each holding the tail of its predecessor and saying piously, "Om, let us eat; Om, let us drink."[2] At that early stage a worldly tendency had also arisen that esteemed personal power, "He who meditates on food as Brahman, he, verily, attains the worlds of food and drink. Oneself is to be waited upon."[3] With such ideas appearing in orthodox scriptures we cannot wonder at the advent of materialism from other quarters.

Materialists were eventually to deny the authority of the Vedic scriptures. They were to distrust all reason, claiming that every inference depends for its validity not only upon accurate observation of facts, but also upon the assumption that the future will behave like the past; and of this, as Hume was to say, there can be no certainty. What is not perceived by the senses, they thought, does not exist; therefore the soul is a delusion. All phenomena are natural; only simpletons trace them to demons or gods. Matter is the one reality. The mind, for them, is merely matter thinking; all phenomena come out of matter. This tendency can be seen in a somewhat late *Upaniṣad* which considered the possibility of there being no god, heaven or hell, no reincarnation or world; of the earlier *Vedas* and *Upaniṣads* being the work of conceited fools; of ideas being illusory and words untrue; of people deluded by flowery speech clinging to gods and temples and "holy men," though there is no difference between Viṣṇu and a dog.[4]

1. *Chānd. Up.* I, 12.
2. S. Radhakrishnan, *Indian Philosophy*, vol. I, p. 149.
3. R. Hume, *Thirteen Principal Upanishads*, p. 65. (*Chānd. Up.* VII, 8–9)
4. It is said that it is set forth in *Svasaṃveda-Upaniṣad*.

In India the most salient materialist was Ajita, who is said to have worn the garment of hair. (A similar instance can be found in Occidental history.[5]) He held the following doctrine: "A human being is built up of the four elements (i.e., earth, water, fire, and air).[6] When he dies the earthy in him returns and relapses to the earth, the fluid to the water, the heat to the fire, the windy to the air, and his faculties pass into space. (Space was not regarded as an element. The faculties, *indriyāni*, mean the five senses and the mind as the sixth.)

"The four bearers, on the bier as a fifth, take his dead body away; till they reach the burning-ground, men utter forth eulogies, but there his bones are bleached and his offerings end in ashes. It is a doctrine of fools, this talk of gifts. It is an empty lie, mere idle talk, when men say there is profit therein. Fools and wise alike, on the dissolution of the body, are cut off, annihilated, and after death they are not."[7]

Based upon such a view, Ajita denounced moral values. "There is no such thing," he said, "as alms or sacrifice or offering. There is neither fruit nor result of good or evil deeds. There is no such thing as this world or the next. There is neither father nor mother, nor beings springing into life without them. There are in the world no recluses or Brahmans who have reached the highest point, who walk perfectly, and who having understood and realized, by themselves alone, both this world and the next, make their wisdom known to others."[8] Such persons were thought to be nothing but composites of elements, the elements alone being real. In India materialists would later be called Lokāyata or Cārvākas.[9]

Other ancient thinkers also thought of things as aggregations of elements (*bhūtāni*, *stoikheia*, *elementa*). In Greece, Empedocles (c. 490–30 B.C.), just as Ajita in India, assumed the four elements to be water, earth, ether and fire,[10] and conceived of them as uncreated.[11] Therefore, re-

5. When on high occasions the pope ordered Cardinal Ximenes to wear his gorgeous robes and cardinal's hat streaming with tassels, Ximenes obeyed, but kept next to his skin a coarse shirt of hair. (Roland H. Bainton, *The Church of Our Fathers*, New York: Charles Scribner's Sons, 1950, p. 124)
6. A classification of the four elements was made according to their greater or lesser density, and corresponding perceptibility. This is indicated in a work of Śaṅkara: "the earth, as capable of being smelt, tasted, seen, felt, is gross (*sthūla*); water, as being tasted, seen, and felt, is subtle (*sūkṣma*): fire, as being seen and felt, is more subtle (*sūkṣmatara*); fire, as only to be felt, is most subtle (*sūkṣmatara*)." (Śaṅkara ad *Brahma-sūtra*, p. 536, 7) As a rule, later Indians added to these a fifth, and still more subtle element, ether (*ākāśa*), with the quality of audibility (also possessed by the other four).
7. *Dīgha-nikāya*, II. 23, vol. I, p. 55.
8. *Ibid.*
9. A detailed explanation of the Lokāyatas etc. is given in Dasgupta: *A History of Indian Philosophy*, Cambridge University Press, vol. III, 1952, pp. 512–550.
10. Empedocles' fragment 71. (According to Freeman's translation.)
11. *Ibid.*, 7.

garding the composition of man, he said: "There is no creation of substance in any one of moral existences, nor any end in execrable death, but only mixing and exchange of what has been mixed;[12] but men, when these [the elements] have been mixed in the form of a man and come into the light, or in the form of a species of wild animals, or plants, or birds, then say that this has "come into being"; and when they separate, this men call sad fate [death]."[13] The elements ". . . never cease their continuous exchange, in this sense they remain always unmoved (unaltered) as they follow the cyclic process."[14]

According to Aristotle, the four terrestial elements are not eternal but are generated out of each other—fire is absolutely light, in the sense that its natural motion is upward; earth is absolutely heavy. Air is relatively light, and water is relatively heavy. This corresponds to the theory set forth in the Buddhist *Abhidharma.* The theory of generation is somewhat similar to the *Trivṛtkaraṇa* (making to three elements threefold), in the *Chāndogya-Upaniṣad* or *Pañcīkaraṇa* (making the five elements fivefold) of later *Advaitins.*

In ancient China the Yin-Yang school offered cosmological theories based on two principles (*yin* and *yang*), the five elements (metal, wood, water, fire and earth), and the orderly rotation of these principles and elements in the formation of nature, man, and the seasons. The five elements were said to be the corporeal essences of the Five Constant Virtues (benevolence, righteousness, propriety in demeanor, wisdom and good faith). These were supposed to induce life and propagation.[15] These concepts were quickly appropriated by the Shintō school in Japan, which originally lacked cosmological theories.

Hsun-tzu's philosophy is said to have had materialistic tendencies.[16] But in ancient China, where the Greek equivalent of a concept of matter was lacking, it does not seem likely that materialism (in the strict sense of the word) existed. However, the teaching of the way of living by Yan-tse can be compared to that of Ajita and the *Lokāyatas*, as will be brought out in the next section.

When Buddhism was introduced into China the Five Elements of Buddhism (*mahābhūtas*) were correlated for explanatory purposes with the Chinese Five Elements (*wu-hsing*), which were supposed to be corporeal essences. In books of the period between the Han and the Chin in China, the Indian concept of four elements (the *mahābhūtas*) was often interpreted

12. *Ibid.*, 8.
13. *Ibid.*, 9.
14. *Ibid.*, 17.
15. Fung Yu-lan, *A History of Chinese Philosophy* (Princeton University Press, 1952), vol. I, pp. 27, 41.
16. Fung Yu-lan: *op. cit.*, vol. I, p. 281.

in terms of the Chinese five elements (*wu-hsing*). Such a comparison or identification of the categories of different traditions may be regarded as an example of *koyi*,[17] the explanation of Indian terms by means of Chinese ones.

2. Materialism (—Atomists—)

ATOMISM appeared at nearly the same time in Greece and India, although in China it did not develop at all. In India, the concept of the atom (*aṇu*, *paramāṇu*[1]) appeared for the first time in Jain scriptures, although we are not yet sure whether it derives from the founder of the school, Mahāvīra. In Greece, Democritus (c. 420 B.C.) was an early representative of atomism. By the unifying of atoms, Democritus was able to develop completely a system of mechanical necessity in nature, every actual event being a mechanism of atoms. Strictly speaking, the Greek Atomist's system would admit only of atoms and the void, and in this regard was almost identical to Jain philosophy.

The Jains bring the whole universe under two everlasting categories.[2] The two classes of things are designated *jīva* and *ajīva*; i.e., the conscious and the unconscious or soul and non-soul. As surely as there is a subject that knows, Jainism says, so surely is there an object that is known. In Greece, Anaxagoras is regarded as the first philosopher who, in contrast to the older hylozoists, made a clear-cut distinction between spirit and matter.

In Jain philosophy the category of non-spirit (*ajīva*) is divided into (1) time (*kāla*), (2) space (*ākāśa*), (3) the principle of motion (*dharma*), (4) that of stability (*adharma*) and (5) matter (*pudgala*). These are all substances (*dravya*).[3] Their essential distinction from the spirit is that they, as such, lack life and consciousness.

17. Tang Yung-Tung, in *Radhakrishnan*; *Comparative Studies in Philosophy* Presented in *Honour of his Sixtieth Birthday* (ed. by W. R. Inge and others. London: George Allen and Unwin, 1951), pp. 278–84.

1. Professor Eliot Deutsch says that the word "atom" is misleading here. One should translate "*aṇu*" as, say, "primordial unit." We have just adopted the conventional English equivalent.
2. Cf. *Menon apeiron*. Zeller, *Die Philosophie der Griechen, op. cit.*, I, 2, 1069, A. 1.
3. The English term "substances" may not be proper. The term "principles" would be much more proper, at least in idiomatic English. In this connection the notion of "substance" held by Aristotle, Descartes, and Thomas Aquinas (substratum versus accident) should be taken into consideration. (Cf. Walter Ruben: Indische und Griechische Metaphysik, Sonderabdruck aus Band 8 (1931) der *Zeitschrift für Indologie und Iranistik*, Leipzig 1931, Deutsche Morgenländische Gesellschaft in Kommission bei F. A. Brockhaus, S. 41–44)

Of these, (1) time is infinite, though the Jains were not agreed as to whether time should be considered a substance. On this issue Aristotle was specific that time at least exists, saying that time is motion and can be the object to enumeration.

(2) Space, which also is infinite, is conceived of as being in two parts —one (*lokākāśa*) where movement is possible and the other (*alokākāśa*) where it is not. All substances exist only in the former,[4] and the latter, thought to be spatially above the former, is mere empty space. Space was apparently twofold also for Aristotle, who, in *On The Heaven*, set forth the simple theory that things below the moon are subject to generation and decay, while from the moon upward, everything is ungenerated and indestructible. The void, which would presumably be the same as the Jain uppermost space, was also controversial in Greek philosophy. Aristotle rejected the void as it had been previously maintained by Leucippus and Democritus.[5]

(3) The principle of motion is explained as that by which motion can take place. It is compared to water for swimming fish, a necessary condition for such an activity to take place.

(4) Stability is the principle by which motion can come to rest. It is compared to the surface of the ground for falling things in that the ground stops their motion. The principles of stability and motion were regarded as substances.

(5) Matter, for the Jains, had four qualities: color, flavor, odor, and touch.[6] (Sound is looked upon not as a quality but as a material mode.[7]) Matter is eternal, consists of atoms and comprises all the things which we experience, including animal bodies, the senses and the mind (*manas*). Atoms, in Jainism are all of the same kind, but they can yet give rise to the infinite variety of things, so that matter, as conceived in the empirical world, is of indefinite nature. Matter may thus have two forms—one, simple or atomic and the other compound (*skandha*). All perceivable objects are of the latter kind. On this point we can compare the somewhat similar distinction in the atomistic views held by Leucippus and Democritus in ancient Greece.

Democritus also admitted empty space and numberless, self-moving, qualitatively similar atoms. These atoms differ only in form and size, and in their union and separation all events are to be explained. However, what makes Democritus' belief different from Jain atomism is that he

4. As the forerunner of this notion, cf. *Chānd. Up.* VII, 12, Yājñavalkya.
5. B. Russell, *A History of Western Philosophy*, p. 206.
6. Umāsvāti, *Tattvārthādhigamasūtra*, V. 23.
7. Guṇaratna, *op. cit.*, pp. 69–70.

considered color, taste and temperatures as belonging to the secondary qualities of the subjective states, not to atoms themselves.[8]

The word "*jīva*" in Jainism, means "what lives or is animate". This concept seems to have been arrived at first by observing the characteristics of life and not through the search after a metaphysical principle underlying individual existence.[9] But as the Jain metaphysics became established, it came to mean the "soul" or "self" as in other religious systems.

The Jain theory of the soul may seem very strange. To understand it adequately, one might view it in the light of relativism, as will be discussed in a following section. In Indian sources there is no clue to make a bridge between the soul theory and Jain relativism. In this context it might be helpful to think of the Western relativism of Protagoras, who could not assume a consciousness without a corresponding existent content of consciousness. He thought that perception is indeed the completely adequate knowledge of what is perceived, but no knowledge of the thing.[10] Admitting that every object is a content of our consciousness, and in that respect partakes of spirituality, it would be natural to arrive at such a conception of soul.

The Jain conception of the soul differs greatly from Democritus' theory, in which the soul is composed of atoms, and its life is really only the motion of such atoms (though the very finest and most nearly perfect of all motions[11]). Epicurus' idea of the atom as having weight and continually falling, not toward the center of the earth, but downward in some obscure sense, was somewhat similar to that of Jainism. But his concept of the material soul composed of, e.g., breath and heat particles (wind and air being separate substances for him) also took a different turn than it did in Jainism. Soul atoms were distributed throughout the body, he thought; sensation being due to thin films thrown off by bodies and traveling on until they touch soul atoms.[12]

A concept of the soul similar to that of the Jains was held, however, by some philosophers of the Hellenistic age. The Stoics held that the soul must be in its nature corporeal. Whatever, they said, influences the body, and is by it influenced in turn, and whatever is united with the body and again separated from it, must be corporeal; and this is the case with the

8. Windelband, *History of Ancient Philosophy*, translated by Herbert Ernest Cushman (Dover Publications, Inc., 1956), p. 162.
9. H. Jacobi, *The Jain Sutras, Sacred Books of the East*, Vol. XXII (Oxford: Claredon Press, 1884), Part I, p. 3, n.
10. W. Windelband, *History of Ancient Philosophy*. Translated by Herbert Earnest Cushman (New York: Dover Publications, Inc., 1956), p. 92.
11. Frederick Copleston, *A History of Philosophy*, Vol. 1 (Maryland, Westminister, The Newman Bookshop, 1946), p. 125; W. Windelband, *op. cit.*, p. 166.
12. B. Russell, *History of Western Philosophy*, pp. 246–47.

soul, since it extends in three directions over the whole body.[13] However, the Stoic conception of the soul seems to be more simple and naive than that of the Jains, for the Stoics described the human soul sometimes as fire, sometimes as breath, at other times as warm breath diffused throughout the body and forming a bond of union for the body.[14]

One of the curious features of the Jain conception of the soul is the belief in the variable size of the *jīva* in its empirical condition; e.g., the soul of an elephant is large, while the soul of an ant is small. "The soul is capable of expansion and contraction according to the dimensions of the physical body with which it is associated for the time being. In this respect it resembles a lamp, it is said, which though remaining the same, illumines the whole of the space enclosed in a small or big room in which it happens to be placed."[15] The very nature of the self in Jainism is perfect enlightenment and infinite intelligence,[16] and its condition of partial or indistinct knowledge marks a lapse from it. The latter respect will recall Plotinus. Porphyry said of his master that Plotinus was like one ashamed of being in a body.

Jainism accepts the common Indian notions of rebirth and *karma.* The natural qualities of the soul—knowledge, intuition, etc.—are spoiled by *karma* and the soul is never completely separated from matter until its final release.[17] *Karma* is the link between its empirical container, the body, and the soul, which is regarded as consisting of extremely subtle matter beyond the reach of the senses.[18] Just as the Jains do, Epictetus thought that while on earth we are prisoners in an earthly body. According to Marcus Aurelius, Epictetus used to say, "Thou art a little soul bearing about a corpse."[19] Accordingly, the Jains justify their practice of naked-

13. Eduard Zeller, *The Stoics, Epicureans, and Sceptics,* translated from German into English by Oswald J. Reichel, a new and revised edition (London: Longmans, Green and Co., 1880), pp. 210–11.
14. *Ibid.*, p. 211.
15. *Sarvadarśanasaṃgraha,* IV, *ll.* 20–21. *Tattvārthādhigama-sūtra,* V. 6.
16. Guṇaratna *ad Ṣaḍdarśanasamuccaya,* p. 74.
17. "The Doctrine of reincarnation can in no sense agree to the assertion that the Universe is not real, but must hold fast to its reality. And further—and this is where the real difficulty begins—it has to make comprehensible how soul and body, if we assume that by their nature they have nothing in common, can stand in any relationship to each other whatever. The doctrine of reincarnation has to do with the same question with which later on in Europe the philosophy based on the definitions of Descartes is busied. For this the problem is to explain how it is that in living creatures the body can receive stimuli from the soul and transform these into reality." (Albert Schweitzer, *Indian Thought and its Development,* Boston: The Beacon Press, 1936, pp. 62–63)
18. References to a physical or quasi-physical conception of sin are traceable in the Vedic literature of A. B. Keith, *Religion and Philosophy of the Veda* (Cambridge, Mass.: Harvard University Press, 1925), Vol. I, p. 245.
19. B. Russell, *A History of Western Philosophy,* p. 263.

ness by saying, "The body is already a bondage for our soul. Why is there any need of doubling bondage by wearing clothes?"[20]

According to Jain teachings, the soul has never been free from this accompaniment of *karma*. Yet dissociation from it is admitted to be possible. The nature of the soul is defiled by its association with *karma* and the consequent lapse of the soul from its pure state is what is called bondage. If through proper self-discipline all *karma* is worked out and there arises "the full blaze of omniscience" in the soul, then it becomes free.

When all *karma* is finally destroyed by the practice of austerities, the soul attains salvation. Salvation results in escape from the round of existence (*saṃsāra*). Enlightenment is reached when all obstacles are entirely broken down. Then the individual soul (*jīva*), while continuing as such, becomes omniscient and knows all objects vividly and precisely as they are. That knowledge is called absolute apprehension without media (*kevalajñāna*) and is described as pure (*kevala*). Mahavira is believed to have attained this state at the end of the long period of his penance.

An ancient Greek philosopher who shared many of the foregoing Jainist characteristics was Empedocles. A priest, prophet, and a physician, he often was seen at magic rites and was said to have worked mighty miracles. Empedocles is said to have had a dislike for flesh as food.[21] Even in his lifetime he considered himself to have purified his soul by devotion, to have purged away the impurities of his birth, to have become in fact what the Indians call "*jīvanmukta*," that is, one liberated in life.

Plato also held that the body is a hindrance in the acquisition of knowledge, and that sight and hearing are inaccurate witnesses.[22] Plato's conception of bondage and deliverance was similar to that of the Jains.[23] The tendency to undermine the body is also quite obvious in early Christianity, for instance, St. Paul's claim that "flesh and blood cannot inherit the Kingdom of God."[24]

In Jainism, when at last the soul escapes at death from the bondage of the body, it rises until it reaches the top of the universe, and there it rests in peaceful bliss forever.[25] This final condition is one of inactivity, and is characterized by complete knowledge and everlasting peace, which is the recovery of the true nature of the soul. This approaches a theory of knowledge not unknown in the West, for instance, Alberuni, describing

20. *Sarvasiddhāntasaṃgraha*, Ch. III, verse 12.
21. R. Garbe, *The Philosophy of India*, p. 35.
22. Russell, *op. cit.*, p. 136.
23. *Ibid.*, pp. 141–42.
24. Romans, XIII, 14. cf. VI, 15–21.
25. *Tattvārthādhigarmasūtra*, X, 6–7; *Sarvadarśanasaṃgraha of Sāyaṇa-Mādhava*. Edited with an original commentary in Sanskrit by Mamhopadhyaya Vasudev Shastri Abhyankar. Government Oriental Series, No. 1. (Poona: The Bhandarkar Oriental Research Institute, 1924), chapter III, *ll.* 345–367, pp. 80–82.

Greek philosophy, said, "Forgetting is the vanishing of knowledge, and knowing is the soul's remembrance of that which it had learned before it entered the body."[26]

Proclus reportedly said, "It is evident that the soul has always existed. Hence it follows that it has always been both knowing and forgetting, knowing when it is separated from the body, forgetting when it is in connection with the body. For, being separated from the body, it belongs to the realm of the spirit, and therefore it is knowing; but being connected with the body, it transcends from the realm of the spirit, and is exposed to forgetting because of some forcible influence prevailing over it."[27] In Platonic language one might say that the embodied soul had become separated from the form of knowledge.

According to Jain philosophy, during the period intervening between enlightenment and the actual attainment of deliverance the enlightened soul dwells apart from flesh and the influence of *karma*. An enlightened person may lead an active life, but his activity does not restrict his soul. The soul, which was in transmigration (*saṃsāra*), rises up when its bonds are dissolved.[28]

Therefore, in Jainism souls, although innumerable, can be classed into two sorts—(1) those bound by a subtle body of deeds (*karma*) to the present world, sullied by contact with nonsentient matter, and (2) the perfected (*siddha*), who are at the summit of the universe, enjoying perfect happiness, incorporeal, invisible. Any soul achieving a blameless life becomes a Paramātman, or supreme soul, and avoids reincarnation for a while; when its reward equals its merit, however, it is born into the flesh again. Only the hightest and most perfect spirits, freed of *karma*, could achieve complete "release"; these were the Arhats, or supreme lords, who lived like deities in some distant and shadowy realm, unable to affect the affairs of men, but happily removed from all chance of rebirth.[29] The Jain doctrine of *karma* leads to unbridled individualism. It fails to see that we all belong to a community, that there is what is called "joint *karma*," corporate evil and guilt. This idea of "joint *karma*" appeared in the Buddhist philosophy of Abhidharma.

At any rate, the primary aim of Jainism is the perfection of the soul, disentangling it from *karma*. Jainism is largely ethical in intent rather than metaphysical. A Jain thinker noted that the forging of the fetter of *karma* around the soul (*āsrava*) and the prevention of that occurence (*saṃvara*)

26. *Alberuni's India*, p. 57.
27. *Ibid.*, p. 57.
28. Śaṅkara ad *Brahmasūtra,* II, 2, 34. *The Sarva-darśana-saṃgraha by Mádhava Áchárya.* Translated by E. B. Cowell and A. E. Gough (London, Trübner and Co., 1892), Trübner Oriental Series, p. 58.
29. Radhakrishnan, *Indian Philosophy*, I, pp. 293; 331.

constitute the core of Jain teaching, the rest being only an amplification of these principles.[30]

Democritus was more secular than the Jains, but we find a similar point in his thought. The main point of his ethics was as follows: we have to strive after well-being (*euesto*) or cheerfulness (*euthymie*), which is a state of soul, and the attainment of which requires a weighing, judging and distinguishing of various pleasures. We should be guided, he thought, by the principle of "symmetry" or of "harmony." By the use of this principle we may attain to bodily calm—health and calm of soul—cheerfulness. This tranquility is to be found chiefly in the goods of the soul.[31] "He who chooses the advantage of the soul chooses things more divine, but he who chooses those of the body, chooses things human."[32] "The best way for a man to lead his life is to have been as cheerful as possible and to have suffered as little as possible. This could happen if one did not seek one's pleasures in mortal things."[33]

30. *Sarvadarśanasaṃgraha*, p. 39.
31. Copleston, *History*, *op. cit.*, I. p. 126.
32. Democritus' fragment, 37.
33. *Ibid.*, 189.

B. The Pursuit of Pleasure

THOUGH this section is broadly titled "The Pursuit of Pleasure," our investigation will take two somewhat different directions. Whereby some men in different ages have at the outset openly advocated pleasure or physical comfort as the highest aim of life, others have begun, perhaps more cautiously, by questioning and sometimes even denouncing established moral theory. The latter approach, which seems to be more basic to the inquiry, is taken up first.

In Indian literature the name of Purana Kassapa immediately comes to mind as a conspicuous advocate of the practice of ignoring moral injunctions. A recluse, Pūraṇa Kassapa taught a theory of non-action (*akiriyā*); however bad an action a man might commit, he did not commit sin: "Were he to go along the south bank of the Ganges striking and slaying, mutilating and having men mutilated, oppressing and having men oppressed, there would be no guilt thence resulting, no increase of guilt would ensue."

Similarly, however good an action a man might perform, he could not acquire merit thereby: "Were he to go along the north bank of the Ganges giving alms and ordering gifts to be given, offering sacrifices or causing them to be offered, there would be no merit thence resulting, no increase of merit."[1] Pūraṇa Kassapa refused to accept moral distinctions and was convinced that the soul was a passive slave to chance.

Another prominent figure in Indian literature who denounced morals was Jābāli, the skeptic, in the Rāmāyaṇa. He scorned ideas of duty and future life and ridiculed Rāma for rejecting a kingdom in order to keep a vow. Jābāli, a learned brahmin and a sophist skilled in words, questioned faith, law and duty, saying to Ayodhya's young prince: "Leading a life of asceticism, do not suffer thy intellect to entertain inanities like any low person. . . . Since a creature is born alone and dies alone, a person that cherishes his father and mother with affection must be looked upon as a madman. No individual hath any one [in this world]. As on the eve of setting out for another country, a person stays somewhere [outside the village he lives in], and the next day goes away, renouncing that abode, even such are a man's father and mother, house and wealth. Worthy people never bear affection towards a mere abode. Therefore, leaving thy an-

1. *Dīgha-nikāya,* II. 18, vol. I, pp. 52–3.

cestral kingdom, thou ought not to abide in the disagreeable forest filled with dangers and difficulties. . . . A father is merely an instrumental cause for birth. People engage in *aṣṭaka* [ancestor worship] in behalf of ancestors and deities. Behold the waste of edibles. Does any dead person feed? . . ." He further adds a reason why the morality he is against exists in the first place: "Works [on morality] enjoining—'Worship', 'Give away', 'Be initiated', 'Observe rites', 'Renounce',—have been composed by crafty persons for inducing people to be charitable. Assure thyself there is no hereafter."[2] One may recall here that in the West by the time of Aristotle doubt had arisen regarding an afterlife. Aristotle suggested that once a man is dead neither good nor evil affects him any more.

Bṛhaspati (date unknown), another well-known materialist, is said to have composed a nihilistic work (*sūtra*) which is no longer extant. A poem ascribed to him exists, however, denouncing the priests of his time. This poem, while ridiculing morals, also serves as a transition to the second area of emphasis in this section in that it distinctly advocates the taking of individual pleasures whenever and however they might be found. In addition, Bṛhaspati, like Jābāli, gives his reasons why the moral traditions he distrusted existed at all:

No heaven exists, no final liberation,
No soul, no other world, no rites of caste, . . .
The triple Veda, triple self-command,
And all the dust and ashes of repentance—
These yield a means of livelihood for men
Devoid of intellect and manliness . . .
While life endures let life be spent in ease
And merriment; let a man borrow money
From all his friends, and feast on melted butter.
How can this body when reduced to dust
Revisit earth? And if a ghost can pass
To other worlds, why does not strong affection
For those he leaves behind attract him back?
The costly rites enjoined for those who die
Are but a means of livelihood devised
By sacerdotal cunning-nothing more . . .[3]

In a similar way Theodorus, a Greek philosopher of the Socratic period, taught that all ethical and legal prescriptions were ultimately

2. *Rāmāyana*, Ayodhā-kāṇḍa, CVIII, *The Ramayana* Translated into English prose from the original Sanskrit of Valmiki. Edited and published by Manmatha Nath Dutt (Calcutta: Girish Chandra Chackravarli, 1892), pp. 476–477.

3. Monier-Williams, *Indian Wisdom*, or *Examples of the Religious, Philosophical and Ethical Doctrine of the Hindus* (London: Allen, 1875), pp. 120–2.

merely institutions valid for the mass of men; he bore the surname "the atheist", and put aside all religious scruples that were opposed to devotion to sensuous enjoyment.[4]

Pleasure-oriented views appeared quite early in Greece; Pindar wrote that there are only two things in life worthy of being cherished —to have good success and to win for it a fair share of fame. He said that one should not seek to be like a god but rather that if the above two honors should befall one he already has everything. To Pindar it was the things of mortals that best befit mortality. There were some, like Aristippus, who advocated a hedonism in which pleasure was the only thing to be considered, and virtue depended upon one's ability for enjoyment. Later, Epicurus developed a hedonistic philosophy of a different type, one that was primarily designed to secure tranquility. This attitude was shared by many Indian recluses but was rarely thought of as hedonism.

Epicurus, however, was a philosopher brought up in a time deeply affected by Platonism. Plato had interpreted "pleasure" consistent with his ethical system. In the *Phaedo* Plato says that "good" means the transcendental form of goodness; and in the *Thaetetus* he attacks the hedonists severely by recommending the avoidance of pleasure. In the *Philebus* he argues that pure pleasures are to be found in the contemplation of the beauty of truth. Pure pleasure is the pleasures of the soul only; the pleasures of the senses and of the bodily functions are secondary. Plato also held that pleasures must take place in both physical and mental health and in a state of harmony and moderation.

The primary Chinese representative of hedonistic thought was Yang Chu (4th century B.C.), who advocated a principle of egoism and complacently remarked, "Each one for himself." Though he might have benefited the whole world by plucking out a single hair, he said he would not have done it.[5] "He did not allow outside things to entangle his person," and condemned the idea of universal love.[6] Following is some typical discourse of Yang Chu:

"Why not enjoy all that is enjoyable while alive? Begone! our doctrinaires, hypocrites, unnatural moralists, and vain aspirants after fame!

"How then is our life to be lived?

"Indulge in what your ear desires to hear; indulge in what your eye desires to see; indulge in what your nose desires to smell; indulge in what your mouth desires to speak; indulge in what your body desires to obtain; and indulge in what your mind desires to do. . . Delicious food and warm clothing are what the body desires to have, and when these are denied, it means the crippling of the sense of comfort. . . . If you cast away the

4. Frederic Copleston, *A History of Philosophy*, vol. I, Part I, p. 143.
5. *Mencius*, VII, 1. 26.
6. Fung Yu-Lan, *Chinese Philosophy*, vol. I, pp. 133–4.

thought of self-molestation, and lightheartedly and joyously indulge your passions and desires, and giving yourself up to the pursuit of pleasure calmly await the coming of death, your life of one day is equal to another's life of one month. Those who are yoked to the thought of self-molestation may have a long life of one hundred, ten hundred, even of ten thousand years, in a depressed state of mind, but what is the use of all that? It is not my way of taking care of life."[7]

Interestingly enough, the assertion was made by a later materialist of India: "The three authors of the Vedas were buffoons, knaves and demons.

"It is only as a means of livelihood that *brahmins* have established here all of these ceremonies for the dead.

"While life remains let a man live happily, let him feed on ghee even though he runs in debt;

"When once the body becomes ashes, how can it ever return again?"[8]

Two other Chinese philosophers of the same period who were thought to have no other goal than the pursuit of pleasure were To Hsiao and Wei Mou. They were described somewhat negatively as those "who give free rein to their passions, are satisfied with indulgence, and act like beasts. They are not qualified to develop culture or conduct government. Nevertheless their views have some foundation and their statements some reason, quite enough to deceive and confuse the ignorant masses."[9]

However a more moderate opinion was prevalent throughout China until recent times as observed in the Taoist way of life. "A more spontaneous enjoyment of life, drawing on the inexhaustible riches of the *Tao*: a looser form of government, permitting greater freedom of human activity; a serene life, extending to the utmost a man's natural span of years—these are the ideals which Taoism opposed to the human cares and concerns of the Confucianists."[10] Confucius had said, "There are three beneficial pleasures and three injurious pleasures. To find pleasure in the discriminating study of the rules of decency and music, to find pleasure in speaking of goodness in others, and to find pleasure in having many worthy friends—these are the beneficial pleasures. To find pleasures in extravagance; to find pleasure in idleness, and to find pleasure in feasting—these are the injurious pleasures."[11]

7. D. T. Suzuki, *A Brief History of Early Chinese Philosophy*, London, Probsthain, 1914, pp. 88–90.
8. The *Sarvadarśanasaṃgraha*, I. *A Source Book in Indian Philosophy*, edited by S. Radhakrishnan and C. A. Moore (Princeton University Press, 1957), p. 234.
9. Hsuan-tzu, Fung Yu-lan, *op. cit.*, vol. I, p. 140.
10. Wm. Theodore de Bary: *Buddhism and the Chinese Tradition*. (A paper read at the International Council for Philosophy and Humanistic Studies, Mexico, Sept. 23–24, 1963. It will be published in *Diogenes*, Paris, UNESCO)
11. *Analects*, XVI, 5 (Legge's translation).

We shall mention another example of the justification of denouncing morals and pursuing pleasure. Or perhaps the metaphysical position used for justification developed first and the denunciation of morals appeared later. Pakudha Kaccāyana in India proposed seven eternal unchanging principles: "The following seven things are neither made nor commanded to be made, neither created nor caused to be created, they are barren (so that nothing is produced out of them), steadfast as a mountain peak, as a pillar firmly fixed. They move not, neither do they carry, they trench not one upon another, nor avail aught as to ease or pain or both.

"And what are the seven things? The four elements—earth, water, fire, and air—and ease, and pain, and the soul as a seventh."[12]

In the West it might be odd to find ease and pain regarded as eternal principles in the same sense as the other five elements. For instance, in Greece, Empedocles, who advocated a very similar doctrine held that "Happiness, like unhappiness . . ." was rather a ". . . property of the soul."[13] But for Pakudha Kaccāyana, ease and pain, or happiness and unhappiness, were considered to be something corporeal. This is simply one of many examples of a traditional tendency of the Indians to hypostatize properties or abstract characteristics.

From this doctrine then, denunciation of morals was drawn out as the conclusion. "So there is neither slayer nor causer of slaying, hearer or speaker, knower or explaincr. When one with a sharp sword cleaves a head in twain, no one thereby deprives any one of life, a sword has only penetrated into the interval between seven elementary substances."[14] Therefore, murder is not a crime. And we can easily see that one may lead his life in any way he might please in that his soul is of an eternally unchangeable character.

12. *Dīgha-nikāya,* II, 26, vol. I, p. 56.
13. Empedocles' fr. 170.
14. *Dīgha-nikāya, op. cit.*

C. Determinism

In India the philosopher Gosāla advocated determinism. He is said to have been born in a cow-pen, where his parents took refuge while on a pilgrimage during a rainy season. Therefore, he was named "Cow-pen" (*Gosāla*). He reportedly asserted: "There is no cause, either ultimate or remote, for the depravity (state of being corrupted) of beings; they become depraved without reason and without cause. There is no cause, either proximate or remote, for the rectitude of beings; they become pure without reason and without cause. The attainment of any given condition, of any character, does not depend either on one's own acts, or on the acts of another, or on human effort. There is no such thing as power or energy, or human strength or human vigour. All animals, all creatures (with one, two, or more senses), all beings (produced from eggs or in a womb), all souls (in plants) are without force and power and energy of their own."[1]

Gosāla considered human efforts to be powerless and, therefore, men completely controlled by fate. "They are bent this way and that by their fate, by the necessary conditions of the class to which they belong, by their individual nature: and it is according to their position in one or other of the six classes that they experience ease or pain."[2]

Gosāla further thought that such destiny could not be altered. "There are fourteen hundred thousand of the principal sorts of birth, and again six thousand others, and again six hundred. There are five hundred sorts of *Karma*, and again (according to the five senses), and again three (according to act, word, and thought); and there is a whole *Karma* and a half *Karma* (the whole being a *Karma* of act or word, the half a *Karma* of thought). . ." etc.;[3] the author continues to enumerate what he thought to be set amounts of various phenomena. Undoubtedly, he thought such numbers existed for all phenomena.

The course and period of transmigration were also considered by Gosāla to be predestined. "The ease and pain, measured out, as it were, with a measure, cannot be altered in the course of transmigration; there can be neither increase nor decrease thereof, neither excess nor deficiency. Just as when a ball of string is cast forth it will spread out just as far, and

1. *Dīgha-nikāya,* II, 20–2, vol. I, pp. 53–55.
2. *Ibid.*
3. *Ibid.*

no farther, than it can unwind, just so both fools and wise alike, wandering in transmigration exactly for the alotted term, shall then, and only then, make an end of pain."[4]

The following opinions mentioned in early Buddhist scriptures were not specifically labelled deterministic, but were rather considered by the Buddhists to be heretical doctrines. However, in that these doctrines denied voluntary actions based upon free will, they have a feature of determinism. They share with Gosāla a view that there exists something that has arisen without a cause. This is totally unacceptable to the Buddhist metaphysics. "There are some recluses and Brahmans. . ." according to the Buddhists, ". . . who are Fortuitous-Originists (*adhicca-samuppannika*), and who in two ways maintain that the soul and the world arise without a cause. And on what ground, starting out from what, do they do so?" By assuming ". . . springing up without a cause."[5]

The first of the two ways that the Buddhists claimed these doctrines to have maintained a spontaneously-originated world and soul was as follows: "There are certain gods called Unconscious Beings (*asañña-satta*). As soon as an idea occurs to them they fall from that state. Now it may well be that a being, on falling from that state, should come hither; and having come hither he might go forth from the household life into the homeless state. And having thus become a recluse, he, by reason of ardour and so on (as in other cases), reaches up to such rapture of heart that, rapt in heart, he calls to mind how that idea occurred to him, but not more than that. He says to himself: 'Fortuitous in origin are the soul and the world. And why so? Because formerly I was not, but now am. Having not been, I have come to be.'

"This is the first state of things on account of which, starting out from which, some recluses and Brahmans become Fortuitous-Originists, and maintain that the soul and the world arise without a cause."[6]

And what is the second?

In this case, some recluse or *Brahman* is addicted to logic and reasoning. He gives utterance to the following conclusion of his own, beaten out by his argumentations, and based on his sophistry. "The soul and the world arose without a cause." This is the second case.[7] Although we are not sure of the content of those "argumentations," we see determinism in India often took a different turn than in the West (stressing no cause rather than everything being caused).

From a purely philological point of view, we can see the extent to

4. *Ibid.*
5. T. W. Rhys Davids, *Dialogues of the Buddha*, Part I (London: H. Frowds, Oxford University Press, 1899), p. 41 n.
6. *Dīgha-nikāya*, I, 2.31, vol. I, p. 28.
7. *Dīgha-nikāya*, I, 2.32, vol. I, p. 29.

which words in use in some Western Indo-European languages reflected one or another form of determinism. For example, the early Greeks and Romans had a number of concepts of the supremacy of destiny (fate) over all existences. Destiny was thought to be the ultimate ground of all earthly and heavenly phenomena. *Moira* was the most outstanding concept of destiny held by Greek poets. Other concepts of a similar kind were variously termed *adrasteisa, aisa, ananke, dike, pronoia, nemesis, tykhe*, and especially *heimarmene*. Ancient Romans called these ideas *fatum* and *fortuna*. In a Nordic saga a king remarked, "The fate [Nordic: *audna*] controls over the life of man, and not a bad spirit."[8] The Indian counterparts to such beliefs were known as *dista* and *daiva*. Finally in the philosophy of the Ajivikas there was necessity (*niyati*). In pre-Islamic times Arabs also held the notions of destiny or fate (*al-himam, al-qadar, al-dahr, az-zaman, al-aijam*), but these notions were wiped out by Islam.[9]

In Greece Democritus (c. 460–370 B.C.) and Leucippus were strict determinists who believed that everything happens in accordance with natural laws and that human purpose did not matter.[10] Leucippus carried on the views of his teacher, Zeno, the Stoic (c. 336–264 B.C.), who had taught that there is no such thing as chance, and that the course of nature is rigidly determined by natural laws. This theory was also maintained by the Ājīvikas who, coincidentally, were flourishing in India at the same time the Stoics, said to have been founded by Zeno,[11] appeared in the West. The real essence of Stoic determinism is expressed in the maxim "nothing can take place without a sufficient cause, nor, under the same circumstances, happens differently from what has happened."[12] Zeno believed that there is no such thing as chance and that the course of nature is rigidly determined by natural laws. Chrysippus (280–209 B.C.) and the Stoics held the doctrine of fate and providence, according to which men and all other creatures are determined in all their external and internal formation and in all that they do and suffer, by the all-animating World-power.[13] According to the Stoics, virtue consists in a will which is in agreement with nature. The wicked, even though they may obey God's law, do so involuntarily; in the simile of Cleanthes, they are like a dog tied to a cart compelled to go wherever it goes.[14]

8. Herman Schneider, *Die Götter der Germonen* (Tübingen, 1938), p. 155. I have cited this passage from Helmuth von Glasenapp, *Buddhisms und Gottesidee* (Wiesbaden: Franz Steiner, 1954), p. 51.
9. Cf. Helmuth von Glasenapp, *Buddhisms und Gottesidee*, p. 51.
10. H. Russell, *History*, pp. 66–67, Cf. Heraclitus' fragment, 20.
11. Copleston, *op. cit.*, vol. I, Part II, p. 71.
12. E. Zeller, *The Stoics, Epicureans and Sceptics*, translated by O. J. Reichel, London, 1880, p. 175.
13. W. Windelband, *History*, pp. 192–93.
14. Russell, *A History of World Philosophy*, p. 254.

Determinism has a difficult problem. The Stoics could not allow freedom of the will, in a strict sense of the term. As a result, opponents would say that if everything is determined by destiny, individual action is superfluous, since what has been once fore-ordained must happen, come what may. The same difficulty of fatalism was solved by Yang Hsiung (53 B.C.–18 A.D.) in a less abstract and more figurative way: "Fate is inexorable. What then of the early deaths of Yen Yuan and Jan Po-niu [Confucius' disciples]? These were inexorable. But a man who deliberately stands under a skaky wall courts injury as he moves and invites death when he walks. Is this fate? So-called 'lucky people' often turn their good luck into bad, while 'unlucky people' turn their bad luck into good."[15] Gosāla shared the same difficulty. His proposed solution to the problem however is not mentioned in his extant writings.

Men who have embraced determinism in the past have usually lived their lives like other men, as though they had options from which to choose. In fact, they have exercised their option to embrace some form of determinism. The consequences of adopting such a viewpoint as a principle on which to live would be self-resignation or complete reliance upon fate. Hence, we might understand determinism better if we compare the function such doctrines had in the lives of representative world thinkers.

The Stoics aimed at realizing imperturbability of mind. Gosāla is said to have formed a religious order which attracted many disciples. These two groups seemed to have sought contemplation or meditation in a serene state of mind, actually indifferent to, and unmoved by, fate. In China, Lao-tzu advocated a somewhat similar doctrine. He described the creative spirit of the universe as working according to the principle: production without possession, action without self-assertion, development without domination. Mencius said, "He who has exercised his mind to the utmost, knows his nature (*hsing*). Knowing his nature, he knows Heaven. To keep one's mind preserved and nourish one's nature is the way to serve Heaven. To be without doubleness of mind, whether one is to have untimely death or long life; and having cultivated one's personal character, to wait with this for whatever there may be: this is to stand in accord with Fate (*ming*)."[16] Mencius held a concept of deterministic heaven[17] (*t'ien*) which was an equivalent to the concept of fate (*ming*), all those events in human life over which man himself has no control.[18] This

15. De Bary, etc., *Sources of Chinese Tradition,* compiled by Wm. Theodore de Bary, Wing-tsit Chan, Burton Watson (New York: Columbia University Press, 1960), p. 248.
16. *Mencius,* VII, a, 1.
17. Fung Yu-lan, *A History of Chinese Philosophy,* translated by Derk Bodde, I (Princeton University Press, 1952), p. 129.
18. Fung Yu-lan, *Chinese Philosophy,* I, p. 31.

is the *t'ien* Mencius refers to when he says, "As to the accomplishment of a great deed, that is with *t'ien.*"[19]

Whereas the Indian fatalism of the Ajivikas was religious, the Chinese fatalism was rather ethical, although the heaven of Mencius was at times personal, at times deterministic, and at times ethical.[20] Mo-tzu was against such a conception. He condemned what he regarded as the tendency towards determinism.[21] Later Wang Ch'ung (27–97?) held the thought of extreme fatalism, which he extended to cover not only individuals but whole nations, leading him by analogical reasoning to the rather curious position that the prosperity or downfall of a dynasty was entirely a matter of its fated span of life.[22]

19. *Mencius,* I. p. 14.
20. Fung Yu-lan, *Chinese Philosophy,* I, p. 284.
21. De Bary, etc., *op. cit.,* p. 36.
22. De Bary, *op. cit.,* pp. 251–52.

D. Skepticism

1. Suspension of Judgment

ALL the works of Western skeptics were lost except those of Sextus Empiricus. In India no works of the skeptics have been transmitted to the present day, and it is unlikely that overt and outspoken skeptics existed in China and Japan either. Yet skepticism is the ever present gadfly to philosophers, challenging them to find some semblance of truth, if they can.

The first skeptic in India appears to have been Sañjaya, according to available records. Whenever he was questioned on a meta physical doctrine, he was elusive. Sañjaya (of the Belattha clan) had a habit of saying "If you ask me whether there is another world—well, if I thought there were, I would say so. But I don't say so. And I don't think it is thus or thus. And I don't think it is otherwise. And I don't deny it. And I don't say there neither is, nor is not, another world. And if you ask me about the beings produced by chance; or whether there is any fruit, any result, of good or bad actions; or whether a man who has won the truth continues, or not, after death—to each or any of these questions do I give the same reply."[1] When asked what was the immediate advantage in the life of a recluse, he also showed his manner of evasion.[2]

Early Buddhism called such men "the eel-wrigglers." Concerning their assertions, the Buddha stated, "There are some recluses and Brahmans who wriggle like eels; and when a question is put to them on this or that they resort to equivocation, to eel-wriggling."[3] Later literature reported such elusiveness on the part of one who said, "I don't take it thus. I don't take it the other way. But I advance no different opinion. And I don't deny your position. And I don't say it is neither the one, nor the other."[4] As to the subject matter that the "eel-wriggler" was prone to avoid, "Thus does he equivocate, and in like manner about each of such propositions as the following:

1. *Dīgha-nikāya*, II, 31, vol. I, p. 58.
2. *Ibid.*, p. 58.
3. *Ibid.*, I. 2.23, vol. I, p. 24.
4. According to Buddhaghosa.

(1) There is another world.
(2) There is not another world.
(3) There both is, and is not, another world.
(4) There neither is, nor is not, another world.

(1) There are Chance Beings (so called because they spring into existence, either here or in another world, without the intervention of parents, and seem therefore to come without a cause).
(2) There are no such beings.
(3) There both are, and are not, such beings.
(4) There neither are, not are not, such beings.

(1) There is fruit, result, of good and bad actions.
(2) There is not.
(3) There both is, and is not.
(4) There neither is, nor is not.

(1) A man who has penetrated to the truth continues to exist after death.
(2) He does not.
(3) He both does, and does not.
(4) He neither does, not does not."[5]

(Such questions are called elsewhere in the same work the common basis of discussion among *Brahmans*.)[6]

Like such "eel-wrigglers," Sañjaya did not want to be involved in metaphysical dispute. The only aim he pursued seems to have been calmness of mind. In terms of epistemology, Sañjaya's attitude can be called "suspension of judgment." In the West also the skeptics advocated that man suspend judgment as far as possible (*epokhē*). They claimed that we can say nothing concerning things (*aphasia*), but can only assert that this or that appears so or so, and in so doing we report only our own momentary states. Furthermore the Greek skeptics were, as was Sañjaya, seeking a calm state of mind (*ataraxia*).

The origins of the Western skeptical attitude can be traced to early days in Greece, e.g., in Heraclitus,[7] Protagoras, Phyrho (c. 365–275 B.C.), and Carneades (c. 155 B.C.). Cicero thought that the heavenly bodies (at least) are outside the ken of knowledge.[8] Protagoras wrote a book that was skeptical as to the existence of the gods, which began, "With regard to the gods, I cannot feel sure either that they are or that they are not, nor what they are like in figure; for there are many things that hinder

5. *Dīgha-nikāya*, I. 2.27, vol. I, p. 28.
6. *Ibid.*, I, 2.28, vol. I, p. 28.
7. Heraclitus' fragment, 20.
8. *Academica*, II (Lucullus) XXXIX, 122.

sure knowledge, the obscurity of the subject and the shortness of human life."[9] But Protagoras' assertion was coherent with his fundamental principle. Protagoras is chiefly noted for his doctrine that "Man is the measure of all things, of things that are that they are, and of things that are not that they are not."[10] Sañjaya's fundamental standpoint is likely to have been quite similar.

The Platonic Socrates professed to know nothing, and though one naturally treats this as irony, it could be taken seriously. Many of the Platonic dialogues reach no positive conclusion, and aim at leaving the reader in a state of doubt. Some, the latter half of the *Parmenides*, for instance, might seem to have no purpose except to show that either side of any question can be maintained with equal plausibility. The Platonic dialectic could be treated as an end, rather than a means, and if so treated it lends itself admirably to the advocacy of skepticism. This seems to have been the way in which Arcesilaus interpreted the man whom he still professed to follow. He carried the dialectic to an extreme purpose. Unlike Plato, who was always seeking true and abiding knowledge, Arcesilaus seemed successfully to bring about only a balanced pro and con on a subject, thereby never being sure of anything.

In contrast to Socrates, who knew that he knew nothing, Arcesilaus was reputed not even to be certain that he was certain of nothing.[11] Arcesilaus maintained no thesis, but would refute any thesis set up by a pupil. Sometimes he would himself advocate two contradictory propositions on successive occasions, showing how to argue convincingly in favor of either.[12]

In later days, the first lecture given by Carneades in Rome expounded the views of Aristotle and Plato on justice, and was thoroughly edifying. His second lecture, however, was concerned in refuting all that he had said in his first, not with a view to establishing opposite conclusions, but merely to show that every conclusion is unwarranted.[13]

Skepticism, which originated in the teachings of the Sophists, found culmination in Pyrrho[14] of Elis (c. 365–275 B.C.), but as he only transmitted his views by word of mouth, a complete collection of the doctrines of the skeptics awaited the works of Sextus Empiricus. Timon, a disciple of Pyrrho, denied the possibility of finding self-evident general principles. Every-

9. Diehls, fragment 80 B 4.
10. The interpretation of Protagoros' famous dictum is controversial. (F. Capleston, *History of Philosophy*, vol. I, part I, p. 108). We have adopted here the interpretation held by Plato in *Theactetus*.
11. *Ibid.*, vol. I, part II, p. 158.
12. Russell, *A History of Western Philosophy*, p. 235.
13. *Ibid.*, pp. 236–37.
14. There is a record that Pyrrho was in India with Alexander's army. If it is true, it is possible that he acquires some of his ideas there.

thing, therefore, would have to be proved by means of something else, and all argument, he held, would be either circular or an endless chain hanging from nothing. In either case nothing would be provable.[15] Accordingly, we can trust neither sense perception nor reason and, therefore Timon held that we must suspend judgment (*epokhē*), avoiding entrapment in theoretical assertions. Remaining so freed from potentially faulty reasoning, a man may then attain to true *ataraxia*, tranquility of the soul.[16] In that this tranquility was the goal of all the schools of Greek skepticism we see skepticism performing the same function as determinism (see previous section).

With regard to action, also, skeptics are faced with difficulties similar to determinists. Skeptics, too, have to make decisions from among various alternatives, insofar as they are alive and acting. Sañjaya, for instance, was surrounded by his followers; tradition has it that he organized a sort of religious order. What then was to be his opinion concerning daily actions? We know he avoided metaphysical dispute. And again the only aim he pursued seems to have been calmness of minu. In the same way, Pyrrho is said to have had no positive doctrines. To be his disciple meant only to lead a kind of life similar to that of Pyrrho. "He wanted to reveal to men the secret of happiness, by showing them that 'salvation' can be found only in the peace of a thought which is indifferent, a sensibility which is extinct, a will which is obedient; and that this quest requires an effort which is, on the part of the individual, an effort to die to himself. . . ."[17]

In China skepticism did not develop, although sophistical argumentations were set forth by dialecticians (*pien che*) such as Hui Shih and Kungsun Lung (next section). Neither did it occur in Japan. Only after the introduction of Western philosophy did the Japanese coin the word "*kaigi-ron*," meaning "skepticism," and his word was introduced into Chinese from the Japanese. So the word meaning "skepticism" in Japanese and Chinese is quite new.

2. Sophistic Dialectic

SOPHISTRY is related to skepticism in the sense that its proponents try to bring to absurdity those ordinary opinions garnered from common sense. If sophistry were to be applied to the entire range of things, the result

15. B. Russell, *op. cit.*, p. 234.
16. Copleston, *op. cit.*
17. L. Robin, *Phyrhon et le scepticisme grec* (Paris: Presses Universitaires de France, 1944), p. 24.

would be tantamount to the conclusions of skepticism. Thus Protagoras' dictum, "Man is the measure of all things," was included in the previous section. Sophistry appeared at nearly the same period in Greece, China and India. As an example of the discussions of the sophists, we shall consider the argumentation involved in their denials of change. In that regard, we choose a philosopher, Zeno of Elea, not usually classed as a sophist but who used what we consider to be exemplary arguments of sophistic dialectic.

Zeno's arguments[1] against motion are well known. Parmenides had derived his determinations of Being directly from the concept of Being. But Zeno tried to prove the same doctrine indirectly by showing that the oppising theories, such as, e.g., the pluralistic hypothesis of the Pythagoreans, involve us in difficulties and contradictions, and that Being does not admit of our regarding it as a plurality, i.e., something divisible and changeable. In other words, he sought to prove the Eleatic doctrine by reducing the prevalent mode of philosophical presentation to absurdity.[2] The following is one short example among many of his arguments against motion.

Consider a moving arrow. According to the Pythagorean hypothesis the arrow should occupy a given position in space. But to occupy a given position in space is to be at rest. Therefore, the flying arrow is at rest, which is a contradiction.[3]

An ancient Chinese philosopher Hui Shih (380–300 B.C.?)[4] was fond of bringing to light just such paradoxes as Zeno's. He (or someone in his tradition) is attirbuted with the sayings, "The shadow of a flying bird never moves," and "There are moments when a flying arrow is neither in motion nor at rest." Mr. Chang Ping-ling and Dr. Hu Shih think that his fourth paradox: "The sun shines obliquely as it is noon. A thing dies as it is born" and his seventh paradox: "I go to Yueh (a State in the South) today and arrived there yesterday," show that time-distinctions are human-made, and have no reality. By showing this, his paradoxes were meant to prove a monistic theory of the universe. The ultimate purpose resulting from them was to teach "Love all things equally; the universe is one." (the tenth paradox). That is, the paradoxes constitute an attempt to establish a metaphysical basis for the Mohist doctrine of universal altruism.

1. E. Zeller, *The Stoics, Epicureans, and Sceptics*. Translated from German into English by Oswald J. Reichel. A new and revised edition (London: Longmans, Green, and Co., 1880), etc., pp. 619 f.
2. *Ibid.*, p. 611.
3. Copleston, *A History of Philosophy*, vol. I, part I, p. 74.
4. Hu Shih, *The Development of the Logical Method in Ancient China* (Shanghai, the Oriental Book Company, 1922), pp. 112–113. Cf. Fung Yu-lang, *A History of Chinese Philosophy*, I, pp. 192 ff.; De Bary: *CT*, pp. 88 ff.

A similar paradoxical opinion was expressed in India at nearly the same time by certain philosophers who were cited for the purpose of refutation by both Buddhist[5] and Jain[6] authorities. They said: "The winds do not blow; the waters of rivers do not flow; pregnant women do not bear children; the sun and moon do not rise and set; they stand firm, as stable as a pillar." This opinion is cited in later Abhidharma literature[7] as the opinion of philosophers who postulated the existence of a minute and eternal *ātman* as a substance. If we admit this tradition, the Indian arguments against motion are also shown to be aimed at establishing a monistic teaching.

To the extent that these arguments were aimed at a sort of monism, the Greek, Chinese and Indian arguments were the same. However, the practical implication of Zeno's dialectic was not clear; Hu Shih's purpose was to establish altruism in an ethical and practical sense; and Indian sophistry probably leads to meditation for the purpose of union with *brahman* as in the cases of most early Vedāntins.[8]

3. Relativism

IF we, admitting the significance of skepticism in any sense, want to justify our actions in any way, we shall be led to the standpoint of relativism. Relationistic doctrines were clearly represented by Jainism in India and by some thinkers in Greece.

The fundamental standpoint of Jainism is logically called "The Maybe Theory" (*syādvāda*).[1] It signifies that the universe can be looked at from many points of view, and that each viewpoint yields a different conclusion (*anekānta*). Therefore, no conclusion is decisive. The Jains enumerate the nature of reality in seven steps. This method is called the

5. *Saṃyutta-nikāya*, XXIV, 1. vol. III, p. 203. The Chinese version corresponding to this passage is in *Tsa a han ching*, S 16 (*Taisho*, XXVI, p. 914 a). The same view is mentioned and refuted in Patñjali's *Mahābhāṣya*, III, 2, 123. Cf. *Udāna*, I, 10, p. 9. The passage in the *Mahābhāṣya* is referred to by Ruben, *Indische und griechische Metaphysik*, S. 47.
6. *Sūyagaḍaṅga*, I, 12, 7.
7. *Abhidharma-jñānaprasthāna-śāstra*, *Taisho*, XXVII, pp. 996 c-997 a; 1022 c. Discussed in detail by H. Nakamura in *Harvard Journal of Asiatic Studies*, vol. 18, June 1955, No. 1–2, pp. 79 ff.
8. Zeno's arguments are usually compared to those of Nāgārjuna. But I compared it here to another opinion which occurred at nearly the same time as in Greece and China.
1. *Syāt* is derived from the Sanskrit root as meaning "to be," and means "maybe" as its form in the potential mode. Substantially it means "Seen from one point of view," "somehow."

"Seven-fold formula" or the "Seven-fold mode of predication" (*saptabhaṅgī*) (*-naya*)):

1) Viewed from one point (or somehow), something is.
2) Viewed from another point (or somehow), something is not.
3) Viewed from another point (or somehow), something is and is not.
4) Viewed from another point (or somehow), something is inexpressible.
5) Viewed from another point (or somehow), something is and inexpressible.
6) Viewed from another point (or somehow), something is not and inexpressible.
7) Viewed from another point (or somehow), something is, is not and inexpressible.

For example, so far as the material cause of an object is concerned, a thing has always existed and will always continue to exist; but the particular form in which it appears here and now has but a limited existence. While the substance remains the same, its modes vary. As a result of this qualification, we get to the third step, which affirms as well as denies the existence of the object concerned. It *is* as well as *is not*, That is, it *is* in one sense, but *is not* in another.

While the opposition between the predicates 'is' and 'is not' can be reconciled when they are thought of as characterizing an object successively, the nature of the object becomes incomprehensible when both of them are applied to it simultaneously. We cannot identify A and not-A as a whole, for that would be to subvert the law of contradiction. So it must be expressible as neither. As Democritus noted, "It has often been demonstrated that we do not grasp how each thing is or is not."[2]

This yields the fourth step, which amounts to saying that reality from one standpoint is inscrutable (no. 4). Hence Jainism insists that in speaking of an object one must state what it is in reference to material, place, time, and state. Otherwise the description of it will be misleading.

It may seem that the formula might stop here. But there are still other ways in which the alternatives can be combined. To avoid the impression that those predicates are excluded, three more steps are added. The resulting description becomes exhaustive,[3] leaving no room for the possibility of dogma in any form.

What is intended by all this is to show that our judgments have only a partial application to reality.[4] The nature of reality is expressed com-

2. Democritus' fragment, 10.
3. These seven are the only ways in which "is" and "is not" can be taken singly and in combination. (cf. *Prameya-kamala-mārtaṇḍa*, p. 205)
4. So far according to Hiriyanna, *Outlines of Indian Philosophy* (London: George Allen & Unwin, Ltd., 1932), pp. 164–65.

pletely by none of them. Every proposition is therefore, strictly speaking, only conditional. Absolute affirmation and absolute negation are both erroneous. Jainism shows extreme caution and anxiety to avoid all possible dogma in defining the nature of reality. According to the Jains, reality is in itself infinitely complex. Permanence and change are equally real. Only human knowledge may be partial and erroneous, and all philosophical doctrines (referring to the ones prevalent in their time) are only partially true, each becoming prejudiced dogma when understood as representing the whole truth about reality. The Jains thought reality to be so complex in its structure that while every one of these views is true for some aspects of reality, none is completely true. Present-day Jains proudly say that it is only they who can stop the conflict of different ideologies in the world, and that war can be prevented by such a standpoint alone.

The seven-fold mode of predication may be compared to some of the ten *tropoi* or arguments for the skeptical position by Aenesidemus of Knossos (c. 43 B.C.), e.g.:

(4) The difference [that exists] between our various states, e.g., waking or sleeping, youth or age. For example, a current of air may seem a pleasant breeze to a young man, while to an old man it is a detestable draught.

(8) Relativity in general.

(10) Different ways of life, moral codes, laws, myths, philosophic systems, etc. Among the five by Agrippa the third argument seems similar.

(3) The relativity involved in the fact that objects appear differently to people according to the temperament, etc., of the percipient and according to their relation whit other objects.[5]

On this doctrine of the seven-fold modes of predication the Vedāntists criticized the Jains as follows: "It is impossible that contradictory attributes such as being and non-being should at the same time belong to one and the same thing; just as observation teaches us that a thing cannot be hot and cold at the same moment. The third alternative expressed in the words 'they either are such or not such' results in a cognition of indefinite nature which is no more a source of true knowledge than doubt is. Thus the means of knowledge, the object of knowledge, the knowing subject, and the act of knowledge become all alike indefinite. How can his followers act on a doctrine the matter of which is altogether indeterminate? The result of your efforts is perfect knowledge and is not perfect knowledge. Observation shows that, only when a course of action is known to have a definite result, people set about it without hesitation. Hence a man who proclaims a doctrine of altogether indefinite contents does not de-

5. Copleston, *History*, vol. I, part II, p. 187 f.

serve to be listened to any more than a drunken man or a madman."[6]

Such a criticism may be fitting. The seven-fold mode of predication (*sapta-bhaṅgī*) stops short of giving one the several partial views put together, without attempting to overcome the opposition in them by a proper synthesis. It is all right so far as it cautions us against one-sided conclusions; but it leaves a certain indefiniteness. Therefore, in order to avoid indefiniteness, the following is a proposed conclusion: it is not quite impossible to make reality known through a series of partially true statements without committing oneself to any one of them exclusively. Actually, based upon this standpoint Jainism went on to build its own metaphysical system.

The standpoint of Aristippus was very similar to that of the Jains. He taught that we know, not things, but only their worth for us, and the states (*pathe*) into which they put us.[7] (Cf. the Jain concept of 'state,' *paryāya*.) These, however, are rest and indifference, violent motion and pain, or gentle motion and pleasure. Of these only the last is worth striving for. Aristippus was led to hedonism, meaning by "pleasure" worldly pleasure, whereas for the Jains "pleasure" meant pure calm of mind.

Possibly the most famous relativist to appear in the history of Western philosophy, however, was Heraclitus (flourished c. 504–501 B.C.). He is best known, perhaps unjustly, for the statement: "You cannot step twice into the same river, for fresh waters are ever flowing in upon you."[8] Aristotle interpreted this statement of Heraclitus as affirming that "All things are in motion, nothing steadfastly is."[9]

The real core of Heraclitus' teaching however is the concrete universal, ". . . the One existing in the many, Identity in Difference."[10] The inseparability of opposites, the essential character of the different moments of the One, comes out in such sayings as: "The way up and the way down is the same," and "It is death to souls to become water, and death to water to become earth. But water comes from earth, and from water, soul."[11] And eventually a certain relativism appears as in the statements that "Good and ill are one"; "The sea is the purest and impurest water. Fish can drink it and it is good for them; to me it is undrinkable and destructive." "Swine wash in the mire, and barnyard fowls in the dust."[12] Heraclitus' relativism, like that of the Jains, applies to the knowledge of men in contrast to a more refined mind: "To God all things are fair and

6. Śaṅkara ad *Brahmasūtra*, II, 2, 33.
7. Windelband, *History*, p. 93 f.
8. Copleston, *op. cit.*, vol. I, part I, p. 55.
9. *Ibid.*
10. *Ibid.*, p. 57.
11. *Ibid.*, p. 58.
12. *Ibid.*, p. 58 f.

good and right, but men hold some things wrong and some things right."[13] Heraclitus' viewpoint, however, in contrast to the Jains, is the result of a patheistic philosophy.

In China and Japan systematized relativism was not advocated with full consciousness. The Chinese and Japanese have been rather practical people, and with regard to religious dogmas they tended to be relativistic. They did not care for metaphysical discussion. Probably due to this reason relativism was not asserted earnestly. This is a paradoxical situation, in that when one is truly relativistic in practice, to make an assertion of relativism earnestly is contradictory. It seems to us that relativism was taken for granted by the ancient Chinese and Japanese and that they did not care to systematize it.

13. *Ibid.*, p. 59.

E. Asceticism

1. Self-mortification

JAINISM is a paradigm among the Indian schools which prescribe strict and rigid austerities.[1] At first, the ascetic should keep the five vows (*vrata*):

(1) not to injure any living being (*ahiṃsā*)
(2) to be truthful (*satya*) (not to lie)
(3) not to steal (*asteya*) (not to take what is not given)
(4) to lead a celibate life (*brahma-carya*) (to preserve chastity)
(5) to renounce pleasure in all external things (*aparigraha*)

In the case of the layman they are nearly the same, the last two being moderated, i.e., he should keep the vows of sexual and moral contentment or strict limitation of his wants. Sense pleasure, they thought, is always a sin, the ideal is indifference to pleasure and pain, and independence of all external objects.

Of the various virtues to be cultivated by the Jains, non-injury (*ahiṃsā*) was regarded as the most essential one. Literally, the word *ahiṃsā* means "non-injury," where "injury"[2] should be understood as encompassing injuring by thought, word or act. Vegetarianism was strictly observed by the Jain devotees of Mahāvīra just as by the followers of Pythagoras in Greece, both traditions beginning in nearly the same period.

Jainism carries the doctrine of non-injury (*ahiṃsā*) of living creatures to an extreme not otherwise paralleled in Indian religions. The Jain

1. In the *Ṛg-veda*, the mightiest god, Indra, is said to have conquered heaven by asceticism (*ṚV.* X, 127). But the dominant note is not one of asceticism. In the hymns we find a keen delight in the beauties of nature, its greatness, its splendour and its pathos. The motive of the sacrifices is love of the good things of the world (Radhakrishnan, *Indian Philosophy*, I, p. 111).
2. Albert Schweitzer (*Indian Thought and Its Development*, translated by Mrs. Charles E. B. Russell [Boston: the Beacon Press, Third Printing, 1960], p. 79 ff) asserts that the Jain *ahiṃsā* is not necessarily based upon compassion, but the general principle of non-activity as it results from Indian world and life negation as such. But I think this is a slightly biased explanation from a Western point of view. Jains occasionally resort to action so as not to kill living beings.

ascetic strains water with a filter lest he destroy creatures lurking in it when he drinks (not for hygenic reasons). He veils his mouth with a white mask for fear of inhaling and killing the organisms of the air. He screens his lamp to protect insects from the flame. In a public highway a Jain monk should walk circumspectly so as to avoid injuring living beings.[3] On lanes he should walk sweeping the ground before him with a broom lest his naked foot should trample out some life. The Jain must never slaughter or sacrifice an animal. So needless to say, the monks as well as laymen are enjoined not to eat meat. The good Jain also rejects honey because it is thought by him to be the life of the bee.

The Jains established hospitals or asylums, as at Ahmedabad or Delhi, etc., for old and injured beasts and birds. It is clear from this that the social or objective side of ethics is not ignored in Jainism; but insofar as its final aim is the perfection of one's personality, the moral life of the individual receives the greater emphasis.

As for the Jain ascetic it is said as follows: "He will not accept food collected (by the faithful in time of drought); Hc will not accept food where a dog is standing by (lest the dog should lose a meal); He will not accept food where flies are swarming round (lest the flies should suffer); He will not accept fish, nor meat, nor strong drink, nor intoxicants, nor gruel."[4]

The ascetic life of the "Great Hero," Mahāvīra, is described in a scripture. "He wandered naked and homeless. In winter he meditated in the shade, in the heat of summer he seated himself in the scorching sun. Often he drank no water for months. Sometimes he took only every sixth, eighth, tenth, or twelfth meal, and pursued his meditations without craving." With Mahāvīra as the ideal, his Jain followers try to take food only once a day, or once every two days, or some up to once every seven days. And some even become accustomed to regularly taking food as few as once every 15 days![5]

The practice of fasting was extolled because this is the greatest victory of the spirit over the blind will to live. The Jain should not destroy life of living beings, the only life he may take is his own. His doctrine highly approves of suicide, especially by slow starvation. The ascetics who committed suicide by fasting were highly praised in religious works and their epitaphs. Many Jains have died in this way, and the leaders of the sect are said to leave the world even today by self-starvation.

Mahāvīra's cardinal virtue is forebearance. "People struck him and mocked at him—unconcerned, he continued in his meditations. In Ladha the inhabitants persecuted him and set the dogs on him. They beat him

3. *Sarvadarśanasaṃgraha* III.
4. *Dīgha-nikāya* VIII, vol. I, p. 166.
5. *Ibid.*, VIII, vol. I, p. 166.

with sticks and with their fists, and threw fruits, clods of earth and potsherds at him. They disturbed him in his meditations by all sorts of torments. But, 'Like a hero in the forefront of the battle,' Mahāvīra withstood it all. Whether he was wounded or not, he never sought medical aid. He took no kind of medicaments, he never washed, did not bathe and never cleaned his teeth."[6]

Pārśva, Mahāvīra's predecessor, allowed his followers two garments, but Mahāvīra permitted his monks none at all. Some Jain monks lived completely naked. This is due to a strict application of the prohibition against possessing property.

After Mahāvīra's death the ascetics strictly observed his prohibition. But about 300 B.C. there developed some who wanted to wear white cloth, and the community split on that issue into two divisions: the Śvetāmbara (white-clothed) and the Digambara (sky-clothed, that is, naked). The division was recognized in 79 A.D. (or 82). These sects have further sects to divide them, the Digambaras have four, the Śvetāmbaras eighty-four.[7] Today both sects wear the usual clothing of their place and time, only their saints go about the streets naked.

Why do the Jain ascetics roam about naked? The Jains answer, "the covering for the soul is the body; this again requires no further covering of cloth, etc., for if it does take such a covering, that will require still another; there will arise no final (*i.e.*, there will be a *regressus ad infinitum*)."[8] The body itself is a bondage for the spirit. If a man wears clothes, the bondage would be doubled. Gandhi was raised in the Western Gujarāt where Jainism is prevailing. He was strongly influenced by the Jain religion, accepting *ahimsā* as the basis of his policy and life, contenting himself with a loin-cloth, and observing fasting very often.

In the Buddhist scriptures also we find some passages where ascetics of the self-mortification type are referred to.[9] Some of them must have been the Jain ascetics. "Dwelling for the most part in the forests, but also in caves in the mountains, the Hermits gave themselves up to renunciation and self-mortification, living on roots and fruits. The professor of self-torture referred to (above) enumerates twenty-two methods of mortifying the body in respect of food, thirteen in respect of clothing, and five in respect of posture."[10]

Some examples of the ascetics' precepts with regard to food are:

"When on his rounds for alms, if politely requested to step nearer,

6. Wintermitz, *Indian Literature* II, p. 437.
7. Sir Charles Eliot, *Hinduism and Buddhism* (New York: Barnes and Noble, Inc. 1921. Reprint 1957), vol. I, p. 112.
8. *Sarvasiddhāntasaṃgraha* II, 12.
9. *Majjhima-nikāya* I, 79; *Jātaka*, I. p. 390.
10. T. W. Rhys Davids, *Early Buddhism* (London; A. Constable, 1908), p. 6.

or to wait a moment (in order that food may be put into his bowl), he passes stolidly on (lest he should incur the guilt of following another person's word):—

He refuses to accept food brought (to him, before he has started on his daily round for alms):—

He refuses to accept (food, if told that it has been prepared especially for him):—

He refuses to accept any invitation (to call on his rounds at any particular house, or to pass along any particular street, or to go to any particular place):—

He will not accept (food taken direct) from the mouth of the pot or pan (in which it is cooked; lest those vessels should be struck or scraped, on his account, with the spoon):—"[11]

Examples of prescriptions regarding wearing apparel are:

"He wears coarse hempen cloth:—

He wears cloths taken from corpses and thrown away:—

He wears clothing made of rags picked up from a dust heap:—

He wears a dress made of a network of strips of a black antelope's hide (cf. John the Baptist):—

He wears a dress made of Kusa grass fibre:—

He wears, as a garment, a blanket of human hair (cf. Ajita Kesakambala, the materialist):—"

Finally, suggestions regarding posture included:

He is a "stander-up," rejecting the use of a seat:—

He sleeps aways on one side:—

He is a "croucher-down-on-the-heels," addicted to exerting himself when crouching down on his heels.[12] (Rhys Davids says about this that this posture is impossible to Europeans, who, if they crouch down on their heels, cannot keep their balance when the heels touch the ground. But natives of India will sit so for hours without fatigue.)

The Buddha taught his disciples that if anybody was addicted to such practices he would be far from the ideal of the true religionist. He said, "But [instead] from the time when a mendicant (*bhikkhu*) has cultivated the heart of love that knows no anger, that knows no ill will, free from the deadly intoxications (the lust of the flesh, the lust after future life, and the defilement of delusion and ignorance), from that time he is called a *samaṇa*, he is called a *brāhmaṇa*!"[13]

11. *Dīgha-nikāya* VIII, vol. I, pp. 166 f.
12. *Dialogues of the Buddha (Sacred Books of the Buddhists)*, translated by T. W. Rhys Davids (London: Oxford University Press 1899), vol. II, p. 231, n.
13. Kassapa-sīhanāda-sutta, *Dīgha-nikāya*, VIII.

It may be rather difficult to find counterparts to the Jains of such a severe self-mortification in Greek civilization. That is why early Greek invaders were so astonished to see the severe practices of some of the Indian ascetics. However, the spirit of controlling oneself was not lacking in Greece, either.

The Pythagorean School (founded in the second half of the sixth century, B.C.) had as a distinguishing characteristic among ancient schools a somewhat ascetic and religious orientation. There is certainly a common ground of influence, though difficult to pin down, between Pythagoreanism and the older sect of Orphism. Common to them both was the doctrine of transmigration of souls,[14] a way of thought that easily lends itself to asceticism. In the Orphic tradition, for example, it was the soul and not the imprisoning body that was the most important part of man, in fact, the "real" man;[15] quite a difference from the concept of the soul as the shadow image of man as found in Homer. Soul-training and soul purification in Orphism included such precepts as the avoidance of flesh-meat.[16]

The religious-ascetic practices of the Pythagoreans centered around the idea of purity and purification. The practice of silence, the effect of music and the appreciation of mathematical manipulation were all looked upon as important parts of culturing the soul. Dictums such as: "abstain from flesh meat and beans," "don't walk in the main street," "refrain from stepping on the parings of your nails," "cover the tracings a pot has made in the ashes of a fire," "do not sit on a bushel," etc., are all more or less accurately attributed to the Pythagoreans. And such dictums, possibly for a variety of reasons, function to deny activities otherwise commonly undertaken.

Pythagoras himself, as described by Diogenes Laërtius, was extremely worried about the maltreatment of other living things, another consequence of the doctrine of transmigration of souls. Diogenes reports that upon seeing a person beating a dog, Pythagoras told him to stop, as the dogs bark reminded him of the voice of a friend. We may recall here the Jain doctrine of non-injury to other living things (*ahiṃsa*).

According to Aristotle, the Pythagorean practice of doing mathematics is intimately associated with their appreciation of music as beneficial to the soul. He wrote, "Since they saw that the attributes of and the ratios of the musical scales were expressible in numbers; since then all other things seemed in their whole nature to be modelled after numbers, and

14. Coppleston, *A History of Philosophy*, vol. I, part I, p. 46.
15. *Ibid.*, p. 48.
16. *Ibid.*

numbers seemed to be the first things in the whole of nature, and the whole heaven to be a musical scale and number."[17]

Regardless of what drew their interest to mathematical forms, a tradition began here that has no highly developed counterpart in the East. The combination of their tendency away from external things plus the discovery of the afore-mentioned properties of mathematics undoubtedly led the Pythagoreans to a practice of working with numbers almost as a form of contemplation. Numbers might be thought to lend themselves magnificently to such an exercise in that they are what they are regardless of the external objects they can be used to enumerate.

The same sort of attitude might be held toward symbolic logic. Disregarding for the moment the extreme usefulness of symbolic logic in the foundations of mathematics and in computer sciences, it has been said that it is "almost entirely irrelevant to philosophy."[18] Yet a goodly portion of the time of Anglo-American philosophers since the turn of the century has been spent in just the sort of activity that was begun in the Pythagorean society some 600 years before Christ. But this is all tangential. The subject at hand is the spirit of moderate ascetism the West inherited from the Pythagoreans through Plato.

Plato probably borrowed from the Pythagoreans at least their doctrine of the tripartite nature of the soul,[19] and their idea of the right way to administer the affairs of the soul. These two combined with the tremendous influence of Socrates prompted Plato to place the rational "part" of the soul (in the sense of a form or principle of action)[20] above the other two divisions which he termed the spirited and the appetitive. Socrates had occupied himself with the excellences of character and his mastery over bodily passions is often stressed.[21] In the apology, Socrates' profession is said to have been ". . . to persuade every man among you that he must look to himself, and seek virtue and wisdom before he looks to his private interest. . . ."[22]

The tripartite nature of the soul as set forth in *Phaedrus*, functions both as Plato's description of the conflict possible in the soul and the impetus for following his moderate ascerticism. In this work is found the famous metaphor of the charioteer (the rational principle of activity in the mind) and the two horses (symbolizing the spirited and appetitive forms of the soul). The spirit-horse causes no trouble (the spirited prin-

17. *Metaphysics*, 985, b 31–986 a 3.
18. Jon Wheatly, *Prolegomena to Philosophy* (Belmont, Calif.: Wadsworth Publishing Co., Inc., 1970), p. 42.
19. Russell, *History of Western Philosophy*, p. 242.
20. *Republic*, 444 b 3.
21. Russell, *History of Western Philosophy*, p. 91.
22. *Apology*, 36.

ciple of action in the soul is naturally akin to reason and ". . . loves honor with temperance and modesty").[23] But the appetitive element is a "friend to all riot and insolence" and, symbolized as an unruly horse which tends to obey passions only, must be constantly restrained by the whip.[24]

In the *Republic*, the soul's evils are set forth as "unrighteousness, intemperance, cowardice, ignorance."[25] It is perhaps passages from Plato like the above that prompted Bertrand Russell to claim that, for Plato, the true votaries of philosophy abstain from fleshly lusts.[26]

Just as Plato had done, Plotinus adopted views of the Orphic-Pythagorean type into what would later be called his Neo-Platonism. For instance, he viewed matter as some Pythagoreans had, as the principle of evil. And, he, like Plato before him, held a tripartite conception of the soul. However, he thought the highest level of soul to be closer to Aristotle's *Nous*, rooted in the intelligible world and uncontaminated by matter.[27]

For Plotinus, when the soul enters into a body, it becomes contaminated by matter. To restore it from this fallen state necessitates an ethical ascent to union with the One. Herein is found the asceticism of Plotinus. The first stage of such an ascent necessitates purification from the body and the senses so the soul can eventually rise to mystical union with the One. It has been said that in the work of Plotinus ". . . the Orphic-Platonic-Pythagorean strain of 'otherworldliness,' intellectual ascent, salvation through assimilation to and knowledge of God, reach their most complete and systematic expression."[28]

The attitudes and practices so far discussed, originating with the Greeks, are obviously much too moderate to compare with those of the Jain monks. Better parallels might be found among early Christian ascetics. "As is well known," we are told by Rhys Davids, ". . . such [ascetic] ideas are not confined to India. Tennyson, in his monologue of St. Simeon Stylites, has given us a powerful analysis of the feelings that lay at the root of similar practices among Christians."[29]

23. Copleston, *op. cit.*, p. 235.
24. *Ibid.*
25. 303 b 8-c 5.
26. Russell, *op. cit.*, p. 41.
27. Copleston, *op. cit.*, vol. I, part II, p. 214.
28. *Ibid.*, p. 215.
29. T. W. Rhys Davids, *Early Buddhism* (London: A. Constable, 1910), pp. 6–7. "Both in the West and in the East such claims were often gladly admitted. We hear in India of the reverence paid to the man who (to quote the words of a Buddhist poet):

—Bescorched, befrozen, lone in fearsome wooes,
Naked, without a fire, a fire within,
Struggled, in awful silence, toward the goal."

(*Majjhima-nikāya*, I, 79, quoted in *Jātaka* I, 390, Rhys Davids, *Early Buddhism*, p. 7)

Some early Christian ascetics thought that the world was bad and also the body was bad. If the body is bad, then, it must be beaten down by hardship. For this reason they lived in caves and slept on rocks. Some lived on pillars.

Clement of Alexandria[30] compared the Indian ascetics who lived in forests and who neither married nor begot children to the Encratities (Enkratetai, literally, the self-disciplined), certain second century Christian ascetics who were regarded as heretics. Describing the life of Dorotheus,[31] Sozomen[32] says that he limited himself to six ounces of bread and a few vegetables each day and drank only water. "He was never seen to recline on a mat or bed, nor even to place his limbs in an easy attitude, or willingly surrender himself to sleep." To the question why he was destroying his body, his reply was, "Because it is destroying me."[33]

A glorification of suffering led to the exaltation of martyrdom in the early church. St. Theresa (1515–1582 A.D.) said, "Suffering alone, from now on, can make life supportable to me. My dearest wishes all lead to suffering. How often from the bottom of my heart have I cried out to God, O Lord, to suffer or die is the only thing I ask."[34] However, later Christianity discouraged self-mortification in geleral. Likewise, self-mortification by the Jains, etc., was refuted as a heterodoxy at least by Buddhism. So in the eyes of universal religions these principles of action became heterodox.

In China there was the ideal of the recluse even in pre-Buddhist times, but the practice of self-mortification did not appear. Confucius said, "He who seeks only coarse food to eat, water to drink, and a bent arm for a pillow without looking for it finds happiness to boot."[35] But the attitude or practice of Chinese philosophers was too moderate to compare with that of the Jain monks. There was not the tendency to despise the human body among the ancient Chinese, and this fact must have accounted for the lack of self-mortification among them. Such a tendency did not appear in Japan either.

30. Megasthenes, *India*, p. 105, fr. XLIII.
31. An Arian bishop of Antioch during the Melitian schism, in succession to Euzoius, A.D. 376.
32. Author of a well-known *Ecclesiastical History*, born about A.D. 400.
33. *Ecclesiastical History*, bk. VI, Chap. XXIX. See also Madame Guyon's Life, by Upham, Chap, XIX, p. 140 (Radhakrishnan, *Eastern Religions*, p. 72).
34. Radhakrishnan, *Eastern Religions*, p. 71.
35. *Analects*, VII, 15.

2. The Seeking of Dishonor

Cynicism appeared in Athens about the beginning of the fourth century B.C. Although the ethical teachings of Cynicism owed much to Antisthenes (c. 446–366 B.C.), it was Diogenes of Sinope (404–366 B.C.) who was first called *kyon*, the dog, from which the name "Cynicism" derives. The popular sermons of the Cynics exerted considerable influence in the days of the Roman Empire until the fifth century A.D.

Antisthenes derived his form of Cynicism from a particularized interpretation of some of Socrates' doctrines. Socrates, we may recall, sought to keep his independence from physical wealth and mass popularity so that he could more freely pursue what he considered to be the higher good of wisdom (*sophia*). For Antisthenes, independence itself was embraced as wisdom or the true good. Self-sufficiency or independence from earthly possessions and pleasures became for him an end in itself.

Antisthenes' interpretation of Socrates' emphasis on ethical knowledge resulted in a contempt for other activities in Greek society, such as artistic and scientific pursuits. Nothing else is needed, he thought, for an individual's happiness except virtue, i.e., independence. Socrates' having been a "gadfly" to the Greek government became in Antisthenes methodology denunciation of government, law and religion.

Diogenes of Sinope believed that Antisthenes had merely held and expounded the above theories but had not lived a life consistent with his beliefs. Diogenes believed that every convention was false and rejected all conventions—whether of religion, manners, dress, housing, food, or of decency. He decided to live like a dog and call himself one. Thereafter he was called a "Cynic," which means "canine." Such animal vows are not without parallel in the Indian tradition, where bull, cock, and sparrow vows as well as dog-vows are referred to.[1] And Buddhist scriptures also mention ascetics who lived like cocks (*kukkuṭika*).

Diogenes of Sinope reportedly advocated forms of communal living (communal wives and children) and free love.[2] He was not satisfied with Antisthenes' mere "indifference" to the products and advances of society and held that freedom could come only from practicing various asceticisms. For instance, it is said that he would roll himself in a tub over hot sand in summer and embrace snow-covered status in winter.[3] The pos-

1. The dog *vrata*, cattle *vrata*, and cock *vrata*. Damodar Dharmanand Kosambi, *An Introduction to the Study of Indian History* (Bombay: Popular Book Depot, 1956), pp. 123–124; *Mahābhārata*, 5, 97, 13–14 noted by Ingalls, *Journal of the American Oriental Scoeity*, vol. 77, 1957, p. 223 a.
2. Diogenes Laërtius, 6, 72.
3. *Ibid.*, 6, 23.

sessions of Diogenes were only a club and a knapsack in addition to the regular dress of the Cynic, the single robe.[4] This style was public evidence of his ascetic way of life and his most popular sermons were those which urged his audience to spurn pleasures and a life of ease. Diogenes and his followers lived by begging, just as the Indian ascetics (*śramaṇa*) did.

Descriptions of the Roman Cynics exist in writings by Lucian, but that he was criticizing their behavior must be kept in mind. Lucian called the Cynics coarse buffoons who lacked culture, with bad manners, vulgar and obscene. He reports that one Peregrinus or Proteus, who had openly declared himself a Cynic, publicly set himself afire at Olympia and burned himself to death. In so doing, the Cynic was supposedly showing his disregard for death. Many Cynics of these later times, however, were simply adopting an ethical position of simplicity and virtue in reaction to the materialism and hedonism of their age.

The Indian counterpart to the Cynics was the Pāśupata sect; a willingness to seek dishonor being common to both the Cynics and the Pāśupatas. The cult of the Pāśupatas seems to have existed before the Christian era. The fundamental text of the cult, the *Pāśupata Sūtras*, thought perhaps to be ascribed to Lakulīśa (c. 100 A.D.), was commented upon by Kauṇḍinya (4th century A.D.). The cult was explained by later theologians such as Bhāsarvajña (10th century A.D.) and Madhava (14th century A.D.). The Pāśupatas, like the Cynics, exposed themselves regularly to scorn and actively sought dishonor even at the cost of blows. Their methods of exciting censure were various: the wearing of filthy garments, the use of violent and indecent language, the imitation of animals, the performance in public of acts that were ridiculous or which gave the impression of madness or which were interpreted by the society as obscene.

The ultimate goal of the Pāśupatas was freedom (*mokṣa*), which they understood to mean not only freedom from suffering but freedom to act without any inhibition. The latter implied omnipotence; being beyond the power of all others within one's powers, i.e., the nature of God (Rudra-Śiva) himself.[5] The Cynics, by undergoing the hardship of dishonor, hoped to equate themselves with the object of their worship, the hero Hercules, who was believed to hold a club, likewise the founder of the Pāśupata cult was called Lakulīśa, the "Lord of the Club." Pseudo-Diogenes urges one to be strong, through poverty and dishonor.[6] What

4. Some of following description concerning Greek and Indian instances of self-degradation we owe to Daniel H. H. Ingalls, "*Cynics and Pāśupatas, The Seeking of Dishonor,*" in *The Harvard Theological Review,* vol. LV, number 4, Oct., 1962, pp. 281–298.
5. *Pāśupata-Sūtra* I, 27–28.
6. Ep. Diog. 31.4.

he meant by dishonor (*adoxia*) is precisely what the Pāśupatas mean by *avamāna* (contempt). The Cynics urged their followers to unsocial actions in order ot gain strength,[7] just as the Pāśupatas sought to gain increase (*vṛddhi*) from similar acts.

However, a difference of intention between the Pāśupatas and Cynics is noticable. The former held the belief that one might transfer one's bad *karma* to another and receive his good *karma* in return, whereas the Cynics claimed that the philosopher who subjects himself to public censure is thereby benefitting the public, effecting an ethical cure of those whom he visits much as a physician effects a physical cure.

Han-shan (Kanzan) and Shih-te (Jittoku),[8] Chinese counterparts of the Cynics and Pāśupatas, were recluses in the Tang period. Han-shan lived in caves and on rocks and Shih-te lived in the precincts of a certain temple. When Han-shan came, Shih-te gave him the remaining scraps of meals forsaken by temple monks. They were given to suddenly shout or revile towards the sky. They wore ragged clothes and acted like mad persons. When a high official came to see them they departed, sending a smile to him in arrogance. It is said that they indulged in gaily sweeping away moonbeams, when they were not telling each other Zen jokes. They were regarded as the ideal of idiot sages. Han-shan, Shih-te and their admirers did not deliberately seek for dishonor, although when it came their way they did not resist it.

The terms free and freedom (*eleutheros, mukta, mokṣa, jizai*) are characteristic of the Cynics, the Pāśupatas, and the Lin-chi school of Zen Buddhism, whose ideal was closely related to that of Han-shan and Shih-te.

7. L. Vit. Auct. 1C; Dio. 8, 20; 9, 12.
8. Cf. *The Biographies of the High Priests of the Sung Period*, vol. 19. Their poems were compiled as *Han-shan-shih-te-shih-chi* (*Kanzan Jittoku Shishu*), compiled around 627–649 A.D.

F. Concluding Words

Heterodoxies in the eyes of universal religions appeared in parallel in both India and Greece and to a great extent in China, probably because these cultural areas reached more or less similar stages in the development of civilization. But in Japan and most other countries of Asia they did not appear. The culture in these countries developed directly from the stage of primitive religion to that of universal religion. That is, Buddhism was imported full-blown into their countries and was accepted by eminent unifying rulers, thereby eliminating any intermediate stages of aspects.

Those systems of thought which were later to be called heterodox have a number of things in common which may now be enumerated:

(1) Adherents thought very freely, minimizing or protesting against the traditions of the past, especially those of the already established religions of the people. In doing so they were advocating new theories which seemed very strange, even dangerous, to the people of their times.

(2) There were similarities in their proponents' ways of living. Generally they spent a great deal of time each year traveling. Some of them taught techniques of argument (which came to be thought of as the art of proving anything). Others sought to demonstrate the non-existence of God and afterlife or the uselessness of commonly held notions of virtue. But whatever their teaching, because they were controversial large crowds gathered wherever they lectured or debated, great halls being built to accommodate them, and sometimes royalty offered rewards to the victorious in the intellectual jousts.[1]

(3) They were all condemned as heterodox[2] by other ideologies or religions which were later more or less officially adopted by their respective societies.

(4) With the exception of Jainism, their traditions were lost except

1. Fairbanks and Reischauer, *East Asia*, pp. 62–63; cf. Sir Charles Eliot, *Hinduism and Buddhism*, 3 vols. (New York: Barnes and Noble, Inc., first published 1921, reprinted 1957)
2. Incidentally the word by which "heterodox" is usually translated into Chinese and Japanese actually means "different origins." (*Seirimondo Dialogue on Human Nature and Natural Order*. Tr. by Poplo Beonio-Brocchieri [Roma: Istituto per il Medio ed: Estremo Oriente, 1961], p. 47)

as transmitted by literary or religious works of other (usually later) scholars. In China some heterodox writings are extant, but as their traditions are lost, they are not easy to understand. Ordinarily, however, only fragments are left from which to conjecture defective and uncertain reconstructions of the major tenets of their systems.

Regardless of the extent to which the above characteristics may hold true, the sayings of the so-called "heterodox" thinkers of history are invaluable. The breadth of their creativity knew no barriers and hence because of their efforts, philosophical speculation is done within much more comfortable boundaries.

IV. CONCLUDING COMMENTS

One cannot over-emphasize the creativity and importance of the thinkers whose works were discussed in this chapter. They have had untold effect on our present ways of life and thinking. Their speculations laid the groundwork upon which the great religions (to be discussed next) were built. In addition, most modern-day schools of analytic and existentialist thought, as well as meditational or contemplative schools, can trace to them at least germinal forms of their respective ways of thought.

In the introduction to this chapter mention was made of intellectual ferment and social change, such as political instability and power struggles which often led to destruction and exile. The influence of these factors on the breakdown of old intellectual and religious traditions in favor of new principles for new times was stressed. But as a final tribute to the extent of accomplishment in this period mention must be made of the extreme tolerance that existed at least in some places under certain rule. By "tolerance" here allowing others freedom of thought and expression is especially meant.

Although unrest toward prevailing customs may trigger man's searching out new ways, the blossoming of various philosophical thoughts and religious systems is also largely due to the possibility for free thought within the society concerned. In addition freedom of thought is an indication of the respect given to each individual. In India such recognition of each person being an individual man worthy of respect occurred very early. Freedom of both thought and expression was permitted not only to hermits and philosophers, but to everyone else. Probably never before, and seldom since, has there been any place where such absolute liberty of thought was allowed. "In India, religious and philosophical thought enjoyed almost absolute freedom. Anyhow, it is certain that it enjoyed freedom so large as had never been found elsewhere in the West before the most recent years."[1]

Of course in India, as elsewhere, when mighty monarchs appeared, freedom of thought was threatened and thinkers often became wary of those in power. When the great Greek king Menander (2nd century B.C.) wanted to discuss metaphysical problems with a Buddhist monk,

1. Max Weber, *Hinduismus und Buddhismus. Gesammelte Anfsätze zur Religionssoziologie,* Bd.
2. Tübingen: J. C. B. Mohr (Paul Siebeck), 1923, p. 4.

Nāgasena, the latter demanded that the former agree to a principle of freedom of thought before entering into discussion.[2] Nāgasena explained:

"When scholars talk a matter over one with another then is there a winding up, an unravelling; one or other is convicted of error, and he then acknowledges his mistake; distinctions are drawn; and contradistinctions; and yet thereby they are not angered. Thus do scholars, O King, discuss."

"And how do kings discuss?"

"When a king, your Majesty, discusses a matter, and he advances a point, if anyone differ from him on that point, he is apt to find him, saying: 'Inflict such and such a punishment upon that fellow!' Thus, your Majesty, do kings discuss."

"Very well. It is as a scholar, not as a king, that I will discuss. Let your reverence talk unrestrainedly, as you would with a brother, or a novice, or a boy disciple, or even with a servant. Be not afraid!"[3]

This represents the situation in a much later period than that of the days when philosophy and heterodoxies arose in the cities. However, we assume that such freedom of thought as is pointed out in the above was, albeit inchoate, beginning to occur as a prerequisite for the initial appearance of philosophy and heterodoxy. For instance, the slave of a king in a very early Buddhist scripture is represented as having thought, "Would that I were like him that I too might earn merit! Why should not I have my hair and beard shaved off, and don the yellow robes, and going forth from the household state, renounce the world?" Thinking so, he entered a religious order. Thereafter even the king could no longer treat him as a slave, but rather greeted him with reverence and rose up from his seat out of deference to him.[4] One can see it taken for granted here that anyone who had devoted himself to the religious life, whatever the views or opinions he held or the association he had joined, would be treated with equal respect and courtesy, in accordance with the remarkable tolerance of that age and country.

In China, also, thinkers enjoyed considerable freedom of thought until it was suddenly cut short by the Ch'in dynasty (221–206 B.C.). What is commonly known as the Ante-Ch'in period is the period in which most varieties of thought appeared which were systematized throughout

2. *The Milindapañha*, ed. by Trenckner (London: Williams and Norgate, 1880), pp. 28–29.
3. Cf. Henry Clarke Warren, *Buddhism in Translations* (Cambridge, Mass.: Harvard University Press, 1896), p. 128.
4. *Dīgha-nikāya*, II, 35–6, vol. II, p. 60.

the entire subsequent history of Chinese philosophy. Chuang-tzu's social and political philosophy, for example, was one of complete liberty.[5]

Of Ionia, the birthplace of Western thought, and Greece, the area of its incubation, it has been said that when social life was settled, men could turn to rational reflection. Ionian philosophy was the fruit of an already mature civilization which is only thought of as "early" in relation to the Hellenic splendor to come in Athens.

Of course, the social settings posited herein have been oversimplified because of an emphasis, not on history as such, but rather on ideas. All the cultures discussed were in a state of flux and therefore conditions were subject to rapid reversal. Nowhere is this more true than Greece, where there had evolved a wide range of possibilities within the personality of the citizen: "As beneath the splendid achievements of Greek culture we see the abyss of slavery, so beneath the dream-world of Olympian religion and Olympian art we see the abyss of Dionysian frenzy, of pessimism and of all manner of lack of moderation."[6] One may recall the Athenian pattern of conquest which, at the height of Athenian splendor, resulted in, e.g., the enslavement of the women and children of the Melians as well as the death of all men of military age (undoubtedly including military-aged philosophers as well).

Of course the latter case was purely political and had nothing to do with the censorship of ideas. Of later days it is said, "When political power passed into the hands of the Macedonians, Greek philosophers, as was natural, turned aside from politics and devoted themselves more to the problem of individual virtue or salvation. They no longer asked: how can men create a good State? They asked instead: how can men be virtuous in a wicked world, or happy in a world of suffering?"[7] In the end, perhaps the most one can say is that urban centralization brought about civilizations in ancient days where even under changing rule men were able (unlike in some modern societies) to continue their philosophical pursuits. As the above quotation illustrates, the political change often tempered the resulting philosophical ideas. But very infrequently in ancient times were total restrictions placed upon a man's right to make his thoughts public.

5. Fun Yu-lan, *A History of Chinese Philosophy*, Princeton University Press, 1952, vol. I, p. 230 f.
6. Copleston, *A History of Philosophy*, Part I, p. 35.
7. B. Russell, *History of Western Philosophy*, p. 230.

CHAPTER THREE

Early Universal Religions

I. INTRODUCTORY REMARKS

This chapter is limited primarily to an examination of early Buddhism as compared with some major Occidental traditions, including early Christianity. "Early," however, is a relative term and one might suggest that Mohammedanism is also an early universal religion, the lifetime of its founder having extended from about 570–632 A.D. But Islam assumes a great deal that was already present in Christianity. Arabic thought is not neglected however but rather emerges with a discussion of the Middle Ages.

For a religion to attain universal (international) proportions it must have universal appeal. But in addition to such popular appeal, in order for any religion to spread there must exist within the supporting of a culture a certain amount of dissatisfaction with the religious or social status quo. This background, so far as early community thought as well as philosophical developments is concerned, has been partly established in the preceding chapters. In pre-Buddhist India such figures as the hedonist Pūraṇa Kassapa, the determinist Gosāla, the materialist Ajita Kasakambala, and the atomist Pakudha Kaccāyana emerged; while in the Greco-Roman world Jesus was preceded by cosmological thinkers such as Heraclitus, ethico-mystics such as the Pythagoreans and Platonists, and more contemporary to his time, Epicureans and Stoics.

Gotama the Buddha was perhaps more affected by previous ways of thought than was Jesus. In the Pāli Nikāyas are found references to many of the Indian thinkers mentioned above; however, in the New Testament one is more likely to encounter the names of political groups (politics and religion being inseparable at that time in the Hebrew world). Anyone who has read the New Testament will recall such groups as the Saduccees, Pharisees, and Samaritans.

Gotama and Jesus each encountered their environment in considerably different ways. Gotama was raised and educated isolated on his father's palace grounds much in the manner of the young Alexander of Macedon, though probably on a less grandiose scale. His first contact with the "outside world" affected him profoundly. Jesus, on the other hand, was brought up in a small town as a carpenter's son. In that area there was considerable intermixing of Jewish and Gentile peoples, who were all a politically conquered lot. While they were legally under Rome's jurisdiction, the nearest seat of strong Roman power was some distance away in Jerusalem. There the leaders of the Jewish tribes had opportunistically accepted Roman rule for some time and were reaping the political rewards thereof. This political favor never reached far into the hands of the common folk, however who resented such obvious sell-outs to Rome. Jesus' youth was spent in Galilee, where people such as the Zealots, whose strength was centered in that area, were actively resisting Roman control. Thus writings such as the following suggest that Jesus expected to see the beginnings of the realized Kingdom of God among the poor:[1]

> "Blessed are you poor, for yours is the Kingdom of God.
> "Blessed are you that hunger now, for you shall be satisfied.
> "Blessed are you that weep now, for you shall laugh."[2]

Perhaps Jesus foresaw how the great political strength of Rome would prevail in Galilee (67 A.D.) and, after the Zealots had fled there to defend her, in Jerusalem also (70 A.D.). For he recommended not violent resistance but rather: ". . . Love your enemies, do good to those who hate you, bless those who curse you, pray for those who abuse you. To him who strikes you on the cheek, offer the other also; . . . and of him who takes away your goods do not ask them again. And as you wish that men would do to you, do so to them."[3]

Gotama did not encounter societal hardship until later in life than Jesus, although when he did, it affected him momentously. Rather, Gotama's formative years seem to have been spent in an environment of the conflict of ideas, most of which he was later to reject. Pantheism in the early Upaniṣads (already existing in his time), hedonistic ethics an also ethics of extreme asceticism, primitive animism, annihilistic and eternalistic philosophies (the latter including the Brahmanic religious goal of absolute Being-Knowledge-Bliss, *sat-cit-ānanda*) were all thriving in the Gotama's youth. He was to reject most of these on philosophical grounds but there were other reasons as well.

Philosophical Hinduism was highly speculative and served the elite of Indian society. Naturally the Brahmanic priesthood was serving the same elitist interests (which, like the priesthood of Christ's time, coincided with their private interests). Hence they had little more to offer a religious visionary than a costly and tiresome ceremonialism in which the practitioners' claims that their charms were stronger than the gods had resulted in a general lack of priestly credibility.

Already disenchanted with the intellectual milieu of his time, Buddha came to the major turning point in his life when at age 29 he became

1. Luke 6:20–26.
2. *Ibid.*
3. Luke 6:27–31.

aware of suffering and death. His subsequent teachings stressed Impermanence (Sanskrit *anitya*, Pāli *anicca*) and Non-ego (Sanskrit *anātman*, Pāli *anattā*) in opposition to the Brahmanic ideals of Being (*sat*) and Self (*ātman*).

As a result, much in the same way that the early Christians were called "atheists"[4] by the Romans, the Buddhists (and the Jains) were called "nihilists"[5] (*nāstikas*) by orthodox Hindus. But the people who heard the messages of Jesus and Gotama were for the most part prepared to accept their teachings due to the social and ideological reasons sketched above. In addition, these two founders perfectly embodied the overwhelmingly positive ideals they taught, a factor that became more important perhaps in Christianity than in Buddhism.[6] Hence, despite condemnation and resistance from the "establishment" of their times, Buddhism and Christianity took root and flourished.

Irrespective of whatever comparisons it is possible to make, there are still vast differences between these major world religions. These differences stem largely from (1) the philosophical background into which they were articulated (e.g., the major Western view of the tripartite nature of the soul as discussed in the previous chapter) and (2) the significance of the death of the founder in each tradition.

4. E.g., to the common charge against the early Christians, based on the fact that Christians refused to offer sacrifice to the pagan idols and imperial statues, Saint Justin the Martyr asserted that Christians are not atheists ("The First Apology," chapter 6, as given in *The Fathers of the Church*, vol. 6, *Writings of Saint Justin Martyr*, translated into English by Thomas B. Falls and edited by Ludwig Schopp [New York: Christian Heritage, 1948], pp. 38–39).
5. In Hindu synoptical works of Indian philosophy such as the *Sarvasiddhāntasaṃgraha*, *Sarvadarśanasaṃgraha*, *Sarvamatasaṃgraha*, *Prasthānabheda*, etc., Buddhism was placed next to materialism (*Lokāyata*), which means that Buddhism was regarded as the second worst teaching in the world in the eyes of Hindu orthodoxy. This tendency has now disappeared in India, where Hindus have gradually elevated Buddhism to a branch of Hinduism.
6. Although it would be difficult to overestimate the influence on his followers of the Buddha's life and enlightenment.

II. THE IDEAL IMAGE OF THE FOUNDERS

A. Their Lives

1. Birth and Youthful Days

THE legend that arose quite early concerning the birth of the Buddha is to a surprising degree similar to that of the birth of Christ. Oliver Wendell Holmes once remarked that, "If one were told that many centuries ago a celestial ray shone into the body of a sleeping woman, as it seemed to her in her dream; that thereupon the advent of a wondrous child was predicted by the soothsayers; that angels appeared at this child's birth; that merchants came from afar, bearing gifts to him; that an ancient saint recognized the babe as divine and fell at his feet and worshipped him; that in his eighth year the child confounded his teachers with the amount of his knowledge, still showing them due reverence; that he grew up full of compassionate tenderness to all that lived and suffered; that to help his fellow-creatures he sacrificed every worldly prospect and enjoyment; that he went through the ordeal of a terrible temptation, in which all the powers of evil were let loose upon him, and came out a conquerer over them all; that he preached holiness and practiced charity; that he gathered disciples and sent out apostles, who spread his doctrine over many lands and peoples; that this 'Helper of the Worlds' could claim a more than earthly lineage and a life that dated from long before Abraham was, of whom would he think this wonderful tale was told? Would he not say at once that this must be another version of the story of One who came upon our earth in a Syrian village, during the reign of Augustus Caesar, and died by violence during the reign of Tiberius? What would he say if he were told that the narrative was between five and six centuries older than that of the Founder of Christianity?"[1] He was speaking of the legend of the Buddha.

1. Arthur Christy, *The Orient in American Transcendentalism, A Study of Emerson, Thoreau and Alcott* (New York: Columbia University Press, 1932), pp. 255 f.

Gotama was born at Kapilavatthu (Sanskrit, Kapilavastu), the principal town in the territory of the Sākiya clan (Sākiya or Śākya means "powerful"). This area is situated about one hundred and fifty miles nearly due north of Benares, at the foot of the Himalayan range in the southeast of what is now Nepal. He was born the son of a local prince at a date believed to be 463 B.C.[2] His father's name, Suddhodana (lit. "Pure Rice"), is suggestive of the occupation followed by the clan. They cultivated the peaceful arts of agriculture in a small territory, not exceeding about nine hundred square miles in extent, partly on the lower slopes of the Himalayas, partly on the plains below. In later India the Buddhists were called "Sauddhodani" (descendants of Suddhodana).[3]

Legend has it that with the births of both the Gotama and Jesus unnatural events occurred. At the moment of birth of the Buddha the ordinary course of all activity of mankind and nature was said to have been suddenly interrupted with auspicious and miraculous phenomena.[4] A non-canonical work claims similar happenings at the time of Christ's birth.[5]

Many miracles are associated with these two religious leaders. But whereas Jesus "performed" them, miracles are linked with the very birth of Gotama. It is said that the blind received their sight by longing to see the coming glory of the Lord; the deaf and dumb spoke with one another

2. The birthdate of Buddha mentioned here is different from the general assumption which is chiefly based on Theravāda sources. The late Hakuju Ui fixed the dates of the Buddha at 466–386 B.C., adopting legends set forth in the Sanskrit, Tibetan, and Chinese versions of Buddhist scriptures, such as the *Samayabheda-uparacana-cakra* (Hakuju Ui, *Indo Tetsugaku Kenkyū*, vol. 2 [Tokyo: Koshisha, 1926], pp. 1–113). Because the date of King Aśoka, the starting point for chronological investigations, should be altered in the light of recent research, Hajime Nakamura proposed that H. Ui's chronology should be modified to 463–383 B.C., following him on the main points of his studies (Hajime Nakamura, "The Date of the Mauryan Dynasty," in *Tōhō Gakuhō*, No. 10, 1955, pp. 1 ff.; also in his *Indo Kodai shi* [Ancient History of India] [Tokyo: Shunjusha, 1966], vol. 2, pp. 409–437). Studies by Japanese scholars exerted influence on scholars who are native Chinese. Rev. Yin-shun, the Chinese scholar and priest, criticizing the dates of the Buddha adopted by Western and South Asiatic scholars, set the date of the Parinirvāna as 390 B.C. The reasons are not very different from those adopted by Ui.
3. Cf. 'Sons of Abraham', Galatians 3:7.
4. *Lalitavistara* VII and *Buddhacarita* I, 25–44. Some of these phenomena had already been mentioned in *Suttanipāta*, vv. 697–700 (*Nālaka-sutta*).
5. The moment of the birth of Jesus is described as follows: "I looked up unto the pole of the heaven and saw it standing still, and the fowls of the heaven without motion. And I looked upon the earth and saw a dish set, and workmen lying by it, and their hands were in the dish: and they that were chewing chewed not, and they that were lifting the food lifted it not. . ." (Book of James 18:2, as given in *The Apocryphal New Testament*, translated by M. R. James [Oxford: Clarendon Press, 1953], p. 46). Also in the same source it is claimed that when Jesus was born "a bright could [was] overshadowing the cave . . . and a great light appeared in the cave" (19:2).

of the good omens indicating the birth of the Buddha. The crooked became straight; the lame walked. All prisoners were freed from their chains and the fires of all the hells were extinguished.[6] In the New Testament we find the following description: "The blind receive their sight and the lame walk, lepers are cleansed and the deaf hear, and the dead are raised up, and the poor have good news preached to them."[7]

The Buddhist canon declares that at the time of Gotama's birth, kings,[8] as they had before paid honor to former Buddhas, now went to meet Gotama. They scattered before him *mandāra* flowers, rejoicing with heartfelt joy to pay their homage.[9] When Jesus was born, wise men came from the east to Jerusalem to worship the babe, saying, "Where is he who has been born King of the Jews? For we have seen his star in the East, and have come to worship him."[10]

In a later Buddhist legend, the queen mother, beholding her child and the commotion which his birth created, felt in her timorous woman's heart the pangs of doubt. But at her couch stood an aged woman imploring the divine beings to bless the child.[11] Likewise, the New Testament relates that when Christ was born, near Mary the mother was one Anna, a prophetess, said to have been of great age. This woman reportedly never departed from the temple, worshipping with fasting and prayer night and day. At the moment Simeon (below) was proclaiming his faith that Jesus was the Christ child, she came up and "gave thanks to God, and spoke of him to all who were looking for the redemption of Jerusalem."[12]

When the Buddha was born, Asita, a seer who lived in Kapilavatthu, came to see him and foretold that the babe would become a great saint or king. According to an ancient Buddhist ballad,[13] Asita, seeing the flocks of Tidasa gods rejoicing, asked them why they were glad. They replied:

"The Wisdom Child, that jewel so precious,
That cannot be matched,
Has been born in Lumbini, in the Sakiya land,

6. *Buddhist Birth Stories, or Jataka Tales.* The oldest collection of folk-lore extant, being the *Jātakatthavaṇṇanā*, for the first time edited in the original Pali by Michael Viggo Fausböll and translated by Thomas William Rhys Davids, vol. 1 (London: Trübner, 1880), p. 64. Cf. Henry C. Warren, *Buddhism in Translations* (Cambridge, Mass.: Harvard University Press, 1896), pp. 38–48.
7. Matthew 11:5. Cf. Mark 7:32–37.
8. The serpent (*Nāga*) kings.
9. The *Fo-sho-hing-tsan-ching*, vv. 22–24.
10. Matthew 2:1–2.
11. The *Fo-sho-hing-tsan-ching*, vv. 39–40.
12. Luke 2:36–37.
13. Nālaka-sutta in the *Suttanipāta.*

For weal and for joy in the world of men."[14]

Subsequently, as the story goes, the old sage went there, and seeing the baby, prophesied: "The topmost height of insight will he reach, this child, he will see that which is most pure, and will set rolling the chariot wheel of righteousness, he who is full of compassion for the multitude. Far will his religion spread."[15] Asita may be termed the Buddhist equivalent of the Christian Simeon.

After the birth of Christ, Simeon, a just and devout man, took him up in his arms, and blessed God, crying,

"Lord, now lettest thou thy servant
depart in peace,
according to thy word;
for mine eyes have seen thy salvation
which thou hast prepared in the
presence of all peoples,
a light for revelation to the Gentiles,
and for glory to thy people Israel."[16]

The Buddha was brought up in Kapilavatthu, the capital of the Sākiyas, by the second wife of Suddhodana, Mahapajāpatī, for his own mother had died seven days after his birth. In later legend he was depicted as a youth of genius. When the kinsfolk of the city gathered to test the prowess and scholarship of the prince, he proved himself manly in all the exercises both of the body and of the mind. There was no rival among the youths and men of India who could surpass him in any test, bodily or mental. He replied to all the questions of the sages; but when he questioned them even the wisest among them were silenced.[17]

Jesus, when he was a boy, is depicted in much the same way in the New Testament. "After three days they found him in the temple, sitting among the teachers, listening to them, and asking them questions; and all who heard him were amazed at his understanding and his answers."[18] Trees were said to have bent down before the young Jesus and dragons to have adored him. At school he supposedly convicted his teacher of ignorance.[19]

14. *Suttanipāta*, 683; Rhys Davids, *Early Buddhism* (London: A. Constable, 1910), p. 29.
15. Rhys Davids, *ibid.*, p. 30.
16. Luke 2:25–32.
17. Paul Carus, *Gospel of the Buddha, According to Old Records* (Chicago: Open Court Press, New York, 1894; Reissue 1930), pp. 10–11.
18. Luke 2:46–47.
19. "In the hearing of many the young child saith to Zacchaeus: Hear, O teacher, the ordinance of the first letter and pay heed to this. . . . Now when Zacchaeus the teacher heard such and so many allegories of the first letter spoken by the young child, he was

When the Buddha was taken to the temple for Hindu baptism, he pointed out that it was unnecessary, as he was superior to the gods, though he conformed to the practice of the world. In the West, "Jesus came from Galilee to the Jordan to John, to be baptized by him. John would have prevented him, saying, 'I need to be baptized by you, and do you come to me?' But Jesus answered him, 'Let it be so now; for thus it is fitting for us to fulfill all righteousness.' " Thereupon he consented, and Jesus was baptized.[20] Hindu baptism, however, never came to have the significance it was given in Christianity.

Even incidental events in the legends of Jesus and Buddha sometimes show a remarkable similarity. For instance, when Gotama and his retinue passed by the palaces of the nobility, Kisā Gotamī, a young princess and niece of the king, saw Siddhārtha and observing the thoughtfulness of his countenance remarked, "Happy the father that begot you, happy the mother that nursed you, happy the wife that calls husband this lord so glorious." The prince, hearing this greeting, responded, "Happy are they that have found deliverance. Longing for peace of mind, I shall seek the bliss of Nirvāṇa." And handing her his precious pearl necklace as a reward for the instruction she had given him, he returned home.[21]

In the life of Jesus one finds a similar incident: "As he said this, a woman in the crowd raised her voice and said to him, 'Blessed is the womb that bore you, and the brests that you sucked!' But he said, 'Blessed rather are those who hear the word of God and keep it!' "[22]

These comparisons from the writings on the early lives of Jesus and Gotama the Buddha are probably legendary. However, as in the next section, without going deeply into problems of historical authenticity, they are offered not as history but for their comparative value in showing the descriptions their followers have given of two of the world's foremost religious leaders.

---

perplexed at his answer and his instruction being so great, and said to them that were there: Woe is me, wretch that I am, I am confounded" (Gospel of Thomas VI, 4–VII, 1, as given in *The Apocryphal New Testament*, p. 51). It is an interesting coincidence that in Vajrayana Buddhism also the first letter, i.e., *a*, was regarded as the fundamental principle of the universe, and this has been conveyed to Japanese Vajrayāna Buddhism. Cf. *Lalitavistara* X.

20. Matthew 3:13–15.
21. *Buddhist Birth Stories*, pp. 79–80; *The Life of the Buddha and the Early History of his Order. Derived from Tibetan works in the bKah-hgyur and bsTan-hgyur. Followed by notices on the early history of Tibet and Khotan*, translated by William Woodville Rockhill (London: Trübner, 1884), p. 23.
22. Luke 11:27–28.

2. Spiritual Activities

ACCORDING to legend, when Gotama decided to leave his father's palace for the life of a mendicant, *Māra*, the Evil One, stood in the gate and stopped him: "Depart not, O my Lord," he exclaimed, "in seven days from now the wheel of empire will appear, and will make you sovereign over the four continents and the two thousand adjacent islands. Therefore, stay, my Lord." To this Gotama replied: "Well do I know that the wheel of empire will appear to me; but it is not sovereignty that I desire. I will become a Buddha and make all the world shout for joy."[1] The Evil One could not dissuade him from his intention.

Gotama became a wanderer and devoted himself to severe asceticism for six years in the jungles at Uruvela. During that time he lived on seeds and grass, and for one period he fed on dung. Gradually, it is said, he reduced his food to a grain of rice each day. He wore hair cloth, plucked out his hair and beard for torture's sake, stood for long hours, or lay upon thorns. He let the dust and dirt accumulate upon his body until he looked like an old tree. He frequented a place where human corpses were exposed to be eaten by birds and beasts, and slept among the rotting carcasses. And he reportedly said, "My body became extremely lean. The mark of my seat was like a camel's footprint through the little food. . . . When I thought I would touch the skin of my stomach I actually took hold of my spine."[2] Nearly at the point of death he came to believe that this method was not the right path; no new enlightenment had come to him from his austerities. "By this severity I do not attain super-human, truly noble knowledge and insight." He abandoned his asceticism, bathed in the river of Nerañjanā, and began to eat again.[3]

After ceasing the practice of austerities, legends account that many Evil Ones (*Māra*) wanted to distract Gotama's attention from his meditation and turn him from his purpose. They threatened him with violent assaults and tried to seduce him with alluring temptations. The Evil One said, "Thou art emaciated from fasts, and death is near. What good is thy exertion? Deign to live, and thou wilt be able to do good works." But the Evil Ones did not succeed. Instead Gotama replied, "O thou friend of the indolent, thou wicked one; for what purpose hast thou come? Let the flesh waste away, if but the mind becomes more tranquil and attention more steadfast. What is life in this world? Death in battle is better to me than that I should live defeated."[4] And the Evil One left Gotama, saying,

1. *Buddhist Birth Stories*, p. 84.
2. Edward Jasper Thomas, *The Life of Buddha as Legend and History* (New York: Barnes and Noble, 1952), p. 54.
3. *Majjhima-nikāya* I, 247; Rhys Davids, *Early Buddhism*, p. 35.
4. *Suttanipāta* 425, 439.

"For seven years I followed the Blessed One step by step, but I found no fault in the Enlightened One."[5] Perhaps the temptations of the Evil One in the legends allegorize the struggle in Gotama's mind.

We have reports in the New Testament, though not in such vivid detail as those in the legend of Gotama, of Jesus' also having undergone austerities. Subsequent to his baptism by John he apparently had a vision of his own religious significance. Thereupon he retired to "the wilderness"[6] where he stayed for "forty days and forty nights"[7] and from time to time "was with the wild beasts."[8] And as the story goes, he became quite hungry, for it was not until after his temptations (below) had ceased that "angels came and ministered to him."[9]

Jesus, like Gotama, encountered many temptations, including great wealth, which threatened a disruption of his solitude. Having withdrawn from the world to the wilderness for fasting, at a time when his resistance was particularly low, the temptor came to him and said, "If you are the Son of God, command these stones to become loaves of bread." But Jesus answered, "It is written, Man shall not live by bread alone, but by every word that proceeds from the mouth of God."[10]

Eventually the temptor led Jesus to a towering mountain "and showed him all the kingdoms of the world and the glory of them;" and he said to Jesus, "All these I will give you if you will fall down and worship me." But Jesus' reply is said to have been: "Begone, Satan! for it is written, 'you shall worship the Lord your God and him only shall you serve.' "[11] Whereupon the temptor, having failed in all attempts to corrupt Jesus, left him. Subsequently, angels were said to appear and minister to his hunger.

Having prevailed over *Māra*, Gotama's meditation could then bear fruit. Seated under the "Bo-tree" on a bed of grass, he remained facing the east, steadfast and motionless, with his mind fixed to a purpose: "Never will I leave this seat until I have attained the supreme and absolute wisdom." He spent seven weeks under the tree, concentrating his mind on meditation. At last, with an effect of abrupt illumination, he realized the truth. In his deeply meditative mood, a new light broke upon his mind. He experienced the Great Awakening, and afterwards was known as Buddha, the "Awakened One."

5. *Suttanipāta* 445.
6. Mark 1:12.
7. Matthew 4:2.
8. Mark 1:13.
9. Matthew 4:11.
10. Matthew 4:3–4. Cf. Luke 4:1–4; Mark 1:13.
11. Matthew 4:10.

In the life of Jesus there is no detailed description of an event corresponding to the Buddha's enlightenment. However, after his earlier baptism with the assistance of John, it was said of Jesus, "the heavens were opened" to him.[12] Although there are textual problems regarding the New Testament (just as with the Buddhist canon) as to what has been added at later times, there is an account of Jesus fulfilling a prophecy from Isaiah. In Matthew the prophecy Jesus is said to have fulfilled (by going to the places mentioned therein) is:

> The land of Zeb'ulun and the land of Naph'tali, toward
> the sea, across the Jordan, Galilee of the Gentiles—
> the people who sat in darkness have seen a great light,
> and for those who sat in the region and shadow of death
> light has dawned.[13]

It was after his odyssey to those places that Jesus began to preach.

If more were known about it the apostle Paul's experience on the road to Damascus might be comparable to the Buddha's experience of enlightenment. The New Testament account includes the statement, "I saw on the way a light from heaven, brighter than the sun, shining round me and those who journeyed with me."[14] However, from the available evidence, the Damascus experience as well as Jesus' past baptismal experience has a considerably different feeling than the Buddhist enlightenment because of the God of Christianity. A large part of the account of Paul's experience, for instance, includes the voice of Jesus giving him instructions for the future. In Jesus' baptismal experience a dove came down from heaven and Jesus heard the voice of his heavenly father praising his actions. On the contrary, the Buddha had no awareness of any superior entity having influence on him. What he became aware of was the *dharma*, the universal law.

When the resolve to teach the *dharma* had become manifest in Buddha's mind,[15] in a deer park near Benares he gave his first discourse, which people later called the "Foundation of the Kingdom of Righteousness." Therein Buddha summarized his views for the five who were present, and he tried to persuade them to give up their belief in penance. Only one of them, Kondañña by birth, was at first convinced. But in the course of a few days all of them gave way and became his disciples. Here the Buddhist Order (*saṅgha*) was first established.

Soon residents in the neighboring townships came to listen to the new teacher. The number of adherents, laymen and laywomen, monks and

12. Matthew 4:16. Cf. Mark 1:9–11; Luke 3:21–22; John 1:31–34.
13. Matthew 4:12–17.
14. Acts 26:13.
15. *Mahāvagga.* Rhys Davids, *Early Buddhism*, pp. 39–40.

nuns, increased, and Gotama said to them that he and they "were free from snares, whether human or divine." He told them to "go forth as wanderers for the sake of the many, for the welfare of the many, out of compassion for the world, for the good and the weal and the gain of gods and men." No two were to go together. They were to make the teaching "lovely in its origin, lovely in its progress, lovely in its consummation, both in the spirit and in the letter; to explain the higher life in all its fullness and in all its purity."[16]

Both the Buddha and his disciples spent nine months of each year wandering from village to village, making the new teaching known to those who cared to hear. They held no public meetings, gave no set discourses; the word was spread by means of conversation alone. His discourses took the form of Socratic-like questioning, moral parables, courteous controversy, or succinct formulas whereby he sought to compress his teaching into convenient brevity and order. A disciple extolled him as follows:

> The Buddha has told the causes
> Of all things springing from causes,
> And also how they find their rest;
> Tis this the mighty sage proclaims.[17]

Jesus, in teaching his disciples, praised the poor and suffering in the world, the meek and hungry, and those who make peace.[18] Like the Buddha, he stressed "the law," from which "not an iota, not a dot" would pass until "all is accomplished."[19] He embraced the same moral commandments that Moses had reportedly received, according to the Old Testament.[20]

The traditional number of the first group of Jesus' disciples, as reflected in the New Testament,[21] was twelve. Therein it is written that these twelve were counselled to carry their message to only a select group, as Jesus sent them out charging them: "Go nowhere among the Gentiles, and enter no town of the Samaritans, but go rather to the lost sheep of the house of Israel. And preach as you go, saying, 'The Kingdom of heaven is at hand.' Heal the sick, raise the dead, cleanse lepers, cast out demons. You received without pay, give without pay. Take no gold, nor silver, nor copper in your belts, no bag for your journey, nor two tunics, nor sandals,

16. *Suttanipāta* I, 105; *Vinaya* I, 21.
17. Cf. Warren, *Buddhism in Translations*, pp. 87–91.
18. Matthew 5:1–9.
19. Matthew 5:18.
20. Matthew 5:21.
21. Matthew 10 is a convenient summary of their names and authority.

nor a staff; for the laborer deserves his food. And whatever town or village you enter, find out who is worthy in it, and stay with him until you depart. . . ."[22] It is natural then that in the beginning the number of disciples multiplied greatly in Jerusalem, including in their number many of the priests.[23]

Later on, the disciples began to travel more widely (partly because they were scattered by persecution).[24] And though they travelled as far as Phoenicia and Cyprus, they still spoke their message to none but Jews.[25] But some who came to Antioch began introducing the words of Jesus to the Greeks.[26] When they were received formally be great numbers of the Greeks, Paul went to Antioch, ultimately remaining for a year. Thereafter, the New Testament records that "in Antioch the disciples were for the first time called Christians."[27]

The sanction for the disciples to spread eventually their doctrine to non-Jews is now contained in the New Testament. Whether or not it was added at a later time is too large a problem to treat adequately here. In his meeting with the disciples after his reputed resurrection, Jesus' words were recorded as follows, "All authority in heaven and on earth has been given to me. Go therefore and make disciples of all nations, baptizing them in the name of the Father and of the Son and of the Holy Spirit, teaching them to observe all that I have commanded you; and lo, I am with you always, to the close of the age."[28]

Among many disciples of the Buddha, Sāriputta was esteemed as the foremost one. The Buddha said, "Sāriputta is like the first-born son of a world-ruling monarch who assists the king as his chief follower to set the wheel of the law a-rolling."[29] In like manner, the Christ said, "You are Peter, and on this rock I will build my church and . . . I will give you the keys of the kingdom of heaven."[30] Citing this, Roman Catholics claim that the Master gave to Peter a power which Peter passed on to the bishops at Rome. In contrast, no Buddhist order claimed its lineage from Sāriputta alone. Incidentally, as St. Paul was most effective in spreading the Gospel in the Hellenistic world, so Mahā-moggallāna, who was often extolled

22. Matthew 10:5–11.
23. Acts 5:7.
24. Acts 11:19.
25. *Ibid.*
26. Acts 11:20.
27. Acts 11:26.
28. Matthew 28:18–20.
29. *Vinaya,* Mahāvagga I, 23. *Vinaya Texts.* Translated from the Pâli by Thomas William Rhys Davids and Hermann Oldenberg. 3 parts, *Sacred Books of the East,* vol. XIII (Oxford: Clarendon Press, 1831), pp. 13–14.
30. Matthew 16:18–19.

side by side with Sāriputta, was most influential in spreading the teaching of the Buddha throughout India and finally to Ceylon.

Many disciples gathered around Buddha and his fame as a sage spread through the cities of northern India. When his father heard that Buddha was near Kapilavatthu, he sent a messenger to him with an invitation to come and spend a day in his boyhood home. According to a legend, the Buddha entered his native city triumphantly.[31] As he approached, marvelous rays proceeded from him, lighting up the gates and walls, towers and monuments. The city, like the New Jerusalem illumined by the lamp, was full of light, and all the citizens went forth to meet him. But the Buddha remained unmoved.

A legend in the West relates that when Jesus entered a temple in Etypt the images prostrated themselves before him. This also occurred to the young Gotama in the temple at Kapilavatthu.[32]

For forty-five years after attaining enlightenment, Buddha travelled up and down the Gangetic plains of northern India and into the neighboring highlands of Nepal. It was very much as Jesus did in Judea and Galilee. And just as, in later legends, Jesus is said to have once left Galilee and journeyed to Egypt, so the Buddha is said by his native authorities to have visited Ceylon, but such statements are generally considered legendary.

The influence of the Buddha increased with the assistance and support of kings, landowners, merchants, and people of other classes. It is said that he was extolled by men and even the gods took refuge in him. The following is an account of Buddha's triumphant entry into Rājagaha: "Now the honoured one and all his followers go forward to the royal city. . . . King Bimbisāra hearing thereof, with all his company of courtiers, lords and ladies all surrounding him, came to where the master was. Then at a distance seeing the Buddha seated, with humbled heart and subdued presence, putting off his common ornaments, descending from his chariot, forward he stepped. . . . With different mouths, but in language one, they magnified and praised this wondrous spectacle . . . (exclaiming) 'The Buddha is our great teacher! We are the honoured one's disciples.' "[33]

In the life of Jesus a similar kind of cheering and jubilation is depicted. When Jesus entered Jerusalem, the royal city of his area, "Most of the

31. Cf. Luke 2:41 f.

32. "Jesus said he would shorten the way—and even as he spoke they began to see the hills and cities of Egypt. They arrived at Hermopolis and entered a city called Sotinen, and had to lodge in a temple where were 365 gods. When Mary and the Child entered, all the idols fell. . . . When he [governor of the city] saw them fallen he adored the child" (Gospel of Pseudo Matthew XXII-XXIV, as given in *The Apocryphal New Testament*, p. 75); *Lalitavistara* 8.

33. The *Fo-sho-hing-tsan-ching*, vv. 1335–1356 (cited from *Sacred Books of the East*, vol. XIX, pp. 187–190, with slight alteration).

crowd spread their garments on the road, and others cut branches from the trees and spread them on the road. And the crowds that went before him and that followed him shouted, 'Hosanna to the son of David! Blessed be he who comes in the name of the Lord! Hosanna in the highest!' And when he entered Jerusalem, all the city was stirred, saying, 'Who is this?' And the crowds said, 'This is the prophet Jesus from Nazareth of Galilee.' "[34]

Neither the Buddha nor Jesus was welcomed always by everyone. Devadatta, his cousin, followed Buddha at first but later became jealous of him and sent a fierce elephant against him. But Buddha "pervaded it with love," and it become subdued.[35] Such an act is reminiscent of Jesus' reaction to his betrayal by Judas Iscariot who brought the Roman soldiers upon him. However, the sufferings experienced by the Buddha at the hands of his society were not so great as those of Jesus, as is most clear from the deaths of both. In spite of the many remarkable similarities that have been pointed out, the ways of dying of both founders were vastly different, the one calmly surrounded by his disciples and followers, and the other crucified amidst the vilification of rulers and "establishment" priests. This difference was decisive in the later development of both religions.

34. Matthew 21:9–11. Cf. Mark 11:1–10; Luke 19:28–38; John 12:12–15.
35. E. J. Thomas, *op. cit.*, p. 134.

B. Faith

1. Significance of Faith

PRELIMINARY to a more specific discussion of faith in early Buddhism and Christianity, a short mention of some different general uses of the word "faith" might be useful. Beginning with the least relevant to the present emphasis, one may distinguish the use of "faith" to mean sincerity, honesty, or with good motives.[1] The word "bonafide" as used in English reflects this meaning, i.e., "genuine." In Latin, of course, it is "*bona fide,*" corresponding to the English phrase "(in) good faith."

A second usage of "faith" in English which is less important here but subsidiary to the main discussion is the use of the word to mean a religion or body of teachings. If one says of someone, "He belongs to the Christian faith," he is referring to a body of doctrine which that person has embraced.

This section deals primarily with what it means to embrace a doctrine in Christianity and Buddhism. That is, emphasis is on usages of the word "faith" in the sense either of belief or hope (the latter thought of as desire plus expectation). Attention will be given to the role that faith (in either sense) plays in each of the two religions. These preliminary delineations are sketchy but will be expanded as their applications become more specific.

Consider the question, "If faith is the devotion of a man to that which commands his trust, what ways are there that he is in this sense commanded?" If he is commanded by (i.e., follows) his intellect or rationality one might correctly say that his faith is a *belief* in the object of the faith. On the other hand, if he is commanded, that is, overwhelmingly drawn by his reaction to an object of faith, one might accurately say he is disposed toward that object in such a way that he would be greatly surprised if his initial reaction was inconsistent with fact. The latter is close to *hope.* Though faith and hope are thought to be different in the New Testament[2] both of these "commands" are found in Christianity as well as Buddhism.

1. "My views have often been grossly misrepresented, bitterly opposed and ridiculed, but this has been generally done, as I believe, in good faith" (Autobiography of Charles Darwin).
2. I Corinthians 13:13.

Part of the difference, however in the two religions is in their emphasis on one instead of the other conception of faith.

In Buddhism, faith or confidence (*saddhā*; Sanskrit *śraddhā*) is not specifically mentioned as a part of the prescribed Eightfold Path. But one of the steps therein is "right volition," that is, man directing his own intellect toward the Four Noble Truths of Buddhism. The Buddha hoped to encourage this by commanding man's reason,[3] thus giving him confidence in the Buddhist path. Philosophically, the Buddha's tactic was an appeal to experience[4] (his own), in which he claimed, by virtue of his *nirvāṇa* that knowing (*jānaṃ*) based on "seeing" (*passaṃ*) proved everything to be causally and dependently in flux (i.e., origination and dissipation). From this experience he was able to "induce" the major Buddhist concept of *karma*[5] (doing or the energy for doing). The reasoning of many Buddhists is undoubtedly captured sufficiently by explanations by the Buddha of creation and experience (especially with regard to *karma*[6]) to follow the Buddha's path with the end in mind of experiencing his truths themselves. The Buddha promised that a sincere, intelligent, honest and straightforward person conducting himself on the Enlightened One's instructions, ". . . before long . . . would himself know and see."[7]

So it seems that ideally Buddhist faith is meant to be provisional. It represents a person's confidence enough in the Buddha's teachings of his experience to start on the Buddhist path for himself. The end of the path is the enlightened "blowing out" (*nirvāṇa*) of attachment to things. Rather than having absolute significance, faith in Buddhism is preliminary, the key that unlocks the door of the ideal state. In the scriptures it is sometimes likened to a seed,[8] sometimes to a part of the chariot of salvation,[9] some-

3. Buddha is not being thought of here as a rationalist in the sense of the Continental Rationalists of modern Western philosophy, attempting to find truth by reasoning from self-evident first principles.
4. Though Buddha thought of experience as being that which is commonly verifiable by the senses, he also often meant that experience which is extraordinary, individual, and therefore not often occurring to groups of people at the same time. The latter is being used here.
5. K. N. Jayatilleke, *Early Buddhist Theory of Knowledge* (London: George Allen & Unwin, 1963), p. 460. Wing-tsit Chang says the following about *karma*: "Karma, which to the Brahmins was hardly more than a mechanical, superstitious, fatalistic operation of retribution was transformed by the Buddha to mean moral energy with which man may exercise his free will, break the Chain of Causation, chart the course of his future, and produce the meritorious fruits of his own conduct." (*An Encyclopedia of Religion*, edited by Vergilius Ferm [New York: The Philosophical Library, 1945], p. 95)
6. K. W. Morgan, editor, *The Path of the Buddha* (New York: The Ronald Press Company, 1956), p. 93.
7. K. N. Jayatilleke, *op. cit.*, p. 427.
8. *Suttanipāta* I, 172. *Studies in the Origins of Buddhism*, Govind Chandra Pande (Depart-

times depicted as the great helper (*dutiya*) of man[10] and "the best treasure of man" by which use one can withstand the "flood,"[11] and it is said that faith opens the gateway to immortality.[12] The Buddhist devotee believes in order that he may know. However, as on most subjects, the scriptures are ambiguous with regard to faith, and there are statements attributed to Buddha such as "Those who have merely faith and love toward me are sure of deliverance hereafter,"[13] and "Those who believe in me are all assured of final salvation."[14] On the basis of such statements various later Buddhist schools placed more emphasis on faith than it was given in the religion of the founder, some even came to hold faith as the supreme value.[15] However, the faith that one needs in adopting the Buddhist philosophy of life was early described as a "rational faith" (*ākāravatī saddhā*) as opposed to a blind or "baseless faith" (*amūlikā saddhā*).[16]

In Christianity, the emphasis is on the followers' emotional reaction to or disposition toward such teachings as the miraculous birth of Jesus, his proclaiming himself the son of God, and Simon Peter's declaration, "You are the Christ, the Son of the living God."[17] In addition, the New Testament seems to resound with statements to the effect that one's belief in Jesus is sufficient for salvation, ". . he who believes in me, though he die, yet shall he live, and whoever lives and believes in me shall never die."[18] A jailer guarding Paul and Silas awoke to find the prison door open but his prisoners still inside. Astounded at this, he asked how he could be saved; and though he was given no rationale to do so was counselled, "Believe in the Lord Jesus, and you will be saved, you and your household."[19]

Some, beginning as early as Tertullian (c. 160 A.D.), have interpreted the more or less "blind" faith or obedience in Christianity as anti-ration-

ment of Ancient History, Culture and Archeology, University of Allahabad, 1957), p. 522 fn.

9. *Ibid., Suttanipāta* V, 6.
10. *Ibid., Suttanipāta* I, 25, 38; IV, 70.
11. *Ibid., Suttanipāta* I, 214.
12. *Ibid., Suttanipāta* I, 138.
13. *Majjhima-nikāya* 22.
14. *Aṅguttara-nikāya* 64.
15. Pure Realm Buddhism and the Nichiren sect of Japan held faith as supreme and regarded it as the highest virtue. Pure Land Buddhism stressed faith in Amitabha Buddha, whereas Nichiren stressed faith in the Eternal Śākyamuni as is taught in the Lotus-sutra. According to Shinran (1173–1262) one is saved at the moment of faith, not at the moment of death.
16. *Majjhima-nikāya,* vol. II (P. T. S. edition), p. 170. Cf. K. N. Jayatilleke, *The Principles of International Law in Buddhist Doctrine* (Leyden: A. W. Sijthoff, 1967), p. 456.
17. Matthew 16:16.
18. John 11: 25–26.
19. Acts 16:31.

alist. Nietzsche said, "If faith is quite generally needed above all, then reason, knowledge and inquiry must be discredited: the way to truth becomes the *Forbidden* way."[20] But there are few if any passages to be found in the New Testament which are obviously opposed to reason. There is even one passage written by Paul that suggests the contrary.[21] And Jesus asked a multitude, "Why do you not judge for yourselves what is right?"[22] thereby suggesting reliance on their own mental faculties for moral direction.

The "blind-faith alone" theory is not as simple as it seems, for as was pointed out in the previous section, Jesus' teachings are mindful of ethics. By their acts men are to be measured, as Jesus preached, at the time of judgment. Men will even be able to judge others "by their fruits," so as not to succumb to "false prophets"[23] (a function at least partly of reason). Peter wrote to the Christians of future generations to ". . . make every effort to supplement your faith with virtue, and virtue with knowledge, and knowledge with self-control, and self-control with steadfastness, and steadfastness with godliness, and godliness with brotherly affection, and brotherly affection with love."[24] The last portion of these verses is noteworthy, for in addition to stressing the morality of the Old Testament, Jesus also put new importance on love (Greek *agape*, not *eros*), saying, "This I command you, to love one another."[25] Furthermore, Paul in one place ranks love above faith, "So faith, hope, love abide, these three; but the greatest of these is love."[26]

In summary, neither in early Buddhism nor early Christianity is faith held sufficient for individual perfection or salvation. In the two teachings, however, one can safely say that their emphasis on faith differs. Generally, faith in early Buddhism is a preliminary step to entering the path to final enlightenment, which will hopefully come in this life. In Christianity, however, faith supplemented by virtue and love is generally thought to be the important sustaining attitude necessary for doing the good works that will allow entry into the Kingdom of God whether in this world or the beyond. This is especially well supported in the New Testa-

20. Friedrich Nietzsche, *The Antichrist*, The Portable Nietzsche, selected and translated by Walter Kaufmann (New York: The Viking Press, 1954), p. 591.
21. I Corinthians 14:6–12; see also verses 15, "I will pray with the spirit and I will pray with the mind also," 20, ". . . in thinking be mature," and 33, "For God is not a God of confusion but of peace."
22. Luke 12:57.
23. Matthew 7:15–16.
24. I Peter 1:5–7.
25. John 15:17.
26. I Corinthians 13:13.

ment book of Hebrews, where the faith of Christianity is interpreted in the framework of the faith of the Old Testament prophets.[27]

2. Worship of the Founder

In both Christianity and Buddhism (or Jainism) there is an element of faith in the founder. References may be found to the founder's personality and character as well as his teaching. In both cases the founder is regarded as specially qualified to give instruction, the Buddha as the Enlightened One, the Christ as the revealer of the One God. In this respect, most religions differ from philosophy, where it is generally thought that teachings are valued and accepted for their own sake. In many religions, an outstanding founder has much to do with its appeal.

Originally the word "Buddha" meant merely "awakened" and in old texts it is doubtful the word ever meant anything more than "awakened." At the beginning of Buddhism, the Buddha was a great man and nothing more. But with the passing of time the Buddha came to be more and more highly esteemed until eventually he came to have a supernatural existence in the eyes of many of his followers.

Early scriptures indicate the Buddha himself to have been very modest in personality. He did not want to be worshipped as a deity but eventually his followers came to deify him. The beginning of this process is noticed in the following dialogue where the Buddha rebuked a disciple for looking upon him as the greatest man in the world. The venerable Sāriputta came to the place where Gotama was, and having saluted him, took his seat respectfully at his side, extolling, "Lord, such faith have I in the Exalted One that methinks there never has been, nor will there be, nor is there now, any other, whether Wanderer or Brahmin, who is greater and wiser than the Exalted One. . . as regards the higher wisdom." "Grand and bold are the words of your mouth, Sāriputta," . . . answered the Master, ". . . verily, then, you have burst forth into a song of ecstasy! Of course, then, you have known all the Exalted Ones of the past, . . . comprehending their minds with yours, and aware what their conduct was, what their wisdom, . . . and what the emancipation they attained to." "Not so, O Lord!" "Of course, then, you have perceived all the Exalted Ones of the future, . . . comprehending their whole minds with yours?" "Not so, O Lord!" "But at least, then, O Sāriputta, you know

27. Hebrews 11. Soren Kierkegaard chose only one of these Old Testament stories to write into a book, *Fear and Trembling*, and launch an entire modern movement back to "existentialist" fiath, unquestioning in character and distinctly against systematic or rationalistic philosophy.

me, . . . and have penetrated my mind? . . ." "Not even that, O Lord," "You see, then, Sāriputta, that you don't know the hearts of the Able, Awakened Ones of the past and of the future. Why, therefore, are your words so grand and bold?"[1]

In Mark, the oldest of the Gospels (though not without textual difficulties), Jesus asked his disciples who they thought he was. When Peter answered, "You are the Christ," Jesus ". . . charged them to tell no one about him."[2] And in the same source, when a man ran up and asked him, "Good Teacher, what must I do to inherit eternal life?" Jesus replied, "Why do you call me good? No one is good but God alone,"[3] All through this Gospel Jesus refers to himself not as the Son of God but the son of man. Not until the very end of the story of his Gospel according to Mark, when asked, "Are you the Christ, the Son of the Blessed?" did he answer "I am."[4] But the authenticity of this statement is disputed.

Such humility is characteristic of most great moral leaders. Confucius said, "In literature perhaps, I may compare with others, but as to my living the noble life, to that I have not yet attained."[5] And again, "As to being a sage or a man of virtue, how dare I presume to such a claim? But, as to striving thereafter unwearyingly, and teaching others therein without flagging—that can be said of me, and that is all."[6]

Neither in the Gospels nor in the oldest Sūtras is there any preaching concerning the worship of the founder, but within one or two generations of the passing away of each founder first reverence and then worship of him arose. "I take refuge in thee, O Buddha," was a very early confession, and Sakyamuni was soon linked with the Order and the Doctrine as one of the three fundamental elements, corresponding to Christ, the Church and the Gospel. The Buddha, the Order and the Doctrine were called the Three Jewels.

Disciples extolled the Buddha with such epithets as the Exalted One, the Wayfarer, the *Arahat*, the Fully-enlightened One, Wise, Upright, Happy, World-Knowing, Supreme, the Bridler of Man's Wayward Hearts, the Teacher of Gods and Men, the Awakened One. Thus glorified, the Buddha finally came to be deified, just as was the Christ.

By way of progressive exaltation Jesus the son of man became transfigured into the Son of God, and then into God incarnate. From the precarious savior of the world, his image for his followers evolved into the living God. His believers say that people who believe in the Christ

1. *Mahāparinibbāna-suttanta* I, 61. *Dialogues of the Buddha,* III, p. 57.
2. Mark 8:29–30.
3. Mark 10:17–18.
4. Mark 14:61–62.
5. *Analects,* VII, 32.
6. *Ibid.,* 33.

are saved in virtue of being twice-born in the spirit of resurrection. The traditional theocentric faith of Judaism was superseded by the new Christ-centered faith and the old belief in the One God, at least in some denominations, receded before a belief in Christ.

Later Buddhists came to believe as follows: "Thy Buddhas are beings whose words cannot fail: there is no departure from truth in their speech. For as the fall of a stone thrown into the air, as the death of a mortal, as the sunrise at dawn, as the lion's roaring when he leaves his lair, as the delivery of a woman with child, as all these things are sure and certain . . . even so the word of the Buddhas is sure and cannot fail."[7] In the New Testament also similar sayings are attributed to Jesus: "Heaven and earth will pass away, but my words will not pass away."[8] "But it is easier for heaven and earth to pass away, than for one dot of the law to become void."[9]

The Buddha is said to have proclaimed, "I am a King . . ." not of political dominion, but rather, ". . . an incomparable king of *dharma*."[10] Jesus reportedly made a similar statement at his "trial" before Pilate, "My kingship is not of this world; if my kingship were of this world, my servants would fight, that I might not be handed over to the Jews; but my kingship is not from the world."[11] The Buddha is said to be the light of the world (*lokacakkhu*, literally, eye in the world).[12] In the New Testament, also, Jesus is depicted as saying, "I am the light of the world; he who follows me will not walk in darkness, but will have the light of life."[13] Again Jesus said, "As long as I am in the world, I am the light of the world."[14]

A number of birth stories were ascribed to the Buddha in previous existences. Tales composed in this manner are called the *Jātakas*. In these stories the details of the Buddha's supposed previous existences were given. Aided by the traditional belief in transmigration and *karma*, "There thus sprung up this idea of the Buddha, the man, who through countless ages of heroic struggle in many different births, had at last attained to such perfect purity and perfect wisdom, that he was able, when goodness was dying out on earth, and men had become more and more wicked and depraved, to extinguish by his teaching the fires of their passions, to lead them along the way of escape from the net of transmigration, and thus in that evil time to save a lost world from impeding ruin."[15]

7. *Buddhist Birth Stories*, p. 18.
8. Matthew 14:35; Luke 221:33.
9. Luke 16:17.
10. *Majjhima-nikāya* 92.
11. John 18:36.
12. *Dīgha-nikāya* 16.
13. John 8:12.
14. John 9:5.
15. T. W. Rhys Davids, *Lectures*, etc., p. 142.

Stories of the former births of a sage may be peculiarly Indian and Buddhist; however in the West also one can find a similar conception. There is a curious Irish legend, recorded in the so-called Book of Balimote (the latter half of the 14th century), which strongly resembles a *Jātaka* tale of transmigration. "The poet is excusing himself for beginning his history a thousand years before his hero was born. It seems that the hero was really alive all the while.

1. Tuan, son of Cairill, as we are told,
Was freed from sin by Jesus;
One hundred years complete he lived;
He lived in blooming manhood.
2. Three hundred years in the shape of a *wild ox*
He lived on the open extensive plains;
Two hundred and five years he lived
In the shape of a *wild boar*.
3. Three hundred years he was still in the flesh
In the shape of an *old bird*;
One hundred delighful years he lived
In the shape of a *salmon* in the flood.
4. A fisherman caught him in his net,
He brought it to the king's palace;
When the bright salmon was there seen,
The queen immediately longed for it.
5. It was forthwith dressed for her,
Which she alone ate entire;
The beauteous queen became pregnant.
The issue of which was Tuan.

Tuan seems to have been a convert of Solumkill (Columbia), a sixth-century Irish saint."[16]

Many miraculous powers also were ascribed to the Buddha. Early in the scriptures of Buddhism so-called magic powers (*siddhi*) are mentioned, such as supernormal memory, levitation, and the like. One example offers a description that fire steamed forth from the upper part of the body of the Buddha and from his lower body proceeded a torrent of water. In addition, there is a story about the Buddha feeling his five hundred brethren at once with a small cake left in his begging bowl (with a good deal left over to be thrown away),[17] which is similar to the story of Jesus feeding the five thousand with five loaves of bread and two fish.[18]

Almost surely added at a later date is this comparable account in the

16. *Ibid.*, pp. 76–77.
17. *Jātaka*, 76.
18. Mark 6:34–44.

New Testament of a miracle regarding Jesus: ". . . Jesus took with him Peter and James and John, and led them up a high mountain apart by themselves; and he was transfigured before them, and his garments became glistening, intensely white, as no fuller on earth could bleach them. And there appeared to them Elijah with Moses; and they were talking to Jesus . . . . And a cloud overshadowed them, and a voice came out of the cloud, 'This is my beloved Son; listen to him.' And suddenly looking around they no longer saw any one with them but Jesus only."[19]

Similarly, the concern to raise the Buddha out of the ordinary world of men, to make him not the teacher of the gods but the god of gods, is intimately connected with the rise of Mahāyāna (next chapter). Formerly scholars wished to infer a Christian influence in this change of attitude towards the founder of Buddhism, but their efforts have not proved convincing to everyone, and this subject awaits further research before anything definite can be said on the matter. This very concern shows to what extent even the most textually oriented scholars have been struck by certain resemblances between these two universal religions.

19. Mark 9:2–8.

C. Concluding Words

MANY points of comparison between Buddhism and Christianity have been included above, indeed too many to summarize here. But one must reiterate that at the present time there is little evidence to support any influence of one religion upon the other at the early stage considered in this section. On this subject, T. W. Rhys Davids has said, "I can find no evidence whatever of any actual and direct communication of any of these ideas from the East to the West. Where the Gospel narratives resemble the Buddhist one, they seem to me to have been independently developed on the shores of the Mediterranean and in the valley of the Ganges—The similarities of ideas are evidence not of any borrowing from the one side or the other, but of similar feelings engendered in men's minds by similar experiences.—The lessons drawn from the study of early Buddhism may be found as useful for the true apprehension of early Christianity as the Vedas are useful for the true appreciation of classical mythology."[1] In addition, a clarification of some of the differences and shifts of emphasis in these two world religions has been attempted herein.

As discussion shifts to some of the basic philosophical standpoints of Buddhism, more areas of comparison will be included, thereby covering a larger area in the west than just Christianity. This is desirable because, for reasons pointed out above, there was less emphasis on philosophical considerations in early Christianity than there was in early Buddhism.

Whereby it was convenient to compare the religious traditions of Buddhism and Christianity, the next section can be introduced by stating that in terms of his historical position in philosophy the Buddha might be more successfully compared with Socrates. These two philosophers flourished at the same time, Buddha dying around 383 B.C. (according to one theory), and Socrates being forced to drink poison around 399 B.C. In both their philosophies a distinctly practical and moral intention constantly comes to the fore. Of course, the actual content of their philosophies differs considerably. Both, however, went on to affect the change of the societies into which they were progressively introduced for centuries to come. And interestingly enough, their respective starting points, philosophically, were quite similar because both began by refuting materialists, hedonists, skeptics and sophists, who in their time of unrest and

1. T. W. Rhys Davids, *Lectures* etc., pp. 151–152.

spiritual confusion were threatening to assume predominance. Therefore, thinkers of the days of Socrates through those of the days of early Christianity should be taken into consideration for comparison with Early Buddhism, as will be done in the following.

III. FUNDAMENTAL ATTITUDES

A. Attitude toward Thinkers and Their Systems

1. Cognizance of Variation

GOTAMA, the founder of Buddhism, took note of the fact that many of the systems of philosophy prevalent in his day were contradictory to each other and that philosophers disputed with each other on various philosophical problems. Each of the philosophers claimed that his own doctrine was absolutely true and that the other doctrines contained falsehoods based on various fallacies. "What some say is truth, the reality that others say is void, false; so having disagreed they dispute. Why do not the thinkers [*Samaṇas*] say one [and the same thing]?"[1] "Here they maintain 'purity'; in other doctrines [*dhamma*] they do not allow purity; what they have devoted themselves to, that they call good, and they enter extensively upon the single truths."[2] "Because, he holds another [to be] a fool, therefore he calls himself expert; in his own opinion he is one that tells what is propitious; others he blames."[3]

The same situation was pointed out by Heraclitus. "For many men —those who encounter such things—do not understand them, and do not grasp them after they have learnt; but to themselves they seem [to understand]."[4] In the Hellenistic age also, people observed the diversity of schools and the acerbity of their disputes, and decided that all alike were pretending to knowledge which was in fact unattainable. Many thought, "Why trouble about the future? It is wholly uncertain. You may as well enjoy the present; 'What's to come is unsure.' For these reasons, Scepticism taught worrying people how to spend life."[5]

1. *Suttanipāta* 883.
2. *Suttanipāta* 824.
3. *Suttanipāta* 888.
4. Heraclitus, fragment 17.
5. Bertrand Russell, *A History of Western Philosophy* (New York: Simon & Schuster, 1945), p. 234.

Early Buddhists thought that if one apart from any particular philosophical standpoint viewed these conflicting ideas objectively, each philosophical system would appear relative and partial in those respects in which it conflicts with and opposes another philosophical system. Then just where shall men find the truth? Despite postulates such as "the truth is one, there is not a second,"[6] many still suffer from seemingly unending contradictions. How can this fact be explained?

Gotama commented on this dilemma as follows: these philosophers get into disputes over various unsolvable metaphysical problems, and are entangled in adhesion or clinging, henceforth they are apt to fall into moral evils. "Saying that there is something firm in his own way, he holds his opponent to be a fool; thus he himself brings on strife calling his opponent a fool and impure."[7] "They are inflamed by passion for their own [philosophical] views."[8] And, "So having got into a contest they dispute 'The opponent [is] a fool, an ignorant [person]' so they say. Which one of these, pray, is the true doctrine [*vāda*]? for all these assert themselves to be the only experts."[9] It is said of Buddha that ". . . he overcame such disputes,"[10] believing that, "having left all resolutions, nobody would excite strife in the world."[11]

2. Partial Veracity of Thoughts

EARLY Buddhism held the theory of partial veracity (truthfulness) of various thoughts. Concerning metaphysical views prevalent in his day the Buddha said:

> On such points Brahmins and recluses stick;
> Wrangling on them they violently discuss;
> Poor folk! They see but one side of the shield.[1]

6. *Suttanipāta* 884.
7. *Suttanipāta* 893.
8. *Suttanipāta* 891.
9. *Suttanipāta* 879.
10. *Suttanipāta* 907.
11. *Suttanipāta* 894.

1. *Udāna* VI, 4. Cf. "The beliefs which we have most warrant for have no safeguard to rest on, but a standing invitation to the whole world to prove them unfounded. If the challenge is not accepted, or is accepted and the attempt fails, we are far enough from certainty still; but we have done the best that the existing state of human reason admits of; we have neglected nothing that could give the truth a chance of reaching us; if the lists are kept open, we may hope that if there be a better truth, it will be found when the human mind is capable of receiving it; and in the meantime we may rely on having attained such approach to truth as is possible in our own day. This is the amount of certainty attainable by a fallible being, and this the sole way of attaining it" (John S. Mill, *On Liberty*).

This means that all metaphysical views are nothing but partial apprehensions of the whole truth which lies beyond our area of cognition, beyond rational analysis. In another scripture the same point is stressed by the famous parable of the blind men and the elephant,[2] which was occasioned by some ascetics and Brahmins who met together and began to quarrel. Some said: "The world is eternal," and the others: "The world is not eternal"; some declared: "The world is finite," and the others: "The world is infinite"; again some taught: "Body and soul are separate," and others: "Body and soul are but one." Some said: "The perfect man *is* after death," others maintained: "The perfect man is not after death" and so forth. Finally all this led to a quarrel, and to harsh and insulting words. The monks told the Buddha of this quarrel, and he related the following parable:

There was once a king who brought together all those who had been born blind. When they were all assembled, the king commanded that an elephant be led before them. The beast was brought and he told some of them to feel his head, others his ear, others his tusk, others his trunk, etc., and the last one the elephant's tail. Then the king asked them: "How does an elephant look?" Those who had touched the elephant's head, replied, "An elephant is like a pot"; those who had touched the ear answered, "An elephant is like a winnowing basket"; those who had touched the tusk declared: "An elephant is like a plough-share"; those who had touched the trunk said: "An elephant is like the pole of a plough," etc.; and those who had felt the tail maintained: "An elephant is like a broom." A great tumult now arose. Each one maintained: "An elephant is like this, and not otherwise; he is not like that, he is like this"; until at last they came to blows, at which the king was mightily amused.

Even so, concluded the Buddha, is the case of the ascetics and Brahmins, each of whom has only seen a portion of the truth, and who then maintain: "Thus is truth and not otherwise; truth is not thus, but thus."[3] The parable of the blind men and the elephant which has been widely popular in both East and West was interpreted as representing the assertion of partial veracity of thoughts of various schools in the eye of early Buddhism. Ordinary teachers, who have grasped this or that small part of the truth, dispute with one another. And rational analysis is useful in making clear the limitations of rationality. But it is by detaching oneself from metaphysical oppositions that one is able to grasp the whole truth.

Ancient Western philosophies nearest to Buddha's doctrine of partial

2. *Udāna* VI, 4, pp. 66–69; the Chinese version of the *Arthavargīya-sūtra* (*Taisho Tripitaka*, vol. 4, p. 178 a–c). This parable of the blind men and an elephant (*andhagajanyāya*) is a favorite one for both Brahmin and Jain philosophers (M. Winternitz, *A History of Indian Literature* [University of Calcutta, vol. II, 1933], p. 88, n).
3. M. Winternitz, *ibid.*, II, pp. 87–88.

veracity of thoughts would probably be those of Aristippus and Heraclitus (see Chapter II-Relativism). And later Pascal embraced a similar doctrine though he eventually expressed his wholehearted devotion to Christianity. Interestingly enough, some 20th century Western thinkers have also been close to the Buddha on this point. F. Harrison has said, "Everything depends on our recognizing as the substratum of our philosophy, that all knowledge is relative; relative in respect of its having no absolute certainty, and relative as respects its harmonizing with the mental and moral nature of man."[4] And more recently, a fundamental thesis of L. Wittgenstein is that it is impossible to say anything about the world as a whole, and that whatever can be said has to concern bounded portions of it.

Bertrand Russell explains Wittgenstein's standpoint as follows: "According to this view we could only say things about the world as a whole if we could get outside the world, if, that is to say, it ceased to be for us the whole world. Our world may be bounded for some superior being who can survey it from above, but for us, however finite it may be, it cannot have a boundary, since it has nothing outside it. Wittgenstein uses, as an analogy, the field of vision. Our field of vision does not, for us, have a visual boundary, just because there is nothing outside it, and in like manner our logical world has no logical boundary because our logic knows of nothing outside it."[5]

According to a scripture, Gotama would not say "[my doctrine] is true," nor would he say "[your doctrine] is false,"[6] thereby avoiding conflict with other philosophers.[7] This was an expression of his distrust of those that adhere to a definite standpoint. He said, "I do not fight with the world, but the world fights with me, for one who knows about the truth [*dharma*] never fights with the world."[8] The teaching of the Buddha is said to transcend comparison; it is neither inferior, nor equal, nor superior to other doctrines.[9] "After investigation there is nothing amongst the doctrines which such a one [as I would] embrace, and seeing [misery] in the [other philosophical] views, without adopting [any of them], searching [for truth] I saw 'inward peace.' "[10]

In the ancient West also one finds similar assertions. The Sophists, notably Protagoras and Gorgias, had been led by the ambiguities and apparent contradictions of sense-perception to a subjectivism not unlike

4. Frederic Harrison, *Philosophy of Common Sense* (London: Macmillan, 1907), p. 41.
5. Bertrand Russell's Introduction to Ludwig Wittgenstein's *Tractatus Logico-philosophicus* (London: Kegan Paul, Trench, Trübner, 1922), p. 18.
6. *Suttanipāta* 843.
7. *Suttanipāta* 847.
8. *Saṃyutta-nikāya* III, p. 138 f. Cf. *Suttanipāta* 73.
9. Cf. *Suttanipāta* 8422 ff. Cf. 855, 860.
10. *Suttanipāta* 837.

that which Hume later expressed. Pyrrho seems to have added moral and logical skepticism to that regarding the senses. He is said to have maintained that there could never be rational ground for preferring one course of action to another. In practice, this meant that one conformed to the customs of whatever country one inhabited. It is possible to speculate that on certain matters regarding his followers (*saṅgha*) the Buddha would have expected similar conformity to customs in the lands to which his doctrine was to travel, for he left not hard and fast rules for the governing of his *saṅgha* but rather rules by which they could democratically govern themselves.

3. Tolerance

Tolerance, to an extent prompted by recognition of the partial veracity of thoughts, has been an outstanding characteristic of Buddhism from earliest times. The feeling that in spiritual matters we are at best blind beggars fighting with one another in our native darkness is not conducive to a narrow and fanatical bigotry. Early Buddhism was filled with the spirit of tolerance. Babbitt alleges that the Far Eastern doctrine most free from undesirable elements is probably the authentic teaching of the Buddha.[1] Buddhism has attempted to arrive at the truth, not by excluding its opposites as falsehood, but by including them as one aspect relevant to truth.

This attitude of tolerance is quite evident in Buddha's sayings. He taught his disciples to think over matters in a calm state of mind, saying, "Brethren, if outsiders should speak against me, or against the Doctrine, or against the Order, you should not on that account either bear malice, or suffer heart-burning, or feel ill-will. If you, on that account, should be angry and hurt, that would stand in the way of your own self-conquest. If, when others speak against us, you feel angry at that, and displeased, would you then be able to judge how far that speech of theirs is well said or ill? But when outsiders speak in dispraise of me, or of the Doctrine, or of the Order, you should unravel what is false and point it out as wrong, saying: 'For this or that reason this is not the fact, that is not so, such a thing is not found among us, is not in us.' "[2]

Similarly, the Buddha was unwilling to accept uncritical praise. "But also, brethern, if outsiders should speak in praise of me, in praise of the Teaching, in praise of the Order, you should not, on that account,

1. Irving Babbitt, *Buddha and the Occident, An Appendix to His Work: The Dhammapada* (London: Oxford University Press, 1936), p. 69.
2. *Dīgha-nikāya* I, 1, 5. vol. I, pp. 2–3.

be filled with pleasure or gladness, or be lifted up in heart. Were you to be so, that also would stand in the way of your self-conquest. When outsiders speak in praise of me, or of the Doctrine, or of the Order, you should acknowledge what is right to be the fact, saying: 'For this or that reason this is the fact, that is so, such a thing is found among us, is in us.' "[3]

Rather than protesting, attacking or proselytizing, in many of the discourses the Buddha is represented as arguing with his interlocutors in a more or less Socratic manner. In the first place he admits the assertion or position of the interlocutors, then he leads them to an appreciation of different positions. With regard to the Buddha's way of dealing with his peers, Dr. Radhakrishnan has said, ". . . the Buddha was more definitely opposed to Vedic orthodoxy and ceremonialism than was Socrates to the State religion of Athens, or Jesus to Judaism, and yet he lived till eighty, gathered a large number of disciples, and founded a religious order in his own lifetime. Perhaps the Indian temper of religion is responsible for the difference in the treatment of unorthodoxies."[4] However, the most important reason for his long and successful religious career may have been the Buddha's attitude of objecting to the assertion of his opponents, not obviously and directly but euphemistically. "Buddha was more prone to humor than most religious teachers. The contrast in this respect between certain portions of the Pali canon and the Christian Bible is striking."[5]

The Buddha condemned the tendency prevalent among the religious disputants of his day to make a display of their own doctrines and damn those of others.[6] He encouraged gifts by Buddhists to non-Buddhists as well[7] and also admitted the right of non-Buddhists to heaven, mentioning that a particular Ājīvika gained heaven by virtue of his being a believer in *karma.*[8] In addition he held in high respect the Brahmins who led a truly moral life.

Such a spirit of tolerance is displayed in the edicts of King Aśoka (two and a half centuries before the birth of Christ); these also reflect, in a simple manner, the spirit of the founder of Buddhism. Although Buddhism was predominant in many Asiatic countries, there is no record of any Buddhist persecution of the followers of another faith. They waged no religious war. Buddhism is probably the only world religion which has spread by persuasion alone, not by resorting to force. It is very dif-

3. *Ibid.*, I, 6. vol. I, p. 3.
4. S. Radhakrishnan, *The Dhammapada,* with introductory essays, Pali text, English translation and notes (London: Oxford University Press, 1950), p. 15.
5. *Ibid.*, p. 71.
6. *Suttanipāta*, v. 782.
7. *Aṅguttara-nikāya* III, 571.
8. *Majjhima-nikāya* I, 483.

ficult to have a firm conviction and at the same time to be tolerant. Many have deemed it almost impossible. Yet not only the Buddha himself but many of his followers achieved such tolerance.[9]

9. It would be very interesting to compare the attitude of early Buddhism with the Maitreyan Way advocated by Prof. Charles Morris of the University of Florida. He says: "Men have long pondered on the question of how to live. For ages they have asked themselves what they should become and how they might become what they choose to be" (*The Open Self* [New York: Prentice-Hall, 1948], p. 73). He mentions thirteen ways to live, some of which various persons at various times have advocated and followed. Morris asked many American college students to indicate by numbers which they liked most. He wanted to see how Americans would like to live. He considered the reactions of almost a thousand young people in colleges throughout the country—colleges in New York, Minnesota, Chicago, Albama, and California. The number of them per hundred that gave first choice to each alternative is as follows:

Way 1–17 ("nothing in excess")
Way 2–1 ("independent of persons and things")
Way 3–4 ("sympathetic concern for others")
Way 4–3½ ("festivity and solitude in alternation")
Way 5–5 ("group activity, group enjoyment")
Way 6–7 ("man the eternal maker and re-maker")
Way 7–40 ("dynamic integration of diversity")
Way 8–10 ("carefree wholesome enjoyment")
Way 9–1 ("wait in quiet receptivity")
Way 10–4 ("vigilant manly self-control")
Way 11–1 ("meditation on the inner self")
Way 12–5 ("active, daring adventuresome deeds")
Way 13–11½ ("let yourself be used")

The seventh way was most popular among them. Forty out of every hundred of them gave it first choice, a higher number than any other way. This seventh way, just as the other ways, is described in full detail on the questionnaire as follows: "We should at various times and in various ways accept something from all other paths of life, but give no one our exclusive allegiance. At one moment one of them is the more appropriate; at another moment another is the most appropriate. Life should contain enjoyment and action and contemplation in about equal amounts. When either is carried to extremes we lose something important for our life. So we must cultivate flexibility, admit diversity in ourselves, accept the tension which this diversity produces, find a place for detachment in the midst of enjoyment and activity. The goal of life is found in the dynamic integration of enjoyment, action, and contemplation, and so in the dynamic interaction of the various paths of life. One should use all of them in building a life, and no one alone" (*ibid.*, p. 77).

In the thirteen paths of life way 7 was called the Maitreyan Path. Maitreya was, in India's history, the name of an enlightened friendly sage, a future Buddha who would one day appear on earth to save suffering human beings. This name of one-yet-to-come was borrowed by Prof. Morris "because it seemed a fitting symbol for a way of life still struggling for birth, a way of life friendly to personal diversity under which Orient and Occident might find kinship" (*ibid.*, p. 84). The data offered protection for whatever potentialities a person has, and so evokes diversified allegiance. And it protects the elasticity of man, also (*ibid.*, pp. 119–120; Prof. Morris more recently developed his thoughts further in *Varieties of Human Values*, University of Chicago Press, 1956). Buddhism is well known for its elasticity. In this manner the Maitreyan personality ideal points to the ideal of a society abundant in contrasting personalities, unified in its acceptance and support of diversity.

Buddhists are generally noted for their liberal attitude toward other religions whether polytheistic, monotheistic, or pantheistic. This feature is found in all Bud-

Lastly, Buddhism has displayed a spirit of acceptance to the various primitive faiths native to the different Asian countries where it has become the prevalent religion. The amalgamation of popular native beliefs is very strong in southern (Theravāda) countries. Thereabouts, many Hindu gods and goddesses have been included in the religious ceremonies of the Buddhist community, and many Buddhists still observe festivals and customs associated with the nature spirits of each country. These spirits are known as "*nats*" in Burma and as "*phis*" in Thailand. Some are thought to be spirits dwelling in trees and houses, others heroes who have passed away and live on a higher plane. Although the canons do not exhort such a form of popular belief, they have been integrated with Hindu beliefs and the worship of the *nats*. So one finds worship of *nats* as well as stars even in pagodas, though this feature is more conspicuous among Mahāyāna Buddhists.

Such attitudes of tolerance were not totally lacking in the ancient West, at least as represented in John Stuart Mill's interpretation of early Christianity. "The Gospel always refers to a pre-existing morality, and confines its precepts to the particulars in which that morality was to be corrected, or superseded by a wider and higher; expressing itself, moreover, in terms most general, often impossible to be interpreted literally, and possessing rather the impressiveness of poetry or eloquence than the precision of legislation. To extract from it a body of ethical doctrine, has never been possible without eking it out from the Old Testament, that is, from a system elaborate indeed, but in many respects barbarous, and intended only for a barbarous people. St*l* Paul*l*, a declared enemy to this Judaical mode of interpreting the doctrine and filling up the scheme of his Master equally assumes a pre-existing morality, namely that of the Greeks and Romans; and his advice to Christians is in a great measure a system of accommodation to that; even to the extent of giving an apparent sanction to slavery."[10] It was natural that the Romans at first did not understand that Christianity was a different religion from that of the Jews; Jesus had been a Jew, and his followers also were Jews. They thought their religion must be a form of Judaism. But as time went on, the Romans found that Christianity was a new religion. Oscar Wilde ironically said, "There were Christians before Christ, for that we should be grateful. The unfortunate thing is that there have been none since."[11]

---

dhist countries. Buddhists admit the truth of any moral and philosophicl system, whether primitive or developed, provided only that it is capable of leading men at least part way toward their final goal. That is why other religions are not so seriously attacked by Buddhists.

10. John Stuart Mill, *On Liberty* (London: Longmans, Green, Reader, and Dyer, 1871), p. 28.

11. Oscar Wilde, *De Profundis* (London: Methuen and Co., 1905), p. 116.

B. Attitude toward Philosophy in General

1. Silence on Metaphysical Problems

The Buddha refused to give a definite answer on most metaphysical problems discussed in his day. Many ascetics were fond of asking questions concerning:

Whether the world is eternal or not,
Whether the world is infinite or not,
Whether the soul is the same as the body, or different from it,
Whether a saint exists in any way after death or not, and so on.

To all questions of this kind, the Buddha did not answer. Because he claimed it was not edifying nor connected with the essence of the norm (law), nor did it tend to the turning of the will, to the absence of passion, to cessation, to peace, to the higher faculties, to supreme wisdom, nor to *nirvāṇa*.[1]

The answering of all such questions, the Buddha held, would leave no time for finding the way to salvation or to liberation from suffering. He illustrated this by means of the following parable: A man is hit by a poisoned arrow. His friends hasten him to a doctor. The latter is about to draw the arrow from the wound. The wounded man, however, cries, "Stop! I will not have the arrow drawn out until I know who shot it, whether a warrior or a Brahmin, a common man (*Vaiśya*) or a slave (*Śūdra*), to which family he belonged, whether he was tall or short, or what kind the arrow was and its description,"[2] and so on. But the Buddha claimed that before all these questions were answered, the man would surely die. In the same way the disciple who wished for answers to all his questions about the beyond and such, would die before he knew the truth about suffering.

The attack thus made on this sort of metaphysical speculation was the most formidable attack so far on theology and metaphysics. As to Buddha's silence, we find two motives: (1) not to discuss things on which we have not good evidence, and (2) not to discuss things which are of no

1. *Majjhima-nikāya* no. 63, I, pp. 431, 385. M. Winternitz, *A History of Indian Literature*, pp. 70–71. Rhys Davids, "Dialogues of the Buddha," vol. I (*Sacred Books of the Buddhists*, vol. II, London, 1899), p. 186 f.
2. H. Warren, *Buddhism in Translations*, pp. 117–128.

use, no good, but possibly the contrary, for us. With regard to both, Gotama was perfectly firm. He refused not only to answer, but even to discuss such points, though they were of course being constantly raised.

The Buddhist way of practice is designed to lead to the understanding that there is no permanent substantial self to anyone or any object, but rather everyone and everything is subject to causal origination and destruction. Since this view itself was subject to its own principle, the Buddha immediately stopped all further metaphysical discussion in favor of preparing men to be able to end their own insecurity.

The Indian attitude of refraining from metaphysical discussion finds parallels in Greece. Heraclitus deplored the abstruseness of men's statements regarding the truth. "You could not in your going find the ends of the soul, though you travelled the whole way; so deep is its Law (*Logos*)."[3] "Let us not conjecture at random about the greatest things."[4] Epicurus remarked that the phases of the moon have been explained in many different ways; any one of these, so long as it does not bring in the gods, is as good as any other, and it would be idle curiosity to attempt to determine which of them is true. Of this, Bertrand Russell said, "It is no wonder that the Epicurians contributed practically nothing to natural knowledge."[5] Russell undoubtedly would have felt the same about the fact that later Buddhists also did not work to develop natural sciences.

A similar attitude toward certain forms of speculation can be found in early Christianity. Jesus exhibited a strong reaction against the Pharisaism, asceticism, formalism, and speculative theology of the Jews. One might say that the religions of both Jesus and the Buddha were at the outset partly an attempt at simplification. St. Paul admonished, "See to it that no one makes a prey of you by philosophy and empty deceit, according to human tradition, according to the elemental spirits of the universe, and not according to Christ."[6] But God, together with Christ, is the center of all Christian faith, while the Buddha did not assume God as the Creator. For the latter the problem of God was one of many metaphysical subtleties against which he protested.

Buddha was clear about where the emphasis lay in his teachings. "Not only by discipline and vows, not only by much learning, not by entering into a trance, not by sleeping alone, do I earn the happiness of release which no worldling can know. Bhikshu, be not confident as long as thou hast not attained the extinction of desires."[7] Very early, in Greece, Hippon of Samos (5th century B.C.) had voiced similar criticism against

3. Heraclitus, fragment 45.
4. *Ibid.*, 47.
5. Russell, *A History of Western Philosophy*, p. 247.
6. Colossians 2:8.
7. *Dhammapada* 271, 272.

learning: "Nothing is more empty than much learning."[8] "Much learning does not teach one to have intelligence; for it would have taught Hesiod and Pythagoras, and again, Zenophanes and Hecataeus."[9]

In China Confucius would not indulge in speculations about the future. He insisted on the formation of good character issuing in good action. When asked about the worship of the celestial and the earthly spirits, Confucius answered, "We do not know yet how to serve men, how can we know about serving ghosts and spirits?" When asked about death, he replied, "We don't know yet about life, how can we know about death?"[10] "The Master would not discuss 'prodigies', prowess, lawlessness, or the supernatural."[11] In light of Confucius' other comments on ancestral spirits and the proper observances for them, it is not necessary to conclude that he thereby expressed a completely agnostic or rationalistic attitude. Rather one should recognize both his skepticism toward prevailing superstitions concerning the spirit-world and his more positive belief that true respect for the dead implies service of the living.[12]

Though Confucius avoided discussion of the subject, he did not deny a future life, for his command to worship the ancestral spirits implies their existence after death. He commended the observance of the rites, not because they would please the deity but because they had come down to us from antiquity. On these points the attitude of Confucius is very similar to that of the Buddha, they differ in that Confucius was more secular, while Buddha wanted to penetrate more deeply into the existence of man.

The same problem which the Buddha confronted was discussed [in the West] by Kant. Portions of *The Critique of Pure Reason* are occupied with showing the fallacies that arise from applying space and time or Kant's categories to things that are not experienced. Human reason in its natural function must necessarily encounter such fallacies.[13] Hence, Kant maintained, we find ourselves troubled by "antinomies," that is to say, mutually contradictory propositions each of which can claim to be proved. Kant specified four such antinomies, each consisting of thesis and antithesis. For example, in the first antimony, the thesis is: "The world has a beginning in time, and is also limited as regards space." The antithesis is, "The world has no beginning in time, and no limits in space; it is infinite as regards both time and space."[14]

With regard to such subjects outside man's experience it is apparent

8. Hippo, fragment 3.
9. Heraclitus, fragment 40.
10. *Analects* XI, 11.
11. *Ibid.*, VII, 20.
12. DeBary, *Buddhism in Chinese Tradition.*
13. Kant, *Critique of Pure Reason*, translated by Max Muller, 2nd edition (New York: Macmillan, 1925).
14. Russell, *A History of Western Philosophy*, p. 708.

that conflicting theses can easily arise and have been doing so throughout the history of philosophy. One example among many from ancient philosophy is Cleanthes' maintaining that all souls survive until the next conflagration (when everything is absorbed into God) while Chrysippus held that this situation was true only for the wise.[15]

In 20th century philosophy, Wittgenstein's standpoint shows a great similarity to that of the Buddha. Wittgenstein claimed that most propositions and questions that have been written about philosophical matters are not false, but senseless. One cannot, therefore, answer questions of this kind at all, but can only state their senselessness. Most questions and propositions of philosophers, according to Wittgenstein, result from the fact that we do not understand the logic of our language. (They are of the same kind as the questions as to whether the Good is more or less identical with the Beautiful.) And so it is not to be wondered at that the deepest problems are really not problems at all.[16]

According to Wittgenstein, human nature is susceptible to a disease.[17] And in the same way the Buddha conceived his own role to be that of the physician. Both their doctrines were presented as therapies, treatments or cures for those who wanted to follow them—a method and a process of healing.

Buddha offered his advice in the practical manner of a spiritual physician; the art of Indian medicine seems to have been adopted by him into the sphere of spiritual problems. So Gotama's doctrine (like Wittgenstein's) can be regarded as rather practical.

It may be noted that the statement of the Buddhist Path begins with the diagnosis contained in the Four Noble Truths. Much the same might be said about Christian teaching, which starts from a view of man's sinful condition. Both the Buddha and the Christ were portrayed as physicians. "Those who are well have no need of a physician, but those who are sick [do],"[18] says Christ in a passage which suggests that in "calling sinners to repentence" he was addressing himself to men who were conscious or could be made conscious of their need for a physician.

Among the followers of the Buddha were such famous physicians as Jīvaka. Buddhism was closely connected with medicine for many years.[19] In the West also, the interest of skeptics centered on the problem of

15. *Ibid.*, p. 258.
16. Wittgenstein, *Tractatus Logico-philosophicus* (London: Kegan Paul, Trench, Trübner, 1922), 4. 003, p. 63.
17. Wittgenstein's claim is that a philosopher treats a question as though it were an "illness." *Philosophical Investigations*, G. E. M. Anscombe, trans. (New York: Macmillan, 1969), p. 123.
18. Matthew 11:12.
19. Julius Jolly, *Medicin* (Strassburg: K. J. Trübner, 1901), pp. 15–16. Hokei Idzumi, *Shūkyō Kenkyū*, Tokyo, N.S., vol. IV, no. 4.

practice. Especially later skeptics, such as Aenesidemus and Agrippa, were physicians.[20] It is noteworthy that the attitude of eliminating metaphysical assertions, of being connected with positive medical science, was established upon the same social basis in nearly the same period both in India and the West.

The practical value of Gotama's position in modern life can be seen from the description of a similar view held by Frederic Harrison in modern Europe. "When men of high moral and intellectual power assure us that they find rest, unity, and fruit in . . . conceptions about themselves, their own natures, the external world, its origin, construction, and maintenance, the future state of what they conceive to be some part of, or the essence of, themselves . . . far be it from us to dispute the value and reality of this knowledge. . . . If we do not adopt them, it is not because we believe them to be false, but because they fail to interest us. We can get no practical good out of them."[21] Or compare this, from a very different school. William James says, "Is the world one or many? fated or free? material or spiritual?—Here are notions either of which may or may not hold good of the world; and disputes over such notions are unending. The pragmatic method in such cases is to try to interpret each notion by tracing its respective practical consequences."[22] In Buddhism, everything is to be set aside which does not make for "quiescence, knowledge, supreme wisdom, and nirvāṇa."

2. Rigorous Examination

In a reaction against sacerdotal ceremonialism and theology, Buddha aimed at establishing his religion by means of free thinking independent of the Brahmanistic tradition. Hence the central tenets of Buddhism were drawn up so as to exclude any reference to the ultimacy of gods or souls. Buddhists asserted that even the existence of Brahma, the supreme god in those days, could not be proved; therefore they assumed no creator.

A young Brahmin, Vāseṭṭha, asked, "Just, Gotama, as near a village or a town there are many and various paths, yet they all meet together in the village; just in that way all the various paths are taught by various Brahmins,—are all these saving paths? Are they all paths which will lead him who acts according to them into a state of union with Brahma?"

20. W. Windelband, *A History of Philosophy*, vol. I (New York: Harper & Row, Torch Books, 1958), p. 160.
21. Frederic Harrison, *Philosophy of Common Sense* (London: Macmillan, 1907), p. 40.
22. William James, *Pragmatism, A New Name for Some Old Ways of Thinking; Popular Lectures on Philosophy* (London: Longmans, 1907), p. 45.

Gotama asked the youth in reply, "Is there a single one of the Brahmins versed in the three *Vedas*, or of their puipls, or of their teachers, or of their forerunners up to the seventh generation, who has ever seen Brahma face to face?" To each of these questions, Vāseṭṭha answered "No."

"Then you say, Vāseṭṭha, that not one of the Brahmins, even up to the seventh generation, has ever seen Brahma face to face. Even they did not pretend to know, or to have seen where or whence or whither Brahma is. Then, the talk of these Brahmins, versed in their three *Vedas*, turns out to be ridiculous, mere words, a vain and empty thing."

The Buddha introduced another parable: "Suppose a man should say so, 'How I long for, how I love, the most beautiful woman in this land!' And people should ask him, 'Well, good friend! this most beautiful woman in the land, whom you love and long for, do you know whether that beautiful woman is a noble lady, or a Brahmin woman, or of the trader class, or a slave?'

"And when so asked, he should answer, 'No!'

"And when people should ask him, 'Well, good friend! this most beautiful woman in all the land, whom you so love and long for, do you know what her name is, or her family name; whether she be tall or short, dark or of medium complexion, black or fair; or in what village or town or city she dwells?'

"But when so asked, he should answer, 'No!'

"Now what do you think of him? Would it not turn out that the talk of that man was foolish talk?

"Just in the same way, Brahma, the highest god, cannot be seen. Therefore he must not be believed in."[1]

These analyses of situations by the Buddha are indicative of an empiricism on his part which has only modern counterparts in Western philosophy. The Buddha's rigorous attitude, as evidenced by analyses such as the above regarding the most beautiful woman in the land, is comparable to the modern tradition that began with Hume and continued through the 20th century "Oxbridge" school right up to present-day language discussions in philosophy. For the Oxbridge philosophers "the most beautiful girl in the land" was a certain mysterious white rabbit. After considering its characteristics of being invisible, inaudible, odorless, weightless, and intangible, the consensus was that if one still believed such a rabbit existed, at the very least he would be using the word "rabbit" in quite an uncommon way.

Among Chinese philosophers a somewhat similar rigorous attitude is seen in Confucius. "What Confucius expected of his favorite students was the exercise of the right to doubt, to question, and not to be pleased

1. Tevijja-sutta. Rhys Davids, *Indian Buddhism*, pp. 56–60.

or satisfied with whatever a great master or authority might say. Confucius himself fully exemplified this right to doubt in his teaching."[2]

The Buddha's conception of religion was purely ethical; his primary concern was daily conduct, not ritual, worship, metaphysics, or theology. When a Brahmin proposed to purify himself of his sins by bathing at Gaya, the holy place, Buddha suggested, "Have your bath here, even here, O Brahmin. Be kind to all beings. If you don't speak false, if you don't kill life, if you don't take what is not given to you, secure in self-denial, what would you gain by going to Gaya? Any water is Gaya to you."[3]

The Buddha repudiated all religious customs that were observed only conventionally. "What is the use of matted hair, O fool, what of the raiment of goatskins? Your inward nature is full of wickedness; the outside you make clean."[4] To the same end Jesus exclaimed, "Woe to you, scribes and Pharisees, hypocrites! for you are like whitewashed tombs, which outwardly appear beautiful, but within they are full of dead men's bones and all uncleanness. So you also outwardly appear righteous to men, but within you are full of hypocrisy and iniquity."[5] In the same spirit, Jesus opposed magical rites and sacrifices. At Jerusalem there stood a great altar, a stone on which animals were killed as an offering to God. The Jews who came to the temple from all parts of the world could not bring with them the oxen, lambs, and doves to sacrifice, and so had to buy them on the spot. The sellers of the animals and the moneychangers made a big profit thereby, which went into the purses of the rich and high priests. Jesus condemned the practice, driving out the men and animals and overturning the money tables.[6]

Sacrifices were virtually abandoned in both of these universal religions. In early Buddhism, including that of King Aśoka, the terms "blessing" (*maṅgala*) and "sacrifice" (*yañña*) were interpreted to have ethical meaning.[7] In Christianity sacrificial forms were symbolically represented, for example, in the layout of a basilica. Even funerals, at which priests commonly officiated, were also discouraged by early Buddhist monks and early Christians alike.[8]

2. Hu Shih, "The Right to Doubt in Ancient Chinese Thought," *Philosophy East and West*, vol. XII, no. 4 (Jan. 1963), pp. 295–300.
3. S. Radhakrishnan, *Indian Philosophy*, vol. I (London: George Allen and Unwin, 1923), p. 421.
4. *Dhammapada* 394.
5. Matthew 23:27–28. Cf. Luke 11:39.
6. Matthew 21:12.
7. E.g., *Suttanipāta* 238–251; Aśoka's edicts.
8. "When one of his [Jesus'] followers asked leave to go and bury his father, 'Let the dead bury the dead,' was his terrible answer. He would allow no claim whatsoever to be made on personality" (Oscar Wilde, *The Soul of Man under Socialism*). Cf. Matthew 8:21–22, Luke 9:59–60.

The Greeks generally put their trust in reason, and were prepared to act in any case according to the dictates of reason. "Thither let us follow, whither the argument (*logos*) leads."[9] This was not only the motto of Plato, but also the fundamental characteristic common to all the Greek thinkers. "Whither the argument blow, thither we go."[10] Some thinkers of the Hellenistic Age were also rationalistic with regard to religious rites. For instance, Epicurus, whose ethics has some features in common with Buddhist ethics, was exceptionally hostile to traditional religion.

Concerning the assertions of early Buddhists it is possible to say that their attitude was highly positivistic.[11] But this does not mean that the scriptures of early Buddhism do not contain anything miraculous or supernatural. In order to mollify the common people concessions to various forms of popular faith were included. Miracle stories and legends of the Buddha and the saints are frequently mentioned, but they are not essential to Buddhist philosophy.

3. Universal Norms

In Buddhism the teaching of the partial veracity of various thoughts (seen above) in some ways still presupposes universal norms of human existence. However skeptical a man may be about anything, the phenomenon of skeptical thinking itself presupposes the existence of some kind of universalizable norms (e.g., in the sense of language rules) although they may be difficult to grasp. Without such accepted laws (or rules) men could not engage in consecutive thinking and communication. Early Buddhists thought that in our human existence there work many universal laws and contiguous norms, which they named *dharmas* (Pāli, *dhammas*). The word *dharma* etymologically means "that which keeps." Gotama was called *dhamma-vādi*, one who reasons according to the law (that is, not on the basis of the authority of the *Vedas*, or of tradition). The Buddha stated, "He who sees not the *dharma* sees not me—He who sees *dharma* sees me."[1]

9. Plato, *Laws*, II, 667 A (Jowett's translation, vol. V, p. 46).
10. Plato, *Republic*, III, 394 D (Jowett's translation, vol. III, p. 79).
11. Nietzsche said: "Buddhism is a hundred times more realistic than Christianity: posing problems objectively and coolly is part of its inheritance, for Buddhism comes after a philosophic movement which spanned centuries. The concept of 'God' had long been disposed of when it arrived. Buddhism is the only genuinely positivistic religion in history" (Friedrich Nietzsche, *The Antichrist. The Portable Nietzsche*, Selected and Translated by Walter Kaufmann [New York: Viking Press, 1954], pp. 586–587).
1. *Itivuttaka* 92.

In a like manner Jesus remarked, "I am the way, and the truth, and the life; no one comes to the father but by me."[2] According to early Christians the law had already been given—the law of Moses. Jesus brought to it the concepts of grace and truth.[3] According to Paul, Christians gain knowledge of what is sinful by means of the law[4] and the coming of Jesus signified "the end of the law," the justification of those who have faith.[5] But in these cases the significance of "law" differs with both religions. Jesus stressed a personal relationship to God, while the Buddha stressed the universal validity of his truth or *dharma*. The teaching of Christ is rather non-rational and personal, while that of the Buddha is more rationalistic. Man, in Buddha's viewpoint, is accountable to law and not to divine will.

Buddhist *dharmas* are not rigid and strict rules. They are flexible and adaptable to places and occasions. The *Book of Discipline* officially admits that rules can be changed according to the differences of places where they are practiced. Christians have done the same for practical reasons, as is admitted by Western thinkers.[6]

According to the Buddha, personal relations should be brought into harmony with the universal norms. When the Buddha was about to die, he admonished his attendant Ananda that the brethren should rely upon the norms. "It may be, Ananda, that in some of you the thought may arise, 'The word of the master is ended, we have no teacher more!' But it is not thus, that you should regard it. The Truths (*Dhamma*), and the Rules of the Order (*Vinaya*), which I have set forth and laid down for you all, let them, after I am gone, be the Teacher to you."[7] And further, "In whatever doctrine and discipline the Noble Eightfold Path is not found, neither in it is there found a man of true saintliness."[8] Jesus had also told his disciples, "Heaven and earth will pass away, but my words will not pass away."[9] The Buddhist motto "Rely upon the law, not on a person" has a Greek counterpart in Heraclitus, who said, "When you have listened, not to me but to the Law (*Logos*), it is wise to agree that all things are one."[10]

2. John 14:6.
3. John 1:17.
4. Romans 3:20.
5. Romans 10:4. Cf. Galatians 2:19 and 3:24.
6. "By Christianity I here mean what is accounted such by all churches and sects—the maxims and precepts contained in the New Testament. These are considered sacred, and accepted as laws, by all professing Christians. Yet it is scarcely too much to say that not one Christian in a thousand guides or tests his individual conduct by reference to those laws. The standard to which he does refer it, is the custom of his nation, his class, or his religious profession" (J. S. Mill, *On Liberty*, p. 24).
7. *Mahaparinibbāna-suttanta* 6, 1. *Dīgha-nikāya*, vol. II, p. 154.
8. *Ibid.*, 5, 27. *Dīgha-nikāya* II, p. 151.
9. Luke 21:33.
10. Heraclitus, fragment 50.

In China, Taoism viewed human life in relation to a transcendent, all-pervading Way (or Tao) which was the ultimate principle of all life. Lao-tzu said, "The Man follows the ways of Earth, the Earth follows the ways of Heaven, Heaven follows the ways of the Taok, Tao follows the ways of itself."[11]

Confucius, too, affirmed worldly life, but for him "this world" was not opposed to heaven. Indeed, the common term for this world was "All-under-heaven," reflecting both man's dependence on the physical heavens and the supremacy of the heavenly order in the affairs of men. For Confucius, if this order were recognized and followed, it would be possible to achieve good government and world peace. The perfectibility of the individual in society, and of society through the cultivation of the individual, would bring about something very much like heaven-on-earth.[12] Of the more common religious view, which sees an afterlife in heaven as the end of personal salvation, Confucius would not try to speak. Heaven for him was not an afterlife, a separate sphere or state of being; it was the moral order, the ruling power in *this* world. And it is in this life that salvation, personal or social, comes about.[13]

In Buddhism the world "*dharma*" is often used to mean the doctrine or path of the Buddha that is the universal norm for mankind. On this point extreme similarity is noted between the assertions of Confucius and Mencius. "The master [Confucius] said, Heaven begat the power (*te*) that is in me. What have I to fear from such a one as Huan T'ui?"[14] Mencius reiterated the master's principle, saying "Constantly strive to be in harmony with the [divine] will and thereby get for yourself much happiness."[15] The Buddha affirmed that *dharma* or righteousness is the only way to welfare on earth as in heaven. On this point also there is close proximity to the assertions of Chinese thinkers. Confucius proclaimed that the will of heaven shall prevail; and Lao-tzu declared that there is no getting past the Tao. They all mean that against the rock of moral law the world's exploiters hurl themselves, eventually to their own destruction.

The Western counterpart of the concept of *dharma* can be said to be *logos*, (although in the sense of "word," it occasionally corresponds with the Indian *śadba* or *vāk*). The rhythm of events in the universe or the uniformity of nature under law, which alone is permanent, was termed by Heraclitus the destiny, the order (*dike*), the reason (*logos*) of the world.[16]

11. T'ang Chün-i, "Four Levels of 'Imitation of the Tao' in Laotze's Sayings," *Journal of the Institute of Chinese Studies of the Chinese University of Hong Kong*, vol. I (1968), pp. 206–207.
12. De Bary, *Buddhism in Chinese Tradition.*
13. T'ang Chün-i, op. cit.
14. *Analects* VII, 22. Huan T'ui was a Minister of War in the Sung.
15. *Mencius* II, 1, 4; I, 2, 5, 6, etc.
16. W. Windelband, *History*, p. 36.

Just as Buddha wanted to teach deliverance to all men with the idea of universal laws, Heraclitus regarded *logos* as universal in the same way. "One must follow (the universal law, namely) that which is common (to all). But although the Law is universal, the majority live as if they had understanding peculiar to themselves."[17]

However, universality does not contradict the need for obedience to a person who represents authority. This was evident in the practice of early Buddhists. And Heraclitus also said, "To obey the will of one man is also Law (political law, *Nomos*)."[18] The authority in man is based upon universal law, and not vice versa. Buddhists said from the earliest stage that "whether a Buddha appears in the world or not, law is eternally valid." Voiced in his own metaphysics, Heraclitus' counterpart to this is: "This ordered universe (*cosmos*), which is the same for all, was not created by any one of the gods or of mankind, but it was ever and is and shall be everliving Fire, kindled in measure and quenched in measure."[19]

Law as the basis of human existence was explained by Buddhists as "deep, profound" (*gambhira*), and "difficult to understand" (*duranubodha*). This compares to Heraclitus' statement, "The Law (of the universe) is as here explained; but men are always incapable of understanding it, both before they hear it, and when they have heard it for the first time. For though all things come into being in accordance with the Law, men seem as if they had never met with it."[20] Heraclitus warned that, "We must not act and speak like men asleep."[21] This statement recalls to mind a similar metaphor utilized in naming the Buddha—"the Awakened One."

In the philosophy of Plato, the idea of the Good, which is the source of all ideas, is supreme. The truly real and truly good are thought to be identical; the idea of the God is the *Logos*, the cosmic purpose. The universe is conceived by him as a logical system of ideas, an organic unity, governed by a universal purpose, *Logos*. It is the function of philosophy, by the exercise of reason, to understand the inner order and connections of the universe, and to conceive its essence by logical thought.[22]

Later Western philosophers who recognized a universal norm were the Stoics, who believed that law rules all. Marcus Aurelius, for example, taught that "life in harmony with the universe is what is good; and harmony with the universe is the same thing as obedience to the will of God."[23]

17. Heraclitus, fragment 2.
18. *Ibid.*, 33.
19. *Ibid.*, 30.
20. *Ibid.*, 1.
21. *Ibid.*, 73
22. Frank Thilly, *A History of Philosophy*, revised by Ledger Wood (New York: Henry Holt and Company, 1952), p. 81.
23. B. Russell, *History of Western Philosophy*, p. 265.

Buddha accepted nearly the same harmony, but felt it could be accomplished through "conformity to *dharma*."

The *logos* doctrine of Heraclitus became a central point of the Stoic metaphysics. The Stoics asserted that all life and movement have their source in the *logos*: it is god; it contains the germs or seess (*spermata*) of life; in it the whole *cosmos* lies potential as the plant in the seed. The entire universe forms a single, unitary, living, connected whole, and all particular things are the determinate forms assumed by a divine primitive power which is in a state of eternal activity. An actively productive and formative power, the deity is the *logos spermatikos*, the vital principle or creative reason, which unfolds itself in the multitude of phenomena as their peculiar, particular *logoi spermatikoi*, or formative forces.[24]

Philo was to interpret the Stoic conception of the *Logos* as the sum total of the divine activity in the world. The *Logos* is on the one hand the divine wisdom, resting within itself, the Supreme Being's rational power of production. On the other hand, *Logos* is reason coming forth from the self-subsistent image of the deity, the not yet arisen first-born son (not to be without origin as is God), the coming *second God*.[25]

24. W. Windelband, *History*, pp. 180–181, 186.
25. *Ibid.*, p. 223.

IV. HUMAN EXISTENCE

A. Analysis

1. Suffering

The first trait of existence which the Buddha traditionally discerned is that certain aspects of human life are characterized by pain, discomfort, or suffering (*dukkha*). Buddha's enlightenment is said to have shown him beyond doubt the efficacy of the Four Noble Truths. The first of these as traditionally represented makes clear that there is suffering in the world. In his first sermon, the Buddha is thought to have given his analysis of the sorrowful aspects of life: "Birth is suffering; decay is suffering; sorrow, lamentation, grief, and despair are suffering; not to get what one desires is suffering; in short, the five aggregates of existence [forms, sensations, perceptions, psychic disposition, and consciousness] are suffering."[1]

The Buddha's contention was that man shall never be at ease until he has overcome his basic anxiety.[2] He sought to teach a way of terminating the suffering that prompts such anxiety. People who are busy all the time, who must always think of something, must always be doing something, are incessantly running away from this experience of the basic or original anxiety. But looking at the inner life, it cannot be denied that there remain many things which can be called suffering. No sooner has the body arisen, taught the Buddha, than disease and decay begin to act upon it. Individuality involves limitation, and limitation ends in suffering. All sorts of suffering are each simply a result of individuality.

Buddhists have especially stressed the fear of death, which overcomes all men. Every moment man is threatened by the depth of death, although he is generally not conscious of it. "Not in the sky, nor in the depths of

1. *Saṃyutta-nikāya*, 5, 421ff.
2. Conze says that the similarity between Buddhism on the one hand and Bergson and Western existentialists does not constitute a parallel (*Philosophy East and West*, vol. XIII, no. 2 [June, 1963], pp. 109–113).

the ocean, nor having entered the caverns of the mountain, nay such a place is not to be found in the world where a man might dwell without being overpowered by death."[3] None can resist the universal supremacy of death. Death, as stressed in Buddhism, is the law of all life, though people have generally attempted to distract themselves from the fear. "How is there laughter, how is there joy, as the world is always burning? Why do you not seek a light, you who are surrounded by darkness?"[4] "This body is wasted, full of sickness and frail; this heap of corruption breaks to pieces. Life indeed ends in death."[5]

Chang-tzu's mysticism seems to be as close as any in China to the Buddhist concept of sorrow, but his experience is of the absurdity of life, not its pain or anguish. Also in China, among the Confucianists, Hsun-tzu argued the evil nature of man from the anarchic state of his selfish desires. However, he was still optimistic that human desires could be educated, refined, and harmonized, without the need to extinguish them.[6] In the latter respect the Buddhist standpoint was similar.

Asceticism (as discussed in Chapter II) shares with Buddhism an assessment of man's human characteristics (i.e., his ordinary bodily state) as inconducive to higher spirituality. In contrast to most asceticisms however, Buddha claimed his experience showed there to be no enduring self in matter. On this point Buddhism differs considerably from the dualistic conception of a perfectable soul capable of separation from its fallen state, the body (as in Pythagorean, Platonic, and Neo-Platonic doctrines). The latter belief is close to the Christian conception, whereby all varieties of suffering are to be endured if necessary in the furtherance of the soul. The Christian tenet that man is in a fallen state from which a return to true religion can elevate him once again is reminiscent of a diagnosis of man found in religion in general. Buddhism puts forth a similar analysis but tells the story slightly differently: man is in a state of suffering or discomfort because of his own ignorance.

Among Western thinkers who came to an understanding of life's condition by a method similar (at least superficially) to Buddha's was Kant. Kant, refuting the optimism of Leibnitz, asks: "Would any man of sound understanding who has lived long enough and has meditated on the worth of human existence care to go again through life's poor play? I do not say on the same conditions, but on any conditions whatever?"[7]

3. *Dhammapada* 128.
4. *Dhammapada* 146.
5. *Dhammapada* 148.
6. De Bary, *Buddhism in Chinese Tradition* (a paper read in Mexico Conference, 1963), p. 4.
7. Kant, *Failure of Every Philosophical Attempt in Theodicy,* 1791 (cited from Radhakrishnan, *Indian Philosophy,* I, p. 364).

Whereby Buddha discerned the prominence of suffering and anxiety in man's psycho-physical existence, it is difficult to think of him as pessimistic, considering his belief in the liberating power of religious discipline and the perfectability of human nature. The Buddha's doctrine was not one of despair; for instance, the concept of eternal damnation is not found in his thought (nor in any of the religions of ancient India). Everyone, he believed, can be saved finally.[8]

2. Ignorance—The Cause of Suffering

GIVEN the impermanence of phenomena (see section immediately below), the cause of craving and ultimately of suffering must be ignorance. Ignorance is the main cause from which false desires (or cravings) spring. Ignorance and false desires respectively are the theoretical and the practical sides of one fact. Purely from a theoretical viewpoint false desires are seen to be ignorance; on the other hand, the Buddha's concrete realization of ignorance was that it is false desires. In actual life, according to Buddhism, the two are one.

New Testament Christians held a similar belief, that ignorance contributes to separation from God. "They are darkened in their understanding, alienated from the life of God because of the ignorance that is in them, due to their hardness of heart; they have become callous and have given themselves up to licentiousness, greedy to practice every kind of uncleanness."[1]

To the Buddhist, as to Indian thinkers in general, knowledge and will are so closely related that a distinction is hardly ever drawn between them. The same word, "*cetanā*," is often used to signify both thinking and willing. So when knowledge in this sense is attained, the will is controlled and suffering comes to an end. The name "Buddha," "Enlightened One," signifies a person who has solved the riddle of existence and discovered the means for the cessation of suffering. The Buddha's virtue (*kuśala*) was based upon knowledge (*jñāna*, *vidyā*).

A close connection between virtue and knowledge is also characteristic of Socrates and Plato. It may be seen that in the Platonic dialogues true knowledge is knowledge of the form of the Good. Ancient Greeks commonly held the belief that virtue is knowledge and knowledge is the gateway to a craft, a skill, a science, and moral excellence.[2]

8. The only exceptions to it were the theology of Madhva who admitted non-eligibility of the wicked and the Hosso school of China and Japan which practically admitted non-eligibility of some persons.

1. Ephesians 4:18–19.

2. *Lysis*; 210. Laches. Cf. the discussion on sophrosyne (moderation) in the *Charmides*.

In Christian ethics, on the other hand, a pure heart is essential and at least as likely to be found among the ignorant as among the learned. But even in Christianity quasi-epistemological explanations of ethics are found. As a counterpart to the Buddhist saying: "When the Brahmin has reached the other shore, to him who knows all bonds vanish,"[3] compare this statement by Jesus: "You will know the truth and the truth will make you free."[4] This is a somewhat isolated statement and Christians relied more on grace than on their own ability to win "truth." In contrast, Buddha was known as *Vidyācaraṇasampanna*, one who has mastered both wisdom and practice. For Buddha, wisdom meant partly knowledge of the chain of occurrences (Dependent Origination or chain of causation)[5] that result in our ignorance. Seeing that chain sequentially, from beginning to end and back again resulted in the Buddha's insight (at the time of his enlightenment) that: (1) because of ignorance (lack of knowledge), we suffer, and (2) because of knowledge (disappearance of ignorance), we do not suffer.

Between the two extremes of ignorance and suffering, Buddhist thinkers have found and set up several causes in the chain. But the fundamental theory which applies to all formulae is that "When this exists, that exists. When this appears, that appears. When this does not exist,

3. *Dhammapada* 384.
4. John 8:32.
5. The most advanced formula of Dependent Origination is as follows:
   1. Because of Ignorance, Will-to-Action (*Saṅkhāras*)
   2. Because of the Will-to-Action, Consciousness
   3. Because of Consciousness, Psycho-physical Existence
   4. Because of Psycho-physical Existence, the six organs of sense (eye, ear, nose, tongue body [the sense of touch], and mind)
   5. Because of the six organs of sense, Contact
   6. Because of Contact, Sensation (or Feeling)
   7. Because of Sensation, Craving
   8. Because of Craving, Attachment (or Grasping)
   9. Because of Attachment, Becoming (or Worldly Existence)
   10. Because of Becoming, Birth
   11. Because of Birth, decay, and death, grief, lamentation, (physical) suffering, dejection, and despair (All of these constitute suffering in general.)

   In the *Upaniṣads* the chief stress was laid on deliverance from natural ignorance (*avidyā*) by the knowledge of *ātman* (e.g., *Bṛhad. Up.* III, 4, 2; III, 5, 1; III, 7, 23; *Chānd. Up.* VII, 1, 3).

   It is noteworthy that the law of Dependent Origination was taught regardless of the authority of Buddhas. As expressing a universal truth, it was considered as valid eternally and from eternity, independently of the advent of a Buddha, not to mention any action by a diety. "Whether the Perfect Ones (*Tathāgatas* Buddhas) arise or not, this elemental datum stands as the establishing of things as effects, as the cause of this and that. Concerning this, a Perfect One (*Tathāgata*) becomes enlightened and penetrates it, and he declares, makes it manifest" (*Samyutta-nikāya* II, 25, 3).

that does not exist. When this disappears, that disappears."[6] Insofar as theory is concerned, this corresponds to Hippocrates' (460–377 B.C.) definition of disease, that "those in whose existence a disease must appear thus must be regarded as the cause (*aitia*) of the disease."[7] The Buddhist concept of inter-relational origination (the chain of Dependent Origination) is called *nidāna*, which can mean pathology in Indian medical science. The Four Noble Truths set forth by Buddhism correspond respectively to diagnosis, etiology, prognosis, and therapy.

This formula of "Dependent Origination" or "Origination through Dependence" (Pāli, *paṭiccasamuppāda*, Sanskrit. *pratītyasamutpāda*, see fn. 5) is repeated in many passages of the scriptures, and elaborate explanations are given for the terms used both in the scriptures and commentaries. According to the *sūtras*, the Buddha found that birth is the cause of such suffering as decay and death, and he traced the chain back to ignorance. Then he contemplated the way in which ignorance gives rise to will-to-action (*karmic* formations), which in turn produces consciousness and so on through the chain of causation until he came to birth as the cause of decay and death. Working backward, he saw that causation of birth is the cause of the cessation of suffering and, finally, he discovered that the cessation of ignorance is the ultimate cessation of the whole chain.

The extinguishing of ignorance which brings about the perfection of one's own existence is called wisdom (or knowledge, *paññā*, Sanskrit *prajñā*). Such a supreme ideal of wisdom was greatly esteemed by Plato and Socrates. For Plato the Good lies in seeking to become "like the divine so far as we can, and that again is to become righteous with the help of wisdom."[8]

Then, what is this ignorance? It is a lack of the right intuition. Then, intuition of what? Technically, the scriptures are silent on this point, but it became the issue for the development of the concept of Dependent Origination in later days. At the outset the laws of impermanence and non-self have the highest degree of certainty of being the objects of ignorance and knowledge.

6. Th. Stcherbatsky, *The Conception of Buddhist Nirvāṇa* (Leningrad: The Academy of Sciences of the USSR, 1927), p. 39, n. 2. H. Ui, *Indo Tetsugaku Kenkyū* (Tokyo: Kōshisha, 1926), vol. 2, p. 318.
7. *Peri arkhaiēs iētrikēs* XIX. Cited from Walter Ruben, "Indische und griechische Metaphysik," in *Zeitschrift fur Indologie und Iranistik* (Leipzig, 1931), p. 17, fn. 1.
8. *Theaetetus*, 176 b 1–3.

3. Impermanence of Phenomena

Why are we subject to so many kinds of suffering? Why are we seemingly so doomed? Buddha taught that it is because of our ignorance of the transiency and impermanence of our human existence. Suffering is one with transiency since what we desire is impermanent, changing, and perishing. The Buddha asked his disciples, "That which is transient, O monks, is it painful or pleasant?" "Painful, O Master."[1] Our dreams, our hopes, our wishes, our desires—all of them will be forgotten as if they had neve been. Buddhism holds this to be a universal principle common to all things. "Whatever is subject to origination is subject also to destruction."[2] Necessary and inexorable is the death of all that is born, Buddha claimed; the difference is only in the degree of duration. A few may last for years, and others for a brief while only. But all must vanish. As man becomes aware of this fact of impermanence and its implications, Buddha expected he would naturally wish to substitute for the ignoble craving of worldly things the noble aspiration to the "imcomparable security of *Nirvāṇa* free from corruption."

> O transient are our life's experience!
> Their nature 'tis to rise and pass away.
> They happen in our ken, they cease to be.
> O well for us when they are sunk to rest![3]

In the Buddhist metaphysics there is no substance which abides forever.[4] There is only becoming; the individual is unstable, temporary, sure to pass away. Even form and other material qualities in things are found to be impermanent. (In later days these sentiments of impermanence became peculiarly Indian rather than Buddhist.) In Greece, Heraclitus also held the same opinion, saying, "All things are in a state of flux," and "Reality is a condition of unrest."[5] He represented life in the world of time and space as a condition of incessant change. Plato asks: "How can that be a real thing which is never in the same state?"[6] Plato, how-

1. *Majjhima-nikāya* III, 19.
2. *Vinaya*, Mahāvagga I, 23.
3. *Theragāthā* 1159, translated by Mrs. Rhys Davids, *Psalms of the Early Buddhists*: *Psalms of the Brethren* (London: The Pali Text Society, 1909–13), p. 385.
4. Criticizing the theory of Aristotle, Bertrand Russell says, " 'Substance,' when taken seriously, is a concept impossible to free from difficulties. A substance is supposed to be the subject of properties, and to be something distinct from all its properties. But when we take away the properties, and try to imagine the substance by itself, we find that there is nothing left" (*History of Western Philosophy*, p. 201).
5. Heraclitus, fragments 56 and 84.
6. *Cratylus* 439 (Jowett's translation).

ever, posited a real world of forms within change; and this the Buddha never did.

In the Old Testament the beginnings of a Christian conception of an impermanent condition are seen, "Then I considered all that my hands had done and the toil I had spent in doing it, and behold, all was vanity and a striving after wind, and there was nothing to be gained under the sun."[7] New Testament Christians continued the assessment of the phenomenality of the world in such sayings as, "The things that are seen are transient, but the things that are unseen are eternal."[8] There is probably a difference in the origins of the Buddhist and Christian ideas of impermanence, however. The Christian origins probably go back to an inchoate Hebrew conception of the greatness of God, and later the role of insignificant human beings separated from God came to be stressed; whereas in Buddhism the fragile and weak existence of human beings was first stressed, and then something beyond was sought for. The fragility of human life prompted pagan conversion to Christianity[9] and was decried in Romantic literature by modern intellectuals.[10]

Once man has become convinced of the efficacy of Buddha's diagnosis that suffering is caused by cravings and cravings are caused by ignorance, he must then walk very carefully on the middle path, avoiding desires, if he wishes enlightenment from his ignorance: "Knowing that this body is (fragile) like a jar, making this thought firm like a fortress, let him attack Māra (the temptor) with the weapon of wisdom, protect what he has conquered and remain attached to it."[11] A similar

7. Ecclesiastes 2:11.
8. II Corinthians 4:18. Cf. the Indian concepts of *sat* and *māyā*.
9. "When a pagan king in England asked his advisers what they thought of the Christian faith, one of them replied: 'O King, the life of man is like the flight of a swallow thought our banquet hall, out of the dark and the cold for a moment through the light and warmth and into the cold and dark again. A religion which can tell us more about that dark beyond certainly ought to be followed'" (Roland Herbert Bainton, *The Church of Our Fathers* (New York: Charles Scribner's Sons, 1950), p. 78).
10. "At this breakneck hurry, we are no sooner boys than we are adult, no sooner in love than married or jilted, no sooner one age than we begin to be another, and no sooner in the fullness of our manhood than we begin to decline towards the grave. It is in vain to seek for consistency or expect clear and stable views in a medium so perturbed and fleeting" (Robert Louis Stevenson: *Virginibus Puerisque*).
    Shelly set the idea to poetry:

    Worlds on worlds are rolling ever
    From creation to decay,
    Like the bubbles on a river,
    Sparkling, bursting, borne away (*Hellas*).
11. *Dhammapada* 40.

caution was expressed by Paul: "Let anyone who thinks that he stands take heed lest he fall."[12]

It is noteworthy that the awareness of transience or change gave impetus to a display of strong will among the Stoics. Epicterus instructed, "Remember that you ought to behave in life as you would at a banquet. As something is being passed around it comes to you; stretch out your hand and take a portion of it politely. It passes on, do not detain it. Or it has not come to you yet; do not project your desire to meet it, but wait until it comes in front of you. So act toward children, so toward a wife, so toward office, so toward wealth; and then some day you will be worthy of the banquet of the gods. But if you do not take these things even when they are set before you, but despise them, then you will not only share the banquet of the gods, but share also their rule. For it was by so doing that Diogenes and Heracleitus, and men like them, were deservedly divine and deservedly so called."[13]

The Buddhist canons co ntain the following story that is remarkably akin to the Greek spirit in herited by Epictetus. When the Buddha was going to die, Ānanda went into the monastery (*vihāra*) and stood leaning against the lintel of the door, and weeping at the thought. "Alas! I remain still but a learner, one who has yet to work out his own perfection. And the Master is about to pass away from me—he who is so kind!" The Buddha called Ānanda and said, "Enough! Ānanda! Do not let yourself be troubled; do not weep! Have I not already, on former occasions, told you that it is in the very nature of all things most near and dear unto us that we must divide ourselves from them, leaving them, sever ourselves from them? How, then, Ānanda, can this be possible—whereas anything whatever is born, brought into being, and organized, contains within itself the inherent necessity of dissolution.—how, then, can this be possible, that such a being should not be dissolved? No such condition can exist! For a long time, Ānanda, have you been very near to me by acts of love, kind and good, that never varies, and is beyond all measure—you have done well, Ānanda! Be earnest in effort, and you too shall soon be free from the Intoxications [sensuality, individuality, delusion, and ignorance]."[14]

It is easy to see that Epictetus metaphor of the banquet was indicative of an assessment of human nature close to the Buddha's. For Epictetus in another passage, offered advice similar to that given by Buddha to Ananda. He said, "When you see someone weeping in sorrow, either because a child has gone on a journey, or because he has lost his property, beware that you be not carried away by the impression that

12. I Corinthians 10:12.
13. Epictetus, *Encheiridion* 15 (Walter Arnold Kaufman, comp., *Philosophic Classics*, vol. 1 (Englewood Cliffs, N. J.: Prentice-Hall, Inc., 1963), p. 558.
14. *Mahāparinibbāna-suttanta* 5, 13–14. *Dīgha-nikāya*, vol. II, 143–144.

the man is in the midst of external ills, but straightway keep before you this thought: 'It is not what has happened that distresses this man (for it does not distress another), but his judgement about it.' Do not, however, hesitate to sympathize with him . . . but be careful not to groan also in the centre of your being."[15]

This teaching not to weep is the same between Buddhists and Stoics, but the Buddhist attitude was always based upon selfless compassion, whereas the sympathy of the Stoics retained an awareness of the distinction between individuals. The Buddha expressed not individual advice but universal compassion when, on the moment of death, he exhorted the brethren with his last words, "All composite bodies are decay prone so work out your salvation diligently" (*Vayadhammā saṅkhārā appamādena sampādetha*).[16]

4. The Theory of Non-Ego

Early Buddhists set forth the teaching that since everything is transient, one should not cling to anything in the objective world; nothing should be regarded as "mine" (*mama*) or "belonging to me." This teaching was set forth in the oldest poems[1] of the scriptures without theoretical support and was shared by early Jains.[2] As prose sections came to be added to the scriptures, based on their poetic counterparts, the theory of Non-Ego became systematized. Admitting the transitory nature of everything, Buddhists did not want to assume any metaphysical substances. They reduced substances, things and souls to forces, functions, movements and processes, and adopted kinetic (see next section) conceptions of reality. Life was considered to be nothing but a series of manifestations of becomings and extinctions, in short, a process of becoming.

The Buddha repudiated the popular conception of the individual ego. The objects with which man identifies himself, he thought, are not the true Self. Fortune, social position, family, body and even mind are not the true Self. In this sense the Buddhist theory can be called "the theory of Non-Self," ie., anything perceived is not the Self. In addition, all the then current theories about "souls" were discussed and rejected in the scriptures, and in this sense as well Buddha's theory can be called "the theory of Non-Soul or Non-Ego."

The "ego" or "soul" translates into Pāli as "*attan*," in Sanskrit

15. Epictetus, *Encheiridion* 16 (Kaufman, *op. cit.*, p. 558).
16. *Mahāparinibbāna-suttanta* 3, 51; 6, 7. *Dīgha-nikāya*, vol. II, p. 120.
1. This thought is especially clear in the poems of the *Suttanipāta*.
2. This is most clear in the first half of the *Āyāraṅga*.

"*ātman.*" It is more literally rendered "self." But occasionally the word "ego" is used to distinguish it from the "true Self" which is stressed even in early Buddhism. There is nothing permanent, and if only that which is permanent deserves to be called the Self or *Ātman*, then nothing on earth is Self. A sermon was delivered to the five ascetics in Benares, headed by Koṇḍañña, on the non-perceptibility of the soul: "The body is not the eternal soul, for it tends towards destruction. Neither feeling, nor perception nor disposition nor consciousness, together constitute the eternal soul, for were it so, feeling, etc., would not likewise tend towards destruction."[3] And again, "So it must be said of all physical forms whatever, past, present, or to be, subjective or objective, far or near, high or low: 'this is not mine, this I am not, this is not my eternal soul.' "[4]

The following chart makes clear how human existence, the totality of mind and body, was divided into five parts, components or aggregates (*skandhas*)[5] by early Buddhists:

REALITY	FICTION
Physical Form (pertaining to body) Feeling (pleasant, unpleasant, neutral) Perception (sight, etc.) Dispositions (latent, formative, phenomena) Consciousness	Ego (self)

Excluded was the traditional conception of a substance called "soul" or "ego" which had hitherto dominated the minds of the superstitious and intellectuals alike.

As one may observe, in daily life it is common to assume that "something is mine," or that "I am something," or that "something is myself." To make this teaching slightly more tangible, the example of a toothache may serve as a comparison. Normally one simply says, "I have a toothache." But to Buddhist thinkers this would have appeared as a very unscientific way of speaking. Neither "I" nor "have" nor "toothache" are

3. *Dhammacakkapavattana-sutta.*
4. *Vinaya*, Mahāvagga I, 21. Cf. *Majjhima-nikāya* I, pp. 135, 300, etc.; *Samyutta-nikāya*, II, pp. 94, 124, and III, p. 66.
5. Many Buddhist terms are very difficult to translate into English. Certain technical terms that were used have no exact equivalents. In Western languages these equivalents have been chosen as means to let Westerners roughly understand what they mean. Such is the case with "*skandhas*," translated variously as: the confections (T. W. Rhys Davids); the predispositions (Warren); the constituent elements of character (T. W. Rhys Davids). Hume's assertion that our mind is "nothing but a bundle or collection of different perceptions, united together by certain relations" is reminiscent of the theory of the Five Skandhas. Cf. Edward Conze, Philosophy East and West, XIII, No. 2 (June 1963), pp. 111–113.

counted among the ultimate facts of existence (*dharmas*). In the Buddhist literature personal expressions are replaced by impersonal ones. Impersonally, in terms of ultimate events, this experience would be divided into:

1. There is the physical *form* (i.e., the tooth as matter).
2. There is a painful *feeling*.
3. There is a sight-, touch-, and pain-*perception* of the tooth.
4. By way of *volitional* actions there is: resentment at pain, fear of possible consequences for future well-being, desire for present physical well-being, etc.
5. There is *consciousness*—an awareness of all the above.[6]

The "I" of common sense speech has disappeared; it is not the ultimate reality. One might reply, of course, that an imagined "I" is a part of the actual experience. In that case, it would be subsumed under the category of consciousness.

Properly applied, the method of reflection must have a tremendous power to disintegrate unwholesome experience. Meditation on these component elements by itself alone obviously cannot uproot all the evil in men's hearts. It is not a panacea, a cure-all, but just one of the remedies in the medicine chest of the Great Physician. Meditation, however, is bound to contribute to one's mental development to the extent that, when repeated often enough, it may set up the habit of viewing all things impersonally. (This way of thinking might be applied with efficiency by modern psychiatrists.)

In most European and all Indian systems except the Buddhist, souls and the gods are considered exceptions to the Law of Impermanence. To these spirits is attributed a substantiality, an individuality without change. But the Buddha did not want to assume all these exceptional substances (cf. Wittgenstein). In early Buddhism the traditional conception is torn away from its ancestral stem and planted in a purely rational argument. Phenomenalistic doctrines (like the above with regard to *skandhas*) which are reminiscent of Hume are developed with great skill and brilliance in the early Buddhist scriptures. Hume had rejected berkeley's theory of spiritual substance (and Locke's "something I know not what"), thereby extending the phenomenalistic interpretation of things from bodies to souls or minds. In proposing a consistent phenomenalism Hume analyzed all complex ideas into impressions, with an attempt to treat spiritual substance the same as material substance.

The views of the soul to which Hume gave his strictest critical attention were more or less theological or scholastic concepts of extended and

6. These illustrations were taken from Edward Conze, *Buddhism: Its Essence and Development* (New York: Harper Brothers, 1959), pp. 107–108. Cf. *Samyutta-nikāya* III, 46, etc.

unextended substances. He said "The question concerning the substance of the soul is absolutely unintelligible [cf. unanswerable questions in Buddhism]. All our perceptions are not susceptible of a local union, either with what is extended or unextended; there being some of them of the one kind, and some of them of the other."[7] The suggestion here is that the problem of the substantiality of the soul would be better dismissed because it doesn't make sense.

On the subject of personal identify, Hume was to deny that we have any idea of a personal self distinct from our perceptions. But where does this lead? Hume wrote, "Self or person is not any one impression, but that to which our several impressions and ideas are supposed to have reference. If any impression gives rise to the idea of self, that impression must continue invariably the same, through the whole course of our lives; since self is supposed to exist after that manner. But there is no impression constant and invariable . . . and consequently there is no such idea."[8] In addition, Hume claimed to have tried to introspect the self, to find it in his own experience. The following is his reported result: "When I enter most intimately into what I call *myself*, I always stumble on some particular perception or other. . . . I never catch myself at any time without a perception. . . . I am certain there is no such principle in me."[9]

One only attributes identity to the mind, for Hume, because the component parts of the aggregate (cf. Buddhism) are changing gradually and are intimately related to each other. The chain has an apparence of a continued and persistent object. Memory is a prime ingredient in this phenomenon.

Some have suggested that the comparisons to be made between the Self-doctrines of Buddha and Hume (such comparisons, being the subject of much recent scholarship, will be treated in no further detail here) are more than mere coincidence.[10] Others suggest that such comparisons "should be treated *at the present state of our knowledge* as nothing more than a cluster of coincidences, just so many curios in the emporium of human ideas."[11] All are in accord, however, that there are substaintial differences to be noted between the two great thinkers, notably the difference of intent. Conze stresses the Buddha's soteriological purpose in contrast to Hume's "sciential" one.[12] Jacobson believes that Hume was especially

7. *A Treatise of Human Nature*, ed. by L. A. Selby-Biggs (Oxford, 1951), 1, 4, 5, p. 234.
8. *Ibid.*, 1, 4, 6, pp. 251–252.
9. *Ibid.*
10. N. P. Jacobson, "The Possibility of Oriental Influence in Hume's Philosophy," *Philosophy East and West*, XIX, No. 1, pp. 17–37.
11. L. Stafford Betty, "The Buddhist-Humean Parallel: Postmortem," *Philosophy East and West*, XXI, No. 3, p. 253. See also K. Inada's comparison of *Anātman* with Whitehead's "actual entity" in this same issue.
12. Edward Conze, "Buddhist Philosophy and Its European Parallels," *Philodophy East and West*, XIII, No. 1 (April 1963), pp. 11–14.

struck by the importation of Confucian ideas by Jesuit monks to the England of his day. As a result, Hume's emphasis, according to Jacobson, is on "social interchange in which he believed the 'ultimate propensities' of human nature to be rooted."[13] On the other hand, "The Buddha's thought" as Jacobson sees it, "leads to a loosening of the individual's social involvement . . . into a type of metalingual meditation which frees the individual from ego-centered and social drives . . . so that the outline of a fundamentally more humane social order may arise spontaneously from the activity of the liberated man."[14]

In early Buddhism those who got rid of the notion of "ego" were highly praised. This kind of denial, however, does not mean nihilism or materialism. The Buddha clearly delineated what the self is not, but he did not give any definitive account of what it is. It is quite wrong to think that there is no self at all according to Buddhism.[15] The Buddha did not embrace materialism (cf. Aristotle).

The wandering monk Vacchagotta once asked whether there is ego or not. The Buddha was silent, whereupon the monk rose from his seat and went away. Then Ānanda asked Buddha, "Wherefore, sire, has the Exalted One not given an answer to the questions put by that monk?" The Buddha replied, "If I had answered: 'The ego is,' then that would have confirmed the doctrine of those who believe in permanence. If I had answered: 'The ego is not,' then that would have confirmed the doctrine of those who believe in annihilation."[16] As in some portions of the presentation of Hume (above), the Buddha neither wanted to affirm nor deny the existence of *Ātman*. He exhorted his followers to be philosophical enough to recognize the limits of philosophy. As "body" is a name for a system of functions, even so "soul" is a name for the sum of the dynamic states which constitute our mental existence. Outside of those states there can be admitted no soul, for we are entering the realm of the senseless.

This Non-Self theory was modified in later days. Hīnayāna teachers explained the theory as follows: things are names; "chariot" is a name

13. N. P. Jacobson, *op. cit.*, p. 25.
14. *Ibid.* L. S. Betty (*op. cit.*, p. 251) points out the further contrast of the Buddha from Hume, that the former exhibited extreme belief and conformity to the doctrine (*dhamma*) whereas Hume "loathed" his conclusions regarding the self (and other skeptical doctrines) as " 'monstrous offspring' and a 'malady' " and wished to be delivered from it by "carelessness and in-attention."
15. That the teaching of "No-Self" (different from "Non-Self") is a Buddhist doctrine is not being denied here. What is meant is that this teaching was maintained in later days by Theravada and other schools of conservative Buddhism (Hīnayāna), and that the original teaching in early scriptures was different from the developed one. The teaching of "No-Self" is held as genuine by southern scholars and some Western scholars who adopt it (e.g., Walpola Rahula, *What the Buddha Taught* [New York: Grove Press, 1959], pp. 51–66).
16. Warren, *Buddhism in Translations*, p. 134.

as much as "Nāgasena" (the name of a Buddhist elder). These is nothing more real, beneath the properties or the events. The immediate data of consciousness do not verify the existence of a unity which cannot be denied. In like argumentation, from the silence of the Buddha on the question of the "soul" Nāgasena drew his negative inference that there was no soul.[17] This opinion became the orthodox teaching of Hīnayāna Buddhism. The original teaching of the Buddha, however, seems to have been slightly different, as was discussed above.

From the investigation done so far, it is clear that the assertion of the denial of the Ego appeared in a later period and that the Buddha did not deny the soul, but was silent concerning it. Moreover, he seems to have acknowledged the true Self in our existence which is to appear in our moral conduct as conforming to universal norms. It is likely that he admitted the Self in the higher sense, although it is very difficult to diversify 'self' into upper and lower cases always (see section of True Self, below). The Buddha did not want to assume the existence of souls as metaphysical substances but in a quite similar way to that of Hume, he admitted the function of the self as the subject of action in a practical and moral sense.

5. The Individual—Kinetic Existence and Transmigration

In general, Indian philosophies and religion have upheed a doctrine of "transmigration" (*saṃsāra*), or "rebirth": that every soul, subject, or personality repeats an endless series of worldly existences. After one dies, he is reborn to live out his temporary existence for a time, and again die. So far as this doctrine is concerned, Buddhism was no exception. And Buddha's message of enlightened release addressed itself to this problem also, as did other Indian philosophies.

On the last journey of the Buddha, his disciple Ānanda went up to him and, mentioning the names of the brethren and sisters who had died, anxiously inquired about their fate after death, whether they had been reborn as animals or in hell, as spirits, or in any place of woe. The Buddha replied, "Those who have died after the complete destruction of the three bonds of lust, of covetousness and of the egoistical cleaving to existence, need not fear the state after death. They will not be reborn in a state of suffering; their minds will not continue as a *karma* of evil deeds or sin, but are assured of final salvation.

"When they die, nothing will remain of them but their good thoughts,

17. *Milindapañha* Edited by V. Trenckner (London: Williams and Norgate, 1880), pp. 25–27.

their righteous acts, and the bliss that proceeds from truth and righteousness. As rivers must at last reach the distant main, so their minds will be reborn in higher states of existence and continue to be pressing on to their ultimate goal which is the ocean of truth, the eternal peace of *Nirvāṇa.*

"Men are anxious about death and their fate after death; but there is nothing strange in this, Ānanda, that a human being should die. However, that you should inquire about them, and having heard the truth still be anxious about the dead, this is wearisome to the Blessed One. I will, therefore, teach you the mirror of truth:

"Hell is destroyed for me, and rebirth as an animal, or a spirit, or in any place of woe. I am converted; I am no longer liable to be reborn in a state of suffering, and am assured of final salvation.

"Then, what is this mirror of truth? It is the consciousness that the elect disciple is possessed of faith in the Buddha, the Truth and the Order."[1]

The dialogue quoted above can be compared to one of Paul's statements in the New Testament: "O death, where is thy victory? O death, where is thy sting? The sting of death is sin and the power of sin is the law. But thanks be to God, who gives us the victory through our Lord Jesus Christ."[2] And Buddha's mirror of truth can be compared to the following, "He who believes in the Son has eternal life; he who does not obey the Son shall not see life, but the wrath of God rests upon him."[3] In the sayings of Paul wrath and protest against wickedness is clear, whereas the Buddhist concept of eternal bliss was supposed to transcend such vehement feelings. Of course there is also a great difference between Buddhist transmigration and the eternal life doctrine of the Christian faith.

The concept of transmigration, however, had appeared earlier among the Greeks. It is a well-known fact that the followers of Pythagoras (ca. 572–500 B.C.) and even Plato believed in transmigration. This belief, however, did not become prevalent among the Greeks, but instead was rather foreign to their original way of thinking. It is supposed that the Pythagoreans adopted it from the Orphic Order, which could have been influenced by Oriental thought.

However, it was natural that the concept of transmigration without a permanent subject was much more difficult for the Greeks to understand than for the Indians. Menandros,[4] a Greek king who invaded India, questioned the Buddhist monk Nāgasena on this point, "He who is born,

1. *Mahaparinibbāna-suttanta* II, 9.
2. I Corinthians 15:55–57.
3. John 3:36.
4. Milinda in Pāli.

O venerable Nāgasena, does he remain the same or become another?" Nāgasena replied according to the doctrine of "Non-Soul" of conservative orthodox Buddhism: "Neither the same nor another." This answer was difficult for the Greek to understand. Obeying the request of the king to give him an illustration, the monk began with the following dialogue:

"Now what do you think, O King? You were once a baby, a tender thing, and small in size, lying flat on your back? Was that the same as you who are now grown up?"

"No. That child was one, I am another." Having drawn out this answer, the monk pointed out the contradiction contained in it: "If you are not that child, it will follow that you have had neither mother nor father nor teacher. You cannot have been taught either learning, or behavior, or wisdom. What, great King. . . . Is the mother of the baby a different person from the mother of the grown-up man? Is the person who goes to school one person, and another when he has finished his schooling? Is it one person who commits a crime and another who is punished by having his hands or feet cut off?"

"Certainly not. But what, Sir, would you say to that?"

"I should say that I am the same person, now that I am grown up, as I was when I was a tender, tiny baby, flat on my back, for all these states are included in one by means of this body."

"Give me an illustration."

"Suppose a man, O King, were to light a lamp, would it burn the night through?"

"Yes, it might do so."

"Now, is it the same flame that burns in the first watch of the night, Sir, and in the second?"

"No."

"Or the same that burns in the second watch and in the third?"

"No."

"Then is there one lamp in the first watch, and another in the second, and another in the third?"

"No. The light comes from the same lamp all the night through."

"Just so, O King, is the continuity of a person maintained.[5] One comes into being; another passes away; and the rebirth is, as it were, simultaneous. Thus neither as the same nor as another does a man go on to the last phase of his self-consciousness. . . . It is like milk, which, when once taken from the cow, turns, after a lapse of time, first to curd, and then from curd to butter, and then from butter to ghee."[6]

5. *Dhammasantati.* This means the continuity of elements which constitute a person.

6. *Milindapañha,* pp. 40 f. In regard to this dialogue, I followed the translation of Rhys Davids (*Sacred Books of the East,* XXXV, 63 f.), making alterations only when the translation seemed inadequate. Warren, *Buddhism in Translation,* pp. 148–152.

This is an expression of the view of the transitoriness of personal existence, one of the main tenets of Buddhism. Yet at the same time a view is held (apparently paradoxically) that individuality is maintained kinetically, i.e., in motion, one state giving way to the next, then the next, etc. The comparison of mundane existence to a burning fire expresses the thought that human life is dynamic, vibrant, and constantly in motion. That such motion doesn't cease at the moment of death is in a sense comparable to the law of conservation of matter and energy.

This same problem is the subject of one of the paradoxes of Heraclitus in his famous saying, "We bathe and do not bathe in the same stream. We are and yet are not."[7] The stream is never quite the same because it is incessantly moving. But of course it is the stream of the same name as the one we entered. Likewise the individual who steps into the stream "is not" in the sense of anything steadfast, for he, like the stream, is constantly moving, i.e., changing. But he is the individual of the same name as the one who just stepped into the stream. No one would deny that.

Plato explained Heraclitus' thought by the phrases, "Nothing eixsts, everything only becomes" and "Everything flows and nothing abides,"[8] and Aristotle by the phrase, "Everything is in motion."[9] In stressing incessant change Heraclitus agrees with Buddhism's opposition to the notion of unchangeable being, the concept of being held by the Elastics. Buddhism also rejected the notion of the permanent, immutable self (*ātman*) advocated by Upaniṣadic philosophers. Here one must not, however, overlook a difference between them. Heraclitus was interested in change primarily for the purpose of setting forth a cosmology; for the Buddha such a purpose could only be considered secondary to his ethical intent, which relied on showing man the kinetic character of human nature. Additionally, of course, Heraclitus was able to make ethical recommendations based on his metaphysics, that the fiery element being best, the "dry" state of the soul is "wisest and best."[10]

As is noticeable in many later dogmatic works, beginning with the *Questions of Milinda*, Buddhists began asserting that the incessant continuity (*saṃtāna*) of elements constituting human existence apparently shows a false aspect of one and the same personality, and compared it to a stream of water.[11] This notion was arrived at through a critical ana-

7. Fragment 49. Cf. fragment 91. Eduard Zeller, *Geschichte der Philosophie der Griechen* (Leipzig: O. R. Reisland, 1920), I, 2, p. 634, note.
8. Plato, *Theaetetus* 152 E 1; *Cratylus* 401 D 5, 402 A 8. It has been made clear by philological study that the famous epigram "Everything flows" was not expressed by Heraclitus himself (though it is somewhat consistent with his other fragments).
9. Aristotle, *Topics* 104 b 22; *De Caelo* 298 b 30; *Physics* 253 a 25.
10. Heraclitus, fragment 118.
11. *Tac ca vartate srotasaughavat* (Vasubandhu, *Triṃśikā*, v. 4). Theodor Stcherbatsky always translated *saṃtāna* with the word "stream" (Th. I. Stcherbatsky, *The Central*

lysis of human internal psychic phenomena. By comparing similar Indian and Greek concepts the difference of interest or objects of knowledge held by both groups can be clarified.

Heraclitus and the Buddha were in agreement in that they explained actual aspects by means of the notion of fire. To Buddha, however, fire was essentially nothing but a simile, while to Heraclitus fire was the permanent substance of everything, viz., the ultimate principle, in one sense, of all the universe. He said, "Neither any god nor any man has created this world which is equal to all beings. One the contrary, it always was, is, and will be eternal living fire, burning according to rules and vanishing according to rules."[12] According to the *Biography of Philosophers* by Diogenes Laertes (ca. 240 A.D.) one of Heraclitus' theories was that "everything originates from fire and dissolves into it again," "fire is an element; everything that becomes is nothing but an interchange of fire; it changes by rarefaction and condensation of fire."[13] These assertions seem to have been rooted in the hylozoistic conception of the world; they might have been remnants of the Milesian way of thinking. The process of an interchange of fire was defined as follows: (1) the way downward, by which fire becomes everything; in which fire first becomes water, and then water becomes earth; and (2) the way upward, by which everything becomes fire, in which earth first becomes water, and then water becomes fire.[14] In this explanation, fire must be characterized as the "first cause," as was asserted by the Milesian school. For Heraclitus, fire seems to have been not only a primordial material cause, but also *cause efficiens* and *causa formalis*. His words are not very clear on this point, however.

In the scriptures the Buddha gave a discourse on fire to show that the world is nothing but the ceaseless flux of becoming. Though the flame maintains itself unchanged in appearance, every moment it is another and not the same flame. The seeming identity from moment to moment consists in a continuity of moments which might be called the continuity of an ever-changing identity. The individual is only a bundle of changing *skandhas*, changing from moment to moment, from life to life, and only *nirvāṇa* (the blowing out of the flame) can bring about his final dissolution. It is assumed that his personal identity remained to such an extent that he could come to remember his former existences. Holding any view

---

Conception of Buddhism and the Meaning of the Word "Dharma" [London: Royal Asiatic Society, 1923] and *The Conception of Buddhist Nirvāṇa* [Leningrad: The Academy of Sciences of the USSR, 1972], passim).

12. Heraclitus, fragment 30.
13. Takashi Ide, *Shijin Tetsugakusha* [Poet-philosophers)] (Tokyo: Koyama-shoten, 1944), pp. 66 f.
14. Zeller, *Geschichte*, I, 2, p. 846, note 2.

of the identity of things or of human existences over a period of time would be erroneous, becaust it would arouse adhesion to the ego as something other than a practical expedient, and this error would result in suffering of grief. The comparison of mundane existence to a burning fire expresses the thought that human life is transient and full of suffering. This comparison was inherited by Mahayana Buddhism also.

In the Lotus Sutra (*Saddharmapuṇḍarīkasūtra*), a verse runs as follows: "This triple world is an dreadful as that (burning) house, overwhelmed with a number of evils, entirely inflamed on every side by a hundred sorts of birth, old age, and disease."[15] This verse was recited with affection by ancient and medieval Japanese nobles.

Nāgārjuna (ca. 150–250 A.D.), the founder of the Mādhyamika philosophy of Mahāyāna Buddhism, compared the continuity of an individual to a burning fire, and the five kinds of elements constituting an individual to fuel, explaining that just as fire and fuel are neither different from nor identical with each other and neither separable nor inseparable, so are an individual and its constituents.[16]

15. III, gāthā 86, translated by Hendrik Kern in *Sacred Books of the East*, vol. XXI (Oxford: Clarendon Press, 1909), p. 88.

16. *Madhyamaka-śāstra*, ch. X: "The Investigation of the Relation of Fire and Fuel." This chapter has been translated into German by Stanislaw Schayer, "Feuer und Brennstoff," *Rocznik Orientalistyczny* VII (1930), pp. 26–52.

In later days the idea of transmigration was discussed by Ogigen. It was also referred to in *The Life of Apolonius of Tyana* by Philostratus. Ernst Benz: *Indische Einflüsse auf die frühchristliche Theologie*. Akademie der Wissenschaften und der Literatur. Abhandlungen der Geistes-und sozialwissenschaftlichen Klasse, Jahrgang 1951, Nr. 3. Wiesbaden: Verlag der Wissenschaften und der Literatur in Mainz, 1951, pp. 17–28.

B. The Aim of Human Existence and the Path toward the Aim

1. The Aim

WHAT is the condition of the man who has attained the ideal state? What will become of him? This is a basic question in Buddhism as well as other traditions, and like all basic questions it has had various answers. In explicating *Nirvāṇa* it becomes apparent that often the explanations given in the past reflect the personalities of those who held them more faithfully than they represent the ideas of Buddhism. So that while some Western scholars, such as Childers and Pischel, have seen *Nirvāṇa* as an eternal death, others, such as Barth and Oldenberg, see it as something extremely blissful. In all honesty it must be admitted that even the Buddhist authors themselves have not been unanimous on this point. Perhaps the best solution may be that suggested by the Christian author of the *Imitation*: to avoid the byways of difficult problems and to walk in the sure paths. If the goal is not crystal clear, at least the path that leads there *is*—a point on which all Buddhists agree to the extent that Buddhism is universally equated with the path to *Nirvāṇa*.

Although in the scriptures there are many teachings, the aim of Buddhist religious practice is to get rid of our delusion of ego. A sage is a man who has eliminated his infatuations about the existence of ego. A sage is extolled as follows:

His sum of life the sage renounced,
The cause of life immeasurable or small;
With inward joy and calm, he broke,
Like coat of mail, his life's own cause![1]

By getting rid of this ignorance or delusion, Buddhists hope to be untroubled by the transitoriness of worldly life.

They're transient all, each being's parts and powers,
Growth is their very nature, and decay.
They are produced, they are dissolved again:
To bring them all into subjection—that is bliss.[2]

1. *Dīgha-nikāta* II, p. 107 gāthā.
2. *Mahāparinibbāna-suttanta* 6, 10. *Dīgha-nikāya* II, p. 157.

Many poetic terms are used to describe the state of the man who has been made perfect according to Buddhist doctrine. One or another name for this many-sided conception is stressed: the harbor of refuge, the cool cave, the island amidst the floods, the place of bliss, emancipation, liberation, safety, the supreme, the transcendental, the uncreated, the tranquil, the home of ease, the calm, the end of suffering, the medicine for all evil, the unshaken, the ambrosia, the nectar, the immortal, the immaterial, the imperishable, the abiding, the further shore, the unending, the bliss of effort, the supreme joy, the ineffable, the detachment, the holy city, and many others. Perhaps the most frequent in the Pāli texts is "the state of him who is worthy" (Arahatship).

In the Christian tradition, too, there are pictural representations comparable to the Buddhist descriptions of the "harbor of refuge," the "island amidst the floods," and the like. For instance, the description in the Book of Revelation of the heavenly city—"the wall was built of jasper, while the city was pure gold, clear as glass"[3]—may be compared with descriptions in later Buddhist tradition of Amida Buddha's Pure Land. What is said of the state of the blessed in this New Testament "holy city" recalls Buddhist texts on the release of *Nirvāṇa*: ". . . and death shall be no more, neither shall there be mourning nor crying nor pain any more, for the former things have passed away. And he who sat upon the throne said, 'Behold, I make all things new.' "[4] Some of the most popular Christian hymns reflect this theme of the heavenly city, "Jerusalem the golden," The same subject inspired the English Puritan John Bunyan to write *Pilgrim's Progress*, a book that was once as widely read in England as the Bible itself.

Yet the Christian tradition, like the Buddhist, included the view that the ultimate goal was beyond imagination or description.

> . . . No eye has seen, nor ear heard,
> nor the heart of man conceived,
> what God has prepared for those who love him,[5]

for

> . . . faith is the assurance of things hoped for,
> the conviction of things *not* seen.[6]

In the Buddhist tradition the difficulty of describing this condition lies in the fact that there is no discrimination. The Buddha declared that just as the great ocean has one taste only, the taste of salt, just so have this

3. Revelation 21:19.
4. Revelation 21:4–5.
5. I Corinthians 2:9.
6. Hebrews 11:1, emphasis added.

doctrine and discipline but one flavor only, the flavor of emancipation. The Buddhist saint, having become perfect, knows no discrimination, but is rather "deep, immesurable, unfathomable like the vast ocean."

Though the actual goal is indesceibable, the results of having reached it are quite apparent. One who escapes from his delusion will be free from the fetters of this mundane world. He is said to have overcome the transmigration of worldly existence and to have attained the supreme goal of the higher life, enlightenment. "He became conscious that birth was at an end, that the higher life had been fulfilled, that all that should be done had been accomplished, and that after this present life there would be no beyond (no worldly existence)!"[7]

These views are reminiscent of the Stoic's theory of the happiness of the virtuous man, which, when stated, sounded more negative than positive. "It consists more in independence and peace of mind than in the enjoyment which moral conduct brings with it. In mental disquietude—says Cicero—consists misery; in composure, happiness. How can he be deficient in happiness, he enquires, whom courage preserves from care and fear, and self-control guards from passionate pleasure and desire? How can he fail to be absolutely happy who is in no way dependent on fortune, but simply and solely on himself? To be free from disquitude, says Seneca, is the peculiar privilege of the wise; the advantage which is gained from philosophy is that of living without fear, and rising superior to the troubles of life."[8] The ideal of *ataraxy* by Hellenistic philosophers is also comparable here.

A sort of enlightenment was admitted by very early Greek thinkers. Plato taught, "Suddenly a light, as if from a leaping fire, will be enkindled in the soul."[9] Plutarch had asserted a principle of knowledge whereby pure and simple flashes throughout the soul occur like lightning and attain to apprehension and vision in a single moment's experience. "The apperception of the conceptual,[10] the pure, and the simple, shining through the soul like a flash of lightning, affords an opportunity to touch and see it but once. For this reason Plato and Aristotle call this part of philosophy the epoptic or mystic part, inasmuch as those who have passed beyond these conjectural and confused matters of all sorts by means of Reason proceed by leaps and bounds to that primary, simple, and immaterial principle; and when they have somehow attained contact with the pure truth abiding about it, they think that they have the whole of philosophy completely, as it were, within their grasp."[11]

7. *Mahāparinibbāna-suttanta* 5, 30. *Dīgha-nikāya* II, p. 153.
8. Eduard Zeller, *The Stoics Epicureans and Sceptics*, trans. by Oswald J. Reichel (London: Longmans, Green & Co., 1880). pp. 239–240.
9. Epistle VII.
10. *tou noētou noēsis.*
11. *De Iside et Osiride,* Chapter 77, translated by F. C. Babbitt, vol. 5, pp. 181–183.

This Buddhist ideal state is called by the Buddhists "*Nirvāṇa*," "extinction of afflictions," and this is the term most often used for it in the West. *Nirvāṇa* was early translated as "dying out," that is, the dying out in the heart of the fierce fire of the three cardinal sins—sensuality, ill-will, and stupidity. But this sense of the word "*Nirvāṇa*" very often conveys a somewhat misleading impression. Contrary to the prevalent Western opinion about *Nirvāṇa*, the craving for extinction in the sense of annihilation or non-existence (*vibhava-taṇhā*) was indeed expressly repudiated by the Buddha. Having attained enlightenment, he was far from dissolving into non-being; it was not he who became extinct but the life of illusion, passions, and cravings. He who has attained *Nirvāṇa* is extolled in Buddhism as being afflicted neither by life nor by death. It is only in the way of explanation that *Nirvāṇa* appears to be negation. Actually "*Nirvāṇa*" is nothing but a word adopted and cherished by Buddhist ascetics and thinkers of old to indicate the ideal state. The cause and source of *Nirvāṇa* is the extinction of selfish desire. It brings on the painless peace nad is almost synonymous with bliss.

Concerning Western confusion about the basic Buddhist experience, Rhys Davids has written, "The choice of this term [*Nirvāṇa*] by European writers, a choice made long before any of the Buddhist canonical texts had been published or translated, has had a most unfortunate result. Those writers did not share, could not be expected to share, the exuberant optimism of the early Buddhists. Themselves giving up this world as hopeless, and looking for salvation in the next, they naturally thought the Buddhists must do the same; and in the absence of any authentic scriptures to correct the mistake, they interpreted *Nirvāṇa*, in terms of their own belief, as a state to be reached after Death. As such they supposed that 'dying out' must mean the dying out of a 'soul'; and endless were the discussions as to whether this meant eternal trance, or absolute annihilation, of the soul. It is now thirty years since I first put forward the right interpretation. But outside the ranks of Pali scholars the old blunder is still often repeated."[12]

The Buddha said clearly that those monks who exert themselves in the religion can be saved; that is, they will never be reborn in the state of suffering. However, the ideal situation should be realized not after death, but now, in this life. "*Nirvāṇa* here and now" was stressed. The "*Nirvāṇa* here and now" (*saṃdiṭṭhikaṃ nibbānaṃ*) of the Buddhist has much in common with the "release in this life" (*jīvanmukti*) of the Hindu philosopher.

Christians, like Buddhists, were also encouraged to press on with earnestness and win the goal in this life. In exhorting his readers to "rejoice in the Lord," St. Paul goes on to observe how he must "press on

12. T. W. Rhys Davids, *Early Buddhism*, p. 73.

toward the goal," asking them "to join in imitating me."[13] These statements suggest that although their reward was heavenly, Christians also were expected to seek for salvation in this life. In Buddhist literature there is a similar intent, "When a brother has, by himself, known and realized, and continues to abide, here in this visible world, in that emancipation of mind, in that emancipation of heart which is Arahatship—that is a condition higher still, and sweeter still, for the sake of which the brethren lead the religious life under me."[14]

Nirvāṇa is only in appearance a cold and negative state of mind. This is probably due to the traditional way of thinking of the Indians, who prefer the negative way of expression. (e.g., they say "not one" [*aneka*] instead of "many," "not good" [*akuśala*] instead of "bad." Cf. "not bad" in English.) *Nirvāṇa* is not mere emptiness. Though the fruit of practice is often represented negatively as "release from sorrow," and so on, it is also represented as happiness. The peace and all-embracing charity that the saint is supposed to attain can scarcely be regarded as merely negative. It is felt consciously as positive in the strongest degree; it exercises a "fascination" by which its followers are as much carried away as are the Hindu and the Christian by the corresponding objects of their worship. *Nirvāṇa* for Buddhists is genuine bliss.

When the knowledge of his emancipation (*vimuttasmiṃ vimuttaṃ iti ñāṇam*) arises, a recluse knows "rebirth has been destroyed. The higher life has been fulfilled. What had to be done has been accomplished. After this present life there will be no beyond!"[15] And this state is called "an immediate fruit of the life of a recluse, visible in this world, and higher and sweeter than the last. . . . And there is no fruit of the life of a recluse, visible in this world, that is higher and sweeter than this."[16] Emancipation is found in a release from habits of mind, in being free from a specified sort of craving that is said to be the origin of specified sorts of suffering. How does one know this?

In a Buddhist scripture, a King asked the monk Nāgaseṇa, "Venerable Nāgasena, does he who does not receive Nirvāṇa know how happy a state Nirvāṇa is?"

"Yes, he knows it."

"But how can he know that without his receiving Nirvāṇa?"

"Now what do you think, O King? Do those whose hands and feet have not been cut off know how sad a thing it is to have them cut off?"

"Yes, Sir, that they know."

"But how do they know it?"

13. Philippians 3:1, 14, 17.

14. *Mahāli-suttanta*. Rhys Davids, *Dialogues of the Buddha*, I, p. 201.

15. *Dīgha-nikāya* II, 97, Voo. I, p. 84.

16. *Dīgha-nikāya* II, 98. Vol. I, p. 85.

"Well, by hearing the sound of the lamentation of those whose hands and feet have been cut off, they know it."

"Just so, great King, it is by hearing the glad words of those who have seen Nirvāṇa that they who have not received it know how happy a state it is."

"Very good, Nāgasena!"[17]

The Buddhist temper, like that of the Christian, is cheerful, and not so rigorous as that of the Stoic. The Buddhist devotee knows intense bliss, pervading the whole being, on the assurance of salvation won. A scriptural passage, after pointing out that the Hindrances (*Nīvaraṇa*)—sensuality, ill-will, torpor of mind or body, worry, and wavering—affect a man like debt, disease, imprisonment, slavery, and anxiety. goes on: "When these five Hindrances have been put away within him, he looks upon himself as freed from debt, rid of disease, out of jail, a free man, and secure. And gladness springs up within him on his realizing that, and joy arises to him thus gladdened, and so rejoicing all his frame becomes at ease, and being thus at ease he is pervaded with a sense of peace, and in that peace his heart is stayed."[18]

The concept of the true cause for happiness held by Indian, Greek, and Chinese sages of ancient times was quite similar although their practical implications were greatly different. The Buddha said, "Health is the greatest of gifts, contentedness the best riches; trust is the best of relationship, nirvāṇa is the highest happiness."[19] Solon, the wise, in turn claimed that "He who possesses great store of riches is no nearer happiness than he who has what suffices for his daily needs, unless it os hap that luck attend upon him, and so he continue in the enjoyment of all his good things to the end of life."[20] Confucius eulogized his disciple Hwuy, "Admirable indeed was the virtue of Hwuy! With a single bamboo dish of rice, a single gourd dish of drink, and living in his mean narrow lane, while others could not have endured the distress, he did not allow his joy to be affected by it. Admirable indeed was the virtue of Hwuy."[21] Describing his own needs, Confucius declared, "With coarse rice to eat, with water to drink, and my bended arm for a pillow;—I have still joy in the midst of these things. Riches and honors acquired by unrighteous-

17. *Milindapañhā*, pp. 69–70.
18. T. W. Rhys Davids, *Dialogues of the Buddha*, vol. I, p. 84.
19. *Dhammapada* 204. This attitude of emphasizing happiness was more predominantly stressed in Mahayana Buddhism, especially in Vajrayana. Observers of such Buddhist countries as Burma and Siam recorded that their inhabitants were spontaneously cheerful and even gay—laymen and monks alike—although their material conditions were not very good.
20. *Herodotus*, translated by Rawlinson, I, 32. vol. I, pp. 141–142.
21. *Analects* VI, 9.

ness are to me as a floating cloud."[22] In this case the Indian and Greek definitions of happiness were given in an abstract way, whereas the Chinese version was very concrete, without setting out any universal proposition.

The Buddha, after he had become enlightened, claimed to have opened the doors to the Undying. The ideal state is often called "the immortal." Although it is true that Buddha tried not to reply to questions of the life or death of the sage after this life, the scriptures include some indications. In one passage he said, "There is an unborn, an unoriginated, an unmade, and uncompounded; were there not, O mendicants, there would be no escape from the world of the born, the originated, the made and the compounded."[23] Provided it is textually accurate, this would suggest that the Buddha believed in something that endures beneath the shifting appearances of the visible world. One can expect that if he did, however, that "substratum" would also be dynamic as well as based on his own experience.

A disciple says, "I find no delight in dying, I find no delight in life: The hour of death do I await, with mind alert and discerning."[24] When the Buddha died, the venerable Anuruddha extolled his death.

> When he who from all craving want was free,
> Who to Nirvāṇa's tranquil state had reached,
> When the great sage finished his span of life,
> No grasping struggle vexed that steadfast heart!
> All resolute, and with unshaken mind,
> He calmly triumphed o'er the pain of death.
> E'en as a bright flame dies away, so was
> The last emancipation of his heart.[25]

The Buddhist concept of *Nirvāṇa* and the Christian concept of salvation may be quite different; but what Christianity aimed at has something in common with the Buddhist ideal, for "the peace of God" was most esteemed by early Christians.[26] Similarly in the Old Testament tradition which the Christians inherited there is some degree of parallel between the Buddhist metaphorical expression of their ideal vision and the visions of the Prophets.[27] *Nirvāṇa* is peace. However, the peace in which the doctrine culminates is not inert, but active, a rest that comes through striving. On the other hand, Buddhist enthusiasm is not of the

22. *Ibid.*, VII, 15.
23. *Udāna* VIII, 3.
24. *Theragāthā* 196; 607. Cf. 20; 1002.
25. *Mahāparinibbāna-suttanta* 6, 10. *Dīgha-nikāya* II, p. 157.
26. Philippians 4:7.
27. Cf. Exodus 33:18 or Isaiah 60:1–5 with Revelation 4.

emotional type with which Westerners and so familiar, but rather of a type which has been defined as "exalted peace," a calm without the slightest trace of languor.

In China the Buddhists final aim came to be linked with one of the Taoists' original ideas, that of spontaneous "non-activity" (*wu-wei*) as an ethical as well as a metaphysical principle. The True Man of Non-activity was extolled as the ideal person. Wang Ch'ung (A.D. 27–ca. 100), the critical scholar, advocated naturalism, saying, "When Heaven moves, it does not desire to produce things thereby, but things are produced of their own accord: such is spontaneity (*tzu-jan*). When it gives forth its ether, it does not desire to create things, but things are created of themselves: such is non-activity (*wu-wei*)."[28] When Buddhism was introduced into China, *Nirvāṇa* was equated with *wu-wei*. And later such a great Zen master as Lin-chi (Japanese: Rinzai) called the ideal person the True Man of Non-activity.

In the West the spirit of God was set forth with metaphorical expressions which point to another, preferable, state of survival. In a Psalm it is said: "We have escaped as a bird from the snare of the fowlers."[29] In Buddhism the final state of deliverance is compared to that of a bird escaped from the net. "This world is blinded, few only can see here. Like birds escaped from the net, a few go to heaven."[30]

The Buddhist life of the Perfect One is difficult for ordinary people to fathom. "Those who have no accumulation [of property], who eat according to knowledge, who have perceived [the nature of] release and unconditioned freedom, their path is difficult to understand like that [the flight] of birds through the sky."[31] Cmpare the Hindu scripture, "As the path of the birds in the air or of fishes in the water is invisible, even so is the path of the possessors of wisdom."[32]

The ideal situation is not something concrete, nor something sizable. It lies only in proceeding towards the aim of the ideal. Proceed a mile, the ideal lies further on. Go on two miles it lies further none the less, like a shadow projected on the way forward. The ideal situation always lies in the direction of putting forth effort to the goal, and the goal should be always elevated. (Effort toward the goal falls under the subject of the next section, *karma*.) The man who has attained deliverance may continue his actions in this world, for actions do not defile him. He naturally works for the welfare of others.

28. Fung Yu-lan, *Chinese Philosophy*, translated by Derk Bodde (Princeton, N. J.: Princeton University Press, 1953), vol. II, p. 152.
29. Psalms 124:7.
30. *Dhammapada* 174.
31. *Dhammapada* 92.
32. *Mahābhārata* XII, 6763.

2. Possibility for Progress

a. Karma and Craving

Karma means "action," "deed." According to the doctrine of *karma*, good conduct brings on a pleasant and happy result, while bad conduct brings on an evil result.[1] It is true that the Buddha finds no center of reality nor unchanging principle in the flux of life, but it does not follow that there is nothing real in the world at all except the agitation of forces (see next section). There is no abiding substance in the world, only change and becoming. In such a state the supreme reality is the law of change, and that is causality. The universe is through and through governed by causality. There is no chaotic anarchy or capricious interference. In this section moral causality is chiefly considered. In order to include the moral cause (free choice), Gotama retained the idea of *karma*.

All acts, whether mental or physical, tend to produce like acts in a continuing series. Good acts increase in a man a tendency to similar good actions, and bad acts create a tendency toward continuing evil acts of a similar nature. *Karma* committed with or without previous intention will come to fruition. Some *karmas* bear fruit in the same life in which they are committed, others in the immediately succeeding one, and others in more remote future lives. The individual is the result of a multitude of causes carried over from his past existences, and is intimately related to all other causes in the world. The interconnection between one individual and the whole universe is stressed in the Buddhist doctrine of *karma*. This much of the doctrine of *karma* has been accepted by all Buddhists through the centuries.

According to the doctrine of *karma*, a man's social position in life and his physical advantages, or the reverse, were the result of his actions in a previous birth. For instance, if a man is blind, it is due to his lust of the eye in a previous birth. But he also has unusual powers of hearing because he loved, in a previous birth, to listen to the preaching of the law. The explanation could always be reversed to correspond to the present fact. It fits the facts because it is derived from them. And it cannot be disproved (though it can be verified by experience),[2] for it lies in a sphere beyond the reach of human inquiry. The reason why this doctrine was

1. K. N. Jayatilleke, *Early Buddhist Theory of Knowledge* (London: George Allen & Unwin, 1963), p. 460. It is the "correlation between god character and a happy state after death, and bad character and an unhappy state after death that is called *Karma*."
2. *Ibid.*

retained in Buddhism is because it thus provided a moral cuase. The Buddha discarded the theory of the presence, within the human body, of a soul, which could have a separate and eternal existence. He instead established a new identity between individuals in the chain of existence, by the new assertion that that which made two beings the same being was not soul but *karma*. He taught that the force of *karma* persisted for more than one existence. The connection of cuase and effect between persons in the present life and persons in past lives was not a physical link between different individuals, but rather a moral one between them. Then by what is *karma* motivated?

According to Buddhism, craving actually causes the birth of the new individual who inherits the *karma* of the former one. "From craving (*chanda*) originates the dear [objects] in the world, and the covetousness that prevails in the world, and the desire and fulfillment originate from it, which are [of consequence] for the future state of a man."[3] Such a notion was adopted by Hinduism also.[4] Heraclitus set forth a similar teaching. "If one does not hope, one will not find the unhoped-for, since there is no trail leading to it and no path."[5] Perhaps Democritus as well had a similar theory in mind with his abstract theory that "Happiness (*eudaimonie*) like unhappiness, is a property of the soul (*psykhe*)."[6]

Plato also found craving or desire to be the true cause of our transmigration. In *Phaedo* Socrates says, ". . . the soul which is pure at departing and draws after her no bodily taint, having never voluntarily had connection with the body, which she is ever avoiding, herself gathered into herself—and making such abstraction her perpetual study . . .—that soul, I say, herself invisible, departs to the invisible world—to the divine and immortal and rational—and is released from the error and folly of men, their fears and wild passions and all other human ills—But the soul which has been polluted, and is impure at the time of her departure, and is the companion and servant of the body always, and is in love with and fascinated by the body and by the desires and pleasures of the body,—do you suppose that such a soul will depart pure and unalloyed?—She is held fast by the corporeal, which the continual association and constant care of the body have wrought into her nature,—is depressed and dragged

3. *Suttanipāta* 865.
4. "Know that wherever there is desire, there in truth is also the worldly existence (*Yatra yatra bhavet tṛṣṇā, saṃsāraṃ viddhi tatra vai, Aṣṭāvakragītā*, 10, 3).
5. Heraclitus, fragment 18.
6. Democritus, fragment 170. Cf. "In diesem Sinne hat auch Meister Eckhart gesagt: Die Tugend und auch die Untugend liegt im Willen," ed. Pfeiffer, p. 552 (Karl Eugen Neumann, *Die Reden Gotamo Buddhos aus der Sammlung der Bruchstücke Suttanipāto des Pāli-Kanons* ubersetzt von Karl Eugen Neumann [Munich: R. Piper and Co., 1911], second edition, p. 286).

down again into the visible world.—These must be the souls—which are compelled—to wander—in payment of the penalty of their evil way of life,—until, through the craving after the corporeal which never leaves them, they are imprisoned finally in another body. And they may be supposed to find their prisons, in the same natures which they have had in their former lives.—What I mean is that men who have followed after gluttony, and wantonness, and drunkenness, and have had no thought of avoiding them, would pass into asses and animals of that sort.—And those who have chosen the portion of injustice, and tyranny, and violence, will pass into wolves, or into hawks and kites. . . . No one who has not studied philosophy and who is not entirely pure at the time of his departure is allowed to enter the company of the Gods, but the lover of knowledge only."[7]

True continence and purity, Plato taught, lie in the purification of the soul from all sensual things, liberation from the passions and desires which "transfix the soul to the body as with a nail" and which compel the soul to endure rebirth in every new form of embodiment. The redeemer from these bonds is philosophy, which alone really prepares one for death. However, Plato asserted the existence of souls within men's bodies, a theory which seems to be diametrically opposed to that of the Buddha. Also, with regard to the action of desire, he does not go as far as the Indian teacher. Gotama held that it was craving which brought about not only a new existence as an animal, but also as a man or a god. Both, though, agreed in attributing to craving a considerable power over future life.

Before Plato, Empedocles ascribed the motivating power for the appearance of things to love. "These [elements] never cease their continuous exchange, sometimes uniting under the influence of Love, so that all become One, at other times again each moving apart through the hostile force of Fate."[8] But in his case the relationship of love to the individual was objective and could not be changed by religious practice.

Some scholars equate the Buddhist concept of craving (*taṇhā*)[9] with the Greek word "*epitjymia*" of the New Testament. But this neglects the fact that both concepts appeared in different contexts, the former in the

7. *Phaedo* 80–82. *The Dialogues of Plato*, translated into English with analyses and introductions by B. Jowett, 5 vols., 3rd edition (Oxford University Press, Humphrey Milford, 1892), vol. I, pp. 223–226.
8. Empedocles, fragment 17.
9. Deussen identifies the Buddhist *craving* with the Greek word *epithymia* of the New Testament. "Es ist im wesentlichen dasselbe, was Buddha als trsna fur den Grund des Leidens, und was Jesus als die *epithymia*, die bose Begierde, fur den Grund der Sünde erklart. Beide haben in ihrer Art recht; die Tṛṣṇā, die *epithymia* oder . . . der Wille zum Leben, ist die tiefliegende Quelle, aus welcher sowohl die Leiden wie die Sunden des Daseins entspringen und mit deren Aufhebung beide aufgehoben sind" (Deussen, *Geschichte*, I, 3, p. 157).

theory of Non-Self, and the latter in connection with the assumption of a soul.

In India before Buddhism, conflicting and contradictory views prevailed as to the precise mode of action of *karma*, and this confusion is reflected in Buddhist theory. The prevailing views are tacked on, as it were, to the essential doctrines of Buddhism without being consistently incorporated into them. Thus in a story of a good layman (whose name is Citta), what determines the position of the individual in the next life is an aspiration expressed on the deathbed,[10] while in another dialogue it is a thought dwelt on during life.[11] In the nemerous stories (in the *Peta-* and *Vimāna-vatthus*) it is some isolated act, and in other passages (e.g., the *Dhammasaṅgāṇi*) it is some mental disposition. They are only alike in that in each case a moral cause is given for the position in which the individual finds himself now, and the moral cause consists of his own past actions. In the popular belief, in contrast to Buddhism, the bridge between the two lives was thought to be a minute and subtle entity called the soul, which left one body at death and entered into the new body. In Buddhism, the craving still existing at the death of one body caused the new set of congregations (*skandhas*) to arise, that is, the new body with its mental tendencies and capacities.

The Buddhist doctrine of *karma* which proposes that whatever a man reaps, that he himself must also have sown appealed as strongly to Eastern ethical natures as the similar parable, "Whatsoever a man soweth that shall he also reap" has appealed to Westerners. These doctrines were retained by Gotama, who also taught the persistence of the force of *karma* for more than one existence. However, he changed the whole aspect and practical effect of the doctrines he retained by removing them from the soul-theory which had been so prevalent before him.

In China before the introduction of Buddhism divine retribution was believed to fall upon families; Buddhism then introduced the idea of *karmic* causation, but this was on more of an individual basis. Finally the two were interwoven into the view that has prevailed since the Sung period: divine retribution works on a family basis *and* through a chain of lives.[12]

The Buddhist notion of *karma* avoids some of the difficulties common to the allied European theories of fate, providence, and predestination. Rhys Davids says: "The heavy hand of the immeasurable past we cannot

10. *Saṃyutta-nikāya* IV, 302.
11. *Majjhima-nikāya* III, 99 f.
12. Cf. Lien-sheng Yang, "The Concept of *Pao* as a Basis for Social Relations in China," in J. K. Fairbank, ed., *Chinese Thought and Institutions* (Chicago, 1957), pp. 291–309. Mentioned in A. F. Wright, *Buddhism in Chinese History* (Stanford, Calif.: Stanford University Press, 1959), p. 105.

escape. A sufferer believing in the soul, and in fate, or providence, can say: 'This was pre-ordained, I must submit,' and he can try to rectify the balance of justice by assuming a remedy in a more satisfactory world beyond the grave. If he believes in *karma* he will think: 'This is my own fault.' And he can try to rectify the balance of justice by assuming an identity between himself and some one else in the past, although he has no evidence for it."[13]

The word "*karma*" covers two distinct ideas: namely, the deed itself, and the effects of that deed in modifying the subsequent character[14] and fortunes of the doer. The Buddhists say that this subjective effect continues after death into the next life: "A swallow's egg cannot hatch out a lark because of the difference in heredity; the countless influences that affected the ancestors of that egg, and the numberless actions performed under those influences are in some mysterious way stored up in that egg, and must bear their own fruit and none other. Therefore a swallow's egg cannot hatch out a lark, because a lark is the result of an entirely different set of conditions; as we might say, its *Karma* is different. But of course the Buddhists do not mean heredity when they use the word *Karma*. '*Karma*' expresses, not that which a man inherits from his ancestors, but that which he inherits from himself in some previous states of existence. But with this difference the Buddhist doctrine and the scientific doctrine of heredity seem very simiar."[15]

Thus, a very curious and instructive parallel can be drawn here between Buddhism and the teachings of modern science. All evolution of animate nature can be characterized as a process of self-integration or assertion of self through countless generations. The Buddhists make a similar statement except that they do not bring in the scientific doctrine of heredity, or inheritance from others, but rather claim that a man inherits from himself.

Babbitt places *karma* in the realm of the unconscious and explains it as the impressions (both the result of present and past "secular" life) "which lie hidden in what the modern psychologist would term the unconscious and tend to give a bias to one's character and conduct both now and in one's secular future. *Karma* thus envisaged is a sort of fate, but a fate of which a man is himself the author and which is not at any particular moment entirely subversive of moral freedom."[16] In any case, according

13. T. W. Rhys Davids, *Indian Buddhism*, p. 92.
14. "I took pleasure where it pleased me, and passed on. I forgot that every little action of the common day makes or unmakes character, and that therefor what one has done in the secret chamber one has some day to cry aloud on the housetop. I ceased to be lord over myself" (Oscar Wilde, *De Profundis* [London: Methuen and Co., 1905], p. 23). See also fn. 1 above.
15. Warren, *Buddhism in Translations*, p. 210 f.
16. I. Babbitt, *The Dhammapada* (London: Oxford University Press, 1936), p. 93.

to Buddhism, the history of an individual does not begin with his birth. He has been through countless aeons and cannot sever himself from the past, not for a moment.[17]

b. *The True Self*

THE Non-self theory in early Buddhism does not mean that the Buddha completely denied the significance of the self. On the contrary, he always admitted the significance of the self in a practical and moral sense as the subject of actions. But the self cannot be identified with anything existing in the outside world nor grasped as some other concrete physical substance. The self can be realized only when one acts according to universal norms of human existence. When one acts morally, according to Buddhism, the true self becomes manifest. (Cf. Spinoza, virtue is its own reward.)

A practical postulate in early Buddhism makes clar that "one who knows the self"[1] was highly esteemed therein.[2] The virtue of relying upon oneself was also stressed considerably. The Buddha taught Ānanda, his disciple, in his last sermon, "Be you lamps to yourselves. Be you a refuge to yourself. Betake yourself to no external refuge. Hold fast to the Truth as a lamp. Hold fast as a regufe to the Truth. Don't look for refuge to any one besides yourself."[3]

According to the Buddha, bad actions hurt oneself,[4] for "the evil done by oneself, self-begotten, self-bread, crushes the foolish, as a diamond breaks a precious stone."[5] Buddha thought "the foolish man bears fruit to his own destruction,"[6] because "he whose wickedness is very great brings himself down to that state where his enemy [Māra, perhaps, or his own worst nature] wishes him to be, as a creeper does with the tree

17. Cf. "Every act rewards itself, or in other words integrates itself, in a two-fold manner; first in the thing, or in real nature; and secondly in the circumstance, or in apparent nature. Men call the circumstances the retribution. The causal retribution is in the thing, and is seen by the soul" (Emerson, "Compensation," in *Selected Writings of Emerson*, Ralph Waldo ed. by Brooks Atkinson [New York: Random House, Inc., 1950], p. 175).

1. Attaññū. *Aṅguttara-nikāya* IV, p. 113; *Dīgha-nikāya* III, 252.
2. Kant remarked in the Preface to the First Edition of his *Critique of Pure Reason*: "It is a call to reason to undertake anew the most difficult of all its tasks, namely, that of self-knowledge" (*Critique of Pure Reason*, trans. by Norman Kemp Smith, A xi).
3. *Mahāparinibbāna-suttanta* II, 26; *Dīgha-nikāya* II, p. 101; "I have taken refuge to myself (*katama me saranam attano*)" (*Dīgha-nikāya* II, p. 120 gāthā).
4. *Dhammapada* 163.
5. *Ibid.*, 161.
6. *Ibid.*, 164.

which it surrounds."[7] In China Mencius expressed a similar thought, "He who is his own enemy cannot be helped."[8]

Rather a man's limited self should be ennobled. In Buddhism a man who is devoted to religious practice is extolled as follows. "He thus abstaining lives his life void of cravings, perfected, cool, in blissful enjoyment, his whole self ennobled."[9] Similarly in the New Testament we find "God did not give us a spirit of timidity but a spirit of power and love and self-control."[10] The Buddha asked a group of young men who were searching for a missing woman, "Which is better for you, to ge seeking the woman, or to go seeking the Self?" He did not say "your selves," for he did not think that each individual had his own self as an entity.[11]

An expression of ambivalence regarding self-knowledge was prevalent in Greece. A Greek writer (Ion) commenting on the famous maxim "Know thyself"[12] remarked, " 'Know thyself' is a short saying, yet it is a task so great that Zeus alone can master it." Taking this literally means interpreting it as "No one can know the self except a god." Yet Heraclitus, the famous denyer of unchanging substance, claimed "I searched into myself."[13]

In a dialogue of Plato (*Charmides*) the problem of self-knowledge was discussed in many ways, and the following agreement was reached: "Then the wise or temperate man, and he only, will know himself, and be able to examine what he knows or does not know, and to see what others know

7. *Ibid.*, 162.
8. Mencius IV, 1, 8. Ishida Baigan, *Seiri Mondo*; *Dialogues on Human Nature and Natural Orper,* trans by Paolo Beonio Brocchieri (Rome: Istitute Peril Medio ed Estremo Oriente, 1961), p. 54. With regard to the Chinese concept of the self, things are not yet so clear as in some other traditions. The following, however, is known: "For the Confucianist 'cultivation of self' (hsiu-shen) was a basic ideal in life. As set forth in the so-called Four Books, especially the *Great Learning*, it meant development of the individual's total personality, with emphasis on his physical growth, intellectual attainment moral training and aesthetic refinement. The ideal of self-renunciation, so strong in Indian religions, had no place here. For according to the strongly ethical view of man in Confucianism, his nature and personality were defined very largely (though not exclusively) in terms of his natural social relationships. Fulfilling his inescapable obligations to his parents, his family, his teacher and his ruler, the individual subordinated to them his personal selfish desires—but never his personality" (Wn. Th. de Bary, *Buddhism in Chinese Tradition*, a memeographed paper read at a Mexico Conference).
9. *Dīgha-nikāya* III, pp. 232–233.
10. II Timothy 1:7.
11. *Vinaya* I, 23, i.e., Mahāvagga 1, 14. Cf. *Visuddhimagga* 393.
12. " 'Know thyself' was written over the portal of the antique world. Over the portal of the new world, 'Be thyself' shall be written. And the message of Christ to man was simply 'Be thyself'. That is the secret of Christ" (Oscar Wilde, *The Soul of Man under Socialism* [Portland, Maine: Thomas B. Mosher, 1905], p. 24).
13. Heraclitus, fragment 101.

and think that they know and do really know; and what they do not know, and fancy that they know, when they do not. No other person will be able to do this. And this is wisdom and temperance and self-knowledge —for a man to know what he knows, and what he does not know."[14] Epictetus taught that we should respect ourselves first and Lucretius emphasised the fact that men seek escape from themselves, "Each man flies from himself (but self from whom, as you may be sure is commonly the case, he cannot escape, clings to him in his own despite), hates too himself, because he is sick and knows not the cause of the malady."[15]

The difference in confidence observed among writers on the self is the same as that found in the group of Greek philosophers above. Those who look for what the self *is* (Ion, Heraclitus) have nothing positive they can say with confidence regarding that entity. Those, on the other hand, who speak about what the self *does* (Plato, Epictetus, Lecretius) are considerably more confident (though sometimes in disagreement with each other) in the tone of their writings.

In early Buddhism two kinds[16] of self were admitted. The one is the self of ordinary daily life, a practical distinction man is led to make by the inherited concepts of language. The other is a latent self. Buddhists felt the former has to be subdued, for man has a tendency to attach linguistic entities to feelings, which can result in such feelings, now having been given a name, being thought to be a self; and this may well be the ignorance which must be overcome. "If a man were to conquer in battle a thousand times a thousand men, and another conquer one, himself, he indeed is th greatest of conquerors."[17] And in a Biblical proverb, "He who is slow to anger is better than the mighty, and he who rules his spirit than he who takes a city."[18] Lao-tzu said, "He who overcomes others is strong; he who overcomes himself is mighty."[19]

A Buddhist saying is "If a man holds himself dear, let himself diligently watch himself."[20] Compare this to a quotation from Mark: "And what I say to you I say to all: Watch."[21] In the Judeo-Christian tradition

14. *Charmides. The Dialogues of Plato,* translated into English by Benjamin Jowett, p. 26.
15. *On the Nature of Things,* III, 1068ff. Translated by H. A. J. Munroe, *Great Books of the Western World* (Chicago: Encyclopaedia Britannica, 1952), vol. 12, p. 43.
16. In the chapter on "The Self" in his *Principles of Psychology,* William James divides the self into an empirical ego and the pure ego. The empirical ego which can be objectively known is subdivided into the Material Me, Social Me, and Spiritual Me, and the pure ego, the agent of the act of knowing and thinking, is what the philosophers call the soul, the transcendental ego, and the spirit (William James, *Psychology* [New York: H. Holt, 1923], pp. 43–83.
17. *Dhammapada* 103.
18. Proverbs 16:32.
19. *Tao-te-ching* XXXIII, 1 (Legge's translation, p. 75).
20. *Dhammapada* 157.
21. Mark 13:37.

one notes a similar tone. The God of Ezekiel reportedly said: ". . . you will loath yourselves for your iniquities and your abominable deeds."[22] The assertion to watch oneself for one's own self sounds paradoxical; however, this reveals the real structure of the existence of the limited self. Another paradoxical assertion is: one should himself know that he is not wise enough. "The fool who knows his foolishness, is wise at least so far. But a fool who thinks himself wise, he is called a fool indeed."[23] (Similar expressions in other traditions have already been examined.[24])

The second type of self, a latent self, was called "the lord of self." "Self is the lord of self, who else could be the lord? With self well subdued, a man finds a lord such a few can find."[25] One should be earnest to carry on his own duty, in compliance with the demand of the true Self. "Let no one forget his own duty for the sake of another's, however great; let a man, after he has discerned his own duty, be always attentive to his duty."[26] To be true to oneself becomes the same as being true to others. In early Buddhism control of oneself was regarded as the starting point for altruistic activities. "If a man makes himself as he teaches other to be, then, being himself well subdued, he may subdue (others); one's own self is indeed difficult to subdue."[27] "And further let each man direct himself first to what is proper, then let him teach others; thus a wise man will not suffer."[28]

The above clarifications should make it possible to see through the apparent contradiction in Buddhism brought about my multiple usages of the term "self," and in addition facilitate explanation of *Nirvāṇa* as "taking refuge to the truth Self of one's own."[29] One must understand that the Buddhist concepts of *anātman* and the "true Self" are not at odds with each other. On the contrary, the former is one of the Buddha's aids to understanding the latter. Through following the Buddha's path and thoroughly understanding the phenomenal nature of existence and awareness (that they are altogether empty of permanent self), one finds that his true Self is nothing other than the unobstructed flow of those events. This true Self is an expression by tne Buddha of his confidence that unobstructed events have the moral character of universal norms (*dharma*) and coincide perfectly with man's duty.

22. Ezekiel 35:31.
23. *Dhammapada* 63.
24. In the second chapter.
25. *Dhammapada* 160.
26. *Dhammapada* 166.
27. *Ibid.*, 159.
28. *Ibid.*, 158.
29. Based upon this thought, the concept of the "great Self" was later developed in Mahāyāna Buddhism.

3. General Principles of Ethics

a. The Value and Equality of Man

Birth as a man is essential for the appreciation of the *Dharma* in Buddhism. Gods are too happy to feel a dislike for conditioned things, and they live much too long to have appreciation for the teachings of impermanence.[1] Animals, ghosts, fighting spirits, and the damned lack clarity of mind. Therefore the Buddhas appear as men, and the human state is in general more favorable than any other for the attainment of enlightenment. According to Buddhism, what distinguishes man from other beings is his aptitude for goodness, observance of the *Dharma*, and consequently compassion for other beings.

In the West, Aristotle said that appetites and desires are shared in common by men and animals. What distinguishes man from the animal is his power of reason. Mencius held that "the faculty of the mind is thinking." He advanced the view of the natural goodness of man, that he cannot bear to see his fellow men suffer. The way these philosophers apprehended the essence of man, however, was rather rationalistic, whereas the Buddhist apprehension was based more upon the mental attitude of sympathy.

Confucius' "way" may be called "life-affirming" in that his whole thought expressed the value of human life, of what it can mean truly to be a "man among men."[2] Unlike Buddha, Confucius did not use the term "gods and men." It seems that Confucian scholars did not set up stages for the spiritual elevation of a person, whereas in Buddhism the Buddhas stood at the very top rung of the ladder for spiritual elevation and were regarded as leading both gods and men alike; the Buddha is very often called "a teacher of Gods and Men."[3]

As for the relationship of man to man, the attitude of compassion and the spirit of human love is stressed strongly in Buddhist thought. If it were up to the Buddha, the castes as in India would have been annulled and abolished. The Buddha asserted that all discrimination between castes should be discarded, and from his time to the present Buddhism has stressed the moral equality of man.[4] The Buddha said, "For worms, ser-

1. *Mahāparinibbāna-suttanta* I, 31 (*Dīgha-nikāya,* vol. II, p. 88).
2. *Analects* XVIII, 6 (De Bary et al., *Chinese Tradition,* p. 24).
3. Even in American Philosophy the concept of "gods (plural) and men" has found occasional voice. Emerson said, "Welcome evermore to gods and men is the self-helping man" (Emerson, "Self-reliance").
4. In pre-Buddhist literature we also find some cases in which the caste distinction was

pents, fish, birds and animals there are marks that constitute their own species. There is difference in creatures endowed with bodies, but amongst men this is not the case; the difference amongst men is nominal only."[5] "What has been designated as 'name' and 'family' in the world is only a term, . . . what has been designated as 'here' and 'there' is understood by common consent."[6]

Buddha's reasoning against the caste claims of the Brahmins is relevant here. A Brahmin youth, Assalāyana, said to Buddha, "The Brahmins say thus: The Brahmins alone are the best caste, every other caste is low; the Brahmins alone are the write caste, every other caste is black, only the Brahmins become pure, not the non-Brahmins; only the Brahmins are the actual sons of the god Brahman, produced out of his mouth, beggotten by Brahman, formed by Brahman, heirs of Brahman. What does the Lord Gotama say to that?" Thereupon, the Buddha asked Assalāyana a series of questions: "What do you think, Assalāyana? Suppose that an anointed king of the warrior race causes a hundred men of different castes to be assembled together; men will come from the families of warriors, or Brahmins, of the nobility, and they will take an upper friction-stick from a Sal tree or Sandal tree or Padmaka tree,[7] produce a fire by turning it (in the lower friction-stick) and bring forth a flame. And there will come men from the families of Caṇḍālas, hunters, basket-makers, chariot-builders, Pukkusas,[8] and they will take an upper friction-stick from a dog's trough or a washing trough, or a stick of ricinus wood, produce a fire through turning, and bring forth a flame. Now, will the fire that the warriors, Brahmins, etc., have produced with the fine wood have flame, brightness and light, and will this fire be useful for all fire purposes? And will the fire which the Caṇḍālas, hunters, etc., have produced with wood from the dog's trough, etc., have no flame, no brightness and no light, and will this fire not be useful for all purposes? Assalāyana naturally had

---

minimized. For example, Kavasa, the son of a slave girl, was accepted as a Brahmin. (*Aitareya-brāhmaṇa* II, 19). Such cases are mentioned in the *Vajrasūcī* of Aśvaghoṣa, Concerning equality of all men, cf. *Vasettha-sutta*, T. W. Rhys Davids, *Indian Buddhism.* pp. 51–55, 62–63. In the first period the brethren addressed each other—with the epithet that is, of "*avuso*" (friend). But afterwards the distinction between the elders and the youngers occurred. A younger brother might be addressed by an elder with his name, or his family name, or the title "Friend." But an elder should have to be addressed by a younger brother as "Sir" (*bhante*) or as "Venerable Sir" (*āyasmā*). (*Mahāparinibbhāna-suttanta* VI, 2. *Dīgha-nikāya*, vol. II, p. 154)

5. *Suttanipāta* 602–611.
6. *Ibid.*, 648.
7. Various kinds of firewood.
8. Sanskrit *pukkaśa*, a very low caste.

to reply that there is no difference between the two kinds of fire, and Gotama concluded that it is the same with the castes."[9]

The Buddha stressed the significance of human virtues instead of the hierarchical order of the castes. "There are these four classes: nobles, brahmins, common people, and slaves. Now here and there a noble deprives a living being of life, is a thief, is unchaste, speaks lies, slanders, uses rough words, is a gossip, or greedy, or malevolent, or holds wrong views. Thus, we see . . . [those] qualities which are immoral and considered to be so, which are blameworthy and considered to be so—And we may say as much concerning brahmins, common people and slaves."

"Again, here and there a noble abstains from murder, theft, inchastity, lying, slandering, gossiping, greed, malevolence and false opinions. Thus we see . . . [those] qualities which are, and are considered, moral, inoffensive—And we may say as much concerning each of the others—brahmins, common people and slaves."[10] This sense of equality has been preserved throughout most Buddhist orders ever since the time of the Buddha and is ardently stressed nowadays as motivating social reform among the Indians of the lower status who have been looked down upon in the Hindu society.

The ideal of equality was emphasized in Christianity also. Christ, looking around on those who sag about him, mostly his disciples, said, "Here are my mother and my brothers! Whoever does the will of God is my brother, and sister, and mother."[11] St. Paul said that before Jesus both master and slave are one, "for in Christ Jesus you are all sons of God, through faith. . . . There is neither Jew nor Greek, there is neither slave nor free, there is neither male nor female; for you are all one in Christ Jesus."[12] In Western philosophy of the time of early Christianity, the Stoic Epictetus said that slaves are the equals of other men, because all alike are sons of God.

In China, whereas equality was not so openly advocated, some similarities can be seen. While Confucius gave moral support to the divine authority of the ruling classes, Mencius advocated the moral right to rebel against the ruling classes and justified revolutions, if obedience meant acquiescence in pernicious conditions.

Buddha, it is said, did not discriminate against anyone even to the point of teaching those thought to be wicked or degraded. He converted

9. *Majjhima-nikāya* II, p. 151 f; Winternitz. *Indian Literature*, II, pp. 47–28.
10. *Dīgha-nikāya* XXVII, 6. Cf. *Sacred Books of the East*, XX, p. 304. The Bhagavadgita also admitted the possibility of all men being delivered by Grace of God. "For those who take refuge in me, though they are lowly born, women, Vaisyas, as well as Sudras, they also attain to the highest goal" (IX, 32). However, their idea of equality was relevant to religious deliverance alone.
11. Mark 3:34–35.
12. Galatians 3:26–29.

the robber Angulimala, for example, and was treated to dinner by Ambapali, a harlot, and gave a sermon to her.[13] A similar attitude is seen in the life of Jesus. The scribes of the Pharisees, when they saw Jesus eating with commoners, some of whom collected taxes for a living, asked Jesus' disciples, "Why does he eat with tax collectors and sinners?" When Jesus heard this, he said to them, "Those who are well have no need of a physician, but those who are sick; I came not to call the righteous, but sinners."[14] In another passage is written, "Truly, I say to you, the tax collectors and the harlots go into the kingdom of God before you. For John came to you in the way of righteousness, and you did not believe him, but the tax collectors and the harlots believed him; and even when you saw it, you did not afterward repent and believe him."[15]

Before Jesus, the Greek Antisthenes had been known for his open-air preaching in a style the uneducated could understand. Likewise the Buddha, in the first attempt to do so in the history of India, preached to any person regardless of his social status or class distinction. Such an attitude contributes greatly to the growth of a universal religion.

b. Compassion and Service to Others

True wisdom in Buddhism consists not in metaphysical sophistication but only in practical knowledge, and its exemplification is the attitude of compassion. Its field of action is one's social life. Compassion or love for one's neighbors was esteemed very highly in early Buddhism. The Sanskrit word "*maitrī*" and the Pali word "*mettā*," which are both derivatives from "*mitra*" (friend) are important words from the scriptures which are translated as "compassion." Both words literally mean "true friendliness." If the virtue of compassion as the Buddhists understood it were allowed to grow in a person, it would not occur to him to harm anyone else any more than he would willingly harm himself. In this way the sentiment and love of ego diminish by widening the boundaries of what is regarded as one's own. By inviting everyone's self to enter into his own personality, man breaks down the barriers which separate him from others.

Early Buddhists thought the ideal form of love was already realized in maternal love: "As a mother at the risk of her life watches over her own child, so also let every one cultivate a boundless (friendly) mind towards all beings. Let him cultivate goodwill towards all the world, a boundless (friendly) mind, above and below and across, unobstructed,

13. *Sacred Books of the East,* vol. XVII, p. 105; XI, p. 30.
14. Mark 2:16–17. Cf. Luke 7:37–39.
15. Matthew 21:31–32.

without hatred, without enmity. Standing, walking or sitting or lying, a long as he be awake, let him devote himself to this mind; this [way of] living they say is the best in this world."[1] In keeping with this belief, even enemies should be loved. Sariputta, a disciple of the Buddha, said:

> Love should be felt for one's own kin,
> And so for enemies too, and the whole wide world
> Should be pervaded with a heart to love—
> This is the teaching of all the Buddhas.[2]

How near this is to Jesus' Sermon on the Mount in which he taught, "You have heard that it was said, 'You shall love your neighbor and hate your enemy.' But I say to you, Love your enemies and pray for those who persecute you, so that you may be sons of your Father who is in heaven."[3]

Meditation on the elements (*dharmas*) which constitute our "ego," for Buddhism, dissolves oneself as well as other people into a conglomeration of impersonal and instantaneous elements, plus a label. If there is nothing in the world except bundles of constituent elements, instantaneously perishing all the time, one might rightly conclude that ultimately there is nothing on which friendliness and compassion could work. Actually, however, this way of meditating or seeing the world abolishes the deep-rooted egoism in human existence and results in natural, spontaneous compassion and love toward others. The whole world and the individuals in it become intimately and indissolubly linked, the whole human family so closely knit together that each unit is dependent upon other units for growth and development. In this sense compassion and love are not a means but a result.

But compassionate, selfless love toward one's fellow man is also a means to further oneself on the path, according to Buddhism. It is the ethical attitude and action par excellence. "All actions, by which one acquires merit, are not worth the sixteenth part of friendliness (*mettā*), which is the emancipation of mind; for friendliness radiates, shines and illumines, surpassing those actions as the emancipation of mind,—just as all the lights of the stars are not worth the sixteenth part of the moon-light, for the moon-light, surpassing them all, radiates, shines and illumines."[4] Love or friendliness could be called the highest virtue in Buddhism, the Buddhist "golden rule." A Buddhist equivalent of the Christian Golden Rule, nearly the same as above, is expressed in the maxim: "Do as one would be done by."[5] In the Bible it is taught, "As you wish that

1. *Suttanipāta,* No. 8, vv. 149–151.
2. *Milindapañha,* p. 394.
3. Matthew 5:43–45.
4. *Itivuttaka,* No. 27.
5. *attānam upamam katvā.* Cf. *Sacred Books of the East,* X, pt. i, p. 36.

men would do to you, do so to them."[6] The concept of the Golden Rule is found to be a universal ideal or norm, discoverable, at least practically, in nearly any religious system. The Hindu epic *Mahābhārata* also contains a version of this doctrine.[7] In the teaching of Mo-tsu (468–376 B.C.) universal love is based upon the idea that all human beings are of the same kind. He teaches also that one should love the father of another man as he does his own. Concerning humanity, Confucius taught, "Do not do to others what you do not want them to do to you." There can be no doubt that this proverb is stated in the negative form, not once but three times,[8] although a negative statement does not necessarily mean a negative idea. The Chinese have always understood it to be positive.

The Confucian ideal of *Jen* is comparable to Buddhist *Maitrī* and Christian love. Love was stressed by Jews also in the Testaments of the Twelve Patriarchs.[9] Many have thought that Jesus condensed the whole of the New Testament into Matthew 22:37–40, "You shall love the Lord your God with all your heart. . . . This is the great and first commandment. And a second is like it, You shall love your neighbor as yourself. On these two commandments depend all the law and the prophets."

In Buddhist practice, love is accompanied by other mental attitudes. The four states are often described as the Sublime Conditions (*brahma-vihāra*). They are love, sorrow at the sorrows of others, joy in the joys of others, and equanimity as regards one's own joys and sorrows.[10] Each of these feelings should be deliberately practiced, beginning with a single object and gradually increasing until the whole world is suffused with such kinds of feeling.

In the days of the Buddha, a sick brother was once neglected by the other inmates of a monastery. The Buddha washed him and tended him with his own hands, saying afterwards to the careless monks, who would have been eager enough to serve him, their leader, "Whosoever would wait upon me, let him wait upon the sick." He claimed oneness with humanity; so services to the sick or to the destitute were considered by him, in reality, to have been rendered to himself.[11] Christ also said, "As you did it to one of the least of these my brethren, you did it to me."[12]

In Buddhist literature a true friend is defined in detail. "Four are the friends who should be reckoned as sound at heart:—the helper; the friend who is the same in happiness and adversity; the friend of good counsel; the friend who sympathizes.

6. Luke 6:31.
7. *Mahābhārata* XIII, 113, 9; XII, 260, 22; V, 39, 72.
9. Russell, *A History of Western Philosophy*, p. 320.
8. *Analects* V, 11; XII, 2; XV, 23; *The Doctrine of the Mean* XIII.
10. *Dīgha-nikāya* II, pp. 186–187.
11. *Mahāvagga* VIII, 26.
12. Matthew 25:40.

"On four grounds the friend who is a helper is to be reckoned as sound at heart:—he guards you when you are off your guard; he guards your property when you are off your guard; he is a refuge to you when you are afraid; when you have tasks to perform he provides a double supply [of what you may need].

"On four grounds the friend who is the same in happiness and adversity is to be reckoned as sound at heart:—he tells you his secrets; he keeps secret your secrets; in your troubles he does not forsake you; he lays down even his life for your sake.

"On four grounds the friend who declares what you need to do is to be reckoned as sound at heart:—he restrains you from doing wrong; he enjoins you to do what is right; he informs you of what you had not heard before; he reveals to you the way to heaven.

"On four grounds the friend who sympathizes is to be reckoned as sound at heart:—he does not rejoice over your misfortunes; he rejoices over your prosperity; he restrains anyone who is speaking ill of you; he commends anyone who is praising you."[13]

The virtue of giving to others[14] was also highly stressed in Buddhism and it was said, "To him who gives shall virtue be increased."[15] It was the Buddha's contention that the charitable man is loved by all; his friendship is prized highly; in death his heart is at rest and full of joy, for he suffers not from repentence. The charitable man was metaphorically thought of by the Buddha as he who receives the opening flower of his reward and the fruit that ripens from it. "Hard it is to understand," he said, "By giving away our food, we get more strength; by bestowing clothing on others, we gain more beauty; by founding abodes of purity and truth, we acquire great treasures."[16] In Paul's charge to the elders, he asserted, "In all things I have shown you that by so toiling one must help the weak, remembering the words of the Lord Jesus, how he said, 'It is more blessed to give than to receive.' "[17]

The spirit of brotherly love should be expressed in all phases of our life, according to Buddhism. One should refrain from hurting others, and put away the killing of living beings. "The cudgel and the sword he has laid aside, and ashamed of roughness, and full of mercy, he dwells compassionate, and kind to all creatures that have life."[18] One should not offend others even by speech. "Our mind shall not waver. No evil speech

13. *Sigālovāda* 21–25.
14. "Those who have much are often greedy; those who have little always share" (Oscar Wilde, *De Profundis*, p. 27).
15. *Mahāparinibbāna-suttanta* 4, 43. *Dīgha-nikāya*, vol, p. 136.
16. *Fo-sho-hing-tsan-ching*, vv. 1516–1517.
17. Acts 20–35.
18. *Dīgha-nikāya* II, 43, vol. 1, p. 62.

will we utter. Tender and compassionate will we abide, loving in heart, void of malice within."[19]

To nurture friendliness, one should reflect upon oneself. "Not the perversities of others, not their sins of commission or omission, but his own misdeeds and negligences should a sage take notice of."[20] Buddhists noted that the fault of others is easily perceived, but that of oneself is difficult to perceive. ". . . A man winnows his neighbor's faults like chaff, but his own fault he hides, as a cheat hides the bad die from the gambler."[21] Confucius also lamented, "I have not yet seen one who could perceive his faults, and inwardly accuse himself."[22] To understand this as a norm of ethics in universal religions one need only read the Lord's Prayer in the New Testament.

One should also not worry about bitter and sarcastic comments by others. The Buddha gave a valuable instruction regarding this, that among men there is no one who is not blamed. "People blame him who sits silent and him who speaks, they also blame the man who preaches the middle path."[23] In the Bible we find a similar saying confirming Buddha's thought. "John came neither eating nor drinking, and they say, 'He has a demon'; teh Son of man came eating and drinking, and they say, 'Behold, a glutton and a drunkard, a friend of tax collectors and sinners!' "[24]

The meek and compassionate character at the same time firm in his own convictions was exemplified in the life of Gotama as well as Jesus. In reading the Pali scriptures one is impressed with the strong personal influence exercised by the Buddha over the hearts of his fellowmen. He was regarded as a very meek and compassionate man by others. All that he did represented ways of peace. Anger, in fact, had no place in his character and played no role in his teachings. The birth stories of the Buddha often extravagantly exalt his great compassion and renunciation.[25] Such descriptions might seem to be fantastic, yet their purport is characteristically altruistic.

The distinction between the Buddhist and Christian concepts of love is still of contemporary significance. Westerners, generally speaking, base the love concept on individualism,[26] whereas Easterners, under Buddhist and Hindu influence, tend to base love and compassion on the concept

19. *Majjhima-nikāya* I, 129.
20. *Dhammapada* 50.
21. *Dhammapada* 252. Cf. 253.
22. *Analects* V, 26.
23. *Dhammapada* 227. Cf. *Fo-sho-hing-tsan-ching*, vv. 1713–1734.
24. Matthew 11:18–19.
25. *Jātaka*, No. 316, etc.
26. "It is love and the capacity for it that distinguishes one human being from another" (Oscar Wilde, *De Profundis*, p. 113).

of non-duality of individuals, although Westernized Asiatics hold the Western concept, and some Western intellectuals influenced by Eastern thought have spoken about love as Eastern thinkers have.[27]

c. The Concepts of Evil and Conscience

In the world's two major universal religions there were highly developed concepts of evil (sin) as well as some form of retribution for evil. The latter led to the concept (and concrete actualization) of conscience. The Buddhist scriptures claim that "Not in the sky, not in the midst of the sea, not if we enter into the clefts of the mountains, is there known a spot in the whole world where a man might be freed from an evil deed."[1] A similar expression is found in the New Testament: "Nothing is covered up that will not be revealed, or hidden that will not be known."[2] In Christianity providence is implied as the medium of retribution, whereas in the Buddhist verse *karma* is suggested. The Christian expression had inherited the Old Testament tradition. "If I ascend to heaven, thou art there! If I make my bed in Sheol, thou art there! If I take the wings of the morning and dwell in the uttermost parts of the sea, even there thy hand shall lead me."[3] The Buddhist concept was based on a belief in the efficacy of causal sequence.

In classical literature[4] of India (i.e., Buddhist, Jain literature, the great epics and law-books), man's action (*karman*) is set forth as threefold: action by body, action by speech, and action by mind. Similar expressions were shown to exist in the *Zend-avesta* and among the Manichaeans. There is no ground for supposing that this formula found its way into the Christian liturgy from Persia, for Greek writers such as Plato employ very similar expressions.[5] The idea of sin committed by thought was not a new idea, for in the Old Testament it was said, "The thought of foolishness is sin."[6]

27. "Love reduces them as the sun melts the iceberg in the sea. The heart and soul of all men being one, this bitterness of *His* and *Mine* ceases. His is mine. I am my brother, and my brother is me" (Emerson, "Compensation," is *Selected Writings*, p. 189).

1. *Dhammapada* 127.
2. Luke 12:2.
3. Psalms 139:8–10.
4. See F. Max Muller in *Sacred Books of the East*, vol. X, pp. 28–29, note. In Jain literature also the same classification can be found.
5. "For all men who have a companion are readier in deed, word, or thought" (*pros hapan ergon kai dianoēma*) (Plato, *Protagoras*. *The Dialogues of Plato* translated by B. Jowett, 5 vols., 3rd edition, [Oxford University Press, 1892, Humphrey Milford Reprint, New York, Random House], vol. I, p. 172).
6. Proverbs 24:9. The King James Version has been used here. "The divising of folly is sin" (Revised Standard Version).

The most dangerous obstacles to man are the Ten Bonds, according to early Buddhism. These bonds are:

1. Delusions about the soul (*sakkāya-diṭṭhi*)
2. Doubt (*vicikicchā*)
3. Dependence on works (*sīlabbata-parāmāsa*)
4. Sensuality (*karman*)
5. Ill-will (*paṭigha*)
6. Desire for rebirth on earth (*rūpa-rāga*)
7. Desire for rebirth in heaven (*arūpa-rāga*)
8. Pride (*māna*)
9. Self-righteousness (*uddhacca*)
10. Ignorance (*avijjā*)

These evil dispositions must be conquered in order for man to progress in this life. The conquering of ignorance, the last one, which is the fundamental principle motivating our mundane existence, will finally lead men to release. The disciples of the Buddha, both monks and laymen, must get rid of these evils gradually through their own efforts. To have broken the first three bonds corresponds to what Christians call conversion and what Buddhists call "the entrance into the stream." Having attained the final "assurance," there can then be no permanent relapse. Sooner or later, in this birth or another, final salvation is assured, according to the teaching of Southern Buddhism. So adherents are encouraged to avoid evil dispositions. "Evil deeds are done from motives of partiality, enmity, stupidity and fear. But inasmuch as the Noble Disciple is not led away by these motives, he does no evil deed through them."[7]

The fact that man is defiled by vices was lamented by ancient sages in other countries as well. Confucius noted that the things that made him sad were "that virtue is not cultivated, that knowledge is not made clear, that people hear of duty and do not practise it, that people have evil in themselves and do nothing to improve."[8] The Gospel of John reads, "This is the judgment, that the light has come into the world, and men loved darkness rather than light, because their deeds were evil."[9]

The following is a story that illustrates the Buddhist view of sin. King Ajātasattu killed his father in order to occupy the throne of the king. But having heard the sermon of the Buddha, he expressed the feeling or repentance before the Buddha. "Sin has overcome me, Lord, weak and foolish and wrong that I am, in that, for the sake of sovereignty, I put to death my father, that righteous man, that righteous king! May the

7. *Sigālovāda* 5.
8. *Analects* VII, 3.
9. John 3:19.

Blessed One accept it of me, Lord, that do so acknowledge it as a sin." The Buddha replied, "Verily, O king, it was sin that overcame you in acting thus. But inasmuch as you look upon it as sin (*accaya*), and confess it according to what is right, we accept your confession as to that. For that is the custom in the discipline of the noble ones, that whosoever looks upon his fault as a fault, and rightfully confesses it, shall attain to self-reatraint in the future."[10]

In the New Testament, sins or evil amount to willfully breaking the laws[11] inherited from the Old Testament prophets (the Ten Commandments, etc.), plus the failure to abide by them in keeping with the new emphasis in Jesus' interpretation of the religious life (love God and your neighbor,[12] etc.). As in Buddhism, however, a person was thought to have regenerative possibilities, for "if he has committed sins, he will be forgiven."[13] The procedure, again as in Buddhism, is to ". . . confess our sins, he is faithful and just, and will forgive . . . and cleanse us from all unrighteousness."[14] Jesus' own forgiving nature with regard to breaches of the law was never better represented than in the New Testament story of a woman brought to him by the scribes and Pharisees and accused of adultery. They reminded him that Moses' law "commanded us to stone such." While they were stating their charges, Jesus was bent over, writing with his finger in the dust. "And as they continued to ask him, he stood up and said to them. 'Let him who is without sin among you be the first to throw a stone at her.' And once more he bent down and wrote with his finger on the ground. . . . They went away, one by one, beginning with the eldest, and Jesus was left alone with the woman standing before him. Jesus looked up and said to her, 'Woman, where are they? Has no one condemned you?' She said, 'No one, Lord.' And Jesus said, 'Neither do I condemn you; go, and do not sin again.' "[15]

A major difference between Buddhism and Christianity is that in the Buddhist faith there is no conception of original sin; nor are there any who will be damned forever. Eternal damnation is absolutely inconceivable for the Buddhists; even such hideous crimes as patricide are believed by Buddhists to be forgiven by deep repentance.

Since universal religions were usually involved in the problem of discriminating "good" from "bad" they developed a consciousness of moral values which gave rise to the concept (and existential awareness)

10. *Dīgha-nikāya*, vol. I, p. 85. I have cited with slight change from T. W. Rhys Davids' *Dialogues of the Buddha*, part I (London: Luzac and Co., 1956), p. 94.
11. ". . . but sin is not counted where there is no law" (Romans 5:13).
12. In the first letter of Peter 4:8 is found "Above all hold unfailing your love for one another, since love covers a multitude of sins."
13. James 5:16.
14. I John 1:9.
15. John 8:3–11.

of "conscience." In the West the problem of conscience was usually discussed in relation to God. For instance the first letter of Peter admonishes, ". . . keep your conscience clear, so that, when you are abused, those who revile your good behavior in Christ may be put to shame. For it is better to suffer for doing right, if that should be God's will, than for doing wrong."[16] In the East, though the relationship to God was not ignored, conscience was discussed in other contexts as well.

Buddhist texts and traditional Hindu texts such as the *Code of Manu*[17] or *Mahābhārata*[18] taught that if you commit an evil act, your *Ātman* will know it;[19] your *Ātman* will be the witness; your *Ātman* will blame you.[20] As is well known, the Indian concept of "*Ātman*" is a counterpart to the Christian God. In some Buddhist texts of India it is said that, although you might try to conceal your bad acts, gods know it;[21] Tathāgatas (the perfected sages) know it.[22] An equivalent of the Western concept of *cum scio*, i.e., "knowing with somebody else" or "common knowledge," is certainly evident in these ideas; however the entity(ies) with whom "common knowledge" is shared are different from the Western God.

A Far Eastern equivalent of "conscience" is "Good Mind." This term was first mentioned in *Mencius*; it developed in the Neo-Confucianism of China and Japan and in the Wang-ming school of those countries in later days. "Good Mind" was regarded as a universal principle, but different from God as a personal existence.

In colloquial Japanese the expression "the torture of conscience" or "the prick of conscience" is quite common. It can be interpreted as the pangs or sting of a guilty conscience. In this case the words "torture," "prick," "pangs" or "sting" are used in the metaphorical sense, i.e., in the mental sense. The Japanese concept seems to be an interesting combination of the Chinese term "Good Mind" and the Buddhist idea of "the torture by the Wardens of Jail in Hells," although no one has ever tried to trace the origin of this expression. In Japanese the phrase, "Heaven knows; Earth knows; man knows; one's Self knows" is in quite common use.

In the philosophy of the ancient West concepts related to conscience also often came under discussion. In the philosophy of Neo-Platonists the *synesis* is at the same time *syneidesis*, meaning conscience, i.e., man's knowledge not only of his own states and actions, but also the criterion of their ethical worth. As a result of Plotinus' conception of conscience, ". . . the

16. I Peter 3:16–17.
17. *Manu* II, 12; VIII, 84 f; 91.
18. *antaḥpuruṣa, Mahābhārata* III, 207, 54.
19. *Aṅguttara-nikāya*, vol. I, p. 149 gāthā.
20. *Majjhima-nikāya*, vol. I, p. 361.
21. *Theragāthā* 497.
22. *Aṅguttara-nikāya*, vol. I, p. 150 gāthā.

doctrine of self-consciousness is developed in the doctrine of the Church-Fathers, not only as man's knowledge of his sins, but also as repentance (*metanoia*) in actively combating them."[23] According to Abelard, the essence of morals consists in the resolve of the will (*animi intentio*). Then according to what norm is the will's resolve to be characterized as good or bad? "He [Abelard] finds the norm of judgment solely within the deciding individual, and it consists in the agreement or non-agreement with the conscience (*conscientia*). That action is good which is in accord with the agent's own conviction; that only is bad which contradicts this."[24] In Thomas'view, conscience (*synteresis*) was a means for knowledge of God *sub ratione boni*.[25]

Concepts of evil and conscience are inseparably linked if one holds out hopes for spiritual progress. That is, man must be able to know and feel what is "wrong," in order to be able to help himself. Responsibility is placed squarely upon the mind of man; he cannot rely upon his actions alone (he may be fooling other people), his mind must be pure as well.

Viewed from the religious standpoint, good action as such is never a means to the final end. Prince Sumana once asked the Buddha what would be the difference between two men, one of whom had been generous in a former life and one not. He replied that there would be no difference at all after they have attained release.[26] Devout Buddhists, it is thought, practise good actions spontaneously, without considering the result of such actions. The concept of conscience instills in man the belief that he is responsible to his own inner sense (which cannot be fooled) for his movement toward a religious goal.

Many ascetics in the days of the Buddha observed the vow of not eating meat[27]. The Buddha denounced this practice as insignificant. Eating meat is not foul, he asserted; rather the vices of one's mind should be called impure. "Destroying life, killing, cutting, binding, stealing, speaking lies, fraud and deceptions, worthless reading, intercourse with another's wife—this is defilement, but not the eating of flesh."[28]

Similarly Christ said, "Not what goes into the mouth defiles a man, but what comes out of the mouth, this defiles a man."[29] Here the thoughts

23. Windelband, *History*, p. 234. "The mystic of the neo-Platonic type is less concerned than the Buddhist with his spiritual indolence felt as a positive evil. The neo-Platonic mystic reminds one of the Buddhist in that his ultimate is indefinable. The Buddhist holds, however, that in order to achieve his ultimate he needs to exercise the sharpest discrimation" (Babbitt, *The Dhammapada*, p. 106).
24. Windelband, *History*, p. 308.
25. *Ibid.*, p. 333.
26. *Aṅguttara-nikāya*, vol. III, p. 32.
27. *Suttanipāta* 241.
28. *Suttanipāta* 244.
29. Matthew 15:10. Cf. Mark 7:15.

of Buddha and Jesus are in exact agreement. Based upon such a standpoint, Theravada Buddhists did not observe vegetarianism. However, in later days, vegetarianism came to the fore owing to the spirit of compassion towards all living beings. Today in South-Asiatic countries some Buddhists are vegetarians, whereas in Tibet and Japan there are just a few vegetarians.

The path of religion leads through morality, but when one approaches the goal, one enters into an entirely different element. The saint who has attained the calm of *Nirvāṇa* is said to be beyond good and evil. What is called "good" in daily life is a very often defiled with worldly desire.[30] The ideal situation should be perfectly pure, so it is said to transcend secular notions of good and evil. In a situation like this there are no differences between the release of one person and that of another, because all are purified.

d. The Mean and the Character of Effort

EXAMINING evil, it was apparent that there are many interrelated concepts involved. In order for man to transgress (sin) and be unrighteous there must be some form of law from which he lapses. There may be all sorts of bane that occurs in the form of affliction, pestilence, etc.; but religion generally recognizes evil (or sin) by its adherents that is done voluntarily or willfully. On the basis of such action alone (fully conscious of import) can one be blamed for reprobacy or transgression of the law.

Such conceptions as these which come up in discussions of morality are not new. On the contrary, they go back to the very beginnings of Indo-European language as we now know it. The origin of the word "sin" has been traced to the Indo-European root *es-, "to be," which in the beginning probably signified an existence and then later an actual occurrence of a negative quality. The word "evil," however, is more interesting for the subject at hand. "Evil" has been traced to the Indo-European root *upo, the most important meaning of which for our purposes was simply "over." In proto-Germanic an important derivation was *ubilaz, "excessive." Later relatives were the Old English "ufel" and finally "evil." Considering these original usages, as meaning "over" and "excessive," it is not too surprising that some of the world's greatest traditions developed concepts of a "mean" (nothing to excess) as the absence of evil.

It is an interesting coincidence that the teaching of the "middle way" or "mean" was advocated at nearly the same period in India, Greece, and China. What was considered to be the mean or the middle way, however,

30. This fact was especially emphasized by Shinran, whose thought will be discussed in the fourth chapter.

came out to be substantially different with historical and social context.

In Buddhism universal norms (*dhamma*; see section on universal norms) were thought to be applicable to everyone (a tautology) and not to conflict with human nature. The way to come into harmony with these norms was termed the Middle Path by early Buddhists because it avoided extremes (excesses). One extreme was the outright pursuit of worldly desires; and the other, the severe, physically exhausting discipline of the ascetics.[1] Thus the trait of Buddhist ethics is thought to be humanistic.

In China, Confucius also advocated a doctrine of a mean. Mencius tells us that "Confucius was one who abstrained from extremes."[2] The *Mean in Action*, attributed to the Confucian Hsün Tsŭ, is one of the great Chinese classics.

In the West the famous saying "Nothing too much" is attributed to Solon, and the virtue of moderation was set forth by Heraclitus[3] in earlier days. But the greatest Western advocate for the doctrine of a mean was undoubtedly Aristotle. One of Aristotle's most famous doctrines was called the "Golden Mean." Every virtue, he taught, is a mean between extremes, each of which is a vice. Courage is a mean between cowardice and rashness; liberality, between prodigality and meanness; proper pride, between vanity and humility; and so on. Aristotle considered how to bring the ideal of the mean into practice very concretely, "Since to hit the mean is hard in the extreme, we must as a second best, as people say, take the least of the evils."[4] Further, "how far . . . a man must stray before he becomes blameworthy, it is not easy to state in words; for the decision depends on the particular facts and on perception (*aisthesis*)".[5]

On the other hand *The Book of Mean*, the Chinese classic, lacks such a consideration of man's activities and the mean in concrete practice. It says: "Sincerity is the way of Heaven. The attainment of sincerity is the way of men."[6] When it is realized in rulers, the four seasons become favorable and things proceed smoothly. But when Aristotle speaks of "human virtue" or "human good" in connection with the mean, he is thinking not so much of the ruler's virtue as of each individual citizen's. Conversely, the thought such as expressed in the *Book of the Mean* helps toward the

1. *Dhammacakkappavattana-sutta*, etc.
2. *Mencius* IV, 2, 10. Cf. IV, 2, 7, 20; *Analects* XI, 15.
3. Heraclitus said: "Moderation is the greatest virtue" (fragment 112) and "All men have the capacity of knowing themselves and acting with moderation" (fragment 116).
4. *Nicomachean Ethics* 1109, a 34 (Ross's translation).
5. *Ibid.*, 1126 b 3 (Ross's translation).
6. *Chung-yung* XX.

preservation of the ruler's position, and develops a political system which has been thought of as despotism.[7]

The Buddhist teaching is somewhat different in emphasis than either of the above. The doctrine of the Middle Path that the Buddha proclaimed is related even in religious life to the fundamental attitude of Buddhism, which is mainly represented as the absence of special dogmas. The universal norms of human life are lawlike, although the ways of applying them vary. Therefore in each case they must be applied in the most auspicious way. The general principles must be adjusted to the infinitely varying circumstances of actual life. Otherwise, there would be a danger that minute outer regulations may encroach unduly on the moral autonomy of the individual. In order to avoid this danger, the Buddha advised his disciples to resort to the spirit of the Middle Path. This fundamental character has been preserved up to the present throughout the Buddhist world, although its application differs with periods and people. Even today[8] each Buddhist subscribes to the principle of the Middle Path.

The doctrine of the mean in Buddhism also has a metaphysical variation (best seen in the Buddha's silence, see section by that name, above). It has been represented as close to Heraclitus' (and Hegel's) "becoming" as the synthesis of the antitheses "being" and "non-being." Buddha's metaphysics however was never far from his ethics; and it might be better said that his "Madhyama Pratipad sought to resolve the opposition of being and non-being, not by synthesizing the two categories but by transcending them both."[9] Metaphysically and ethically "the Buddha 'without falling into two extremes preaches the *dhamma in the middle*' (*ete ubho ante anupagamma majjhena . . . dhammam deseti*). . . . The 'middle way' (*majjhimā paṭipadā*) which is a mean both in the mater of belief as well as of conduct is said to 'make for knowledge . . . and bring about intuition and realization' (*ñāṇa-karaṇī . . . adhiññāya sambodhāya . . . saṃyattati*)."[10]

7. Discussed in detail by Motozo Mocegi in his "Meson and Chung-yung: A Comparative Study of the Mean, Greek and Chinese, and Some Related Problems," in *The Bulletin of the Yokohama City University Society*, vol. XIV, Spiritual Science No. 1 (January, 1963), see especially pp. 16ff., 25–27.
8. In the West also we find a similar notion. "For what man has sought for is, indeed, neither pain nor pleasure, but simply Life. Man has sought to live intensely, fully, perfectly. When he can do so without exercising restraint on others, or suffering it ever, and his activities are all pleasurable to him, he will be saner, healthier, more civilized, more himself. Pleasure is Nature's test, her sign of approval" (Wilde, *The Soul of Man under Socialism* [Portland, Maine: Thomas B. Mosher, 1905], p. 89).
9. G. C. Pande, *Studies in the Origins of Buddhism* (Department of Ancient History, Culture and Archaeology, University of Allahabad, 1957), p. 420.
10. *Majjhima-Nikāya*, vol. I, p. 15. K. N. Jayatilleke, *Early Buddhist Theory of Knowledge* (London: George Allen & Unwin Ltd., 1963), pp. 359f. Neither Jayatilleke nor Pande (fn. 9 above) use italics for the Pali.

In the ethical realm the primary emphasis was on right action. Buddhist adherents were to strive to be "full of confidence, modest in heart, ashamed of wrong, full of learning, strong in energy, active in mind, and full of wisdom;" they were to "live in the practive, both in public and private, of those virtues which, when unbroken, intact, unspotted the unblemished, make men free, and which are untarnished by the belief in the efficacy of any outward acts of ritual or ceremony, by the hope of any kind of future life."[11] In the same spirit of careful ethical regulation for the sake of spiritual advancement, Marcus Aurelius cautioned that since it is possible man may depart from life at any moment, he should regulate every act and thought accordingly.

The Buddha distinguished between expansive desires and the will to refrain from them. In that one (psychological) respect he was an uncompromising dualist.[12] By exercising this quality of will a man may gradually put aside what is impermanent in favor of release from impermanence altogether. A chief virtue for early Buddhism is therefore the putting forth of this quality of effort, spiritual strenuousness, as one may say. His last exhortation to his disciples was to practice this virtue, spiritual strenousness (*appamāda*) unceasingly. And if spiritual strenuousness is a supreme Buddhist virtue, then spiritual slackness is an unpardonable offense. One must constantly keep in mind, however, that both the perseverance and its opposite have reference primarily not to the outer world but to meditation. Considering that early Christianity also stressed constant effort toward the goal (one could cite the example of St. Jerome),[13] hard spiritual work may be said to have universal appeal in universal religions. And as has been seen, spiritual effort is nearly always geared away from personal material gain.

From this characteristic a noteworthy conclusion can be drawn: monks and nuns do well to be meek and mild. This trait might be called, as was the case in Buddhism, their main strength. The Buddha said "There are here, O monks, eight powers! Which are they? Crying is the power of child, scolding is the power of women, weapons are the power of robbers,

11. *Mahāparinibbānna-suttanta.* Rhys Davids, *Buddhist suttas Translated from Pali, Sacred Books of the East,* vol. XI (Oxford: Clarendon Press, 1881), pp. 8, 10.
12. The absence in Buddhism of metaphysical dualism (or pluralism) is not to be taken as automatic evidence for monism; ". . . reason cannot and should not be used as an apogogic device, i.e., the rejection of a view does not automatically mean acceptance of another" (K. Inada, *Nāgārjuna* [Tokyo: The Hokuseido Press, 1970], p. 9). "This world, O Kaccāna, is addicted to dualism, to the 'it is' and to the 'it is not.' He who perceives in truth and wisdom how things arise in the world, for him there is no 'it is not' in the world. And O Kaccāna, he who perceives in truth and wisdom how things in the world pass away, for him there is no 'it is' in the world" (*Saṃyutta-nikāta* II, 17).
13. Russell: *A History of Western Philosophy*, p. 341.

sovereignty is the power of kings, pride is the power of fools, humility is the power of sages, reflection the power of scholars, meekness the power of ascetics and Brahmans."[14] To the brethren this strength is quite in opposition to force.

That the Buddhist dualism is psychological and not metaphysical is quite easily seen in the fact that to control one's mind one must control one's body. The Buddha declared, "Herein, O mendicants, a brother continues, as to the body, so to look upon the body that he remains strenuous, self-possessed and mindful, having overcome both the hankering and the dejection common in the world. (And in the same way) as to feelings (*vedanā*)—moods (*cittāni*)—ideas (*dhammā*), he continues to look upon each [such] that he remains strenuous, self-possessed, and mindful, having overcome both the hankering and the dejection common in the world."[15] More often in the West a strict dualism was maintained and the soul was to be purified from its bodily cage by various ascetic practices.

The Buddhist dualism is psychological (and ethically practical), because Buddhist analyses were highly introspective. Unfortunately, the terms used by early Buddhists with considerable precision have no exact Occidental equivalents. Translators seem at times to have given up in despair the task of rendering into English all the discriminations of a subtle and unfamiliar psychology. (It is estimated that a European scholar has translated fifteen different Pali words by the one English word "desire.") In spite of this difficulty, however, the Buddhist attitude can be seen to suggest a peculiarly modern method of study. As is well known, modern thinkers are tending more and more to discard speculative philosophy in favor of psychology; and therein they are at one with the Buddha. Buddhists have always been attentive to the inner life of man, and modern psychoanalysts also deal with it, though from different angles. Buddhist psychology will be contributive to the solutions of psychological problems, even (or perhaps especially) for moderns who live in a purely industrialized and mechanized society.

Introspective psychology in Buddhism went hand in hand with a very close attention to calming various passions which produce negative mental results. Purity of mind was stressed. "There is no fire like lust, there is no spark like hatred, there is no snare like folly, there is no torrent like greed."[16] Lao-tzu also expressed nearly the same thought: "There is no greater sin than to look on what moves desire; there is no greater evil than discontent; there is no greater disaster than covetousness."[17]

In the Buddhist analysis sensuous pleasure belongs to man, but it is

14. *Aṅguttara-nikāya* VIII, 27. Winternitz, *Indian Literature* II, p. 65.
15. *Mahāparinibbāna-suttanta* II, 100.
16. *Dhammapada* 251.
17. *Tao-te-ching* XLV, 2.

not what makes man as such. The Buddha said, "A man who has learnt but little grows old like an ox; his flesh increases but his knowledge does not grow."[18] Amos of the Old Testament tradition addresses the fat and undisciplined women of his day as "You cows of Bashan,"[19] i.e., massive in body but small in mind. Heraclitus also noted, "If happiness lay in bodily pleasures, we would call oxen happy when they find vetch to eat."[20] These various traditions commonly stress the simple fact that peace is a result of body-mind harmony. Buddhism stressed an inner apprehension of such harmony.

Buddhists thought that only the external appearance was pure in the case of traditional ritualists (e.g., the ritualists who flourished just prior to Buddha's time). In contrast Buddhism came to place value on the inner significance of purity. For instance, in a Buddhist sceipture is found, "Reverence shown to the righteous is better than sacrifice."[21] Jesus also insisted less on sacraments and more on the opening of oneself in faith.[22] An interesting paradox is seen in the fact that for Buddhism, the man who is outwardly ideal may be at once more strenuously and more assiduously engaged in religious cultivation than the man who is outwardly hyperactive.[23]

Although the Buddhist emphasis was laid chiefly upon inward effort, early Buddhists in general did not minimize the necessity of outward effort, as is seen in the case of King Aśoka. It is said the King Aśoka came to be converted, hearing a monk reciting the second chapter of the present *Dhammapada* which stresses the importance of effort. Aśoka proclaimed to his subjects: "Let all joy be in effort"; "Let small and great exert themselves." He said, "For the welfare of the whole world is an esteemed duty with me. And the root of that, again, is this, namely, exertion and dispatch of business. There is no higher duty than the welfare of the whole world."[24] Aśoka was active in every sense of the word, in religious activities and in administrating political and economic affairs. However, generally speaking, the outward efforts by Buddhists towards the natural world seem to have been less than those by ancient Westerns.

18. *Dhammapada* 394.
19. Amos 4:1.
20. Heraclitus, fragment 4.
21. *Dhammapada* 109.
22. *Mahāparinibbāna-suttanta. Sacred Books of the East* XI, p. 109; Introd. to *Sacred Books of the East,* vol. XIV; Matthew 3:14; John 4:2.
23. Cf. the dialogue between Buddha and a Brahmin peasant in *Suttanipāta* 18–33.
24. Rock Edict, VI. D. R. Bhandarkar, *Aśoka,* 3rd ed. (University of Calcutta, 1955), p. 227.

4. Ethics in the Order

a. Establishing of the Order

THE Buddha established a religious order which has continued to the present day as one of the oldest and most influential orders of religious brethren in the world. In his place in history, in his methods of exposition, in many of his personal qualities, Gotama stands side by side with Socrates. But in one significant particular he was much more important than Socrates. He established a completely elaborated scheme of practical life, a carefully thought-out system of inward self-culture, a comprehensive system of philosophy, and regulations for a monastic order.

It is noteworthy that the Buddha organized an order of nuns also.[1] The Buddhist Order thus consisted of four kinds of followers: monks, nuns, laymen, and laywomen. The *upāsaka* or layman, who held different moral and ethical obligations, is comparable to the Christian "Third Order" of later times. But the place of women in Buddhism is a complicated question and by no means free from ambiguity. Today in Southern Asiatic countries there are very few women monastics.

A Western counterpart which arose at nearly the same period as Buddhist monasticism was the Orphic brotherhoods which were organized around 600 B.C. and worshipped Dionysos under various mystic names. The preachers of the Orphic doctrines were the first propagandists or missionaries that can be traced in the pre-Christian Mediterranean world. But their influence was limited. Admission to the brotherhood required the possession of Greek speech, which limited the scope of Orphic expansion, compared with other universal religions. Initiation into the Orphic brotherhood, however, was open to women and sometimes even to slaves.

In later days a distinction between *electi*, i.e., intelligent people who are chosen, and *auditores* (hearers), i.e., lay believers, was made in Manichaeism, corresponding to the distinction between the monks (*bhikkhus*) and the laymen (*upāsakas*) as represented in the *Gāthā*, portions of the early Buddhist scriptures. (In Jainism lay believers were called "hearers," *sāvakas*.) The main characteristic of the *electi* was not that they had the

1. Yielding to many soft entreaties, the Buddha allowed women to enter the Order as nuns, but he never completely reconciled himself to this move. "If, Ānanda," he said, "women had no received permission to enter the Order, the pure religion would have lasted long, the good law would have stood fast a thousand years. But since they have received that permission, it will now stand for only five hundred years" (*Vinaya*, Cullavagga X, 1, 6).

exclusive right to perform certain acts, but rather that they possessed a fuller knowledge of religion and abstained from certain practices which were allowed to other members of the religious order.[2]

The Buddhist Order amounted to a form of republic. All its proceedings were settled by resolutions that were agreed upon in regular meetings of the members. These meetings were held subject to the observance of certain established regulations and to the use of certain fixed forms of words. Many of the rules were introduced from the republics and guilds existing in those days. The forms of words under which the meetings were conducted, and the resolutions passed, were called *Kammavācās*, i.e., the "Words of the Act." They were naturally regarded with great reverence by the members of the Order and were handed down with scrupulous care.

In the established orders of early Buddhism, monks and nuns were required to shun all amusements, all music, dances, shows, games, luxuries, idle conversation, argument, or fortune-telling; they were to have nothing to do with business or with any form of buying or selling. A similar phenomenon is noticed in ancient Greece. In the society that Pythagoras founded, men and women were admitted on equal terms; property was held in common, and there was a common way of life.[3] The Pythagoreans, however, engaged in scientific and mathematical research, while Indian believers did not.

Christians also established a similar order. The early Roman Catholic Order had many features in common with the Buddhist Order.

2. A. A. Bevan in *Encyclepedia of Religion and Ethics*, vol. VIII, p. 399 a.
3. Russell, *History*, p. 32.

"True,—as one of the more recent historians of these Greek developments has already observed —the segregation of these sectaries from the world was of a much milder character in Greece than in India, corresponding to the differences in the national characters. . . . In Greece, there is greater moderation. True, the communities searching for redemption, in Greece too, consider the present world as a place of uncleanness, of imprisonment; but there is no very great seriousness in their efforts to escape from this thraldom. Outwardly they continue to observe the duties and enjoy the pleasures of every-day life, and are satisfied with the practice of securing inwardly a release from the limitations of such a life by the secret power of the mystic doctrine and mystic cult" (H. Oldenberg, *Ancient India* [Chicago: Open Court Publishing Company, 1896], pp. 88–90).

"This world appears to all of them [Buddhism and the Orphic order] as a gloomy domain of dissension and suffering. The symbolism of the Orpheans has it that Dionysus, the divinity, is torn to pieces by Titans: the blessed unity of all Being undergoes the evil fate of disintegration. Another Greek conception, of the sixth century B.C., discerns in the material existence of things a guilt; all heavens and all worlds, issuing from unity and infinity, having become guilty of wrong, must pay the penalty and do penance therefor, resolving themselves again into the components from which they originally came into being" (*Ibid.*, pp. 90–91).

These were not only monks and nuns but also novices (*sāmaṇeras*), rites of tonsure, repentence, etc. Some monks were out to solicit alms. The possessions of the monks were strictly limited and diet was frugal.[4] They worshipped religious symbols, and practiced meditation.

Peace and harmony among members of the Buddhist Order was highly esteemed. "Blessed is concord in the Order."[5] In early Christian orders harmony among the brothers was undoubtedly in keeping with the spirit of such scriptural saying as, "Behold, how good and pleasant it is when brothers dwell in unity."[6] However, in Christian orders of later times concord was kept by means of force, whereas Buddhist orders never resorted to this practice and hence were sometimes easily divided.

Unlike Jesus, the Buddha himself instituted his own order, corresponding to ones that developed later in the Western Church. He followed the way of other spiritual teachers in his day and in the course of his forty-five year ministry, when the occasion arose, he gradually made many regulations for the guidance of the Order. But, unlike the Catholic Church, the Buddhist Order was not strictly organized. Buddhist followers of all types have been comparatively individualistic. They have not, on the whole, submitted to a rigid outer authority. Indian Buddhism has never known any strong regulative body comparable in elaborateness and effectiveness to that of Roman Catholicism (itself modeled in important respects on the Roman imperial organization). This corresponds with the fact that ancient India lacked a rational unity in the political sense.

Gotama's system of self-training was one that all persons were invited to adopt; it could be carried out irrespective of residence at any particular place or in any particular company. So the disciples were not confined only to those who could remain with the master, but isolated followers could form their own body of companions. Gotama's disciples were allowed to receive new disciples into the society without consulting or referring the matter to him. By this method the existence of the Order was assured, even after the passing of its founder. Thus Buddhists formed the oldest

4. Early Buddhism allowed meat-eating under some conditions, as is described in the *Suttanipāta* and the *Vinaya*. "Paul, in the 8th Chapter of the First Epistle to the Corinthians, solves the question whether Christians may eat of the meat from heathen sacrifices. He decided that if one is told that this is its origin, one should not eat of it, for this would be a sin. But if meat is served when heathens invite one to a meal, or if one buys meat in the market, one need not enquire about its origin and can eat it without troubling" (Schweitzer, *Indian Thought and its Development*, trans. by Mrs. Charles E. B. Russell [Boston: Beacon Press, 1960], p. 102). [The editor's note:—I wonder at Schweitzer's interpretation of Paul's words. It doesn't seem to me to be what Paul is saying in I Cor. 8]

5. *Dhammapada* 194.

6. Psalms 133:1.

and one of the most influential orders of religious brethren in the world. Indeed, the Buddhist community is one of the oldest surviving institution of mankind. It has survived longer than any other institution with the exception of the kindred sect of the Jains. Christianity, though a few hundred years younger, quickly acquired supremacy among religions in the West and has held it ever since.

b. Moderate Asceticism

1) Away from the World into the Order

THE opinion is widely prevalent that Western religion is "this-worldly," while Indian religions are "other-worldly." (The phrases "this-worldly" and "other-worldly" are used primarily ethically here and not metaphysically, though the two senses are often difficult to distinguish.) But as for the ancient phases of religions in both civilizations, one cannot summarize them with such ready-made categories. Throughout the East and West, ancient sages wanted to *transcend* worldly life, even while being amidst the life of the world. But Buddha asserted, ". . . Even as a blue lotus, a water rose, or a white lotus is born in the water, grows up in the water, and stands lifted above it, by the water undefiled: even so, monks, does the Perfect One [=Buddha] grow up in the world, by the world undefiled."[1] In Christianity Jesus is said to have given a "ministry of reconciliation," that is, God in the person of Jesus was "reconciling the world to himself."[2]

"Other-worldliness" may be regarded as a salient feature common to both Eastern and Western religions of antiquity, and some similar instances can be cited from the philosophical history of the West. For Plato (an other-worldly metaphysician as well as ethicist), the ordinary world of common sense held little significance. Truth and complete satisfaction were obtainable only in the realm of eternal ideas, where the soul, fallen from its bright estate, homesick, wants to return. Plotinus pronounced all worldly things to be vain and void of value, and called upon the man seeking perfection to throw off the influence of the phenomenal world. Other-worldliness and ascetic pmphasis can be perceived in the original doctrine of Jesus also. Dr. Radhakrishnan has clarified the latter's position toward "this world" as follows: "The eschatological teaching of Jesus that the end of the world was at hand reveals an attitude of world and life negation insofar as he did not assume that the Kingdom of God would be realized in this natural world but expected its sudden

1. *Saṃyutta-nikāya* XXII, 94.
2. II Corinthians 5:18–19.

and startling inauguration by supernatural power. In the coming Kingdom the State and the other earthly institutions and conditions shall either not exist at all or shall exist only in a sublimated form. The only ethic that Jesus can preach is a negative one, to enable man to free himself from the world and fit himself for the Kingdom. It is a penitential discipline and not a humanistic ethic."[3]

Withdrawal from the life of the "householder" was considered almost a prerequisite if one wished to devote himself to following the Buddhist Path. The life of the homeless ones was the ideal; it was based on the belief that involvement in ordinary worldly affairs was an obstacle too great to be overcome. In the Buddhist scriptures is found, "Full of hindrances is a household life; it is a path for the grime of passion. Free as the air is the life of him who has renounced all worldly things. How difficult it is for the man who dwells at home to live the higher life in all its fullness, in all its purity, in all its bright perfection! Let me then cut off my hair and beard, let me clothe myself in the orange-colored robes, and let me go forth from the household life into the homeless state."[4] A Buddhist nun defiantly said, "Know me as one who saw, and therefore fled from, the perils rising from the life of sense desires."[5] Since the Buddha had initiated the order of monks and nuns himself, as well as providing a philosophical analysis which showed the ordinary sense world to be fraught with suffering, it was natural for monasticism to flourish even in his own time.

Finding the seeds of monasticism in the New Testament, however, is a difficult, if not impossible, task. Jesus did not live in a religious order, though his tendency away from the life of what Indians would call the "householder" was pronounced. Jesus did not hold much with the things men usually cherish, such as wealth and family.[6] Nor did he ever marry; and Paul suggested that "he who refrains from marriage will do better."[7]

3. S. Radhakrishnan, *Eastern Religions and Western Thought* (New York: Oxford University Press, 1959), pp. 68–69.
4. *Dīgha-nikāya* II, 41, vol. I, p. 62.
5. *Therigāthā* 346.
6. Matthew 12:48.
7. I Corinthians 7:38. Cf. "A man's foes will be those of his own household" (Matthew 10:36). "... Go, sell what you have, and give to the poor, and you will have treasure in heaven; and come, follow me" (Mark 10:21). "It is easier for a camel to go through the eye of a needle than for a rich man to enter the kingdom of God" (Mark 10:25). "... Whoever of you does not renounce all that he has cannot be my disciple" (Luke 14:33). "Do not love the world or the things in the world. If any one loves the world, love for the Father is not in him.... The lust of the flesh and ... of the eyes and the pride of life, is not of the Father but is of the world. And the world passes away, and the lust of it; but he who does the will of God abides for ever" (I John 2:15–17). "That which is born of the flesh is flesh, and that which is born of the Spirit is spirit" (John 3:6; cf. *Itivuttaka* 100).

However, elsewhere Paul seemed to discourage "rules and regulations" against the use of sense objects, since he felt "they [regulated orders] are of no value in checking the indulgence of the flesh."[8] Submitting to such rules and activities, he apparently thought, was behaving as though one "still belonged to the world," which should not be the case if one were fully converted to Jesus' teachings.[9] And indeed, it was not until ca. 300 A.D. that some hermits began to gather together as cenobites, i.e., in community life, around such great saints as St. Pachomius and St. Anthony.

However, the very core of the Buddhist movement consisted of monks. The Brahmin institution[10] stipulated that one should give up one's family life and retire in a forest when one became old. But Buddhism encouraged one to join the order while still young. If we wait till we become old they thought, it is too late. The Buddha taught that the pursuit of earthly desires could be likened to a man running against the wind with a torch of hay, whose flame would burn him up unless he threw it away at once.[11] This attitude is reminiscent of Diogenes, the Cynic, who said in a different context, "To give medicines to a dead man and to teach an old man are the same."[12] Even young people took to the Buddhist order, "I who was young and filled with happiness and vigor, became a homeless wanderer apart from home life against my parents."[13]

An aspirant to the Buddhist Order, forsaking his portion of wealth and his circle of relatives, would cut off his hair and beard, clothe himself in the orange-colored robes and go forth from the household life into the homeless state. The life of a recluse was highly extolled in such writings as the following: " . . . Uprightness is his delight, and he sees danger in the least of those things he should avoid. He adopts, and trains himself in, the precepts. He encompasses himself with good deeds in act and word. Pure are his means of livelihood, good is his conduct, guarded the door of his senses. Mindful and self-possessed he is altogether happy."[14]

In the monasteries monks could devote all their time to meditation and study; attachment to food and clothing could be curbed, sexual activity could be eliminated, all actions could be guarded. The full code of the discipline (*Vinaya*) could be followed. Begging was encouraged as a

8. Colossians 2:20–23.
9. *Ibid.*
10. *Manu* VI, 1f.
11. *Majjhima-nikāya* 54, *Potaliya-suttanta.* Cf. the corresponding Chinese *sutta, Taisho,* vol. I, pp. 773–774.
12. Translated from the citation in K. E. Neumann, *Die Lieder der Mönche und Nonnen Gotama Buddhos* (Berlin: Ernst Hofmann, 1899), p. 69.
13. *Majjhima-nikāya* 26, *Ariyaparyesanā-sutta.* Cf. the corresponding Chinese version, *Taisho,* vol. II, p. 72.
14. *Dīgha-nikāya* II, 42, vol. I, p. 62.

foundation for many virtues, and was practiced in the spirit of Teles, a Cynic of the Hellenistic age, who said to a rich man, "You give liberally and I take valiantly from you, neither grovelling, nor demeaning myself basely nor grumbling."[15] This was exactly the attitude of the early Buddhists and this demeanor has been observed in South Asiatic countries. Even nowadays, a monk will not say "thank you" to a donor.

2) Disciplines

In the Buddhist tradition, various disciplines have been followed by which evil passions may be calmed, the senses restrained, and constant awareness of one's feelings and desires developed. The extant Pali scripture of such disciplines contains 227 rules for monks, and 305 rules for nuns.[1] They are of a prohibitive nature. It is said, however, that the Buddha permitted the adoption of certain changes in the precepts if the Order should so wish. He reportedly told the brethren at his last sermon, "When I am gone, Ananda, let the Order if it should so with, abolish all the lesser and minor precepts (*sikkhāpadāni*)."[2] So disciplines changed with subsequent places and times.

Generally, purity of mind was stressed. Of the Buddhist devotee we find in a Buddhist scripture, "Putting away the hankering after the world, he remains with a heart that hankers not, and purifies his mind of lusts. Putting away the corruption of the wish to injure, he remains with a heart free from ill-temper, and purifies his mind malevolence. Putting away torpor of heart and mind, keeping his ideas alight, mindful and self-possessed, he purifies his mind of weakness and of sloth. Putting away flurry and worry, he remains free from fretfulness, and with heart serene within, he purifies himself of irritability and vexation of spirit. Putting away wavering, he remains as one passed beyond perplexity."[3]

Buddhist devotees observed a discipline that required monks to eat only between sunrise and noon, and total abstinence from intoxicating drinks was obligatory. The usual mode of obtaining food was for a monk to beg from house to house every morning with his begging-bowl in his hands.

Buddhists highly revered the practice of begging. The monk had no sense of inferiority about this mode of livelihood. He felt that he was not

15. *The Hellenistic Age* (Cambridge, 1923), p. 86. Cited from B. Russell, *A History of Western Philosophy*, p. 233.

1. Some later schools of conservative Buddhism kept 250 rules for monks and 348 rules for nuns.
2. *Mahāparinibbāna-suttanta* VI, 3.
3. *Dīgha-nikāya* II, 68, *The Dīgha-nikāya*, 3 vols., edited by T. W. Rhys Davids and J. E. Carpenter (London: Pali Text Society, 1890–1911), vol. I, p. 71.

idle by any means, but led a strenuous life, controlling his desires and developing his meditations. Since generosity was considered one of the prime virtues, the monks felt that by accepting alms they gave the householder an opportunity for gaining religious merit. The practice of the Buddhist monks was to some extent paralleled by that of St. Francis of Assisi, who had once been a prosperous man, "dainty in his father's home." After his great renunciation of all property, he took a bowl and begged scraps of food from door to door.

Therefore, if one finds the begging custom of the Buddhists strange, he might remember that all through Europe during the Middle Ages, monastic orders maintained themselves by begging. It was only after the economic system of rising industrialism had found that begging was incompatible with its needs for industrial workers that vagrancy laws came into general use. Begging rules and practices, however, have been strictly observed to the present day in South Asiatic countries, whereas they have generally been abolished in those to the north.

Buddhism prescribed that monks should be very circumspect in their actions. "How is the recluse (*bhikkhu*) guarded as to the doors of his senses? When he sees an object with his eye he is not entranced in the general appearance or the details of it. He sets himself to restrain that which might give occasion for evil states, covetousness and dejection. He keeps watch upon his faculty of sight [and the other senses in turn], and he attains to mastery over it. . . ."[4] In directing men toward the disciplining of themselves, Buddha in one instance utilized a metaphor that has become very famous in Western philosophy. He said, "Even the gods envy him whole senses are subdued like horses well tamed by the charioteer, who is free from pride and free from taints."[5] In a similar way, Plato's ethical metaphor in *Phaedrus* of the charioteer and two horses may be thought of as Reason (the Charioteer) and Appetite and Spirit (the two horses), as he later developed them in *The Republic*.[6]

The Buddhist disciple, in whatever he did—whether going or coming, standing or walking, speaking or silent, eating or drinking—was to keep clearly in mind what is involved in such actions: the temporary character of the act and its ethical significance, that is, the thought that behind the act there is no actor (goer, seer, ester, speaker, etc.) that is an eternally persistent entity. "In this manner the recluse in going forth or in coming back keeps clearly before his mind's eye (all that is wrapt up therein—the immediate object of the act itself, its ethical significance, whether or not it is conducive to the high aim set before him, and the real facts underlying the mere phenomenon of the outward act). And so

4. *Dīgha-nikāya* II, 65. vol. I, p. 70.
5. *Dhammapada* 94. Cf. *Kāṭhaka-Up*., III, 3; *Milinda-pañha* 26–28.
6. *Phaedrus* 246, 253, 254. Cf. *Republic* 439, 440.

in looking forward, or in looking round; in stretching forth his arm, or in drawing it in again; in eating, or drinking, in masticating or swallowing, in obeying the calls of nature, in going or standing or sitting, in sleeping or waking, in speaking or in being still, he keeps himself aware of all it really means. Thus it is that the recluse becomes mindful and self-possessed."[7] In the West, St. Paul said to the same effect, "So, whether you eat or drink, or whatever you do, do all to the glory of God."[8]

In early Buddhism monks and nuns strictly kept the vow of celibacy. Monks had to be very cautious about women and tried not to excite lustful thoughts. Ānanda, a favorite disciple of the Buddha, asked him:

"How should we conduct ourselves, lord, with regard to women?"
"Do not see them, Ānanda."
"But if we should see them, what should we do?"
"Don't talk, Ānanda."
"But if they should speak to us, lord, what should we do?"
"Keep wide awake, Ānanda."[9]

The Buddha further counseled, "If, after all, you must speak with her, let it be with a pure heart, and think to yourself, 'I as a monk will live in this sinful world as the spotless leaf of the lotus, unsoiled by the mud in which it grows.' If the woman be old, regard her as your mother, if young, as your sister, if very young, as your child. The monk who looks at a woman or touches her as a woman has broken his vow and is no longer a disciple of the Śākyamuni."[10]

In the West also, early Christian monks were so strict that they would not even look at women. An ancient picture shows a monk being visited by his mother and some of her friends. He has to keep his hand over his eyes during the entire talk, though he looks as if he were peeking.[11] In the same way Jesus had taught, "Every one who looks at a woman lustfully has already committed adultery with her in his heart. If your right eye causes you to sin, pluck it out and throw it away; it is better that you lose one of your members than that your whole body be thrown into hell."[12]

Buddhists supposed that a well-disciplined man did not even dream of defilements. "He who was the best of them, a strong Brāhmaṇa, did not

7. *Dīgha-nikāya* II, 65, vol. I, p. 70.
8. I Corinthians 10:31.
9. *Mahāparinibbāna-suttanta* 5, 9. *Dīgha-nikāya,* vol. II, p. 141.
10. Sūtras of Forty-two Sections (*Taisho,* vol. XVII, pp. 722–724), *Fo-sho-king-tsan-ching,* vv. 1757–1766.
11. R. H. Baiton, *The Church of Our Fathers* (New York: Charles Scribner's Sons, 1950), p. 48. This book is primarily for children, but a certain American professor strongly recommended it and I found it very interesting.
12. Matthew 5:27–29. Cf. Mark 9:47; Matthew 18:9.

[even] in sleep indulge in sexual intercourse."[13] Plato notes that a "wild beast" latent in man can come forth in sleep: ". . . The wild beast within us, gorged with meat or drink, starts up and having shaken off sleep, goes forth to satisfy his desires; and there is no conceivable folly or crime—not excepting incest or any other unnatural union, or parricide, or the eating of forbidden food—which at such a time, when he was parted company with all shame and sense, a man may not be ready to commit. . . . But when a man's pulse is healthy and temperate, and when before going to sleep he has awakened his rational powers, and fed them on noble thoughts and enquiries, collecting himself in meditation, . . . then he attains truth most nearly, and is least likely to be the sport of fantastic and lawless visions."[14] That adherents were to be alert in their disciplines even while asleep shows to what extent importance has been placed on such disciplines.

c. Mission Work

Just as Christianity expanded westward, becoming the dominant religion of Europe while in Palestine itself it was only the religion of a minority, so Buddhism expanded eastward while it declined in its own Indian homeland. For the past twenty-five centuries, all sects of Buddhism have recognized their mission to spread the teachings of the Buddha throughout the world. Buddhists felt that the doctrine should be known to all and not concealed; "the Doctrine (*Dhamma*) and Discipline (*Vinaya*) proclaimed by the Buddha shine forth when they are displayed and not when they are concealed."[1] In the West Jesus also said, "Let your light so shine before men, that they may see your good works and give glory to your Father who is in heaven."[2]

An unselfish teacher, the Buddha had no reservations about disclosing his findings. He talked freely to his disciples, concealing nothing. "Ānanda asked the Buddha to leave instructions as touching the Order before he passed away. The Buddha answered: 'What, then, Ānanda? Does the Order expect that of me? I have preached the truth without making any distinction between exoteric and esoteric doctrine; for in respect of the truths, Ānanda, the Buddha (*Tathāgata*) has no such things as the closed fist of a teacher, who keeps some things back' "[3] Confucius also explained in the same way, "My disciples, do you think that I have

13. *Suttanipāta* 292.
14. *Republic* IX, 571.
1. *Aṅguttara-nikāya* III, 124. vol. I, p. 283.
2. Matthew 5:16.
3. *Mahāparinibbāna-suttanta* II, 25; vol. II, p. 100.

any secrets (concealments)? I have no secrets from you. It is my way to do nothing without communicating (showing) it to you."[4]

The Buddha's compassion in sharing his knowledge with his followers was significant in spreading the new religion. "He proclaims the *Dhamma*, the Truth, both in letter and in spirit; he makes known the higher life in all its purity and in all its perfectness."[5] The gift of the *Dhamma* was the most esteemed of all gifts. In Christian writings also, Christ was represented as the manifestation of God to men, the *Logos*, the Word of God made flesh, the Bread of Life. —

With this tender compassion for all beings, the Buddha set forth "to establish a kingdom of righteousness, to give light to those enshrouded in darkness and to open the gate of immortality to men."[6] So, soon after the founding of the Order, the Buddha sent out twelve followers on missionary journeys with the command: "Fare ye forth, brethren, on the mission that is for the good of the many for the happiness of the many; to the compassion to the world; to work for the profit and good and happiness of gods and men."[7] In the New Testament, Jesus is represented as also having actively started the Christian missionary effort. Calling his twelve disciples together, he gave them power and authority over all demons and to cure diseases, and sent them out to heal and preach the kingdom of God.[8]

Christians and Buddhists alike concurred that the spiritual gift should be distributed to everyone. But they realized that it should not be given indiscriminately, regardless of the qualifications of the recipient. In the Buddhist canon is found the warning, "Let not this Dhamma so full of truth, so excellent, fall into the hands of those unversed in it, where it would be despised and condemned, treated shamefully, made a game of, and found fault with. Nor let it fall into the hands of the wicked who would deal with it in all respects as badly as they." Thus the recitation of the *Pāṭimokkha* is, to that extent, kept secret out of reverence for the Doctrine (*Dhamma*).[9] In a *Book of Disciplines* it is prescribed that "when monks are reciting rules of disciplines (*pāṭimokkha*) on the Uposatha day, if a robber or a king should come in, they should stop recitation of the rules, and instead, recite other texts, "because kings do unfavorable things to people."[10] In early Christianity is found a similar teaching in a succinct form: "Do not give dogs what is holy; and do not throw your

4. *Analects* VII, 13.
5. *Tevijja-suttanta* I, 46.
6. *Vinaya*, Mahāvagga I, 6, 8.
7. *Dīgha-nikāya* XIV, 22. Cf. Mahāvagga I, 12, i; *Fo-sho-king-tsan-ching*, vv. 1297–1300.
8. Luke 9:1–6.
9. *Milindapañha*, p. 191 (*Sacred Books of the East*, vol. XXXV, p. 266).
10. *Mahāsaṅghika-vinaya* (*Taisho*, vol. 22, p. 447 c).

pearls before swine, lest they trample them underfoot and turn to attack you."[11]

The acceptance of the Buddha's "Doctrine and Discipline" was open to all. Of course many, including the Brahmins, did not accept it. However, the Buddhist gospel spread among all sorts of men. "A householder (*gahapati*), or one of his children, or a man of inferior birth in any class, listens to that faith."[12] This conviction appeared in China also. Once, when Fan Ch'e, a disciple, asked about virtue, Confucius responded, "In private life be courteous, in handling public business be serious, with all men be sincere. Even though you go among rude uncultivated tribes, you may not neglect these virtues."[13]

In early Buddhism, monks were considered to be the leaders of householders (laymen). The former were given a means of living by the latter and the latter received spiritual guidance from the former. Consequently, the Buddha condemned misdemeanors by his disciples because they had to set an example. Seeing that some in the monastic community were not showing a proper level of respect for their teachers, Buddha first observed that, "Even the laymen, O monks, . . . for the sake of some handicrart that they may procure them a living, will be respectful, affectionate, and hospitable to their teachers." Then Gotama told the transgressing monks why such behavior could not be tolerated in the community at large—because "this will not conduce to the conversion of the unconverted, and to the augmentation of the number of the converted, but it will result in the unconverted being repulsed (from the faith), and in many of the converted become estranged."[14] Christ also bade his followers, "Love your enemies and pray for those who persecute you. . . . For if you love those who love you, what reward have you? Do not even the tax collectors do the same? And if you salute only your brethren, what more are you doing than others? Do not even the Gentiles do the same? You, therefore, must be perfect, as your heavenly Father is perfect."[15]

5. Ethics for Laymen

From the very beginning of Buddhism the distinction was made between those who would become monks, leaving the household life in favor of

11. Matthew 7:6.
12. *Tevijja-suttanta*, 47.
13. *The Analects of Confucius*, XIII, 19.
14. *Vinaya*, Mahāvagga V, 4, 2 (*Sacred Books of the East*, vol. XVII, p. 18).
15. Matthew 5:44–48.

the Sangha, and the lay devotees of the Buddha. Naturally, then, in addition to the *Vinaya* rules for the Order there developed ethics for laymen who would remain householders. These laymen were expected to obey at least the following five precepts:[1]

1. One should not destroy life.
2. One should not take what is not given.
3. One should refrain from unlawful sexual intercourse.
4. One should not tell lies.[2]
5. One should not drink intoxicating liquors.[3]

(In Tantric Buddhism in India and also in Japanese Buddhism the fifth precept is often minimized; Japanese priests call liquor "Wisdom Water.") These precepts are more or less included in the Ten Command-

1. At the outset of Buddhism four, not five, vices of conduct were enumerated: "(1) slaughter of life, (2) theft, (3) lying, (4) adultery. To these no word of praise the wise award" (*Dīgha-nikāya* III, p. 182 gāthā). "(1) Let him not commit theft, (2) let him not speak falsely, (3) let him touch friendly what is feeble or strong, (4) what he acknowledges to be the agitation of the mind, let him drive that off as a partisan of Kaṇha [i.e., Māra the Evil One]" (*Suttanipāta* 967). It seems that later the precept of "not taking to liquor" was added, making up the five. Cf. "A man, when he gets drink, is led stumbling along by an immature boy, not knowing where he is going, having his soul wet" (Heraclitus, fragment 117).
2. This precept involves a difficult problem. A scripture of early Buddhism says: "An ennobled person does not tell anything which does not give benefit to another person, even if it is true." "However, occasionally he tells it, when it is true and to tell it is beneficial to another, even if to tell him is unpleasant to the latter" (*Majjhima-nikāya*, no. 58, vol. I, p. 395, etc.). Similar notions are expressed in *Manu*, VIII, 104; Winternitz, *Indian Literature*, vol. I, p. 395, etc.; *Mahābhārata* VII, 69, 53; Hopkins, *Great Epic of India*, p. 381. "A lie may be told by a truth, or a truth conveyed through a lie. Truth to facts is not always truth to sentiment; and part of the truth, as often happens in answer to a question, may be the foulest calumny. . . . You never speak to God; you address a fellow-man, fgll of his own tempers; and to tell truth, rightly understood, is not to state the true facts, but to convey a true impression; truth in spirit, not truth to letter, is the true veracity" (R. L. Stevensin, *Virginibus Puerisque*). A Japanese proberb says: "Uso mo hoben" [Even lies are for expediency, if out of sincerity]. In the West there are "white lies."
3. Especially being addicted to drinking is severely admonished:

   "The tippler of strong drink, poor, destitute,
   Athirst while drinking, haunter of the bar,
   As stone in water, so he sinks in debt;
   Swift will he make his folk without a name." (*Sigālovāda* 13 G.)
   "One who by habit in the day doth sleep,
   Who looks upon the night as time to arise,
   One who is ever wanton, filled with wine,
   He is not fit to lead a household life." (*Sigālovāda* 13 G.)

   So Buddhists in Southern Asia even today don't drink, but Japanese Buddhists for the large part do not prohibit drinking.

ments and practised by Christians also. In addition, early lay Buddhists observed abstinence (*uposatha*) on the eighth, fourteenth, and fifteenth days of the half-month, in which they practised eight vows: (1–5), the above-mentioned five vows; (6), not to eat untimely food at night; (7), not to wear wereaths nor to use perfumes; and (8), to lie on a couch spread on the earth.[4] The only other requirement for Buddhist laymen was that they place their faith in the three Treasures (*Buddha, Saṅgha* and *Dhamma*).

When Buddhism was introduced into China the five normative virtues of Confucianism (*wu-ch'ang*) were equated with the five precepts for the behavior of Buddhist lay adherents, and this was inherited by the Japanese. The Confucian expression *hsiao-hsun,* "filial submission and obedience," was used to translate the more general and abstract Sanskrit word *śila*, "morality," reflecting the traditional morality of the patriarchal family system of the Chinese.

In the Northern Wei (386–535 A.D.) a priest named T'an-Ching, between the years 454–464, wrote a spurious sutra called *T'i-wei-po-li-ching*, in which the Chinese five cardinal virtues (*Wu-ch'ang*) were compared and equated with the five precepts of the Buddhist lay believers:[5]

Five Virtues	*Five Precepts*
Humaneness	Not to take life
Righteousness	Not to commit adultery
Propriety	Not to drink intoxicating liquor
Wisdom	Not to steal
Sincerity	Not to lie

Admitting the essential oneness of Confucian and Buddhist ethics, the Chinese master Kukai admitted only a slight difference betwen the two. "A nation in observance of the (Confucian) virtues shall be blessed with peace, and a home in observance of them shall be blessed with no wrong-doings.[6] The observance of the virtues is a profound art which gives one fame and glory: it is the virtue which protects the nation and safeguards its people. Outwardly, it is called the (Confucian) five virtues; inwardly, it is referred to as the (Buddhist) five precepts. The names are different but their essence is one (lit. conflationary). The five virtues are the criterion on which one can determine evil, which is to be severed, and good, which is to be observed. The (Buddhist) five precepts and the

4. *Suttanipāta* 399–400.

5. Tang-Yung Tung, *Radhakrishnan Comparative Studies*, ed. by Inge et al., pp. 278–284. Cf. Jiun's *Jūzen Hōgo* (A sermon preached in 1773 by Katsuragi Ji-un. *Transactions of the Asiatic Scoeity of Japan*, vol. XXXIII, pf. 2, 1905), p. 56.

6. Literally, not to pick up that which is left on the road. It therefore means not to commit wrong and implies a high standard of moral conduct.

basis on which spiritual liberation and mental happiness are to be realized."[7]

In many religions the precepts for the laymen were far less strict and severe than those for monks and nuns. In Buddhism as well this was generally the case, but the qualifications of laymen for *Nirvāṇa* were uncertain in the early scriptures. Occasionally it was admitted that a layman can also win *Nirvāṇa*, but it was expected that he must then either enter the Order, or die.[8] In one passage, it is said that a layman could attain *Nirvāṇa* in this life only if he had pursued a monastic life in some former existence.[9] It is mostly believed in Theravāda and other schools of conservative Buddhism that what is most feasible for laymen, with regard to their final attainment, is to be born in one of the heavens.

Concerning daily life a similar teaching is found in both Buddhism and Christianity. In society one should be a man of careful speech and action. Buddhists say, "Better than a thousand utterances composed of meaningless words is one sensible word on hearing which one becomes peaceful."[10] In Christianity, "Nevertheless, in church I would rather speak five words with my mind, in order to instruct others, than ten thousand words in a tongue."[11] And again, "The scribes and the Pharisees sit on Moses' seat; so practice and observe whatever they tell you, but not what they do; for they preach, but do not practice."[12]

One should not find faults with others, according to Buddhism.[13] Buddhists say, "The fault of others is easily seen; our own is difficult to see."[14] Jesus said, "Why do you see the speck that is in your brother's eye, but do not notice the log that is in your own eye?"[15]

With regard to human relations, early Buddhism stressed in a systematic way the duties between (1) parents and children, (2) pupils and teachers, (3) husband and wife, (4) friend and friend, (5) master and servants, and (6) laymen and monks.[16] These reciprocal obligations are at once recognizable as comparable to the five relationships of Confucian morality. Three of the latter are identical with the Buddha's scheme: parents and childredn, husband and wife, and friend to friend. Buddhists, unlike the Chinese, were more religious than politicalminded and so

7. *Hizō Hōyaku*, vol. I (*Taishō*, vol. 77, pp. 363–374).
8. *Milindapañha*, p. 265.
9. *Ibid.*, p. 353.
10. *Dhammapada* 100.
11. I Corinthians 14:19.
12. Matthew 23:2–3.
13. *Dhammapada* 50, 253.
14. *Ibid.*, 252.
15. Matthew 7:3.
16. *Sigālovāda-suttanta* (*Dīgha-nikāya* 31).

emphasized the relations of teachers and pupils, and laity and clergy, and omitted the mutual duties of sovereigns and subjects.

With regard to such relationships, Jesus spoke to the common people, cautioning them to perpetuate the law (Ten Commandments) given them by Moses: honor thy father and mother, etc. Most of these commandments have to do with man's relationships to his fellowmen, proscriptions against stealing or killing, and so forth. Jesus interpreted even divorce to come under the commandment against adultery.[17] But as stressed above, Jesus' strongest conviction and message was that the commandments regarding man's relationship to God as well as to his fellowman could be fulfilled by love[18] (Greek, *agape*, not *eros*). In no way could it be said (as it might in Confucianism) that for Jesus family relationships came first. Rather, those who leave family for the sake of Jesus are told they will receive "a hundredfold now in this time . . . and in the age to come eternal life."[19]

In Buddhism the virtue of diligence was highly stressed for laymen.

> But he who reckons cold and heat as less
> Than straws, doing his duties as a man,
> He nowise falls away from happiness.[20]

Through the virtues of diligence and thrift Buddhists thought one may accumulate riches (—The philosophy of success!)

> To him amassing wealth, like roving bee
> Gathering its honey (and hurting naught),
> Riches mount up as ant-heap growing high.
> When the good layman has so amassed wealth
> Able is he to benefit his clan.
> In four portions let him divide that wealth.
> So binds he to himself life's friendly things.
> One portion let him spend and taste the fruit.
> To conduct his business let him take two (portions).
> And the fourth portion let him reserve and hoard;
> So there'll be wherewithall in times of need.[21]

Although Buddhist monks and nuns were strictly prohibited from touching money or engaging in economic activities, Buddhism never denounced the accumulation of riches by laymen, on the contrary, it encouraged them to do so. In Buddhism there was no prohibition of

17. Mark 10:11.
18. Matthew 22:37–40.
19. Mark 10:30.
20. *Sigālovāda-suttanta* 13, gāthā (*Dīgha-nikāya* 31).
21. *Ibid.*, 26.

receiving interest[22] on invested capital, contrary to the medieval West; interest was justified, and debts should be paid.[23] By this attitude early Buddhism could have become the religion of the newly-risen traders of medieval times, had not the Muslim invasion destroyed the *Saṅgha* in India.

Riches, however, must not be accumulated by other than lawful means (in keeping with the *Dharma*). "To live by means of unlawful measures and to die owing to actions by means of lawful measures, the latter is superior to the former."[24] In trade "unlawful coins, unlawful scales, and unlawful measures"[25] were denounced. "Not to violate law"[26] was the ideal of Buddhists. To keep to righteous deeds was strictly enjoined by Confucius also. "Any thought of acoepting wealth and rank, by means that I know to be wrong, is as remote from me as the clouds that float above."[27]

The New Testament is slightly ambiguous on the subject of wealth for laymen. If the following were interpreted materialistically it might suggest a positive attitude: "Take heed what you hear; the measure you give will be the measure you get, and still more will be given you. For to him who has will more be given; and from him who has not, even what he has will be taken away."[28] But Jesus, as we have seen, was much more concerned for the welfare of the soul. The ambiguity is probably a result of the fact that he had but one message for everyone and made no distinction between the religious community and laymen. As mentioned above, he cautioned all (the multitude) to "deny himself and . . . follow me. . . . For what does it profit a man to gain the whole world and forfeit his life?"[29]

The Christian laity since the beginning have adopted Jesus' teachings both th the multitudes and to his disciples (as found in the New Testament) as their own. His teachings regarding faith, how to pray, baptism, the One God, giving a monetary offering to the church, and the symbolic gestures of the last supper, have all become part of the lives of most Christians.

22. The Chinese version of the *Madhyamāgama-sūtra*, vol. 33 (Taisho, vol. I, p. 642 a). Cf. *Aṅguttara-nikāya* III, p. 351f. The Chinese version of the *Madhyamāgama-sūtra*, vol. 29 (The Sutra on Poverty).
23. *Suttanipāta* 120.
24. *Theragāthā* 670. A similar thought was expressed in *Manu* IV, 170–171.
25. *Dīgha-nikāya* III, p. 176. A like idea in the early modern West was discussed by R. H. Tawney: *Religion and the Rise of Capitalism* (New York: New American Library, Mentor Books, 1947), p. 184.
26. *Aṅguttara-nikāya*, p. 18 gāthā.
27. *Analects* VII, 15.
28. Mark 4:24.
29. Mark 8:34–36.

Such an "economic ethic" as the Buddha's however, was probably not advocated in the West until the advent of Calvin in modern times.

6. Further Practice

a. The Use of Philosophy as a Path

The Buddha taught many doctrines which came to be elaborated by his followers. Some of these doctrines were contradictory to each other; however, all are in agreement on the point that they aim at teaching the way to realize an ideal selfless life. In Buddhism considerable stress lies on the mode of living,[1] on the righteousness of life, and on the removal of vices. A merely theoretical proposition, such as "there is no ego" would be regarded as utterly sterile and useless. In Buddhism, a philosophical sentence is no more than a tool and its justification lies in its products. That is why there are so many teachings even on one subject, such as "Dependent Origination," "the Four Noble Truths," etc.

The Buddha's doctrine is called a "vehicle" in the sense that it is like a ferryboat. To enter the Buddhist vehicle means to begin to cross the river of life, the shore of the worldly experience of non-enlightenment, the state of spiritual ignorance (*avidyā,*) craving (*kāma*), and suffering, to the other shore of transcendental wisdom (*vidyā*), which is liberation (*mokṣa*) from bondage and suffering. Buddha offered a useful analogy: suppose a man builds a raft and by this means succeeds in attaining the other shore. "What would be your opinion of this man?" he asked. "Would he be a clever man, if, out of gratitude for the raft that carried him across the stream to safety, he, having reached the other shore, should cling to it, take it on his back, and walk about with the weight of it?" The monks replied, "No." The Buddha then conclude, "In the same way the vehicle of the doctrine is to be cast away and forsaken, once the other shore of Enlightenment (*Nirvāṇa*) has been attained."[2] Spiritual teachings such as the Buddha's can be compared to rafts. Once the goal has been attained, they become useless. Just as differences in shape, weight, and material among rafts matter little, differences in teachings matter little. This point of view is set forth both in Theravāda and Mahāyāna Buddhism.

Buddhism for all sects is nothing but "the path leading to release," (*nibbāṇagamana-magga*). A statement from the Old Testament bears similarity: "This is the way, walk in it."[3] As for the use to which one should

1. In the case of the Eightfold Path, "seeing rightly" was the first step. Cf. "O taste and see that the Lord is good" (Psalms 34:8).
2. *Majjhima-nikaya* I, 3, 2, No. 22.
3. Isaiah 30:21.

put the scriptures, the New Testament contains the following suggestion: "Be doers of the word, and not hearers only, deceiving yourselves. For if any one is a hearer of the word and not a doer, he is like a man who observes his natural face in a mirror; for he observes himself and goes away and at once forgets what he was like. But he who looks into the perfect law, the law of liberty, and perseveres, being no hearer that forgets but a doer that acts, he shall be blessed in his doing."[4] Exactly such an attitude, it seems, bore fruit abundantly for early Buddhists who pursued the way. Vāseṭṭhī, a Buddhist sister, wrote,

> I heard his teaching (*dhamma*) and left the world
> And all its cares behind, and gave myself
> To follow where He taught, and realize
> Life in the Path to great good fortune bound (*padam sivam*).[5]

The rules of the doctrine, according to Zimmer, are intended for beginners and advanced pupils alike; but for the perfect they become useless. Doctrines "can be of no service to the truly enlightened, unless to serve him, in his role of teacher, as a convenient medium by which to communicate some suggestion of the truth to which he has attained."[6] The attitude of earlier Buddhists, then, can be seen to be rather practical; it was later medieval monk-scholars who developed Buddhist metaphysics. Early Buddhists stressed what might be called proficiency, which is never a merely physical skill but also a "wisdom" (*kauśalya*, in Buddhism). This stress on wisdom as proficiency is also noticeable in the concept of the Greek word "*sophia*", of which the basic meaning is precisely "expertise."

In Buddhism if something is said, it is justified only by what is called "skill in means." Words like "enlightenment," "ignorance," "freedom" and "attachment," are preliminary aids, referring to no ultimate reality, mere hints or signposts for the traveler on the path, which serve only to point out the goal. This kind of philosophical knowledge was called in later Mahayana "the Perfect Wisdom" or "the Transcendental Wisdom" (*Prajñāpāramitā*). The wisdom which is sought in Buddhism is not the wisdom of conflicting metaphysical systems, but the wisdom of Enlighten-

4. James 1:22–25.
5. *Therīgāthā* 137.
6. H. Zimmer, *Philosophies of India* (New York: Pantheon Books, 1951), p. 478. Deussen disagrees as follows: "Philosophy is originally based on a pure desire for knowledge, and knows no other aim than the search for truth. Only when this desire is weakened does philosophy become a mere means to an end, a *remedium* for the suffering of existence. This was the case in Greece in the schools that succeeded Aristotle; it was so also in India in the Samkhya system and in Buddhism" (P. Deussen, *The Philosophy of the Upanishads*. Authorized English translation by A. S. Geden [Edinburgh: T. and T. Clark, 1906; New York: Dover Publications, 1966], p. 255).

ment as to the true nature of human existence. This was especially stressed in Zen Buddhism.

The acceptance of rational analysis of the nature of human existence has been a continuing characteristic of Buddhism, but it should be noted that metaphysical speculation concerning problems not related to human activities and to the attainment of enlightenment has not been considered to be a proper part of that analysis. Considering these features, one might say the doctrine of the Buddha is not a system of philosophy in the traditional Western sense (though, as pointed out above, it is close to some 20th century philosophies) but is rather a path. A Buddha is simply one who has trodden this path and can report to others on what he has found. The appellation *Tathāgata* ("one who has gone thus," wayfarer) can be interpreted in this sense.

Regardless of the modern sound of some of the Buddha's thinking (some readers may still say, "Why, that sounds just like X," one or another language philosopher), the major difference must be pointed out that Buddha's fame as a great leader of mankind was not built on his written word alone, nor even on his reports of having attained enlightenment (great though the effect of that has been). Rather it was the way all of these factors manifested themselves in his character (cf. Jesus, with the addition of crucifixion and martyrdom) that resulted in the development of Buddhism as a universal religion.[7] Professor Conze has pointed out that nowadays it just would not do to "refute" a philosopher by pointing out that he is insufferably rude to his wife, envies his more fortunate colleagues, or gets flustered when contradicted. Those who look to Buddhism for startlingly new and unheard-of ideas on philosophical problems, he says, will find little; however, those who look to it for advice on how to lead a selfless life may learn a great deal.[8] Conze is correct about the latter emphasis, which points out a great difference between the Buddha and 20th century philosophers, though some may be more startled than others at the freshness of some of the Buddha's ideas.

b. Meditation

Earliest records of meditative practices indicate that they were always carried out privately, in solitude. Buddhist recluses generally spent their lives in lonely, secluded places in the early days.[1] "He chooses some lonely spot as in the woods, at the foot of a tree, on a hillside, in a mountain

7. S. Radhakrishnan, *The Dhammapada* (Oxford University Press, 1950), p. 24.
8. E. Conze, *Buddhism: Its Essence and Development* (New York: Harper and Brothers, 1959), p. 20.
1. Noticed in *Suttanipāta*, passim.

glen, in a rocky cave, in a charnel place, or on a heap of straw in the open field, and returning after his round for alms, he seats himself, when his meal is done, cross-legged, keeping his body erect, and his intelligence alert and intent."[2] The *Bhagavadgītā* says, "Let the *yogin* try constantly to concentrate his mind (on the Supreme Self) remaining in solitude and alone, self-controlled, free from desires and longing for no possession."[3] To retire into a quiet place was encouraged by Christianity also: "When you pray, go into your room and shut the door."[4] But with the rise of monasticism, which occurred early in Indian Buddhism and later in the West, monks came to practise meditation in the solitude of monasteries.

Because of the introspective character of the Buddhist path, monks especially esteemed calmness of mind. In order to acquire this calmness, the practice of meditation was stressed. A necessary discipline for the path to enlightenment and also for the ethical life, meditation was the means for developing the awareness which checks attachment to the senses. This practice of mental concentration was called *yoga* throughout India. The word *yoga* is related to the Latin *jugum* and the English word "yoke." Metaphorically, a man practices *yoga* when he "yokes" or reins the impulses of his natural state, though the term generally means the putting forth of this special quality of will in meditation. The yoking of self in meditation is at times compared to the actual yoking of horses or oxen. The Buddha himself is described with some justification as the great *yogi*.

In the very early times of the most remote animism, one can find the belief that a person, rapt from all sense of the outside world, possessed by a spirit, acquired a degree of sanctity. He was supposed to have attained a degree of supernatural insight which was denied to ordinary mortals.

Such a view, of course in a much more highly developed form, is not unfamiliar in Western philosophy, where it is usually classed as intuition. The Platonic Socrates advocated a method (which he may have inherited from some mystery religion of his day or the Pythagoreans) that sounds much like meditation. "And he attains to the purest knowledge of them who goes to each with mind alone, not introducing or intruding in the act of thought, sight or any other sense together with reason, but with the very light of the mind in her own clearness searches into the very truth of each; he who has got rid, as far as he can, of eyes and ears and, so to speak, of the whole body, these being in his opinion distracting elements which when they infect the soul hinder her from acquiring truth and knowledge—who, if not he, is likely to attain the knowledge of the true being?"[5]

2. *Dīgha-nikāya* II, 67, vol. I, p. 71.
3. VI, 9.
4. Matthew 6:6.
5. Phaedo, 66. B. Jowett, *The Dialogues of Plato* (New York: Random House, n.d.), VI, p. 499.

The solitude of meditation, practiced first in the mountains and then in the monasteries, is also reminiscent of a Western mystical tradition that began with Plotinus and extended "so far apart in time as Eckhart, Boehme, and Blake."[6] Though man may lapse from his state of unity with the One, according to Plotinus he may yet "awaken to the virtue which is in him, again know himself made perfect in spendour; and he again may be lightened of his burden, ascending through virtue to the intelligence, and thence through wisdom to the Supreme."[7] Such a life Plotinus describes as "beyond earthly pleasure, a flight of the alone to the Alone."[8]

Plotinus' path was made up of four stages which are too detailed for inclusion here. For comparison's sake, however, some salient features deserve mention. The first stage consists of practice of the four cardinal virtues (*protos kalos*), the highest of which is *phronesis*, correctness of mental direction. The second stage is a turning away from sense perception to the supreme. The third stage is a conquering of discursive thought. Though all these three, man remains conscious of his own self-identity. The fourth stage, however, is the culminating, ecstatic, mystical union with the One, in which all subject-object duality (caused by separation) has vanished. Both Plotinus' ethical system as well as his experience (though couched in language of a different culture) show themselves to possess the high ideals and attainment of the Buddha's own such precepts and experience.

The search after *Nirvāṇa*, or release from the miseries of rebirth by means of meditation, was not even a peculiarity of Gotama in India, but was a common striving of the age and country in which he lived, and many methods of acquiring the desired end were in vogue. It is clear from the Buddhist scriptures[9] that belief in meditation was in full force when Buddhism arose, and that the practice was followed by the Buddha's teachers. It is likely that the Buddha adopted meditation from his teacher Āḷāra Kālāma. A story regarding this early teacher of the Buddha has been included in the Buddhist canon. Though the descriptions of the meditative state of mind may lack some accuracy (they sound more like trance than Buddhist meditation) they correctly describe the external demeanor of the meditator. "Formerly, Āḷāra Kālāma was once walking along the high road; and leaving the road he sat himself down under a certain tree to rest during the heat of the day. Now five hundred carts passed by one after the other, each close to Āḷāra Kālāma. And a certain man, who was following close behind that caravan of carts, went up to the place where Āḷāra Kālāma was, and when he was come there he

6. Babbitt, *The Dhammapada,* p. 105.
7. Enneads 6, 9, 11.
8. *Ibid.*
9. *Majjhima-nikāya* I, 163–166.

spoke as follows to Āḷāra Kālāma . . . 'though you were both conscious and awake, [you] neither saw, nor heard the sound of five hundred carts passing by, one after the other, and each close to you. Why, lord, even your robe was sprinkled over with the dust of them.' " And Āḷāra Kālāma answered, "It is even so, sir." The thoughts of the observer are then included as follows, "How wonderful a thing is it, and how marvelous, that those who have gone forth out of the world should pass their time in a state of mind so calm!"[10]

While such stories present an accurate psychological picture of Buddhism from a behavioristic viewpoint, some additional introspective evidence is necessary to round out the picture. Since evidence of this kind is difficult to find in the most ancient scriptures, there has been confusion over the nature of Buddhist meditation (among those other than actual practitioners) until recent times and the advent of the spirit of scientific investigation into almost every field. Such investigation has occurred recently in Japan with regard to Zen meditation. Hence (in addition to laboratory tests on Zen masters) there have come to be descriptions of the meditative state that are much more careful in their wording than those of past times. Richard de Martino, for example, has offered the following analysis based on his own experience with *zazen* (Zen meditation), of the meditative condition of mind just prior to the onset of the breakthrough into enlightenment. Beginning negatively, he says, it is not ". . . either the pre-ego-consciousness of the infant, the abortive ego-consciousness of the idiot, the retarded ego-consciousness of the 'wolf-child,' the deteriorated ego-consciousness of the psychotic, the numbed ego-consciousness of the anesthetized, the lethargic ego-consciousness of the stupor, the quiescent ego-consciousness of dreamless sleep, the suspended ego-consciousness of the trance, or the inert ego-consciousness of the coma. This is rather ego-consciousness itself, in and as its own radical contradiction, stayed and impacted. It is neither vacant nor blank, nor does it cancel itself and dissolve. . . . It is, indeed, most sensitive. Moreover, being as yet unresolved, its struggle continues, although no more by or of the ego merely as ego."[11]

10. *Mahāparinibbāna-suttanta* 4, 27–28. *Dīgha-nikāya* II, pp. 130–131. The Buddha reportedly related a similar incident from his own life: "Now on one occasion, I was dwelling in one place called Atuma and was at the threshing floor. And at that time the falling rain began to beat and to splash, and the light rings to flash forth, and the thunderbolts to crash; and two peasants, brothers, and four oxen were killed. But the Buddha, being conscious and awake, neither saw, nor heard the sound thereof when the falling rain went on beating and splashing, and the light rings were flashing, forth, and the thunderbolts were crashing" (*Mahāparinibbāna-suttanta* 4, 30–34, *Dīgha-nikāya* II, pp. 131–132).

11. *Zen Buddhism and Psychoanalysis*, D. T. Suzuki, Erich Fromm, Richard De Martino (London: George Allen and Unwin Ltd., 1960), p. 165.

In order to practice the Buddhist method to its fullest degree of effectiveness, it is necessary to carry on this awareness throughout all of one's daily activities such that no extraneous misconceptions can enter the purity of one's mind. This process was clearly set forth by the Buddhist scriptures. "In what is seen there must be just the seen; in what is heard there must be just the heard; in what is sensed (as smell, taste or touch) there must be just what is sensed; in what is thought there must be just the thought."[12] An account of the practice of the Buddha himself in his daily life found that, "going begging from house to house, watching the door (of the senses), well restrained, he quickly filled his bowl, conscious, thoughtful."[13]

The states of deep meditation or rapture are occasionally called Conditions of Bliss, and are regarded as useful for the removal of mental obstacles to the attainment of the ideal state.[14] However, early Buddhists did not give trance an important place in religion. Like Confucius, early Buddhists maintained an extreme reserve with regard to it,[15] and even condemned trances as unsatisfactory.[16] Also seeking for the ideal state (*Arhatship*) in the practice of meditation alone was considered a deadly heresy.[17] This practice is both pleasant in itself, and at the same time useful as one means to the end proposed. It is not the end, but the end cannot be reached without it.[18] Nor, however, would the Buddha have led anyone to believe the end could be reached without walking a straight ethical path.

Some early Buddhists also admitted that it is possible for man to acquire super-normal powers such as levitation and the like by developing certain psychic capacities that have become atrophied through long disuse. But these effects were generally minimized in favor of meditation as "a footstep to the realization of higher learning (*vijjā*) culminating in Bodhi."[19]

As indicated by the above, Buddha aws dissatisfied with what had been taught him by other ascetics as to their methods of meditation. He realized that although the many ways of meditation led one from the

12. *Udāna* I, 10.
13. *Suttanipāta* 412. Translated by V. Fausböll, *The Sacred Books of the East*, vol. X (Oxford University Press, 1881), pp. 67–68.
14. *Aṅguttara-nikāya* III, 119.
15. *Analects* VII, 20.
16. *Saṃyutta-nikāya* XXXVI, 19.
17. *Dīgha-nikāya* I, 38.
18. The most ancient form is recorded in Dialogues I, 84–92. Later and much more elaborate forms are given in the Yogāvacara's *Manual of Indian Mysticism as Practiced by Buddhists*.
19. G. C. Pande, *Studies in the Origins of Buddhism* (Department of Ancient History and Archaeology, University of Allahabad, 1957), p. 532.

dominion of the senses into the realm of calmness, yet as long as ignorance remained, craving, and hence misery, was liable to recur. He therefore improved on previous disciplines to imbue deeply in the minds of his followers the conviction that everything is transient and nothing seizable is Self. However, without the act of spiritual concentration, he stressed, religious life cannot subsist at all.

Meditation, it must be remembered, is to be undertaken only in conjuction with the practice of the Buddhist ethical precepts. The Buddha claimed that the strong aspiration of a good man takes effect after the destruction of the cardinal vices. Then if he should wish to realize "by his own transcendent knowledge in this present world initiation into, and abode in, the viceless deliverance of heart and intellect it will come to pass."[20] In Christianity also is found. "The prayer of a righteous man has great power in its effects."[21] In Christianity the "effect" is the answer of God to a petition, whereas in early Buddhism it was the response of cosmic law.

At present, society is inclined to regard contemplatives as parasites. From the point of view of traditional universal religions, however, the existence of contemplative persons is the only justification of human society. It is not certain whether religion itself can be considered useful unless men retain some sense of the wisdom that may be won by sitting in quiet recollection: On this point Radhakrishnan offered a remark: "The soul in solitude is the birthplace of religion. Moses on the lonely Mount of Sinai, Buddha under the *bodhi* tree lost in comtemplation, Jesus by the Jordan in the stillness of prayer, Paul in the lonely sojourn in the desert, Mohammed on a solitary mount at Mecca, Francis of Assisi in his prayers in the remote crags of the highlands of Alverno, found the strength and the assurance of the reality of God. Everything that is great, new, and creative in religion rises out of the unfathomable depths of the soul in the quiet of prayer, in the solitude of meditation."[22]

20. *Majjhima-nikāya* 41.
21. James 5:16.
22. S. Radhakrishnan, *Eastern Religions*, p. 53.

V. THE IDEAL OF THE UNIVERSAL STATE

A. States and Kings

CONCERNING the problem of state administration, early Buddhists held a particular political thought which is reminiscent of the theory of *social contract*. According to their theory, the authority of sovereignty was not conferred upon kings by gods, but was given to them by the people through the process of election. A Buddhist scripture contains the following speculation regarding how the election process came about: "From our evil deeds, sirs, becoming manifest, inasmuch as stealing, censure, lying, punishment, have become known, what if we were to select a certain being, who should censure that which should rightly be censured and should banish him who deserves to be banished. But we will give him in return a proportion of the rice. Then those beings went to the being among them who was the handsomest, the best favoured, the most attractive, the most capable and said to him: Come now, good being, be indignant at that him who deserves to be banished. And we will contribute to thee a proportion of our rice. And he consented, and did so, and they gave him a proportion of their rice."[1] So *Māhasammata*, meaning "chosen by the whole people," was the first standing phrase to be applied to such a king, because Buddhists thought that the king was originally elected by the populace. Accordingly, the rights of a king were not considered to be sacred or conferred by the gods.

In the India of those days there were some small republics governed by a body of nobles. For example, the people of Kusinārā,[2] where the Buddha died, made it a custom to assemble in the council hall in order to discuss their public affairs. The Buddha is said to have heartily ap-

1. *Dīgha-nikāya* XXVIII, 17f.
2. Now at that time the Mallas of Kusinārā were assembled in the council hall on some public affairs. And the Venerable Ānanda went to the council hall of the Mallas of Kusinārā (*Mahāparinibbāna-suttanta* V, 20. *Dīgha-nikāya* V, p. 147).

proved of such a republican form of government,[3] in which the sovereignty of the kings was delegated by the people.

But the republican form of government did not come to prevail in India. Monarchy was predominant at that time and kings were very powerful, some being extremely despotic and oppressive toward their subjects. Buddhists disliked them intensely. In mentioning the many kinds of disaster, the Buddhists enumerated fire, earthquakes, thunder, floods, robbers and kings, robbers and kings being classified in the same category. A similar idea is noticed in ancient China also. Mo-Tzu said, "If a ruler attacks a neighbouring country, slays its inhabitants, carries off its cattle and horses, its millet and rice and all its chattels and possessions, his deed is recorded on strips of bamboo or rolls of silk, carved upon metal and stone, inscribed upon bells and tripods, that in after days are handed down to his sons and grandsons. 'No one,' he boasts, 'ever took such spoils as I have done.' But suppose some private person attacked the house next door, slew the inhabitants, stole their dogs and pigs, their grain and their clothing, and then made a record of his deed on stips of bamboo or rolls of silk and wrote inscriptions about it on his dishes and bowls, that they might be handed down in his family for generations to come, boasting that 'no one ever stole so much as he, would that be all right?' 'No,' said the Lord of Lu. 'And looking at the matter as you have put it, I see that many things which the world regards as all right are not necessarily right at all.'"[4]

St. Augustine, who regarded the church as high above the state, asked, "Without Justice what are kingdoms but great bands of robbers? What is a band of robbers but a little kingdom?" He further concurred with the reported statement of a pirate who spoke in the manner of Mo-Tzu: "Because I do it with a little ship, I am called a robber, and you, because you do it with a great fleet, are called an emperor." The pirate's saying was supposedly a reply to none other than Alexander the Great.[5]

3. The Buddha extolled the confederacy of the Vajji people. Among them there were no kings; people decided political and communal affairs by holding meetings. "So long as the Vajjians foregather thus often, and frequent the public meetings of their clan; so long may they be expected not to decline but to prosper.

"So long as the Vajjians meet together in concord, and rise in concord, and carry out their undertakings in concord—So long may the Vajjians be expected not to decline, but to prosper" (*Mahāparinibbāna-suttanta* I, 4. *Dīgha-nikāya* II, p. 73).

"When I was once staying at Vesali at the Śarandada Shrine, I taught the Vajjians these conditions of welfare; and so long as these conditions will continue to exist among the Vajjians, so long as the Vajjians will be well instructed in those conditions, so long may we expect them not to decline but to prosper" (*Mahāparinibbāna-suttanta* I, 5. *Dīgha-nikāya* II, p. 73).

4. Arthur Waley, *Three Ways of Thought in Ancient China* (London: George Allen and Unwin, Ltd., 1939), p. 175.

5. F. Copleston, *A History of Philosophy* (Garden City, New York: Doubleday & Co., Image Books, 1962), vol. II, part I, p. 102.

Early Buddhists sought to avoid all conflicts with kings. They saw no necessity for arguing with them, feeling that kings were like venomous serpents—one should not make them angry. It is better not to come into contact with them at all. Such was the instruction of the Buddha. The Buddhist attitude was rather apolitical, or perhaps anti-political. The Buddha not only discouraged members of the order from participating in political life, he went further and banned all discussion of politics. He made a distinction similar to that of Jesus between the things of God and the things of Caesar.

But in disregarding the existing despotism it was virtually impossible to establish the ideal Buddhistic society. So gradually Buddhists tended more and more to teach ways in which kings should manage their political affairs. This kind of instruction is expounded in various forms in the scriptures. For instance, a Brahmin who was a chaplain said to a king, "Whosoever there be in the king's realm who devote themselves to keeping cattle and the farm, to them let his majesty give good and seed-corn. Whosoever there be in the king's realm who devote themselves to trade, to them let his majesty give capital. Whosoever there be in the king's realm who devote themselves to government service, to them let his majesty give wages and food. Then those men, following each his own business, will no longer harass the realm; the king's revenue will go up; the country will be quite and at peace, and the people, pleased one with another and happy, dancing their children in their arms, will dwell with open doors."[6] Then the king, it is said, accepted the word of his advisor and did as he had instructed. And subsequently those men, following each his business, harassed the realm no more. And the king's revenue went up. And the country became quiet and at peace. And the people, pleased one with another and happy, dancing their children in their arms, dwelt with open doors.

Confucius also taught to the same purport, saying, "People despotically governed and kept in order by punishments may avoid infraction of the law, but they will lose their moral sense. People virtuously governed and kept in order by the inner law of self-control will retain their moral sense and moreover become good."[7] Confucius again said that a king should be one of integrity. "If a man can reform his own heart, what should hinder him from taking part in government? But if he cannot reform his own heart, what has he to do with reforming other?"[8]

Finally the ideal of the universal monarch (Pāli, *Cakkavatti*; Sanskrit,

6. *Kūṭadanta-sutta* 11. *Dīgha-nikāya*, vol. I.
7. Lionel Giles, *The Saying of Confucius*. A new translation of the greater part of the Confucian Analects with introduction and notes by Lionel Giles (London: John Murray, 1907), p. 39.
8. *Ibid.*, p. 45.

Cakravartin) appeared among Buddhists, Jains, and Hindus. He is said to have ruled the people of all the world by his virtuous personality and benevolent governance. It has often been explained that the *Cakravartin* is the reflection of an actual monarch of the Mauryan Dynasty on a mythological plane. Under the rulership of Western tribes (e.g., *Śakas*, *Kuṣāṇas*, etc.), the Buddha was invoked for the protection and prosperity of the states.

Some scholars assert that the ideal monarch of the *Cakkavatti* must have derived from the ancient glory of the sun-god. This idea is comparable to that of the Messiah among the Jews. The *Cakkavatti* and the Buddha were to the early Buddhists what the Messiah and *Logos* were to the early Christians. In both cases, the two ideas overlap and supplement one another. As the Jewish ideal of a Messiah influenced the minds of the early Christians, in a similar way the early Buddhist applied the ideal of *Cakkavatti* to Gotama. However the divine and solar elements in the Buddhist ideal king distinguish him from the ideal Messiah of the later pre-Christian Jews.[9]

Except among monarchs[10] Western thought of this period centered not around kings, but states. The mystery religions had little to say about government (and before Christianity hardly any other religion was given much philosophical play). But ethics was a major subject among the ancients, and this very often resulted in discussions concerning life in the state. Western philosophers of that time were generally not restricted from stating their views on such subjects and were granted a good deal of freedom to speculate on the relationship of citizen to state. So much so that groups of thinkers such as the Cyrenaics and Cynics, before Plato, could agree on such apparently anti-social precepts as that all fixed thought (rules) set up by the social conventions of law and morality are limitations of man's natural right to enjoyment. The wise man, they thought, goes on about his enjoyment without troubling himself with such conventions. Oddly enough, after Plato and Aristotle, the Epicureans and Stoics were also to reach a very similar conclusion that the wise man, self-sufficient in his own virtue, needs the state as little as he needs any other society. In certain circumstances, they felt, he may even avoid those two for the greater interest of his own enjoyment or duty. Equally strange is the fact that the ideas of the latter two (Stoics and Epicureans) came much closer to actualization (through Cicero into Roman jurisprudence) than did the glowing ideals set forth by Plato.

Plato's ethical ideal lay not in the ability and happiness of the in-

9. Rhys Davids, *Indian Buddhism*, pp. 130–139; also *Buddhist Suttas*, p. 253.
10. Alexander asserted his ideal of "one world, one king." Antiochus IV called himself Antiochus *Epiphanes* (revelation of God). (B. Russell, *A History of Western Philosophy*, pp. 181, 313)

dividual but in the ethical perfection of the human species. The doctrine of ideas seemed to logically lead him to assume mankind as being truly real in the ethical domain; and the form this truly existent humanity takes is the organic unity of individuals, the state. His view of the state was distinctly not empirical, then, but rather was an attempt to provide direction for the state through an *a priori* rationalization of society's task. Plato thought society (as man enlarged) would function best if it possessed the characteristics present in his psychology of the individual man. The three parts of the soul became the three parts of society—the teaching class, warrior class, and working class governed by their respective virtues of wisdom, fearless performance of duty, and industry—so that the true virtue of the state, justice, may come to the fore. Not until the rise of the medieval priesthood did such a hierarchy as Plato recommended find historical actualization.

Aristotle adopted his teacher's viewpoint that moral excellent finds its fulfillment only in community life. Hence he too believed the true end of society is the ethical training of its citizens. A constitution is proper if it provides this and has failed if it does not. Any kind of rule may be either good or bad, according to Aristotle, depending on its direction. Although he agreed with Plato then, that society must provide public education, he could never have gone into the detail Plato did in setting forth the ideal system of government. Aristotle's views through St. Thomas had great effect on the centralized church of later times.

As previously noted, Cicero is thought to have been responsible for many of the formative principles of Roman jurisprudence.[11] Through Cicero, Attic ethical philosophy attained to political realization in the following way. The relationship between rational beings, he held, is universally determined by moral world order and the command to reason inseparably connected with the instinct toward self-preservation. Human reason is innate in all men equally. From the universally valid natural moral law are derived the commands upon man in the moral society. This may sound like a totally rational basis for society, but it is that only to an extent; for Cicero also included in his conception of the state an investigation not only of what it should be, but of what it is. It is a product of history; and therefore there must be laws of nature already discernible, such as the laws structuring the life of historical institutions, individual states (domestic law), laws of confederation between states, etc. Seen here is the basis for the soon to be developed analyses of such institutions into a developed study of law as such.

The thought of St. Thomas probably represents the highest point reached in the West of the integration of religion and state. Though his

11. W. Windelband, *A History of Philosophy* (New York: Harper & Row, Torch Books, 1958), vol. I, p. 177.

thought exercised influence for a time, there has been a steady increase in the popularity of separation of religion and state from his time to the present. Because of the power of the Church (and undoubtedly because of their own religious convictions), great Western rulers after St. Thomas' time could not help but be struck by his viewpoint, derived from Aristotle, that the end of the state is to realize virtue in the individual. In so adopting this viewpoint, very close also to that of Cicero, Aquinas avoided going the way of his great predecessor St. Augustine, whose City of God was obviously contrasted to the state (a result of the fall from divinity), metaphorically represented as the city of Babylon. St. Thomas in some ways was much closer to Aristotle.

Aquinas' great difference from Aristotle, though, was that he did not see civic virtue as the highest end of man. Since man's true fulfillment is a supernatural one which only the direction of the church can provide, the church was considered more important than the state. From the viewpoint of their ultimate goal, the church is a society superior to the state and, for Aquinas, the state must subordinate itself to the church where supernatural matters are concerned. Hence from a latter day point of view Thomas may be regarded as an upholder of the "indirect power" of Church over state.[12] The true aim of man, for Aquinas, bears on the duties of the monarch, whose business it is to facilitate the attainment of that end. In terms of natural virtue the state may be a "perfect society" in an Aristotlean sense; "but the elevation of man to the supernatural order means that the State is very much a handmaid of the Church."[13]

Because Western heads of state were very infrequently leaders and propagators of universal religion, the next three sections are devoted to the comparative effects Eastern rulers had on their respective societies. In the East several great leaders were also the religious inspiration of their populace, and through their agency Buddhism came to be the universal religion it is today. In contrast the church as an institution in the West became the most powerful force among the people. This made it necessary for political leaders to grant much authority (but never, voluntarily at least, control of the kingdom) to church leaders. Only Constantine, in the period under consideration, can be compared with the Asian Buddhist rulers taken up next, and he only in limited ways.

12. Copleston, *op. cit.*, vol. 2, part II, p. 136.
13. *Ibid.*

B. Attempts at a Universal State Based on a Universal Religion

1. Universal States

THE term "universal state" here refers to a state founded by a monarch who believed in the existence and validity of universal laws or a universal mission which should be realized beyond the differences of races, peoples and ages. States which can be so designated came into existence at a certain stage in the history of mankind. Universal religions, which in their first stages were religions of only certain races or groups, could develop as they did only through universal states, i.e., after being adopted and encouraged by monarchs or rulers who professed universal religions. So between the incipient stage of universal religions and that of medieval thought, in which universal religions had already been granted their overwhelming authority, it is necessary to consider a major agency in their dissemination, the universal state or the universal monarch. Even before the rise of universal religions the image of the ideal hero who unified a country was not lacking. According to Japanese legend, for example, Jimmu, the first emperor of Japan, conquered most of Japan. Jimmu may be compared with the Indian hero Kṛṣṇa who played a leading part in the great Kurukṣetra war, which decided the fate of India. It is said that Jimmu started his conquest at the age of forty-five; Kṛṣṇa also began his political action fairly late in life. Jimmu and his wife claimed all the great *Kami* (gods) among their ancestors. Kṛṣṇa, the ninth *avatāra* (nearly a god himself) is called the Perfect Avatāra (*pūrnāvatāra*). In the Chinese tradition, the legendary Yellow Emperor (Huang-ti) may be their counterpart. But these historical figures do not come into the present framework for reasons taken up below.

When political military confrontations were abolished among tribes of antiquity comprising a single cultural area, and the political and military unity of that cultural area was established, changes typically occurred as follows: (1) A mighty monarch (or ruler) appeared and ruled the whole cultural area as a unit; his dynasty was firmly established. (2) The need of an ideology which could not be found in the ages of conflicting tribes was keenly felt. (3) The ideology, ideas, or at least the spiritual basis of the ideology was provided by a universal world religion. (4) The ideology or ideas were officially expressed to the public in the form of fixed statements (e.g., edicts in the case of Aśoka).

These political and cultural phenomena can be found at a certain stage in the history of various countries of antiquity. King Aśoka (3rd century B.C.) of ancient India is well known to have been the first such example. Then Prince Shōtoku of Japan (ruled in 592–622) and King Songtsan-Gampo of Tibet (Sron-btsan sgam-po., 617–651 A.D.)[1] gave a firm foundation to their respective states and cultures at nearly the same time. Each of them was the founder of a unified state and the greatest promoter of the resulting culture. In South Asia monarchs of similar historic significance appeared still later. King Anawrahta (1044–1077 A.D.) of Burma and King Jayavarman VII (1181–1215) of Cambodia belong to the same type. Chronologically these monarchs do not belong to the same period, but it is assumed that they are located approximately in the same developmental stage of their civilizations.

King Aśoka is very famous as the unifier of nearly the whole of India, as well as some adjacent districts.

Less well known perhaps is Japan's Prince Shōtoku, who laid the foundation of a unified culture in his country. Before his time Japan was torn by independent provincial magnates or hereditary local rulers who were masters of their own peoples and enforced their own laws. They were suppressed first by Prince Shōtoku and finally by the Reform of Taika (645 A.D.). The autonomous local governors were abolished, and their "property," including "their people and slaves," was confiscated by the central State. Not long after the death of Prince Shōtoku, King Songstan-Gampo appeared in Tibet. He unified the whole of his country and accelerated the practice of Buddhism there.

In Burma it was only when Anawrahta, King of Pagan and the first great name in Burmese history, ascended the throne that the course of events in that country became clear and coherent. A man of arms, he conquered Thaton in 1057 and transported many of its inhabitants to his own capital. He also subdued the nearer Shan states and was master of nearly all Burma as we now understand the term.[2] In Siam his counterpart appeared still later. An inscription probably composed about 1300 A.D. relates how the monarch called Rāmarāja or Rāma Khomheng extended his domain during a period when the Siamese states became acquainted with Pāli Buddhism. The king states that hitherto his people had no alphabet but that he invented one, a script that subsequently developed into the modern Siamese script. The king also speaks of religion, saying that his court and citizens were devout Buddhists, and that they observed the season of Vassa and celebrated the festival of Kaṭhina with

1. The date of King Songstan-Gampo is based on my work *Early Vedānta Philosophy* (in Japanese), pp. 105 ff. Dr. Roerich places him at c. 650 A.D. (George N. Roerich, *The Blue Annals*, part I [Calcutta: Royal Asiatic Society of Bengal, 1949], pp. iii, 49).
2. Eliot, *Hinduism*, III, p. 48.

processions, concerts and reading of the scriptures. In the city were to be seen statues of the Buddha and scenes carved in relief, as well as large monasteries.[3] In Cambodia things were slightly different. Buddhism had already been established before Jayavarman VII. However, his ideal has some features in common with those of the above-mentioned monarchs.

In China it is somewhat difficult to find a mighty king who held the same historic significance as those previously mentioned. One perhaps might be Emperor Wu-ti (464–549) of the Liang dynasty or Emperor Wen (reigned 581–604) of the Sui dynasty. The latter especially can be compared to the above-mentioned kings of other countries, for he united the whole area of China after long civil war and immediately restored Buddhism, which had declined due to suppression by previous kings. "The Sui founder presented himself to the populace as a universal monarch, a pious believer and a munificent patron of the church (*mahādāna-pati*).[4]

In the cases of these monarchs the universal religion was Buddhism. In the West, however, it was Christianity. A figure corresponding to the above Eastern monarchs was Emperor Constantine (306–337 A.D.), but the situation was considerably different, representing virtually the difference between Eastern and Western thought and cultures, and also that between Eastern and Western societies. In order to explicate this differences as well as to evaluate the significance and comparative traits of these "ideal" monarchs, the case of Prince Shōtoku may serve as a convenient starting point.

Prince Shōtoku, the real founder of the centralized state of Japan, proclaimed the Seventeen Article Constitution in 604 A.D. This was the first legislation in Japan—the characteristic expression of the original and creative development of the Japan of the time, adopting to a great extent the civilizations and thoughts of China and India, chiefly based upon the spirit of Buddhism. This is, so to speak, the "Magna Carta" of Japan. The Constitution prescribed rules of conduct which the officials of the Imperial Government should obey, thereby perchance revealing how badly needed such rules were. The Constitution was proclaimed about forty years prior to the Reform of Taika (645 A.D.), confirmed by scholars as a close spiritual relative of Shōtoku's Constitution, which ushered in the political regime that accomplished the unification of Japan as a state.

In contract to Prince Shōtoku's Seventeen Article Constitution, King Songtsan-Gampo, the founder of the centralized state of Tibet, proclaimed the Sixteen Article Law at nearly the same time; and, further back in early history, King Aśoka of India published many Pillar

3. *Ibid.*, pp. 80–81.
4. Wright, *Buddhism in Chinese History*, p. 67.

Edicts which proclaimed various precepts (the number of which has not been fixed). The common characteristic of these laws is that they represented moral precepts, but did not in practice function as positive laws.

The Tibetans were especially conscious of this point. According to them, the Sixteen Article Law was men's Law (*mi-chos*), which was different from Gods' Law (*Iha-chos*).[5] The former was an ethical law, whereas the latter was a religious one. Both of them together constitute the System of Laws (*chos-lugs*). King Aśoka included both of them in just the one word 'Law' (*dharma*).

On the basis of such fundamental laws, practical laws were instituted. The Tibetans called them 'Laws or Ruling' (*rgyal-khrims*). Songtsan-Gampo is said "to have instituted laws to punish murder, theft and adultery."[6] This corresponds to the laws and rules from the Taika Reform in Japan. The laws which were in practice in the Mauryan Age around Aśoka seem to have been more or less incorporated in the *Arthaśāstra* of Kauṭilya. Due to later interpolation in the work, however, it is very difficult to identify those that were composed in the Mauryan age.

There is, however, one difference. Songtsan-Gampo's Law taught popular morals meant for the common people, whereas Shotoku's Constitution proclaimed the "Ways of the Public," i.e., mental and moral attitudes of officials about state affairs. The edicts of Aśoka were mostly meant for the common people, thought some were intended for officials. This difference indicates that bureaucracy was very strong even at the outset of Japan's centralized state, and it harbingers the supremacy of bureaucrats in the later history of Japan.

Because these centralized or universal states were established after overcoming conflicts among various tribes, what was stressed initially was "concord" as the principle of a community. The first article of the Sixteen Article Law (as set forth in the Chronicle of Tibet) declared: "Whosoever quarrels, is punished severely." Aśoka also stressed the spirit of concord (*samavāya*). In the same way Prince Shōtoku emphasized "harmony" in human relations. Showing deep self-reflection, the first article of his Constitution advocated: "Above all else esteem concord; make it your first duty to avoid discord. People are prone to form partisanships, for few persons are really enlightened. Hence there are those who do not obey their lords and parents, and they come in conflict with the neighbors. But

5. Taishun Mibu, "Buddhist Thought in the Tibetan Law," *Journal of Indian and Buddhist Studies*, vol. V, no. 2 (March, 1957), pp. 414–418.

"The king introduced a legal code and established punishments for murder, robbery and adultery. He taught his subjects writing and the good law, such as sixteen laws (mi chos), etc." (Roerich, *The Blue Annals*, p. 40).

6. Roerich, *The Blue Annals*, I, 20 b5.

when those above and those below are harmonious and friendly, there is concord in the discussion of affairs, and things become harmonious with the truths. Then what would there be that could not be accomplished?" (Article I)

The main problem seemingly being addressed is that men are apt to be bigotted and partial; within a community or between communities conflicts easily occur. Such conflicts must be avoided and concord must be realized in order for a harmonious community to be formed in an ideal way. The spirit of concord is stressed throughout all the articles of Prince Shōtoku's Constitution. Concord between lord and subject, superior and inferior, among people in general or among individuals, is repeatedly taught. This does not imply strict obedience. Prince Shōtoku did not teach that men were only to follow or obey, but that discussion should be carried on in an atmosphere of harmony so that one could attain right views. Earnest discussion was highly prized.

Concord between ruler and subject received the most emphasis in ancient China; for example, by Mencius: "When a ruler rejoices in the joy of his people, they also grieve at his sorrow. Rejoicing with all under Heaven, grieving with all under Heaven, he cannot but become King over all."[7]

In the case of Emperor Constantine, after his political and military success, what caused him the most concern were quarrels on religious issues in the Church. He wielded his influence in religious affairs. When the trouble of the Donatists occurred, Constantine ordered an investigation of the incident.[8] The quarrel threatened the unity of the Church which he deemed essential. Constantine therefore sent his chief ecclesiastical adviser, Bishop Hosius of Cordova, in Spain, to Alexandria with an imperial letter, counselling peace and describing the issue involved as "an unprofitable question." He called a council of the entire Church. Constantine was then master of all the empire, and therefore bishops of all the empire were summoned. The principle was the same, but the extent of Constantine's enlarged jurisdiction made the gathering in Nicaea the First General Council of the Church.[9] In the case of Constantine the prestige of the Church had already been established and its influence was very strong, so his endeavor centered on religious issues. But in Eastern countries religious orders were not so strong, therefore these latter monarchs promulgated edicts of a general form.

In the edicts of the Eastern monarchs it was taught that demeanor or

7. *Mencius* I p. 4.
8. Reinhold Seeberg, *Text-book of the History of Doctrines*, translated by Charles E. Hay, vol. 1 (Grand Rapids, Michigan: Baker Book House, 1961), p. 314.
9. Williston Walker, *A History of the Christian Church*, revised edition (New York: Charles Scribner's Sons, 1959), p. 108.

language which is detrimental to concord should be avoided. King Aśoka said: "It should certainly be looked into thus: these [passions], indeed, lead to depravity, such as violence, cruelty, anger, conceit, envy."[10] Songtsan-Gampo also taught "to be equal to everybody and not to be jealous," "to be gentle and not extravagant (modest) in speech," and "to be noble in behaviour, and tolerant in mind."

Prince Shōtoku went further. He said that giving up anger in debate was only possible by way of self-reflection on the relativity of men, that we are all ordinary men. "Let us cease from wrath, and refrain from angry looks. Nor let us be resentful just because others oppose us. Every person has a mind of his own; each heart has its own leaning. We may regard as wrong what others hold as right; others may regard as wrong what we hold as right. We are not unquestionably sages, nor are they assuredly fools. Both of us are simply ordinary men. Who is wise enough to judge which of us is good or bad? For we are all wise and foolish alternately, like a ring which has no end. Therefore, although others may give way to anger, let us on the contrary dread our faults, and though we may be sure that we are in the right, let us act in harmony with many others." (Article X) Shōtoku advised discussing affairs in a calm mind, with a feeling of harmony, desisting from anger. He thought that thereby difficult problems with be settled spontaneously in the right. In this way alone is it possible for decisions to be reached at conferences.

The above-mentioned attitude has often been regarded as peculiarly Eastern but it is not lacking in the West of antiquity, either. Christians would not go to law courts, since the apostle Paul had taught that when people quarreled they should settle things among themselves. This is said to be the reason why the practice arose of letting the bishop decide disputes. It may involve contempt for secular justice, but it seems to be something similar to the above.

The attitude of broad-mindedness or self-reflection is noticed in the case of Constantine also. "Acesius, Bishop of an insignificant Roman Church, was eager to make his community consist solely of pure saints, and to exclude all others from future blessedness. Constantine, whose sanctity was not of the strictest kind, laughed at him. 'Take your ladder, Acesius, and climb up alone to heaven.' "[11]

Meanwhile, Eastern universal monarchs thought that at the bottom of the activities of a community led by a monarch with modest self-reflection, there should be religion. So Prince Shōtoku said in the second article. "Sincerely revere the Three Treasures." Songtsan-Gampo said

10. Pillar Edict III, D. R. Bhandarkar, *Asoka,* third edition (Calcutta: University of Calcutta, 1955), p. 302.
11. Ernest Edward Kellet, *A Short History of Religions* (Middlesex: Penguin Books, 1962), p. 167.

in the first article:[12] "Have faith in, and pay respect to, The Three Treasures," and in the second article: "Seek for the True Religion and accomplish it."

Further back in history, in the Rock and Pillar Edicts proclaimed to the subjects in general, King Aśoka expressed freedom of thought, and did not teach that Buddhism alone should be esteemed. However, in an edict (Bhabru inscription) proclaimed to a Buddhist order he declared his faith in the Three Jewels, i.e., Buddha, the Law and the Order. "King Priyadarsin of Magadha, having saluted the *Saṃgha*, wishes them good health and comfortable (bodily) movement. Ye know, Reverend Sirs, how great are my respect and kindliness towards Buddha, *Dharma*, and *Saṃgha*." One may be reminded of the well-known expression "a servant of the Three Treasures" by Emperor Shomu, a Japanese king of antiquity.

Some scholars say that the conception of concord (*wa*) was adopted from Confucianism, for the word "*wa*" is used in the *Analects* of Confucius. But the term "*wa*" was used in connection with propriety or decorum in that work[13] and concord was not the subject. Prince Shōtoku, on the contrary advocated concord as the chief principle of human behavior.[14] His attitude was derived from the Buddhist standpoint of benevolence, which should be distinguished from the Confucian one.

Then why had the Japanese in those days to resort to Buddhism? Prince Shōtoku said: "Sincerely revere the Three Treasures. The Three Treasures, viz. Buddha, the Law and the Congregation, are the final ideal of all living beings and the ultimate foundation of all countries. Should any age or any people fail to esteem this truth? There are few men who are really vicious. They will all follow it if adequately instructed. How could the crooked ways of men be made straight, unless we take refuge in the Three Treasures?" (Article I) According to Prince Shōtoku, the "Law" is "the norm" of all living creatures, the "Buddha" is in fact "the Law embodied," which "being united with Reason" becomes *Saṃgha*. So according to his teaching, everything converges upon the one fundamental principle called the "Law."

The then Empress Suiko issued an Imperial edict to promote the prosperity of the Three Treasures in the year 594. It is said that, at that time, all the ministers vied with one another in erecting Buddhist temples for the beatitude of their lords and parents. Thus the Buddhist culture came to take root, grew and blossomed. A new epock in the cultural

12. The Sixteen Article Law conveyed in the *Mani bkah hbum.*
13. The Analects of Confucius I, 12: "In practising the rules of propriety, a natural ease is to be prized." Here "a natural ease" is the translation of the Chinese word *ho*. Confucian Analects. James Legge's *The Chinese Classics*, vol. 1 (Worcester, Mass., 1855), p. 15.
14. In the Chinese versions of Buddhist scriptures such words as *wakyō* or *wagō* are frequently used.

history of Japan began. It is likely that other Asiatic kings adopted Buddhist thought in a similar way.

In the case of King Aśoka, however, what he resorted to was *dharma*, which is valid beyond the confrontation of various religions, and not necessarily for Buddhism alone. Buddhism was only one of many religions which received his protection, along with Brahmanism, Jainism and the Ajivikas, although it is certain that Aśoka particularly patronized and supported Buddhism. Things being so, it may seem that there was a fundamental difference between Aśoka and other Asian monarchs, including Prince Shōtoku.

Investigating, however, the fundamental ideas which brought these historical facts to realization, reveals that there was not much difference. For Prince Shōtoku, there was only one philosophical system which taught universal laws; that was Buddhism. It was natural that he termed Buddhism "the final ideal of all living beings and the ultimate foundation of all countries." In the case of Aśoka, however, many religious systems had already become highly developed, and there were many other religions which claimed to be universal philosophical systems. So he had to deal with many religions. By examining the matter more deeply, one finds that the quintessence of Buddhism consists, at least according to some texts, in acknowledging the universal laws taught by all religions and philosophies, as is evidenced in early and Mahāyāna Buddhism. So one may conclude that there is no actually fundamental difference between King Aśoka and Prince Shōtoku. They had this in common, that they wanted to found their kingdoms on the basis of universal laws or the truth of the universe.

Because of this characteristic of Buddhism, neither Prince Shotoku, King Aśoka, nor King Songtsan-Gampo suppressed indigeneous faiths native to their respective peoples, although they themselves esteemed and revered Buddhism. That is why Shintoism in Japan and the Bon religion in Tibet have been preserved as their respective religions, up to the present. In Burma the faith of Nats is prevalent even now among common people. In view of such an attitude, one can understand why the following kind of edict was proclaimed in the reign of Prince Shōtoku (607 A.D.): "In my reign, why should we be negligent of practising the worship of Shintoist gods? All my officials should worship them sincerely."

In the reign of the Cambodian king Jayavarman VII (c. 1185 A.D.), Mahayana Buddhism seems to have been professed frankly as the royal religion. However, the King did not neglect the Brahmanic gods, nor was Hindu mythology discarded. The king's chaplain (presumably a Sivaite) received every honor.[15]

The rational basis for such a spirit of tolerance and conciliation in

15. Eliot, *Hinduism* III, pp. 121, 123.

the case of Prince Shōtoku is to be sought in the tendency, conspicuous among the Japanese, to recognize absolute significance in everything phenomenal. It leads to the acceptance of the *raison d'être* of any view held by men, and ends up with an adjustment to any view in a spirit of tolerance and conciliation.

Such a way of thinking appeared from the earliest days of the introduction of Buddhism into Japan. According to Prince Shōtoku, the *Saddharmapuṇḍarīka-sūtra*, supposed to contain the ultimate essence of Buddhism, preached the doctrine of the One Great Vehicle and advocated the theory that "any one of thousands of the good leads to the attainment of Enlightenment.[16] According to the Prince, there was no innate difference between the saint and the most stupid.[17] Every one of them is primarily and equally a child of the Buddha. Prince Shōtoku regarded secular moral teaching as the elementary gate by which to enter Buddhism. He used expressions of a heretical doctrine and a pagan religion, but these expressions were borrowed rather from the traditional Indian terminology. He did not mean by them the doctrines of Lao-tsu and Chuang-tzu or Confucianism.[18] His interpretation of Buddhism was characterized by its all-inclusive nature. Only through taking into consideration such a philosophical background is one able to understand the moral idea of the Prince when he said, "Harmony is to be honored."[19] It was this spirit that made possible the emergence of Japan as a unified cultural state.

When one compares these facts with those in the West, one finds a fundamental difference. Christianity gradually came to the fore in spite of various persecutions. Finally, freedom of faith was assured by Emperor Constantine with the edict of Milan in the year 313. Probably late in 312 Constantine and Licinius published in Milan the great edict which gave complete freedom to Christianity. The new policy was no longer, as in 311, one merely of toleration; nor did it make Christianity the religion of the empire. It proclaimed absolute freedom of conscience, placed Christianity of a full legal equality with any religion of the Roman world, and ordered the restoration of all church property confiscated in the recent persecution.[20] Later, Christianity attained the position of a state religion on the occasion of the unification of the state by Emperor Theodosius in the year 394. Emperor Justinian of the Eastern Roman Empire forbade, in 529, the worship of any gods except the Christian God. These

16. Shinsho Hanayama, *Hokke-gisho no Kenkyū* (Tokyo: Toyo Bunko), p. 464 f. Prince Shotoku's philosophical standpoint is represented by expressions like "The One Great Vehicle" or "The Pure Great Vehicle," which are supposed to have originated from the *Saddharmapuṇḍarika-sūtra*.
17. *Ibid.*, p. 117 f.
18. *Ibid.*, p. 460.
19. In his Seventeen Article Constitution.
20. Walker, *Christian Church*, p. 101.

measures characterized the later development of Western culture, which has differed greatly from that in Eastern countries. A Western counterpart to *Cakravartin* could be found in the longing on the part of people for the unity which had once existed in the old Roman Empire. To meet this wish, Charles the Great founded the Holy Roman Empire.

2. The Ideal of the Management of the Centralized State

THESE universal states were formed after fundamentally abolishing the hereditary privilege of heads of clans (nobles) and their political rulership based upon the social order of clans. The powerful clans or nobles could preserve their political power only by qualifying as officials of the newly established centralized state. In India and China this step was taken earlier than adoption of a universal religion by the universal states, whereas in other Asian countries both steps were taken at the same time by the same rulers.

Between the state of the Mauryan dynasty and that of Ch'in there exists a parallel which extends to the whole social and cultural history of the two. Each state was the ultimate victor after a long period of war. The ancient political framework of Indian society underwent an important change. The older division into clans, some of them patriarchal, some aristocratic republics, passed into the more wide-range division into nations. A new kingly power arose and made itself very clearly felt. At the end of the fourth century B.C., the first great sovereign of India, Chanddragupta, appeared.

The new Dynasty of the Mauryas swept across the whole of northern India in 317 B.C.,[1] just 96 years before the Ch'in state accomplished a similar hegemony throughout China. "The victory of both states seems to have been due to the same causes: a ruthless foreign policy, an efficient, highly centralized administration, and an emphasis on the army. In both kingdoms the doctrine of the total state became popular. Every inhabitant should subserve the interests of the king. Every social action should be regulated by precise laws. These should be made clearly knowon to the inhabitants and enforced even at the cost of cruelty."[2] This doctrine was expressed in the *Arthaśāstra* of Kauṭilya in India and by Ch'in legalists such as Shang Yang (who was a minister of Ch'in between 359–338 B.C.),[3] and Han Fei-tzu in China.

1. The date is based upon my own article published in *Tohogaku*, Tokyo, vol. X.
2. Daniel H. H. Ingalls, Supplement to *Journal of the American Oriental Society*, 1954, no. 17, p. 45.
3. For Shang Yang see *The Book of Lord Shang* translated by J. J. L. Duyvendak (London, 1928).

However, in both states failure soon followed success. The dynasty of Ch'in fell in a few decades, execrated by every Chinese author whose works have been preserved. And the founder of the Han dynasty abolished all the precise laws of the Ch'in dynasty, simplified them, and adopted a lenient policy.[4] In India King Aśoka, who appeared nearly at the same time as the founder of Han, had to face a critical point; the *Machtpolitik* of the dynasty had to be altered. This was done by him, and he was highly admired and respected by later Indians.

After the disappearance of the Ch'in dynasty many of its principles[5] of empire were taken over, willingly or not, by later dynasties, and these principles continued to function in the later political history of China. In India, on the other hand, the principles of Kauṭilya were soon almost forgotten. It seems that in later times strong dynasties occasionally tried to revive the 'Arthaśāstra' state, but the main stream of Indian history ran in a very different channel. From the end of the Maurya dynasty the whole of India became politically decentralized. A religious orientation has been

4. The Han empire before the introduction of Buddhism and the Roman Empire before the spread of Christianity had many similarities. This fact has already been pointed out by scholars.

"Han China was expansive, full of bustling life, extroverted. Alexander Soper suggests the spirit of Han life:

Han was a time of empire-building, of immense new wealth and power, of enlarged political and economic responsibilities. The realistic mood of the age gave small encouragement to anti-social dreaming. . . . For the articulate man of Han—courtier, soldier, or official, city-dweller absorbed in the brilliant pageant of metropolitan life in a busy and successful empire—the most insistent stimulus to the imagination came from the palace, the prime symbol of human greatness, erected now on an unimaginable scale of splendor, vastness, and multiplicity.

This sensuous satisfaction in the new prosperity of China was not limited to those who contemplated the splendors of the capital. Here is an official speaking of life on his estate, to which he retired after being dismissed from office in 56 B.C.:

When the proprietor has finished his labor and when the season is late summer or the holidays of year's end, he cooks a sheep, he roasts a lamb, he draws a measure of wine, and thus rests from his work. I am from Ch'in and know how to make the music of Ch'in; my wife is from Chao and plays the lute very well. Many of our slaves sing. When after drinking the wine I am warm to the ears I raise my head toward heaven, beat the measure on a jug, and cry 'Wuwu,' I swing my robe and enjoy myself; pulling back my sleeves. . . . I begin to dance.

If such were the preoccupations and pleasures of Han officialdom and gentry, it is scarcely surprising that the thought of the Han has been characterized as a sort of imperial pragmatism in the Roman manner." (Wright, *Buddhism in Chinese History*, pp. 9–10)

5. "Now they had to be rationalized; and the new order was of such growing complexity that the simple dicta of Confucius, uttered in an earlier period, were clearly inapplicable or inadequate. This suggests why the formulators of Han Confucianism drew so extensively on non-Confucian traditions to develop the structure of ideas which the times and the demands of their own intellects required." (*Ibid.*, p. 11.)

typical of Indian society. The *Machtpolitik* was forgotten there.[6] As evidence of the religious orientation of government one could cite a world wide phenomenon (also found in India), the divine right of kings. For example, the kings of the Seleucid and Ptolemaic dynasties were deified. They usually enjoyed divine honors after death, and sometimes bore divine titles such as 'Savior' (*Sōtēr*), and 'God' in their lifetime. This tendency familiarized the Graeco-Roman world with the idea of the incarnation of the Man-God. These titles were imitated by kings of northwestern India in the period from the second century B.C. to the second century A.D. They claimed to be 'Savior' (*trātar*) and 'God' (*iśvara*). This corresponds to the imperial title of 'Son of Heaven' in ancient China, which was also applied to Japanese emperors. Kings of ancient Persia assumed the title 'King of kings' (*basileus basileon*) according to Greek records, and kings of ancient India took the title *rajatiraja*, corresponding to the above. The glorification of kings appeared in a similar way at nearly the same period.

Contrary to the above-mentioned tendency in India and China (i.e., the disappearance of a *Machtpolitik*), Prince Shōtoku, King Anawrahta of Burma, and King Songtsan-Gampo realized the unification of their countries and the adoption of a universal religion at the same time. Emperor Wen of the Sui dynasty somewhat shared the same achievement.

Prince Shōtoku established a new official organization, reforming the old regime under which the higher court ranks had been occupied only hereditarily. In this new regime anyone could attain promotion according to his ability and merit without distinction of birth. This new system of appointment was called the Twelve Court Ranks (603 A.D.). The same measures seem to have been taken up by the Mauryan dynasty, due to the advice of Kauṭilya,[7] and by the Ch'in dynasty, due to the thought of Legalists, as was mentioned above.

As it was the officials who acted as the central figures in the newly established centralized states, morale had to be firmly kept among them. The spirit of esteeming the good and hating the bad had to be cherished. To this end, Prince Shōtoku taught: "Punish the vicious and reward the virtuous. This is the excellent rule of antiquity. Do not, therefore, let the good deeds of any person go concealed, nor the bad deeds of any go uncorrected, when you see them. Flatterers and deceivers are like the fatal missile which will overthrow the state, or the sharp sword which will destroy the people. Likewise sycophants are fond of dilating to their superiors on the errors of the inferiors; to their inferiors, they censure the

6. "There are literally thousands of manuscripts of Manu, Yajnavalkya and Vasistha; while there have been found only three manuscripts of Kautilya's Arthasastra" (Ingalls, *Journal of the American Oriental Society*, 1954, no. 17, p. 45).
7. Kauṭilya's *Arthaśāstra*, p. 14 (ed. by Ramaskastry).

faults of the superiors. Such are the kind of men who are never loyal to the lord, nor benevolent toward the people. All this is the source from which grave civil disturbances occur." (Article VI) This spirit can also be traced in the case of King Aśoka of old. He lamented that "good is difficult to perform," whereas bad is easy to do. "The good is difficult to perform. He who initiates the good does something difficult to perform. Hence by me much of the good had been done. If my sons, grandsons, and my descendants after them, until the aeon of destruction, follow similarly, they will do what is meritorious, but in this respect he who abandons even a part (here), will do ill. Verily, sin is easy to commit."[8] In the scripture of early Buddhism it is also taught: "Evil deeds, deeds which are harmful to oneself, are easy to do. What is beneficial and good, that is very difficult to do."[9]

Prince Shōtoku wrote: "Light crimes should be embraced by our power of reforming influence, and grave crimes should be surrendered to our power of strong force."[10] He did not avoid resorting to force in order to punish the severely wicked.

Considering these historical facts, the assertion made by some scholars that Westerners are keen on the distinction between good and bad, whereas Eastern peoples are not, is an untenable oversimplification.

With regard to judicial administration, the impartiality and speed of justice was urgently required. Prince Shōtoku admonished as follows: "In hearing judicial cases of common people judges should banish avaricious desires and give up their own interests. Deal impartially with the suits brought by the people. Of the cases to be tried there are a thousand each day. If so many in one day, there will be immense numbers of disputes to be settled in a series of years. Nowadays it is alleged that some judges seek their own profit, and attend to the cases after having taken bribes, which has given rise to the saying: 'The suits of the rick men are like the stone cast into the pond, whereas the suits of the poor men are like water thrown upon a rock.' Hence the poor people do not know where to betake themselves. Such a state of affairs, if brought about, would mean a deficiency in the duty of officials." (Article V)

King Aśoka also taught officials that they should aim at the happiness and welfare of people, and for that purpose they should observe the utterances of *dharma*, the ordinances and the instructions of *dharma*. He esteemed forbearance and lightness of punishment.[11] This require-

8. Pillar Edic V (D. R. Bhandarkar, *Aśoka*, p. 270).
9. *Dhammapada*, v. 163 (The Dhammapada with introductory essays, Pāli text, English translation and notes by S. Radhakrishnan [London, New York, Toronto: Geoffrey Cumberlege, Oxford University Press, 2nd impression, 1954], p. 113).
10. Prince Shotoku's *Shōmangyō-gisho*, ed. by Shinsho Hanayama (Iwanami, 1948), p. 34.
11. The Rock Edicts XIII.

ment went further. Officials, he said, should be men of integrity. A good regime does not necessarily guarantee the welfare and safety of the country, if the persons who manage administration are wicked. "Each person has a duty to perform, let not the spheres of duty be confused. When wise and capable persons are entrusted with high offices, there will arise a unanimous voice of pleased approval; but when wicked persons hold high offices, disasters and disturbances are multiplied. In this world there are few who are endowed with inborn wisdom; sainthood is the goal attained after long self-discipline. All matters of State, whether great or small, will surely be well ordered, when right persons are in the right positions; in any period. whether critical or peaceful, all affairs will be peacefully, settled when wise men are secured. In this way will the State be lasting and the realm be free from dangers. Therefore the wise sovereigns of the ancient times sought good men for high offices, and not good offices for favored ones." (Article VII)

It is noteworthy that Prince Shōtoku admonished officials against jealousy, which is a hindrance to the wholesome development of a community or society. Monarchs of the universal states did the same thing (e.g., Pillar Edict III of Aśoka; the thirteenth article of Songtsan-Gampo's Law), but it is interesting that Prince Shōtoku wrote in great detail on the subject: "All officials, high and low, should beware of jealousy. If you are jealous of others, others in turn will be jealous of you and thus is perpetuated a vicious circle. So if we find others excell us in intelligence, we are not pleased; if we find them to surpass us in ability, we become envious. Really wise persons are seldom seen in this world—possibly one wise man in five centuries, but hardly one sage in ten centuries. Without securing wise men and sages, wherewith shall the country be governed in good order?" (Article XIV)

Setting forth the multifarious mental attitudes of rulers and officials, Prince Shōtoku denounced dictatorship and stressed the necessity of consultation and discussions at the end of his Constitution. "Decision on important matters should not be made in general by one person along. They should be discussed with many others. But small matters are of less importance, and it is unnecessary to consult many persons concerning them. In the case of discussing weighty matters you must be fearful lest there be faults. You should arrange matters in consultation with many persons, so as to arrive at the right conclusion." (Article XVII) This is the beginning of Japanese democratic thought. This article corresponds to the first article, which stated that discussion should be carried on in a spirit of concord. This trend developed into an edict after the Taika Reform, which denounced the dictatorship of a sovereign, saying: "Things should not be instituted by a single ruler:" Such denunciation of dictatorship was inherited from an ancient way of ruling represented in Japanese mythology not as dictatorship by a monarch or by "the Lord of All," but as a conference on the shore of a river. Where public opinion was not esteemed, conferences could not have been held successfully. So the spirit of primitive Shintoism must have been inherited and developed by Prince Shōtoku. On the other hand it is possible that the rules of the Buddhist Order influenced the thought of the Prince. The rules of the Buddhist Order were set forth in full detail in the scriptures, including the rules of decision by majority. The fact that consultation with many others was not explicitly encouraged by Ashoka, nor by Songtsan-Gampo, but by Prince Shōtoku, is noteworthy. This attitude was preserved in the days when the Emperors were in power. Japanese monarchy developed as something different from dictatorship, although it was utilized arbitrarily by the military in later days.

In the case of the Prince, an intention different from those of monarchs of other countries was expressed. "When you receive the orders of the Sovereign, you should listen to them reverentially. The lord is like the heaven and the subjects are like the earth. With the heaven above and the earth below united in performing their functions loyally in their respective positions, we shall see the world ruled in perfect good order, as in the harmonious rotation of the four seasons. . . . If the earth should attempt to supplant the heaven, all would simply fall in ruin. Therefore when the lord speaks, let his subjects listen and obey; when the superiors act, the inferiors comply. Consequently when you receive the orders of the Sovereign, you should be attentive in carrying them out faithfully. If you fail in this, ruin would be the natural consequence." (Article III)

The desire to have his edicts observed among the common people was very strong in the case of Aśoka also. Having edicts inscribed on stone pillars erected by him or on the polished surface of rocks, he intended that they be read by the common people. He said, "Since my consecration twelve years ago, I have caused Edicts of dharmas to be written for the welfare and happiness of the people, so that without violation thereof, they might attain to this and that growth of dharma."[12] Needless to say, those who could read and understand the edicts in those days must have been limited to only the classes of rulers and intellectuals. However, those who were impressed by the sentences of the edicts must have amounted to a considerable number. Moreover, Aśoka urged people to propagate the *dharma*. "Relatives should propagate [the teaching] appropriately to their own relatives."[13] He saw to it that the edicts were recited on fixed days and that their intention was effected. "This document should be heard on the Tiṣya day every fourmonthly season; and, indeed, on every festive occasion in between the Tiṣya days it may be

12. Pillar Edicts VI.
13. Yerragudi Edict.

heard even by one [official]. By acting thus, endeavour to fulfil [my instructions]."[14]

But Aśoka did not command the prestige of a monarch solely by reason of being a sovereign. His words were said to be esteemed because they expressed universal laws. In the Sixteen Article Law of Songtsan-Gampo also, loyalty to the monarch was not taught at all.

What was stressed by Prince Shotoku, however, was the relation between lord (emperor), officials and the common people in the centralized monarchical state. Officials ruled the common people in compliance with the command of the emperor. The principle of governing the state was propriety, morale or morals in a wider sense. Prince Shōtoku counseled that if superiors are lacking in morals, the common people cannot be ruled; if the common people are lacking in morals, many crimes and delinquencies will occur, however much an endeavor may be made to prevent or punish this. So management by the officials should be based upon propriety and morals. The relationship between the emperor, his officials and the common people was described after the model of ancient China, which was formulated by State Confucianism, but was implanted on the soil of Japan. It seems that this concept of government was closely connected with the abolishment of big clans' ownership of land and people by the Taika Reform.

The thought of esteeming the prestige of the emperor is especially conspicuous in the Constitution of Prine Shōtoku: "Provincial governors and district administrators should not levy exacting taxes on their respective peoples. In a country there should not be two lords; the people should not have two masters. The people of the whole country have the Sovereign as their sole master. The officials appointed to administer the local affairs are all his subjects. How can they levy arbitrary taxes on the people in the manner of public administration?" (Article XII) This article is assumed to bespeak the centralized administration in the territory under the Imperial Court, and to foretell the abolishment of ownership of land and people which occurred later on a nation-wide scale. The power entrusted to officials would be greatly diminished. The phrase "In a country there should not be two lords; the people should not have two masters," is conspicously Japanese, and harbingers the absolutism of the later emperor institution which was characteristic of Japan. Such a way of esteeming the prestige of the emperor can hardly be illustrated in the abundant classical literature of India, although the situation may have been similar in ancient China. In the West, where Christianity was the predominant factor, it may also be difficult to find counterparts, although this point needs further investigation.

When the sovereign of a state preserves the prestige of the chieftain

14. Separate Kalinga Edicts II (D. R. Bhandarkar, *Aśoka*, p. 329).

of the tribes, the monarch who adopts a universal religion comes to be regarded as a manifestation of a god-like being. Thus, there grew a legend that Prince Shōtoku was a re-incarnation of Eshi, the Zen master of the Chinese Tientai sect, and the legend was conveyed to China.[15] Still more popular was the belief that he was an incarnation of Kwannon (*Avalokiteśvara*) Bodhisattva, as shown in a poem by Shinran:

> Bodhisat Avalokita
> Showed his self as Prince Shōtoku.
> He was kind—a father to us—
> And with us walked like [a] mother, too.[16]

In Tibet also, King Songtsan-Gampo was worshiped as an incarnation of Avalokiteśvara Bodhisattva, who is said to have manifested himself in the person of the king.[17] Such legends cannot be found in the vaious tales of Aśoka, nor in the records about Wen-ti. With regard to Western kings it is quite impossible, in view of the dogmas of Christianity. Then why is it that such legends were formed in Japan and Tibet alone? Probably it was due to the fact that in both countries the prestige of the ruler as a chieftain was very strong, and Buddhism developed there in combination with it alone. In Tibet religious prestige was identical with secular prestige. The prestige of the emperor of Japan could find its parallel probably in the person of the czar of Russia. Taking this fact into consideration, some ancient ways of thinking of the Japanese may be examined carefully.

3. Religious and Cultural Policy for the Populace

The universal monarchs who wanted to realize universal laws in politics did not wish to isolate their respective states. King Aśoka sent envoys to such remote countries as Egypt, Syria, Macedonia, Cyrene and Epirus to spread his ideals, and his dynasty received envoys from these countries, as evidenced by literature and inscriptions. The despatch of envoys may possibly have been of political importance, but according to his edicts, it was aimed at conveying the religious and ethical ideals of Aśoka. In

15. Keidō Ito, "A Legend that Prince Shotoku Was a Re-incarnation of Nangaku Eshi and Tosan-Daishi," *Dōgen Zenji Kenkyū* (Tokyo: Daito Shuppansha), vol. I, pp. 319–332.
16. Hymns in Praise of Prince Shotoku, in *The Shinshū Seiten. The Holy Scripture of Shinshū*, compiled and published by the Hompa Hongwanji Mission of Hawaii, Honolulu, Hawaii, 1955, p. 247.
17. E.g., *The Path of the Buddha. Buddhism Interpreted by Buddhists*, ed. by Kenneth W. Morgan (New York: Ronald Press Co., 1956), p. 239.

compliance with his endeavor, the Buddhist Order also sent missionaries to various countries, as is described in chronicles. It is said that in his reign Buddhism spread to Ceylon, Burma and the mountainous districts of the Himalayas. According to his edicts and historical works, Aśoka's activities for interchange of culture were carried on between East and West on a world-wide scale. He was also to open the passage for the first world-wide spread of a universal religion (Buddhism).

In the age of Prince Shōtoku, also, intercourse with Korea was very active. He sent many envoys there and received Koreans who were later naturalized in Japan. Moreover, he sent envoys directly to the mainland of China, as is set forth in the *Chronicles of Japan* (*Nihon-shoki*). Emperor Wen, who founded the empire of the Sui dynasty was Shōtoku's Chinese counterpart. The Sui and Tan dynasties were those of the most international character in the entire long history of China.

King Songtsan-Gampo of Tibet also was a man of international scope. He married two wives, one from China and the other from Nepal, both of whom were Buddhists. Prior to him there was no tradition of literacy, and he sent to India Thonmi-Sambhota and sixteen other students, who learned letters and returned with Buddhist scriptures. Aparting India characters to the Tibetan language, Thonmi-Sambhota invented Tibetan characters and composed eight grammatical works.

In Burma, King Anawrahta was introduced to the Buddhist faith by a monk called the Arahanta Thera, who came from Thaton and enjoyed Anawrahta's confidence. Anawrahta sent envoys to the king of the Mons and asked him to give him the Buddhist scriptures. As his request was contemptuously declined, he sent troops and brought the king, the scriptures and all the monks and nobles to the capital of Pagan. Anawrahta also sent to Ceylon for other texts. Toward the end of his reign Anawrahta made rather unsuccessful attempts to obtain relics from China and Ceylon and commenced the construction of the Shwe Zigon pagoda. His successors, who enjoyed fairly peaceful reigns, finished the work and constructed a thousand other buildings.

Jayavarman VII of Combodia built the surrounding walls of Ankhor-Thom, and expanded his territory. Being himself a devout Mahāyāna Buddhist believer, he introduced conservative Buddhism from Ceylon, and built many temples, monasteries and hospitals.

These monarchs who adopted a universal religion, in order to have it spread (1) built many temples and monasteries, (2) allowed applicants to take order, and gave political and economic protection to monks and nuns, (3) donated land to temples and monasteries, (4) procured scriptures and statues. Such features are common to all these monarchs. Aśoka, moreover, made pilgrimages to the places which were famous for having a connection with Śākya-muni, and built many *stūpas*. For Emperor Wen-ti of the Sui dynasty, these activities were carried on in the form of a revival of Buddhism after the suppression by Emperor Wu-ti of the Northern Chon dynasty. There is a conjecture that Wen-ti began to establish many *stupas*, being stimulated by the legend that King Aśoka built "eighty-four thousand" *stūpas*.

These universal monarchs each had their respective spiritual teachers. For King Aśoka it was Upagupta. Wen-ti revered Chi-i, the Tientai master, and Hui-yuan (523–529) of the Ching-yang temple. Songtsan-Gampo had no specific spiritual teacher, as the introduction of Buddhism was just under way, but King Trisong-Detsan (Khri-sron Ide bcan) (738–786) had Kamala-śīla, the great scholar of India, as his spiritual preceptor. In the case of Prince Shōtoku, it is likely that Eji and Eso, who came from Korea, were his teachers. Constantine had no permanent instructor, but ". . . was at the mercy of any theologian who happened to catch his ear at an opportune moment."[1] At first he was persuaded by Eusebius of Caesarea, afterwards his eulogistic biographer. But later his attitude changed.

In spite of so many similarities in these ancient monarchs there were nevertheless great differences between them.

Prince Shotoku himself lectured on Buddhism, and his "Commentaries on the Three Sutras" (i.e., the *Saddharmapuṇḍarīka-sūtra*, the *Vimalakīrtinirdeśa-sūtra* and the *Śrīmālādevīsiṃhanāda-sūtra*) have been handed down to posterity as authoritative works. Among Japanese classical works these are the oldest ones extant. How can this fact be explained? Was the Prince very enthusiastic about the spread of Buddhism? Or was he highly erudite? How was Prince Shōtoku self-assured that he was qualified to give religious lectures? It is hard to imagine a monarch lecturing on the Bible in the final stage of ancient Rome. Such a practice would have been impossible in the West, for society would not have allowed a monarch to give a sermon or a lecture on the Bible. One could not give a sermon or a lecture on religion in the Medieval West uness one was ordained. How much more so in the countries of Southern Asia, where a king worships monks with great respect from the bottom of his heart, but the monks sit stolidly without showing any sign of salutation! Among an immense number of Buddhist religious works composed in ancient India, there have been preserved hardly any authoritative works composed by kings. But in Japan, such a way of composing works was possible and was actually done. Probably the Chinese practice of kings lecturing on Buddhist scriptures was introduced into, and imitated in, Japan. In China, however, the kings' lectures on Buddhist scriptures were not so significant and not so influential on posterity, whereas in Japan Prince Shōtoku has borne absolute and decisive significance in Japanese Buddhism. There is an as-

1. Kellet, *A Short History*, p. 212.

sumption among scholars that his Three Commentaries are spurious, and that his passage in the *Chronicle of Japan* on Buddhism scriptures is also spurious, but even in that case, the fact that these were later ascribed to him is undeniable. This was an event suggestive and symbolic of the destiny of the Japanese, that religions could develop only by posing as being protected by the prestige of the emperor, although the emperor was not made the head of all Buddhist Orders as the czar was made the head of the Russian Orthodox Church.

In the Roman Empire, the power of Constantine seems to have been chiefly limited to the political and administrative affairs of the Church. "The emperor deemed it his duty to give legal force to the decrees of the council, demanding obedience to them and punishing those who opposed them. . . . The emperor summons the councils; the state guarantees traveling expenses and entertainment; the emperor, or an imperial commissioner, opens the councils and regulates the proceedings; and imperial edict gives legal force to the decrees."[2] It has been said that the emperor assumed a power in ecclesiastical affairs which was ominous for the future of the Church.[3]

The desire to realize universal religions in politics caused rulers to deal with people affectionately and compassionately. Aśoka remarked, "All people are my children." Prince Shōtoku noted, "As the disease of infatuation of the common people is endless, the compassionate measures taken up by bodhisattvas also are endless." "Proper ties are what can save people from poverty and affliction. So Buddhas save living beings in various areas with the Four All-Embracing Virtues, the Four Virtues of Infinite Greatness, and the Six Perfections." Shōtoku's Constitution stressed esteem for the welfare of the people, and its fifth article taught sympathy with suffering people in lawsuits. Hence the common people came to have some significant role in the consciousness of the ruling class. This role could not be wiped out in later history, and this trend might be regarded as the first step in the gradual development of beneficial government.

The monarchs who professed a universal religion carried on humanitarian activities based upon a philanthropic spirit. For example, Aśoka established the post of Officials of Religions (*dharmamahāmātra*) which administered charity and social programs. His imperial court was enthusiastic about donations, and established groves and houses for charity. It showed special consideration to the lonely, destitute and aged. The Shitenno-ji Temple in the city of Osaka, founded by Prince Shōtoku, was famous as an original enterprise of social relief. It was divided into four parts: Kyoden-in (the great central hall to receive training), Hiden-in (a

2. Seeberg, *Doctrines*, I, pp. 217–218.
3. Walker, *Christian Church*, p. 111.

hall to relieve the poor), Ryōbyō-in (a hall to cure the sick free of charge) and Seyaku-in (a hall to dispense medicine also with charge). Prince Shōtoku also built the Compassion House (Hiden-in) in Shitennō-ji Temple to save the poor and destitute. There is a legend that he pitied and helped a starving man at Kataoka Hill. This spirit was inherited by later emperors of Japan.[4]

King Aśoka also endeavored greatly to promote the cultivation of medicinal herbs. "Wherever medicinal herbs, wholesome for men and wholesome for animals, are not found, they have everywhere been caused to be imported and planted. Roots and fruits, wherever they are not found, have been caused to be imported and planted."[5] Prince Shōtoku also, together with his officials, carried on the "hunting of medicinal herbs," and established dispensaries.

Moreover, Aśoka established hospitals for men and even some for animals in various places of his domain. Rulers of countries in Southern India and Greek kings in the West followed his example.[6] Jayavarman VII of Cambodia also issued a decree for establishing charity houses, and built many hospitals. An inscription of his time proclaimed that there were 102 hospitals throughout his kingdom. He seems to have regarded such facilities as being a natural part of a well-ordered state and expended much care and money on them.[7]

In the West, also, it was only with the adoption of a universal religion by monarchs that institutions for the sick were organized. In Christian days no establishments for the relief of the sick were founded until the reign of Constantine. Late in the fourth century Basil founded a leper hospital at Caesarea, and St. Chrysostom established a hospital at Constantinople. A Law of Justinian (527–65 A.D.) recognized *nosocomia* or hospitals among ecclesiastical institutions. The Maison Dieu or Hotel Dieu of Paris is sometimes alleged to be the oldest European hospital, dating from the seventh century.[8] Hence one might say that such institutions appeared rather late in the West. However, there is no difference in this respect, that these institutions were made possible only by the influence of a universal religion.

4. As an example of it, Emperor Daigo devoted his energies to public welfare, and on winter nights he divested himself of his robes and tried to get an idea of the sufferings of the people. He always showed himself benevolent and serene towards the vassals who came to report to him. He always listened attentively to whatever was reported to him.
5. The Fourteen Rock Edicts, II (D. R. Bhandarkar, *Aśoka*, p. 261).
6. The Fourteen Rock Edicts, II.
7. Eliot, *Hinduism*, I, p. 124.
8. Vincent A. Smith, *The Early History of India from 600 B.C. to the Muhammadan Conquest Including the Invasion of Alexander the Great*, 4th ed. (Oxford: The Clarendon Press, 1924), p. 313, n.

VI. CONCLUDING REMARKS

Many similar expressions and descriptions can be found with regard to the images of founders of universal religions; they shared a great deal. But as to ethical problems, early Buddhism and Indian religions of the same period shared similar thoughts not only with Christianity, but also with Greek philosophy on the one hand and Chinese philosophy on the other. Although at the beginning of this chapter, Buddhism and Christianity were seen to be distinctly comparable in view of the lives of those founders, many of their ideas were so universal in scope that it was impractical just to compare the two.

On some problems, such as the theory of Non-Ego, Buddhism shared very little with other religions and philosophies in both the East and West. On the other hand, many Eastern and Western religions and philosophies bear similarities on such concepts as that of the soul. A possible conclusion here is that in some areas, the dichotomy of "East and West" does not hold.

Whether man's nature is good or bad has been controversial[1] in world philosophy but most of the thinkers discussed above agreed on the possibility for human progress. Mencius held that human nature is fundamentally good, asserting that if there is evil in man's conduct it is because his original nature is not developed, or is obscured. Hsun-tzu, another follower of the Confucian school, felt that non-rational impulses are born with the rational. In spite of his difference betwen these two thinkers, they agreed that evil in human conduct can be overcome by knowledge or education. A conviction common to both Greek and Chinese philosophers was that the soul, or the mind, can be ordered and harmonized under the control of reason or some higher principle. In the Christian heterodoxy man's possible salvation from his sins (original and otherwise) through the agency of the Holy Trinity became the central concern. In Buddhist literature one does not find the term "human nature." Buddhism taught the deliverance of all living organisms, not that of human existence alone. The Buddhist teaching implies the possibility that all living beings will be delivered eventually by wisdom and practice. In Mahāyāna Bud-

1. The original goodness of human nature was discussed by Vincent Y. C. Shih, *Philosophy East and West,* XII, No. 4 (Jan. 1963), pp. 328–339.

dhism this principle became more explicitly expressed: "All living beings have Buddha-nature (latently)."[2]

Contrasts, some of which have been already noted, cannot but be noticed when one surveys the literature of universal religions in the period just covered.

Buddhist teachings were to be made known to all men for their enlightenment. This spread of Buddhism was accomplished by the devotion of monks and laymen, and conversion took place only by persuasion. There is no known case of conversion to Buddhism by the use of force. Even King Aśoka, one of the most ardent Buddhist rulers, renounced the use of force and sent out missionaries to persuade men to accept the universal truth of the Buddha's teachings. Western religions (as well as other Eastern ones) sometimes spreas through political force even to the point of war. Relevant here is the fact that the teaching of Confucius did not attain universal proportions at all, whereas Buddhism and Christianity did. This may have been due to an intrinstic idea of Confucianism which admited the hierarchical system of society.

Also, when the Buddha said to his converts, "Come (*ehi*), be my disciple," he told them to expect to get rid of suffering; i.e., to stamp out suffering by stamping out cravings. In an opposite manner, when Jesus said to his disciples, "Come, follow Me," he expected them to glory in their sufferings, to seek for the perfection of their character through suffering.

A further area of difference lies in the conception of the self. In Greek thought the self was usually identified with reason. It was assumed that reason not only separated man from animal, but also related man to the divine. This presents a striking contrast to the Indian concept of self which sees the unity of life as the common ground of man, animal, and even plants. In Western thought, man came to value his rational soul quite highly, while in India various concepts of metaphysical soul substance (not considered rational or otherwise) evolved, the less subtle of which were a point of departure for the Buddha's *anātman* theory.

By way of transition to some reflections on the Middle Ages (in the next chapter), a brief look at concepts of the universe as such may be in order. Whereby previously in this chapter interest has focused on the universal as that term applies to the widespread incidence of similar ideas, the focus will now be shifted to cosmology. In doing this, a corner is being turned to another time if mention is not made that the ways of nature did not matter essentially to the early Buddhists. The Buddha was mainly concerned with matters of human conduct. As for their attitude toward the natural world, monks of early Buddhism observed strictly the attitude

2. This was especially stressed in the *Mahāparinirvāṇa-sūtra* of Mahāyāna. This is available in two Chinese versions alone nowadays.

of non-attachment. Their reference to the structure of the natural world was rather exceptional and casual, as shown in the following passage: "This great earth is established on water, the water on wind, and the wind rests upon space. And at such a time as the mighty winds blow, the waters are shaken by the mighty winds as they blow, and by the moving water the earth is shaken."[3]

Strange to say, Empedocles spoke of elements (though some were undoubtedly thought of differently by him than by Buddhists) in the same order as early Buddhists: "Come now, I will first tell yot of (the sun) the beginning, (the elements) from which all the things we now look upon came forth into view: Earth, and the sea with many waves, and damp Air, and the Titan Aether which clasps the circle all around."[4] The world in which human beings live, then (the world of desire), is made up of four elements—earth, water, heat, and wind—according to the scriptures of both Theravāda and Mahāyāna. The Tantric theories added space and intelligence to the list of elements, making six.

Because the philosophers of the Middle Ages were affected in the West by Aristotle and the East by Buddhism, a comparative (including contrastive) glance at these two cosmologies may be in order.

To begin with there is an area of considerable contrast. With regard to the structure of the universe (i.e., the number of the worlds), there is a great difference between the Greek and Buddhist assumptions. The Greek assumption was very simple. According to Aristotle, the universe is divided into two halves of opposite character—"the one terrestrial, and the other celestial."[5] However, there is only one world for Aristotle.[6] On the other hand, the idea of the universe maintained by later Buddhist dogmatists of the *Abhidharma* was highly complicated.[7] According to them, the world consists of the realm of desire (*kāmadhātu*) and the first heaven of the realm of form (*rūpadhātu*), including a sun and a moon which move. One thousand times one thousand times one thousand worlds makes one billion worlds, which constitute the domain of a Buddha and there are many domains of other Buddhas as well.

In spite of such a tremendous difference between Aristotle and Buddhists concerning the framework of the universe, there are many similarities in terms of the concept of one world. According to Aristotle, "In the middle of the whole lies the earth—a solid sphere, but in extent a relatively small portion of the world." In addition he believed there to

3. *Mahāparinibbāna-suttanta* III, 13. *Dīgha-nikāya*, vol. II, p. 107.
4. Empedocles, fragment 38.
5. E. Zeller, *Aristotle and the Earlier Peripatetics*, translated by F. C. Costelloe and J. H. Muirhead, 2 vols. (New York: Russell and Russell, 1962), vol. I, p. 472.
6. *Ibid.*, p. 485.
7. The theory is elaborated in the 11th volume (Hsuang-tsang's version) of the *Abhidharmokośa-śāstra*, etc.

be a lower world of spherical form.[8] In the Buddhist theory, underneath the earth there is a spherical layer of metal, and underneath the latter is a spherical layer of water, and still underneath at the bottom there is the spherical layer of air. Even here Aristotle's assumption was somewhat similar. "The hollows on the surface of the earth are filled with water, the upper surface of which is spherical. Around the water and the earth are hollow spheres—first of air, then of fire."[9] Aristotle thought that heaven is also of spherical form. This idea, though maintained in the Vedic and Hindu literature also, disappeared in Buddhist cosmography.

According to Aristotle, all the heavenly bodies seem daily to move from east to west, but seven of them move in longer periods of very unequal lengths in the opposite direction (i.e., from west to east) around the earth.[10] The Buddhists also thought that the sun and the moon move, although their orbits were not clearly mentioned.

For Aristotle, the heavenly bodies were not dead masses but living beings; he conceived that there must be as many "souls" to preside over their motions as there are spheres.[11] This idea was held by Buddhists as well as Hindus. So, a common ground of cosmological discussion is seen as bequeathed to the thinkers of both Buddhist and Christian traditions in the Middle Ages.

Both Buddhism and Christianity, as well as other religions, admitted damnation and (the existence of) hells. These are further areas that are not forgotten in medieval times. In Buddhism the hells were numerous, and were usually divided into hot and cold ones. Since life in hell eventually comes to an end the Buddhist conception was more like the purgatory of the Catholic Church than like any eternal hell. On the other hand, poetry drew all kinds of pictures of the horrors of the infernal world.[12] There was a "voyage to the lower world in poetry among the Orpheans, and another of the same name among the Pythagoreans; the Buddhistic literature is fairly overrun with innumerable moral-pointing descriptions of the descents of holy men into the infernal regions and of the horrors there observed by them."[13]

A creation myth also evolved in the later phases of early Buddhism and a highly developed form of creation-myth was set forth in a Buddhist *sūtra*: "Now at that time, all had become one world of water, dark, and of darkness that makes blind. No moon nor sun appeared, no stars were seen, nor constellations, neither was night manifest nor day, neither

8. E. Zeller, *op. cit.*, pp. 487–489.
9. *Ibid.*
10. *Ibid.*, pp. 491–492.
11. *Ibid.*, pp. 495–496.
12. Plato, *Republic* X, 614. Cf. C. Scherman, *Materials for a History of the Indian Literature of Visions*, 1892 (*The Realm of Yama*).
13. H. Oldenberg, *Ancient India*, p. 96.

months nor half months, neither years nor seasons, neither female nor male, Beings were reckoned just as beings only. And to those beings, sooner or later after a long time, earth with its savour was spread out in the waters. Even as a scum forms on the surface of boiled milky rice that is cooling, so did the earth appear."[14] The process of genesis is set forth in full detail[15] elsewhere for those who would like to compare it to the Book of Genesis in the Bible. Conspicuous in Buddhism, of course, will be the absence of a creator.

14. *Dīgha-nikāya* XXVII, Aggañña-suttanta 11.
15. *Dīgha-nikāya,* vol. III, p. 85 f.

CHAPTER FOUR

Features of Medieval Thought

I. GENERAL THOUGHTS ON DEVELOPMENTS IN THE MIDDLE AGES

A. Introduction

THE "medieval thought" in this chapter is drawn from approximately the period after the rise of universal religions, especially Christianity, and the beginning of what is considered by philosophers as "modern thought." Considered first are similar situations or socio-political conditions to which philosophical and religious thought of this period is related.

In the West the period between the origination of Christianity and the rise of modern thought is very broadly divided into the Hellenistic Age and the Middle Ages. Roughly speaking, the former was rather cosmopolitan, whereas in the latter the focus became centered on single cultural areas of individual races or otherwise commonly oriented peoples. Each of these latter groups then developed its own distinctive features while having in common their position under the authority of the Catholic Church.

In the same way, India of the corresponding period can be roughly divided into a cosmopolitan period and a culture-area-oriented period.[1] The former is the period of the Parthian and Kusana rules, and the latter is the post-Gupta period. The Gupta period seems to have been transitional, i.e., it possessed some features of both characters. In China the same period may be divided into the pre-Sung age and the time from the Sung dynasty on, the former being highly cosmopolitan and the latter particularly esteeming the culture and institutions of Chinese origin. Chi-

1. Walter Ruben, in *Indisches Mittelalter* (Istanbul: Robert Anhegger, 1944), reviewed the culture of medieval India in comparison with the medieval West. Helmuth von Glasenapp's work (*Buddhismus und Gottesidee.* Die buddhistischen Lehren von den überweltlichen Wesen und Mächten und ihre religionsgeschectlichen Parallellen. Akademie der Wissenschaften und der Literatur. Abhandlungen der Geistes- und sozialwissenschaftlichen Klasse, Jahrgang 1954. Nr. 8 Verlag der Akademie der Wissenschaften und der Literatur in Mainz in Kommission bei Franz Steiner Verlag GMBH [Wiesbaden, 1954]) gives us suggestions and materials concerning medieval thought. Herein will be found some results of my own independent studies on these times.

nese pride in their own race was not greatly emphasized in the pre-Sung period due to the influence of Buddhism, but it revived conspicuously in later days.[2] In Japan cultures of the Asuka and Nara[3] periods also had a cosmopolitan flavor, while that of the Kamakura period and onward followed the indigenous culture-oriented trend of preceding periods. During the former period, the Japanese, or at least their intellectual leaders, imitated the culture of the continent. But from the Kamakura period on, their attitude became rather nationalistic, and even among Buddhists staunch nationalists appeared such as Nichiren (1222–82).[4]

The question now arises, considering the rough general similarities, why such distinct characters evolved in the history of each people. It is likely that this was partly caused by the invasions of barbarians and the decline of ancient, universal empires in East and West. Throughout the continent of Eurasia, in both East and West, the collapse of the centralized imperial states of antiquity which ruled wide areas was caused by the influx of Hun invaders and other barbarian tribes. Kingdoms of ancient China also were often threatened by these same invaders. The subsequent decline of the Chinese Empire affected Japanese leaders toward increasing independence from Chinese ways.[5]

India was invaded by Huns (*Hūṇa*) from the northwest in the middle

2. The Chinese insisted on the greatness and superiority of their own race. The racial pride and haughtiness of the Chinese were established on this point. They discriminated foreign countries from their own country, calling their land "Chung-kuo" (the central or superior country), but believing that other countries belonged to their own country.

   However, the Chinese monks who traveled to India to look for the doctrines of Buddhism claimed that China was only a "remote country" before the splendor of Indian culture, and used the term "Chung-kuo" instead for India. Cf. *The Biography of Fa-hien*, Taisho, vol. 50, p. 470 b–c.

   Later on though, as Buddhism spread in China, Chinese Buddhists also came to call their country "Chung-hua" or "Chung-hsia." (*Ch'an-yüan-chu-ch'üan-chi-tu-hsü*, Zengen Shosen shū Tojo, ed. by Hakuju Ui [Tokyo: Iwanami], pt. 1, pp. 5, 29, 83) This tendency was naturally connected with nationalism.
3. When Nara was made the capital of Japan in 710 A.D., the "configuration of hills and waters was considered to be auspicious and essential for the site of a national capital. The idea is of Chinese origin, formulated in the theory of 'Air and Waters.' " (Masaharu Anesaki, *History of Japanese Religion with Special Reference to the Social and Moral Life of the Nation* [London: Kegan Paul, Trench, Trübner and Co., 1930], p. 86, n)
4. Masaharu Anesaki, *Nichiren. The Buddhist Prophet* (Cambridge: Harvard University Press, 1916).
5. In the reign of Emperor Uda (reigned 887–897) the Japanese embassy to T'ang (China) was suspended. Emperor Daigo (reigned 897–930) made Japanese civilization independent of China. From this time on Japan's own literature began. The four early Japanese official chronicles were compiled after the pattern of the *Shu-king*, the writings of Han, by Ssse Ma Chien, but later chronicles, the *Montoku Jitsuroku* and *Sandai Jitsuroku*, differ from the preceding four. China as the model for historical compilation was minimized, and historical works of especially Japanese style came into existence. The *Eiga Monogatari* and the *Ōkagami* took further steps.

of the fifth century; they attacked the Gupta kingdom (the then unified state of India), in 455 A.D. The Gupta dynasty, one of the most flourishing throughout the long history of India, declined after 480 A.D. Around 500 A.D., Toramāṇa, the Hun king, was enthroned. Hun rule lasted for half a century in some parts of India. Later, King Harśa (in the first half of the seventh century) unified India again, ruling a wide area. But after his death Indian unity was again destroyed, and the land was ruled under many major and minor dynasties. Political chaos continued until Kutubuddin Aibak, the Mohammedan king, unified northern India in 1206 A.D.

In the West, Attila, the Hun chieftain, having crossed the Danube River in 441 A.D., invaded Italy in 452 A.D. Attila had much in common with Toramana in that both were cruel destroyers of civilization. A short time later an invasion by the Vandals occurred and the western Roman Empire was destroyed in 476 A.D.

With the advent of these successful barbarian invasions came the decline of universal empires in both East and West and much past glory disappeared. In China such destruction was lamented as follows: ". . . the last Emperor—so they say—fled from Saragh (Loyang) because of the famine, and his palace and walled city were set on fire. . . . So Saragh is no more, Ngap (the great city of Yeh, further north) no more!"[6] With these words, a Sogdian merchant writing back to his partner in Samarkand, recorded the destruction of the Chinese capital—an imposing city of 600,000—and the shameful flight of the Son of Heaven before the oncoming Huns. The year was 311, and it marks a turning point in Chinese history comparable to the sacking of Rome by the Goths in 410.

St. Jerome's letters express the feelings produced by the fall of the Roman Empire very vividly. In 396 he wrote, "I shudder when I think of the catastrophes of our time. For twenty years and more the blood of Romans has been shed daily between Constantinople and the Julian Alps, Scythia, Thrace, Macedonia, Dacia, Thessaly, Achaia, Epirus, Dalmatia, the Pannonias—each and all of these have been sacked and pillaged and plundered by Goths and Sarmatians, Quadi and Alans, Huns and Vandals and Marchmen. . . . The Roman world is falling." Seventeen years later, three years after the sacking of Rome, he again reported, "The world sinks into ruin: yes! but shameful to say our sins still live and flourish. The renowned city, the capital of the Roman Empire, is swallowed up in one tremendous fire; and there is no part of the earth where Romans are not in exile. Churches once held sacred are now but heaps of dust and ashes."[7]

6. Arthur F. Wright, *Buddhism in Chinese History* (Stanford, Calif: Stanford University Press, 1959), p. 42.
7. Bertrand Russell, *A History of Western Philosophy* (New York: Simon & Schuster, 1945), pp. 343–344.

Despite her small geographical area, comparable reports are found in Japan when rule by the nobility disappeared at the hands of a victoriously emergent warrior class. The Empress, having become a nun, said, "I was a daughter of Premier Taira, and the mother of the former Emperor. All the world was in my hand. But now, alas! I have nobody to rely on. . . . The Empress, carrying the former Emperor (who was a child) in her hand, sank into the sea. The sight I cannot forget, even if I try to forget it. The navy soldiers were clamoring and shouting. Even the shouting and groaning in the flame of the Avīci hell would not surpass this cruel and terrible scene!"[8]

Perhaps partly nurtured by the insecurity of the times, the attention of much of the world's populace shifted from their place in the state to their inner, spiritual welfare. This was the period during which universal religions spread widely and became established among such peoples. Buddhism became a universal religion beyond the range of India and Ceylon and extended its influence into Central Asia, China, then to Tibet, Mongolia, Korea and Japan on the one hand, and the South Asian countries on the other. As Western political leaders, picking up the pieces of the Roman empire, recognized the advantages of allying with the power of the Church, Christianity took a firm hold in Britain, the present France, Spain, Scotland and Ireland.

Buddhism had to change, when transported from one country into another, because of differences in climate, temperament, living conditions, traditional values, etc., between the old and new societies. In China this remodelling of Buddhist practice and teaching was accomplished in the Sui-T'ang dynasties, and in Japan during the period of transition from the Heian to the Kamakura periods.

The weakening of the Han imperial line was largely responsible for the successful spread of Buddhism in China. Han Confucianism had made the emperor a cosmic pivot, but in later Han days he often became in fact the puppet of rival factions, a pitiful pawn in a rapacious struggle for power. The great estates were economically self-sufficient, centers of commerce and manufacturing as well as of farming. They commanded hordes of dependents who did their farm work, kept their sumptuous houses, and could be armed for defense or to carry out their masters' vendettas.[9] Many peasants chose to become dependents of powerful landlords and work as laborers or sharecroppers on large estates,[10] signalling the complete breakdown of Han authority and permitting the spread of Buddhism throughout the Chinese world.[11]

8. *Heike Monogatari*, the section "Ōhara Gokō."
9. Wright, *Buddhism in Chinese History*, p. 18.
10. *Ibid.*, p. 19.
11. *Ibid.*, pp. 27–28. The Confucian ideal of the perfect man came under severe criticism

The advance of early Christianity had already met with a degree of success in the days of the "universal" Roman Empire. Early Christianity originally flourished in the empire's commercial centers, "largely because there were synagogues, or at least Jewish quarters, in them, and the Christian message could make its best appeal in places where the Jewish religion was already known. But when the orthodox Jewish communities rejected the new faith, and refused to harbor it, independent Christian communities sprang up among the tradesmen and working people of the great cities and towns, first among the Greek-speaking citizens and then among those who spoke other languages."[12]

In China Taoist communities may have served to spread certain Buddhist symbols and cults, thus playing a role somewhat analogous to that of the Jewish communities which at first helped propagate early Christianity in the Roman world.[13]

---

during this period. As for your "princely man" (*chun-tzu*), it was asked of the Confucians, how does he differ from a louse living in a pair of trousers? (*Ibid.*, p. 29)

12. John Boyer Noss, *Man's Religions* (New York: Macmillan Co., 1949), p. 612.
13. Wright, *Buddhism in Chinese History*, p. 33.

B. Supremacy of Religion

1. Otherworldliness

In India the preference for isolation from the secular world in favor of a totally religious life was displayed very early, several hundred years before the Christian era, as has to an extent already been discussed. In the period from the Christian era to the beginning of the modern era, however, this same otherworldly tendency (otherworldly primarily in an ethical sense) came to be very conspicuous in China and neighboring lands such as Japan, on one side, and the West on the other. Discussion will center in this section, then, on these geographical areas.

In the China of early centuries A.D., the confidence of the declining aristocrats was shaken and could not be restored. Men began to seek something immutable in a time of disaster, or perhaps an escape into nature from an inhuman scene they found intolerable. A characteristic southern Buddhism developed in this period of disunion in China. Among the literati,[1] the early optimism reflected in classical Chinese literature yielded to a generally more pessimistic view of life during and after the Han dynasty (from about the second century B.C.). The experience of early Chinese buoyancy and the onset of a more pessimistic mood sensitized the Chinese to Buddhism, making them more receptive to this foreign religion in the third and fourth centuries than they had been earlier or were to be much later.[2]

Gradually more and more Chinese came to subscribe to Buddhism, a religion at first alien to them; many even eventually believed that conformity to the Buddhist way of celibacy and ritual acts of bodily mortification rendered a higher service to their parents than the Confucian ideals of preservation of the body and perpetuation of the family. This could not help but influence the Neo-Confucian traditions to follow.[3]

1. Much of the discussion of Buddhist ideas was carried on in Neo-Taoism's favored mode: the dialogue or colloquy known as ch'ing-t'an (literally "Pure Talk"). Wright, *Buddhism in Chinese History*, p. 45.
2. W. T. DeBary, "Buddhism in Chinese Tradition," a paper read at the International Council for Philosophy and Humanistic Studies, Mexico, Sept. 23–24, 1963.
3. Wei-ming Tu, "The Creative Tension between Jen and Li," *Philosophy East and West*, vol. XVIII, nos. 1–2 (Jan.–April, 1968), p. 32.

Because of many of the aforementioned cultural developments the otherworldly attitudes of some thinkers took on more and more of a metaphysical context.[4] Some Buddhist masters in China emphasized the terrible aspects of human life. Shan-tao, explaining the human predicament in his parable of the White Path, showed man beset on all sides by evil beasts, poisonous vermin and vicious ruffians, symbolizing the sense organs, consciousness, and the various psychic and physical constituents of the ordinary human self. The White Path is "comparable to the pure aspiration for rebirth in the Pure Land which arises in the midst of the passions of greed and anger."[5] Lin-chi, the Zen master, emphasized the emptiness of this life: "Followers of the Way, do not acknowledge this dream-like, illusory world, for sooner or later death will come. . . . Seeking only the barest minimum of food, make do with it; spend your time in the shabbiest of garments and go to visit a good teacher."[6]

Monks were enjoined to spend a calm and quiet life, having secluded themselves from secular activities. Master T'ien-t'ai said, "There are four things in which people ply. Monks in monasteries should not engage in these things. These four are: first, worldly life; second, worldly customs; third, various techniques, e.g., medicines, fortune-telling, sculpture, painting, chess, calligraphy, sorcery, etc.; forth, sciences, e.g., study on scriptures, discussion and debate."[7] This ideal was inherited by the T'ien-t'ai sect of China and the Tendai sect of Japan. Even such a man of letters as Monk Kenkō[8] in medieval Japan admired such a life.

As an escape from worldly life a peculiar kind of practice appeared in medieval Japan. The worship of local mountain deities in medieval Japan became very much influenced by the popular Buddhism that was founded on the forms of worship of a variety of Shingon Buddhism known as "Shugendō" or "The Way of the mountain anchorites" or "Yamabushi," a special sect syncretic of Buddhism and Shintoism. Well-known examples were Mt. Katsuragi and Kimbusen in Yamato, Hakusan in Kaga, Futara-san at Nikkō in Shimotsuke, and Gassan, Yudono-san and Haguro-san, the Three Mountains of Dewa. In these places the influence of the Yamabushi made itself felt in very early days.

4. In early Japanese Buddhism the belief in Maitreya, a future Buddha but one still belonging to this world, was predominant. But in eighth-century Japan an increase in statues of Amida, a Buddha of a world hereafter, overtook and passed the incidence of Maitreya statues. This is parallel to changes in China evidenced by a predominance of Amida statues over those of Śākyamuni and Maitreya in the Yun-kang Cave sculptures. Out of such a spiritual atmosphere Pure Land Buddhism took firm root among the common folk of both countries.
5. *Taisho*, XXXVII, p. 273 a.
6. *Taisho*, XLVII, p. 498 a.
7. *Mo-ho-chi-kuan*, vol. 4, a (Taisho, vol. 46, pp. 36 a, 42 c–43 a). Cf. Taisho, vol. 46, p. 265 b.
8. *Tsurezuregusa*, paragraph 75.

In the medieval West there were many traces of otherworldliness. The homeless life was highly esteemed and praised by such Christian fathers as St. Basil, who said, "We consider this human life of ours to be of no value whatsoever; not do we think or call anything absolutely good which is profitable to us while we are here—but we run forward in hope, and act in everything with a view to another life."[9]

Jerome invited his fellow Christians to join the order, exhorting them, "What do you, Brother, in secular life, who art greater than the world? How long shall the shadows of roofs oppress you? How long shall the prison-house of smoky cities enclose you? Believe me, I know not how much more light I gaze upon. It is well, having cast off the burden of the body, to fly off to the pure effulgence of the sky. Do you fear poverty? Christ calls the poor blessed. Do you dread labour? No athlete is crowned without sweat. Do you think of diet? Faith fears not hunger. Do you fear to lay your body, wasted with fasting, on the naked ground? The Lord will lie down with you. Do you shrink from the undressed hair of a neglected head? Your head is Christ. Are you fearful of the boundless extent of the solitude? You mentally walk in paradise. As often as you ascend thither in contemplation, you will not be in Solitude."[10] Augustine, in his *City of God*, "comforted himself and the people of the Empire with the thought that the destruction of our earthly cities [Rome, etc.] was a matter of no importance, since there was a spiritual city of God triumphant here and in the world to come, which was destined to endure for ever."[11]

Such an attitude persisted among some religious people in both East and West throughout the whole medieval age. "There was a period, approximately between 400 and 1500 A.D., when a similar world-and-life-negation seemed widespread throughout Europe." For example, "Medieval London had an anchorite or anchoress (the equivalent of a *Sadhu*) attached to practically every one of its numerous parish churches, almost one per street. Some were walled-in in an 'ankerhold,' others itinerants."[12] The anchorite way of living remained as an ideal into much later days,[13]

9. *A Monument to St. Augustine: essays on some aspects of his thought written in commemoration of his 15th centenary*, by M. C. D'Arcy etc. (London: Sheed & Wood, 1930), p. 133.
10. Jerome, Ep. ad Heliodorum (Op. ed. Erasm. I, f. 2), cited from T. W. Rhys Davids, *Lectures on the Origin and Growth of Religion as Illustrated by Some Points in the History of Indian Buddhism*, second edition (London: Williams and Norgate, 1891), p. 169.
11. Radhakrishnan, *Eastern Religions and Western Thought* (New York: Oxford University Press, 1959), pp. 70–71.
12. A. C. Bouquet in *Radhakrishnan: Comparative Studies in Philosophy Presented in Honour of His Sixtieth Birthday* (London: George Allen & Unwin, 1951), p. 154, n.
13. "The typical Christian attitude in this matter is beautifully set forth in Bunyan's *The Pilgrim's Progress*. In this text-book of Christian faith the hero of the story, significantly named Christian, discovers that he is living in a city which is doomed to imminent destruction. Filled with alarm, he wonders what he shall do and encounters a man named Evangelist, who counsels him to fly. Immediately Christian

and still has a large following as manifested in contemporary Catholic monasticism. When Catholicism spread in Japan in the sixteenth and seventeenth centuries, the faith of Kirishitan people was called "simple and sincere, they believed in the future destinies, Paraiso or Inferno, just as taught by the Church, as if these were tangible realities at hand."[14]

Even in Islam, originally a religion much concerned with things of this world, an otherworldly tendency developed. Some companions of the prophet Mohammed lived in isolation practicing self-mortification and meditation. About the end of the eighth century the name Sufi came to be applied to these ascetics. The Sufi ideal of life was renunciation, self-abnegation and poverty. They practiced fasting and communion with God. Al-Ghazali (1058–1111), thought to have been born as a great renewer of the faith of Islam, renounced his successful teaching career for a time in order also to seek in the desert for union with God.

In any of the above-discussed cultures giving up one's home was likely to inflict hardship upon one's family. This was to be of no concern, however, and men were counselled to deny their families in favor of their own salvation. "St. Jerome writes to the priest Heliodorus bidding him break away from all contact with the world and leave his mother's house, adding these words; 'Should your little nephew hang on your neck, pay no regard to him. Should your mother, with ashes on her head and garments rent, show you the breasts at which she nursed you, heed her not. Should your father prostrate himself on the threshold, trample him underfoot and go your way.' "[15] In medieval Japan a disciple asked Master Dōgen, "My mother is very old, and I am the only son. If I should become a recluse, she cannot live for even one day. What shall I do?" The master replied, "If you are surely aspiring for the Way of Buddha, you should take [the Buddhist] orders, having prepared for the livelihood of your mother. However, if it is difficult, you should take orders immediately. Even if your old mother should starve to death, her merit of letting her only son enter the Way of Buddha is very great, isn't it? Her merit will cause her to attain Enlightenment in an after-life in the future."[16]

---

begins to run away. His wife and children, frightened at his precipitate departure, 'began to cry after him to return', but Christian 'put his fingers in his ears, and ran on crying "Life! Life! Eternal Life!" '. His friends and neighbours tried to stop him, but Christian would not so much as even pause for a moment to tell them the doom that was upon the city and bid them to fly as well. He was thinking only of himself, of his own salvation. So far as the city was concerned, it might disappear together with his wife and children, and all his friends and neighbours, but there was no need to worry if only he were saved." (Radhakrishnan, *Eastern Religions and Western Thought*, p. 71)

14. M. Anesaki, *History of Japanese Religion*, p. 251.
15. Radhakrishnan, *Eastern Religions and Western Thought*, p. 72.
16. *Shōbō-Genzō-Zuimonki*, vol. III, *Dōgen Zenji Zenshū*, ed. by Doshu Okubo (Tokyo: Shunjūsha, 1930), p. 34.

Otherworldliness, when adopted in the extreme, may even lead to the denial of one's own existence. The more suggestible and overly zealous of believers in otherworldly doctrine have sometimes ended their own lives. The extreme type of self-sacrifice for the sake of rebirth into the Pure Land took the form of self-immolation and drowing.[17]

Throughout the history of Buddhist China, it was common practice for a monk to burn his thumb, his fingers, or even his whole body, as a form of merit in emulation of the supreme sacrifice of the Bodhisattva Bhaiṣajyarāja, the deity of medicine in Mahāyāna Buddhism. Each of the three great Buddhist biographical series (e.g., *The Biographies Liang Dynasty*) devoted one section to biographies of Chinese monks who had burned themselves to death, or otherwise committed suicide as the supreme sacrifice. This section is entitled "Those who gave up their lives,"[18] and it contains detailed stories of hundreds of such suicides. Usually a monk would announce the date of his self-destruction, and on that day would tie his whole body in oiled cloth, light the faggot pyre and his own body with a torch in his hand, and go on mumbling the sacred names of the Buddhas until he was completely overpowered by the flames. Very often such human sacrifices were witnessed by thousands of Buddhists whose plaintive wailings would accompany the slow burning of the pious monk. It is little wonder that many people committed suicide in order to be born in the Pure Land among the followers of Shan-tao who taught the doctrine "Loathe this defiled world and desire to be reborn in the Pure Land." Such a custom was imitated by some Japanese Buddhists in the medieval age. Some burnt themselves, and others set sail on the ocean never to return, for the purpose of reaching the Pure Land (*Fudaraku, Poṭalaka* in Sanskrit) of Kannon Bodhisattva, which was supposed to be located in the southern sea. Such an attitude was not unknown in the medieval West either. For instance, the Catharis "regarded matter as essentially evil, and believed that for the virtuous there is no resurrection of the body. . . . They saw no objection to suicide."[19] However their opinion was banned as heresy, and it did not prevail in the West.

The otherworldly tendency in Buddhism was severely criticized by Kumārila in India, and by Fu-i in China. Kumārila[20] (650–700) said that Buddhism was destructive to the social order (sacrifices, etc.) set up by Brahmanism and practiced from the immemorable past. Su-i complained, "The myriad functionaries darkly brood on the crimes of their past lives and vainly seek to make provision (through religious faith and

17. Examples are found in such works of biographies of Pure Land believers as the *Jūi-ōjō-den, Sangai-ōjō-ki*, and *Honchō-shinshū-ōjō-den.*
18. Hu Shih, *The Indianization of China*, pp. 227–228.
19. Russell, *History of Western Philosophy*, p. 447.
20. In *Ślokavārttika* and *Tantravārttika.*

works) for future felicity. They talk wildly of heavens and hells. They revile things Chinese."[21] Such preoccupations, he thought, were demoralizing, unworthy of members of a Chinese government of a Chinese empire. The Buddhist doctrines of heaven and hell and retribution beyond the grave he considered to have terrorized and deluded the masses. Because of Buddhism, he believed that, no longer contented with their lot and in their quest for salvation, they had become contemptuous of temporal law. Attacks upon Buddhism to the same effect were continued by Neo-Confucianists of the Sung Period (and beyond) and some centuries later in the Tokugawa period by Confucianists and scholars of national lore in Japan.

So otherworldliness may be called common to both the religion of the East and that of the West. But there was a difference between these two kinds of otherworldliness. Buddhism indeed, at least in its original form, was more frankly eudaemonistic than Christianity. Traditionally the motive suggested to the Christian for renouncing the world has been love of God, whereas the Buddha would have one make a similar renunciation with an eye primarily to one's own spiritual advantage. And this action was, at the same time, regarded as advantageous to others also. According to Buddhism the self that one loves is not only a higher self, but a self which is related to, and inseparable from, other men.

2. The Establishment of Religious Authority

That religions were spread through individual persons is undoubtedly true, but that common people needed spiritual leaders is also a situation that has consistently been evident in both East and West. Śaṅkara said, "As here in this world hungry children sit round their mother, so sit all beings round the fire-sacrifice (brought by him, who has the knowledge of Brahmin)."[1] As pointed out in an earlier chapter, the teachings of Jesus that inspired all later Christianity were in their inception directed toward the common, laboring, almost slave class of his time. The suffering and heavily burdened were counseled to come to him for help.[2] Naturally the later leaders of the Church, considered to be the instruments of God on earth, were accorded the highest respect. An attitude of complete devotion to specific persons was manifested by medieval Catholics toward the saints; such reverence is comparable to that of the Hindus toward the

21. Arthur F. Wright, "Fu I and the Rejection of Buddhism," in *Journal of the History of Ideas*, 12 (1951), 34–47.
1. Śaṅkara's interpretation on *Chānd. Up.* V, 24, 4.
2. Cf. Romans 8:19.

guru. In medieval Japan it can be noticed in the worship of the founders and chief abbots of respective sects.

The admiration of believers for their spiritual leaders gave rise to religious orders, which, in turn, further increased the prestige of the religious leaders. The orders were given lands and were extended special support by kings and feudal lords. The lands owned by religious orders were tax-exempt. Moreover, the right of asylum was honored and anyone who had fled into the precincts of the orders could not be apprehended. A chain of these phenomena could be seen in the West, India, China, Tibet, and Japan, although in India these privileges were infringed upon by the Mohammedan invasions and by the persecutions of anti-Buddhist kings.

When the world was in grave difficulties, the monks of the West undertook to build a new, more secure world. This could be done in two ways: first, by building monasteries in safe places, such as in mountainous areas and on islands, where they could get away from the roughness of the barbarians; secondly, by planting among the barbarians themselves monasteries from which the light of Christianity could shine in the surrounding darkness.

In Eastern countries monasticism had existed among Buddhists and Jains several hundred years before the Christian era. However, a Buddhist monasticism which was similar to that in the West occurred at nearly the same period in Zen Buddhism.

The period of preaching by Bodhidharma, the founder of Chinese Zen Buddhism, was c. 470–532 A.D. He inherited the Buddhism of the Gupta period. Until this period, Indian monasteries claimed to accommodate monks "from the four directions." This practice was propagated by early Zen Buddhists of China. However, with Tao-hsin (580–651), the fourth patriarch, a remarkable change in the way of life occurred in the Zen order. He resided on Double Peak Mountain for thirty years, and did not go to any other place, but around him more than five hundred people lived constantly. The tradition of a great number of monks living together became customary since then. This custom may be considered a Buddhist transformation of a traditional Chinese way of life, for from the end of the civil war period until the Han dynasty Chinese recluses lived together in groups on mountains and had their own ideal of life. This seems to have been inherited by Zen Buddhists.

The establishment of group life in monasteries by Tao-hsin can be compared to the founding of the first Christian monastery by Pachomius, an Egyptian, in about 315 or 320 A.D. In the monasteries derived from Pachomius, "the monks did much work, chiefly agricultural, instead of spending the whole of their time resisting the temptations of the flesh."[3]

3. Russell, *A History of Western Philosophy*, p. 376.

This method is identical with the Zen revolution in the life of Buddhist monasteries.

Zen Buddhists in mountain retreats had to work to sustain themselves. They often came to engage in economical production, not for the sake of selling their produce on the market, but only for self-sufficiency; however it was none the less commercial production. Formerly Buddhist monks had refrained from worldly labor and had only practiced meditation without working physically. This attitude has still been preserved throughout Eastern countries except China and Japan because the Book of Disciplines (*Vinaya*) in traditional Buddhism forbade monks to dig in the ground or to cut grasses and trees.[4] This provision was also common to Jainism. It was only from Tao-hsin's time on that Zen priests came to cultivate fields attached to their temples in order to secure food. Master Po-chang (720–814) said that to dig in the ground and to cut grasses and trees did not necessarily cause sins.[5] His motto, "If one did not work a day, one should not eat on that day," has become a favorite among Zen Buddhists. Master Po-chang developed rules for Zen monasteries in detail, which became the standard of later Zen monasteries. They might be easily compared with the rules of St. Benedict.

It was St. Benedict (c. 480–542), in Italy, who adapted monasticism to meet the needs of the new world of the West. When the barbarians were disturbing the country, he provided a place of safety for religious refugees by building his monastery high on a mountain cliff. At that place, called Monte Casino, a way of living was perpetuated similar to that of Tao-hsin and other Zen masters. And like Po-chang's for the Eastern counterparts, the rules of St. Benedict became the charter of Western monasticism.

Among these rules there was a new requirement that monks should stay at home. This stricture was no doubt a reaction against the hermit monks who had sometimes made a nuisance of themselves by wandering about like tramps. The monks of St. Benedict could not leave without special permission. For that reason the monastery had to provide, as far as possible, everything necessary for life: a garden, a mill, fields and rivers, a well, a bakery, and a kitchen. The monks had to do all their own work: farming, cutting down trees, cooking and serving, and all the necessary clerical and workshop labor.[6] Their day was divided among handwork, prayer and meditation by oneself, songs and readings together,

4. *Pācittiya* 10 and 11.
5. *Collected Saying of Master Po-chang* (The Chinese text in *Kokuyaku Zengaku Taisei*, vol. 9 [Tokyo: Nishōdō, 1929], p. 6).
6. Cf. F. Cabral in *Encyclopaedia of Religion and Ethics*, ed. by James Hastings (Edinburgh: T. & T. Clark, 1908), vol. 8, p. 792.

study, meals and sleep. The monks also took in children, taught school and copied books.[7]

In Zen monasteries monks also kept gardens, fields, and rice paddies. Not only meditation, religious services, and reading, but also such manual labor as sweeping and cooking, as well as less menial but equally time-consuming activities such as receiving guests, etc., were required of the monks. In Japan Zen temples have been well known, especially for cleanliness, due to the labor of the monks. Monks of some Japanese sects went so far as to engage in such economic activities as constructing roads, rest houses, hospitals, ponds, harbors, developing new fields, and so on. Such kinds of work were approved as rendering service to others, which was claimed to be the essence of Mahāyāna. For laymen all sorts of productive work was encouraged, although slaying animals, selling wines, weapons, and so on, were occasionally held to be controversial.

With the parallel development of monastic life in East and West also came many parallels in religious services and ceremonial behavior. Clerical celibacy, tonsure, confession, altar rituals including incense, flowers, lights and singing, veneration of relics, the use of rosary and bells, have been observed since those days among Roman Catholicism, Buddhism, as well as some Hindu sects.

With this emphasis on religious action, ceremonialism, and labor came an attendant marked decline in scholarship and learning in the Middle Ages. Gregory I was no friend to secular learning, and "St. Francis once said that a great scholar, when he joined the Order, ought in some sort to resign even his learning, in order that, having stripped himself of such a possession he might offer himself to the arms of the Crucified."[8] As a further example, among medieval English Franciscans, ignorance of the clergy (*ignorantia sacerdotum*) has been described as an undeniable phenomenon.[9]

The characteristic of being against secular scholarship, though sometimes overemphasized as such, was certainly present also among Zen Bud-

7. The copying of books had to be done by hand in the Medieval Ages. The monks gave the most loving care to their work and made letters with colored inks of exquisite loveliness. The first letter of the page often had a picture inside. This was called an "illuminated initial." In India and south Asiatic countries pictures representing religious scenes were added to the first sheet of manuscripts of scriptures. In Japan manuscripts of scriptures illustrated with beautiful pictures were made in the Medieval Ages.

On the other hand, throughout the Medieval Ages the attitude of hostility to pagan literature was held. Cf. Russell, *A History of Western Philosophy*, pp. 342–343.

8. A. G. Little, *Franciscan Papers. Lists and Documents*, 1943, p. 55. Cited from S. Rad= hakrishnan, *The Principal Upaniṣads*, (London: George Allen and Unwin, 1953) p. 222. Cf. "Paul, you are mad; your great learning is turning you mad." (Acts 26:24)
9. A. G. Little, *Studies in English Franciscan History* (Manchester: University Press, 1917), pp. 158–162.

dhists of the same period. Master Dōgen, as one example among many, ordered his disciples: "You should give up useless things such as *belle lettres*, poems and so on. You should solely concentrate on practicing the Way of Buddha."[10] "You should not read books of the other sects, secular books and so on. If you feel like reading, collected works of Zen masters are allowed."[11] However, it does seem that this prohibition was enforced more leniently in the East than in the West, and especially among Japanese Buddhist priests, who maintained a higher level of scholarship than Chinese priests due to the fact that persecutions and wars caused Chinese Buddhist scholarship to be interrupted and uneven. In Japan internal wars involved monasteries and temples very little, thereby allowing them to carry on any scholarly activities which from time to time might catch the monks' interest.

The emphasis away from scholarly activities in favor of labor and silent meditation in some cases gave way almost completely to practical considerations related to their labors. This ushered in a low ebb for monasticism in both East and West. A partial explanation of why the Buddhist monasteries in India were sacked to the extent that Buddhism there never recovered afterwards was that very early Buddhist monasteries acquired huge amounts of land and money. Their wealth began in the form of donations of land for monasteries and money for perpetuating the order. The money which was donated by their believers was invested in guilds of various kinds, from which the monasteries received interest regularly, as is evidenced in inscriptions.

In Brahmin orthodoxy every sin could be atoned for by the performance of a penance, and these penances were an important source of profit for the Brahmins much in the same way as dispensations were to the Roman Catholic Church during the Middle Ages in Europe. Religious gifts to Brahmins (frequently in monetary form) were greatly recommended as penances. In medieval Japan feudal lords who often engaged in warfare and killing donated lands and funds to Buddhist temples as expiation for their sins.

In the medieval West the Church came to be especially wealthy. People had long been giving lands to the Church and the pope had to manage the farming of these lands. Clerks were retained to look after the accounts and slaves who had been donated with the lands did the manual labor. The Church did not free them, but at least tried to treat them well.

However, not all religious persons in the Middle Ages accepted this material aggrandisement of established religious organizations as a salutary development. Some Western monks were so disgusted with what happened to Christianity after the world became Christian that they fled

10. *Shōbo-Genzō-Zuimonki*, vol. I, in *Dōgen Zenji Zenshū*, p. 7.
11. *Ibid.*, vol. II, in *Dōgen Zenji Zenshū*, p. 18.

to the desert to get away from the world entirely. Similarly, in Japan at the end of the Heian period and the beginning of the Kamakura period the established religious orders supported by the royal court and feudal knights became so corrupt that many monks fled from the orders. Some lived as recluses in forests; others preached their own faiths as individuals among the people.

3. Approach to Common People

WITH the rise of their standard of living and the gradual expansion of the scope of freedom among common people in the later Middle Ages, higher levels of culture began to spread among them, and at the same time became transformed to be more acceptable to them. Various aspects of culture underwent such metamorphoses. In the domain of philosophical literature, leaders both East and West came to give up classical languages and adopt languages of the common people. Especially some who were not exactly the most orthodox churchmen related their religious beliefs or experiences in the vernacular. Meister Eckhart (1260–1327), Tauler (died in 1361), and Ruysbroeck (c. 1293–1381), for instance, related their mystical experiences in popular languages.

The same tendency appeared in Japan also and at nearly the same period with Buddhist leaders of new movements in the Kamakura period. The last vow by St. Hōnen was written in 1212 in Japanese; Master Dōgen, who introduced Sōtō Zen into Japan, wrote many works in Japanese rather than in Chinese as had been the previous custom.

In the India of this period religious and philosophical works of various kinds were written not only in Sanskrit (the language of the literati), but also in vernacular dialects. Saints in Southern India, for example, left their religious songs in Tamil and Telugu; leaders of Sahajiya Buddhism in Bengal composed their works in Bengali. After the Mohammedan invasions the tendency especially arose to write in modern Indian languages of the common people. Such religious leaders of the common people as Visoba Khecar (at the end of the thirteenth century), Rāmānanda (c. 1299–1411), and Kabīr (fourteenth century), deliberately avoided classical languages and wrote only in contemporary languages. In this respect of popularization these Indian leaders were in advance of Western mystics who still partially used Latin, or Japanese Buddhist leaders of nearly the same period who used the classical Chinese language for official and formal writing.

In China it seems that a definite turning point in the historical development is not so clear and distinct, but by investigating the style of literary works carefully, one can find a change corresponding remarkably to that in the above-mentioned cultures. Just as the style of Neo-Confucian works of the Sung period differed greatly from that of previous Confucian works, so a change of style occurred in Zen works of the Sung period and afterwards. *The Blue Cliff Writings* (*Pi-yen lu, Hekigan-roku*) was compiled by K'o-chin (1063–1135), the *Gateless Gate* (*Wu-men-kuan, Mumonkan*) by Wumen (1182–1260), and *Composedness* (*Tsung-jung-lu, Shoyo-roku*) by Wansung (1166–1247); these authors belong to the same period as the German mystics or leaders of new religious movements in Japan. These works were immediately conveyed to Japan and easily accepted there, probably because the social and historical background for the rise and spread of such texts was nearly the same in both countries.

The Chinese Zen works in and after the Sung period shared two features. First, both show some traces of the diction and vocabulary of modern vernaculars, even if not those of Peking and Mandarin. In this respect they are similar to the works of German mystics, reformers of Indian religion (prior to the advent of Western civilization), and Japanese religious reformers of the Kamakura period; their style and vocabulary are closely related to modern languages. Because of this fact alone it is natural that modern Chinese people have faithfully preserved Zen Buddhism although they have forsaken other sects. Second, sayings of early Zen works are rather rational and logical and occasionally even systematic in the way of discussion. The logical context of their sayings is clear, whereas sayings in later Zen works are very difficult to follow, almost enigmatic, as in the case of *kōans* or *mondōs*, and upon casual first reading they do not easily convey their purport.

A similar change occurred in India also. The Tantric religion, which is said to have arisen in the sixth or seventh century, nearly corresponds to the development of Zen Buddhism in China in terms of chronology. It incorporated the dialect and vocabulary of common people, especially the Bengalis. Moreover, Tantricism made much use of enigmatic expressions. Moreover just as collections of words of Zen masters came to have as much authority in China as the original Indian Buddhist scriptures, so also later Indians came to assert that revelation (*śruti*) is twofold, Vedic and Tantric. In fact, as popular knowledge and belief, Tantric ideas have practically superseded the Vedas over a large part of India.[1] More specifically, Tantric Buddhists hold that their own literature should constitute the fourth section of the scriptures (*Vidyādhara-piṭaka*) in addition to the former three, admitted by both Hīnayāna and Mahāyāna Buddhists.[2]

1. A. S. Geden in *Encyclopaedia of Religion and Ethics*, edited by James Hastings (Edinburgh, T. & T. Clark, 1908), vol. XII, p. 193 a.
2. Or *Dhāraṇīpiṭaka*. Louis de La Vallée Poussin in *Encyclopaedia of Religion and Ethics*, vol. XII, p. 197 a.

An allegorical moral drama of medieval India, the *Prabodhacandrodaya* (*The Moonrise of Intelligence*), composed at the end of the eleventh century by Kṛṣṇa-miśra, extols the spirit of universal tolerance and love of mankind, saying, "Even a Śūdra deserves respect who knows and does his duty well," and "Noble-minded men regard the whole world as their kin."[3] The value of true friendship and of the interrelatedness of good men are often dwelt on. The Tantras, as well, were generous and broad in their sympathies and recognized no distinction of caste or sex, "for men and women equally compose humankind." In addition they forbade the practice of *Satī*.[4]

In the *Subhāṣitaratnakośa*, a Sanskrit anthology compiled in northern Bengal by a Buddhist scholar named Vidyākara, there are poems of village and field. They differ markedly from the verses of the courtly and priestly tradition, which minimized the life of common people. An anonymous author wrote of cattle grazing after the rains and one can almost smell the mud. In the same work, Yogeśvara (850–900 A.D.), a Bengali, writes with great sympathy for the poor and sad. Śatānanda, Vāgura, and Vākpatirāja, who lived shortly before or during the ninth century, belong to the same school. The majority of Yogeśvara's verses are of the rustic and realistic type: "The children of the poor come to a house and put their little hands to the door, leaning forward. Their voices are hushed with shame, but they are hungry. They look with half-glances at him who eats within."[5] The poverty of common people was often sung of in the *Subhāṣitaratnakośa*.[6] One poem describes the children chasing fish in the rain in a flooded paddy field. Pigeons, shying clear of the scarecrows, are picking seeds from the corner of the field. In winter the farmhouse is gay with the songs of women pounding rice.[7] The style is simple. "The double and multiple meanings, the subtle use of rhetorical figures, the utterly untranslatable suggestiveness (*dhvani*)—these elements are generally lacking."[8]

This change of style exactly corresponds to that from the court poems of the Heian nobility to the poems and songs by people in general in the medieval ages of Japan. Novels by Heian court ladies dealt solely with the life of the nobles, whereas those in the late medieval ages came to relate

3. Macdonell, *Lectures on Comparative Religion* (University of Calcutta, 1925), p. 71.
4. Mentioned earlier as *suttee*, widow suicide, A. S. Geden in *Encyclopaedia of Religion and Ethics*, vol. XII, p. 193 b.
5. The *Subhāṣitaratnakośa*, compiled by Vidyākara, edited by D. D. Kosambi and V. V. Gokhale, with an introduction by D. D. Kosambi. Harvard Oriental Series, vol. 42 (Cambridge: Harvard University Press, 1957), v. 1320.
6. Daniel H. H. Ingalls, "A Sanskrit Poetry of Village and Field: Yogeśvara and His Fellow Poets," in *Journal of the American Oriental Society*, vol. 74, no. 3 (1954), p. 128.
7. *Subhāṣitaratnakośa*, vv. 226, 264. Ingalls, *ibid.*, p. 120.
8. *Ibid.*, p. 122.

the life of the common people. The pictures of scrolls in the Heian period extolled the life of nobles and glorified huge temples, but early in the medieval ages some scrolls appeared, such as "Playing Scenes of Birds and Animals" (*Chōjū Giga*) ascribed to Bishop Toba, in which the demeanor of priests was sarcastically painted in the figures of birds and animals. Such comical descriptions of priests as animals and birds appeared at nearly the same time in the medieval West also.

As a further approach to their populace, some religious authorities became more lenient towards women. For example, St. Jerome was not as strict as earlier monks had been in his attitude toward women. Some noble-women of Rome came to his monastery at Bethlehem and established a nunnery nearby. They helped him with his translations, and he is also known to have taught women. In Japan as well, a similar change occurred in this area. In the Heian period there had been established some holy places or large temples where women were not allowed. Master Dōgen denounced this situation, saying, "In the country of Japan there is a laughing stock. What is claimed to be a limited holy place or an asylum (place for practice) of Mahāyāna, does not allow nuns and women to come in. This bad custom has been existing for many years, and yet people do not know it is a bad thing. . . . Was there any convention in the lifetime of Lord Buddha which nuns and women did not attend? . . . Those would-be holy places, on the other hand, welcome kings, premiers, ministers, and officials! What a corruption!"[9]

The progression throughout this long span of history was, as has been seen in this section, then, a constant movement toward the populace as a whole.

9. The chapter of "Raihai Tokuzui" in the *Shōbō Genzō*, included in *Dōgen Zenji Zenshū*, pp. 44–51. Master Dōgen said such a custom did not exist either in India or in China (*Ibid.*, p. 48).

II. TWO TYPES OF RELIGION

A. Introductory Words

Both Buddhism and Christianity have contained two types of religious thought and practice, the one characterized by self-reliance or self-power (*jiriki* in Japanese), the other marked by a dependence on grace or other power (*tariki* in Japanese). The former is a way of "self-saving," whereas the latter resorts to "saving of another." In each tradition, these two concepts are discernable, and it is misleading to identify any one religion with one type only.[1]

Buddhism, especially Southern or so-called Hīnayāna (*Theravāda*) Buddhism that has been largely referred to in previous chapters, is typically a religious tradition which in teaching and practice encourages self-reliance. In the teachings of the Buddha, "Work out your own salvation" is very much emphasized, and monks who leave the household life to accept monastic discipline and follow the Path by resolutely pursuing meditative exercises may be seen as pursuing the way of self-reliance or self-power. In the Christian tradition, as previously observed, there is comparable teaching and practice of monastic disciplines. But Christianity is more generally regarded as a religion of grace, emphasizing a dependence on other power. This way of grace was strongly favored by St. Augustine against the contrary teaching of Pelagius who advocated the exercise of human will power, teaching more in the direction of self-

1. As Paul Tillich observed, following his visit to Japan: "The establishment of types . . . is always a dubious enterprise. Types are logical ideals for the sake of a discerning understanding; they do not exist in time and space, and in reality we find only a mixture of types in every particular example. But it is not this fact alone which makes typologies questionable. It is above all the spatial character of typological thinking; types stand beside each other and seem to have no interrelation. They seem to be static, leaving the dynamics to the individual things, and the individual things, movements, situations, persons (e.g., each of us) resist the attempt to be subordinated to a definite type. Yet types are not necessarily static; there are tensions in every type which drive it beyond itself." (Paul Tillich, *Christianity and the Encounter of the World Religions* [New York and London: Columbia University Press, 1963], pp. 54–55)

reliance. St. Augustine's view prevailed, however, and has had a profound influence on Christian thought and practice ever since (though certain Pelagian tendencies remained nevertheless). At the time of the Reformation, Martin Luther and others criticized Catholic practice and teaching as amounting to a dependence on "works" of faith rather than an unquestioning belief in divine grace (other power). Luther's doctrine of "justification by faith alone" put Protestant Christianity completely in the category of dependence on other power. The same might also be said of Catholics who rely entirely on the Christian sacraments for the furtherence of their religious life.

To the extent that Pelagius' ideas remained, however, the two types of religion, the self-reliant type and the type which emphasizes other help, are apparently in tense combination in the Christian tradition.

Some Christian churches have been described as semi-Pelagian in their doctrine and practice. Much the same can be said of Buddhism, especially in its Mahāyāna form. The Mahāyāna form came, in course of time, to embrace a number of different schools and sects along with new scriptures and new interpretations of the Buddhist faith in the schools or sects of the Buddhist Pure Land tradition. A remarkable development was the appearance of the type or religion which emphasized dependence on other power comparable with the Christian religion of grace. But within the Mahāyāna tradition there was also a continuance of monastic disciplines along with teachings which stressed resolution in the Path (meditation, etc.) in much the same way as did southern Buddhism.

In Buddhism also, then, the two types of religion were found side by side, though in most cases the proportion of followers of the self-help doctrine was greater than those who sought release through an appeal to other power. But Buddhism also had patterns of thought which might be described as mixed. Sōtō Zen Buddhism is a case in point. Zen exercises may seem to demand the same self-effort, the same resolute striving as the monastic disciplines of southern Buddhism. Yet Master Dōgen counselled his novices to eschew worry and entrust themselves to the "home" of Buddha, promising that everything then will be "conducted by Buddha" —advice which suggests some dependence on other power.

With the change of focus in the Middle Ages to the salvation of the common man, there naturally arose a shift of emphasis (with corresponding change in religious ideas) to the belief that all have been destined for salvation from the very beginning. This was interpreted in various ways. Some said that man is the imperfect creature he is simply to serve as an example of the compassion of some savior to guide him to a paradise. Others claimed that man is saved from the beginning and only his ignorance leads him to believe otherwise. Others held their own versions of what seemed to be views that man need not strive after his own salvation but can rely either on what is inherent in him or on the inevitable intervention of a divine helper. The following sections will discuss some of these approaches to the problem of man's ultimate release: (1) the compassion and love of the divine helper and those who aspire to be like him; (2) the various conceptions of the roles played by these saints and bodhisattvas in helping men; (3) the occurrence of "vicarious sacrifice" by savior figures for the sake of lesser lives; and (4) the belief that man incurs sin which results in a need for "grace"; hence, what "grace" is variously thought to consist of and bring about.

It is equally natural that some men would be eager to find some sort of verification in their own experience of their progress toward their aim. Consequently some of these men sought to reach the level of mentality that the founders of their chosen religions had professed. Accordingly, various meditational practices were utilized and various interpretations of the experiences reached thereby were also offered. In subsequent sections, then, meditation schools are examined as to: the object of contemplation in meditation; some problems of interpreting the resulting experience(s) of meditation; and the practical significance of meditation.

B. The Themes of Compassion and Love

1. Compassion-Love Doctrine

In India when the conservative Buddhist Order (so-called *Hīnayāna*) became a large organization with huge endowments, some of the monks no longer felt obliged to render much service to the common people. It was thought by some that the monks of conservative Buddhism were very complacent and self-righteous and that, being fond of solitude, they despised the common people. This somewhat negative view of the Buddhism of the Elders is supportable by certain interpretations of verses from the Buddhist canon, such as: "When the learned man drives away vanity by earnestness, he, the wise, climbing the terraced heights of wisdom, looks down upon the fools, serene he looks upon the toiling crowd, as one that stands on a mountain looks down upon them that stand upon the plain."[1]

By way of protest against this assumedly Hīnayāna attitude in India, some religious leaders advocated a new form of Buddhism, which was called Mahāyāna (the Great Vehicle). These monks were in close contact with the common people and felt their needs. They vehemently attacked the complacent and self-righteous attitude of conservative Buddhists. This situation seems to be similar to the rise of Christianity against Stoicism, Epicureanism, and other ideological systems. On the other hand, just as St. Paul was opposed by Judaic conservatives, so Mahāyāna was opposed by conservative Buddhists.

1. *Dhammapada* 28. As a similar comment, Lucretius said: "It may be sweet when on the great sea the winds trouble its waters to behold from land another's deep distress; not that it is a pleasure and delight that any should be afflicted, but because it is sweet to see from what evils you are yourself exempt. It may be sweet also to look upon the mighty struggles of war arrayed along the plains without sharing yourself in the danger. But nothing is more sweet than to hold the lofty and serene positions, well fortified by the learning of the wise, from which you may look down upon others, and see them wandering all abroad, and going astray in their search for the path of life, see the contest among them of intellect, of rivalry, of birth, the striving night and day with surpassing effort to struggle up to the summit of power, and be masters of the world. O miserable minds of men! O blinded breasts! in what darkness of life and in how great dangers is passed this term of life, whatever its duration!" (Lucretius, Book II ad init. "Suave mari magno," Munro's version, cited from T. W. Rhys Davids, *Indian Buddhism*, pp. 165–166)

In Greater Vehicle (*Mahāyāna*) Buddhism the virtue of compassion[2] was more heavily stressed than in Hīnayāna, although Mahāyānists are quick to admit that a compassion motif was not entirely absent in Hīnayāna doctrine either. But Mahāyānists claimed that compassion was a chief characteristic of Mahāyāna. "To those whose intelligence is low and whose mind is quiet the Way of Śrāvaka (*Hīnayāna*) is taught to have them get out of suffering. To those whose intelligence is slightly keener and clearer and who hanker for the teaching of the Interdependent Origination the Way of Pratyekabuddha (an ascetic who practices by himself) is preached. To those whose intelligence is excellent and who aspire to benefit living beings out of Great Compassion the Way of Bodhisattva (*Mahāyāna*) is taught."[3] "Great Compassion" was regarded as the essence of Buddhism by Mahāyānists who noted: "The Buddha-Mind is nothing but Great Compassion."[4]

When Buddhism was introduced into China, the Taoist term for immortals, "*chen-jen*," served as a translation of the Buddhist word "*Arhat*," "the worthy one", which is tantamount to "the fully enlightened one." "*Wu-wei*," "non-action," was used to render the Buddhist term for ultimate release, "*Nirvāṇa*." Because men of non-action had been praised by Taoists, early Chinese Buddhists thought this a natural phrase by which to translate the idea of the man of *Nirvāṇa*. When Mahāyāna teachings began to come to the fore in China, these earlier concepts of the ideal men were criticized as being aloof from and lacking compassion for the common man.

The Mahāyāna protest against Hīnayāna is somewhat akin to the change in the history of Judeo-Christian thought; both occurred at roughly the same time. It is occasionally said that Christ abrogated the Mosaic Law and stressed love, although the love motif was not entirely absent from Mosaic Law in Judaism. John especially had much effect on later Christianity by simplifying Christ's doctrine to faith in God and love for one's neighbor. According to John, faith and love are awakened in man's heart by the spirit; and true love is the practical, active brotherly love which works according to the commandments of God.[5] Among the

2. The Sanskrit word for "compassion" is *maitrī or karuṇā* or *dayā*. *Maitrī* can be translated as "friendliness" also, because the word derives from the word "*mitra*" meaning "friend." The word "*karuṇā*" was translated into Chinese with the word meaning "sorrow." In Sanskrit literature also, the sorrow of a lady who has no prospect of seeing her lover again is expressed with the word "*karuṇā*." (*Sāhityadarpaṇa* III, 213)
3. The Chin version of the *Buddhāvataṃsaka-sūtra*, vol. 27; *The Book on the Hua-yen Five Teachings* (*Kegon Gokyō-sho*) ed. by Kannō, vol. 1, p. 50 b. In the *Lotus Sūtra* a similar thought is found. (*yo vīryavantaḥ sadā maitracitta bhaventi maitrīm iha dīrgharātaṃ*, Chapter 2, ed. by Ogihara and Tsuchida [Tokyo: Seigo-Kenkyūkai, 1935], p. 93; cf. p. 248)
4. *Amitāyurdhyāna-sūtra* (*Taisho Tripiṭaka*, vol. 12, p. 343 c).
5. II John.

very early apostolic fathers love continued to hold this high position. Ignatius (flourished c. 110 A.D.), for example, perpetuated the doctrine that faith (the beginning of Christian life) and love (the culmination of same) are divine when united. Further, all other elements of a Christian life are consequences of these two. For him, love was the way drawing up to God. For Polycarp, another apostolic father, the Christian who loves his neighbor is far from sin. Whereby in later Christianity faith came to be the main requisite for man's salvation, the apostolic fathers held good works and exhibiting love for one's neighbor to also be a great aid. What seems clear at this point is that both Mahāyāna and Christianity laid greater stress on love than previous religions and philosophies and that both movements appeared in nearly the same period. The compassion of the Buddha, like that of the ideal Christian, was to be offered to everyone equally. In the Lotus Sūtra Buddha's compassion is compared with rain: "All those grasses, shrubs, and trees are vivified by the cloud that both refreshes the thirsty earth and waters the herbs. In the same way . . . I preach with ever the same voice, constantly taking enlightenment as my text. For this is equal for all; no partiality is in it, neither hatred nor affection." And again, "I recreate the whole world like a cloud shedding its water without distinction; I have the same feeling for respectable people as for the low."[6]

God was, of course, the ideal of compassion and love in the Christianity of this period. Indeed it is sometimes said "God is love." Clement, one of the most famous Alexandrian fathers, compared God to the physician who can help those who work with him to attain health. Those who work with God, Clement thought, are given the compassionate gift of his salvation. God's greatest compassionate act, for any Christian, would certainly be his assumption of human form for the sake of mankind's salvation. St. Paul says, "You know the grace of Our Lord Jesus Christ, that though he was rich, yet for your sake he became poor, so that by his poverty you might become rich."[7]

At least as late in time as St. Augustine, love was given a supreme place, even above belief, in the life of a Christian seeking his soul's salvation. Augustine asserted, "When it is asked whether anyone is a good man, it is not asked what he believes or hopes, but what he loves. . . . He who does not love, believes in vain, even though the things which he believes are true."[8]

6. The *Saddharmapuṇḍarīka-sūtra* V, vv. 6, 11, 21, 24. Cf. "Society, as we have constituted it, will have no place for me, has none to offer; but Nature, whose sweet rains fall on unjust and just alike, will have clefts in the rocks where I may hide, and secret valleys in whose silence I may weep undisturbed." (Oscar Wilde, *De Profundis* [London: Methuen and Co., 1905], pp. 150–151)
7. II Corinthians 8:9.
8. *Enchiridion ad Laurentium* 28.117.

One of the illustrations of God's compassionate nature that is a great favorite among Christians of all times is the parable of the prodigal son, from the New Testament.[9] At nearly the same time that this parable was being recorded (first or second century A.D.) another prodigal son was being described in the Mahāyāna Buddhist scripture the Lotus Sutra. In the Buddhist parable of the prodigal son, Buddha is represented as the good, wealthy father who means well towards his sons, the human beings. As the story goes, a rich man has an only son, who roams about in foreign lands for fifty years. While the father grows richer and richer, and has become a great man, the son lives in foreign parts, poor and in reduced circumstances. At last as a beggar, he returns to his home, where his father has been yearning for him all the while. The beggar comes to the house of his father, whom, however, he does not recognize as that great man, who, like a king surrounded by his retinue, sits before his mansion. Seeing the pomp and splendor, he flees for fear that he, a ragged beggar, might be ill-treated. His father, however, recognizes him at once and sends out servants to bring the beggar in. Trembling and shaking with fear, he is dragged in and falls unconscious. Then his father commands that he be released. Gladly the beggar gets up and leaving the house, he goes to the poor section of town.

Presently the rich man decides on a plan whereby he may win the confidence of his son. He sends workmen to hire him for the humblest work in his house. As time goes by, he sometimes chats with his son and gradually becomes intimate with him. In this way twenty years pass without the father making himself known. Not until the hour of his death does he call all his relatives together and announce that the beggar, who has now become a trusted servant, is his own son. Then he makes him the heir to all his wealth. Of course, the rich man is Buddha; The son who was lost and is found again represents human beings, whom Buddha, as the wise father, gradually draws to himself, and finally appoints as his fortunate heirs.[10]

The parable of the prodigal son was related in later India by early Vedāntins such as Dravida (c. 550 A.D.), Bhartṛprapanca (c. 550 A.D.) and Sundarapāndya (c. 600 A.D.), with whom the father represented the highest self (*paramātman*) and the son the individual self (*jivātman*).[11] The story was interpreted as representing the renunion of individual souls with the highest one. In a *Mahātmya* on Kāncīpuram (i.e., a book depicting

9. Luke 15:11–32.
10. Chapter IV of the *Lotus Sūtra, Sacred Books of the East*, ed. by F. Max Müller (Oxford University Press, 1879–1927), 21, p. 98 f.; with slight changes from M. Winternitz, *A History of Indian Literature* (University of Calcutta, 1933), vol. II, pp. 298–299.
11. Mentioned in Sureśvara's *Bṛhadāraṇyakopaniṣadbhāṣyavārttika*, etc. Discussed in H. Nakamura, *Vedānta Tetsugaku no Hatten* (Tokyo: Iwanami Shoten, 1955).

the "glory" of the holy place of Viṣṇu and recording the legends associated with his great temple), there is another version[12] of the prodigal son parable in even more detail than in the fragments of early Vedāntists.

The ideal of compassion-love evokes an altruistic attitude. Of course, all Mahāyānists did not engage in purely altruistic deeds. But some stressed especially the altruistic spirit. For instance, Śāntideva (7th century) made these vows:

By the merit which I have ever acquired,
By good deeds, may I bring to all beings
Relief from all their sufferings!
I desire to serve as medicine, doctor and nurse
To all the sick as long as their sickness lasts.
I desire to be a protector to those who need protection,
A guide to those who wander in the desert,
And a ship, a landing-stage and a bridge
To those who seek the shore.
A lamp to those who need a lamp,
A couch to those who need a couch,
A slave to all beings who need a slave."[13]

and:

"I must destroy others' suffering, for it hurts like one's own pain;
I must do good to others, as they are beings like myself."[14]

Santideva's poems are often compared to *The Imitation of Christ*, traditionally ascribed to Thomas a Kempis. The latter work praises love, saying that there is nothing sweeter than love, nothing stronger, nothing better in heaven nor in earth; that love feels no burden and takes account of no labor. However, whereas it is said that this book bears the mark of the distrust of scholasticism spread by the modern school of devotion (*devotio moderna*),[15] Santideva still, at least to some extent, adhered to traditional scholarship.[16]

As an interesting paralled to this, love came to be emphasized in China even among anti-Buddhist scholars. For Neo-Confucianists the natural affections constituted the basis of human relations. The perfection of virtue—humanity or benevolence—which Neo-Confucianists like

12. Rudolf Otto, *India's Religion of Grace and Christianity Compared and Contrasted*, translated from the German by Frank Hugh Foster (New York: Macmillan, 1930), pp. 136–141.
13. *Bodhicaryāvatāra* III, 6, 7, 17, 18. Winternitz, *Indian Literature*, II, p. 371.
14. Winternitz, *ibid.*, p. 372.
15. Etienne Gilson, *History of Christian Philosophy in the Middle Ages* (New York: Random House, 1955), p. 446.
16. Śāntideva wrote a book called *Śikṣāsamuccaya* which is full of quotations from scriptures.

Ch'eng Hao (1032–85) and Chu Hsi (1130–1200) raised to the level of a cosmic principle, was often defined as "love" (*ai*).[17]

It is often reported that Buddhism has softened the rough warrior races of Tibet and Mongolia, and nearly effaced all traces of their original brutality. In Japan also, according to statistics, cases of murder or assault are relatively rare in districts where Buddhist influence is strong.

The attitude of compassion also motivates one to esteem highly the natural disposition of man. Japanese Buddhism tends to be most conspicuous in that respect. Even Buddhist ideas were preached with a close reference to matters of love, and sexual love is not considered in Japan to be incompatible with religious love.

Though Zen Buddhism in China does not seem to have emphasized the ideas of compassion (there is not a single reference made to the word "compassion" in the well-known scriptures of Chinese Zen Buddhism), after Zen Buddhism was brought into Japan, deeds of benvolence began to be accorded a high degree of moral importance.

The spirit of tolerance and compassion engendered by Buddhist ideals made deep hatred, even toward sinners, a near non-reality. Hardly any cruel punishment existed in times when Buddhism flourished. Such a situation was reported by Chinese pilgrims to ancient India and this fact also holds true in most of the Buddhist countries of Southern Asia. In Japan of the Heian period, a time when Buddhism was actively practiced, capital punishment was not practiced for a period of nearly three hundred and fifty years.[18]

17. Cf. Wm. T. DeBary et al., *Sources of Chinese Tradition* (New York: Columbia University Press, 1960), pp. 530–531, 556–557, 559.
18. However, the esteem of the compassion and love did not go together with the esteem of faith in a parallel way. In the West the Christian practice of love suffered restriction in some cases. The teaching "Love your enemies" was not put in practice in relation to persons holding opinions different from those of the ruling Church. Even the Christian God is not supposed to be kind to non-believers. St. Augustine believed that while God was merciful to mere moral wickedness, He could not extend forgiveness for error of dogma. The chief weapon for persecution was excommunication and the chief excuse for excommunication was "heresy."

    In India intolerance of other faiths also characterized some of the Vaiṣṇava writers. The rival creeds were depicted with malice. Some Vaiṣṇava writings exhibit great intolerance of the Jaina and Buddhist faiths. (N. K. Devaraja, *Hinduism and Christianity* [Bombay: Asia Publishing House, 1969], pp. 101–103) Some rulers who maintained Śaiva faith persecuted Jain monks, to the extent that some were boiled in hot water.

    These facts involve a difficult problem of incompatibility of faith and tolerance in some cases.

2. The Role of Saints and Bodhisattvas

ALONG with the development of a compassion motif in Mahāyāna Buddhism, the worship of Bodhisattvas came into existence. "Bodhisattva" had originally been the name used for the Buddha before his enlightenment (that is, before he became Buddha, the enlightened one); but later anyone who aspired to the ideals of enlightenment and willingly rendered help to suffering creatures was called a "Bodhisattva." In nearly the same period that the latter usage came into vogue, the worship of saints appeared in the West. Because the saints themselves had lived such impeccable lives, their prayers were supposed to have more weight with God. Bodhisattvas also, being so compassionate, were supposed to extend hands of help willingly. The practice of the Bodhisattva required vigor and endeavor. In Tibetan, the word "Bodhisattva" is translated as "heroic being" (*byan-chub sems-dpaḥ*). The Catholics also have made a practice of canonizing only those who have exhibited virtues in *gradu heroico*.

It is sometimes said that in the case of Mahāyāna Buddhism the historic Buddha (*Śākyamuni*) fades into the background and Amida and other Buddhas and Bodhisattvas virtually take his place. In some forms of Christianity there has been comparable preference for the saints over Christ. Believers often sought the aid of the Virgin Mary or St. Anthony when it might be expected that they would appeal directly to Christ. In both cases the explanation may be given that such forms of belief do not mean that faith in the founder is absent, it is included or implicit in the appeal to the saints and bodhisattvas.

Buddhist art of the earliest period represented Buddha by an empty place or a symbol (such as a wheel, a Bodhi tree, footprints, etc.), which was only later replaced by a divine figure of the Apollo type. In the art of Gandhāra the nimbus is also given to gods and kings. It is said that Christian art adopted that symbol in the fourth century, although in early Christianity there were no visual representations of Christ either. Later on however, women and monks especially adored Christ and saintlike images, and compared iconoclasts to the Roman soldiers who crucified Christ.

Perhaps the use of symbols for Christian worship first became popular among eighth-century Greek congregations. Regarding symbolic representations, Pseudo Dionysius the Areopagite thought that in order to imitate Christ one's mind needs to be refreshed by "recollection of the most holy works of God."[1]

In Mahāyāna Buddhism the worship of images, in addition to the existing worship of *stūpas*, came to be strongly encouraged. A Mahāyāna

1. *De Ecclesiastica Hierarchia* 3.3.

scripture urged the making of symbols for worshipping Bodhisattvas as follows: "All who caused jewel images to be made and dedicated, adorned with the thirty-two characteristic signs, reached enlightenment. Others who had images of Sugatas (Buddhas) made of the seven precious substances, of copper or brass, have all of them reached enlightenment. Those who ordered beautiful statues of Sugatas to be made of lead, iron, clay or plaster have '&c' (a sacred symbol). Those who made images (of the Sugatas) on painted walls, with complete limbs and the hundred holy signs, whether they drew them themselves or had them drawn by others, have '&c'. Those even, whether men or boys, who during the lesson or in play, by way of amusement, made upon the walls (such) images with the nail or a piece of wood, have all of them reached enlightenment."[2] Various legends and stories[3] extolling Buddhas, Bodhisattvas and devout believers came into existence, even as tales of saints and martyrs were related in the medieval West.

As for the Mohammedans, they were able to resist idol worship for a long time. Alberuni, the Arabian scholar, criticized all kinds of idol worship in India and the West, saying that although Westerners claimed that their religions do not practice idol worship, in the eyes of the Mohammedans, Western and Indian worships were not different. Describing idol worship among the common people of India, he wrote, "As common people will only acquiesce in pictorial representations, many of the leaders of religious communities have so far deviated from the right path as to give such imagery in their books and houses of worship, like the Jews and Christians, and, more than all, the Manichaeans."[4] He claimed that idol worship was restricted to the low classes of people. "For those who march on the path to liberation, or those who study philosophy and theology, and who desire abstract truth which they call *sara*, are entirely free from worshipping anything but God alone, and would never dream of worshipping an image manufactured to represent him."[5] But Alberuni was forced to admit the prevalence of idol worship even among some Mohammedans. "Even in Islam we must decidedly disapprove, e.g., of the anthropomorphic doctrines, the teachings of the Jabriyya sect, the prohibition of the discussion of religious topics, and such like."[6]

In Mahāyāna, Bodhisattvas were sometimes worshipped for their alleged magical powers of bringing forth fortune, wealth, the healing

2. *Saddharmapuṇḍarīka-sūtra* II, vv. 82–87.
3. A genre of Buddhist literature, *avadāna*, a legend, originally meant a pure and virtuous act, *aristeia.* (Max Müller, ed., *Sacred Books of the East* [Oxford University Press, 1879–1927], vol. X, part I, p. 50, n)
4. Edward C. Sachau, *Alberuni's India* (London: Trübner and Co., 1888), p. 111.
5. *Ibid.*, p. 113.
6. *Ibid.*, p. 32.

of diseases, the dispelling of disasters, etc. In the West, also, followers of the Greek section of the Church kissed the icons, put them down dry wells to restore the water and trusted them to perform other feats of magic. Such features can be seen among some Roman Catholics nowadays. But a great difference was that, whereas Christian saints were originally historical persons, Buddhist Bodhisattvas are not historical individuals, although they are thought by believers to be repeatedly born in this world to help suffering beings.

Another analogy, however, concerning the elevation of holy personages in both East and West is possible between the cult of the goddess of mercy in Mahāyāna lands and worshippers of the Virgin Mary in the West. The comparison is especially noticeable in the worship of the Bodhisattva Avalokiteśvara (Kwan-yin in Chinese and Kannon in Japanese), who is a mother-like figure. Avalokiteśvara has probably been the most worshipped divine being throughout Asian countries. Conversely, the Virgin Mary was the friend of souls and all alike, lord and lady, serf and maid, took refuge under the protection of Mary. The similarities Avalokiteśvara shares with Mary are so very convincing that in the days when Catholics were persecuted for political reasons in feudal Japan, Japanese Catholics worshipped images of Mary secretly under the pretense that they represented the Buddhist Kannon. Such idols were called "Maria-Kannon."

In spite of obvious similarities, there are remarkable differences between the Virgin Mary and Avalokiteśvara. Avalokiteśvara was by origin a male, although his aspect became female. Moreover, whereas Mary was a historical individual, Avalokiteśvara was not supposed to be a mortal, for his real personality was regarded as eternal.

A parallel may also be drawn between the Buddhist tradition and the Hellenistic cult of Asklepios, the god of medicine, who as healer and savior called all mankind to himself. In a treatise called *Asklepios*, a long address and prayer to this deity are preserved, of which the tone is strikingly Christian-like. A Buddhist counterpart to Asklepios is found in the figure of the Healing Teacher (Bhaiṣajyaguruvaiḍūryaprabhāsa).

Even transcendental wisdom came to be deified as an object of worship, being proclaimed Sophia in the West and "the Holy Goddess Wisdom" (Bhagavatī Prajñā-pāramitā) in India and other south Asian countries. There were wisdom speculations in western Asia between 200 B.C. and 300 A.D. Their conception of *chochma* and *sophia* is closely analogous to that of *prajñā-pāramitā*, and similarities between them are said to be considerable.[7] However, the iconographies of Sophia and Prajñā-pāramitā

7. E. Conze refers to his review of H. Ringgren, "Word and Wisdom," in *Oriental Art*, I, no. 4 (Spring, 1949), 196–197.

seem to have evolved independently. The Holy Goddess Wisdom was, like the Virgin, a mother and yet was "untouched" by defilement.[8] Pilgrimages to locations associated with holy personages were popular in many areas. In the medieval West pilgrimages to Jerusalem became common. On their way the pilgrims entertained each other with stories which Geoffrey Chaucer gathered together in verse as the *Canterbury Tales*. In India, Hindus made pilgrimages to holy places (*tīrtha*) or temples which were well known as meritorious. Buddhists in India made pilgrimages to the places especially related to the life of the Buddha.[9] Jains also made such pilgrimages. In Japan Buddhists made pilgrimages to places especially related to the life of the founder of each sect. That such activity has continued to the present day is an expression of the veneration among the world's populace for their saints and Bodhisattvas.

3. Vicarious Suffering

One striking expression of the compassion-love motif is the idea of "vicarious suffering" such as found in the crucifixion of Christ. Christians frequently call this phenomenon "vicarious atonement."[1] The cross sub-

8. In the Mediterranean world, we meet, at the same period, with Sophia, who is modelled on Ishthar, Isis, and Athene; she represents a fusion between the idea of wisdom and the idea of the Magna Mater, and is placed by the side of the supreme male being. Like Isthar and the Virgin Mary, the *prajñā-pāramitā* was in essence both mother and virgin. She is the "Mother of all the Buddhas" i.e., she is not barren but fertile, fruitful of many good deeds, and her images lay great stress on her full breasts. Like a virgin, on the other hand, she remains 'unaffected, untouched', and the scriptures emphasize her elusiveness more than anything else. The Sophia (Wisdom) of the Gnostics and the Neo-Platonists "plays a definite role at the creation of the world, while the Prajñā-pāramitā [Transcendental Wisdom of the Mahāyāna] has no cosmic functions, and remains unburdened by the genesis of this universe. The iconographies of Sophia and Prajñā-pāramitā also seem to have evolved independently. . . . [There is] a Byzantine miniature of the 10th century (Vat. Palat. gr. 381 fol. 2) which is said to go back to an Alexandrian model. There, the right hand of Sophia makes the gesture of teaching, while the left arm holds a book. This is not unlike some Indian statues of the Prajñā-pāramitā." (Based upon Edward Conze, *Buddhism: Its Essence and Development* [New York: Harper & Brothers, 1959], p. 143)
9. They are: Lumbinī, Buddhagayā, Migadāya (Benares) and Kusinārā. Pilgrimages to these places are still customary among Buddhists.
1. The thought of vicarious atonement has a long history in the West. For example, Abélard (1079–1142) asserted that we are redeemed from sin and fear, since Christ works love in us. "Our redemption, therefore, is that supreme love in us, through the sufferings of Christ, which not only liberates from the servitude of sin, but acquires for us the true liberty of the sons of God, so that we fulfill all things from love." (R. Seeberg, *Textbook of the History of Doctrines* [Grand Rapids, Michigan: Baker Book House, 1951], II, p. 71)

sequently became a symbol of Christ's martyrdom in taking the sufferings of men upon himself. In this connection, there is a widespread opinion that the concept of such vicarious sacrifice is confined to Christianity alone. Recently even a Hindu swami remarked, " 'His [Christ's] life is spiritually inspiring. To us in India, however, the end is just tragedy. . . . The deaths of our own spiritual heroes, Śrī Rāma and Śrī Kṛṣṇa, were near tragic: but we did not build our religion on them.' But this is what Christians have done with the death of Christ, and the consequence has been calamitous. In place of 'the life-giving message of Jesus' came grim dogmas of atonement from sin."[2] But contrary to opinions such as this the notion of vicarious atonement is indeed found in Hinduism as well as Buddhism, although it is correct to say that the significance is slightly different. In Christianity vicarious atonement was carried out by Christ alone, whereas in Buddhism, for instance, it is the duty and privilege of any Bodhisattva (or aspirant to Bodhisattvahood) to do so. "To take over the sufferings of others by oneself"[3] was held as a supreme ideal of Mahāyāna ascetics.

A Buddhist conception of vicarious sacrifice was expressed, for example, by Nāgārjuna. In his work *Ratnāvalī* he expressed the wish that his merits might go to others and that the sufferings of others might be taken over by him. "May the evil acts produced by another ripen their fruits (i.e., cause retribution) upon me! May the good acts produced by me ripen their fruits (i.e., cause retribution) upon him!"[4]

Whereas medieval Christians found the ideal image of vicarious atonement in Christ on the cross, Northern Buddhists especially revered Kṣitigarbha (or Jizō in Japan). The name of Kṣitigarbha means "Earth-Womb" or "Earth-Storehouse." The original meaning of the title is not very clear, but it was interpreted as "he who is lord of the nether world." Some scholars think that the belief in Kṣitigarbha first appeared in central Asia. Legend has it that he vowed to save all creatures from hell and that he visits them in their places of suffering to seek their deliverance. In Japan he is the special protector of dead children. Whenever someone died to save others, people in Japan would erect an image of Jizō in honor of him, calling it "Lord Jizō in Vicarious Atonement" (Migawari Jizō-son). It is said that Jizō will never enter *nirvāṇa* so long as there remains even one person suffering from afflictions, but rather that he stays on in the mundane world to help sinners.

Hindu literature contains some stories expressing this ideal. For ex-

2. Robert Lawson Slater, *Can Christians Learn from Other Religions*? (New York: Seabury Press, 1963), p. 26.
3. *Boddhisattvabhūmi*, ed. by Unrai Ogihara, p. 249, 1. 6.
4. The Chinese version of the *Ratnāvalī*, the Sanskrit text of which is lost for the most part. *Taisho*, vol. 32, p. 504, c. Cf. *Boddhisattvabhūmi*, *ibid.*, pp. 367–368.

ample, the *Mārkandeya-Purāṇa* relates the story of the pious king Vipaścit[5] who expressed this wish to Yama the King of Death:

> If through my presence, racking torture
> Of these poor ones is alleviated,
> Then will I stay here, my friend,
> Like a post, I will not move from this spot.

At the story's end, the king grants him his wish, and as he ascends to heaven, all the inmates of hells are released from their pain.

The figure which represents the ideal of vicarious atonement most conspicuously in Hinduism seems to be that of Toṇḍar-aḍi-poḍiy-āḻvār, a Vaiṣṇava saint, a historical person, who lived about 830 A.D.[6] But he was regarded as an incarnation of the chaplet (*vanamālā*) of Viṣṇu.[7] His image was always represented in a standing posture with a burden on the right shoulder, whereas the images of other *avatars* or saints are of sitting posture. In this respect one is reminded of the images of Amitābha in the Shinshū Buddhism of Japan, which are always of standing posture, illustrating his readiness to help suffering people.

The idea of vicarious suffering is naturally closely related to human needs and implies ideas of sin which must be remedied by compassionate grace. Such ideas will be discussed in the following section.

4. Sin and Grace

a. Faith and Deliverance in the Pure Land or Paradise

Belief in sin and grace probably could not be maintained without a corresponding belief in a pure state, unsullied by sins, and faith in the possibility of achieving or regaining that state. This section contains thoughts on the subject of such beliefs and on the faith in some deity capable of interceding on man's behalf for his attainment of such a pure state. Pure Land[1] Buddhism is a good subject with which to begin. Scrip-

5. Winternitz, *Indian Literature*, I, pp. 562 ff.
6. Surendranath Dasgupta, *A History of Indian Philosophy*, vol. III (Cambridge University Press, 1952), p. 64.
7. *Ibid.*
1. The Pure Land is sometimes called the Buddha Land, or Buddha Field, or Pure Western Land. Professor Kenneth Morgan thinks that Pure Realm is preferable since it avoids the erroneous connotations of a geographic location or a material world. (*The Path of the Buddha*, edited by Kenneth W. Morgan [New York: Ronald Press, 1956], passim) This is especially true with Hōnen and Shinran. Here I followed the ordinary, conventional translation.

tures of early Pure Land Buddhism were compiled in an age of spiritual unrest, probably at the end of the Indian Kuṣāṇa dynasty (second century), a time of deep spiritual crisis. One scripture states that the teaching was meant for people in such a degenerated age: "The Buddha taught the Law which all the world is reluctant to accept, during this corruption of the present *kalpa*, during this corruption of mankind, during this corruption of belief, during this corruption of life, during this corruption of passions."[2] At such a time it must have been obvious that fewer and fewer were willing to put forth the effort required to follow the path of so-called "primitive" Buddhism.

The followers of the Pure Realm sects of Buddhism seek Buddhahood (i.e., enlightenment) through rebirth in Amitābha Buddha's[3] Pure Land of the Supreme Happiness. Rebirth in the pure realm is attained through faith[4] in the power of Amitābha's vows to save all beings. These vows are recorded in the Great Sūtra of the Endless Life, the *Sukhāvatīvyūha-sūtra*, which claims to be the discourse between Śākyamuni Buddha and Ānanda, his disciple. The sūtra tells us that the monk Dharmākara, the future Amitābha, made a number of vows which were to be assured of fulfillment before he would become a Buddha. Since he did become the Buddha Amitābha, these vows are believed to be a power which can save human beings regardless of the law of *karma*. Amitābha supposedly now dwells in the Western Paradise of the Pure Realm (Sanskrit *Sukhāvatī*, in Japanese *Jōdo*), where he helps believers to be born after death as the reward for their faith and/or good works. The Pure Realm of Amitābha is depicted in a gorgeous manner: prosperous, good to live in, fertile and lovely. It is said to be fragrant with several sweet-smelling scents, abundant with flowers and fruit, adorned with gem trees, and frequented by flocks of sweet-voiced birds.

The idea of a Pure Realm in the West finds counterparts in other countries also. The Egyptian "Fields of Reeds," or the Paradise of Osiris, the Iranian "Var," the Greek "Islands of the Blessed" and "Gardens of the Hesperidae" also lie in the West. Chinese folklore possesses the notion of a "fairy palace in the Kun-lun mountains, inhabited by Hsi-wang-um," the "Royal Mother of the West." The Pure Land has something in common with the paradise of Christianity also. "Jesus represents the kingdom of heaven as a festal gathering, where they sit down to table,[5] and drink

2. *Smaller Sukhāvatīvyūha-sūtra* 18. *Sacred Books of the East*, vol. 49, p. 102. In the Chinese version of the *Larger Sukhāvatīvyūha-sūtra* by Saṅghavarman the consciousness of crisis and sin is set forth with great emphasis.
3. Japanese Amida, Sanskrit Amitābha, literally, "Immense Light," and Amitāyus, literally, "Eternal Life."
4. T. Unno thinks that "faith" is a misleading translation for the central experience of Pure Land teaching and it might better be rendered "awakening" or "awareness."
5. Matthew 8:11.

wine;[6] and . . . even a Dante or a Milton could not choose but borrow all the colours for their pictures from this world of earth."[7] The Apostolic fathers of the earliest Church especially cherished and perpetuated the idea of paradise in the afterlife. And one reason why the Gnostic movement in the Church was never accorded much popularity was because it rejected the idea of resurrection. Subsequently, the Church never again wavered on this point and Christians to this day are characterized by their faith in a heavenly reward.

In the Pure Land in the West, beyond numberless Buddha lands where he casts his light in all ten directions, Mahāyāna Buddhists believe Amitābha Buddha upholds his vow to save countless sentient beings. Therefore, Śākyamuni, as represented in Pure Land scriptures, taught that one should always concentrate on Amitābha. The *Smaller Sukhāvatīvyūha-sūtra* does not stress self-effort so much as the importance of final thoughts: "Beings are not born in that Buddha country as a reward and result of good works performed in the present life. No, all men and women who hear and bear in mind for one, two, three, four, five, six or seven nights the name of Amitābha when they come to die, Amitābha stands before them in the hour of death, they will depart from this life with quiet minds, and after death they will be born in paradise."[8]

A similar thought is expressed in the *Bhagavadgītā*: "Whatsoever being a man at his end in leaving the body remembers, to that same he always goes, O son of Kuntī, inspired to being there in."[9]

In the West Origen noted that magicians invoked the "God of Abraham," often without knowing who He was; but apparently this invocation was especially potent.[10] Names are essential in magic; in each different culture the spirits were addressed by their proper Jewish, Egyptian, Babylonian, Greek or Brahman names. Magic formulae were thought to lose their efficacy when translated. One is led to suppose that the magicians of the time used incantations from all known religions, but if

6. Matthew 26:29.
7. Paul Deussen, *The Philosophy of the Upanishads*, translated by A. S. Geden (Edinburgh: T. and T. Clark, 1906), p. 320.
8. The original text runs as follows: "Not on account of a mere root of goodness are beings born in the Buddha country of the Tathāgata Amitāyus. Whatever son or daughter of good family shall hear the name of the Lord Amitāyus, and having heard it shall reflect upon it, and for one, two, three, four, five, six, or seven nights shall reflect upon it with undisturbed minds, when they come to die the Tathāgata Amitāyus attended by the assembly of disciples and followed by a host of bodhisattvas will stand before them, and they will die with unconfused minds. After death they will be born even in the Buddha-country of the Tathāgata Amitāyus, in the world Sukhāvati." (*Smaller Sukhāvatīvyūha-sūtra* 10)
9. *Bhagavadgītā* VIII, 6.
10. Origen, *Contra Celsum*, Bk. I, Ch. XXVI, cited in Russell, *History of Western Philosophy*, pp. 328–329.

Origen is right, those derived from Hebrew sources were the most effective. (The argument is the more curious as he points out that Moses forbade sorcery.) Augustine also set forth a similar opinion: "As many as received Him, to them gave He power to become the sons of God, even to them that believed on His name."[11]

In Japan devotion to Amida is observed in the practice of repeating the phrase "*Namu Amidabutsu*" (Adoration to Amida Buddha), which is called the Title of Six Syllables.

In Tamil Saivism the constant repetition of the five syllables (*pañcākṣara*), i.e., "Namas Śivāya" (literally, Adoration to Śiva) was very important. In Śaivaite catechisms a whole capter is devoted to its uses.

> Those who repeat it while love's tears outpour,
> It gives them life, and guides them in the way.
> The Lord's great name, wherefore "Hail Śiva" say.[12]

Tulsī Dās said that the name of Rāma is more important than Rāma himself.

Some devout believers of Japanese Pure Land Buddhism thought that the more they repeated the efficacious phrase (*Namu Amidabutsu*) the more merit one could obtain. A legend grew that Saint Hōnen repeated the phrase a million times; however on this point, Hōnen's opinion does not seem to be clear. He simply said, "It is very good to believe in the grace of Buddha with the heart, and repeat the name of Buddha with the mouth."[13] Shinran thought that both faith and repetition of the name were required. "Though you have faith, and do not repeat the name of Amida Buddha, it profits you nothing. Though you repeat the name of Amida Buddha, and do not have faith, you will not be able to be born into the Pure Land. Therefore, you should believe in the grace and repeat the name of Amida, and you will undoubtedly be born into the Buddha's Land."[14] But he did not want to separate these two; "Faith and adoration are not two different things but one, for there is no adoration without faith, and no faith with adoration."[15]

As for Christianity, it is not immediately evident whether such an oral practice is essential. However, the fact that such a tendency existed in Christianity should not be overlooked. Paul said, ". . . if you confess with your lips that Jesus is Lord and believe in your heart that God raised

11. *Confessions* VII, 9. *The Works of Aurelius Augustine, Bishop of Hippo*. A new translation. Edited by Rev. Marcus Dods. Vol. XIV, *The Confessions of Saint Augustine* (Edinburgh: T. and T. Clark, 1876), p. 154.
12. F. Kingsbury and G. E. Philips, *Hymns of the Tamil Saivite Saints* (London: Oxford University Press, 1921), p. 25.
13. *The Life of Hōnen*, vol. 28.
14. *Mattōshō*, 12th letter.
15. *Ibid.*, 11th letter.

him from the dead, you will be saved. For man believes with his heart and so is justified, and he confesses with his lips and so is saved."[16] He said clearly that salvation is accomplished when the two—belief with the heart and confession with the mouth—are combined. And further, "Every one who calls upon the name of the Lord will be saved."[17] However, oral confession was not as simplified in Christianity as in Pure Land Buddhism but rather gradually became complicated and afterwards mingled with the articles of creed.[18] The practice maintained in Catholicism of reciting "Hail Marys" is however close to that of Amidism.

The *Larger Sukhāvatīvyūha-sutra* tells how Dharmākara, when he was still a Bodhisattva striving to become a Buddha, made his forty-eight vows to help ordinary people be reborn to his selfless Pure Land. There, he maintained, they could attain enlightenment by hearing, believing and rejoicing in the merit of Amitābha which is above the natural world, and unthinkable. Oddly, Mahāyāna Buddhists supposed that in the Pure Land there are no human women, although they admitted the existence of heavenly nymphs (*apsaras*). Amitābha Buddha, before attaining Buddhahood, made a vow: "If, after I have obtained Enlightenment, women in immeasurable, innumerable, inconceivable, incomparable, immense Buddha-countries on all sides, after having heard my name, should allow carelessness to arise, should not turn their thoughts towards Enlightenment, should, when they are free from birth, not despise their female nature; and if they , being born again, should assume a second female nature, then may I not obtain the highest perfect Enlightenment." The idea that a woman is born as a man in afterlife is often set forth in Buddhist literature. A teaching to an extent comparable with this was held by John the Scot in the medieval West, who proposed that man was originally without sin, and in that original state was also without distinction to sex. "According to John, it was only as the result of sin that human beings were divided into male and female. Woman embodies man's sensuous and fallen nature. In the end [the Scot speculated] distinction of sex will again disappear, and we shall have a purely spiritual body."[19]

The doctrine of self-cultivation and the worship of a Bodhisattva, which are both preached in Buddhism, may seem contradictory to each other. Be that as it may, both have arisen from the same source. According to Buddhist philosophy man should endeavor to realize his "true self" in a moral and religious sense; this ideal is quite compatible with the worship of one who has already realized his "true self" in a perfect

16. Romans 10:9–10.
17. Romans 10:12–13.
18. Fumio Masutani, *A Comparative Study of Buddhism and Christianity* (Tokyo: The Young East Association, 1957), pp. 138–139.
19. Russell, *History of Western Philosophy*, p. 406.

way. In Mahāyāna Buddhism many Buddhas and Bodhisattvas were revered, but the worship of Amitābha Buddha has played a particularly important role, especially in Chinese and Japanese Buddhism.

Pure Land Buddhism took root gradually among the peoples of China. According to the inscriptions on the Buddha-images in Yunkang and Lung-men, the motives behind the creation of these images were: (1) to attain enlightenment; (2) to achieve rebirth in the Pure Land of Amitābha; (3) to express gratitude to the Buddha for the fulfillment of certain wishes, such as recovery from illness, completion of a certain enterprise, etc.; and (4) to realize material benefits such as prosperity, longevity, power, influence, or prestige.[20] Obviously, there are mixed objectives here, a psychological situation which persisted for some time in the Far East. Shan-tao proposed a new method of Pure Land worship which he called the Five True Practices, consisting of: (1) chanting, (2) contemplation, (3) worship, (4) reciting the name, and (5) praise and offering.[21] He counseled, "Exclusively repeat the Name of Amida with a single-hearted devotion, whether walking, standing, sitting, or lying down, without question of the length of time, never ceasing for even one moment. This is the truly determined practice which unfailingly results in deliverance, for it is in accord with the Original Vow of Buddha.[22]

Genshin (alias Eshin Sōzu, 942–1017), a leader of Japanese Pure Land Buddhism, engaged in contemplation of the mind on the Lord (Amitābha) of the Western Pure Land, and his visions were written down in a treatise on "Birth in Pure Land." Of the religious art produced by him it has been said: "As writer on the vices and miseries of life, on the varieties of existence and on the states of perdition or spiritual beatitude, he may be compared to Dante; while as a painter of paradise [Pure Land] and saints he may be called the Fra Angelico of Japanese Buddhism."[23]

Pure Land Buddhism, it has been seen, is definitely an otherworldly religion. In it stress is placed principally on faith (exhibited by repeating a vow) in a superhuman "other-power." Hōnen, the founder of Japanese Buddhism, for instance, believed that disciplines definitely constituted an auxiliary path; they should be set aside in favor of seeking entrance into the Pure Land. "True meditation is none other than the recitation of the Name of Buddha. If we recite the Name, rebirth is guaranteed, because it is in accord with the Buddha's Original Vow."[24]

20. Kenneth K. S. Ch'en, *Buddhism, The Light of Asia* (Woodbury, New York: Barron's Educational Series, 1968), pp. 148–149.
21. *Shinshū Shōgyō Zensho*, Hensansho Compilation (Kyoto: Kōgyō Shoin, 1940), I, pp. 535–537.
22. Shan-tao's *Kuan-chin-su* (Kangyo-sho), translated by Taitetsu Unno, *ibid.*, p. 538.
23. Anesaki, *History of Japanese Religion*, p. 153.
24. *Hōnen Shōnin Zenshū*, compiled by Kyōdō Ishii (Tokyo: Jōdoshū Shūmonsho, March, 1955), p. 990.

When this way of thinking is drawn to its furthest consequence, even the simple act of faith is removed from the purview of the will of man and relegated to the compassionate being. For instance, in Japan it is believed that the value of *Nembutsu* (repeating the "*Namu Amidabutsu*" for mala) is the virtue of true compassion, and it is not the meritorious act of man. The act of *Nembutsu* itself is guided and effected by the grace of Amitābha. One's own will is not causal in this respect. Therefore no relative value can be fixed to the recitation of Amida Buddha; for everyone has already been saved by the faith resulting in *Nembutsu.*

> By the blessings of the Unhindered light
> The awakening of faith, both magnificent and spacious, is realized.
> The ice of blind desire will melt without fail,
> To become the pure water of enlightenment.[25]

The thought that faith is not acquired by one's own endeavor, but is rather given by God the Absolute, was expressed in the early West by Paul, who said, "So faith comes from what is heard, and what is heard comes by the preaching of Christ."[26] This thought was inherited by later Christian thinkers, for instance, St. Thomas Aquinas, who wrote, "The works of a man who is led by the Holy Ghost are the works of the Holy Ghost rather than his own."[27]

b. Sense of Sin and Need for Divine Grace

In the Middle Ages some thinkers came to solidify a belief in the deep-rooted sinfulness of human existence. Shinran (1173–1262), the Japanese Buddhist who carried the idea of Buddha's grace to its furthest extreme, is an Asian paradigm of this way of thinking. He became the founder of the Shinshū sect which has the largest membership among Japanese Buddhists at the present time. Shinran has often been compared to Luther, not only in the respect of the breadth of his following but also in that he married a nun and spent his life as a married priest. Since he lived in nearly the same period as Thomas Aquinas, which corresponds with the beginning of the Medieval Age of Japan, it would not be inappropriate to discuss his thought in the framework of Medieval thought. At about the same time in India, Rāmānuja and other Hindu leaders of the Bhakti religion advocated salvation by the grace of God Viṣṇu or Śiva. So their thought is also relevant here.

Shinran deeply felt that calamity is involved in the mere fact of our

25. Kōsō Wasan, *Shinshū Shōgyō Zensho*, II, p. 505.
26. Romans 10:17.
27. *Summa Theologica* II, 1, 93, 6.

being alive; that all living beings are sinful; and that we cannot live without committing sins because we are all *karma*-bound. Hōnen, Shinran's master, saw "man with blind eyes, capable of doing nothing."[1] Shinran candidly lamented humanity's propensity to sin:

> Though I seek my refuge in the true faith of the Pure Land,
> Yet hath not mine heart been truly sincere.
> Deceit and untruth are in my flesh,
> And in my soul is no clear shining.[2]

It is no wonder that a devout Buddhist might consider non-believers capable of committing various wicked acts. However, Shinran considered even those who were already practicing the teachings of Buddhism as committing sins. This fact was a starting-point of reflection for him. "I am already neither a priest nor a layman. Therefore my surname should be 'Bald-headed fool' (*Gutoku*, i.e., outwardly shaven, inwardly secular, polluted)."[3]

Sambandhar, the Śaiva saint (7th century) of southern India, likewise cried:

> No righteousness have I, I only speak in praise of Thee.
> Come, Valivalam's Lord, let no dark fruit of deeds, I pray,
> Torment thy slave who with his song extols Thee day by day.[4]

This character of openly admitting a sinful nature was present from earliest days in Christianity. Paul had said, "For I do not do the good I want, but the evil I do not want is what I do."[5] St. Augustine carried the same humble spirit into the Middle Ages: "Behold my heart, O my God; behold my heart, which Thou hadst pity upon when in the bottomless pit. Behold, now, let my heart tell Thee what it was seeking there, that I should be gratuitously wanton, having no inducement to evil but the evil itself. It was foul, and I loved it; I loved to perish, I loved my own error—not that for which I erred the error. Base soul, falling from Thy firmament to utter destruction—not seeking aught through the shame but the shame itself!"[6]

1. Hōnen, *Ōjō-taiyō-shū* (The Outline of the Way to Salvation), in *Shōwa Shinshū Hōnen Shōnin Zenshū*, edited by Kyōdō Ishii (Tokyo: Jōdoshū Shumusho, 1955), Masutani, p. 67.
2. *Hitan-jutsukai-wasan* (Wherein with Lamentation I Make My Confession), v. 327, as given in S. Yamabe and L. A. Beck, *Buddhist Psalms Translated from the Japanese of Shinran Shōnin* (London: J. Murray, 1921), p. 86.
3. *Kyō-gyō-shin-shō*. For comparison, cf. Paul O. Ingram: Shinran Shōnin and Martin Luther: A Soteriological Comparison, *Journal of the American Academy of Religion*, vol. XXXIX, No. 4, Dec. 1971, 430–447.
4. Kingsbury and Philips, *Hymns of the Tamil Saivite Saints*, p. 21.
5. Romans 7:19.
6. *Confessions*, Bk. II, Ch. IV.

In Indian Buddhism the concept of sin distinguished from the concept of "bad" or "evil" is not clear. The words *akuśala* or *pāpa* could mean either. Such terms as *agha, kilbiṣa, enas,* etc. were used from antiquity and inherited by Buddhists, but it is unlikely that they had any significance in Buddhist dogma as being different from evil, one reason being that Buddhism did not presuppose the concept of God. But when Shinran used the term "*zaiaku*" or "*zaishō*," it bespoke keener self-reflection on the innate sin of man.

Shinran did not systematize his concept of sin. In his main work (called "*Kyō-gyō-shin-shō*") he conveyed the traditional concept of the Ten Sins or Evil Deeds (*Jūaku*) and the Five Deadly Sins (*Gogyakuzai*). The Ten Sins are: (1) to kill, (2) to steal, (3) to seek unlawful lust, (4) to tell lies, (5) to flatter, (6) to slander, (7) to use a double tongue, (8) to be greedy, (9) to become angry, (10) to hold wrong views. The Five Deadly Sins are: (1) patricide, (2) matricide, (3) killing of *arhats,* (4) causing disorder to the Buddhist Brotherhood, (5) causing blood to come out of the Buddha's body. Obviously, his sin consciousness was deep.

Augustine's pre-occupation with sin seems to have been based upon a simple childhood action: plucking some pears from a tree in a boyish prank although he was not hungry.[7] He continued throughout his life to consider this an act of almost incredible wickedness. Shinran, on the other hand, did not especially describe each kind of wicked act he had committed. Perhaps he was ashamed of mentioning individual cases, a phenomenon in religious confession parallel to the difference between the mental attitude of many Western artists who describe the cruel scenes of battles vividly and most Japanese painters who depict them vaguely.

According to Shinran, sin is implied in human existence.[8] As it is deeply rooted in human existence, he believed the committing of sins to be unavoidable. He expressed this situation as follows:

> In their outward seeming are all men diligent and truth speaking,
> But in their souls are greed and eager and unjust deceitfulness,
> and in their flesh do lying and cunning triumph.

7. Augustine pointed out that he sinned, not only as a schoolboy when he told lies and stole food, but even earlier; that even infants at the breast are full of sin—gluttony, jealousy, and other horrible vices. When he reached adolescence, the lusts of the flesh overcame him. "Where was I, and how far was I exiled from the delights of Thy house, in that sixteenth year of the age of my flesh, when the madness of lust—which to the human shamelessness granteth full freedom, although forbidden by Thy laws—held complete sway over me, and I resigned myself entirely to it?" (*Confessions,* Bk. II, Ch. III, 4, p. 27)
8. The existentialist penetration of the plight of human existence: "Human life is thus only a perpetual illusion: men deceive and flatter each other. No one speaks of us in our presence as he does of us in our absence. Human society is founded on mutual deceit." (B. Pascal, *Pensées,* no. 100. Translated by W. F. Trotter [New York: Random House, Modern Library, 1941], p. 40)

Too strong for me is the evil of my heart. I cannot overcome it.
Therefore is my soul like unto the poison of serpents,
Even my righteous deeds, being mingled with this poison, must be named the deeds of deceitfulness.[9]

Shinran felt that he must surely be destined to hell.[10] With regard to his belief that human sinfulness is exceedingly strong, Shinran was unique in the history of Buddhism. But his concept of sin, as illustrated in the following, was still derived from the traditional one. "Though sin hath no substance in itself, and is but the shadow of our illusion, and soul [literally, the essence of mind] is in itself pure, yet, in all this world is there no sincere man."[11] In Christianity the idea of original sin was kept alive throughout the Middle Ages to the present day. All descendants of Adam are thought to be of a perverted or depraved nature. Paul may be responsible for perpetuating this ancient Hebrew doctrine in Christian thought. The Hebrew version, however, had probably not presupposed that the original sin of Adam was bequeathed to all his ancestors as did Paul and later medieval thinkers such as Tertullian. Augustine was the first of the Church fathers to develop a full-blown theory explaining man's inherited sinfulness. Against Pelagius, who claimed that sin is a fault of the free will, not nature, the result of long practice or habit, Augustine held that man's will is perverse by nature. Directly from the epistle to the Romans he developed a view that whereby free will was the root of the human race's being a "mass of sin," it was only the free will of Adam, not his descendants. The "defect" (*vitium*), for Augustine, was "of the seed."[12]

Shinran's explanation of the sinful state of man's mundane existence was that it is a product of *karma* which begins in the profound and deep past; in fact, it is so deep-seated that it is no longer a matter of temporal consideration, but only an existential reality. He designated this *karma* "*shukugō* (*karma* in the unperceivable past) or "*zaigō*" (sinful *karma*). Shinran's thought, which was otherwise very similar to Christianity, differed considerably from that of, e.g., Augustine in that he did not entertain the idea of original sin. Shinran stressed solely the salvation of common men by the grace of Amitābha Buddha. "Take refuge in the ultimate Strength, for His pure radiance is above all things. He who perceiveth

9. *Hitan-Jutsukai-Wasan*, vv. 328–329. Yamabe and Beck, *Buddhist Psalms*, p. 86.
10. *Tannishō* 2.
11. *Hitan-Jutsukai-Wasan*, vv. 340. Yamabe and Beck, *Buddhist Psalms*, p. 88.
12. *De Nuptiis et Concupicentia* ii, 8, 20. For a while after Augustine, Roman Catholicism combined some Pelagianism with his doctrine, holding that sin is a "staining" of man's rational nature and freedom (that makes him different from beasts). Later, however, the church went back to the Augustinian position of radical sinfulness of a humanity totally dependent on God's grace for salvation.

the Light is set free from the fetters of Karma."[13] And again, "Take refuge in the Mighty Consoler. Wheresoever His mercy shineth throughout all the worlds, men rejoice in its gladdening light."[14] Further, "Without His Compassionate Vow how can we wretched beings be liberated from the fetters of birth-and-death?"[15]

Augustine also felt that he had to cry for salvation from the abyss into which he had fallen, declaring, "There is no other means for man than to know his weakness, and cling to God, being tired out."[16] And further, "When man learns that in himself he is nothing and that he has no help from himself, then arms in himself are broken in pieces, then wars in himself are ended."[17]

Christianity inherited also the concept of grace from the Hebrew tradition, which held that God bestows kindness upon man much greater than that deserved. This idea was heavily stressed in the New Testament, especially as a result of the belief expressed therein that Christ was another supreme act of grace given by God to man and through Christ such grace continues to be freely offered. The sole condition for receiving grace is believed to be faith in God, since no other act will earn such merit. Once again in opposition to Pelagius, Augustine's concept (actually, he held several concepts of grace) was that man's very will by which he attains grace is itself supplied by grace. St. Thomas picked this up—at least to the extent that he believed man's will needs the support of God's grace.

Shinran in a similar way felt that the grace of Amitābha is so subtle that we may not even know the extent of its workings in and through us.

"Though we are covered with illusion,
And cannot see the light of salvation,
Untired is He who always shines upon me!"[18]

Through meditating on the reflection that we are sinful, we come to feel compassionate towards others; yet the attitude of compassion in this instance and in all others can be founded only by grace. Shinran taught, "We are wicked and sinful, but through the virtue of faith we try to do good for the welfare and peace of the world—yet not through our own power, but through that of another (i.e., Amitābha)." All men, whether

13. *San-Amidabutsu-ge* (Lauding the Infinite One), v. 5. Yamabe and Beck, *Buddhist Psalms*, p. 20.
14. *Ibid.*, v. 8.
15. *Tannishō* 14.
16. *Confessions* VII, 18.
17. Theodore E. Mommsen, "St. Augustine and the Christian Idea of Progress," in *Ideas in Cultural Perspective*, edited by Philip P. Wiener and Aaron Noland (New Brunswick, New Jersey: Rutgers University Press, 1962), p. 533.
18. *Shōshin-ge.*

they are honest or criminal, are, without any distinction, believed to be admitted to Amida's Pure Realm. Like the Christian belief, faith in Amida's grace is the one and only condition of admission. Men are equally sinful, and Amida is a being of compassionate love in the genuine form comparable to the highest God, but unlike the Christian God, he is not a judge. There is no conception of punishment by Amida. The Shin sect holds the view that the evil also are rightfully eligible for salvation by Amida Buddha.

Shinran carried the idea of Buddha's grace to its extreme logical conclusion. A saying of Hōnen's is: "Even a bad man will be received in Buddha's Land, but how much more a good man!" Shinran reversed this: "Even a good man will be received in Buddha's Land, but how much more a bad man!"[19] To elaborate on this, a good man may be able to save himself by his own merit; but it is not expected that a bad man can save himself by his own merit; having no other means, he needs the grace of the Buddha. The sinner has only to believe in the grace of Amitābha and the Pure Realm will be his. Here faith became the sole requisite to salvation; all of the other Buddhist moral philosophy was swept away.

Thomas Aquinas, who flourished at nearly the same time as Shinran, propounded a corresponding doctrine of the need for divine grace. Russell describes Aquinas' theory as follows: "By mortal sin a man forfeits his last end to all eternity, and therefore eternal punishment is his due. No man can be freed from sin except by grace, and yet the sinner is to be blamed if he is not converted. Man needs grace to persevere in good, but no one can *merit* divine assistance. God is not the cause of sinning, but some He leaves in sin, while others He delivers from it. As regards predestination, Saint Thomas seems to hold, with Saint Augustine, that no reason can be given why some are elected and go to heaven, while others are left reprobate and go to hell."[20] Aquinas, however, held that no man could enter heaven unless he had been baptized, while for Shinran no ceremony was necessary for salvation except genuine faith.

In medieval Hindu sects *bhakti*, i.e., faith[21] with the added ingredient

19. *Tannishō* 3. Cf. "While to propose to be a better man is a piece of unscientific cant, to have become a deeper man is the privilege of those who have suffered. And such I think I have become." (Oscar Wilde, *De Profundis*, pp. 124–125)
20. Russell, *History of Western Philosophy*, p. 460.
21. Another Indian word meaning 'faith,' *śraddhā*, is etymologically traced back to the conception of knitting together and means the link between man and the beyond. Sáṅkara defines it as "causes for good actions" (*śubha-karma-pravṛtti-karma*, ad *Praśna-Up.*, p. 250, 6). This may bring to mind the etymology of 'religio.' But "recent studies have assembled reasons for believing that the root is neither that of *ligare* 'to blind' nor *legere* 'to gather, to study, to read' but a third root *lig-*, meaning 'to pay attention, to give care,' and appearing also in the Latin correlative (*nec-legere*) *neglegere*, 'to neglect.' " (Wilfred Cantwell Smith, *The Meaning and End of Religion* [New York: American Library, 1964], p. 205)

love, was emphasized. *Bhakti* was first clearly taught in the *Bhagavadgītā*, and finally it became almost a catchword of Hinduism. Even the traditional Hindu concept of *dharma* was modified according to the tendency of the times. "*Dharma*" was defined in the *Bhāgavata-purāṇa* as the "motiveless and natural flow of devotion to God by which the spirit attains supreme contentment."[22] Tantric religions (both Hindu and Buddhist) preach solely the way of devotion (*bhaktimārga*).

A controversy occurred in religions of grace in different traditions with regard to grace and faith. Western theologians expressed both standpoints, i.e., *gratia cooperativa* and *gratia sola*. In the Vaiṣṇava religion of *Bhakti*, the school of Rāmānuja divided over the doctrine of grace into two separate factions, and there arose a bitter dispute about the exclusiveness of grace. The differences between these two schools were illustrated metaphorically as the "ape way" and the "cat way." For, they said, when a mother ape falls into danger, her young immediately cling fast to her. When she makes a leap to safety, they are saved by the act of the mother, it is true, but in such a way that the young cooperate a little, because they cling to their mother *by their own act*. By this action, the young ape is therefore classed as a synergist. However, when danger threatens a cat with her litter, the mother cat immediately takes the young in her mouth. The kitten does nothing for its own salvation but remains merely passive. All cooperation is excluded.[23]

In the Pure Land Buddhism of China and Japan the relation between faith (*shin*) and work (*gyō*) was also an issue of heated debate. Many leaders thought that both should cooperate. Hōnen seems to have admitted the significance of "work" (that is *nembutsu*, the invocation Amitābha Buddha) even on the behalf of others. He said, "Think in love and sympathy of any beings who have an earnest desire to be born in the Land of Purity; repeat Buddha's name for their sake, as if they were your parents or children, though they may dwell at any distance, even outside the cosmic system. Help those who are in need of material help in this world. Endeavour to quicken faith in anybody in whom a germ of it may be found. Deem all these deeds to be services done to Amida Buddha."[24] Against this opinion some teachers of Jōdo pietism taught that such "work" was useless, even injurious, to an exclusive faith in the grace of Amida Buddha (see previous section). Shinran firmly believed that faith is also required and that one should not rely upon work alone. However when the "work" consists of repeating the name and can be classed as adoration, it and the grace are not separate.

Among the later followers of Shinran there appeared some people

22. Dasgupta, *History of Indian Philosophy*, IV, p. 11.
23. Otto, *India's Religion*, p. 56.
24. A letter sent to the widow of Yoritomo. Anesaki, *History of Japanese Religion*, p. 176.

who boastfully said that they were not afraid of committing sins, an allegiance called "Pride in the Original Vows (of Amitābha)." On the contrary, only for the reason that we are wicked persons, some said, are we qualified to be saved by the grace of Amitābha. (In this connection one might compare Western antinomianism.[25]) Thus the problem of the "eligibility of wicked persons" was formed. In India, the Tengalais had adopted the dangerous doctrine of *doṣabhogya*,[26] i.e., that God enjoys sin, since it gives a larger scope for the display of His grace. The thought that sins give opportunities for salvation appeared very early in the West also. Paul was of the opinion that "law came in, to increase the trespass; but where sin increased, grace abounded all the more."[27]

The teaching of the eligibility of wicked persons was not meant to encourage bad actions. Such a thought was forbidden as heresy by the Shinshū sect which taught that out of pure faith good deeds arise spontaneously. "Unto us hath our Father given those two spiritual gifts. Of these the first is the Virtue whereby we attain unto His Kingdom, and the second is the Virtue whereby having so attained we return into this world for the Salvation of men. By the merit of these two gifts are we initiates of the true faith and of its deeds."[28] In the West also, to sin under the excuse of grace was not justified. "Are we to continue in sin that grace may abound? By no means!"[29]

A rather more neutral opinion of Shinran regarding sin was that it is *devoid* of reality in itself, and that this is the reason man has a possibility of being liberated. Such a Buddhistic concept of sin can also be found among medieval Christian thinkers, such as John the Scot, who believed that, "Sin has its source in freedom: it arose because man turned towards himself instead of towards God. Evil does not have its ground in God, for in God there is no idea of evil. Evil is not-being and has no ground, for if it had a ground it would be necessary. Evil is a privation of good."[30]

With these various concepts of sin being considered, a certain degeneration of the clergy became noticeable and was a topic of heated debate in both East and West nearly at the same time. Shinran wrote:

> Being of one accord with the many minds of the heathen,
> They bow in worship before devils,

25. Antinomianism was first advocated by John Agricola, the German theologian, in the sixteenth century. There were some who subscribed to it. "Mortality does not help me. I am a born antinomian. I am one of those who are made for exceptions." (Oscar Wilde, *De Profundis*, p. 30.)
26. S. Radhakrishnan, *Indian Philosophy* (London: George Allen and Unwin, 1923), II, p. 669.
27. Romans 5:20.
28. *Thanksgiving for Donran*, v. 150. Yamabe and Beck, *Buddhist Psalms*, p. 49.
29. Romans 6:1–2.
30. Russell, *History of Western Philosophy*, p. 405.

While yet wearing the robe of the Buddha.[31]

With all his emphasis on the sinfulness of even those of the Buddhist path, sacerdotalism was still stressed by Shinran, who asserted that a monk, even if degenerated and only outwardly a monk, should not be despised, but respected, for he may yet assist laymen to receive Buddha's grace. "May they yet bring offerings with homage unto the priests, even as you do unto Śāriputra and Mahāmaudgalyāyana [Sāriputta and Moggallāna, the two great disciples of the Buddha]; though they are priests but in name and without discipline, for this is the time of degeneration and of the last days."[32] This opinion was shared by Master Dōgen[33] also, whose standpoint otherwise was quite opposite to that of Shinran. On the other hand, the opinion officially adopted by the Catholic Church in the Medieval Ages was that the sacraments were valid even when dispensed by wicked ministers.

31. *Hitan-Jutsukai-Wasan*, v. 336. Yamabe and Beck, *Buddhist Psalms*, p. 88.
32. *Ibid.*, v. 339, with some corrections.
33. *Shōbō-Genzō-Zuimonki* III, 9.

C. Mystical Schools

1. Methodology

An approach different from those just discussed is that of mysticism. Mystics believe in taking action on their own behalf, i.e., in some form of self-help. In addition, unlike some so-called "faith schools," mystics usually hold an opinion that the nature of man, rather than being basically sinful, is in some way representative of the highest good.

The word "mysticism" was probably first used in the Middle Ages, by Pseudo-Dionysius the Areopagite (c. fifth century) to refer to an approach to theology. Hence some, such as D. T. Suzuki, have been hesitant to refer to experiences of Buddhism as "mystical" because "mysticism" has for so long been applied to an experience somehow relevant to man's relationship with God. Others, such as Father Heinrich Dumoulin, are convinced that encounters with descriptions of the Buddhist experience (especially in Zen), convince one that old concepts of mysticism must now be expanded to accommodate the Buddhist counterpart.[1] Herein, for comparison's sake, Eastern and Western religious experiences are discussed side by side without denying that the question of the unity (i.e., identity) of those experiences is still (and perhaps forever must remain) open. Such discussion begins with methodology.

The requirements for meditation were more or less the same in var-

1. H. Dumoulin, *A History of Zen Buddhism* (Boston: Beacon Press, 1969), p. 4. According to the comments of Mrs. Ruth Sasaki, who studied Zen at length in Japan, the Zen monasteries in present-day Japan are not monasteries in the Catholic or Western sense of the word. They are primarily what might be called "theological seminaries to which students come to engage in Zen study and practice under the direction of a Zen master." After two or three years, the majority of these monks will be ordained as priests and go to their own temples. Only a few of the more serious stay for the many years necessary to complete their Zen practice.

In China, in olden times at least, it would seem that a Zen student was free to go to a Zen master for a time, remain perhaps several years, then go on to another master, and later to still another. In the end, the student seems to have been considered the disciple or heir, as the case may be, of the teacher under whom he completed his attainment. Such freedom as this does not exist in Japanese Zen today. Once a student is accepted as a disciple by a Zen master, he remains that master's disciple until the relationship is terminated by the death of one or the other, or by some unusual circumstance.

ious advanced religions. Practitioners needed composure of mind, abstinence from sensual enjoyments, quietude, and persistent mental concentration. But the method differed with religions. In the West meditation meant the reverent, intense, and sustained contemplation of God or of some religious theme or ideal.

Meditation, as pointed out in the chapter on heterodoxies above, is a very old practice in the West, extending back at least to the Orphic and Pythagorean practices that influenced Plato. Plato's theory of knowledge denied that truth could be found by looking outward through the senses for reality, for he felt "the eye and ear and other senses are full of deception. . . ." Instead, in order to practice philosophy, Plato thought the soul would do better "to retire from them [the senses] and abstain from all but the necessary use of them, and be gathered up and collected into herself, bidding her trust in herself and her own pure apprehension of pure existence, and to mistrust whatever comes to her through other channels and is subject to variation."[2]

Through Neo-Platonism, chiefly that of Plotinus, this particular method of Plato's found its way into Christianity by way of St. Augustine and Pseudo-Dionysius. So influenced were these writers by the accounts of Plotinus' experience of the one (see Chapter III above) as reported by Porphry that they were inspired to base theologies on Plotinus' hierarchical metaphysical system, itself one of the first attempts at mystical systematization. Because of the influence of Plotinus through Augustine and Pseudo-Dionysius, it seems safe to say that all subsequent Western mysticism is in some sense Neo-Platonic.

In the meditations (*upāsanas*) of the Upaniṣads and many early Vedāntins, meditation was often directed toward symbols. The Indian word for symbol was *pratīkam* (from *prati-añc*). Deussen has pointed out that the word "originally denoted the side 'turned towards' us, and therefore visible, of an object in other respects invisible." An example given of such an invisible "object" of adoration is the Hindu supreme, Brahman as "turned toward" the warshipper under some form perceptible by the senses, e.g., as name, speech, etc., as *manas* [mind] and *ākāśa* [ether],[3] as *āditya* [the sun],[4] as the fire of digestion,[5] or even as the holy syllable *oṃ*[6] . . . In comparison, Deussen relotes that the ancient Western writers understood a symbol[7] to be "the visible sign of an invisible object or cir-

2. *Phaedo*, 83.A.
3. *Chānd. Up.* III, 18.
4. *Chānd. Up.* III, 19.
5. *Bṛhad. Up.* V, 9; *Chānd. Up.* III, 13, 8.
6. *Chānd. Up.* I, 1.
7. On pratimā, areā, Cf. Deussen, *Philosophy of the Upanishads*, pp. 99–100. Cf. Śaṅkara ad *Brahmasūtra*, pp. 147, 14; 189, 8; 217, 10; 835, 9; 1059, 6; ad *Chānd. Up.* pp. 9, 8; 10, 1; 21, 3 (Bibliotheca Indica).

cumstance. The word ["symbol"] itself may be derived from the piecing together (*symballein*) of a broken ring or the like carried by guests, messengers, etc., as their authorisation, . . . or simply from the mutual understanding (*symballein*) on which the recognition of this visible token depended."[8] The similarity between Indian and Greek symbols was pointed out and discussed by Alberuni, the Arabian.[9]

The main current of meditation in India was provided by yoga. The word "yoga"[10] in philosophical usage has two meanings: (1) contemplation based on a special technique of mental exercise, and (2) the special system which gave it a philosophical basis and ranks as one of the philosophical systems of India. Yoga contemplation exercises for the attainment of higher awareness are very old in India and were of great influence in the practice of Buddhism.

Zen Buddhists today practice Zen meditation in the cross-legged posture, and Hindu sects also practice a cross-legged yoga that probably dates back as far as the Indus civilization fifteen hundred to twenty-five hundred years before Christ.

In addition these exercises have even influenced some twentieth century Western thinkers.[11] Yoga as a philosophical system had its rise in a later period than the contemplation exercises of the same name. The scriptures of this school, the *Yoga-sūtras*, are supposed to have been composed after 450 A.D. by a philosopher named Pantañjali. In the *Yoga-sūtras* the final goal is described as the cessation of the functions of mind (*citta-vṛtti-nirodha*), meditation upon the highest good being a preliminary step. Psychological reflections in the system offer sound good suggestions even to modern thinkers.[12] The ultimate situation of yoga is somewhat

8. Deussen, *Philosophy of the Upanishads*, p. 99.

9. "The ancient Greeks, also, considered the idols as metaphors between themselves and the *First Cause*, and worshipped them under the names of the stars and the highest substances. For they described the First Cause, not with positive, but only with negative predicates, since they considered it too high to be described by human qualities, and since they wanted to describe it as free from any imperfection. Therefore they could not address it in worship." (Sachau, *Alberuni's India*, p. 123)

10. The Yoga is fully discussed in Mircea Eliade, *Yoga: Immortality and Freedom*, translated by W. R. Trask (New York: Pantheon Books, 1958). The *Bhagavadgītā* (II, 53) says, "When your intelligence, which is bewildered by the Vedic texts will stand unshaken and stable in spirit (*samādhi*), then you will attain to insight (*yoga*)."

11. Thoreau's living at Walden as a spiritual retreat is very similar to a Yogi's complete abstention from all worldly objects. He himself said, "Even I am a yogi." The fact that Thoreau thought of himself in this way is noteworthy, and more than once he affirmed it, saying "I would fain practice the *yoga* faithfully." (Arthur Christy, *The Orient in American Transcendentalism* [New York: Columbia University Press, 1932], pp. 199 f)

12. We find opinions similar to it in Spinoza. "If we imagine a certain thing to possess something which resembles an object which usually affects the mind with joy or sorrow, although the quality in which the thing resembles the object is not the efficient

similar to the well-known Buddhist *nirodha-samāpatti* which is another an example of how Buddhism introduced the popular practice of yoga into its own system.

Meditating on a symbol was easy for Indian thinkers who were influenced by the pantheism of certain portions of the *Upaniṣads* (all things are God, Ātman, Brahman; therefore one might pick anything as a symbol with which to meditate on him). However another trend in the *Upaniṣads*, particularly the *Bṛhadāraṇyaka Upaniṣad*, also became quite popular among Hindu mystical methods, namely, the "*neti neti*" ("it is not, it is not") doctrine. Like the mystical, negative theology of Pseudo-Dionysius, the *neti neti* phrase originally began as a rational representation of the unknowability of a totally transcendent deity. But, again comparable to negative theology, the negative phrase later became a method to be utilized in meditation. When seeking for the mystical union, the Hindu devotee would greet any thought or image with a tense "not this, not this," because of the belief that any representation could not possibly be the "object" of his quest.

As for Pseudo-Dionysius, thinking he was a disciple of Saint Paul, possibly even privy to some esoteric teachings of Jesus, all later Christian theologians are "indebted to him for some aspect of their own thought."[13] However, because his thought often resorted to the monism of the Neo-Platonists (Plotinus and Proclus) he was prone to the same reasoning as that behind the negative approach of the *Bṛhadāraṇyaka-Upaniṣad*. There are two elements in this approach, "first that since reality is one and knowledge is dual, we cannot have knowledge of reality and second that the subject of knowledge cannot be known since it is never the object and 'thou canst not know the knower of knowing.' "[14] These are similar to the background thought of Dionysius who became quite negative regarding knowledge of God, and lamented, "all things are but a parable—the insufficient here is that which occurs."[15]

Dionysius' thought was but confirmation for the first real founder of systematic mystical theology, Gregory of Nyssa (c. 335–395 A.D.). Gregory

---

cause of these effects, we shall nevertheless, by virtue of the resemblance alone, love or hate the thing." (*Ethics* III, 16. Translated by William Hale White [London: Trübner, 1883], p. 121) "If we imagine that a thing that usually affects us with the affect of sorrow has any resemblance to an object which usually affects us equally with a great affect of joy, we shall at the same time hate the thing and love it." (III, 17, p. 121) "A man is affected by the image of a past or future thing with the same affect of joy or sorrow as that with which he is affected by the image of a present thing." (III, 18, p. 122)

13. Gilson, *History of Christian Philosophy*, p. 85.
14. K. N. Jayatilleke, *Early Buddhist Theory of Knowledge* (London: George Allen and Unwin, 1963), p. 40.
15. Seeberg, *History of Doctrines*, p. 292.

had also utilized Neo-Platonic language and had reasoned ecstatic love to be the pinnacle of the soul's endeavor. Dionysius described "Absolute Truth" in negative terms exclusively, for the cause of all things is neither soul nor intellect, nor can it be spoken or thought. He held the Absolute to be without number, order, and magnitude; in it is no equality, inequality, similarity, or dissimilarity. It is beyond any description. Dionysius denied qualifications not because the truth falls short of them, but because they are all excelled by it. "Truth," as he called the ultimate, must be above them.

Another Eastern counterpart of Pseudo-Dionysius' negative theology was Nāgārjuna's doctrine of the void. Nāgārjuna (c. second-third centuries A.D.) in combination with the *neti neti* doctrine of the *Bṛhadāraṇyaka-Upaniṣad* gave impetus to Śaṅkara,[16] the great Vedāntist, and thereby affected most of later Hindu thought down to the present. Nāgārjuna's method was a fourfold negation. In an attempt to set out a correct interpretation of Buddhist doctrine, he submitted all the basic Buddhist concepts—*Karma, pratītya-samutpāda*, the middle path, four noble truths, etc., even *nirvāṇa*—to his fourfold negation and found they were not existing, not non-existing, not both existing and non-existing, nor neither existing nor non-existing. Therefore they were *śūnya*, void of characterization. Experience for Nāgārjuna was simply "such as it is" (*yathābhūtam*). His "method" was not purely a result of reason but of *prajñā*, Buddhist "mystical" wisdom, as advocated in the *Prajñāpāramitā Sūtras*.

In Pseudo-Dionysius' *Mystical Theology*, the concluding series of negations is followed by negations of negations. Meister Eckhart (1260–1327) was also to perpetuate this insight of denial of denial, "the *nihtesniht, daz ê was denne niht*."[17] Nāgārjuna believed exactly the same rigorous attitude must be applied to his method if the right insight were to be effected; consequently, even the principle of "Voidness" must also be negated. Negation itself must be negated, and denial of denial is required.[18]

16. This was assented by T. Stcherbatsky in his *Buddhist Nirvāṇa, op. cit.* Prof. R. C. Pandeya shares this opinion.
17. Deussen, *Philosophy of the Upanishads*, p. 149.
18. The question whether relativity is itself relative is mentioned by Russell and dismissed with the remark that it is absurd. "A certain type of superior person is fond of asserting that 'everything is relative.' This is, of course, nonsense, because, if *everything* were relative, there would be nothing for it to be relative to. However, without falling into metaphysical absurdities it is possible to maintain that everything in the physical world is relative to an observer." (*The ABC of Relativity* [London: Kegan Paul, Trench, Trubner, 1925], p. 14) Russell's comment hinges on the ambiguity of the word "everything." It seems Russell was particularly deaf to ordinary usage in this instance. The "superior person" (haven't we all used the phrase "everything is relative" at least once?) actually means "each thing is relative to some other thing which is itself relative to some other thing which is—etc., *ad infinitum*." Russell misinterpreted the superior person's phrase to mean "the class of everything is relative."

Nāgārjuna said, "If something non-relational (not 'void') did really exist, we would then likewise admit the existence of the relational, but there is absolutely nothing non-relational, how then can we admit the existence of the relational (or the truth of 'Void')."[19] If the void does not exist, Voidness itself ceases to be "Voidness." Inheriting this idea, the T'ien-t'ai school of China set forth the principle of harmony of the threefold truth as its basic doctrine. According to this principle, all things (*dharmas*) have (1) no ontological reality (void) but (2) only temporary existence; the fact that they are simultaneously unreal and temporarily existing is (3) the middle state or the middle truth. Any existing thing should be viewed from these three standpoints.

In keeping with the above, the philosophy of "Voidness" has no fixed dogma and the *Mādhyamika* philosophers therefore held the conviction that they had no standpoint to be refuted.[20] Of this position, Nāgārjuna wrote:

> "If I have theses (of my own to prove),
> I may commit mistakes just for the sake (of proving)
> But I have none. I cannot be accused in any way."[21]

Āryadeva, Nāgārjuna's famous pupil, similarly declared:

> If I neither admit a thing's reality,
> "Nor unreality, nor both (at once),
> Then, to confute me
> A long time will be needed."[22]

Nāgārjuna's thought was quite prevalent at the time when Buddhism

---

He then rightly (but trivially) observes that this is absurd because anything outside the class of everything, to which the class could be related, has been stipulated to be within the class.

19. *Mādhyamaka-kārikās* XIII. 7.

20. Murti has pointed out some analogies between Kant and Mādhyamika. Although his approach met the objections raised by May, Murti's main point seems to be of significance. (T. R. V. Murti, *The Central Philosophy of Buddhism* [London: G. Allen and Unwin, 1955]. Jacques May, "Kant et les Mādhyamika," *Indo-Iranian Journal*, vol. III [1959], pp. 102–111) E. Conze asserts that the parallelism between the Mādhyamikas and Kant is spurious, fully discussed "Spurious Parallels to Buddhist Philosophy," in *Philosophy East and West*, vol. XIII, no. 2 (June, 1963), pp. 105–115. The apparent similarity between Kant's antinomies and the Buddhist treatment of speculative questions (*avyākṛtavastūni*) cannot be doubted.

21. A verse of the *Vigrahavyāvartanī*, cited in *Prasannapadā* (*Madhyamakavṛttiḥ*: *Mūlamadhyamakakārikās* de Nagārjune avec la *Prasannapadā* commentaire de Candrakīrti. Publiée par Louis de la Vallée Poussin. St-Pétersbourg, L'Académie Impériale des Sciences, 1903–1913. Bibliotheca Buddhica, 4), p. 16.

22. *Catuḥśataka* XVI, 25. Cited in *Prasannapadā*, p. 16. Stcherbatsky, *The Conception of Buddhist Nirvāṇa* (Leningrad: The Academy of Sciences of the USSR, 1927), p. 95.

was being transmitted into China; hence his doctrine helped mold Chinese Buddhism and through it, the Japanese counterpart. His *Mādhyamika* philosophy found great sympathy among some of the most prominent Taoists of that time in China. Such Buddhist converts as Seng Chao and Tao Sheng combined Nāgārjuna's thought with Taoism to produce a Chinese form of Buddhism that Fung Yu-lan has noticed was very near to Zen. An isolated instance of Nāgārjuna's influence in this area (among many) is the tendency in Seng Chao (374–414), affected by Nāgārjuna, to attempt demonstrations that the conditions of "existent" and "inexistent" cannot be absolutely and universally predicated of anything.[23]

The unique contribution of Zen to higher religion is its method of reaching and presenting the truth. Many different methods of instruction have been used by Zen masters but, whatever the method of instruction, Zen intuition cannot be attained arbitrarily. The true law of the Buddha according to the Zen school must be transmitted from mind to mind and from personality to personality. The Zen motto: "A special transmission outside the classified teachings" means that systems of teachings based upon the Sūtras are not relied upon, and that the true law is transmitted by other means. Therefore, to attain the goal of Zen one must begin by receiving guidance from a true master of Zen who has synthesized understanding and action. Under the guidance of the master, the transmission from mind to mind takes place. Plotinus said to the same effect: "Out of discussion we call to vision, to those desiring to see we point the path; our teaching is a guiding in the way; the seeing must be the very act of him who has made the choice."[24]

In the Rinzai sect practitioners are directed to concentrate on enigmatic or paradoxical, non-logical[25] questions called "*kōans*."[26] *Kōans* were substantially based upon *mondōs* and a considerable part of Zen literature consists of *mondō*, brief dialogues between masters and disciples. These dialogues illustrate the peculiar method of instruction which evolved in Zen of pointing to the truth, the real now, without interposing ideas and notions about it. For example, a monk asked Tung-shan, "How do we escape the heat when summer comes and the cold when winter is here?" The master replied, "Why don't you go where there is no summer, no winter?" "Where is such a place?" "When the cold season comes, one is thoroughly chilled; when the hot summer is here, one swelters." There are

23. R. H. Robinson, "Mysticism and Logic in Sêng-chao's Thought," *Philosophy East and West*, vol. VIII, pp. 99–120.
24. *Enneads*, VI, 9, 4.
25. Professor Paul Wienpahl believes the Zen *kōan* is logical—once one has gone through it.
26. "Kung-an" in Chinese. It literally means "official document." The meaninglessness of kōan was discussed by Paul Wienpahl, "On the Meaninglessness of Philosophical Questions," *Philosophy East and West*, vol. XV, no. 2 (April, 1965), pp. 135–144.

some *kōans* which logically do not seem to make any sense. Answers do not reply to questions. "Once a monk asked Tung-shan: 'What is the Buddha?' Tung-shan replied: 'Three pounds of flax.' "

Zen sometimes attacks human concepts quite violently. Thus its technique has often the appearance of spiritual shock-tactics. Paradoxes are used because it is difficult to express pure experience in the form of ordinary, formal logic. How paradoxical these dialogues can be is illustrated in the following: The Zen master Nan-ch'üan was asked "What is the Tao?" He replied, "Everyday life is the Tao." "How," pursued the enquirer, "does one get into harmony with it?" "If you try to get into harmony with it, you will get away from it."

A rather explicit Zen saying runs as follows:

> Like unto space it knows no boundaries:
> Yet it is right here with us, ever retaining its serenity
>   and fulness;
> It is only when you seek it that you lose it.
> You cannot take hold of it, nor can you get rid of it;
> While you can do neither, it goes on its own way;
> You remain silent and it speaks; you speak and it is silent;
> The great gate of charity is wide open with no
>   obstructions whatever before it.[27]

For Zen masters, the best way to express deepest experiences is by the use of paradoxes which transcend the opposites. For example, these are typical paradoxes[28] to be used for meditation: "Where there is nothing, there is all." "To die the great death is to gain the great life." "Drop into a deep chasm and live again after your death." "We have been separated for a long time and have never been apart. We meet each other throughout the day, and do not meet a moment." Paradoxes like these bring objective thought to a deadlock and from there it is possible to uncover the vital way of turning around.

Sometimes the *kōan* seem to contradict each other. When asked, "What is Buddha?" Ba-so answered, "This mind is Buddha," but on another occasion he said, "This mind is not Buddha." But both assertions are no less than ferryboats which lead one to enlightenment.[29]

27. Hsuan-chiao, *Cheng-tao Ke* 34. In D. T. Suzuki, *Manual of Zen Buddhism* (London: Rider, 1950), p. 115.
28. Reiho Masunaga in *The Path of the Buddha*, edited by Kenneth Morgan (New York: Ronald Press Company, 1956), pp. 341–342.
29. Professor Charles Morris explains as follows: "As an example of this language [of paradox and contradiction] Dr. Suzuki in his *Introduction* [*to Zen Buddhism* (London: Rider, 1960)] gives the following Zen Utterance, an esteemed gatha from the sixth century by Shan-hui:

Some *kōans* can be translated into less metaphorical expressions. A famous *kōan* is: "Before father and mother were born, what was your true nature?" Many think it can be worded: "Beyond time and space, what is reality?"[30]

The way of resorting to *kōans* can be compared to the religions of Tantric Sahajiyas in medieval India, who taught by riddles and enigmatic expressions, partly to guard the secrets of their thoughts, partly to avoid abstractions by concrete imagery.

Kōan work was usually carried out in Zen monasteries taking advantage of the same meditation practices Indian masters had learned from yogis. Master Po-chang exhorted devotees towards the goal in the following manner: "Cling to nothing, crave for nothing."[31] This he impressed

---

> Empty-handed I go, and behold the spade is in my hands:
> I walk on foot, and yet on the back of an ox I am riding;
> When I pass over the bridge
> Lo, the water floweth not, but the bridge doth flow.

. . . To be sure, no one of them taken singly need have this quality: to imagine oneself on the moon looking down upon oneself on the earth may be interesting, but it is hardly mystical. Suppose, however, that the interpretants of these various symbolic processes are aroused simultaneously or nearly simultaneously. If the interpretants of signs are (or involve) neutral processes, then . . . there is no reason why the interpretants of contradictory signs cannot be aroused simultaneously, though the corresponding reactions could not simultaneously be performed. In this way, one can be symbolically both here and not here, in the past and in the future, can be both the fish that swims and the gull that dives. It is suggested that this simultaneous, or nearly simultaneous, arousal of the complex and often contradictory role-taking processes made possible by language constitutes an essential part of the mystical experience." "Comments on Mysticism and Its Language," (*ETC. A Review of General Semantics*, vol. IX, No. 1 (Autumn 1951), pp. 4–6) Morris concludes, "Having undergone the process of symbolic identification with everything available to him, a person is a changed person; symbolically he is no longer merely one object among objects. As one object existing among other objects he is small and fragile, empty-handed, on foot, walking on a bridge. But having roamed afield symbolically, he rides the cosmic ox, and digs with the cosmic spade; and as the water, he sees the flowing bridge. The commonest things are henceforth perceived at both the old and the new levels; a spade is still a spade, water is water, and a bridge a bridge; and yet they are more than they were, for they now are seen through symbolic eyes enlarged by cosmic wandering. The experience is liberating." (*Ibid.*, p. 8)

30. In this connection a comment by Emerson seems apt: "These roses under my window make no reference to former roses or to better ones; they are for what they are; they exist with God today. There is no time to them. There is simply the rose; it is perfect in every moment of its existence.—But man postpones or remembers; he does not live in the present, but with reverted eye laments the past, or, heedless of the riches that surround him, stands on tiptoe to foresee the future. He cannot be happy and strong until he too lives with nature in the present, above time." (*Essays*, First Series, "Self-Reliance")

31. Heinrich Dumoulin, *The Development of Chinese Zen after the Sixth Patriarch in the Light of Mumonkan*, translated from the German with additional notes and appendices by Ruth Fuller Sasaki (New York: First Zen Institute of America, 1953), pp. 15, 62.

upon his disciples as being fundamental. Thus the *kōan* of "nothing" was highly esteemed in later days. "When you forget the good and the non-good, the worldly life and the religious life, and all other things, and permit no thoughts relating to them to arise, and you abandon body and mind—then there is complete freedom. When the mind is like wood or stone, there is nothing to be discriminated."[32] This is similar to Eckhart's conception of the correct action of the soul: "It must renounce not only sin and the world, but itself also. It must strip off all its acquired knowledge, and all present knowing of phenomena; as the deity is 'Nothing,' so it is apprehended only in this knowledge that is a not-knowing—*docta ignorantia*, it was later called by Nicolaus; and as that 'Nothing' is the original ground of all reality, so this not-knowing is the highest, the most blessed contemplation."[33] This ultimate situation is not realized by petty deliberation of man, but by the absolute itself, according to Eckhart. It is, he thought, "no longer an act of the individual, it is the act of God in man; God begets his own essence within the soul."[34] This last point seems to be quite dissimilar to the thought of Zen Buddhism, especially of the Lin-chi or Rinzai sect. But a similar echo is seen in another branch of Zen Buddhism, i.e., the Sōtō sect founded by Master Dōgen.

The way of practice in Sōtō Zen is significantly different from that of the Rinzai sect; but Master Dōgen also made meditation the essential practice. "Why do you encourage others to practise meditation? The answer: This is the right gate to the teaching of Buddha. . . . Meditation is the gate to comfort and happiness."[35] However, Sōtō Zen went still further than Rinzai Zen, it was thought, by rejecting even *kōans*. Sōtō practitioners were instructed not to endeavor to concentrate on anything. Master Dōgen said, "In meditation, if mind is distracted, don't try to suppress it. Let it be as it is!" He disliked the term "Zen sect"[36] and claimed to convey the right path of religion, believing that if one limits the Way with the word "Zen-sect," one loses the Way. Sōtō Zen emphasized silent sitting and meditating on the illumination or insight received while waiting thus in silence.

Dōgen's teaching for the practice of meditation was: "Abandon your body and soul into the abundance of light sent from above and give no thought to them. Do not seek for enlightenment nor reject illusion; do not try to avoid distractions nor attach yourself to them nor dwell on

32. *Keitoku Dentōroku*, Vk. VI: Words of Po-chang. Cf. Dumoulin, *Ibid.*, p. 63.

33. W. Windelband, *A History of Philosophy with Special Reference to the Formation and Development of Its Problems and Conceptions*, translated by James H. Tufts (New York: Macmillan and Co., 1893), p. 337.

34. *Ibid.*

35. *Shō-bōgenzō*, chapter "Bendōwa," in Tamamuro, *Dōgen Zenji Zenshū*, ed. Doshu Okubo (Tokyo: Shunjūsha, 1930), pp. 17–20.

36. *Ibid.*, p. 19 f., etc.

them. Just sit with perfect composure. If you do not prolong distractions voluntarily, how should they occur by themselves? Only sit like the great void or fire, breathing naturally; do not concern yourself with anything whatever; just keep sitting . . . if you take no heed of them and leave them alone, every distraction will be turned into the divine light of Wisdom (*prajñā*). This principle applies not only to the state of sitting but also to that of walking. You would be led by light at every step."[37] This passage is well known to many Japanese Buddhists and its Western counterpart can be found in *The Cloud of Unknowing*, by an unknown English author of the fourteenth century. This author says that the seeker's quest will become easier with the passage of time: "Travail fast but awhile, and thou shalt soon be eased of the greatness and of the hardness of this travail. For although it be hard and strait in the beginning, when thou hast no devotion, nevertheless afterwards, when thou hast devotion, it shall be made full restful and full light unto thee, that before was full hard. And thou shalt have either little travail or none."[38] The coincidence is considerable. Master Dōgen (1200–53) and the author of *The Cloud of Unknowing* were almost synchronous and their ways of practice bore great similarity to each other. The author of *The Cloud of Unknowing* belonged to a mystical trend known as "*apophatic*" because of its tendency to emphasize (in accordance with the entire history of Western mysticism that went before him) that God is best known by negation. He asserted that man can know much more about what God is *not* than about what He is.

2. Interpretation of Experience

Mahāyāna Buddhism found in the theory of relational origination (*pratītya-samutpāda*) the basis for the interpretation of experience as emptiness, *śūnyatā*. "*Śūnya* means swollen and anything swollen is void inside. The little circle which is known nowadays as zero was called "void" (*śūnya*) in Sanskrit. This was originally an Indian invention which was introduced into the West by the Arabs about 1150 A.D. Mahāyāna philosophers, especially those of the Mādhyamika school, advocated as follows: there is no real existence; all things are but appearance and are in truth empty, "devoid" of their own essence. Even "non-existence" (the void somehow considered an entity) is not reality; everything which occurs is conditioned by everything else. Voidness or emptiness is neither nothingness nor an-

37. Ejō, *Shōbō-Genzō-Zuimonki*. Cited from William Johnston, *The Mysticism of "The Cloud of Unknowing": A Modern Interpretation* (New York: Desclee Co., 1967), p. 24.
38. *The Cloud of Unknowing*, C. 84:20. Cited from Johnson, *ibid*., p. 214.

nihilation, but that which stands in the middle between affirmation and negation, existence and non-existence, eternity and annihilation. So "voidness' means the "relationality"[1] of all things.

The Mādhyamika philosophers also denied change as a reality in the phenomenal world, and set forth the theory of the ineffability of the basic Buddhist experience. Nāgārjuna, the great Mahāyāna philosopher, asserted at the beginning of his major work:[2] "The Buddha has proclaimed the principle of Dependent Origination (Relationality), the principle that nothing (in the universe) can disappear, nor can (anything new) arise, nothing has an end, nor is there anything eternal, nothing is identical with itself, nor is there anything differentiated (in itself), there is no motion, neither towards us, nor from us."[3] Here the word "relationality" means the same as "the void." One should know, according to Nāgārjuna, that fundamentally nothing whatsoever is happening to the true essence of one's nature, nothing to give cause for either distress or joy. He denied change itself. A scriptural passage of a Mahāyāna sūtra runs as follows: "Just as, in the vast ethereal sphere, stars and darkness, light and mirage, dew, foam, lightning and clouds emerge, become visible, and vanish again, like the features of a dream—so everything endowed with an individual shape is to be regarded."[4]

There are Western parallels to this way of thinking: the kindred Gnostic and Neo-Platonic modes of thought, especially the later Neo-Platonists, like Proclus and Damascius,[5] and also their Christian form in Origenes and in Dionysius Areopagita, who in some passages of his *Mystical Theology*[6] gives what may well be called a Christian version of the *Heart Sutra.* Pseudo-Dionysius' equivalent of Nāgārjuna's "void" might be what he called the "super-essential Darkness."[7] The parallel

1. The term "*sūnyatā*" was translated as "relativity" or "contingency" by Stcherbatsky (*The Conception of Buddhist Nirvana* [Leningrad: The Academy of Science of the USSR, 1927], passim). Aristotle also took the notion of relativity in a generalized sense. In his *Metaphysica* he treated *Ad aliquid*, not as one among the distinct categories, but as implicated with all the categories. (Cf. George Grote, *Aristotle*, edited by Alexander Bain and G. Croom Robinson [London: John Murray, 1872], p. 88) He does not maintain that the relative in unreal, but he declares it to be Being (*Ens*) in the lowest degree (*Ibid.*, p. 85). The question of whether Being (*Ens*) is itself relative he leaves unsolved. (Stcherbatsky, *Buddhist Nirvāṇa*, pp. 42–43) But still the term "relativity" is misleading. I followed the suggestion of Professor Philip P. Wiener that it be translated "relationality."
2. The opening verse of the *Madhyamaka-karikās*.
3. *Madhyamaka-karikās* I, 1. (Stcherbatsky, *Buddhist Nirvāṇa*, p. 93)
4. *Vajracchedikā-prajñāpāramitā-sūtra*, 32.
5. J. Rahder, *Indogaku Bukkyōgaku Kenkyū* IX, no. 2 (1961), p. 754.
6. I. 2, II. 1, III. 1, chapters 4 and 5. Conze says, "The translations are apt to obscure the parallel, which becomes strikingly obvious as soon as the Greek text is consulted." (*Philosophy East and West*, XIII, no. 1 [April 1963], p. 17, fn. 61)
7. *Mystical Theology*, 2.

is especially apt of Dionysius if the mystical experience, as he suspected, floods that darkness once such experience is reached.

The doctrine of the void (*śūnyatā*) is not nihilism. On the contrary, Mahāyāna Buddhists asserted that it is the true basis for the foundation of ethical values. There is nothing in the void, but everything comes out of it. Compare a mirror. The void is all-inclusive; having no opposite, there is nothing which it excludes or opposes. But virtually speaking, the real character of *śūnya*, according to the Mādhyamika, is fullness of being rather than emptiness. It is the basis upon which all phenomena can be realized. It is living void, because all forms come out of it, and whoever realizes the void is filled with life and power and the Bodhisattva's love (*karuṇā*) for all beings. Love is the moral equivalent of all-inclusiveness, which is nothing but the "void."

A set of the two, i.e., love and knowledge, was not necessarily limited to Buddhism alone. The Mahāyānistic conception of substantial identity of knowledge and compassion is implied with sophisticated argumentations by Thomas Aquinas. According to him, "God alone is good through His own essence."[8] "God loves all existing things,"[9] and also at the same time, "in God there exists the most perfect knowledge."[10]

Dante (1265–1321), the great poet of the *Divine Comedy*, generally assumed this notion. He implied that God is the love and knowledge which bind together all things in the universe. However, in the *Divine Comedy*, the identity of love and knowledge is not clearly expressed in a systematic way, which is somewhat natural in a poetic work.

> O light eternal who only in thyself abidest, only thyself dost
> understand, and to thyself, self-understood self-understanding,
> turnest love and smiling!

And again,

> To the highest fantasy here power failed; but already
> my desire and will were rolled—even as a wheel that moveth
> equally—by the Love that moves the sun and the
> other stars.[11]

According to Mahāyāna, the fundamental basis upon which everything occurs is the "void." So knowing the "void" means having omniscience. The void resembles a crystal ball, which is visible to our eyes only because of what it reflects. Hold it up before a flower, and there within

8. *Summa Theologica* I, vi, 3, p. 29.
9. *Ibid.*, I, xx, 2, pp. 121–122.
10. *Ibid.*, I, xiv, 1, pp. 75–76.
11. Dante Alighieri, *The Divine Comedy*, the Carlyle-Wicksteed translation (New York: Random House, 1932), Paradiso, Canto XXXIII, the end of the entire work.

it is a flower. Hold it up before the empty sky, and there seems to be nothing in it, but only because it is reflecting the emptiness of the sky. Its true nature remains unknown. As the crystal ball reflects images, the manifold phenomena appear spontaneously within the void. When man realizes the void, good acts come spontaneously.[12]

A similar thing can be said of the "negative theology" of Christianity. Rudolf Otto says: "This 'negative theology' does not mean that faith and feeling are dissipated and reduced to nothing; on the contrary, it contains within it the loftiest spirit of devotion, and it is out of such 'negative' attributes that Chrysostom fashions the most solemn confessions and prayers. He thereby shows once more that feeling and experience reach far beyond conceiving, and that a conception negative in form may often become the symbol (what we have called an 'ideogram') for a content of meaning which, if absolutely unutterable, is none the less in the highest degree positive. And the example of Chrysostom at the same time shows that a 'negative theology' can and indeed must arise . . . from purely and genuinely religious roots, namely, the experience of the numinous."[13] The negative descriptions of Dionysius the Areopagite, the *nescio* of Bernard, "the dim silence where all lovers lose themselves" of Ruysbroeck, Eckhart and Boehme, followed on this line. Ruysbroeck, a follower of Meister Eckhart, spoke of the "God-seeing man" whose spirit is undifferentiated and without distinction, and who therefore feels nothing without the unity. This may correspond to the "knowledge without differentiation" (*nirvikalpaka-jñāna*) of Mahāyāna Buddhism.

Voidness (*śūnyatā*) corresponds to the "desert of the Godhead," to Ruysbroeck's "idle emptiness," to Eckhart's "still wilderness where no one is at home," to the "naked orison," the "naked intent stretching unto God" which becomes possible with entire self-surrender, and also to the "fathomless abyss" of Ruysbroeck and Tauler (another of Eckhart's followers).[14] This "abyss" is wholeheartedly welcomed by those steeped in self-negation, which corresponds to the import Mahāyānists give the

12. "A perfectly good will would therefore be equally subject to objective laws (viz., laws of good), but could not be conceived as *obliged* thereby to act lawfully, because of itself from its subjective constitution it can only be determined by the conception of good. Therefore no imperatives hold for the Divine will or in general for a holy will; ought is here out of place, because volition is already of itself necessarily in unison, with the law." (Kant, *Metaphysics of Morals*, in *Critique of Pure Reason and Other Works on the Theory of Ethics*, translated by T. K. Abbott [London: Longmans, Green and Co., 1963], p. 31)
13. Rudolf Otto, *The Idea of the Holy* (Oxford University Press, 1928), p. 189.
14. Cf. Tauler, "Sermon on St. John the Baptist," in *The Inner Way: Thirty-six Sermons for Festivals*, new translation, edited with introduction by Arthur Wollaston Hutton (London: Methuen and Co., Ltd., 1901), pp. 97–99. Cf. St. John of the Cross, *Noche Oscure*, vol. I, Book 2, chap. 17. Based upon Conze, *Buddhism*, p. 18.

teaching of "Non-Self." In the *Theologica Germanica* (an anonymous work of the same tradition as the above German mystics) are many words reminiscent of Buddhist technical terms such as non-attachment, the perverted views, self-deception, suchness, the One, emptiness, desire, etc. (Their Buddhist equivalents would be *asaṅga, viparyāsa, avidyā, tathatā, eka* or *advaya, śūnyatā* and *tṛṣṇā*, respectively.)

The Taoist conception of the void, to which the Buddhist counterpart was later fused, also compares, though not exactly, with the Mādhyamika one. "Wang Pi refers to the Way of *Tao*[15] as 'non-being' (*wu*), without, however, explaining very clearly what he means by this term. But when we turn to the *Chang-tzu Commentary*[16] it becomes apparent that 'non-being' is there interpreted as actually signifying a state of nothingness. In other words, it is equivalent to what we would today describe as a mathematical zero. Hence *Tao*, since it is 'non-being,' cannot be regarded as the first cause or prime mover for things in the world of being. On the contrary, we are told that all things are the way they are simply because of an inherent natural tendency which causes them to be thus."[17]

Later Taoists held the doctrine of "self-transformation" (*tu hua*), discarding the necessity of the original concept of *Tao*. This doctrine was set forth by Hsian Hsiu and Kuo Hsiang. "According to these statements, what we call the Way or *Tao* is simply a designation for the principle that 'everything produces itself and does not issue from anything else.' . . . For in actual fact, 'being' as such eternally exists."[18]

Chang Tsai (1020–77) opposed the Buddhist doctrine of *sunyata* which was interpreted as "nothingness." He employed his key metaphysical concept of *ch'i* (vital force) to prove the existence of the objective universe, drawing his arguments from empirical data which he had painstakingly gathered and subsequently reflected upon. This is not to say, however, that Chang Tsai was an epistemological empiricist in the sense that sense-perception was for him the source of knowledge nor that the existence of the external world was reduced to the awareness of the mind.[19]

15. "What Lao Tzu symbolizes by the term '*Tao*' corresponds to Whitehead's Creativity as the metaphysical ultimate." (Arnolds Grava, "Tao: An Age-old Concept in Its Modern Perspective," *Philosophy East and West*, vol. XIII, no. 3 [October 1963], p. 248)
16. Joint interpretation by Hsiang-Kuo.
17. Fung Yu-lan, *A History of Chinese Philosophy*, translated by Derk Bodde (Princeton, New Jersey: Princeton University Press, 1953), vol. II, pp. 207–208.
18. *Ibid.*, p. 209.
19. Siu-chi Huang, "Chang Tsai's Concept of Ch'i" *Philosophy East and West*, vol. XVIII, no. 4 (October 1968), p. 256. Chang Tsai was a methodological sceptic. He said, "If one can doubt what seems to others not to be doubtful, he is making progress." He would doubt the reliability of any proposition until it could be proved to be so. (*Ibid.*)

In the medieval West there appeared a number of mystics who taught that their mystical experience was of the absolute. Among Buddhists of India, China and so on, and Neo-Confucianists of the Sung and Ming periods of China, are found mystics who also resorted to this line of thought. There will be no attempt here to comprehensively treat this trend as a historical phenomenon. But as an example of the approach to the problem, a variation of this phase of mysticism as found in Zen Buddhism will be discussed in reference to other systems. This is not affirmation that all Zen Buddhists have patently affirmed the existence of an absolute. One Zen saying, however, does state that, "Seeing into one's own nature" means that the seeing of this "Buddha-mind" is the same as becoming the Buddha—that one is the Buddha.

The Western counterpart of this trend in Zen mysticism can be found in Angelus Silesius, a Christian mystic, who said, "If Jesus should be born in Bethlehem a thousand times, and yet if he is not in you, you will remain lost for ever."

> Though Christ a thousand times
> In Bethlehem be born.
> If He's not born in thee
> Thy soul is still forlorn.[20]
> The Cross on Golgotha
> Will never save thy soul,
> The Cross in thine own heart
> Alone can make thee whole.

Jabal-ed-din Rumi, a Muslim mystic, also said, "Get the knowledge of the Prophet in your heart without a book, without a teacher, without a guide."[21]

The *Theologia Germanica*[22] (c. 1425) constantly emphasized that "I-hood and selfhood," or "I, me, and mine" is the source of all alienation from true reality, and that there is the need to undo that "blindness and folly." "Self-will" is repeatedly repudiated in the work (cf. *anātman* theory in Buddhism). Self-will underwent the same demotion at the hands of the Zen master Dōgen.[23] According to the *Theologia Germanica*, the "deified man" is activated by both "cognition" and "love" wherein there neither is nor may remain any I, Me, Mine, Thou, Thine, and the like. Such a man may be compared to the Bodhisattva, as depicted in Mahāyāna Buddhism, who is motivated by cognition (*prajñā*) and compassion (*karuṇā*).

A well-known motto of Zen, "Direct pointing to the mind of man,"

20. *Cherubic Wanderer* I, 61.
21. Glasenapp, *Buddhismus und Gottesidee*, p. 98.
22. New York: Pantheon Books, 1949.
23. *Shōbō-Genzō-Zuimonki*, passim.

may be interpreted that man originally has the Buddha-mind and needs the actual experience of it. That is, the master points to the Buddha-nature, or reality itself. Zen practioners believe deeply in the original Buddha-hood of each man and express this through meditative disciplines which can bring out the Buddha and the patriarchs in everyone. Because of this Zen masters often stressed that one must rely on living experience rather than the words and letters of the *sūtras*.

Zen teaching claims a special lineage of transmission from Mahākāśyapa, the great disciple of Śākyamuni. Adherents of Zen say that when the Buddha conveyed the teaching, all stood nonplussed save Mahākāśyapa, whose understanding smile brought this recognition from his master: "I have the most precious treasure, spiritual and transcendental, which this moment I had over to you, O venerable Mahākāśyapa!"[24] Tradition asserts that this knowledge was handed down from Mahākāśyapa through a line of patriarchs to Bodhidharma, who brought it to China, where it continued to be passed from teacher to teacher. Because this knowledge can never be written down, Zen does not rely on scriptures, even though it may use them as expedients for instruction.

Western mystics, it may be recalled, did not deny the mission conveyed from Jesus Christ through Peter. However, in this respect one notices a similarity rather with the religion of the *Tantras* in medieval India. The Tantric form of Indian mysticism is claimed by its adherents to be the secret teaching and rites which were told by Śiva, the primordial god of the world, to his consort (Durgā or Kālī). The *Tantras* were supposed to be the scriptural authority and rule for the present degenerated age, the *kaliyuga*. The rites and doctrines which they inculcate are to prevail until the close of the *kaliyuga*. The awareness that they were living in an age of dissipation and degeneration was very strong among peoples in different countries during the Medieval Ages.

The division of the whole Buddhist period into "true dharma" and "simulated dharma" existed in several texts of Indian Buddhism. Hui-ssu (515–577) set forth the idea of the five hundred years of true law, one thousand years of simulated law, and ten thousand years of corrupt law. This theory prevailed in Chinese Buddhism,[25] and was inherited by Japanese Buddhism. The names for the three periods are: *Saddharma* (*Shōbō*), *Pratirūpa-dharma* (*Zōbō*), and *Paścima-dharma* (*Mappō*), respectively.[26] Ji-en (1155–1225), the learned Tendai priest who set forth a kind of philosophy of history, regarded the historic period of Japan as one of deterioration,

24. Perhaps the first occurrence of this story was in *T'ien-sheng kuang-teng lu*, compiled in 1036. It may be found in *Dainihon zokuzōkyō* 22:8. 4. 306 b–d (Kyoto: Zōkyō Shoin, 1905–1912).
25. *Taisho*, vol. 46, p. 786 c.
26. Anesaki, *Nichiren*, pp. 4–5.

following the three-state pattern of Buddhist history. For his evaluation of historic events, Ji-en depended on the criterion of *dōri* (*justice immanenta, des choses*), a concept greatly influenced by the ideas of the Chinese historian Liu Hsin.

3. Practical Consequences of Mysticism

AMONG popularizers of religion an important practical consequence of mysticism has always been certain supernormal by-products of the preliminary stages of the "ascent." Supernatural worlds and powers, designated *siddhis* and *abhijñās*, were believed by Indian mystics to be attainable much in the same way that Christians believed holy persons became capable of various miracles. The latter Neo-Platonist Abammon (flourished c. 300 A.D.) asserted that people who become filled with a certain holy enthusiasm can attain miraculous powers. This trend has been for the most part played down, however, by the most eminent mystics in favor of the supreme characterless experience that the highest form of mysticism nearly always seems to represent.

One of the most important practical consequences of the mystical experience is that it provides a metaphysical basis for personal morality. As pointed out above, descriptions of thc cxperience differ and yet at the same time suggest commonality. The Indian religionists spoke of a "deliverance" due to the knowledge of reality[1] which brought about "liberation from sufferings."[2] Alberuni pointed out how this feature was similar to Greek and Hellenistic mystics (such as Plotinus),[3] and also noted likenesses in practical significance between Christian and Sufi mystics.[4] It has been said that the *ekstasis* or *haptosis* ("the union with the deity")

1. *jñānād muktiḥ* (Kapila, *Sāṃkhya-sūtra* 3, 23).
2. All the names *mokṣa, apavarga, niḥśreyasa* are essentially negative and not redeem (*apolytrosis, exagorasmos, redemptio*) in the Christian sense, but sheer liberation.
3. "Others (some Greeks) thought that he who turns with his whole being towards the First Cause, striving to become as much as possible similar to *it*, will become united with *it* after having passed the intermediate stages, and stripped of all appendages and impediments. Similar views are also held by the *Sufi*, because of the similarity of the dogma." (Sachau, *Alberuni's India*, p. 34)
4. Having described the eight spiritual powers which can be attained by Yogis, Alberuni said. "The terms of the Sufi as to the *knowing* being and his attaining the *stage of knowledge* come to the same effect, for they maintain that he has two souls—an eternal one, not exposed to change and alteration, by which he knows that which is hidden, the transcendental world, and performs wonders; and another, a human soul, which is liable to being changed and being born. From these and similar views the doctrines of the Christians do not much differ." (*Ibid.*, p. 69)

of Plotinus corresponds to the *pratibhā* or the *pratibhāṃ jñānam* of the Yoga system.[5]

Sometimes, however, a consequence of mystical experience is that the person who had it refuses to interpret it at all. St. Thomas, for instance, reportedly experienced prolonged ecstasy during the last year of his life, but despite the entreaties of his secretary Reginald, he refused to write any more.

Just as there were different reactions to the mystical experience, there were different views of its relationship to moral problems. Justification of moral virtues is possible by the fundamental supposition that human beings in their innermost are good and pure. In Zen Buddhism a common saying is, "Living beings are by origin (essentially) Buddhas." Eckhart also said that "beneath the garment of goodness" the essential nature of God is latent; intellectualism in the mediaeval age taught the *perseitas boni*, the rationality of the good.[6] Zen speaks of an "effortless, purposeless, useless man who, because he doesn't exert his limited self desires, is in accord with Buddha-nature." This would seem to correspond to Eckhart's man of freedom, defined as "one who clings to nothing and to whom nothing clings."[7] (It must be added, however that the "nothing" of Zen Buddhism is not often give a metaphysical interpretation.) Eckhart admitted the "natural light," a basic part of the nature of all man, which makes moral principles known.[8] He believed that if the soul would know God, it must be God, it must cease to be itself, i.e., cease its limited separate selfishness. Dōgen said, "When you follow the process, you will became free from the suffering of life and death, and become Buddha."[9] This is quite similar to the method of attaining enlightenment in Zen Buddhism, namely, to sever the bonds of man's petty, selfish ego. Zen masters called it metaphorically "to break down a lacquer-painted pail" or "the collapse of mind and body."

Sometimes mystics rely on their experience as a reason to be moral and thereby an impetus to integrate their experience by their own efforts into all phases of their lives. According to the teachings of the Shingon of Kūkai, "the body, speech, and thought of the Great Illuminator [Japanese *Dainichi*, Sanskrit *Vairocana*] make up the life of the universe, whether as a whole or in parts, and the aim of Shingon ritual amounts to evoking the vitality of the 'three mysteries' in the body, speech, and thought of

5. *Yoga-sūtra* III. R. Garbe, *Philosophy*, of Ancient India (Chicago: The Open Court, 1899), p. 51.
6. Windelband, *History of Philosophy*, p. 332.
7. D. T. Suzuki, *Mysticism: Christian and Buddhist* (New York: Harper, 1957), p. 43.
8. Windelband, *History of Philosophy*, p. 332.
9. *Shōbō-Genzō*, Shōji, *Dōgen Zenji Zenshū*, edited by Doshu Okubo (Tokyo: Shunjūsha, 1930), p. 440.

every one of us. . . . This threefold category is common to all the systems of Hinduism, and to Manichaeism. Probably through the latter channel it influenced Augustine and entered the West, in the phrases 'thought, word, and deed.' "[10]

To other mystics, however, the import of their experience is such that the recipient can no longer do any wrong; his morality is more or less insured. According to the philosophy of Al-Ghazali (1058–1111), who has been regarded by some as the greatest thinker of Islam, the entire being of man is transformed in the practice. "Desire and passion are extinguished, consciousness is purged of objects of the world and concentrated upon God, and finally the mystic is blessed with the beatific vision, so that he passes away . . . from the self and abides in . . . the Divine Reality."[11] Milarepa, the Tibetan mystic poet, said that righteousness is not so much the immediate goal of the holy man as it is a by-product of enlightenment.

Another prevalent moral consequence of the mystical experience seems to be that, with regard to vast portions of the mystic's life, he considers himself to be amoral, somehow beyond morals; his actions no longer affect him personally. A typical statement of this opinion runs as follows: In the state of liberation, future *karmas* would not bind the practitioner of the mystic discipline and the result of past *karmas* will be exhausted in course of time. Thus the period between the realization of the perverse nature of desire and the deceptive nature of worldly objects and complete exhaustion of the results of past deeds provides an opportunity for the existence of a liberated but bodied soul. Such a person does not regard the world as world (i.e., as separate) but lives in the world as a part of it. Advaita Vedānta[12] would call this type of person a *jīvanmukta* and Mahāyāna Buddhism would name him a bodhisattva with a great deal of difference in connotation. Sureśvara[13] explains the existence of the body after a person is liberated as a phenomenon of the effect outliving its cause. He says that just as the fear of snakes continues for some time although the snake has vanished, the body, as an effect of perversion, continues for some time although perversion does not exist anymore.[14]

10. Anesaki, *History of Japanese Religion*, p. 125, text and n. 2.
11. Tara Chand, "Growth of Islamic Thought in India," in *History of Philosophy Eastern and Western*, vol. I, edited by S. Radhakrishnan and others (London: George Allen and Unwin, 1952), p. 498.
12. Although Fichte and Śaṅkara were far removed from each other in time, space, and cultural background, their theories are so remarkably similar that they should be both considered when idealism itself is discussed. (Leta Jane Lewis, "Fichte and Śaṅkara," *Philosophy East and West*, vol. XII, no. 4 [Jan. 1963], pp. 301–309).
13. *Naiṣkarmyasiddhi*, ed. by M. Hiriyanna, p. 199. According to R. C. Pandeya, *Indian Philosophical Annual*, 1969, p. 6.
14. In the state of liberation the individual is not annihilated or destroyed; it disappears

To the same effect (amorality), some mystics interpret their experience as confirmation of the illusory character of life as we usually perceive it, the domain of ordinary morality. This attitude exactly corresponds to that of the Sāṃkhya philosophers. According to it the Spirit (*puruṣa*) is never in fact bound to the world. "Nothing is bound: nothing is released. Nothing transmigrates."[15] "As a dancer ceases from the dance after having been seen by the audience; so also Matter (*prakṛti*) ceases after having manifested herself to the Spirit (*puruṣa*)."[16] "The Spirit is indifferent (*upekṣaka*).[17] He is a spectator (*draṣṭṛ*)".[18] "The Soul does not worry about troubles of the world, just seeing quietly."[19]

After the process of religious practice, the contemplative, however grateful for the gift of being in the world to have been able to attain the mystic state, nontheless wishes to remain immune from the effects of such being. In *The Cloud of Unknowing* it is said, "And yet in all this sorrow he desireth not to un-be; for that were devil's madness and despite unto God. But he liketh right well to be; and he giveth full heartily thanks unto God for the worthiness and the gift of his being, although he desire unceasingly for to lack the knowing and the feeling of his being."[20] This is exactly the spiritual situation which Master Dōgen and other Zen masters professed.

The consequence of this way of thinking has been that some mystics have seemed not even to care for the suffering of others. Looking at the corpses of war-dead, Kṛṣṇa in the *Bhagavadgītā* remarked, "You have grieved for those whom you should not grieve for, and yet you speak words about wisdom. Wise men do not grieve for the dead or for the living."[21]

A similar ideas was expressed by Plotinus: "Murder, death in all its disguises, the reduction and sacking of cities, all must be to us just such a spectacle as the changing scenes of a play; all is but the varied incident of a plot, costume on and off, acted grief and lament. For on earth, in all the succession of life, it is not the Soul within but the Shadow outside of the authentic man, that grieves and complains and acts out

in the Absolute; it is, as Bradley says, "merged," "blended," "fused," "absorbed," "run together," "dissolved," "or lost." (Ram Pratap Singh, "Radhakrishnan and Śaṅkara Vedānta, "*Philosophy East and West*, vol. XVI, nos. 1–2 [Jan.–April, 1966], p. 26)

15. *Sāṃkhya-kārikā* 62.
16. *Ibid.*, 59.
17. *Ibid.*, 66.
18. *Ibid.*
19. Gerald Larson, *Classical Sāṃkhya* (Delhi, Banaras, and Patna, 1969), pp. 279–280.
20. *The Cloud of Unknowing*, C. 84:20. Cited from Johnston, *Mysticism of The Cloud of Unknowing*, p. 214.
21. II. 11.

the plot on this world stage which men have dotted with stages of their own constructing."[22]

Certain Zen writings suggest a like attitude. Morality (at least if purposefully carried out) requires a certain amount of bifurcation of the world; i.e., a self capable of a moral action must be separate from the world as the domain of his action. Seng Tsan, the second patriarch of Zen, warned against such bifurcation:

> Abide not with dualism,
> Carefully avoid pursuing it;
> As soon as you have right and wrong,
> Confusion ensues and Mind is lost.[23]

And further,

> . . . The Enlightened have not likes and dislikes.
> All forms of dualism
> Are contrived by the ignorant themselves.[24]

For a certain type of Zen master, then, mental direction in decision-making can only lead to a separation of a world that is complete just as it is. The question of how Zen masters seem to be so perfectly in accord with socially acceptable moral standards requires explanation too detailed to be appropriate here.

4. Ecumenical Thinking

The religious experiences of some men through the ages have suggested to them that an explanation of such experience emphasizing its universal character would be appropriate. Thinking that their experience was somehow indicative of the nature of the Absolute, such men have stressed that no matter what method was used to arrive at such an experience, if it is of similar description, it also has the saving effect of having touched the Absolute. This is an aspect of what in this section is referred to as "ecumenical thinking." Generally, for doctrinal reasons, such a way of thinking was unpopular in the clericalism of the medieval West and perhaps still is today. When it has been seen how universally and among what caliber of thinkers this opinion has been held, it is hoped that the approach of this section (as well as the comparative approach of the entire work) will promote tolerance of such an opinion.

22. *Enneads*, III. 2. 15.
23. D. T. Suzuki, *Manual of Zen Buddhism* (New York: Grove Press, 1960), p. 78.
24. *Ibid.*, p. 79.

As stressed above, Buddhism from the very beginning was quite tolerant of other paths leading to what was assumed to be the same goal. And of course this must be said for the general trend of Hindu thought, which successfully absorbed most of the ideas of Buddhism throughout its history. A great many gods, based on natural phenomena, had been admitted in the Vedas; and this must have fostered a great tolerance for each of the various gods worshipped in India. The *Laws of Manu* contain a poignant saying which expresses this tolerance: "All gods verily are the Self."[1] In the *Bhagavadgītā* the attitude arose which implied the possibility of the existence of various religions. This became a very popular trend in subsequent Hindu thought. "But whatever form a devotee with faith wishes to worship, I make steady that faith of his."[2]

In the West, despite the unpopularity among clerics of the attitude of many paths to the same goal, mystics favored this viewpoint. Two possible reasons for this immediately come to mind. The first reason is the strongest: that such a viewpoint seems to be a natural consequence of the mystical experience. As a mystical sympathizer, inspired by the descriptions of an earlier triumphant follower of a path, tries to use similar methods, he finds the introspective nature of the path leads him toward his own individualized version of it. And further, when the experience occurs to him, he finds himself describing it in the same negative (i.e., characterless) way his predecessors had. These factors certainly must contribute to his belief that any path leading to a similar experience is as good as any other. A second reason, especially among all the mystics of the Middle Ages, must surely be the effect of Plotinus.

Plotinus admitted the possibility of various paths leading to the absolute in the following way. "There are different roads by which this end (of spiritual apprehension) may be reached; the love of beauty which exalts the poet; that devotion to the one and that ascent of science which make the ambition of the philosopher; that love and those prayers by which some devout and ardent soul tends in its moral purity towards perfection. These are the great highways conducting to that height above the actual and the particular, where we stand in the immediate presence of the Infinite, who shines out as from the deeps of the soul."[3]

Such a tendency did not vanish in the West, but was maintained by some church fathers of early Christianity. They at least had considered that previous studies in different traditions had done them no harm. Justin Martyr, for instance, sought divine knowledge in the schools of Zeno, Aristotle, Pythagoras, and Plato before he turned his attention to

1. *Manu* XII, 119.
2. VII, 21. This passage was cited from Eliot Deutsch's translation (New York: Holt, Rinehart, and Winston, 1968), p. 75, to make clear the philosophical implication.
3. Letter to Flaccus. This passage was cited from S. Radhakrishnan, *The Bhagavadgita* (New York: Harper and Brothers, 1948), p. 54, n. 1.

the study of the Jewish prophets. Clement of Alexandria acquired much from reading the works of Greek scholars and also from studying Tertullian in Latin. Julius Africanus and Origen possessed a very considerable share of the learning of their times.[4]

Even in the Islamic tradition, which is noted for its exclusiveness, a tendency of tolerance appeared; as one example, Ibn al-'Arabi' believed in the unity of all religions. According to him, all paths meet in one 'straight path' (*al tariq al'amam*) which leads to God. Monotheism and polytheism, philosophic religion and the crudest forms of idolatry are all beliefs regarding one God, are aspects of one universal religion. For the *Qurân* says, 'for each one of you have we made a religion and a pathway.' And then, God is the essence of everything including gods that are worshipped, and therefore in every form it is He who is worshipped.[5] Such an attitude continued in the West at least into the nineteenth century. Louise Claude de St. Martin boldly expressed the opinion that "all men who are instructed in fundamental truths speak the same language, for they are inhabitants of the same country."[6]

In the East, as mentioned above, there appeared many ways of thought that incorporated other methods.[7] The most conspicuous one, however, is the Shingon philosophy of Kūkai in Japan. Kūkai was a philosopher of all-absorbing syncretism. "In him," it has been said, "were combined the dialectic mind of a Hegel, the theosophic tendency of a Philo, the syncretic mind of a Manu. Indeed, the affinity or connection of Shingon Buddhism with Manichaeism or the Alexandrian theosophy is a question of great interest."[8] And further that, "In embracing the deities and demons, saints and goblins, Hindu, Persian, Chinese and others, into the Buddhist pantheon, Shingon Buddhism interpreted them to be but manifestations of one and the same Buddha."[9]

Kūkai took a conciliatory attitude toward Shinto, and it provided the theoretical basis for Ryōbu ("Two Aspects") Shinto, a Shinto-Buddhist amalgamation. This development brought about a popular belief that the Shinto gods (*kami*) are nothing but manifestations (*suijaku*) of the Buddhas and Bodhisattvas who are the original realities (*honji*).

4. Edward Gibbon, *The Decline and Fall of the Roman Empire, Great Books of the Western World*, vol. 40 (Chicago: Encyclopedia Britannica, 1952), pp. 204–205.
5. Tara Chand, "Growth of Islamic Thought in India," in *History of Philosophy Eastern and Western*, vol. 1, p. 501.
6. Quoted by W. Major Scott, *Aspects of Christian Mysticism* (London: John Murray, 1907), p. 61. This comes from Joseph Politella, "Meister Eckhart and Eastern Wisdom," *Philosophy East and West*, vol. 15, no. 2 (April, 1965), p. 133.
7. Hajime Nakamura, *Ways of Thinking of Eastern Peoples: India, China, Tibet, Japan*, edited by Philip P. Wiener (Honolulu: East-West Center Press, 1964), pp. 284–294, 383–405.
8. Anesaki, *History of Japanese Religion*, p. 130.
9. *Ibid.*, p. 125.

III. THEOLOGY AND ITS COUNTERPARTS

A. Reasoning and Philosophy

THEOLOGICAL systems were developed concurrently with the establishment of social supremacy by religious orders. Universal religions in the Medieval Ages had early systematizers of their respective doctrines in Augustine (354–430), Buddhaghoṣa (c. 400 A.D.) of Southern Buddhism, and Vasubandhu (c. 320–400) of Northern Buddhism. Catholic scholasticism reached its highest synthesis in the work of Thomas Aquinas (1224?–74). In the same period Chu Hsi (1130–1200) in China completed the system of Neo-Confucianism which served as the ideological basis of the Sung period and later dynasties and of the Tokugawa government in Japan. Medieval scholasticism found all-comprehensive exponents in Mādhava (c. 1380) of India and Gyōnen (1240–1321) of Japan.

As a systematizer of Hīnayāna doctrine, Buddhaghoṣa knows no peer. He was brought up in India in the learning of the Brahmans, was converted to Buddhism, went to Ceylon, and became an exceedingly prolific writer. He is regarded as the highest authority of Southern Buddhism and is the author of a commentary on each of the four great collections of *Nikāyas* which are said to be the very teachings of the Buddha. But his greatest work is the *Way of Salvation* (*Visuddhimagga*), an encyclopedia of Buddhist doctrine. Indeed, it is proper in some ways to compare him with the most illustrious of the Latin fathers. One might call him the Saint Augustine of India. Both lived at nearly the same age. Both were converts, the one to Buddhism, the other to Christianity; both were men of majestic intellect and wide learning; both were prolific writers and authors of works which have been very influential even to the present day. Buddhaghoṣa employed citations from the Sacred Texts in his writings, quite after the manner of the fathers of the Christian Church.

In the Middle Ages after 1000 A.D. and before the fifteenth century what is called Scholasticism appeared. Medieval Christian philosophy tried to prove that the absolute Christian truth was revealed in scripture and developed as Catholic doctrine by the Church fathers, and that it could be ascertained in the human mind by philosophical thinking. In India of the same period, Vaiṣṇava teachers like Rāmānuja, Madhva, Nimbārka, etc., and Śaiva teachers of different faiths produced elaborate systems based upon *śruti* (revealed texts, i.e., the *Veda*), *smṛti* (traditional texts), and their own scriptures (the *Āgamas, Sunchitas,* etc.). The endeavor by Neo-Confucianists who appeared in China at nearly the same time was similar to the above. They endeavored to show that their particular opinions could be proven by scripture and reason alike, the result of reasoning being shown mostly in their commentaries upon fundamental texts, and not so much in their own independent books.

The principal subjects to which great Christian theologians from Anselm to Thomas Aquinas and Meister Eckhart devoted their interest were, as has been seen, such subjects as the existence of God, the relation of God and man, and the role of faith in the process of salvation. Also evident is that these topics are exactly the same as were discussed by great Indian theologians who taught sectarian theism. For Chinese Neo-Confucianists, heaven was discussed instead of God, and ethical problems and mental disciplines instead of salvation.

The work of Vedāntins, such as Bādarāyana, Śaṅkara,etc., stands to the *Upaniṣads* in the same relation as the Christian dogmatics to the New Testament. Both investigated teachings about the absolute—Brahman in the Vedānta dogmatics, and God in the Christian theology. Vedāntins pondered the world and the soul in its conditions of wandering and deliverance, and Christians theorized about conditions of life, death, and salvation. Both tried to remove apparent contradictions in the doctrines and bind them systematically together in a coherent way. Both were concerned especially to defend their systems against the attacks of opponents. This trend is noticed among Buddhist, Jain, and other Hindu orthodox systems as well.

In the Islamic world, also, theological speculation eventually came to the fore. The companions of the Prophet (*Sāhāba*) were so close to him and his message that they refused to apply reason to the revelation. But among the followers (*Tabi'ūn*) questions arose and people began to discuss the nature of God and His relation with man. Finally the Mutakallamīn (scholastics, dogmatics) endeavored to justify religious dogmas by the use of reasoning. The writers on *Ilm-i-Kalām* were concerned with finding philosophical support for religious dogmas.

An opposing feeling that existed early in the Middle Ages and continued throughout, was that basic religious dogma is somehow defiled if submitted to the mundaneness of rational argumentation. In the West after St. Thomas, this way of thinking eventually won out in the Church, bringing about the decline of Scholasticism as well as the gradual secularization of philosophy. In the early days especially, when new religions were rising, the followers did not care much for theology. In early Buddhism and Mahāyāna, for instance, teachings were compared to rafts. (This thought is noticed in a Mahāyāna *sūtra*.[1]) When the raft is finally left behind, and the vision of the two banks and the separating river is lost, then there is neither the realm of suffering nor that of deliverance. Moreover, there is no raft—no Buddhism—and there is no raftsman—no Buddha. Buddhism is nothing but the proceeding of the Path.

A notion somewhat similar to that of "the raft" can be found in the early Christianity of nearly the same period. According to Justin Martyr (c. 125–165) we need not accept any particular creed; it is enough if we live the life. "And those who live reasonably, (i.e., according to *logos*) are Christians even though they have been called atheists."[2] The seeds of Western theological thinking on this point however, are to be found among the Greeks. Before the existence of the established order of universal religions, some thinkers pointed out the possibility of at least two ways for acquiring knowledge. Plato said, "A man should persevere until he has achieved one of two things: either he should discover the truth about them for himself or be taught by some one else; or if this is impossible he should take the best and most irrefragable of human theories and make it the raft on which he sails through life."[3] This attitude was systematized by theologians of universal religions of the Medieval Ages.

It seems that the decay and fall of the Roman Empire in the West and of the Kuṣāna and Gupta dynasties in India (both characterized by continual wars) were not favorable to the development of philosophical thinking. Instead, fixed dogmatic methods and dogmas flourished and tended to hinder free thinking. This situation may be similar to that of Confucian orthodoxy in China. The examination system in education, for instance, was inevitably established with a Confucian curriculum, despite the generally strong Taoist and Buddhist sympathies of the Sui and T'ang rulers, because Confucianism provided the only available *corpus* of political theory, ritual precedents, and normative rules for the conduct of court and official affairs.

In India the *Vedas* were the sacred scriptures of orthodox Brahmanism and were known as the revelation (*śruti*). Brahmanic scholars held that the *Vedas* were not the work of man but revelations from time immemorial acquired by various sages (*ṛṣis*) through mystic inspiration and handed down by them from generation to generation. In order to differentiate between the *Vedas* and the compositions of the later sages, the latter were called *smṛti* and were supposed to be based on the *śruti*, i.e., the *Vedas*. Both

1. *Vajracchedikā-prajñāpāramitā-sūtra.*
2. Gilson, *History of Christian Philosophy*, p. 13. Cf. Radhakrishnan, *India and China* (Bombay: Hind Kitabs, 1944), p. 13.
3. I have expanded upon Jowett's translation of *Phaedo* 85.

śruti and *smṛti* were handed from father to son in an unbroken chain through many ages, and the Indians in general accorded to both authority and veneration. Concerning just what authority the instruction with regard to the sacrifice and its consequences commands, the Mīmāṃsā said that the *Veda* needs no authority, but is eternal and uncreated; its revelation concerns only things existing from eternity, and self-evident. For the Vedāntins the sentences of the *Upaniṣads* and similar passages were of absolute authority. Other philosophical schools also acknowledged the authority of the *Vedas* at least nominally. Bhartṛhari,[4] the Vedāntin and grammarian, accepted this view of the orthodox Brahmins, regarding the *Vedas* as the absolute source of all knowledge. He studied them diligently and was well versed in them.

Such an attitude toward basic scriptures can be found in other traditions also. Al-Mansur, a Muslim caliph, published an edict in which he declared that God had decreed hellfire for those who believed that truth could be found by means of unaided reason. During his reign, all books on logic and metaphysics were burnt. Al-Ghazali, the great Muslim philosopher, wrote a book called *The Destruction of the Philosophers* pointing out that, since all the truth necessary to life is to be found in the *Koran*, speculation independent of revelation is pointless. Abelard in his famous book, *Sic et Non* (*Yes and No*) states that nothing outside the scriptures is infallible; even apostles and fathers may err.

According to Bhartṛhari even something which is rejected by the public or considered to be contrary to all reason should nevertheless be obeyed and carried out if it is so stated in the sacred scriptures. In addition, he held that even if a phenomenon's existence is thought to be quite impossible, it must nevertheless be acknowledged if its existence is claimed in the sacred *Āgama*.[5] His veneration of the sacred scriptures may be regarded as conservative in the extreme, even blindly enthusiastic. Another point he wished to make was that in actual life no inference can exist which will meet with the approval of everyone. "A fact verified after much thought by those skilled in inference may be interpreted in quite a different way by those who are even more skilled in inference."[6] Thus, with regard to other than revealed "knowledge," Bhartṛhari maintained an attitude of relativism or scepticism. His arguments refuting inference became famous in later years, and various writings of the Vedānta school refer to these arguments.[7] Having assumed an attitude of relativism,

4. Hajime Nakamura, "Bhartṛhari the Scholar," in *Indo-Iranian Journal*, vol. IV, no. 4 (1960), pp. 282–305.
5. *Vākyapadīya* I, 42.
6. *Vākyapadīya* I, 34.
7. *Bhāmatī* ad *Brahmasūtra* II, 1, 11; *Sarvadarśanasaṃgraha* XVI, 11, 820–821. The statement is also quoted in the Anumānaparīkṣā of the *Tattvasaṃgraha of Śāntarakṣita*,

Bhartṛhari declared inference to be as a consequent, incapable of persuading: "When a person does not doubt his knowledge even as he does not doubt his senses, how can anyone persuade him?"[8] This brand of relativism or scepticism was not new in India but had been propounded by Sañjaya as early as Buddha's time, and the Jain belief had had similar philosophical inclinations from its inception. But the fact that an orthodox Brahmin should take up this attitude is remarkable indeed.

It is interesting to note in passing that what portions of Bhartṛhari's philosophy Śaṅkara accepted, he adopted as they were. This can be seen from the tone in which he propounded Bhartṛhari's doctrine in the following extracts from his writings. Śaṅkara said, "In matters to be known from Scripture mere reasoning is not to be relied on for the following reason also. As the thoughts of man are altogether unfettered, reasoning which disregards the holy texts and rests on individual opinion only has no proper foundation. We see how arguments, which some clever men had excogitated with great pains, are shown, by people still more ingenious, to be fallacious, and how the arguments of the latter again are refuted in their turn by other men; so that, on account of the diversity of men's opinions, it is impossible to accept mere reasoning as having a sure foundation." And again, "But that cognitions founded on reasoning do conflict is generally known; for we continually observe that what one logician endeavors to establish as perfect knowledge is demolished by another, who, in his turn, is treated alike by a third."[9]

Bhartṛhari's doctrine had influence on the later school of Advaitins as well. Mādhava, for example, accepted his view unreservedly.[10] (It might also be mentioned that a similarity exists between the view of Bhartṛhari, and Śaṅkara, and those of the French philosopher Blaise Pascal as expressed in his *Pensées*, where he asserted that the philosophical reflections of men are always one-sided and contradictory, and hence that people should revert to Christian truth.)

Regarding Bhartṛhari's own argument, one might notice that his conclusion "Therefore one should not rely on inference" is evidently derived from inference. For the proposition "One should not rely upon that which is not accepted by all" is presupposed as the major premise to the above statement. Here one comes face to face with the interesting case of a philosopher who negates inference, by making use of it himself.[11]

---

edited by Embar Krishnamacharya (Baroda: Central Library, 1926), as a doctrine of Bhartṛari (p. 426, v. 1462).

8. *Vākyapadīya*, I, 39.
9. Śaṅkara ad *Brahmasūtra* II, 1, 11 (Ānandāśrama Sanskrit Series, no. I [Poona: Ānandāśrama Press, 1900], pp. 449, 452).
10. *Sarvadarśanasaṃgraha* XVI, 11. 818 ff.
11. Eubalides said as follows: "Wenn ich sage: ich luge,—luge ich dann oder sage ich die Wahrheit? Wenn ich dabei die Wahrheit sage, so luge ich; wenn ich aber luge,

However, Bhartṛhari's real aim in refuting the power of inference is easily discernible; it was to minimize its importance and exalt the sanctity of the orthodox Brahmin *Āgama.* Thus all his statements quoted above point to the one conclusion that all inferences include falsehood, and he really believed this.

As to the status of the apparent contradiction, Bhartṛhari proposed the following solution: "When one wishes to convey to others that what one said was untrue, when one declares that one's sayings were nothing but lies, one does not mean the actual stating of that statement. For if the saying itself be false, the words fail to convey the meaning they were meant to convey."[12] This argument can be taken to mean that he repudiates the statement that "an assertion that all is falsehood is self-contradictory and therefore cannot exist." In other words, an assertion "all is false" can be either true or false.

Thus Bhartṛhari addressed himself to a philosophical problem that has plagued philosophers from the earliest time to the present day. Though it has many variations, some quite relevant to the philosophy of mathematics, the form closest to Bhartṛhari's problem is known as "the liar's paradox." Russell's theory of types and ramified counterpart addressed such problems. But Frank Ramsey's solution in the form of the simple theory of types has been given the most credence today. In the case of the liar's paradox it requires the supposition that notations for the naming relation and for truth (with formal properties as defined) do not occur in the domain of the paradoxical situation as constructed and in principle should not occur. Unfortunately Ramsey's solution is impossible to discuss in a short amount of space and requires a background in symbolic logic on the part of the reader. One can only hope this will be the subject of a scholarly study in the near future comparing Ramsey's solution with Bhartṛhari's.

It is indeed true that many of the interpretarions of words and phrases in the sacred books contradict each other. Even those who profoundly venerate the sacred books have to admit this. When confronted with such problems,[13] theologians had to resort to their mortal reasoning to decide

so sage ich eben die Wahrheit. Die Losung liegt darin dass in diesem Falle die Form des Urteils, welche den Anspruch involviert, etwas als seiend als wahr auszusagen, zufalligerweise mit dem Inhalt des Urteils in Widerspruch steht. Als Curiosum mag in Erinnerung gebracht werden, dass es . . . von den Kretern heisst. . . . Die Kreter sind immer Lugner." (Paul Deussen, *Allgemeine Geschichte der Philosophie*, II, 1 [Leipzig: F. A. Brockhaus, 1911], p. 212)

12. *Vākyapadīya* III, 3, 25, p. 108.
13. Pascal said: "If he had only reason without passion . . . if he had only passion without reason . . . But having both, he cannot be without strife, being unable to be at peace with the one without being at war with the other." (*Pensées*, no. 412, Libraire Hachette, p. 457)

which interpretation to use. The following words written by Bhartṛhari illustrate this clearly: "Logical argument (*tarka*) which does not contradict the sacred *Vedas* is as an eye to those who have not yet seen the truth. For the meaning of the sentences cannot be construed from the color (that is the tangible, material contents of the sacred books) alone."[14] Even as color which is a material thing can be perceived by the eye, so can the contents of the sacred books only be comprehended by rational reflection. Therefore, though he appears to be a profound venerator of the sacred books, Bhartṛhari was conscious of the eventual need to resort to rationality. Bhartṛhari's fellow countryman, Puṇyarāja, also makes this point quite clear in the following lines: "Logic which does not conflict with the *āgama* is indeed a proper foundation on which to build knowledge. And contrarily *āgama* which is not tempered with logic is meaningless." Interesting to say, the argument which Bhartṛhari employed to advocate the scriptures was used by the materialists to refute them.[15]

Western thinkers had the same problems of trying to reconcile seemingly contradictory parts of their scriptures or their interpretations of same. It is well known, for instance, that Avicenna's philosophical dogma of the supremacy of reason conflicts with his view of the "transcendent faculty" of the prophet.[16] In such a case a tactic that was employed in India by Bhartṛhari and Śaṅkara was utilized. Averroes made the point that "each time there appears any conflict between the religious text and demonstrative conclusions, it is by interpreting the religious text philosophically that harmony should be re-established."[17] According to the [Muslim] mystics, says Russell, every text of the Koran had 7 or 70 or 700 layers of interpretation, the literal meaning being only for the ignorant vulgar. It would seem to follow that a philosopher's teaching could not possibly conflict with the Koran; for among 700 interpretations there would surely be at least one that would fit what the philosopher had to say.[18] Among early Buddhist theologians of China also, the attainment of harmony among different scriptural statements was of the utmost concern.

In this respect it seems that Western theologians generally tried harder to be literal, and in the direction of detailed technical discussions, made more effort, whereas Eastern theologians were quite free with their interpretations. When Indian theologians found a contradic-

14. *Vākyapadīya* I, 137.
15. *Vākyapadīya* I, 137. Cf. I, 138.
16. W. Montgomery Watt, *Muslim Intellectual: A Study of Al-Ghazali* (Edinburgh: Edinburgh University Press, 1963), p. 54.
17. Gilson, *History of Christian Philosophy*, p. 218.
18. Russell, *History of Western Philosophy*, p. 426.

tion to a sentence of a scripture, they simply said, "Here the word 'not' is missing."

Faced with these and similar problems of discussing religious experience in terms of rational phrases (not always designed for the purpose they were being stretched to serve), many authors in the Middle Ages resorted to stratified conceptions of knowledge and/or truth. Bhartṛhari's fragmentary views regarding knowledge reveal that he recognized three ways in which knowledge could be obtained:

1. Perception through the senses (*pratyakṣa*)
2. Thinking by inference (*anumāna*)
3. Intuition of the Brahman (*āptavacana*)

The first and second methods are those applied by ordinary men, and according to one viewpoint of his, perception is stable and inference subsists on it.[19] While emphasizing, however, the fact that inference is unstable, he resorted to it in his own writings (as seen earlier). The three kinds of knowledge, as set forth by Bhartṛhari, were mentioned in nearly the same way by Thomas Aquinas. In his conception, "there are three ways of knowing God: by reason, by revelation, and by intuition of things previously known only by revelation. Of the third way, however, he says almost nothing."[20]

With regard to such stratified conceptions of truth, some asked if it was not possible that a thinker, accepting a traditional teaching, might still hold a different opinion of his own. Thinking that this was indeed possible, theories such as those of the "twofold truths" and the distinction of the "three orders of the teaching" cropped up. Averroes, as a case in point, thought that it was advisable to establish the distinction of three orders of interpretation and teaching: "at the peak, philosophy, which gives absolute knowledge and truth; immediately below that, theology, the domain of dialectical interpretation and of mere probability; and at the bottom of the scale, religion and faith, which should be left carefully to those for whom they are necessary." According to him, "theology is the worst type of speculation precisely because it is neither faith nor philosophy, but, rather, a corruption of both."[21]

Already, in Pyrrhon's philosophy, the distinction between conventional truth, the appearances (*phainomena*) on the one side, and the ultimate truth (*adela*) on the other, had been made. The ultimate truth, he felt, is completely hidden. "I do not know that honey is sweet, but I agree that it appears to me so." The doctrine of the twofold truth was expressly proclaimed by bold dialecticians such as Simon of Tournay, or John of Brescia, and was all the more rigidly condemned by the power of

19. *Vākyapadīya* III, 13, 12, p. 436.
20. Russell, *History of Western Philosophy*, p. 460.
21. Gilson, *History of Christian Philosophy*, p. 219.

the Church. However, the leading minds could not evade the fact that philosophy, as it had developed under the influence of Aristotle and the Arabians, was, and had to remain, alien to those doctrines of the Christian religion.[22]

A similar situation occurred with Buddhists, also. The idea of the two truths was held by some Sarvāstivādins—one truth for ordinary people, the other for philosophers. Vasubandhu in a more metaphysical context, admitted at least two kinds of existence. "If something exists by itself (as a separate element), it has an actual existence, as for instance color and other (ultimate elements of matter and mind). But if something represents a combination (of such elements) it is a nominal existence, as for instance milk."[23] Nāgārjuna admitted the two kinds of truth (or reality) which he termed absolute reality (*paramārtha-satya*) and empirical reality (*saṃvṛti-satya*, literally, the "surface reality").[24] By the latter he meant the traditional teaching of Hīnayāna, above which he placed his own doctrine. Mahayanists made a distinction between the conventional truth (*neyārtha*) and the real, perfect truth (*nītārtha*).

Inheriting the Buddhist conception, Advaita Vedāntins later set up the theory of the three truths:[25] i.e., the highest truth (*pāramārthika-satya*), the truth in daily life (*vyāvahārika-satya*), and the illusory truth (*Prātibhāsika-satya*). When one assumes that a rope is a snake, it is the illusory truth which is true insofar as illusion goes. When one realizes that what appeared to be a snake is nothing but a rope, it is the truth in daily life. However, even the rope is illusion, viewed from a metaphysical standpoint. This is, for the Vedāntins, the highest truth.

22. Windelband, *History of Philosophy*, pp. 320–321.
23. Th. Stcherbatsky, *The Soul Theory of the Buddhists* (Leningrad: Bulletin de l'Academie des Sciences de Russie, 1919), p. 829.
24. E.g., *Madhyamaka-kārikā* XXIV.
25. *Sarvadarśanasaṃgraha* XVI.

B. Frequently Discussed Problems

1. The Nature of the Absolute

a. Threefold Characterizations

THE sections that follow will be concerned with various ramifications that have occurred in the development of concepts of absolute(s). Christianity obviously began with a concept of an absolute, namely God. But Christ as the "Son of God" also claimed some right to absolute status in the eyes of theologians and believers. And later on, Mary as (in a sense) mother of God, along with various saints, seemed to have a more than average degree of immanent deification as considered by later writers. (This was discussed in an earlier section.) In India, from early days orthodox religious believers wholeheartedly accepted the idea of an immanent and transcendent God. Part of the heterodoxy of Buddhism is that it seemed, for a long time, to resist such an idea (at the very least remaining entirely silent on the question of the existence of such entity(ies).) Before too long had passed, however, the Buddha became more and more magnified and deified until he was no longer regarded as a man but as, so to speak, the living God.[1] Mātṛcata, the poet (second century A.D.) addressed the Buddha, "Only you yourself can know yourself who are beyond measure, beyond number, beyond thought, beyond comparison."[2]

Since each of the major traditions eventually developed concepts of an absolute, this subject will now be discussed, beginning with a short examination of the triune divisions of the absolute in various traditions.

The immediate successors of the Christian apostles were not concerned with inquiry into the relationship between Father, Son and Spirit. But in later days theologians concentrated on this problem, and it became an issue of heated debate. The Western problem of trinity is close to the Three Forms of God (*trimūrti*) in Hinduism,[3] especially as the former was

1. The God of the "Kirishitans" (the Japanese Catholics in feudal days) was properly called *Deus-Nyorai. Nyorai* is the Japanese equivalent of the Sanskrit *tathāgata* (Buddha).
2. *Adhyardhaśataka* 151.
3. "For Eckhart and Ruysbroeck, there is an Abyss of Godhead underlying the Trinity, just as Brahman underlies Brahma, Vishnu and Shiva." In the diagrammatic picture

formulated by Jacob Boehme, who claimed that creation was the act of the Father, and the incarnation that of the Son, while the end of the world would be brought about through the operation of the Holy Ghost. Roughly speaking, the Self in its transcendental (*adhidaivam*), cosmic (*adhibhūtam*) and individual (*adhyātman*) aspects as mentioned in the *Upaniṣads* corresponds to the Christian Trinity of Father, Son, and Holy Ghost, although there remains a great difference. The idea of the Self in its three aspects appeared in early *Upaniṣads*[4] and was maintained throughout the long history of Vedānta. It stood the test of time and existed throughout nearly the same time period as the comparable idea in the West.

A similarity between the Christian and Hindu conceptions of a threefold absolute was noticed by Alberuni. He cited a theory in which the first cause, called Brahman, Prajāpati, and many other names, brings forth the creation of the world; the second force, called Nārāyaṇa, preserves that which has been created; and the third force, called Mahādeva or Rudra, destroys the world. He continued: "Here there is an analogy between Hindus and Christians, as the latter distinguish between the Three *Persons* and give them names, Father, Son and Holy Ghost, but unite them into one substance."[5] The relation between Brahman, Īśvara, and Māyā in Advaita Vedānta is also somewhat similar to the relation between Father, Son, and Holy Ghost. But the notion of salvation, the primary function of the Christian trinity, is lacking in Advaita Vedānta.

A similar theory is found in Mahāyāna, which considers the Buddha under three aspects, which are essentially one:

(1) The essential body (*dharmakāya*), which is the pure and undifferentiated one. It is the same as the "Void."

(2) The enjoyment body (*saṃbhogakāya*), which is the perfect figure of the Buddha who is enjoying the results of his religious practices in the past. It might be called the Buddha as an ideal and accomplished personality provided with every kind of virtue.

(3) The transformation body (*nirmāṇa-kāya*), by which the Buddha works for the good of all creatures. The person of the historical Buddha is counted as one example of this.

The second aspect in particular became the object of worship among the

---

left by Suso "a chain of manifestation connects the mysterious symbol of the Divine Ground with the three Persons of the Trinity." (Aldous Huxley, *The Perennial Philosophy* [New York: Harper, 1945], Introduction, p. 14)

4. E.g., *Bṛhad. Up.* III. 7. 14 f.

5. Sachau, *Alberuni's India*, p. 94. In a picture of early Christianity the Trinity was shown with one head and three faces. (Roland H. Bainton, *The Church of Our Fathers* [New York: Charles Scriber's Sons, 1950], p. 42)

followers of Mahāyāna. The first concept, "the essential body," became the pivot of Buddhist philosophy and culminated in the Shingon (Vajrayāna) school. The main idea of Shingon is cosmotheism (not quite the same as pantheism) in which the whole universe is regarded as the body of the supreme Buddha Vairocana, being composed of the six elements (i.e., earth, water, fire, air, ether, and consciousness).

The concept of a set of three principles was also conceived, consisting of Amitāyus, Avalokiteśvara and Mahāsthāmaprāpta (i.e., "the one who has attained great strength"). Conze has found counterparts to this Trinity in Iranean religion as well "in the Mithras cult and in Zervanism, a Persian religion which recognised Infinite Time (Zervan Akarana= Amita-āyus) as the fundamental principle." Assimilated by Buddhism, Conze states further, "Avalokiteśvara became a great Bodhisattva, so great that he is nearly as perfect as a Buddha."[6]

Discussions of this abtruse problem are difficult, but one difference can be easily pointed out: both Christians and Hindus regarded God as being, whereas Mahāyāna Buddhists regarded the absolute Buddha as the "void" beyond being and non-being.

Among Western conceptions of trinity, the creator aspect has been given a goodly degree of emphasis. According to Christian orthodoxy, God is the maker of heaven and earth. A debate of grave consequence developed in the Hellenistic period because certain gnostics thought the earth was bad and God the Father did not create it. In India the same problem was discussed by the Hindus, who asserted the world's creation by Brahman, Viṣṇu or Śiva on the one hand, and the Buddhists and Jains who denied this theory. In China and Japan this problem was not discussed, for both peoples gave up the notion of world-creation as held in earlier days.

However, of the three aspects in the Christian trinity, the son has received the most emphasis in theological argumentation. In a sense the other two parts of the triadic explanation of the Godhead are but further (sometimes metaphysical) explanations and authentication of the most important representation, and the historical incarnation. Because of differences of opinion in the New Testament as to whether or not the Son of God could have undergone suffering and death on the cross, a sect of Christian gnostics (whose thought was later held to be heretical[7]) came to hold a view of Christ's incarnation known as "docetism." Christian docetism asserted that Christ was too divine to suffer agony and death,

6. Conze, *Buddhism*, p. 147.
7. The 'Gospel of Peter' gave the incidents of the life of Jesus a 'Docetic' tinge. This was condemned. (E. E. Kellet, *A Short History of Religion* [Middlesex: Penguin Books, 1962], pp. 172–204) The Albigenses, who were called Catharis or Puritans, were Docetists, and held, like Mani, to the principle of dualism. (*Ibid.*, p. 278)

and that he only seemd (Greek: *dokeo*) to do so. They claimed that the Christ descended on the man Jesus at baptism and left him again on the cross, at the point where Jesus cried, "My God, my God, why hast Thou forsaken me?" Clement sought, although without success, to avoid docetism.[8] In some respects docetic thought passed over into Islam.[9]

For example, a touch of docetism appeared in the Islamic thought of Ash'ari (born 873 A.D.). "The universe is contingent (*mumkin*), he held, as the substance and quality that make it up are both contingent. Qualities are merely subjective relations, and as no substance can exist apart from qualities, the universe of things is a system of appearances, a 'mere show of ordered subjectivities.' [This assumedly would apply to the physical form of the prophet.] Substances with their accidents constitute indivisible elements or atoms, which are continuously created and destroyed by the Will of God."[10]

In Eastern countries also, teachings comparable to docetism were of great influence. In Mahāyāna Buddhism the *Lotus Sūtra* proclaimed as follows: people believe that the Buddha was born in Kapilavastu, attained enlightenment, taught the Law, and died in Kusinagara; however, his birth, life, teaching, and death are but an appearance, and his passing away is but a device to lead men to accept the teachings of the Buddha. His essence or real body is eternal. The Mahāyāna thereby substitutes for the historical Buddha the eternal Buddha. According to its doctrine, his existence in the earthly form is not his true and proper mode of being. In the *Lotus Sūtra* the Buddha said:

> An inconceivable number of thousands of *koṭis* of Aeons, never to be measured, is it since I reached superior enlightenment and never ceased to teach the law.
>
> I show the place of extinction, I reveal to all beings a device to educate them, albeit I do not become extinct at the time, and in this place continue preaching the law.
>
> There I rule myself as well as all beings, I. But men of perverted minds, in their delusion, do not see me standing there.
>
> In the opinion that my body is completely extinct, they pray worship, in many ways, to the relics, but me they see not.

8. Seeberg, *History of Doctrines*, p. 143.
9. Mahomet "adopted the view of the Docetics (a Gnostic sect), according to which it was a mere phantom that hung upon the cross, upon which, impotently and ignorantly, Jews and Romans wreaked their ineffectual vengeance. In this way, something of Gnosticism passed over into the orthodox doctrine of Islam." (Russell, *History of Western Philosophy*, p. 325)
10. Tara Chand, "Growth of Islamic Thought in India," in *History of Philosophy Eastern and Western*, p. 492.

> I was not completely extinct at that time; it was but a device of mind; repeatedly am I born in the world of the living.
>
> Such is the glorious power of my wisdom that knows no limit, and the duration of my life is as long as an endless period.[11]

These verses were regarded by the Nichiren sect of Japan as representing the supreme and essential teaching of Buddhism.

In Hinduism also a similar teaching arose. In no less important a scripture than the *Bhagavadgītā* can be found:

> Though I am unborn, and My self is imperishable, though I am the lord of all creatures, yet establishing Myself in My own nature, I come into birth through My power (*māyā*).
>
> Whenever there is a decline of righteousness and rise of unrighteousness, then I send forth (create incarnate) My self.
>
> For the protection of the good, for the destruction of the wicked and for the establishment of righteousness, I come into birth age after age.[12]

To the thinkers who share the docetic turn of thought, the question of historical existence seems to be quite irrelevant. In this respect theological-style thinking took similar direction in all the major religions. The main difference between traditions is that unlike in Christian docetism and gnosticism, the eternal Buddha in Mahāyāna and God in Hinduism become incarnate repeatedly to save suffering people.

b. Interrelational Existence

A discussion of interrelatedness may seem strange under a large heading dealing with absolute(s). Anything absolute is usually opposed, in philosophical circles, to relativism of all sorts. Strictly speaking, it may be better not to label some of the ways of thinking included in this section as absolutism (and indeed many adherents of some of the thought included herein would repudiate such a label), because to do so might add concepts to those ways of thinking which are not there. Herein are included some of the beliefs of philosophers who held that every thing in the universe is so related one to the other as to constitute one indivisible whole; that is why this thought has been included under discussion of the absolute. This way of thinking has had vast consequences up to the present time. It survived in nineteenth century Western philosophy and flourished as

11. *Saddharmapuṇḍarika-sūtra* XV, vv. 1–18. Cf. *Sacred Books of the East*, vol. XXI, pp. 307–309.
12. *Bhagavadgītā* IV, 6–8.

German Idealism; and, principally as expounded by Hegel, it has been one of the chief points of departure, usually be way of reaction, in the twentieth century. Perhaps the most advanced metaphysical system yet proposed in the West, that of Whitehead, will come to the minds of many as they read this section. Interrelatedness (for want of a better term to call this way of thinking) is considered in turn from a metaphysical, ethical, and then epistemological viewpoint although these three are themselves so interrelated that a neat division one from the other, especially in such subject matter as this, is always very difficult.

According to the concept of Interdependent Origination of Mahāyāna Buddhism, all existences and phenomena are interrelated. Even a flower is closely connected with all the universe, having no separate existence in the metaphysical sense. The tiny violet droops its fairy head just so much and no more, it is balanced by the universe. It is a violet, not an oak, because it is the outcome of the interrelational existence of an endless series of the past. One cannot sever himself from the past. This can be said of everything in the universe.

The interconnection between one individual and the whole universe was especially stressed by the *Buddhāvataṃsaka-sūtra* of India which became the central scripture of the Hua-yen sect in China and the Kegon sect in Japan. The *Buddhāvataṃsaka-sūtra* says, "Within one pore of the body all living beings are accommodated,"[1] or "All things appear in one pore,"[2] and "The visible body of a Buddha teaches the ocean of merits of all Buddhas."[3] This idea was not limited to Buddhism alone. In the *Mahābhārata* also it is said, "The world of mortals is an interdependent aggregate."[4] Among Christian mystics Eckhart clearly expressed th same idea. "Here all blades of grass, wood and stone, all things are one." . . . Black is still black, white is still white, and yet the opposites coincide. "In the Kingdom of Heaven all is in all, all is one, and all is ours."[5]

The idea of unification with all creatures had been expressed already in early Christianity,[6] but the idea of unification was limited to the mem-

1. The *Hua-yen sūtra,* vol. 46, p. 245 b.
2. *Ibid.*, p. 403 c.
3. *sarvaromavivara-aśeṣabuddha-guṇasamudra-megha-nigarjana-varṇa* (*Gaṇḍavyūha-sūtra,* edited by D. T. Suzuki and H. Idzumi, p. 347, l. 24). I translated the word in collation with the Tang version (vol. 73, Taisho, p. 398 b).
4. *saṅghātavān martyalokaḥ parasparam apāśritaḥ* (*Mahābhārata* XII, 298, 17). The Sanskrit word for interdependence or interrelational existence is "*parasparopekṣā.*"
5. Rudolf Otto, *Mysticism East and West: A Comparative Analysis of the Nature of Mysticism,* translated by Bertha L. Bracey and Richenda C. Payne (New York: Macmillan Co., 1932), p. 61.
6. "He has put all things under his feet and has made him the head over all things for the church, which is his body, the fulness of him who fills all in all." (Ephesians I: 22–23) The unification with all creatures as a member of the body of Christ is solemnly expressed in the Communion (*tou ta panta en pāsi pleroumenou*).

bers of the church alone. Actually, the Indian idea has a most conspicuous counterpart in Plotinus, who so greatly influenced early church philosophy. According to him, the eternal selves also are in actuality fused with every other and, with a love-without-partition, make together an eternal company-without-partition. With the penetration of a black that is white and of a white that is black, all alike atone with all "without ceasing to be what they are in themselves." Plotinus said, "In this nature inheres all life and all intellect, a life living and having intellection as one act within a unity: every part that it gives forth is a whole, all its content is its very own, for there is here no separation of thing from thing, no part standing in isolated existence estranged from the rest, and therefore nowhere is there any wronging of any other, any opposition."[7]

This parallel is the more interesting considering that, though this theory was expressed throughout all Mahāyāna *sūtras*, it was especially stressed in the *Buddhāvataṃsaka-sūtra* which appeared in India at nearly the same time that Plotinus was writing its counterpart in the West. It is notable that, following Plotinus, Proclus (410–485) also said, "All things are in all, but each is appropriately in each."[8] However a contrast must be noted in that where Plotinus and Proclus admitted one first cause,[9] their way of apprehension was different from the Avataṃsaka philosophy which, according to traditional Buddhist doctrine, denied one first cause. Proclus, after he had admitted the interrelatedness of all things, continued, "For in being there are life and intellect; and in life being and thought; and in intellect being and life. But in intellect, indeed, all things subsist intellectually, in life vitally, and in being all things are truly beings . . . everything subsists either according to cause, or according to hyparxis or according to participation."[10]

The Hua-yen philosophy of China sets forth the theory of interrelation from a spatial viewpoint in fourfold manner as follows:

(1) One is in one;
(2) One is in all;
(3) All is in one;
(4) All are in all.

From the viewpoint of time the following formula is set forth:

(1) When one is taken in by all, one enters into all;

7. *Enneads* III, 2, 1. (*Plotinus*. Psychic and Physical Treatises, comprizing the second and third Enneads, translated from the Greek by Stephen MacKenna [London: Philip Lea Warner, Publisher to the Medici Society, 1921], p. 12)
8. *Proclus' Metaphysical Elements*, translated from the original Greek by Thos. M. Johnson (Osceola, Missouri: Press of Republican, 1909), pp. 77 (proposition 103).
9. *Ibid.*, proposition 11.
10. Proclus' own explanation ad proposition 103 (*Ibid.*).

(2) When all is taken in by one, all enters into one;
(3) When one is taken in by one, one enters into one;
(4) When all are taken in by all, all enter into all.

All things in the universe were brought into existence according to the above-mentioned formulae at the same time.[11] This Hua-yen philosophy, which as Suzuki has pointed out is very nearly the philosophy of Zen, may have reached a synthesis in the thought of Dōgen, who interpreted interdependence in such a way as to state that being is time. Time, for Dōgen, is everywhere. It is interwoven with all things. Buddha as the ultimate reality is nothing but time, of which all things are made. The bamboo is time; the tiger is time; enlightenment is time; man is time.[12] A fourfold formula in a systematized form can also be found in the West though some centuries later than its Eastern counterpart Hua-yen. Eckhart admitted the four intermediate stages:

(1) Many is seen as one (and only thus rightly seen).
(2) Many is seen in the One (where the One is still a form of the many).
(3) The One is seen in the many (as supporting and conditioning reality).
(4) The One is seen.

The One itself becomes the object of intuition as that which is superior and prior to the many. For Eckhart these four also represent the stages of spiritual development (thereby taking on an ethical cast), whereas for the Hua-yen school they represent nothing but modes of being. They were in that sense more in line with Plotinus who was also largely metaphysical with regard to his treatment of relatedness.

Plotinus' metaphysics might be described as one of superabundant emanation. A comparable theory is found in an incipient stage in the Chinese Taoist system and was elaborated in the systems of Neo-Confucianism. In China the idea of interpenetration was preserved by Chu Hsi (1130–1200) in the Confucian disguise. He maintained the idea of the Great Ultimate as the principle of heaven and earth and the "myriad things." With respect to these myriad things, he thought that the Great Ultimate is in each and every one of them. This does not mean however that the "Ultimate" was split up into parts. "Fundamentally there is only one Great Ultimate," said Chu Hsi, "yet each of the myriad things has been endowed with it and each in itself possesses the Great Ultimate

11. *Kegon Gokyō-shō* (*Taisho*, vol. 45, pp. 477–509, especially p. 504 b).
12. Norimoto Iino, "Dōgen's Zen View of Interdependence," *Philosophy East and West*, vol. XII, no. 1 (April, 1962), pp. 51–28. Dōgen's sayings exactly correspond to the title of Heidegger's work, *Sein und Zeit.*

in its entirely. This is similar to the fact that there is only one moon in the sky but when its light is scattered upon rivers and lakes, it can be seen everywhere."[13] Based on these ideas, Chu Hsi developed his own distinctive metaphysical system.

The concept of interpenetration of all things was preserved till late in China. Yen-yüan said, "There is nothing that does not interpenetrate everything else, and nothing that does not undergo evolutionary growth."[14] He held the idea of the original potentiality (*liang neng* 良能).

Kegon, the Japanese counterpart of the Hua-yen (Indian Avataṃsaka) philosophy of interrelatedness, "envisages a vast universe of interrelationship and interpenetration of all existing things such that when one is the subject all other things become its attendants to form a harmonious cosmos. At the same time the one becomes an attendant to each of the others which also becomes the subject. Both functions occur in the self-same instant, and neither takes precedence over the other."[15] This dynamic relationship, called *Shuban-gusoku* (主伴具足), has been rendered as "the subject-attendant constellation."[16] In terms of the *Buddhāvataṃsaka-sūtra* itself this constellation is centralized in the Vairocana Buddha. In Japan the theory is exemplified in the statue of the Great Vairocana Buddha at Nara. The Buddha Vairocana represents the original body of Buddha in the Kegon sect.

According to the scriptures of Kegon, each petal of the thousand-petalled lotus flower upon which the Vairocana Buddha dwells represents a universe, and in each universe there are millions of actual worlds (*jambū-dvīpa*). In each lotus-petal universe is a Śākyamuni Buddha who is a manifestation of the Vairocana Buddha, and in each of the millions of actual worlds is a small preaching Buddha who is, in turn, a manifestation of Śākyamuni. The *Kegon Sūtra* for a time represented the national religion of Japan,[17] because such symbolism was most suitable for the requirements of the State. It was thought that the officials of the government should be manifestations of Vairocana, and the people should be manifestations of the government official, just as small Buddhas of actual worlds are manifestations of Śākyamuni Buddha. As long as there was

13. De Bary et al., *Chinese Tradition*, p. 539.
14. Fung Yu-lan, *History of Chinese Philosophy*, vol. II, p. 637.
15. An explanation by Mr. T. Unno.
16. *Ibid.*
17. In the Nara period of Japan (710–784), the Kegon sect, which put forth a philosophy regarded by some as the highest of all Buddhist philosophies, came to be given the position of a national religion. A Rescript of the Emperor Shomu (747 A.D.) states, "We consider the Kegon Sūtra to be the most authoritative scripture." The Todaiji, the central cathedral of the capital, was also known as the Dai-Kegonji, or the Great Kegon Temple.

harmony among the State, the government officials and the people (as in the cosmology of Kegon) it was thought that there would be peace in the land and the nation would be safe.

According to the Kegon philosophy every existence is a reality in itself, with its own nature and activity. These realities can perfect themselves by realizing their ultimate communion with the cosmic principle embodied in Buddha's person and thereby acknowledge their participation in the grand system of the universe. This is but one of the ways such independent metaphysical philosophies exhibited ethical implications.

A later Japanese theory of interrelational interdependence took another distinctive ethical direction in that it outlined a particular relation between individual persons as well. Ryōnin (1072–1132), the founder of the Yūzū Nembutsu sect of Japan taught that "the *nembutsu* of one man interacts with the *nembutsu* of others and effects salvation." He is said to have seen Amida Buddha appear and presented a poem to him, saying, "One person is all persons; all persons are one person; one meritorious deed is all meritorious deeds; all meritorious deeds are one meritorious deed. This is called deliverance to the Pure Land by the grace of Amida." Dōgen also advocated unification of the self with other selves, claiming, "Oneself and others should be benefited at the same time."[18]

Such an idea was not absent in the West either. The New Testament suggested a metaphysical substratum as a basis for ethics in the phrase "Inasmuch as ye have done it unto one of the least of these my brethren, ye have done it unto me" Plotinus expressed a similar thought. Loving one in all things and all things in one, none can find themselves excluded from the universal meeting. "Those drunken with this wine, filled with the nectar, all their soul penetrated by this beauty, cannot remain mere gazers; no longer is there a spectator outside gazing on an outside spectacle. The clear-eyed hold the vision within themselves."[19] Meister Eckhart also suggested somewhat the same thing when he spoke of the man who knows himself as "seeing thyself in everyone and everyone in thee."[20]

In China later Neo-Confucians of different schools maintained that a man with the complete sentiment of humanity should identify himself with all there is. In love and compassion alienation is extinguished. Life should be exalted to the complete fulfillment. Chang Tsai (1020–77) said, "Heaven is my father and Earth is my mother, and even such a small

18. *Shōbō-Genzō*, Bodaisatta Shishōbō (*Dōgen Zenji Zenshū*, p. 259).
19. *Enneades* V, 8, 10. (Plotinus, the Divine Mind, being the treatises of the fifth Ennead. Translated from the Greek by Stephen Mackenna [London and Boston: The Medici Society, 1926], pp. 85–86)
20. C. de B. Evans, translator, *The Works of Meister Eckhart*, vol. II (London: John M. Watkins, 1952), p. 132.

creature as I find an intimate place in their midst. Therefore that which fills the universe I regard as my body and that which directs the universe I consider as my nature. All people are my brothers and sisters, and all things are my companions."[21]

From an epistemological reference, many of the advocates of an interrelational view of reality expressed themselves metaphorically. And surprisingly, many of them used the same metaphor, that of a mirror. A parable very often used in the Kegon philosophy is as follows: Let there be a mirror set up at the eight points of the compass, at the zenith, and the nadir. When a lamp is placed at the center, it is observed that each one of the ten mirrors reflects the light; now if one of the ten is lifted, it also reflects all the rest of the ten containing the light, together with the particular one that was lifted. Each of the nine is in the one and one is in each one of the nine.[22] In Buddhist Idealism (*Yogācāra*) mirror knowledge (*ādarsajñāna*) was propounded. Eckhart often used a phrase, "the miraculous mirror," to describe the innermost self of the mystic.

Eckhart elaborated his metaphor as follows: "If I knew myself as intimately as I ought, I should have perfect knowledge of all creatures," for, "the soul is capable of knowing all things in her highest power," viz. "as a clear mirror sees all things in one image," and so "not till she [the soul] knows all that there is to know does she cross over to the unknown good."[23] Windelband expresses Nicolaus Cusanus' thought as follows: "A certain infinity belongs . . . to each individual thing, in the sense that in the characteristics of its essence it carries within itself also the characteristics of all other individuals. All is in all: *omnia ubique*. In this way every individual contains within itself the universe, though in a limited form peculiar to this individual alone and differing from all others. . . . Every individual thing is, if rightly and fully known, *a mirror of the universe*."[24] (Incidentally, this thought had been expressed by the Arabian scholar Alkendi.) However individuality, which was also emphasized by Nicolaus Cusanus, is not clearly mentioned in the Kegon

21. Chang Tsai (1020–1077), The Western Inscription. Wing-tsit Chan, *A Source Book in Chinese Philosophy* (Princeton University Press, 1963), p. 497. The Chinese search for Being is "centered around essential human nature and is always existential in its philosophical import. With an enlarged range of sympathy we humans share this existential Being with all creatures and things, inasmuch as all Being is endowed with and sustained by the heavenly power. Human beings partake of the divine Being in a pre-eminent sense; all other beings share the divine Being equally. There is, then, a linkage of Being in all beings." (Thome H. Fang, "The Alienation of Man in Religion, Philosophy, and Philosophical Anthropology," a paper read at the Fifth East-West Philosophers' Conference, p. 18)
22. Daisetz Teitarō Suzuki, *The Essence of Buddhism* (Kyoto: *Hōzōkan*, 1948), p. 56.
23. Evans, *Works of Meister Eckhart*, vol. I (1924), pp. 324, 359, 253, 385.
24. Windelband, *History of Philosophy*, p. 347.

texts. This seems to be an important area of difference between their ways of thinking.

Plotinus, rather than expressing his epistemology metaphorically (at least in this one instance) set forth an epistemology of interdependence based on his Platonic metaphysics: "Those seeing by the bodily sense the productions of the art of painting do not see the one thing in the one only way; they are deeply stirred by recognizing in the objects depicted to the eyes the presentation of what lies in the idea, and so are called to recollection of the truth—the very experience out of which Love rises. Now, if the sight of Beauty excellently reproduced upon a face hurries the mind to that other Sphere, surely no one seeing the loveliness lavish in the world of sense—this vast orderliness, the Form which the stars even in their remoteness display—no one could be so dull-witted, so immovable, as not to be carried by all this to recollection, and gripped by reverent awe in the thought of all things, so great, sprung from that greatness. Not to answer thus could only be to have neither fathomed this world nor had any vision of that other."[25]

The right knowledge of the truth, as proclaimed in Buddhism, is nothing but a recognition of the interdependent relations of various aspects of actual human existence. As expounded by Mahāyānists, the truth of interdependent causation must lie in the principle of negation at the very existence of things that are transient and void—since they, being interdependent, do not exist independently and separately. People suffer as the necessary consequence of attachment to the existence of things and of claiming their unvarying eternity in defiance of the truth. If, on the contrary, one realizes the truth as it is and knows the vanity of the existence of things, one will not be afflicted by suffering when experiencing decay, disease, and death. Śākyamuni is an example of a person who is considered to have freed himself from suffering by thoroughly realizing the truth of interdependent causation in this sense.

c. The Absolute as Phenomena

In this section the primary agent of comparison from the direction of Western philosophy is Meister Eckhart. Eckhart has been the subject of a number of comparisons with Eastern thought, and one can only wonder at the reason for his popularity in this regard. Several possibilities come to mind. One factor is his historical position in Western philosophy, coming just after the culmination of scholasticism, itself the pinnacle of the Middle Ages. Medieval philosophy was largely concerned with religious

25. *Enneades* II, 9, 16 (Mackenna translation, p. 231).

themes; this is relevant because religion and philosophy are usually difficult to separate in Oriental thought as well.

Eckhart studied St. Thomas and many other prominent figures in Western philosophy of the Middle Ages. In addition, he drew on his own personal experience of a mystical nature, the descriptions of which are reminiscent of similar accounts from the East. Hence he was a studied mystic with a highly developed philosophical vocabulary at his command with which to describe his feelings about his experiences. Yet he also had an earthy quality; as with many Eastern philosophers, he wrote in the vernacular of his time and place. Paradoxes (or at least seeming paradoxes) abound giving the mind freedom to explore the richness of Eckhart's experience as well as his flights of speculation about the nature of that experience in relation to the absolute, the thematic impetus of the Middle Ages. Frosting for this cake, from an Oriental point of view, is that Eckhart was just naughty and heterodox enough in the eyes of his peers to make him interesting to thinkers who are often skeptical about the likelihood of academic philosophy contributing to the highest attainments of the human condition. There are probably many other reasons why Eckhart has attracted such attention; but these are enough for the present discussion, where the primary interest is in Eckhart's theory regarding the absolute in phenomena.

An interesting place to begin is a comparison of Eckhart's thought about the absolute with that of Śaṅkara. When Śaṅkara and other Vedāntic philosophers of India characterized the Absolute (Brahman) at all, it was as Being, Intelligence, and Joy (*Sac-cid-ānanda*). However Śaṅkara, although he defined Brahman as Being (*Sat*) according to the traditional conception of Brahman, yet regarded it as above Being and Non-Being. This is especially true as well in Gauḍapāda's *Māṇḍūkya-kārikās*. According to Eckhart, also, "the original ground of all things, the deity, must . . . lie beyond Being and knowledge; it is above reason, above Being; it has no determination or quality, it is 'Nothing.' "[1] Eckhart speaks of godhead as "a pure nothingness" (*ein blossiniht*).[2] Yet he, like Śaṅkara, did not totally reject his tradition's belief in God as being;[3] he merely subordinated

1. Windelband, *History of Philosophy*, p. 335.
2. Suzuki, *Mysticism: Christian and Buddhist*, sets forth comparative studies on Eckhart and Buddhism.
3. Scholars of Eckhart's writings do not believe this to be quite as paradoxical as it seems. Gilson explains Eckhart as follows: that God is first and foremost intellect "seeing." By virtue of this intellect, however, he teaches us that he is "One," hence "Being," and that nothing other than him is "wholly intellect" and "truly one." (*History of Christian Philosophy*, p. 440) Copleston says, "The truth of the matter seems to be that there are various strands in Eckhart's thought," and "Probably it is not possible to harmonize these different strands completely." (*A History of Western Philosophy* [Garden City, New York: Image Books, 1963], vol. 3, part I, pp. 198 f)

it. There is a third area of comparison that needs introduction in this regard, that of Zen, whose adherents also speak of the ultimate condition as "nothingness."

Eckhart and Śaṅkara have many other similar areas of presentation. For example, Eckhart distinguished between *Deitas* (Godhead) and *Deus* (God); For Śaṅkara distinguished between *Brahman* (neuter) and *Brahmā* (masculine), which he also called Īśvara (the Creative God). Both Eckhart and Śaṅkara characterized the absolute (*Deitas, Brahman*) as "nameless," i.e., above all conceptions. "Creation" for Eckhart and for Advaitins (Śaṅkara, etc.) is in reality a seeming, an appearance, a *māyā*. Both Eckhart and Śaṅkara "teach a soteriology which does not bind them to a system of thought, though Eckhart must necessarily speak guardedly, and wander off into areas where his metaphysics is so abstract he cannot be followed." And, for both mystics, "the fruits of contemplation come as the culmination of a mighty effort and lengthy preparation. . . . The purified life must always come before the beatific vision."[4]

"I entered into myself [*Ātmanā ātmānam saṃviśate*] and knew that creatures in themselves are nothing but a passing show. I saw that in the Godhead every creature is faultless [*prabhāsvara-prakṛti*] bliss [*ānanda*], and found that the light [*jyotis*] of God's countenance was formed in me, and realized that endless [*anādi*] joy was locked within my breast [*hṛdi*] and that there was in me a diapsalm and unbroken stillness [*ādiśānta*] of all interior things [*sarvadharmānām*] . . . and my mind was free from images and my spirit free from means [*bandhana-vinirmukta, abaddha*]. . . ."[5] This is not an Indian passage but is from a sermon by Eckhart with Sanskrit equivalents found in the works of Śaṅkara supplied in brackets. Major ideas of Eckhart can be expressed, word by word, in technical terms used by Śaṅkara, both systems are that similar.

Returning to the subject at hand, there were other thinkers who admitted the absolute reality of phenomena in the world. Rāmānuja was one of them. According to Rāmānuja (born in 1017), the phenomenal world is not illusory, as was asserted by Śaṅkara. "The relation between God [Brahman] and the world can be conceived on the analogy of the relation between body and soul. God is the soul of the universe, and the universe is his body. It is because of the presence of God as soul in all these finite beings and changing things that, in spite of their apparent diversities, they are related and are organically united with one another. All things and beings of the world have evolved out of the nature of God; they are guided and controlled by him."[6]

4. Joseph Politella, "Meister Eckhart and Eastern Wisdom," *Philosophy East and West*, vol. 15, no. 2 (April, 1965), pp. 127, 129.
5. Sermon XXI, in Evans, *Meister Eckhart*, vol. II, p. 142.
6. Anima Sen Gupta, "Ramanuja on Causality," *Philosophy East and West*, vol. VIII, nos. 3 and 4 (Oct. 1958, Jan. 1959), p. 142.

Zen adherents dispelled all kinds of ratiocination on the absolute. The Buddha dwells hidden in all inconspicuous things of daily life. To take them just as they come, that is all that Zen amounts to. Zen adherents seek spiritual freedom, the liberation of their true nature from the burden of those fixed ideas and feelings about reality which are accumulated because of fear—the fear that life is ebbing away. *Mondō* (Zen dialogues) may seem puzzling at first glance, but in fact there is nothing obscure or hidden about them. The truth which they indicate is, however, of radical simplicity and self-evidence.

> It is so clear that it takes long to see.
> You must know that the fire which you are seeking
> Is the fire in your own lantern,
> and that your rice has been cooked from the very beginning.

A Zen poet says,

> How wondrous, how miraculous, this—
> I draw water and I carry fuel!
> In spring, the flowers, and in autumn the moon,
> In summer a refreshing breeze, and in winter the snow.
> What else do I have need of?[7]

The sayings of Eckhart are set forth in the form of general propositions, whereas Zen masters expressed their teachings with reference to individual cases, casting away the restrictions of general propositions. But we can see in Eckhart's thought the way of thinking to locate the absolute in phenomena, or particular things. With reference to the statement that God created "in the beginning," Eckhart says that this "beginning" is the "now" of eternity, the invisible "now" (*nunc*) in which God is eternally God and the eternal emanation of the divine Persons takes place.[8] The "here" and "now" have essence, in so far as they are themselves God.[9] Eckhart said, "(. . . in eternity there is no yesterday or morrow): therein it is the present now; the happenings of a thousand years ago, a thousand years to come, are there in the present and the antipodes the same as here."[10] According to Eckhart, Being is God and God gives being. But this Being of Eckhart's is far from a static and changeless characterization, as was Śaṅkara's for example. Eckhart's

7. *Mumonkan* (*Taisho*, vol. 48, p. 295 b).
8. F. Copleston, *A History of Philosophy* (Westminster, Md.: Newman Bookshop, 1946), 3, 1, p. 202. In his *Expositio libri Genesis*.
9. "According to Eckhart all things have essence or substance only in so far as they are themselves God; whatever else appears in them as phenomena, their determination in space and time, their 'here' and 'now' . . . is nothing." (Windelband, *History of Philosophy*, p. 336)
10. Evans, *Meister Eckhart*, vol. I, p. 228.

Being is the eternal living (*vivere*). God is a living process in Himself, not a static being. This process is activity, mighty self-positing, a procreation not under the compulsion of laws or blind impulse but in the creative power and freedom of sublime wonder.[11] The Great Zen master Dōgen held a similar viewpoint but went still further, asserting, "Being is time, and time is being. Everything in the world is time at each moment. To practice religious disciplines and to attain Enlightenment and to enter into Nirvana are nothing but to ascertain that these events are Being, time, and that all time is all Being."[12] And further, "There is no beginning to practice (*shu*), and no end to enlightenment (*sho*)."[13]

A similar idea was maintained in the West also by a German mystic of later days. The combination of a quietistic approach to this world with the possibility of achieving the experience of eternity even in earthly time was one of the major themes of Angelus Silesius:

> Whosoever accepts time without time and cares without care,
> For whom yesterday was like today and today is the same as
> tommorrow,
> Whoever estimates all things alike, he enters already in time,
> Into the desired state of dear eternity.[14]

And in another place,

> Eternity is time and time eternity,
> Except when we ourselves would make them different be.[15]

Eckhart denied a difference between God and time by denying the reality of death. He believed God to be a vigorous life in which dead things revive, and even death itself is changed to life. He said, "To God naught dies: all things are living in Him."[16] Dōgen's assertion seems to be more radical—"Birth and death is the life of Buddha."[17]

The above-mentioned tendency leads one to admit all things and phenomena *as they are*, an idea which is exemplified in the teachings of Shingon Buddhism in Japan.

Although some people stated that the six great elements (earth, water, fire, wind, space, and mind) only symbolize the enlightenment of Vairocana, Kūkai wrote in his *Sokushin-gi* that the six elements are the

11. Otto, *Mysticism East and West*, pp. 170 ff.
12. *Shōbō-Genzō*, Uji (*Dōgen Zenji Zenshū*, ed. by Dōshū Ōkubo [Tokyo: Shunjūsha, 1930), pp. 62–65).
13. *Kegon gokyō-shō*. Translated by Taitetsu Unno (unpublished).
14. J. L. Sammons, *Angelus Silesius* (New York: Twayne Publishers, Inc., 1967), p. 24.
15. *The Cherubinic Wanderer*, I, 47 (Jeffrey L. Sammons: *Angelus Silesius*. New York: Twayne Publishers, Inc. 1967, p. 82).
16. Evans, *Meister Eckhart*, vol. I, p. 207.
17. *Shōbō-Genzō*, Shōji (*Dōgen Zenji Zenshū*, p. 440).

substance of the enlightenment of Cosmic Body Vairocana Buddha.[18] Man has already reached the ultimate situation, he thought. A Tendai scripture states, "The pure and immaculate original enlightenment, from the beginningless beginning to this time, does not require insight through practice, nor does it need the power of another. Its essential virtues are perfect and fulfilled; basic wisdom is already existent."[19]

According to the oral tradition (*Kuden Hōmon*) of Tendai, people are already enlightened just as they are. Inheriting such a tendency of thought, Dōgen claimed of his own enlightenment, "I recognized only that my eyes are placed crosswise above the nose that stands lengthwise, and that I was not deceived by others. I came home from China with nothing in my hand. There is nothing mysterious in Buddhism. Time passes as it is natural, the sun rising in the east, and the moon setting in the west."[20]

Zen masters use *chih-mo* (this) which is taken from the Chinese vernacular to indicate things as they are, and Japanese Pure Land believers speak of *sono-mama* or *kono-mama* (as-it-is) to express truth. These terms correspond with the "is-ness" (*isticheit*) of Eckhart.

In the eyes of mystics, one should transcend even the idea of "the absolute." One should give up the idea of God itself. Chinese Zen masters advised not to adhere to the idea of Buddha. Hui-hai (550–686) said, "He who seeks the Law does not seek it in the Buddha."[21] Neither should one become attached to the likenesses of the Buddha or other idols. The Chinese Zen monk Tan-hsia (?–834), in order to combat the deplorable tendency to become overly attached to an image of Buddha and regard it as the Buddha himself, burned a wooden statue of the Buddha as firewood.[22] Eckhart expressed a similar thought. "Had I a God, whom I could understand, I would no longer hold him for God." He describes the nature of this nonrational element with acute precision. "Now you will ask: How does God work without an image in the depth and essence of the soul? That I cannot know, for the soul has only power to conceive in images, and since the images come always from without, God's work remains hidden to it."[23]

18. *Mikkyō Bunka* (published by the Kōyasan University Press, Wakayama-ken, Japan), vol. 33, p. 9.
19. *Ben-kenmitsu-nikyō-ron, Taishō* vol. 77, p. 275 c. Translated by Taitetsu Unno.
20. Edited by Van Meter Ames.
21. *Tun-yu-yao-men* (Essentials of Immediate Enlightenment), edited by Hakuju Ui (Tokyo: Iwanami Shoten, 1938), p. 61.
22. *Ching-te-chaun-teng-lu* (Transmission of the Lamps of Religion), XV.
23. Rudolf Otto, *Mysticism East and West* (New York: The Macmillan Company, 1960), pp. 42–43.

2. The Absolute and the Individual

a. The Relationship between the Absolute and the Individual

AMONG early Vedāntins who appeared in the period corresponding to the Medieval Ages of the West, the relationship between the absolute (*brahman*) and the individual self (*jīvātman*) was an issue of heated debate. Already, in the period from the composition of the older *Upaniṣads* to that of the *Brahma-sūtras*[1] (c. 400–450 A.D.), there had appeared several such important teachers of Vedānta. Kāśakṛtsna (c. 350–250 B.C.) advocated the theory of identity in difference (*bhedābheda*) and affirmed that the *ātman* is a part or an essential constituent of Brahman. Auḍulomi (third century B.C.) held a special opinion of "identity in difference," i.e., although *ātman* is different from Brahman while man is alive, the former will be united with the latter after one who has attained deliverance by means of perfect knowledge has died and been liberated from earthly (bodily) existence. Āśmarathya (c. 350–250 B.C.) explained the relationship between Brahman and *ātman* as that of *natura naturans* and its evolutionary by-products (*prakṛti-vikārabhava*), which relation may be compared to that between fire and sparks. Bādari admitted only two Brahmans, i.e., the "Brahman as cause" and "Brahman as effect."[2] Finally Śaṅkara strongly asserted that Brahman and *ātman* are the same. After his time this problem also was earnestly discussed among Vedāntins of different sects.

Western counterparts of discussions regarding the relation between the Great Self (*Brahman*) and the individual self (*ātman*) took one form as the problem of the relation between God and the Son. Arius maintained that the Son is not the equal of the Father but was created by Him. Sabellius asserted that they are not discrete but only different aspects of one Being. The former emphasized the distinctness of the Father and the Son and the latter their oneness. The view that was finally adopted was that the Father and the Son were equal and of the same substance but were, however, distinct beings. While the Apostles' Creed laid stress on the human nature of the Son of God, the Nicene Creed added that he "came down from heaven and was made flesh." A comparison to this is to be found in the *Bhagavadgītā* (as in Hinduism in general) where Kṛṣṇa is an incarnation (*avatāra* or *avataraṇa*) or descent of the Divine into the human frame.

1. Many sayings by Western thinkers which seem to be relevant to the thoughts of the Brahmasūtras, in terms of ideas, were mentioned in S. Radhakrishnan, *The Brahma Sūtra* (London: George Allen and Unwin, 1956).
2. The thought of these philosophers are mentioned in the *Brahmasūtras*.

As to the relationship between the divine and creatures, the *Bhagavadgītā* contains the view that all the phenomena and changes of the world depend upon the will of God. Kṛṣṇa (Viṣṇu) states, "If I should cease to work, these worlds would fall in ruin and I should be the creator of disordered life and destroy these living beings."[3] The world also developed from Brahman, according to Vedāntins. The same idea was expressed by Thomas Aquinas, who said, "As the production of a thing into being depends on the will of God, so likewise it depends on His will that things should be preserved in being. . . . Hence if He took away His action from them, all things would be reduced to nothing."[4]

In the same way, Western theologians presented highly developed theories regarding God's creation of the world. For example, according to Augustine, the *Logos*, as the complex of collective ideas (cf. Bhartṛhari and Śaṅkara) which the unenvious God actualized in the world, is the prototype of the world, while the world is the image of divine wisdom. The *Logos*, besides being the world-idea, is also the idea of God, the *alius Dei*, while the world is the *aliud Dei*.

Another Indian Vedantist, Bhaskara, advocated an idea that the absolute and the individual are neither different nor identical. This notion of "neither different nor identical" in terms of the relationship between God and the individual may be quite alien to the West, but still a similar echo is heard in the case of Augustine, who said, "What is that which gleams through me and strikes my heart without hurting it; and I shudder and kindle? I shudder inasmuch as I am unlike it; I kindle inasmuch as I am like it. It is Wisdom, Wisdom's self which gleameth through me."[5]

The Vedāntins characterized Brahman as *Ānanda*, which occasionally means "sexual pleasure or sexual delight." This tendency is conspicuously found in Tantrism and Tantric Buddhism. The idea can be traced already in the *Upaniṣads* and it greatly effects the metaphorical representation between the individual and the Absolute. "This, verily, is his form which is free from craving, free from evils, free from fear. As a man when in the embrace of his beloved wife knows nothing without or within, so the person when in the embrace of the intellect-self (*prājña ātman*) knows nothing without or within. That, verily, is his form in which his desire is fulfilled, in which the self is his desire, in which he is without desire, free from any sorrow."[6]

3. *Bhagavadgītā* III, 24.
4. *Summa Theologica* I, ix, article 2. *Great Books of the Western World* (Chicago: Encyclopedia Britannica, 1952), vol. 19, p. 39 b.
5. *The Confessions* XI, 8, 11, translated by Edward Bouverie Pusey. *Great Books of the Western World*, vol. 18, p. 92.
6. *Bṛhad. Up.* IV, 3, 21.

The tendency to consider purified and consummated love as the supreme state of the spirit was found in the medieval West also. "St. Bernard speaks of the highest contemplation as spiritual marriage which impels the soul to go forth to bear spiritual offspring to the Lord. Richard of St. Victor, St. Bernard's contemporary, dwells upon four phases of spiritual marriage—espousals, marriage, wedlocks, child-bearing. John Ruysbroeck's chief work is called The Adornment of the Spiritual Marriage. St. John of the Cross says: 'The end I have in view is the divine embracing, the union of the soul with the divine substance. In this loving obscure knowledge God unites Himself with the soul eminently and divinely.' "[7] God, for some Sufis, was the Eternal Feminine. "The Muslim poet Wali of Delhi composed two poems, in which the lover is God and the loved one is the human soul invited to unite with God."[8]

In Vaiṣṇava literature the soul pining for union with God is said to be the bride and the divine love which sanctifies, purifies and elevates the soul to itself is said to be the bridegroom,[9] but this attitude is rather exceptional in the history of Indian thought.

Regarding the relationship of Absolute and individual in Chinese thought, Wang Yang-ming, rejecting Chu Hsi's view of the *li*, equated it with mind and interpreted the individual mind as the concrete particularization of the universal mind. His concept of "Prime Conscience" appealed to many Japanese. Notable followers of his school in Japan included Nakae Tōju (1608–48), Kumazawa Banzan (1619–91), Miwa Shissai (1669–1744), Satō Issai (1772–1859), and Ōshio Heihachirō (1793–1837). As a synthesis, Ichijō Kanera (1402–81) attempted, under the influence of Chu Hsi, to reconstruct Shinto along the line of an idealistic monism based on the identification of the cosmic soul with the individual. Although he accepted the existence of many *kami* (gods), he considered them manifestations of the cosmic soul. After him, Yoshida Kanetomo (1435–1511) postulated the existence of the one unique *kami*-nature as the source of the universe.

The relation between Buddha and man in Buddhism, especially when all men are considered to have Buddha-nature, as in the Mahāyāna belief, is not the same as the relation between God and man in Christianity, since Buddhism presents no concept of a Creator-God. The nearest approach in Mahāyāna Buddhism to such a thought occurs in Mahāyāna doctrine when the Eternal Buddha is presented as Father of the worlds, the source of a general, persistent provision and concern for all sentient beings. This is vivid in the parable given in the Lotus sutra (*Saddharma-*

7. *Ascent of Carmel* II, 24.
8. Radhakrishnan, *Principal Upaniṣads*, p. 263.
9. *Ibid.*

puṇḍarīka) of the refreshing rain, falling constantly on all beings everywhere.

b. Immortality of the Self

This section could, in a sense, have been included in the previous section on the relationship between the Absolute and the individual. For the idea of immortality of the self may have occurred when some men, describing the already postulated Absolute in anthropomorphic terms, not unnaturally also postulated a close relationship between themselves and the Absolute. The relationship discussed in this section is one of resemblance to an extent that man should believe himself to have a soul, "a spark of the divine" that never dies. The immortality of the soul was a topic of heated debate among medieval theologians. Thomas Aquinas thought the immortality of the soul could be proved by means of natural reason. Averroes, adhering closely to Aristotle, maintained that the soul is not immortal, but intellect (*nous*) is.[1] A large body of nonprofessional freethinkers who were later called Averroists denied immortality altogether.

Immortality was a popular idea in the West. Stemming from Socrates, it played a large part in Plato's theory of knowledge as recollection. Discussing a knowledge of absolute equality, Plato said, "We must have acquired the knowledge of equality at some previous time. . . . If we acquired this knowledge before we were born, and were born having the use of it, then we also knew before we were born and at the instant of birth not only the equal or the greater or the less, but all other ideas; for we are not speaking only of equality, but of beauty, goodness, justice, holiness, and of all which we stamp with the name of essence in the dialectical process, both when we ask and when we answer questions. Of all this we may certainly affirm that we acquired the knowledge before birth?"[2]

Some Indian philosophers also tried to prove immortality by reasoning that knowledge is nothing but the recollection of what one knew in previous existences. Bhartṛhari said, "(Even for a just born baby) there is motion of senses, vibration of breath, and sounding of voice. They could not occur without the *a priori* impression of words (in his previous existences)."[3] A similar argumentation was also set forth in the *Nyāya-sūtras.*[4]

1. Russell, *History of Western Philosophy*, p. 426.
2. *Phaedo*, 75. Cf. *Meno*, 81. Criticism on it, cf. Russell, *History of Western Philosophy*, p. 139.
3. *Vākyapadīya* I, 123.
4. *Nyāya-sūtras* III, 1, 17–20.

Augustine asserted that the soul knows its existence by immediate self-knowledge. In that I doubt or since I doubt, Augustine thought, I know that I, the doubter, am; thus, only this doubt contains within itself the valuable truth of the reality of the conscious being. So the existence of the soul cannot be doubted. "But from this first certainty, Augustine's doctrine at once leads farther, and it is not only his religious conviction, but also a deep epistemological reflection, that makes him regard the idea of God as immediately involved in the certainty which the individual consciousness has of itself."[5] An argument very much like this was quite important in the modern philosophy of Descartes.[6]

A similar notion was set forth by the Vedāntins, Upavarṣa, (c. 450–500), Śaṅkara (c. 700–750), etc., in medieval India. Śaṅkara said, "For if the Self also (like ether, wind, fire, water, earth) were a modification of something else, then, since the Scripture teaches nothing higher above it, every effect from ether downwards would be without Self (*nirātmaka*, soulless, essenceless), since the Self (also) would be (only) an effect; and thus we would arrive at Nihilism (*śūnyavāda*). Just because it is the Self, it is not possible to doubt the Self. For one cannot establish the Self (by proof) in the case of anyone, because in itself it is already known. For the Self is not demonstrated by proof of itself. For it is that which brings into use all means of proof, such as perception and the like (inference, etc.) in order to prove a thing which is not known. For we can call in question something, which comes to us (*āgantuka*) (from outside), but not that which is our own being. For it is even the own being of him who calls it in question;[7] fire cannot call its own heat in question. And further, when it is said: 'It is I, who now know what at present exists, it is I, who knew the past, and what was before the past, it is I, who shall know the future and what is after the future,' it is implied in these words that even when the object of knowledge alters, the knower does not alter, because he is in the past, future, and present; for his essence is eternally present (*sarvadā-vartamāna-svabhāvatvād*); therefore, even when the body turns to ashes, there is no passing away of the Self, for its essence is the

5. Windelband, *History of Philosophy*, pp. 277–278.
6. Descartes called ego a "thinking thing," including under the term thinking, understanding, affirming, denying, willing, refusing, imagining, perceiving (*Meditation* II). He asserted, "Ego is a thinking substance independent of its own, and other bodies cannot therefore be justified by an appeal to immediate consciousness, psychological analysis, or philosophical reflection." Reflection on Descartes' conception of substance led Spinoza to deny the substantial existence of the Ego. His method was different from that of the English Empiricists. Emphasizing the idea that there is only one Substance—God. Minds and bodies are but modes of its two attributes—thought and extension—respectively. (*Ethics*, ii, prop. 10)
7. Cf. *Brahmasūtrabhāṣya*, Bibliotheca Indica p. 79, 1. i; p. 823, 1. 2.

present. . . ."[8] The denial of Self is impossible, according to Śaṅkara, for the one who denies is of the very nature of the Self.[9]

Buddhists did not admit the soul, yet they tried to prove the immortality of a sort of existence which would be the basis of transmigration. Such philosophical maneuvers relied on the concept of *karma*, which gradually became one of the most important doctrines of Buddhism. In order to defend it from the attack of materialists, Buddhists thought out very interesting justifications. These included a dialogue between King Pāyāsi and the Buddhist monk Kassapa, wherein Kassapa held it to be common knowledge that the moon and sun are in another world, not in this, and that they are gods, not human. He felt this should be sufficient evidence that there is both another world and rebirth assured therein as fruit and result of good or bad deeds done in this world.

The king however argued as follows, "When a bad man was going to die, I asked him thus: 'According to the views of some thinkers those who break the precepts of morality are reborn in hell after their death. If it is true, this will be your fate. If this fate should befall you, come to me and tell me of it.' Whereupon the bad man consented to do so. But he has neither come himself, nor dispatched a messenger after his death. Now this is evidence for me that there is neither another world, nor rebirth."

To this Kassapa replied that felons about to be executed often request postponement of their executions, but the executioners will not grant permission. In just the same way, he argued, the keepers of hell will not grant permission for returning to this world and reporting to us.

Upon hearing Kassapa's reply, the king argued from a different direction: "When a good man was going to die I asked him thus: 'According to the views of some thinkers those who keep the precepts of

8. *Brahmasūtrabhāṣya*, Bibliotheca Indica, work 22, p. 619, 8, in *The Aphorisms of the Vedánta* by Bádaráyaṇa, with the commentary of Śaṅkara Áchárya and the gloss of Govinda Ánanda, edited by Pandita Ráma Náráyana Vidyáratna, 2 vols. (Calcutta: Asiatic Society of Bengal, 1863). Cf. P. Deussen, *The System of the Vedanta* according to Badarayana's Brahmasutras and Çankara's commentary thereon set forth as a compendium of the dogmatics of Brahmanism from the standpoint of Çankara, translated by Charles Johnston (Chicago: Open Court Publishing Company, 1912), p. 127 f.

9. Ānandagiri's ṭīkā on *Gauḍapādīya-kārikās* II, 11; *ātmanirākaraṇasya duṣkaratvān nirākartur evātmatvād ity arthaḥ*. *Ātman* means that which remains if we take away from our person all that is Not-self. In early Buddhism each of the five factors of the psychophysical individual existence is dismissed with the words "That is not my Self" (*na me so attā*). Eliot Deutsch analyzed the ambiguity involved in the argumentation by Śaṅkara and Vidyāraṇya to prove the existence of the Self. "It is the self in waking consciousness who is aware of an 'I' and who . . . is associated with a qualified reality, the *jīva*, and not with Ātman, the non-dual Reality." (*Advaita Vedanta: A Philosophical Reconstruction* [Honolulu: East-West Center Press, 1969], pp. 50–21)

morality are reborn in the heaven after their death. If this is true, such will be your fate. If that fate should befall you, come to me and tell me of it.' Whereupon the good man consented to do so. But he has neither come himself, nor dispatched a messenger after his death. Now this is evidence for me that there is neither another world, nor rebirth."

To this argument Kassapa replied that a man who had been plunged headfirst into a bog of mire and then pulled out of it, would never want to be plunged into such a bog again. Further he explained that, in the eyes of the gods, human beings are in a foul, disgusting, repulsive state. Those who are born again in heaven therefore do not desire to come back to this world.[10]

So it is certain that Buddhists wanted to defend the conception of rebirth against annihilationists. In China Hui-yüan (334–416) expressed the popular Chinese interpretation of the Buddhist theory of transmigration. This was criticized by Confucianists and Taoists who maintained that man's soul is inseparable from his body.[11] Hui-yüan asserted that "Spirit does not perish," admitted transmigration, and said that the concept of spirit is fundamental to the *I-ching*, and accords with the Taoist classics.[12]

3. Problems of More Formal Reasoning

a. Proofs of God's Existence

MEDIEVAL theologians of the West endeavored in various ways to prove the existence of God. Looking back across that period, Immanuel Kant systematically summarized their thought as follows: there are only three proofs of God's existence by pure reason; these are the ontological proof, the cosmological proof, and the physico-theological proof. Approximations of these three as delineated by Kant were also found in India. The latter two were set forth by Śaṅkara in order to prove the existence of Brahman, and a version of the former was at least suggested by Bhartṛhari.

The "physico-theological proof" was Kant's characterization of what others have also called the "teleological argument" for God's existence

10. *Pāyāsi-sutta* 5–9.
11. Fung Yu-lan, *History of Chinese Philosophy*, II, pp. 284–292. Cf. Hu Shih, "The Concept of Immortality in Chinese Thought," being the Ingersoll lecture on the immortality of man for the academic year 1944/1945, Harvard University, delivered in Andorier Chapel, April 10, 1945, *Divinity School Bulletin* 1945–46, pp. 23–42.
12. Richard H. Robinson, *Early Mādhyamika in India and China* (Madison: University of Wisconsin Press, 1967), pp. 99–109.

or the "argument from design." Basically the argument (as it developed in the West) is to the effect that the order pervading the world (in all its inorganic, organic, and human aspects) is indicative of a purpose or end toward which everything moves. Also implied, then, is the all-good purposer or designer who set forth the plan. This architect or artist must be God. The first probable appearance of this argument in the West was in Plato's *Laws*, where it was suggested that there would be no difficulty in proving the existence of the gods. "In the first place" Plato asserted, "the earth and the sun, and the stars and the universe, and the fair order of the seasons, and the division of them into years and months, furnish proof of their existence."[1] But the argument pervaded the Middle Ages and has continued into the twentieth century.

Śaṅkara set forth the physico-theological proof of the existence of Brahman[2] as follows: "When the matter is considered with the help of examples only, it is seen that in the world of non-intelligent objects without being guided by an intelligence brings forth from itself the products which serve to further given aims of man. For example, houses, palaces, beds, seats, pleasure-gardens and the like are (only) contrived in life by intelligent artists in due time for the purpose of obtaining pleasure and averting pain. Exactly the same it is with this whole world. For when one sees, how, for example, the earth serves the end of the enjoyment of the fruit of the manifold works, and how, again, the body within and without by possessing a given arrangement of parts suitable to the different species and determined in detail that it may form the place of the enjoyment of the fruit of the manifold works,—so that even highly skilled artists full of insight are unable to comprehend it through their understanding,—how should this arrangement proceed from the non-intelligent original-matter (or the Sāṃkhyas)? For lumps of earth, stones and the like are in no wise capable of this? Clay also, for example, is formed as experience teaches, to different shapes (only) so long as it is guided by the potter, and exactly in the same way must matter be guided by another intelligent power. He, therefore, who relies on the material cause only as clay, etc., cannot rightly maintain, that he possess the primordial cause; but no objection meets him who, besides it (the clay), relies on the potter, etc., as well. For when this is assumed there is no contradiction, and at the same time the scripture, which teaches an intelligent power as cause, is thereby respected. So that, as the arrangement (of the Kosmos) would become impossible, we may not have recourse to a non-intelligent power as the cause of the world."

1. *Laws*, X. 886, Jowett's translation, *The Dialogues of Plato* (New York: Random House, 1937), vol. II, p. 628.
2. Śaṅkara defines the Brahman as follows: "Brahman is the omniscient and omnipotent cause of the origin, persistence and passing away of the world." Śaṅkara's *Brahmasūtrabhāṣya*, Bibliotheca Indica, p. 90, l. 3. Cf. Deussen, *System of the Vedânta*, p. 123.

In China the great T'ang (618–907) writer Liu Tsung-yuan discussed the purpose of "the Fashioner of Creatures" (*tsao wu che*) in creating startling things. Most often in the history of ideas in China the creator was mentioned with reference to a sport or *lusus naturae*. Han-Yu (768–824) guessed that perhaps divine purposes were sometimes aesthetic and sometimes playful. There was also another way of looking at the natural world in China. This was the notion of nature as *tzu-jan—natura naturans*—a self-determining emergent from the background of the Tao. But usually, in China, this fashioner was seen as a shaper and molder of matter, like the Egyptian god Ptah and his Chinese counterpart Shun. Moreover, unlike the primordial Creator in the Judeo-Christian tradition, the Chinese Fashioner of Creatures' supernatural skill acts continuously and timelessly.[3]

The cosmological proof is a great favorite among Western theologians because it is said to follow from the assumption of the existence of anything. The seeds of this argument, heavily dependent on the notion of causality, are probably to be found in the twelfth book of Aristotle's *Metaphysics*. His thought gave impetus to the argument in the form that a distinction between an imperfect and a more perfect tends to support a position of the reality of a most perfect. A somewhat modern formulation of the argument might run as follows: if there is nothing but the sum of contingent (arbitrary) causes, regardless of whether or not they are infinite in series, then that anything at all exists is purely a matter of accident. Yet this is thought to be impossible since if "nothing exists" were to be a fact at least that fact would exist. Furthermore, all details of being may be arbitrary (accidental) but "that there are details of being" is not accidental. The ground of being such that facts of existence can come into being (however contingent) must be, and must be God. Such arguments pervaded the Middle Ages in the West and tracing them thoroughly would necessitate too much space for the scope of the present work. Thomas Aquinas summarized these arguments as those which consist in reasoning: from motion to a prime mover, from efficient or secondary causes to a first cause, and from contingent existence to a necessary Being. Śaṅkara's cosmological proof is as follows: "But (there is) *no origin of 'the Existent,' on account of the impossibility*."[4] Śaṅkara explained this as follows: "After anyone has been taught from the scripture, that also ether (or space) and air have originated, although we cannot conceive their coming into being, he might come to think that the Brahman also originated from something, for when he perceives how from the ether and the like, which are still only modifications, yet other modifications arise, he might

3. Edward H. Schaffer, "The Idea of Created Nature in T'ang Literature," *Philosophy East and West*, vol. XV, no. 2 (April, 1965), pp. 153–160.

4. *Brahmasūtra* II, 3, 9.

conclude that the ether also sprang into being from the Brahman, as if from a mere modification. The present sūtra 'But (there is) *no origin*' etc., serves to remove this doubt; its meaning is: but one must not think that the Brahman, whose essence is Being (*sad-ātmaka*), could have originated from anything else; why? '*owing to impossibility*!' For Brahman is pure Being. As such it can (*firstly*) not have sprung from pure Being, because (between the two) there is no superiority, so that they cannot be related (to each other) as original and modified;—but also (*secondly*) not from differentiated Being, because experience contradicts this; for we see that from homogeneity differences arise, for example, vessels from clay, but not that homogeneity arises from differences;—further (*thirdly*) also not from non-Being, for this is essenceless (*nirātmaka*); and because the scripture overthrows it, when it says:[5] 'How should the Existent come from the non-Existent?' and because it does not admit a producer of the Brahman, when it is said: 'Cause is He, Master of the Sense's Lord, He has no Lord, and no Progenitor.'[6] For ether and wind on the contrary an origin is shown, but there is none such for the Brahman, that is the difference. And because it is seen how, from modifications, other modifications, arise, there is no necessity for the Brahman also to be a modification. For were this so, then we should come to no primordial nature (*mūlaprakṛti*) but should have a *regressus in infinitum* (*anavasthā*). What is assumed as the primordial nature,—just that is our Brahman; there is thus perfect agreement."[7]

The ontological proof for God received its classical formulation by Anselm (1033–1109). But the major bases for the argument stem from Plato's theory of universals which proposed a hierarchical value system of ideas. The more universal an idea is, Plato thought, the greater would be its causal efficiency and hence the greater its worth. Applying such thinking to the problem of the existence of God, Anselm reasoned that God is generally understood to be that greater than which nothing can be thought. If God did not exist, something with characteristics otherwise equal with his but also existing would surely be greater. Therefore God must certainly exist. It seems that the ontological proof is lacking in Śaṅkara's works.[8] However, an ontological proof was implied in the thought of Bhartṛhari, who asserted that we cannot deny the existence of *ens*, being (*bhāva*) the *summum genus* of all concepts; and that being is the absolute.[9] But he called the absolute the "*mahā ātmā*" (the great Self), and

5. *Chānd. Up.* II, 2, 2.
6. *Śvet. Up.* II, 9.
7. *Brahmasūtrabhāṣya*, Bibliotheca Indica, pp. 627–628.
8. Deussen said, "As it appears, the Indians were never ensnared into an ontological proof." (*System of the Vedânta*, p. 123)
9. *Vākyapadīya* III, 3, 72; III, 1, 32, 34, etc.

in this respect the Indian version was different from its Western counterpart.

There were many other proofs for God found in the West. But Śaṅkara set forth one which doesn't seem to have been utilized in the Occident —the psychological or introspective proof of the existence of the absolute. He argued, "That Being which of its own nature is eternal, pure, wise, free, all-knowing, almighty is Brahman. . . . The existence of the Brahman is demonstrated by the fact that it is the Self (Soul, *ātman*) of all. For everyone assumes the existence of himself, for he cannot say: 'I am not.' For if the existence of Self were not demonstrated, then all the world could say 'I am not.' "[10] So far this is similar to St. Augustine's favorite argument for the existence of God. But without further clarification Śaṅkara's next step was an immediate jump to the proposition: "And the Self is the Brahman." His above-mentioned proof for the existence of the Self was immediately accepted in India as a proof of the existence of the Absolute. Śaṅkara, it seems, took it for granted that the self is identical with the Absolute, whereas Christian philosophers usually tried to avoid what they considered to be such a radical position.

b. Motion

VARIOUS forms of arguments (illustrated below) thought by some to be "sophistic" occurred both in Eastern and Western thought. The denial of the possibility of motion, for example, was expressed several hundred years B.C. in India by some heretical thinkers who were repudiated by Brahman orthodoxy, Buddhism, and Jainism alike.[1] In Greece, Zeno devised the celebrated "sophisms" in order to prove the impossibility of motion and in support of Parmenides' conception of the world as one motionless whole. The Greek sophism made (among other examples) the following statement. "A man cannot cross this room. Because first he must cross half the room, then half of the half that remains, then half of the fourth that remains. In this process, there will always be a remainder of which the man must cross one half before coming to his terminus. Therefore, a man cannot cross this room."

Nāgārjuna, the Indian dialectian (2nd century A.D.), negated the possibility of motion, although it is doubtful whether there was ever any historical connection with the above-mentioned heretics. He argued that "Nothing passes away, because if anything is to come it must be past, present or future. We cannot say the past is, for it no longer is. We cannot say the future is, for it is not yet. We are left then with the present. But

10. *Brahmasūtrabhāṣya,* p. 32, 4. Cf. p. 78, 6.
1. Cf. supra, chapter III.

the present can only be defined as the dividing line between the past and the future. Being a line described by two imaginary entities, it also has no claim to exist. Therefore, nothing passes away."

Compared with the above, Aristotle's argumentation was just to the contrary. It might, Aristotle said, be maintained that time does not exist, since it is composed of past and future, of which one no longer exists while the other does not yet exist. However he rejected this view, claiming that time is motion that admits of enumeration. Russell comments on this "It is not clear why he thinks numeration essential."[2] At any rate, although their ways of approach are similar, the conclusions of Nāgārjuna and Aristotle are contrary to each other.

The two argumentations are typical of the logical traditions within which they occur. The Greek example is based on a problem of mathematics, the Indian one on a problem of grammar. In philosophizing the Greeks made as much use as possible of mathematics. The Indians, curiously, failed to do this, although they were good mathematicians. It was an interesting characteristic of Indian philosophy in general that it developed independently of mathematics. Instead, Indian philosophers relied on grammatical theory and argument.

c. Categories

IN discussing categories the Western example for the Middle Ages comes from the writings of Aristotle, since his treatment of the subject was the primary one until the time of Kant. According to Aristotle, the concepts of the highest generality are called "categories," of which he enumerated ten: Substance (*ousia*), Quantity (*poson*), Quality (*poion*), Relation (*pros ti*), Place (*pou*), Time (*pote*), Position (*keisthai*), Possession (*ekhein*), Action (*poiein*), Passion (*paskhein*).[1]

In India Kanāda (c. 150–50 B.C.), the founder of the Vaiśeṣika school, undertook a classification of things under six categories which he called *padārthas* (word-things, essences or concepts corresponding to words). They were: Substance (*dravya*), Quality (*guṇa*), Action (*karman*), Community (*sāmānya*), Difference (*viśeṣa*) and Inherency (*samavāya*). The theory was

2. The explanation given here is based upon Russell (*History of Western Philosophy*, p. 206).

1. Paul Deussen, criticizing Aristotle, says: "It might be possible to do with three Categories: (1) Substance (*Ousia—dravya*); (2) Quality (*poson, poion—guṇa*); (3) Relation (*pros ti—sāmānya, viśeṣa, samavāya*); for *pou* and *pote*, as Kant observed, are not conceptual but perceptual, and the verbal Categories (*keisthai, ekhein, poiein, paskhein —karman*) can be reduced to the others by separating the copula, which is not a concept but the linguistic sign of a combination of concepts." (*The Elements of Metaphysics*, translated by C. M. Duff [London: Macmillan and Co., 1894], p. 73 f)

expanded to ten categories by Maticandra (c. 550–650), as will be discussed later. The classification of the objects of experience into substances, qualities, and actions derived from the examples set by early grammarians,[2] who had grouped words into nouns, adjectives, and verbs.

Both the Vaiśeṣika thinkers and the Aristotelians were aware of the intimate relation between name and thing. Though Aristotle's treatment was of words, it happens to be a classification of things as well, for whatever receives a separate name is a thing. "Expressions, which are in no way composite, signify substance, quantity, quality, relation, place, time, position, state, action, or affection."[3] Of these ten categories the last nine are predicable of something else, while the first, substance, is *ens*,[4] and cannot be predicated of anything,[5] not even of itself, for then it is no more a substance but becomes an attribute.[6]

The ten categories of Maticandra may be compared with those of Aristotle in the following way:

1)	substance	*ousia*	*dravya* (substance)
2)	quantity	*poson*	*guṇa* (attribute)
3)	quality	*poion*	
4)	relation	*pros ti*	*sāmānya* (*summum genus*, being) *sāmānyaviśeṣa* (commonness) *viśeṣa* (particularity) *samavāya* (inherence)
5)	place	*pou*	
6)	time	*pote*	
7)	position	*keisthai*	
8)	possession	*ekhein*	*śakti* (potentiality) *aśakti* (non-potentiality)
9)	action	*poiein*	*karman* (action)
10)	passion	*paskhein*	
			abhāva (non-existence)

2. Pantañjali's *Mahābhāṣya* I, 1, 1.
3. Aristotle's *Categories*, 4, in *The Basic Works of Aristotle*, edited by R. McKeon (New York: Random House, 1941), p. 8.
4. By the way, *Ens* (or *Entia*) in the doctrine of Aristotle is an equivocal term. It had at least the following four meanings: (1) *ens per accidens*; (2) *ens*, in the sense of Truth; (3) *ens*, potential and actual; (4) *ens*, according to the ten varieties of the categories. (George Grote, *Aristotle*, vol. I [London: John Murray, 1872], pp. 84–90) The Vaiśeṣika philosophers also differentiated their key term, Being, into several meanings.
5. A substantive proper cannot characterize, but is necessarily characterized. "Substance, in the truest and primary and most definite sense of the word, is that which is neither predicable of a subject nor present in a subject, for instance, the individual man or horse." Aristotle's *Categories*, 5, in McKeon, *Basic Works of Aristotle*, p. 9.
6. S. Radhakrishnan, *A Source Book in Indian Philosophy* (Princeton University Press, 1957), vol. II, p. 184.

Comparing the Greek "*ekhein*" with "*śakti*" and "*aśakti*" should be acceptable, for "to have" ("*ekhein*") involves to have power. According to the old theory of the six categories, Aristotle's "*ekhein*" may be included in the concept of "*karman.*"

These two systems of categories coincide fairly well, but there is one great difference. The teaching of categories by Aristotle centered on classification of the ways of existence of individual things in the sphere of the phenomenal or natural world, whereas this feature in Maticandra's system is given considerably less emphasis. The *pros ti* of Aristotle is the relation between individual entities or things in the phenomenal or natural world, whereas the four categories of the Indian system (i.e., commonness (=being), particularity, commonness and particularity, and inherence) corresponding to *pros ti* are relations among genus-concepts or abstract universals. That means the one and same category of relationship was applied to different realms. The categories of Aristotle were rather concerning physical aspects, whereas those of the Vaiśeṣikas, especially of Maticandra, were of the style of conceptual realism.[7] One must consider that this difference between both teachings of categories actually reflects the difference between traditional Indian and Greek ways of thinking.

Plotinus' five highest ideas[8] deserve mention in the context of categories. These can fairly easily be equated with Indian categories as follows:[9]

ousia	*dravya*
statis and *kinesis*	*karman*
tantotes	*sāmānya*
heterotes	*viśeṣa*

d. Controversy over Universals

In the medieval West there was a controversy between realists and nominalists. For medieval realists a universal was an entity whose being is independent of its mental apprehension or actual exemplification. For nominalists, it was a general notion or concept which has no reality of its own in the realm of being. Extreme realism was represented by William of Champeaux, among others, who for a time asserted that the universal alone has real existence, that it is wholly and exhaustively present in each particular example of itself, and that the individuality of these examples is nothing but an accidental variation of the generic essence. Abelard

7. In this connection the philosophies of Bolzano, Husseel, Meinong, etc., should be considered in relation to the Vaiśeṣikas and the Sarvāstivādins.

8. *Enneades* IV, 1–3.

9. Deussen, *Allgemeine Geschichte der Philosophie*, I, 3, 2, 359.

taught a modified nominalism (or moderate realism), distinguishing sharply between the mere word (*vox*) as a physical phenomenon, and the meaningful word (*sermo*). Aquinas summarized and synthesized the ideas of his predecessors by stating that the universal had real existence only as a creative idea in God (*ante rem*). He claimed it existed within experienced reality only in individual things (*in re*), and as a mental fact when abstracted from the particulars in the human mind (*post rem*). Occam is regarded as one of the most prominent of nominalists. He said all that exists in external reality is individual objects; universals exist only in the mind as the last or family names of things, born of our habit of dealing with particulars *en masse*.

Both the Platonic and Indian Vaiśeṣika schools have to their credit that they came to make clear the significance of universals. Therefore, both shared the same difficulty.

The birth of the problem of universals (in the West) occurred in the same place that the beginnings of criticism of such concepts started, in the writings of Plato. In *Parmenides*, Plato reports Parmenides' criticism of the theory of ideas as follows:

> "You mean to say that if I were to spread out a sail and cover a number of men, there would be one whole including many—is not that your meaning?"
>
> (Socrates answers:) "I think so."
>
> "And would you say that the whole sail includes each man, or a part of it only and different parts different men?"
>
> "The latter."
>
> "Then, Socrates, the ideas themselves will be divisible, and things which participate in them will have a part of them only and not the whole idea existing in each of them?"
>
> "That seems to follow."
>
> "Then would you like to say, Socrates, that the one idea is really divisible and yet remains one?"
>
> "Certainly not," he said.
>
> "Suppose that you divide absolute greatness, and that of the many great things, each one is great in virtue of a portion of greatness less than absolute greatness—is that conceivable?"
>
> "No."
>
> "Or will each equal thing, if possessing some small portion of equality less than absolute equality, be equal to some other things by virtue of that portion only?"
>
> "Impossible."
>
> "Or suppose one of us to have a portion of smallness; this is but a part of the small, and therefore the absolutely small is greater, that to

which the part of the small is added will be smaller and not greater than before."

"How absurd!"

"Then in what way, Socrates, will all things participate in the ideas, if they are unable to participate in them either as parts or wholes?"

"Indeed," he said, "you have a question which is not easily answered."[1]

The controversy between nominalism and realism seen in the medieval West has its counterpart in India, where the Nyāya[2]-Vaiśeṣikas[3] and Mīmāṃsakas[4] asserted a conceptual realism and the Buddhists propounded the theory that universals are only abstractions devised by the mind of man. All of the former (except the Buddhists) maintained that words denote both universals and individuals, and that both are real objects (*artha*) to be grasped by the senses.[5] The Nyāya school maintained that the universal connoted three things: an individual, the class in which it resides, and its particular configuration or form.[6]

The Mīmāṃsakas held that a word denoted a genus, and only indirectly referred to the individual. Kumārila said that Being (*sattā*) is the highest universal (*mahāsāmānya*), and every universal is a form of Being and is therefore not a negative principle (*apoha*), as the Buddhists maintain.[7] It may be called universal (*sāmānya*), form (*ākṛti*), genus (*jāti*), and energy (*śakti*, power).[8] No universal can have its own universal; for instance, "cow-ness" cannot have "cow-ness-ness" in it. Some held that a universal is an entity (*vastu*), and so can have in it another universal to be called "entity-ness" (*vastutva*). But Kumārila rejected this view as it leads to infinite regress; for even "entity-ness" will be an entity (*vastu*) and have "entity-ness" again in it.[9]

Also included in the class of Indian realists were the Jainas. They divided the universal into two kinds: the horizontal (*tiryak*) and the

1. *Parmenides* 131. *The Dialogues of Plato*, translated by Jowett, vol. IV (Oxford University Press, 1892), pp. 50–51. Cf. Francis Macdonald Cornford, *Plato and Parmenides: Parmenides' "Way of Truth" and Plato's "Parmenides" translated with an Introduction and a running Commentary* (New York: Liberal Arts Press, 1957), pp. 84–90.
2. *Nyāya-sūtra* II, 2, 68.
3. *Vaiśeṣika-sūtra* I, 2, 3 ff.
4. *Ślokavārttika*, *apoha* section, in *Mīmāṃsāslokavārtikam*, edited by Tailanga Rāmasāstri Mānavallī (Benares: Chaukhambā Sanskrit Book Depot, 1898; Chaukhambā Sanskrit Series, work 3).
5. J. Sinha, *History of Indian Philosophy* (Calcutta: Sinha Publishing House, 1956), vol. I, p. 321.
6. *Nyāya-sūtra* II, 2, 68.
7. *Ślokavārttika*, *Ākṛti* section, verse 4, etc., in *Mīmāṃsāślokavārtikam*, pp. 568 ff.
8. *Ibid.*, p. 255.
9. *Ibid.*, p. 551.

vertical (*ūrdhva*). The horizontal universal is the similarity or similar development in several instances and the vertical universal is the identity that persists between the prior and posterior states of an object. The former is static and the latter dynamic.[10]

Two schools of Indian grammarians also discussed the problem of universals: one consisting of those who believed that the referrent of word was the particular; and the other consisting of those who maintained that it was the universal.[11] Vyāḍi, for example, believed in the former, while Vājapyāyana held the latter view.

As already must be evident, a major format for the discussion of universals developed from the notions of genus and species. The Vaiśeṣikas said, "The notions, Genus and Species, are relative to the Understanding,[12] i.e., a notion can be a genus in relation to a lower species, and a species at the same time, in relation to a higher genus.

In China also the controversy over genus and species was alive. Corresponding to the Vaiśeṣikas, Chuang-tzu's fifth paradox runs as follows: "A great similarity (i.e., genus) differs from a little similarity. This is called the little similarity-and-difference (*ta t'ung i*). All things are in one way all similar, in another way all different. This is called the great similarity-and-difference (*ta t'ung i*)."[13]

Kung-sun Lung had probably initiated the Chinese controversy over universals in the fifth century B.C. by insisting on the difference of meanings between species name and genus name, saying "A white horse is not horse." If genus name is different from species name because it has a wider denotion, it is implied that the lowest class-name still can denote more than one name, and so individuality[14] cannot be expressed by any class-thing as such. Thus the individuality can be pointed out or indicated only by names and not conceptually determined by them. People use universals (*chih*) for pointing out individual things (*wu*). "*Chih*" literally means a finger, to point out, or to designate.[15]

Hsun-tzu later asserted on the subject of the relation between genus

10. *Pramāṇanayatattvālokalaṅkāra* V, 3–5.
11. *Patañjali's "Mahābhāṣya," with Kaiyata's "Pradīpa," Nāgeśa's "Uddyota" and Rudradhara Śarma's "Tattvāloka"* (Banaras: Kashi Sanskrit Series, 1954), pp. 35, 38. Dhirendra Sharma, "Buddhist Theory of Meaning (*Apoha*) and Negative Statements," *Philosophy East and West*, vol. XVIII, nos. 1–2, (Jan.–April, 1968), p. 3.
12. *Vaiśeṣika-sūtra* I, 2, 3.
13. Fung Yu-lan, *History of Chinese Philosophy*, I, p. 198.
14. A voluminous outcome of discussions on the problem of "the individual" is: *The Status of the Individual in East and West*, edited by Charles A. Moore (Honolulu: University of Hawaii Press, 1968). The English term "the individual" can mean either an individual human being or an individual thing in the objective world, and it seems to me that in the above-mentioned discussions the distinction between these two was not made clearly, and this situation caused ambiguity in terms of the use of the term.
15. Fung Yu-lan, *History of Chinese Philosophy*, I, pp. 205–206.

and species, "For although all things are innumerable, there are times when we wish to speak of them all in general, so we call them 'things.' 'Things' is the most general term. We press on and generalize; we generalize and generalize still more, until there is nothing more general. Then only we stop. There are times when we wish to speak of one aspect, so we say 'birds and beasts.' 'Birds and beasts' is the great classifying term. We press on and classify. We classify and classify still more, until there is no more classification to be made, and then we stop."[16] This assertion corresponds to the 'tree of Porphory' in Western formal logic. But the attempt to explain the universal-particular relationship by means of diagrams did not occur in India, nor in China or Japan. This seems to reflect on the fact that Eastern people were rather weak in pursuing the universal-particular relationship in things of the natural, phenomenal world. (The science of classifying flora and fauna did not develop in ancient India.)

Although the above-mentioned Chinese thinkers admitted universals, they did not think that the relation between universal (concept) and the word designating it is eternally or *a priori* fixed. Hsun-tzu stated, "There are no names necessarily appropriate of themselves. Things were named by agreement. When, the agreement having been made, it has become customary, this is called an appropriate designation."[17] In India the Vaiśeṣika and Nyāya schools asserted that the relation between word and its meaning was made by agreement or convention (*saṃketa*), against the doctrine of the Mīmāṃsakas that it is eternally and *a priori* fixed. This is reminiscent of the controversy in the Hellenistic world about the essence of a word, whether it is *physei* or *thesei*.

Most of the non-Buddhist philosophers in India, as pointed out above, contended that a word meant both the particular or individual and the universal. But Buddhist logicians thought that the universals assumed by Vaiśeṣika philosophy were nothing but a sort of substance. They directed almost the same criticism against the conceptual realism of the Vaiśeṣikas. Dharmakīrti began a criticism of universals, in the following manner, reminiscent of the criticism found in Greek philosophy:

> "It [a universal, e.g., called "pot-ness"] does not go there [to a pot]—and it was not there [in a pot] before; and yet it is there afterwards—although it does not have parts, and does not quit its former receptacles! What a series of difficulties!
>
> "It is [of] great dexterity, that what [as a universal] resides in one place [e.g., in a pot, and] resides in what comes to exist in a place other than that place.
>
> "It [i.e., the universal] is joined with this thing (which is now

16. *Ibid.*, pp. 305–306.
17. *Ibid.*, p. 306.

coming into existence) in the place where the thing in question is; and yet it does not fail to pervade the thing which is in that [another] place. Is not this very wonderful?"'[18]

As seen in the above, the greatest Indian opponents of the doctrine of the reality of the universal were the Buddhist logicians, such as Dignāga, Dharmakīrti and others. It is also evident that some of the arguments advanced against the reality of the universal in medieval Western philosophy were set forth by Buddhist logicians against the Nyāya-Vaiśeṣika doctrine.[19] The Buddhists maintained that the universal is only a *vikalpa* (artificial construct of imagination without a corresponding reality), and that its nature is not positive but negative (*apoha*), i.e., it excludes what is not the concept. The function of the so-called universal, like "horse-ness" in a horse, is to differentiate it from other objects like the cow and so to exclude "cow-ness," etc., from it. But the function of a word like horse is also just the same.

The Buddhist theory of "*apoha*" is somewhat similar to the Western view of nominalism. *Apoha*[20] literally means "differentiation" or "exclusion." Words are the result of mental conceptualization, therefore they refer to mental images and cannot be directly associated with external realities. Meaning thus denotes the referend, the instrument of an act of reference, as distinct from the referent, the object toward which the act of reference is directed. Buddhist logicians regarded it as only a logical concept, not an external entity inherently residing in the individual. The Buddhist logicians, therefore, were nominalists. The school of Badhva, as another example, denied the category of inherence (*samavāya*), claiming that substance and quality are identical.[21]

An important peculiarity of the Indian philosophical tradition is that the reality of the universal was upheld by realists and not by idealists for

18. *Pramāṇavārttika*, edited by Rahula Sankrityayana, I, 153–156 ab. They are cited in a different order in the *Sarvadarśanasaṃgraha*, Government Sanskrit Oriental Series, no. 1, chap. 2, 11.135 f. The English translation here has been cited from H. N. Randle, *Fragments from Diṅnāga*, Prize Publication Fund, vol. IX (London: Royal Asiatic Society, 1926), pp. 56–57, with slight alteration and additions.
19. Śāntarakṣita, *Tattvasaṃgraha*, edited by Embar Krishnamacharya (Baroda: Central Library, 1926), I, pp. 236–262. The Nyāya-Vaiśeṣikas gave an elaborate defense of their position. Nyâyamañjarī of Jayanta Bhatta, edited by M. M. Gaṅgâdhara Śâstrî Tailanga (Benares: E. J. Lazarus and Co., 1895), Vijianagram Sanskrit Series, vol. 8, pp. 273–300.
20. *Apoha* was discussed recently by Dhirendra Sharma, "Buddhist Theory of Meaning (*Apoha*) and Negative Statements," *Philosophy East and West*, vol. XVIII, nos. 1–2 (Jan.–April, 1968), pp. 3–10. The controversy over *apoha* was examined by Nagin J. Shah, *Akalaṅka's Criticism of Dharmakīrti's Philosophy: A Study* (Ahmedabad: L. D. Institute of Indology, 1967), especially pp. 76–154.
21. S. Dasgupta, *History of Indian Philosophy*, vol. IV (Cambridge University Press, 1949), pp. 182–184.

the moment, in the modern sense of these words. In Western philosophy, some who upheld its reality were the greatest idealists. But in Indian philosophy, both the orthodox and the Buddhist idealists denied its reality.[22]

Dharmakīrti,[23] the famous Buddhist, and William of Occam (died in 1349 or 1350) played a similar role in the history of logic Indian and Western. Both nominalists shared the following six features: (1) By means of rationalistic thinking both denied the absolute authority of theological knowledge. Dharmakīrti forsook the theological system of Abhidharma literature. (2) Logic held a pivotal place in the philosophical system of both of them. (3) For both logicians "intuitive" knowledge, or the knowledge of perception, is given first, and abstract knowledge always presupposes it. Perception[24] is the source of knowledge and sensation is an intuition. (4) According to Occam, sense perception bears upon singular objects; things are individual. The attitude of Dharmakīrti was very thoroughgoing. He said that sense perception bears upon the thing in itself (*svalakṣaṇa*), which is of the duration of one instant. (5) Universal, genus, and species are not real things. Occam did not believe in "something common" that makes Socrates resemble Plato more than a monkey. He never allowed himself to think of universals as things. Socrates is similar to Plato, he thought, but not in virtue of a *third* thing called similarity. Dharmakīrti denied the reality of universals in a similar way. (6) Their methods of approach made it possible for them to carry on their studies on logic and human knowledge without any close connection to any religious belief.

The reason why so many similar features are noticed between these two systems is that both appeared during the decline in social influence of grandiose theological systems (Catholic scholasticism and Mahāyāna-Abhidharma), although their traditions and dates are different. However, a contrast between them is that whereas Occam's work encouraged British empiricism and scientific research (which provided the basis for modern civilization), the Buddhist logic did not lead in a similar direction. One explanation for this may be that Buddhist logicians' approach to the individual or the singular thing could not break out of the limitations of the idealist school (*Vijñānavādins*).

22. The information about notes 1–4 and 15 I owe chiefly to P. T. Raju's article in *Radhakrishnan; Comparative Studies in Philosophy Presented in Honour of his Sixtieth Birthday*, ed. by W. R. Inge and others (London: George Allen and Unwin, 1951).
23. The logical thought of Dharmakīrti is discussed in Th. Stcherbatsky, *Buddhist Logic*, 2 vols., photomechanic reprint (The Hague: Mouton, 1958).
24. The Indian equivalent of perception is "pratyakṣa," which literally means "towards eyes." Cf. "The eyes are more exact witnesses than the ears." (Heraclitus, fragment 101 a)

IV. CONCLUSION

The discussions that occurred in the Middle Ages both in the East and West were heavily tempered by religious themes. Religious authority was a fact in politics throughout most of the period in both areas. This was influenced by and an effect of the fact that religious leaders of the Middle Ages progressively sought popularity among the common people. This popularization perhaps also contributed to an increased trend toward otherworldliness in all the major world religions during this period. Despite an overwhelming tendency toward otherworldliness, there remained a strong trend, also worldwide, of a religion (or philosophy) of self-help.

The popular otherworldly trend in religion was characterized by dependence on the grace of the powerful transcendent "other." In some theism, for example, complete dependence on the absolute was aimed at as the ultimate state. Kṛṣṇa (Viṣṇu's incarnation) in the *Bhagavadgītā*, promised "Delivered from passion, fear and anger, absorbed in Me, taking refuge in Me, many purified by the austerity of wisdom have attained to My state of being."[1]

An increased role of saints and bodhisattvas naturally arose; they became intercessors on behalf of common people, who needed forgiveness for their basic sinful nature so as to enter the pure land or paradise. It came to be very unpopular after this time, especially in the East, to retire from the world for one's own salvation without taking into consideration the salvation of others.

A "self-reliance" trend of philosophico-religious practice remained strong, however, and was represented in the Middle Ages by the mystics of East and West. Much has been written about these exemplars of mankind's highest possibilities, especially Meister Eckhart and the Zen school of Japanese Buddhism. Because the mystics, to an extent, relied on their own practice to reach sublimity of the human condition, thcy naturally began with a different assumption regarding the nature of that condition. In contrast to those who relied on assistance from a "holy other" (who often considered their basic nature to be sinful) the mystics of the Middle Ages were prone to consider their innermost nature as representative of the highest good. But for mysticism in general, this is already saying too

1. IV. 16.

much; descriptions of the mystical experience, if such are to be found at all, are usually prefaced by an expression of its ineffability.

In Western mysticism one cannot overestimate the influence of Plotinus and the mysterious propagator of his teachings, Pseudo-Dionysius the Areopagite. According to Plotinus, the One is indefinable, and in regard to it there is more truth in silence than in any words whatsoever. This is comparable to the standpoint adopted by Vedantins and Zen Buddhists. Plotinus sometimes refers to the One as God, sometimes as the Good; it transcends Being, which is the first sequent upon the One. The philosopher must not attribute predicates to it, according to Plotinus, but only say "It is." This definition is nearly the same as the idea of *Brahman* in the *Brahmasūtras* (c. 400 A.D.).

The most important practical consequence of the mysticism of this period was its effect upon ethics. One of the most prevalent opinions of mystics regarding ethics, as seen in this chapter, is that their experience often leads them to believe that their natural responses and actions are right just as they are. Any attempt at reasoning out the morality of a proposed action, some mystics believe, would necessitate a splitting or division (dualism) in their view of the world quite unwarranted by their experience.

Another consequence of mystical thinking seen in this chapter is that certain thinkers felt it necessary to propound twofold notions of truth. For instance, in the Indian Buddhist Mādhyamika school, there was a division between the worldly, conventional truth (*samvṛti-satya*) and the highest truth (*paramārtha-satya*). The former is not a lesser truth, in this school, but an essential aspect of the highest truth, i.e., necessary for the understanding on the part of lay people.

Once more it must be emphasized that no attempt was made to draw a sharp line of demarcation between the two types of religion that were suggested for purposes of pedagogy. Perhaps the best that can be said is that certain religions emphasized otherworldliness over self-help or vice versa. But even where the one emphasis predominates, echoes of the other remain, with tension maintained between the two, as is shown in the ape-cat illustration used in the debates concerning the operation of Grace and the degree of human cooperation. Similar tension is exhibited in the difference of Buddhist views regarding the recital of the Nembutsu. It may also be observed that it is difficult to decide whether to place Zen Buddhism in the category of Self-Help or Other help. Such observation means that one needs to be critical, as Paul Tillich has said, of any disposition to present any one religious tradition in narrow, static terms of a particular type, for this implies ignoring movements of life and thought which are not confined to any one type.

Theology became highly developed, to the point of the Scholasticism of St. Thomas, in the Western Middle Ages. There was comparable philosophizing about religious themes in Eastern traditions. Reasoning, which was at times denigrated and at other times came to the fore, was utilized on such problems as the nature of the absolute, and the relationship of the absolute to the individual. These were the subject of much comparison and contrast in this chapter. The absolute was characterized as being surprisingly alike in many traditions.

But the relationship between the absolute and the individual differed with traditions. Western medieval thinkers always looked upon God with awe. Hindu saints called the individual "the slave of God."[2] However, Japanese and Chinese Pure Land leaders never used the term "slave"; rather they called Amida Buddha "parent" (singular). This appelation implies that all believers are his children. As parents want to bring up their children to the same state as themselves, Amida makes all sinners Buddhas like himself. There is no discrimination. If there should be any discrimination, Amida's compassion would not be complete.

Philosophy of a more formal nature was certainly not lacking in the Middle Ages, either in the East or West. Problems of a purely philosophical nature, which are still given a good deal of discussion in the twentieth century, were continued and advanced in the Middle Ages. These problems like others were usually discussed in a religious context. But some of them such as the problem of universals, the problem of the categorization of reality, and problems of motion are of such wide application that they have continued to rate philosophical treatment even after the widespread separation (in the West) of philosophy from religious themes.

In spite of so many striking parallels and similarities which existed in the Middle Ages between East and West, we find remarkable differences. Probably the most important one is the papacy. Eastern countries lacked the idea of church-state in this sense, the only exception being the church-state governed by the Dalai Lamas. Also, in Eastern countries heretics were not tried by court of law. Inquisition or other persecution of heretics did not occur even once due to religious reasons. Such differences are still of contemporary significance.

2. Kingsbury and Philipps, *Hymns of the Tamil Śaivite Saints*, pp. 21–23.

CHAPTER FIVE

Common Features of Modern Thought

I. INTRODUCTORY REMARKS

One conclusion which may be drawn from the comparable attitudes to life observed in Eastern and Western traditions is that human beings face much the same problems of life and have demonstrated comparable responses to these problems. In some cases what may be compared is a view of life, or a response to life, which is that of a minority in one tradition while it may be the view or response of a majority in another. Thus it may be held that the religious response indicated by doctrines of self-help is more prevalent in the Buddhist tradition than in the Christian, where the response indicated by acceptance of doctrines of Divine Grace (other help) is more general. Nevertheless both responses can be observed in each of these traditions, with tension between them, as different aspects of the human situation are encountered.

This conclusion may lead one to question the kind of explanation which accounts for such comparable features by positing the possible influence of one tradition upon another in the course of history. Some historians, for instance, have thought that the emergence of Pure Land teachings of other help, comparable with Christian doctrines of Grace, may be attributed to Christian influence. But such an explanation is not required if it can be observed that, within the Buddhist tradition itself, there are tendencies in this same direction, notwithstanding the Buddhist emphasis on self-reliance. Allowance may indeed be made for the impact of one tradition upon another where there has been some meeting of the two. But before concluding, in any one instance, that it is simply a case of "borrowing from" or taking over what is put forward in the one tradition, one might also ask, in the case of the other, whether there are indigenous movements of life and thought pointing in the same direction.

These considerations may lead to a critical look at views which are widely held regarding the impact of modern Western civilization on the East today. For example, there is the opinion that modern civilization has followed from a view of man and his environment which was only held in the Western tradition as against Eastern valuations. More broadly, people often say that Eastern countries had nothing which could properly be termed a modern outlook before the impact of Western civilization. Their thought and practice remained medieval. Some authors point to India, where the primitive social system of "caste" persisted, and people continued to adhere to superstitions and magical rites. There had not yet appeared what might be called "modern" ways of thinking. Such would be a current estimation of Indian thought during the last several hundred years by many scholars. Concerning China, Japan, and other Asian countries before the introduction of Western civilization, similar evaluations have been made. These judgements appear at first glance to be accurate; but if the history of modern thought in Asian cultural areas is investigated thoroughly, a gradual indigenous development of "modern" conceptions of man and ethical values, corresponding to, yet different from, those in the modern West[1] can be seen. Among the characteristics of the "modern age" may be noted a freedom of thought marked by a skeptical attitude to accepted "authorities"; what may be called ego-consciousness; as well as by empiricism, materialism, and this-worldliness as against the medieval submission to authority, scholasticism, and otherworldliness.

In this chapter some features of the thought in Eastern countries are discussed, of nearly the same period as the modern West; and it will be seen that the East was not so unprepared for this modern age as is sometimes supposed. However, all that is modern in the East today is not just Western or entirely due to the impact of Western civilization. Moreover, the range examined herein is wider than in earlier chapters, with some reference to what may be observed in the East of other traditions besides the Buddhist and reference to Western thought in general rather than to Christian thought in particular.

Medieval thought patterns have indeed remained strong in the Orient throughout what is thought of as the modern period in the West (roughly the seventeenth and eighteenth centuries), especially in highly religious areas. Generally speaking, many religious sects have remained as medieval in their behavior as in their manner of valuation. What is meant by medieval ways of valuation is generally characterized by the following features:

1. John Stuart Mill said about Christianity, "Its ideal is negative rather than positive; passive rather than active; Innocence rather than Nobleness; Abstinence from Evil, rather than energetic Pursuit of Good; in its precepts (as has been well said) 'thou shalt not' predominates unduly over 'thou shalt.' In its horror of sensuality, it made an idol of asceticism, which has been gradually compromised away into one of legality. It holds out the hope of heaven and the threat of hell, as the appointed and appropriate motives to a virtuous life: in this falling far below the best of the ancients, and doing what lies in it to give to human morality an essentially selfish character, by disconnecting each man's feelings of duty from the interests of his fellow-creatures, except so far as a self-interested inducement is offered to him for consulting them. It is essentially a doctrine of passive obedience; it inculcates submission to all authorities found established." (*On Liberty*, [London: Longmans, Green, Reader, and Dyer, 1871]) If this comment is true with traditional or medieval Christianity, it seems to apply almost exactly to traditional Buddhism.

(1) The absolute authority of traditional religions was admitted by people in general who were under their strict control. Traditional symbols were stereotyped for a long period.
(2) Consequently, in the realm of social relations and in repressing scientific evaluations of the world religious orders were extremely influential.
(3) The absolute sacredness of religious scriptures was stressed. Scholarship was no more than the deduction from, and elucidation of, the fundamental dogmas of religions. Learning was, in the main, scholastic. Free thinking was not permitted, heretics were punished, skepticism was abhorred.
(4) The tendency of thought was, generally, otherworldly. Religious life was regarded as noble, secular life as vile and mean.
(5) As for social structure, a feudalistic hierarchy of status was accepted by the common people and was enforced by authority.
(6) Cultural life was limited to the upper classes; common people hardly participated in it.

Such ways of thinking and behavior were characteristic of the medieval West, China, Japan, and India. And it is assumed that modern ways of thinking involve the casting off of them. Western criteria of what constitutes the "modern age" (as mentioned above) cannot always be used when Eastern counterparts are pointed out. Once again, it should be stressed that modern thought in a period corresponding to the modern age of the West if *not* the specific counterpart that is being sought from the East. Nor is the problem at hand exactly whether there was anything like modern thought, philosophical ideas, etc., in the Eastern areas under consideration prior to Westernization, although this is of concern at times. The Eastern criteria of modernity must also sometimes come to light. And they will show differences from Western medieval thought. In addition, being able to state without doubt that there has been no Western influence is not always so simple.

The sections that follow, especially III and IV, are heavily overbalanced in the direction of Eastern material. The Westerner who reads this book probably has modern thought ingrained to the point of its having become part of his basic attitude (presuppositions) toward life. Comparison, especially in those later sections, is both unnecessary and difficult. Difficult because so many Westerners from the sixteenth century to the present have shared common ideas. One Indian thinker discussed in Sections III and IV, Rāmakrishna, is definitely late enough in time to have lived considerably after the advent of Western ideas to India. He indeed was very much affected by the life of Christ, but his thought remained so purely in keeping with the India of his time that the thought of this remarkable man has been included.

Literature written during this period is voluminous. However, focusing the investigation, a main purpose is to point out and discuss some conspicuous features in the change from medieval to modern (or slightly pre-modern) thought, in the works of some Eastern thinkers of the past four or five centuries. As a major motivating power behind the move toward modernization, the critical attitude will be dealt with first.

II. MODERN PHILOSOPHICAL ATTITUDES

A. Nature and Natural Law

Certain attitudes toward nature and natural law, as exhibited in various periods East and West, are more or less the major transition stage from medieval to modern thought. The general esteem for nature and its lawlike consistency has of course existed in each philosophical age. But the modes of explanation for the workings of nature have often been radically different. Specific modes of explanation which were unlike those of a modern or pre-modern cast were those of the Indian Vedāntic period, which generally conceived of nature as directed from without. This way of thinking is also consistent with that of the medieval West, which mainly clung to an explanation of nature heavily dependent on the agency of God's will. Among mystics, more or less worldwide, a similar explanation but from an internal point of view, was expounded, holding that everything is perfectly directed by God who is the self-nature of everything.

Differing from the above ways of thinking about nature, the modern view seems to play down the role of an added constant director of nature either internal or external. (God is sometimes given other interesting roles in modern thought.) Nature conforms to its own laws in modern thought, and interest in these laws has led to scientific thinking, appreciation for methods of measurement of nature (e.g., mathematics, geometry, astronomy), as well as systems of government and jurisprudence in the West. In the East such thinking, while present, remained largely pre-modern and concentrated on metaphysical and ethical issues, though heightened interest in the law as it applies to society was attendant in Eastern areas also.

In Western ancient philosophy Aristotle had especially been interested in observing nature firsthand to try to understand its laws. For Aristotle God was only a prime mover who, so to speak, started the ball rolling, not an ever-present director. His view did not become popular again, however, until the later Middle Ages, when Thomas Aquinas included Aristotelianism in his scholastic synthesis. Scholasticism though conservative was argumentatively rigorous and probably produced the potentiality of philosophical thinking which led to its own demise. Men such as Copernicus, Galileo, Kepler, etc., began to make discoveries about nature through their observational interests, which considerably contradicted established dogma. Naturally these finds had to be very carefully brought to light and many were condemned as heresy. These thinkers included a great deal of metaphysical speculation in their work, so they were not scientific in the twentieth century sense. But their ways of experimentation were the backbone of modern thought.

Francis Bacon (1561–1626) is sometimes thought of as the first modern philosopher in the West. Inspired by the "scientific" discoveries that were finding their way into the open, he advocated an "inductive" method of inquiry to be undertaken by observing analyzing the observed data, then inferring hypotheses and verifying the hypotheses through further observation. The result, he thought, would be a separation of essential from nonessential and the discovery of the underlying structure or form of the phenomena being observed. The result, however, must be considered tentative, he believed, because some contrary instances may have been overlooked. Bacon knew that investigating in this manner would be slow and meticulous. The main objection to this method was not its slowness, however. Rather, Bacon thought, it was obstructed by prejudice. People cling to four idols (prejudices), he said: (1) Idols of the tribe, human nature's inherent tendencies which impair objectivity, e.g., a naively realistic reliance on sense experience. (2) Idols of the den, each man's individuality which can hamper objectivity. (3) Idols of the marketplace, prejudices inherent in our language(s). And (4) idols of the theater, the "plays" that past philosophy has created to explain nature. Bacon's thought is indicative of the direction that the bulk of European philosophy took afterwards. Eastern thought on nature and its laws, however, never took the same turn prior to the influx of Western influence.

Indian thought hardly changed its views of natural law (*dharma* or *sanātana dharma*) from antiquity until the advent of Westernization. Future scholars might discern shifts of meaning that occurred; but that study is too specialized for the present work. The paradigm speculators on nature were the Chinese; many opinions have come to the fore as a result of their work, some of which are only slightly pre-modern in flavor. Much of this thought was transmitted to Japan and subsequently individualized by thinkers there who shared the Chinese preoccupation with nature. All of this speculation, however, remained in the domain of ethics, metaphysics, or social law as related to natural law.

In China one form of the discussion of natural law was undertaken by some materialists who claimed that the world was totally made up of ether. Given that premise they were naturally concerned about the relationship of principle or law (*li*) to the basic metaphysical substance. In these discussions *li*, the supreme subject of Neo-Confucianists of the recently past Sun period, was usually relegated to a subsidiary position. Liu Tsung-chou (1578–1645) held that the ether is the same as principle (*li*), and ether is the more basic, maintaining that, "Some say that the Ether is generated out of the Void (*hsü*), but since the Void is itself the Ether, how can it produce it in this way? . . . There has never been a time when there has not been the Ether." Huang Tsung-hsi (1610–95) had an opinion on the same subject that was at least equally monistic: "In the great process of evolutionary change there is only the single Ether, which circulates everywhere without interruption."[1] Noticeable in this passage is the fact that some Chinese had an inchoate concept of evolution.

For Wang Fu-chih (1619–93), Heaven's principle, *li*, was merely the orderly pattern of the Ether: "The Ether is the vehicle of Principle, through which it derives its orderliness."[2] For Wang Fu-chih, physical substance was believed to embody the Ether, and the Ether to embody Principle. Further, it is because physical substance so embodies the Ether that a given individual possesses life, and ". . . it is because the Ether embodies Principle that this same individual possesses a nature."[3]

This same discussion about the primacy of principle over the physical substance within which it works was carried out in relation to the teachings of the eminent Neo-Confucianist Chu Hsi and was relevant to ethics. Yen Yüan (1635–1704) strongly attacked Chu Hsi's dichotomy between the metaphysical *li* as being wholly good and the physical *ch'i* as being the source of evil. According to Yen Yuan, "*li* and *ch'i* are inextricably bound together into a single continuum, of which, therefore, it is impossible to say that one part is good and another evil. 'How then,' he asks 'can it be said that Principle (*li*) is uniform and single in its goodness, whereas the physical endowment deviates toward evil? This would be like saying that the eye's (non-physical) power of vision is good, whereas the physical eye itself, possessing this power, is evil. In actual fact, however, it is only when its (the eye's) vision is led astray by improper things, or blocked or beclouded by them, that its view of things becomes wrong, so that evil can first be spoken of.' Thus, for Yen, evil is not to be associated solely with the *ch'i*, nor is it a positive quality in itself. Rather, it is simply a deflection from 'Heaven's correct pattern,' caused by 'enticement, delusion, habit, and contagion.' "[4]

The Chinese discussions regarding nature and natural law also became relevant to the problem of the law in society. But as in Western

1. Fung Yu-lan, *A History of Chinese Philosophy*, translated by Derk Bodde (Princeton New Jersey: Princeton University Press, 1953), vol. II, p. 640.
2. *Ibid.*, p. 641.
3. *Ibid.*, p. 649.
4. Derk Bodde ,"Harmony and Conflict in Chinese Philosophy," in *Studies in Chinese Thought*, edited by Arthur F. Wright (University of Chicago Press, 1962), pp. 42–43.

philosophy,[5] a more pluralistic conception was necessary than the monistic ones that equated nature with its law. Huang Tsung-hsi (1610–95) is notable as a thinker who, while still in the Confucian tradition, advanced an almost modern point of view regarding law. In traditional Confucianism if a man's character was correctly developed, his relationships would be in harmony also (a situation capable of expanding to all the relationships in the empire, hence, to perfect government). Huang Tsung-hsi, however, attached importance to the form or system of government, rather than simply to the character of the men administering it. "If men [who govern] were of the right kind," he claimed "the full intent of the law would be fulfilled; and even if they were of the wrong kind, it would be impossible for them to govern tyrannically and make the people suffer. Therefore I say we must first have laws which govern well and later we shall have men who govern well."[6]

The school of the Old Learning or Antiquity (Kogaku of Japan) was in a sense a protest movement against the tradition of Chu Hsi and other Neo-Confucianists. This school asserted that Neo-Confucianists had distorted the Confucian sages' dynamic view of the world and life. The main characteristic of the Kogaku was its monistic philosophy based on the identification of *li* (principle or reason) and *ch'i* (material force). According to this school, everything and every reason is a direct manifestation of the vitality of the cosmos. Thus relating metaphysics to ethics, the Kogaku scholars advocated a universalistic philosophical principle as the basis for practical life. In other words, the aim of life is the realization and fulfillment of one's potentialities by following the law of cosmic life. According to Itō Jinsai (1627–1705), "the moral order is not a mere haphazard law, but a providential rule, based upon the inherent nature of things. The ruling of Heaven is in all things, punishing evil and rewarding good."[7]

Ishida Baigan, the founder of the Japanese Shingaku school, considered nature in terms of its forms, another area of the Neo-Confucianists in which Nature is called the Mind. "It is the Mind," he said "which identifies itself in the Forms. See how the Mind exists even in birds and

5. Many modern philosophers of the West went further with the problem of ego as the main motive in their thinking. Kant held that it is only in the cultivation of one's will that one can "carry the cultivation of his will up to the purest virtuous disposition, in which the law is also the spring of his dutiful actions, and to obey it from duty, for this is internal morally practical perfection" (I. Kant, Preface to the *Metaphysical Elements of Moral Philosophy Metaphysische Anfangsgrunde der Sittenlehre*, Kant's *Critique of Pure Reason*, T. K. Abbott, trans. [London: Longmans, Green and Co., 1954], p. 297)—a perfection resulting in the "harmony" of the will of one's self with that of a "holy and good Author of the world." (*Ibid.*, pp. 226–227)
6. Wm. T. De Bary et al., *Sources of Chinese Tradition* (New York: Columbia University Press, 1960), p. 593.
7. Joseph Spae, *Itō Jinsai* (Peiping: Catholic University of Peking, 1948), p. 205.

animals! Frogs are naturally afraid of snakes. It is not surely a mother who teaches its offsprings that snakes are dangerous and will gobble them up and, of course, tadpoles do not study and do not gradually learn all this. The fact is that if you are born under the Forms of a frog, the fear for snakes comes straight in the Mind from the Forms. Let us consider something analogous: a flea when summer comes clings to man's body. Here again do a flea's parents teach it to live by sucking men's blood? Is it taught if it sees a man's hand approach, it must jump away immediately lest it loses its life? The reason is that when a flea jumps away it acts in accordance with the Forms and not because it has learnt to do so."[8] "Birds and Beasts have no Personal Mind and therefore comply perfectly with the dictates of the Forms."[9] This emphasis on natural law compares with some continental rationalists as well as Hegel.

The final goal of ethical conduct was, according to Baigan, to recover one's own original Mind. "To attain something by following the Law means to attain the Mind."[10] "If you just let yourself go, and become receptive, everything is natural, easy, evident."[11] It is interesting to observe that Baigan wanted to apply his theory to politics. "By ruling without knowing this Order (Principle) a ruler will not be able to govern his country."[12] His thought may sound too idealistic, but perhaps not so much when a highly idealistic Western counterpart such as the recent Western philosopher Fichte is considered.[13]

Master Jiun, the pioneer of Sanskrit scholarship in Japan, stressed the idea of natural law from a rationalistic standpoint. "In this world there are the true Laws which benefit it always. Those who have open eyes can see these Laws as clearly as they see the sun and moon. Whether a Buddha appears or whether a Buddha does not appear (regardless of it) this world exists, and human beings exist. These Ten Virtues will always be manifest along them (i.e., so long as they exist)."[14]

Here one is reminded of the thought of Hugo Grotius (de Groot,

8. Ishida Baigan, *Seiri Mondō, Dialogue on Human Nature and Natural Order*, translated by Paolo Beonio-Brocchieri (Rome: Istituto per il Medio ed Estremo Oriente, 1961), p. 43.
9. *Ibid.*, p. 44.
10. *Ibid.*, p. 56.
11. *Ibid.*, p. 33.
12. *Ibid.*, p. 60.
13. However, the following saying of Ishida Baigan seems highly Buddhistic and different from Fichte. "To say that one has to seek for Absolute of Mind, and to say the Mind of the Saints is No-Mind are not two different things but only the same thing. What makes everything live in Heaven and Earth, is the Mind. Everything which has this life, through the Mind who generates things of Heaven and earth, which makes things live, creates its own mind. However, men being blinded by selfishness can lose sight of such a Mind." (*Seiri Mondō*, p. 62)
14. *Jūzen Hōgo*, p. 44.

1583–1645), whose sharp distinction between inviolable natural law and ever mutable positive or civil law has had great effect on European jurisprudence. He maintained that "natural law . . . originates in principles which are contained in human nature itself (*ex principiis homini internis*), and which would be valid, even were there no God."[15] There is a striking similarity here between the concepts of natural law of Grotius and Jiun. But Grotius was a Westerner and he included in his belief the opinion that God may be called the author of natural law, since He is the author of nature, and therefore He wills this law to be valid. Jiun, on the other hand, held that nature and law are nothing but Buddha himself.

The doctrine of Jiun had considerable ethical consequences, for he found the essence of Buddhism in observing natural law, which could be termed the observance of the Ten Virtues. "It is true of only the teachings of the Ten Virtues that they never change. Throughout all the ages, both ancient and modern, and throughout all lands they constitute the suitable and true Path for both the wise and ignorant, the superior man and the inferior man, and for both men and women."[16] Jiun thought that his concept of natural law was of universal application, just as the law is universal, and that natural law should be the basis for ethical conduct throughout all countries. "Just as heaven and earth exist," he held, "so also are there various countries in existence. Sun, moon, and stars move according to the laws of heaven, while mountains, seas and rivers are governed by the laws of earth. As there are various countries, so there exist men to inhabit them. Human nexus is constituted with the relationships between lord and subject, parents, and children, husband and wife, between brothers, between friends."[17]

Ninomiya Sontoku (1787–1856), the "Peasant Sage" of Japan, stressed the importance of nature to man and further the importance of noting and following the natural in man's relationships with his fellow beings. "Man's true nature, Sontoku taught, consists in pious devotion to the order of nature, which manifests itself in the moral order of human life, especially in the relation between the lord and his subjects, parents and children, benefactor and recipient in general, expressed in grace and gratitude. Nature evolves and changes by itself, but man has to conquer his instinctive selfishness and endeavour to conform to the moral order of life."[18] Contrary to the general trend of naturalism, the ethical effect of

15. Harald Höffding, *A History of Modern Philosophy: A Sketch of the History of Philosophy from the Close of the Renaissance to Our Own Day*, translated from the German edition by B. E. Meyer (Dover Publications, 1955), vol. 1, p. 54.
16. *Jūzen Hōgo*, p. 55.
17. De Bary et al., *Chinese Tradition*, p. 593.
18. Masaharu Anesaki, *History of Japanese Religion with Special Reference to the Social and Moral Life of the Nation* (London: Kegan Paul, Trench, Trubner and Co., 1930), pp. 302–303.

Ninomiya Sontoku's doctrine was that he emphasized frugality, which is an outcome of the sense of indebtedness, gratitude for the benefit bestowed by nature.

B. Mathematics, Logic, and the Movement toward Scientific Methods

MODERN philosophy may be seen primarily as the response to challenging new scientific ideas. A voluminous history of modern philosophy (*The Career of Philosophy*) has been written from the standpoint that "during the modern period, it has been chiefly science that has driven men to the searching thought that is philosophy." The existence of some philosophers who antagonized scientific approach presupposes the fact that they duly admitted the significance of science. "This is true even of those philosophers who have tried to escape from science, like the romantic idealists and the present-day existentialists; they are heavily colored by what they are trying to emancipate themselves from."[1]

The movement toward science has been a long one, however, and its history before the advent of the use of inductive methods in the West was largely promoted by mathematicians and logic. Even after the emergence of the usefulness of induction, deductive methods were still of great use in drawing out the consequences of hypotheses. To begin with, two great figures of ancient times advanced their cultures toward modern thought by their mathematical and logical attitudes. Euclid (c. 300 B.C.) did work in geometry, solely for love of knowledge, that paved the way for the uses of parabolas and elipses in modern studies of projectiles and the motions of the planets. His Indian counterpart, Pāṇini (c. fourth century B.C.) did more to promote the understanding of his country's language within that country than any figure the world has known.

Both Euclid and Pāṇini had precursors whose results are largely lost (on the one hand, Hippocrates of Chios, Leon, Eudoxos, Theudios, etc.; on the other, Āpiśali, Kāśyapa, Gārgya, and the Northern and Eastern schools), but each of the two constructed their own almost complete system by means of a precise method, strictly maintained. It is hardly necessary to emphasize the importance of Euclid's methods in the history of Western science. Since Euclid's time, philosophy had made repeated attempts to become or present itself as a deductive science in the manner in which Pāṇini formulated theorems. But there was a difference between their methods that was characteristic in Euclid's work; i.e., deduction was not conspicuously used by Pāṇini. However his system produced at an

1. John Herman Randall, Jr., *The Career of Philosophy*, vol. I (New York: Columbia University Press, 1962), p. ix.

early date such logical distinctions as those between language and metalanguage, theorem and metatheorem, use and mention, which were discovered much later in Europe.

Euclid's methods inspired nearly all the Western philosophers after him at least until the time of Kant. The preoccupation with mathematical methods led also to astronomical calculations by Copernicus, Kepler, Galileo, etc. In Eastern areas such as India and China, although sciences were pursued in antiquity and the Middle Ages, their development stopped at some periods, and there was no remarkable progress before the introduction of Western sciences. With regard to anatomy, for instance, in the West it began to be developed for the first time during the early Renaissance. Although it is likely that anatomy had already been studied by doctors of ancient India, as is mentioned in Indian medical works of antiquity, it was only after the introduction of Western medical science that some Eastern doctors became inclined to study anatomy.[2]

The natural sciences in India were broadly classified from early days as theoretical knowledge, sources of power (*vidyā*), and art (*kalā*). Techniques and skills (or arts), as suggested by the name, were *done*, while *vidyā* were *known*. The sciences and the arts were distinguished from each other, but both were virtually interconnected creative operations.[3] Indian grammarians tended to use their advances in an introspective way, a way more common to their culture. They were deeply interested in tracing the expressed language to a universal, inward language common to all men.[4] Bhartṛhari,[5] the grammarian, regarded the main function of language as the spiritual liberation of the individual.[6]

In modern India, however, some highly advanced speculation occurred in the field of logical studies. For example, the idea that a number

2. Early Renaissance anatomy is discussed by Charles Singer in his work *Studies in the History and Method of Science* (Oxford: Clarendon Press, 1917), pp. 79–164.
3. "The several branches of natural science in India are classified as theoretical knowledge and source of power (*vidyā*) and as art (*kalā*). Techniques and skills or arts are *done*, while a *vidyā* is *known*. The sciences and the arts are different but interconnected creative operations." Stella Kramrisch, "Natural Science and Technology in Relation to Cultural Patterns and Social Practices in India," in *Philosophy and Culture East and West*, edited by Charles A. Moore (Honolulu: University of Hawaii Press, 1962), p. 156.
4. This problem was discussed by Raju in the light of contemporary philosophy. P. T. Raju, "Indian Epistemology and the World and the Individual," *Philosophy East and West*, vol. XIV, nos. 3–4, (October, 1964), pp. 311–332.
5. *Vākyapadīya*, S. N. Sukla, ed. (Banaras: Chowkhamba Sanskrit Series, 1961), Part I, pp. 24, 141.
6. Cassirer regards language as one of the forms of man's self-liberation from the entanglement in the world of individual objects. (Ernst Cassirer, *An Essay on Man: An Introduction to a Philosophy of Human Culture* [New Haven: Yale University Press, 1944], p. 121)

is a class of classes was discovered by Raghunātha (c. 1475–1550) much earlier than in Europe.[7] However, in Europe this discovery came only within the mathematical tradition and led almost immediately to new developments. In India, it was put to further use, not to solve mathematical problems, but to render more precise verbal statements of the laws of concommitance. Jayatīrtha (fourteenth century) made a distinction between that which does not exist and that of which one can have no notion.[8] This represents a valuable step over the realism of the Nyāya, which held that a nonexistent entity cannot form the content of a valid knowledge and is reminiscent of some aspects of the modern Western epistemology of Kant, and others.

The Chinese were more preoccupied with ethics than Westerners, and so did not develop their logical theories into forms conductive to the growth of science. In particular they failed to apply mathematics to the formulation of regularities in natural phenomena.[9] Of Chinese as well as Indian mathematics three general features can be discerned: "First, with the exception of Wan Wang's the *Yi King*, none of the Oriental mathematical works seems to relate to the concerns of Oriental philosophers. Second, Oriental mathematics lacks the great variety found in Greek mathematics. . . . Third, . . . unlike Greek mathematical works, those of the Indians and Chinese hardly ever contain proofs of the results stated in them."[10]

It has been noted that a new approach by Ku Yen-wu (1613–82) brought with it the use of the inductive method, assembling evidence from the broadest range of sources, not from only a few selected texts, and made

7. "The precise symbolism for quantification invented in 19th century Europe derives from the symbolism of mathematics. On the other hand the Indian system, which was used at least from the time of Gangesa in the 13th century, derives from the elaboration of Sanskrit grammar, in particular from the unnatural and marvellous powers of abstraction and noun-composition which the grammar developed." (Ingalls, *Journal of Oriental Research Madras*, vol. XXII [1954], p. 7) A number is always a class of classes. In Europe this was first clearly pointed out by Frege in the 19th century and almost immediately it led to very interesting logical results. The same principle was found in India by Raghunatha (c. 1475–c. 1550 A.D.). The Indian discovery precedes the European one by more than three centuries. "Raghunatha did not think in terms of classes, he thought in terms of abstracts; but what he says comes to the same thing. There are two sorts of twoness, he says, a twoness which is connected with each of two objects by a relation which he calls inherence; and a twoness which is not connected with each of the two objects but rather with all pairs taken as wholes. This second sort of twoness is connected not by inherence but by what he calls *paryāpti*." (Ingalls, *ibid.*, p. 9)
8. Surendranath Dasgupta, *A History of Indian Philosophy*, vol. IV (Cambridge University Press, 1949), pp. 173–178.
9. Wing-tsit Chan, "Neo-Confucianism and Chinese Scientific Thought," *Philosophy East and West*, vol. VI, no. 4 (Jan., 1957), pp. 309–332.
10. Michael David Resnik in a review of *The Treasury of Mathematics*, *Philosophy East and West*, vol. XIV, nos. 3–4 (Oct., 1964), p. 383.

new hypotheses to test against the evidence. This new method, however, was applied first in the field of phonetics (studying the rhymes of ancient poetry to determine the ancient pronunciations) and led to broader studies of philosophy, etymology, and textual criticism. It was called the method of "empirical research" (*k'ao chu,* literally "search for evidence"). This scholarly work has been hailed by some as an instance in pre-modern China of the "scientific method," but if this term is used it must be understood to apply to the limited field of literary studies, not to the fields of natural science and material technology. The promising early beginnings of scientific lore in China were never consciously rationalized and institutionalized as was modern science in the West.[11]

Also in China, a sort of instrumentalism was advocated by Wang Fu-chih (1619–92). He thought that the Way does not exist outside of its practical application, stating, "The whole world is nothing more than an instrument. . . . What is called the Way is simply the way of using an instrument. . . . If there is no instrument, then there is no Way—this statement is seldom made and yet it is absolutely true. . . . Bows and arrows have never existed without the way of shooting them." Finally he ventured to claim that "the sages of antiquity were able to make use of instruments, but they were not able to make use of the Way, for what is called the 'way' is the use of instruments."[12] This attitude has a modern flavor and is also conducive to the development of science.

A practical character is particularly conspicuous in Japanese Confucianism also. "Japanese Confucianism, spurred on by the practical tendencies of Japanese thought and the people's aversion to mere speculation, even accentuates the practical character of all knowledge and education inherent in continental Confucianism."[13] So Japanese thought was, in important respects, also prepared for the advent of Western scientific advances.

11. J. K. Fairbank, E. O. Reischauer, and A. M. Craig, *East Asia: The Modern Transformation* (Boston: Houghton Mifflin Co., 1958), p. 378 f. Hu Shih, "The Scientific Spirit and Method in Chinese Philosophy," in Moore, *Philosophy and Culture East and West*, p. 216 f.
12. De Bary et al., *Chinese Tradition*, p. 603.
13. Spae, *Itō Jinsai*, p. 55.

C. Revival of Skepticism

1. Rational Doubt and Consciousness of the Ego

ALTHOUGH, as already mentioned, many consider Francis Bacon to be the first "modern" philosopher in the West, most votes would go to Descartes (1596–1650) as being the "father of modern philosophy." Both of these men subjected the opinions of their day to severe rational doubt and would not take for granted even the most sacred traditions and institutions without testing them by reason. Bacon voiced the criticism that "the corruption of philosophy by superstition and an admixture of theology is far more widely spread, and does the greatest harm, whether to entire systems or to their parts."[1]

But Descartes is really the most famous for claiming to be "universal" and "methodic" in his doubt. In a way, it is ironic to include Descartes under a major heading dealing with a revival of skepticism for his purpose was quite the contrary and he considered his chief enemy to be skepticism. In stating his aim he wrote, "I wish to give myself over completely to the search after truth,"[2] and by this he meant certain knowledge. He said that in the past he had studied mathematics, geometrical analysis and algebra and that the methods used therein to achieve clarity and certainty were worthy of adaptation to other fields of study. So Descartes was inspired by mathematical exactitude to apply his reason alone to philosophy and circumvent established authority. He wanted to develop a system of true propositions, and in so doing presuppose nothing which was not self-evident and indubitable. The "most certain routes to knowledge" he held to be the "two methods, . . . intuition and deduction."[3] In the course of his methodical doubt he claimed to follow the precept, "to accept nothing as true which I did not clearly recognize to be so: that is to say, carefully to avoid precipitation and prejudices in judgement, and to accept in them nothing more than what was presented to my mind so clearly and distinctly that I could have no occasion to doubt it."[4]

1. *Novum Organum*, LXV. Walter Kaufmann, *Philosophic Classics, Bacon to Kant* (Englewood Cliffs, N. J.: Prentice-Hall, 1961), p. 20.
2. *Discourse on Method*, 1.
3. *Rules for the Direction of the Mind*, 3.
4. *Ibid.*

Descartes was aware that he was heading in a different direction from that of his expressed purpose. "I thought that it was necessary for me to adopt an apparently opposite course and to reject as absolutely false everything concerning which I could imagine the least ground of doubt, in order to see whether afterwards there remained anything in my beliefs which was entirely certain."[5] But he could not, of course, know that many who came after him would take his doubts quite seriously (in point of fact, Descartes restored most of the things he doubted after he reached his so-called indubitable ground) because of failure to be convinced by some of his initial arguments (such as the existence of God, necessary in his "proof" of the external world).[6]

Descartes' doubt took approximately the following course. The senses sometimes deceive us, so they must be doubted.[7] Even the seemingly most evident perceptions, such as "this is my body," may occur equally as strong to one while dreaming, so these are also deceptive.[8] The propositions of mathematics seem indubitable whether waking or sleeping. Yet one can rationally suppose a condition of the world in which a "malevolent genius" of a metaphysical nature might be employing "his whole energies in deceiving me."[9] No doubt if that same "malevolent genius" did exist, he might even be deceiving one with regard to the existence of God. Quickly Descartes had subjected to his doubt nearly all the things men before him had awarded reality. Where he found his certainty will be discussed shortly; before going on to that, however, it bears mention that Descartes' method was very damaging to the image of Christianity, and many forms of Christian dogma were severely criticized, partly because of Descartes, partly because of the rise of science. Spinoza, a later rationalist and follower of Descartes in some ways, was one of the thinkers who was

5. *Discourse on Method*, 4.
6. Descartes thought not only that man is dependent on God for certainty and validity in knowledge, but also that God is the cause of man's coming-into-being and indeed of his continuing existence from moment to moment in time. (*Meditations*, 3; *Principles*, Pt. I, 21; and *Reply to Objections*, 5) "The knowledge of all other things other than the existence of self or mind depends on the knowledge of God." (*Principles*, Pt. I, 13) An Islamic scholar criticized Descartes as follows, "The scope and value of knowledge, according to Descartes, remain extremely limited as long as knowledge is confined to the existence of the self, for doubt continues to beset all sense perception and mathematical demonstration. It is only with the proof of the existence of God that knowledge of physical reality and abstract principles is made secure. Without the guarantee of God's veracity and good will the epistemological edifice of Descartes remains both empty and shaky." (Sami M. Najm, "The Place and Function of Doubt in the Philosophies of Descartes and Al-Ghazali," *Philosophy East and West*, vol. XVI, nos. 3–4 July–Oct., 1966, p. 139)
7. *Meditations*, 1.
8. *Ibid.*
9. *Ibid.*

critical of, for example, miracles in the Bible. He challenged as follows:—Those who wish to seek out the cause of miracles, and to understand the things of nature as philosophers are soon considered heretical and impious, and proclaimed as such by the conventional interpreters of nature and the gods. For these men know that once ignorance is put aside, that wonderment would be taken away which is the only means to preserve their authority.[10]

There was a similar direction taken by much of the doubt in China and Japan. According to one opinion, many Chinese rejected Christianity in the seventeenth century on rational grounds, posing questions that went right to the heart of Christian theology, questions that could have come from eighteenth century France or even the seventeenth century European rationalists.[11] But according to some scholars, when the Chinese rejected Christianity in the seventeenth century, Confucianism was sufficiently vital for rejection of new ideas to be on the grounds that they were untraditional; it was "the Chinese feeling for a special historical Chinese identity" that made the Christians' claim unacceptable to Chinese. In the twentieth century, however, the Chinese rejected Christianity because it was not modern, not scientific.[12]

In Japan also a similar movement can be traced, but directed against the prevalent Buddhist theories of the day. Miracles had already been repudiated in the Medieval Ages by Master Dōgen who claimed that people commonly believe the occult powers of Buddhas are such as exhaling water and fire from the body or inhaling water from the ocean into the pores of the body. These may be called "small occult powers," but they are not worthy of being termed true occult powers. The true occult powers, that is to say "great occult powers," exist within and only within the simple everyday occurrences of "drinking tea, eating rice, drawing water, and carrying faggots." This is the "occult power of Buddha" or "the occult power of one who aspires to be a Buddha." One who practices this power will eventually become "an occult-power Buddha." By this Dōgen

10. "Hence it happens that the man who endeavours to find out the true causes of miracles, and who desires as a wise man to understand nature, and not to gape at it like a fool, is generally considered and proclaimed to be a heretic and impious by those whom the vulgar worship as the interpreters both of nature and the gods. For these know that if ignorance be removed, amazed stupidity, the sole ground on which they rely in arguining or in defending their authority is taken away also." (Spinoza, Ethics, Part I, Appendix. *Ethic*, translated by W. Hale White [New York: Macmillan and Co., 1894], p. 43)
11. Michael Casster, "The Death and Transfiguration of Confucianism," *Philosophy East and West*, vol. XVIII, no. 3 (1968), p. 210.
12. Joseph R. Levenson, *Confucian China and Its Modern Fate*, vol. I (Berkeley: Univ. of California Press, 1958), pp. 117–125.

meant that the true miracle is the fact that one lives righteously one's own daily life.[13]

Yoshida Shōin (1830–59), the nationalist leader, strongly criticized the miracle stories mentioned in the Kannon Sutra.[14] But in Japan the problem of miracles did not cause much trouble because miracles were not regarded as essential to Buddhism. After Christianity was introduced, Suzuki Shōsan (1579–1655) repudiated those miracles set forth by Catholicism. He charged that there should be no miracle in the true religion, that in Japan the chief miracle workers are foxes and badgers.[15]

During this period (corresponding to the Western modern period) in Japan, certain scholars began to take a critical look at the social sciences. Some were particularly doubtful towards the myths prevalent in the telling of the country's history. This attitude was represented for example, by Arai Hakuseki (1657–1725), an adviser to the government. He criticized the work of the Mito Historical Commission which was supposed to be compiling the most authoritative history of Japan. "I have been expecting that the history of our country being undertaken at Mito would correct errors in the national chronicles, but through contact with the staff of the Mito Historical Commission, I have found that all ancient events are to be left as described in the Nihongi, Shoku-Nihongi, and other chronicles. If that is the case, the true history of Japan . . . will be left unwritten. . . . Concerning Chinese history and Confucianism . . . in Japan there are no books that give a critical examination of historical facts and serve a practical purpose in government."[16] Noticeable here is the modern emphasis on the practical use of ideas.

Returning now to Descartes, it is well known that what he felt to be the indubitable ground of all his philosophy is the fact that "I think, therefore I am (*cogito ergo sum*)." Descartes could not doubt the existence of his self or even consider that his postulated "malevolent genius" could be deceiving him about the existence of his self. For to be deceived, thought Descartes, he must think; and to think, he must exist. It must be noted, however, that in keeping with his methods, Descartes did not consider his indubitable truth to be found by rational means alone. He considered the *cogito* to be a direct appeal to experience and explained this as follows: "He who says, I think, hence I am or exist, does not deduce existence from thought by syllogism, but by a simple act of mental vision, he recognizes it as if it were a thing which is known through itself (*per se*) . . . if it were

13. *Shōbō-Genzō*, chapter 25, Jinzu (*Dōgen Zenji Zenshū*, pp. 160–164).

14. H. Dumoulin, "Yoshida Shōin. Ein Betrag zum Verstandnis der geistigen Quellen der Meijierneuerung," *Monumenta Nipponica*, vol. I, pt. 2 (1938), pp. 73–76.

15. Suzuki Shōsan, *Ha-kirishitan* (Refutation of Christianity).

16. R. Tsunoda, Wm. T. De Bary, and Donald Keene, comps., *Sources of the Japanese Tradition* (New York: Columbia University Press, 1958), pp. 473–475.

deduced syllogistically, the major premise, that *everything which thinks is or exists,* would have to be known previously; but it has been learned rather from the individual's experience that unless he exists he cannot think. For our mind is so constituted by nature that general propositions are formed out of the knowledge of particulars."[17]

Before Descartes, of course, there had been other thinkers who came to a similar conclusion. In the West there were St. Augustine and Al-Ghazali. In India Upavarsa and other thinkers took up similar arguments to prove the existence of *Ātman.* A distinguished patron of the Indian Śūnyavādins (sometimes called nihilists) was Dayaram, the king (*rājan*) of Hatras. Like Descartes, he began his search for truth with systematic doubt. Under his encouragement a work in Hindi verse was composed by Bakhtavar, a religious mendicant, entitled the "Essence of Emptiness (*Sunisar*)," the purport of which was to show that all notions of man and God are fallacies, and that nothing is. In the first place he asserted that everything is void.[18] Theism and Atheism, Māyā and Brahman, were false, full of error, he claimed. The sun and moon, Brahmā, Viṣṇu and Śiva, Kūrma and Śeṣa, the teacher and his pupil, the individual and the species, the temple and the god, the observance of ceremonial rites, and the muttering of prayers, all these were emptiness. Speech, hearing, and discussions were also emptiness in Bakhtavar's poem, and substance itself is no more. The tone of all this is reminiscent of the *Prajñāpāramitā-sūtras* and the treatises of the Mādhyamika school. But whereas these works declared that phenomena and concepts in general did not exist by themselves, here negation is directed toward traditional mythological concepts and religious authority. This can be regarded as reflecting an attitude of protest against traditional authority.

Such a spirit of denunciation of authority comes to assert the absoluteness of ego and, again like Descartes, the result was the idea that what ultimately cannot be doubted is ego, one's own self. The treatise continues: "Let every one meditate upon himself,[19] nor make known his self-com-

17. *Replies to Objections,* 2, 3.
18. "*Śūnyavādin*" was originally an appellation of the Mādhyamika School founded by Nāgārjuna, but in modern India it has become one which nihilists claimed. H. H. Wilson, *The Religious Sects of the Hindus* (London and Madras: Christian Literature Society for India, 1904), pp. 148–150.
19. "Look at Yourself" was a motto of Ignatius Loyola, the founder of the Order of Jesus, although the connotation of this phrase may be different from that in the East. In Zen Buddhism we have a similar saying: "Watch your steps" (literally Throw light underneath your steps), which is rather aimed at ethical or psychological significance. In the thought of Campanella there was an opinion that "all knowledge of the world is rooted in *man's knowledge of himself,*" that man "knows in the proper sense only himself, and knows all else only from and through himself. All knowledge is perception (*sentire*), but we perceive, not the things, but only the states into which these set us." (W. Windelband, *A History of Philosophy,* translated by James H. Tufts

munion to another; let him be the worshipper and the worship, nor talk of a difference between this and that; look into yourself and not into another, for in yourself that other will be found. There is no other but myself, and I talk of another from ignorance. In the same way as I see my face in a glass I see myself in others; but it is error to think that what I see is not my face, but that of another—whatever you see is but yourself,[20] and father and mother are non-entities; you are the infant and the old man, the wise man and the fool, the male and the female; you are the king and the subject. You seize yourself and let go, you sleep, and you wake, you dance for yourself and sing for yourself. You are the sensualist and the ascetic, the sick man and the strong. In short, whatever you see, that is you, as bubbles, surf, and billows are all but water."[21] Readily noticeable is that these arguments are considerably more medieval by Western criteria than the Cartesian counterpart.

Bakhtavar compared all the phenomena in the world to experience in dreams. This is in a way comparable with part of Descartes' method of doubt. Bakhtavar's assertion is also similar to that of Buddhist idealists (*Vijñānavādins*) and consequently his consciousness of ego was not individualistic as in the West, but rather monistic. His notion of one's own self seems to have been derived from that of *ātman* in the olden Vedānta philosophy.

The attitude of Indian skeptics in denying everything developed into an assertion of realism (in the twentieth century sense), although the rational connection between the affirmation of the self and the realistic view is not clear. Common to Indian works of this period are such statements of realism as the following: "Earth, water, fire and wind blended together constitute the body—of these four elements the world is composed, and there is nothing else. This is Brahma, . . . all consists of these elements, and proceeds from them through separate receptacles."[22]

The revival of realism, of course, was one of the most remarkable events in modern Western thought; and in India a similar phenomenon

---

[New York: Macmillan and Co., 1893] p. 370) Jakob Boehme also asserted self-knowledge. (*Ibid.*, p. 375)

20. "Nothing should be able to harm a man except himself. Nothing should be able to rob a man at all. What a man really has, is what is in him. What is outside of him should be a matter of no importance." (Oscar Wilde, *The Soul of Man under Socialism* [Portland, Maine: Thomas B. Mosher, 1905], p. 20)

21. The problem of "*cogito ergo sum*" was dealt with by Śaṅkara with full insight in the medieval age. Paul Deussen, *The System of the Vedanta*, translated by Charles Johnston (Chicago: Open Court Publishing Co., 1912), pp. 127, 289.

22. Such argumentation was common among Indian realists. Cf., e.g., the Sarvadarśana-samgraha I: *Sarva-Darśana-Saṃgraha* or *Review of the Different Systems of Hindu Philosophy* by Mádhava Ácharya, translated by E. B. Cowell and A. E. Cough (London: Kegan Paul, Trench, Truebner & Co., 1914), pp. 2–11.

has been seen, although not as advanced. Hearing the bold assertions of the Indian realists, one is instead reminded of the cosmopolitan Stoic; and in India early Buddhist and Jain thinkers also showed such an attitude.

Just as Descartes' modern philosophy turned out to be metaphysically dualistic, so modern Indian thinkers for the most part voiced protests to the monism (*advaita*) of Śaṅkara which was prevalent in the Middle Ages. Later thinkers such as Madhva, Vallabha, Rāmānanda, and so on, set forth dualistic or pluralistic philosophical forms. A strong protest against monism is most clear in the following verse, naturally characteristic of the intensely religious focus the Indian mind is known for. Rāmaprasāda, the great Śākta poet of nineteenth century Bengal, addressing Goddess Kālī, said, "Mother! I want to taste sugar, not to become sugar."[23]

Another approach to the self was displayed in the modern period of Japan however, where at least in the Zen sect dualism never became popular. Hakuin's (1685–1768) introspection was a kind of auto-suggestion based on the idea that man's body and spirit form a close unity. Hakuin was confident that this method of instropection through which man, in a certain sense, finds his true self would liberate spiritual forces which greatly influence man's bodily well-being.[24]

In Japanese (as well as Chinese) Buddhism, then, the process of the appearance of a heightened ego-consciousness was slightly different. As seen above, critical doubt was indeed present in the Japan of this period; but some, such as Master T'ien-tai (538–597), the founder of the Tientai school, declared that one should not entertain doubt toward one's own master.[25] This way of thinking was also quite conspicuous in later Zen Buddhism, which esteemed transmission from master to disciple. But even some modern Zen adherents exercised freedom of doubt. "To be honest one must declare one's own doubts, if he has any, as I do."[26] A critical assertion of self was expressed towards the "masters." For example, whereas Dōgen (1200–53) denounced the theory of "perceiving one's own nature intuitively" set forth in the Sutra of the Sixth Patriarch, Tenkei, his spiritual descendant, rejected Dōgen's opinion as "absurd sheer non-sense."[27] According to the traditional attitude, "one's own enlightenment should be conveyed face to face, from master to disciple, and it should be approved by a single master." It is likely that this attitude reflected the feudalistic tendency of the Tokugawa period. But Tenkei

23. A. K. Majumdar, *Bhakti Renaissance* (Bombay: Bharatiya Vidya Bhavan, 1965), p. 43.
24. Hakuin's *Yasen-kanna*.
25. *Mo-ho-chih-kuan,* vol. 4 b (Taisho, vol. 46, p. 45 b).
26. Ishida Baigan, *Seiri Mondō*, p. 13.
27. Genryū Kagamishima, *Dōgen Zenji to sono Monryū* (Tokyo: Seishin Shobō, 1961), p. 112.

(1648–1735) held that "master" meant "one's own self"; "disciple" also meant "one's self"; "a single master" meant "one's self." So, the whole phrase was construed as "the attainment of one's own or true self by oneself." There was no need to practice under the guidance of a single teacher, he held. Even by looking at peach blossoms one could make one's own self clear.[28] Master Dōgen taught to learn one's self, and Tenkei explained that it was nothing but the way to follow the "Great Self." To know one's self was interpreted by Tenkei to mean to know one's mind. Knowing one's mind was also emphasized by such Zen priests as Munan (1603–76), Bankei, etc. Ishida Baigan (1685–1744) declared, "To know Mind is said to be the beginning of learning (science)."[29] Zen seekers were counselled that it should be found out by oneself.

As the Japanese concept of the self differs from the Western one of the same period, ethical implications are also different. In the West individualism was regarded as the basis for ethics, but in Japan the removal of the confrontation between different individuals was regarded as the ethical ideal. This was probably due to Buddhist influence, but even among non-Buddhists this thought is noticed. Ishida Baigan, the founder of the Shingaku school, taught that "real learning consists in attaining a whole *freedom from the personal Mind*."[30] "You must conceive this *selflessness* as a Law."[31] Among the thinkers of the modern West egoism and individualism were clearly distinguished; but among Japanese thinkers of the same period this distinction was not so clearly made.

2. Movement toward Reliance on Experience

FRANCIS Bacon has been discussed as an early Western proponent of the scientific method. And that he was. But a century divides the time of his death from that of the birth of the first classical British empiricist. During that century science came more and more to dominate the thinking of the intellectual elite because of the remarkable success of scientific methods. Among the British empiricists, this success had the effect of stimulating and confirming a theory that all knowledge is based on experience, on direct observance of internal and external events. One development to be seen below is that many remnants of medieval philosophical thinking were to go by the board in the wake of this way of thinking. Previous expectations (held by even the modern philosopher Descartes) were that man

28. *Ibid.*, pp. 106, 108.
29. *Seiri Mondō*, p. 57.
30. *Ibid.*
31. *Ibid.*

would sometime establish his philosophy on absolutely certain grounds and then develop a system of information about reality through extension by deductive discovery of new facts. At the end of the modern period the opinion was strong that such hopes were little more than a pipe dream. This did not all happen overnight, however, but was rather a progression from Locke's thesis that all man's ideas come from experience, i.e., from sense-perception and introspection.

John Locke (1632–1704) is generally classified as the first British empiricist. Early in his career he stated his aim to constitute a critical inquiry into, among other things, the source, certainty, and extent of human knowledge. In examining the source of knowledge he launched a heavy attack on the theory of innate ideas[1] (a principle exponent of which was Descartes), universally possessed, inborn, *a priori* ideas, e.g., of God or immortality. Locke claimed that such ideas (in fact all the ideas men have) can be explained by the hypothesis that they originate in sense experience or reflection on sense experience. This asserts the experiential origin of ideas but does not restrict knowledge to the immediate data of experience. Complex ideas are mentally constructed from simple ideas and the latter have objective references. Locke believed such a construction to be the origin of our idea of material substance, the substratum that supports primary qualities (extension, etc.) and the "powers" which produce secondary qualities (color, etc.) in subjects. Locke seemed to have no trouble convincing himself that there indeed exist material substances, something he knew not what, even though man does not perceive them. Kant, too, later affirmed that there must be what he called "things in themselves," though one cannot know them or even know that they exist. An Asian counterpart in certain ways to Locke and his belief with regard to "things in themselves" was the Japanese thinker Hōtan (1654–1738).

What characterizes Hōtan's concept of the individual and also marks his similarity to Locke, is that he thought the "thing-in-itself" was something substantial. He said, "Fire burns the body. Therefore, this fire can be regarded as an individual object. Only the fire that can burn the body is named the thing-in-itself."[2] This characterization of the "thing-in-itself" is conspicuously empirical and makes quite a contrast to the idealistic concept of the "thing-in-itself" held by, e.g., Indian Buddhist logicians such as Dharmakīrti, etc., who belonged to the tradition of Buddhist idealism (*Vijñānavāda*).

The major difference between the thought of Hōtan and Locke is that whereas Locke believed the material substance was a complex idea only derived from sense experience, Hōtan believed ". . . the thing-in-

1. *Nouveaux Essais*, passim.
2. *Immyō Zuigenki* (Sources of Buddhist Logic), vol. 8, published in 1711 (no mention of publisher), p. 13 a.

itself is apprehended by direct perception. Any characteristic which can be found in common throughout various things is an object of inference."[3] "The reality of things is called the thing-in-itself. It is an individual and cannot be in common with others. Genus is found throughout various things, just like a thread piercing flowers. This characteristic can be set up as an object of the mind in an ordinary situation (not in meditation). Genus in Buddhist logic is an object of inference."[4]

The second great British empiricist was Bishop George Berkeley (1685–1753). Since Locke's material substance was contrary to Berkeley's religious beliefs about the spiritual nature of the world, he devised arguments to show where he felt Locke had gone wrong. Some of his arguments have a twentieth century flavor in that he utilized discussions about language to further his points. Addressing Locke's theory of material substratum, he stated, "All significant words stand for ideas. All knowledge [is] about our ideas. All ideas come from without or from within."[5] If from without, they are called sensations; if from within, thoughts. Perceiving then, for Berkeley, meant having an idea. By definition an idea from without, a perception such as a color, is a sensation. Sensations however cannot occur in a senseless thing,[6] he reasoned. Such ideas as sensations, then, could not possibly inhere in inert material substance. "Nothing like an idea can be in an unperceiving thing."[7] Perception implies a perceiver, a "conscious thing," and existence means either to perceive or to be perceived. This is the famous Berkeleyan statement that *esse=percipi or percipere.*

An Asian counterpart to Berkeley on the subject of the above historically important part of his philosophy was the famous Chinese philosopher Wang Yang-ming (1472–1529).[8] "Wang lived more than two centuries before Bishop Berkeley, and yet he already had the insight to see what Berkeley later described as *esse est percipi*. . . . Wang went still one step beyond Berkeley [possibly toward the Kantian synthesis] in stating, not only 'Separated from my intelligence there would be no heaven and earth, ghosts and spirits, and the ten thousand things,' but also, 'My intelligence when separated from heaven and earth, ghosts and spirits, and the ten thousand things, would also be nothing.' For Wang, there is still only one world, a world not to be bifurcated into the inner (subjective) and the outer (objective), the 'what is above shapes' (noumenal) and the 'what is

3. *Ibid.*, pp. 16 a.
4. *Ibid.*, pp. 9 b–10 a.
5. *Philosophical Commentaries*, 378.
6. *Ibid.*
7. *Ibid.*
8. *Instructions for Practical Living and Other Neo-Confucian Writings* by Wang Yang-ming, translated by Wing-tsit Chan (New York: Columbia University Press, 1963).

below shapes' (phenomenal). In his philosophy, the realization of knowledge (*chih-chih*) already implies the investigation of things (*ke-wu*)."[9] Naturally the dichotomy between the two thinkers in terms of religious orientation is great enough to keep a comparison from being carried too far. The point is that Eastern thinkers can be found whose thoughts correspond to those of philosophers in the modern period of the West.

The last great British empiricist of the modern period was Hume (1711–76). Whereby Berkeley's analysis of the world had denied Locke's material substance but retained at the heart of his philosophy a spiritual element that receives and sustains ideas, Hume pressed the analysis on to the spiritual realm as well. Like the empiricists before him, he stressed that ideas are derived from impressions. Complex ideas, are to be put to the test, as Berkeley had proposed, to see if they have objective reference. But Hume appealed to his own experience in stating that there is no impression of a spiritual substratum to our ideas. Looking into himself, he claimed to perceive only the psychic series of events, thoughts, feelings, desires, etc. The underlying permanent spiritual element, the soul or self, was not present in his perception.

As with the other Western empiricists who have come under discussion, there is certainly no very close Eastern correlate. However, in the case of Hume, mention was made in an earlier section of the proximity of Hume's theory on the self with that of earliest Indian Buddhism, precisely, the historical Buddha's philosophy as far as it is known. There are, however, less apt but interesting comparisons to be made with Eastern movements of thought toward empiricism or perhaps some of its more pragmatic offspring.

In India also the attitude of relying solely upon one's own experience was clear in the case of Kabīr (1440–1515). Although not many details can be related regarding this, it is known that he strongly advocated reliance on direct and evident experience.[10] It is difficult to make any further comparison for he was not a professional philosopher, but rather a poet who had much influence on latter Indians. "Kabīr gives utterance to the words of experience; and he knows very well that all other things are untrue,"[11] he said of himself in a poem translated by Rabindranāth Tagore.

Empiricism appeared in China after the Ming period. Yen-yüan[12]

9. Vincent Y. C. Shih in a review of *Instructions for Practical Living. . . .* (see note 8), *Philosophy East and West,* vol. XV, nos. 3–4 (July–Oct., 1965), p. 294.

10. J. Estlin Carpenter, *Theism in Medieval India* (London: Constable & Co., 1926), p. 462.

11. *Songs of Kabīr,* translated by Rabindranath Tagore with the assistance of Evelyn Underhill (New York: Macmillan Co., 1915), I, 79, p. 90.

12. Yen-yüan's philosophy is explained in Fung Yu-lan, *History of Chinese Philosophy,* vol. II, pp. 631 ff.

(1635–1704), Huang Tsung-hsi (1610–95), and Wang Fu-chih (1619–92) "insisted that there were no principles apart from things, and that moral perfection could not be achieved except through the full development of the actual nature in the conduct of everyday life." In their opinion, "what they [the Neo-Confucianists] called 'principle' might be purely subjective, whereas in fact principle could only be found in things and studied objectively."[13]

Li Kung (1659–1733), being a disciple and colleague of Yen Yüan, also stressed the significance of empirical scholarship. In protest to conventional scholarship, he declared: "The mere reading of books is not learning. People who read books in these times merely value the elucidation of unreal 'principles' and the memorization of 'empty words.' On this account their spirits are dissipated; on this account their years of life slip uselessly away. When a time arrives for them to exert themselves and engage in the affairs of the world, they are as though blind. Surely, learning as practiced by the ancient sages was never of this sort! The studies of the ancients—rites, music, military arts and agriculture—served both for the cultivation of the self and for practical application. The proper methods of governing the world and assisting the people were all to be found therein. This is what 'learning' really means. Books should merely be used for investigation into these matters. Making memorizing and reading one's only endeavor is not learning—nay rather, it is a detriment to learning."[14] Lu Shih-yi (1611–72), as well as Yen Yüan, devoted considerable attention to what he regarded as practically important matters such as warfare, agriculture, rituals, music and political institutions. Chang Hsueh-ch'eng (1738–1801) "argued that the scholar's work should be of practical use (viz., to society and to the state) and that it can be of use only if he studies documents . . . and the actual conduct of men in society."[15]

Emphasis upon the practical significance of scholarship was voiced in both China and Japan synchronically, although there was little cultural interchange between these two countries in the seventeenth and eighteenth centuries. One is not quite sure whether such an emphasis was voiced in other countries of Asia. In Japan this idea of "practical learning (*jitsugaku*)" was espoused not only by Satō Nobuhiro (1767–1850) and others, but also by such a novelist as Takizawa Bakin (1767–1848).[16]

Japanese Zen masters of the time corresponding to the modern period

13. De Bary et al., *Chinese Tradition*, p. 615.
14. As cited in David S. Nivison, "'Knowledge' and 'Action' in Chinese Thought since Wang Yang-ming," in *Studies in Chinese Thought* edited by Arthur F. Wright (University of Chicago Press, 1962), p. 124.
15. *Ibid.*, p. 127.
16. Isoji Aso, *Takizawa Bakin* (Tokyo: Sanseido, 1943), p. 297.

in the West continued to rely heavily on experience. Prof. Paul Wienpahl has called Zen "radical empiricism"[17] (an area of twentieth century thought which has inherited the British Empiricist tradition). Of course Zen experience is not of the public nature that Hume was probably referring to. The modern renovator of Zen in Japan, Hakuin (1685–1768), rebelled against the *koan* system in favor of personal experience of the basis of Zen. Satori is communicable in the eyes of Hakuin as seen in his statement, "All former doubts were fully dissolved like ice which melted away. With a loud voice I called out, 'How glorious, how glorious!' We need no escape from the cycle of life and death, nor need we strive after enlightenment. The seventeen hundred koan exercises are not worthy of being posed."[18]

17. *Zen Diary* (New York: Harper & Row, 1970), p. 55. Prof. Wienpahl has also compared Zen with modern thought via the philosophy of Spinoza. Particularly he seeks to show that Spinoza abandoned the concept of substance as being a basic metaphysical concept, in a way not unlike the Chinese Zen master Huang Po. ("Ch'an Buddhism, Western Thought, and the Concept of Substance," *Inquiry*, vol. 14 [1971], pp. 84–101)

18. *Orategama*, vol. 3, in *Hakuin Oshō Zenshū*, vol. 5 (Tokyo: Ryūginsha, 1934), p. 35.

D. Discovery of Antiquity in a Modern Light

AUTHORITIES of the Middle Ages were for the most part damned and forsaken by modern thinkers. But this is not to say that moderns entirely gave up all cultural assets of the past. On the contrary, new movements were given stimulus by the rediscovery of the cultural heritage of antiquity in a modern context. Interest in the ancient cultures was renewed during the Renaissance and the Humanist movements of the West. Of course, Greek philosophy was "discovered" many times in the Western Middle Ages also.

At the beginning of the modern Western age the idea was widespread that the declining world (and Church) needed to be reborn by going back to the great days of old Greece and Rome (as well as the early Church). This rebirth was part of what is now termed the Renaissance. Erasmus (1466?–1536), Reuchlin (1455–1522), etc., were great figures in this movement. A spirit of revival of the old was advocated in the Roman Catholic Church by such Anglo-Catholics as Newman. And some even looked back upon the Middle Ages as an especially rich period of culture, a time of spiritual and social organization following an age of dissolution.

To China the revival of classical studies was brought about in connection with philology in the Chin period. It was generally contended by the followers of the "Han Learning" movement in the Ch'ing dynasty (1644–1911) that "the Sung and Ming Neo-Confucianists, in their interpretations of the classics, had been corrupted by Buddhist and Taoist ideas, and that therefore, in order to understand the true teachings of Confucius and Mencius, it was necessary to go back to the classical commentaries of the Han dynasty."[1]

The age of revival of classical learning was about 1600–1900. Ku Yen-wu, the chief founder of the great Ch'ing school of "Han Learning" sought to restudy the Chinese classical inheritance utilizing writings of the pre-Sung period. The spirit of exact and impartial inquiry, as exemplified in Ku Yen-wu, Tai Chen, Ch'ien Tai-hsin, and Wang Nien-sun gave rise to disciplined and dispassionate research. However, it seems that it did not give impetus to modernization in China. Their approach did not lead to an age of Galileo, Vesalius, and Newton in China.

There was a literary renaissance in Japan three centuries later than

1. Fung Yu-lan, *History of Chinese Philosophy*, p. 630.

that in Europe. Little read ancient scriptures, for example, began to be read again. The ancient culture of Japan was similar to its European counterpart, partial as it was to naturalism and humanism. The return to the fore of past cultural spirit had greatly contributed to the Western renaissance, an ideological basis for the French revolution and subsequently modern culture. In Japan the revival of ancient thought offered revolutionary and innovative elan to the Meiji restoration. The literary pinnacle of the Japanese movement might be found in such an author as Norinaga Motoori (late 18th century). "There developed a relationship between this [Japanese] literary movement of a return to the more natural ancient culture and a revolutionary movement against the feudal rule of the Tokugawa, a relationship quite reminiscent of the ideological relationship between J. J. Rousseau's 'return to nature' and the French revolutionaries."[2]

Among Japanese Confucianists a revival of classics appeared, but a critical approach was taken toward them. Arai Hakuseki (1657–1725), a rationalist, emphasized a critical approach to Japanese history and proposed "a modern interpretation of the Divine Age."[3] The revival of Confucian scholarship was utilized by some nationalists. For example, Tokugawa Nariaki, a feudal lord who encouraged the Confucian revival, noted, "Confucius was a sage by whom the Ways of To (T'ang), Gu (Yu) and the 'There Dynasties' were synthesized to the state of perfection, and we have been nourished with his teachings. Therefore we reverence his virtuous personality, and ardently desire to let the people know that it is quite natural for the Way to become greater and greater, and brighter and brighter. . . . The Way which was re-inforced by the teachings of the Western Land of Cathay, is indigenous to the Divine Kingdom (Japan)."[4] By "the Way" he understood "loyalty and filial piety," which were decidedly feudalistic ideas. However, his ideal was immediately betrayed, because the revival of Confucian studies gave impetus to the overthrow of the Japanese feudal system.

In Japanese Buddhism revivalism (i.e., recovering of lost traditions) also occurred. However, it was carried on with the new spirit of criticism. For example, Gesshū Shūko, who tried to revive ancient disciplines in the Zen order, said, "My institution is neither contradictory to Mahāyāna and Hīnayāna, nor in conformity to Mahāyāna and Hīnayāna. By being eclectic we institute rules, and practice what is *reasonable*."[5] Even Buddhist

2. Seizō Ohe, "Toward a Comparative and Unified History of Human Culture with Special Reference to Japan," in *International Symposium on History of Eastern and Western Cultural Contacts, 1957, Tokyo–Kyoto* (Tokyo: Japanese National Commission for UNESCO, 1959), p. 200.
3. Tsunoda et al., *Japanese Tradition*, p. 473.
4. *Kōdōkwan-ki.*
5. Kagamishima, *Dōgen Zenji to sono Monryū*, p. 182.

revivalism had to be based upon "What is reasonable." To recover the original spirit of Śākyamuni, scholars such as Jogon or Jiun endeavored to read the original Sanskrit texts, resulting in revival of Sanskrit studies (*shittan*). Just as Western Humanists studied non-Christian books, Japanese Buddhists came to study non-Buddhist texts. The *Daśapadārthaśāstra*, the Chinese version of a Vaiśeṣika text of India, was ignored in ancient Japan: only now, at the end of the Tokugawa period did Buddhist monks begin to study it enthusiastically.[6] This was a change from the former attitude of concentrating only on the religion which they professed.

In India a tremendous number of commentaries and systematizing works on the classics were composed in this period. The revival of Sanskrit scholarship was especially conspicuous under the rule of the Vijayanagara dynasty and may have had something to do with a renewed cultural pride based on the victory of that dynasty over the Muhammedans. But whether this revival represented something other than mere conservatism of traditional lore is not clear. It is not likely that the Sanskrit works composed in this period gave any impetus to modernization of the country before the onset of Western influence. The reformative power came out of religious works in written vernaculars.

At any rate, all attempts to revive the spirit of ancient times were inspired by the ideals which new generations held, some of which they discovered in classical works.

6. H. Nakamura, *Kokuyaku Issaikyō*, Ronshūbu, 23 (Tokyo: Daito Shuppansha, 1958), pp. 528–530.

E. Liberty

THERE was a good deal of discussion about freedom and liberty in the Western modern period. Hobbes, Locke, Spinoza, Rousseau, and later the Utilitarians paid great attention to this subject. Hobbes (1588–1679) thought of liberty from the standpoint of the absence of external restraint; as long as man is able to act without external impediments (like an undammed river flowing downhiill) his freedom is expressed. Personally, however, man is obliged to do what God wills and since all our volitions are caused, they are to that extent also obligatory. Locke belonged to a tradition that was to have more effect on later Utilitarians. He held that the foundation of all liberty is the necessity of pursuing true happiness and that liberty, in a sense, can be improved by governing the passions. It was Spinoza, however, who developed viewpoints concerning liberty (freedom) that were comparable to that of modern Eastern thinkers.

Baruch Spinoza (1632–77) had two different views on freedom which are hard to reconcile. One stems from his metaphysics: Since there is only one substance, Nature-God, individuals do not, in reality, exist; hence belief in the ultimate freedom of a separate individual is the result of ignorance of what constitutes individuality. Individuality is in reality a misinterpretation (due to an ignorance of the real causes) of natural events, among which are desires, ideals, choices, actions, etc., of people. To understand the root of these events, for Spinoza, is to be freed from the ignorance that enslaves man to his emotions. "An emotion which is a passion," said Spinoza, "ceases to be a passion as soon as we form a clear and distinct idea of it."[1]

Spinoza's other concept of freedom is difficult to put side by side with the strict determinism his first (metaphysical) view seems to imply. This other is his ethical explanation of freedom. (Its importance might be judged in light of the title of his major work, *Ethics*.) Man is capable of progress toward understanding, so he must "seek means which should lead him to perfection."[2] At the conclusion of *Ethics*, Spinoza expressed the following wish: "If the road I have shown to lead to this [i.e., the power of the mind over emotions, which leads to freedom] is very difficult. it is yet discoverable. And clearly it must be very hard since it is so seldom

1. *Ethics*, Part V, prop. 3.
2. *Tractatus theologico-politicus*, 2, 13.

found. For how could it be the case that it is neglected by practically all, if salvation were close at hand and could be discovered without difficulty? But all excellent things are as difficult as they are rare."[3] A more technical definition of liberty (*libertas*) by Spinoza was "to be in itself" (*in se esse*), probably signifying becoming one with nature, the single substance. Needless to say, this is an unusual definition in the West. In the East, however, the idea of liberty was also expressed by some phrases, the literal translations of which are "to depend upon oneself" or "to be in itself,"[4] quite close to Spinoza's concept.

The term "liberty" was expressed with the words "*jiyū*" and "*jizai*" (pronounced according to the Japanese translation) in works by Chinese and Japanese Zen masters or in the Chinese versions of Buddhist scriptures of India. These words primarily meant spiritual liberation and the concept of freedom held by more recent idealists is more or less the same. Freedom of the individual, according to the Neo-Hegelian T. H. Green (1836–82), lies "in fulfillment of the law of his being . . . in attainment of the righteousness of God."[5] This also corresponds to the idea of freedom held by Tagore, who said, "Freedom can be gained only through the bonds of discipline, through the sacrifice of personal inclinations. . . ."[6]

The idea of liberty in the political sense, however, probably appeared in the East only after the introduction of Western civilization. In Japan during the 1870's people who fought for political liberty derived their inspiration from the political ideas of English Parliamentarism, as well as from the histories of the French Revolution and the American struggle for independence. The word "*jiyū*" (liberty), this time in the political sense, charmed the people like a spell, and the theory of the natural rights of man found a hearing even in the remotest corner of the country. The English *Magna Carta* was circulated in facsimile reprints; the name of Rousseau was repeated like that of a savior; Patrick Henry was well known

3. Part V, prop. 42, note.
4. *Jiyū* in Japanese, *svatantratā, aiśvarya* in Sanskrit. Cf. *asvatantrīkaraṇa, Prasannapadā*, p. 290, *l*. 7.
5. A most comprehensive work on freedom is Mortimer J. Adler, *The Concept of Freedom* (New York: Doubleday and Co., 1958). A detailed review of it from an Indian point of view was given by C. P. Ramaswami Aiyar, *Philosophy East and West*, vol. XI, no. 3 (October, 1961), pp. 153–160. Thomas Hill Green made clear some connotations of the word "freedom." One meaning of freedom is to "express the condition of a citizen of a civilized state," the other is to "express the condition of a man who is inwardly 'master of himself.' " (*Lectures on the Principles of Political Obligations* [London: Longmans, Green and Co., 1955], p. 17)
6. Rabindranath Tagore, *Towards Universal Man* (Bombay: Asia Publishing House, 1961), pp. 87–88. Cf. Shadi Lal Malhotra, "The Social and Political Orientations of Neo-Vedāntism," *Philosophy East and West*, vol. XVI, nos. 1–2 (Jan. –April, 1966), pp. 67–80.

to many and his words "Give me liberty or give me death" became a slogan.

Hiroyuki Katō advocated a theory that "all human rights were not innate in human nature, but an outcome of the struggle for the 'right of the stronger.' This was derived from the German theory of social evolution claiming to be a consequence of Darwinism, opposing the French school standing for innate rights."[7] Katō depended much upon Iehring, Hellwald, Bluntschli, and other German scholars for many of his ideas.[8]

7. Masaharu Anesaki, *History of Japanese Religion with Special Reference to the Social and Moral Life of the Nation* (London: Kegan Paul, Trench, Trubner and Co., 1930), pp. 354–355.
8. Later Katō published his theory in German—*Der Kamp ums Recht des Stärkeren.* (*Ibid.*, p. 355, n. 1).

F. Post-modern Movement toward Dialectics

THE movement toward dialectical reasoning was distinctly of another time than the modern age in the West. It belongs to the period generally referred to as recent thought. But it is worthwhile mentioning that instances of this style of thinking occurred in certain Eastern areas prior to Western influence and even prior to the renewal of the dialectic of the Western philosophy of Hegel. Because it does not wholly belong to the period discussed in this chapter, the presentation below of dialectical thinking amounts to only a brief mention.

For Hegel (1770–1831), the dialectic was the movement in thought toward the real (the Absolute), and all thought, he believed, was descriptive of the real. This movement of thought is propelled from any point of view (thesis) to an opposed point of view (antithesis) in such a manner that a third insight about a new aspect of reality is generated (synthesis). He chose a specific place to begin in his logic, however. He began with "being" as the thesis and was driven to admit that postulating pure being is the same as postulating nothing. "Nothing" in this instance is the antithesis. Completing the triad is the knowledge that the movement from being to nothing constitutes becoming, the synthesis.

There were some earlier dialectical thinkers in the East, just as there had been in the West. The Tendai and Sanron philosophies of ancient China and Japan had some dialectical thinking, but it did not develop fully. And in modern Japan there were individual thinkers who held some dialectical ideas. Ishida Baigan set forth the thought that negative and positive are two things and yet cannot be separated; though seemingly one, they still possess the aspects of motion and quiescence.[1]

There was another Japanese thinker who, independently and earlier than Hegel, developed an interesting Eastern counterpart to Hegel's dialectic (without, of course, any resemblance to Hegel's system). Miura Baien (1723–89) expressed the following theory of dialectic: "The way to understand nature (or the universe) is dialectics (*jōri*). The secret (*ketsu*) of dialectics is to see synthesis (*gōitsu*) in antithesis (*han*). It is to give up one-sided preoccupation and to correct marks (*chōhyō*). Yin and Yan are antithetic to each other, and constitute a battle. As they are antithetic to

1. *Seiri Mondō*, pp. 19–20.

each other they can be brought to synthesis."[2] Further he added, "The way to see things thoroughly (*takkan*) is logic (*jōri*) and the essence of logic is nothing else but the dialectic of antithesis and synthesis (*hankan gōitsu*), setting aside all attachments of mind and following the correct signs."[3] The three elements, then, that go into the full structure of Miura's *jōri* are the dialectic of things, the prerequisite eliminations of bias and preoccupation, and finally the empirical test.[4] Here the thought of dialectics is seen in its incipient stage rather than systematically as in the case of Hegel.

According to Hegelian philosophy, the time process proceeds from the less to the more perfect. However, according to the Indian Vedāntins, "it is not . . . perfection that the universal Spirit or human soul accomplishes through time, since, being already perfect, it cannot be wanting in anything. It seeks only self-revelation." Many Vedāntins hold that "the perfection of the world is merely the result of the full expression of the divine spirit."[5] It is in this direction that leaders of modern India such as Rām Mohan Roy (1772–1833), Swami Vivekānanda (1863–1902), Rabindranāth Tagore (1861–1941), etc., made their way. Traditional Vedānta was brought into modern effectiveness, however, by thinkers after the influx of Western influence.

2. Hiroto Saigusa, *Miura Baien no Tetsugaku* (Tokyo), p. 132; also his *Nihon no Yuibutsuronsha*, p. 93.
3. Miura Baien's thought was discussed by Gino K. Piovesana, "Miura Baien, 1723–89 and his Dialectic and Political Ideas," *Monumenta Nipponica*, vol. 20, nos. 3–4 (1965), pp. 389–443. Cf. p. 402.
4. *Ibid.*
5. Shadi Lal Melhotra, "The Social and Political Orientations of Neo-Vedāntism," *Philosophy East and West*, vol. XVI, nos. 1–2 (Jan.–April, 1966), p. 72.

III. MODERN RELIGIOUS ATTITUDES

A. Protest against Medieval Way of Thinking

1. Introductory Words

MODERN valuation of man begins with the discarding of charismatic authorities in general. Moderns generally do not admit the significance of particular men who are endowed with magical or spiritual powers by birth or by esoteric practice.

To this fundamental attitude there are three corollaries:

a) Denunciation of esoteric religious practices which are regarded as bestowing upon the practitioner charismatic authority. Here "esoteric" means "intended for only a secluded group of disciples who are qualified by a religious authority."

b) Denunciation of the charisma of a particular person who has been given prestige by peculiar practices authorized by something above men. "Charisma" in this case is used to mean "possessing certain extra-ordinary, divine powers which inspire people to follow a specific pattern of behavior laid down by an authority."

c) Denunciation of systems of esoteric religious practices which have tended to be formalistic. The charisma of Brahmins was hereditary and it could not be inherited by people of other castes. They developed their own ritualism and formalism. Moreover, in India the charisma of a particular person was, in many cases, regarded as being acquired by particular religious practices and not necessarily by birth. This feature was conspicuous among *śramaṇas* of ancient times and some priests of Hindu sects. Denunciation of esoteric religious austerities, then, was the starting point for the development of modern thought. As the present work is written for the Western reader and since most of the points mentioned have become common to the lives of Westerners, detailed Western parallels are mentioned only infrequently. Whenever mention is made of a feature of modern thought, the reader should be easily reminded of Western instances.

In addition to these features of modern thought, the change from the medieval other-worldliness to a this-worldly attitude will be noticed as well as a correlative increase in inner-worldly activities and vocational ethics.

2. Denunciation of Religious Formalism and Stress on Inner Devotion

The esteem of religious rites is based upon attention paid to the outer symbolic expression of religious feeling. But stereotyped symbols do not necessarily continue to express human values. The effort, then, to recover oneself as man implies the devaluation of esoteric or formalistic religious rites and symbols in favor of stress on inner devotion. This tendency eventually came to an extreme. "God is dead," was a cry by Nietzsche after the modern period. He wanted the old order of spiritual values to be buried. Many thinkers the world over, though perhaps not so explicitly as Nietzsche, were heading in the same direction.

Rāmānanda (fourteenth century) was probably the first man in modern India to denounce traditional religious rites and ceremonies. Inheriting the thought of Rāmānuja, he stressed the significance of inner devotion (*bhakti*) to the highest God. But whereas Rāmānuja, his spiritual ancestor, accepted highly complicated rites, Rāmānanda stressed the inward character of faith, comporting himself with humility. He preached that all servants of the highest God are brothers; by getting rid of prejudice and bigotry men can become undefiled ones (*avadhūta*). One's sex, caste and social status do not matter, if one has genuine devotion to God.

Caitanya (1485–1533) also condemned the ritualistic system of the orthodox Brahmins. He preached devout faith in Hari and love of him, as well as invocation of his name, as the only effectual ways to salvation.[1] Yet he himself founded a religious ceremony called *kīrtana*, a procession in which the followers proceeded in lines, enthusiastically singing love songs of Kṛṣṇa and his beloved Radha. Thus he eventually expressed a ritualistic interest which had been absent in his earlier thought, although the Gaudiya Vaiṣṇavas, his followers, were not advocates of idolatry either in gross or subtle form.[2]

1. Bhakti Pradip Tirtha, *Sri Chaitanya Mahaprabhu* (Calcutta: Gaudiya Mission, 1947), Appendix II, p. 73.
2. According to the *Upadeśāmṛta* (v. 10), "those who have attained knowledge (*jnānin*) are superior to whose who esteem deeds (*karmin*). . . . The devotees (*bhaktiparama*) who are free from the sphere of knowledge are superior to those who esteem deeds. . . . Those who serve Sri Kṛṣṇa with unswerving sttachment are superior to the aforesaid devotees." Cf. "I have no attachment for castes or stages of life, nor have I any fondness for piety or impiety in this world; yet I have got my physical taber-

But it has been pointed out that those who followed Krishnaite teachers of this time, such as Caitanya (and Vallabha, 1479–1531) were prone to sensualism. (Cf. the similar criticism of the attitude of the followers of Luther in early days.) However, it is also refreshing to note that from time to time there appeared some religious leaders within the Caitanyaises and the Vallabhaises who tried to reform their degenerating religious practices. They attempted to show that the Kṛṣṇa cult is not equivalent to gross sensualism. They also established a monastic order and initiated people who became *sannyāsins* and led a life of *vairāgya* (non-attachment) and devotion to the lord Kṛṣṇa.

But, according to Kabīr, the rite of procession which Caitanya advocated so ardently was of no significance. "If by repeating Rāma's name the world is saved, then by repeating 'sugar' the mouth is sweetened."[3] Kabīr questioned the value of any traditional religious rites. "There is nothing but water at the holy bathing places; and I know that they are useless, for I have bathed in them. The images are all lifeless, they cannot speak; I know, for I have cried aloud to them. The Purāṇa and the Koran are mere words; lifting up the curtain, I have seen."[4] The existence of

---

nacle for the performance of some socioreligious duties enjoined by the Scriptures. But then, I am desirous to perform such devotional practices as are *conducive to pure devotion* (*dharmān sarvān subhajana-sahayann abhilase*)." The rise of the Caitanya school of Bengal can be understood historically only in view of "other products of the 15th-16th century Hindu renascence in Northeast India: the increasing liberalism of Muslim kings, the rise of a Hindu middle class, the importation of ritual and logic from the sheltered retreat of Mithilā, the religious revivalism with its *sankirtans* in which whole villages took part." (Daniel H. H. Ingalls, in a review of Dasgupta's *A History of Indian Philosophy*, vol. IV, Indian Pluralism, *Journal of the American Oriental Society*, vol. 71 [1951], p. 85)

3. J. Estlin Carpenter, *Theism in Medieval India* p. 459.
4. *Songs of Kabīr*, translated by Rabindranath Tagore with the assistance of Evelyn Underhill (New York: Macmillan Company, 1915), I, 79, p. 90.

O servant, where dost thou seek me?
Lo! I am beside thee.
I am neither in temple nor in mosque,
I am neither in Kaaba nor in Kailash:
Neither am I in rites and ceremonies
nor in Yoga and renunciation.
If thou art a true seeker, thou shalt at once see Me
thou shalt meet Me in a moment of time (*Ibid.*, I, 13, p. 45)

The inner veil of the temple of Mecca
Is in man's heart, if the truth be known. (Carpenter, *Theism in Medieval India*, p. 462)

"Better than these stones (idols) are the stones of the flour-mill with which men grind their corn." (Nicol Macnicol, *Indian Theism* [London: Oxford University Press, 1915], pp. 138–139)

God is realized through one's own intuition for Kabīr who emphasized a sincere faith plumbed from the bottom of one's inner heart.[5] Similarly, with Luther each individual is on his own before God; "to be saved by faith alone" (*sola fide*) was the fundamental tenet of Luther.

Evidence of a similar emphasis can be found in other thinkers of the fourteenth, fifteenth, and sixteenth centuries. Nānak (1469–1538), the founder of the Sikh religion, denounced the worship of idols, the use of cemeteries or cremation grounds, and asceticism. "By God's grace," he said, "man obtaineth it [divine knowledge]; skill and order are useless therefore."[6] The thoughts of "God's order" and "the pre-ordained will of the Commander" had a prominent position in his teaching, although they were to be reconciled with a doctrine of *karma*.[7] (Cf. Calvin's doctrine of predestination.)

Tukārām (c. 1608–49), a devotee of Vithobā of Pandharpur, condemned the worship of other gods, goddesses, ghosts, and goblins, and was in this sense a monotheist. Though he worshipped the image at the shrine, he always kept in his mind's eye the great Lord of the Universe. "Without devotion and faith everything else is useless trouble." He asserted God was not to be found by processes of concentration (*yoga*), sacrificial rites, practice of austerities, or any bodily exertions, nor by knowledge. He felt the nature of God was beyond the grasp of the mind or of words and could be attained only by devoted love. Tukārām stressed the "simplicity of the heart."[8] Once again, Western readers will be reminded of the reformative thought of Martin Luther. "After defining 'the noblest of all good works' to be 'to believe in Christ,' he affirmed the essential goodness of the normal trades and occupations of life, and denounced those who 'limit good works so narrowly that they must consist in praying in church, fasting or giving alms.' "[9]

Rāmakṛṣṇa (1836–86), thought by some in India to be the prophet of the new age, held that the practice of charity should not be confined to outward actions alone. One's thought also should be pure and genuine. "Bhakti, love of God, is the essence of all spiritual discipline. Through

5. Kabīr believed that the highest God transcends any form. According to a tradition, he made a pilgrimage to Mecca, and sat among the worshipers in the great mosque. As he lay down to sleep at night he turned his feet toward the sacred stone. An Arab priest angrily kicked the sleeper and asked why he had turned his feet toward God: "Turn my feet," was the well-known reply, "in the direction in which God is not." Carpenter, *Theism in Medieval India*, p. 475.
6. Macnicol, *Indian Theism*, p. 149.
7. *Ibid.*, p. 148.
8. R. G. Bhandarkar, *Vaiṣṇavism, Saivism and Minor Religious Systems* (Strassburg: Truebner, 1913), pp. 95–96.
9. Williston Walker, *A History of the Christian Church*, revised edition (New York: Charles Scribner's Sons, 1959), pp. 307–308.

love one acquires renunciation and discrimination naturally."[10] If in a corner of an ascetic's mind lewd desire was hidden, his observance of sexual precepts would be of no value, Rāmakṛṣṇa thought. What one thinks forms one's character. One should repeat "I am not bound, I am not bound. . . . Who can bind me? I am the son of god, the King of Kings" to be freed. For Rāmakṛṣṇa, bondage and freedom were strictly results of a person's thinking.[11] (It is important to note that Rāmakṛṣṇa was an almost illiterate, simple-hearted Brahmin, for most of his life untouched by Western civilization. By his simple, direct, and captivating talks on God, religion, humanity, and the world, he was recognized as a modern prophet. That he read Vedānta and also some books on Christianity is not so important, because all these he did after he came to be regarded as a religious leader and a man with superior vision.)

Among the Jains, a movement to reject idolatry also appeared. The founder of this movement was an influential merchant in Ahmedabad, Lonka Sha by name, who professed the Śvetāmbara-Confession. Perusing the holy Jain scriptures, he discovered that there was no mention of idolatry and many things did not coincide with Jain doctrine although taught by Jain professional leaders of his day. Under his influence the Lonka sect was established (1467).[12]

Though it is highly likely, historically speaking, that these thinkers appeared independent of religious movements in the West, nevertheless they have Western counterparts.[13] For example, Erasmus (1466?–1536), the preacher, poked gentle fun at the magical religion of the people and villified the deadly sins of churchmen. He illustrated the folly of trusting oneself to the saints by a story of a shipwreck, in which a man who took hold of a wooden, worm-eaten image of the Virgin sank to the bottom, whereas a woman with a little child, strapped to a stout plank, got to shore.

Zwingli (1481–1531), the Swiss reformer, gave up all images and crosses in the church and in this respect was like the iconoclasts. Organs in church also were prohibited. While the Lutherans loved to sing around the organ, the Zwinglians, if they sang at all, did so without any instrument. In Switzerland, at that time, the common folk took things into their own hands and rioted against the images in the churches. In one day every image in the public places of the town of Basel was smashed except

10. *The Gospel of Sri Ramakrishna*, translated into English by Swami Nikhilananda (New York: Ramakrishna-Vivekananda Center, 1942), p. 123.
11. Romain Rolland, *Prophets of the New India*, translated by E. F. Malcolm-Smith (London: Cassel & Company, 1930), p. 195.
12. Helmuth von Glasenapp, *Der Jainismus* (Berlin: Alf Haeger Verlag, 1925), pp. 69–70.
13. To show Western parallels, I have cited some movements of iconoclasm in the West from some elementary works. There were more events of the same tendency.

a statue of the Virgin and her babe on the tower gate. During the time of Cromwell's rule the stained glass windows in the cathedrals depicting Roman Catholic saints were smashed.

Later on, the Mennonite sect asserted that infant baptism was wrong. And the Quakers abolished many of the outward forms of Church worship, such as baptism and the Lord's Supper, pulpits, prayer books, robes, ministers, and so on. In the Quaker service the congregation sits in silence while the Spirit of God stirs the hushed group until one or more may be moved to speak. They have no altars, no pulpit, and no minister. (In their simplicity Quakers can be compared to the Myōkōnins of Shinshū sect of Japan.)

Some early Congregationalists in England claimed that cathedrals where the Mass had once been observed were temples of Antichrist, and barns would do just as well for churches. Some said that pulpits were nothing but tubs. In keeping with these criticisms, they held gatherings outside the churches, which the law of Charles II had outlawed.

Turning to China and Japan, iconoclasm was a trait of Zen priests, especially in ancient China. Tan-hsia (739–824), the Chinese Zen priest, combatted the tendency to be overly attached to images of Buddha and to regard them as the real Buddha himself by burning a wooden statue of the Buddha as firewood.[14] This action was highly praised by Chinese devotees of Zen. In contrast to the attitude prevailing in China, Japanese Zen priests were not so ready to approve, although iconoclasm occurred among Zen followers. As a rule, however, in this period Japanese Buddhists of other sects were more attached to images.

The attitude of iconoclasm was exhibited only by independent individuals in Japan and did not appear as a nationwide movement among Japanese Buddhists. For example, Mokujiki (1718–1810), the itinerant, exclaimed:

> My voice has become hoarse
> Due to repetition of Nembutsu prayers
> But, alas, no reply!
> Amida and Shakya Buddha are taking a siesta![15]

In a work entitled "The Daijingū-Sankeiki" ("Diary of a pilgrim to Ise Shrine") by Saka-Jūbutsu (popularly known by the name of Saka-Shibutsu, father of Jūbutsu), there is a significant criticism of general Buddhist practice: "It is quite usual with us and it is of great significance, that we do not carry with us any rosaries like Buddhists and we do not present any material offerings to the Sun-Goddess at Ise; in other words, there is no selfish desire or petition on our part. This is called inner purity

14. *Transmission of Religious Lamps*, vol. 14.
15. *Yanagi Sōetsu Senshū*, vol. 9 (Tokyo, Shunjūsha).

or heart-purity. We, worshippers, cleanse ourselves with lustrum water ceremonially; we call this outer purity or bodily purity. So purified, outer and inner, we are all-purity itself like Divinity. The deity is immanent in man and man is inherent in the deity; there is neither the divine nor the human; there is no difference in essence at all between them. When I (the author) was so told by the Shinto priest at the Shrine of the Sun-Goddess, I was overwhelmed with tears of pious gratitude."[16]

New Shinto sects which appeared at the end of the Tokugawa period showed the strong tendency to discard all doctrinal subtleties and complicated ritualism, and to establish a religion of the simple pure heart. On the occasion of the Meiji Restoration fanatical nationalists took images of Buddhas and Bodhisattvas and copies of scriptures from Buddhist temples and burned them. This was not a movement which occurred from within Japanese Buddhism itself; it was instigated by aggressive Shinto revivalists. Shinto iconoclasm was carried out within its own tradition without any religious influence from abroad.

Religious rites can be regarded as symbols, in essential respects, expressing and communicating a religious feeling and a will to act in accordance with religious values. But some modern thinkers, Eastern and Western, took the view that these symbols are not to be regarded with the same reverence as that which they symbolize, however long they may have been traditionally observed. If symbols come to bind and hamper men, they cease to be useful, and many people tried to restore the source upon which such religious symbols were based.

3. Denial of Charismatic Authority

In the medieval age, in both East and West, spiritual teachers often claimed special authority over their disciples and followers. Some assumed the role of a superior being and were regarded as higher than common people. Very often they posed as living gods or deputies of God or gods. Such an attitude was not encouraged by some modern Indian thinkers. In the songs of Kabīr no trace of self-veneration is found. Even Rāmakṛṣṇa, who is esteemed nowadays as the object of worship in the mission founded by his followers, is said not to have claimed the authority of a teacher for himself. Up to that time in India the word of the master had been strictly observed and a *guru* (teacher) exacted from his pupils a deeper respect

16. Genchi Katō, *Shinto's Terra Incognita to Be Explored Yet* (Gotenba, 1958) (for private circulation), pp. 1314. Watarai Nobuyoshi (died in 1690) said, "Complete sincerity is the absolute principle of Shintoism." (*Jingū Hiden Mondō*, cited in Katō, *ibid.*)

than that paid to their parents. However, Rāmakṛṣṇa would have none of it and reputedly put himself on a level with his young disicples,[1] never saying to them "You ought to give yourselves no me." Romain Rolland asserts that herein lies one of the main differences between his guidance and that of Christ.[2] If it is true, this probably reflects on the difference of the social conditions in which each religious leader came to prominence. Rāmakṛṣṇa's attitude was a striking deviation from that common to medieval masters.

In a like manner, the other extreme of human self-evaluation was tempered in these times; and those impure or defiling qualities which were thought to inhere in persons of lower castes were denied reality by some modern Indian thinkers. It was common in India for people of high castes to abhor being touched by people of lower castes. But Kabīr, for example, in his thoroughgoing religious reflection attacked such behavior: "When you are touched by other people, you bathe; tell me who is more degraded than yourselves."[3]

In China and Japan Zen masters often denied charismatic authority in their leaders but not necessarily in modern times. One modern Japanese religious leader who is a noteworthy exception in this regard is Suzuki Shōsan (1579–1655) who rejected the authority of the founders and previous masters of various sects. He said, "Looking into written sayings of previous masters, it does not seem that there have been persons who have practised with zeal."[4]

As mentioned in a previous section (on the subject of experience), such attitudes were carried over to leaders who claimed authority based on scholarship. Some modern Indians represented a popular revolt against the learning and pride of learning of the orthodox Hindus. These individuals felt that to boast of lore of religious scriptures was senseless and ridiculous. Kabīr stated, "Rāma and Kṛṣṇa are dead. The four Vedas are fictitious stories."[5] Dadu urged, "What avails it to collect a heap of books? . . . Wear not away your lives by studying the Vedas."[6] This attitude is closely connected with an accelerated approach to the masses, which will be discussed later.

In China a protest against medieval traditional scholarship was evinced by Yen Yüan (1635–1704), who expressed the idea that knowing is doing or that knowledge is experience. Li Kung (1659–1733) also held that "the mere reading of books is not learning." Studies should "serve

1. Rolland, *Prophets of the New India*, p. 151.
2. *Ibid.*, p. 168.
3. Bhandarkar, *Vaiṣṇavism, Saivism and Minor Religious Systems*, p. 71.
4. *Roankyō* I, 134.
5. Macnicol, *Indian Theism*, p. 138.
6. *Ibid.*, p. 156.

both for the cultivation of the self and for practical application." He was against the existing examination system used by the Government. "Making memorizing and reading one's only endeavor, is not learning—nay rather, it is detriment to learning."[7]

Insisting upon the inapplicability of ancient institutions to modern situations, Wang Fu-Chih (1619–92) ignored the authority of the classics or even that of Confucius, saying, "The most effective way of governing is to examine the *Book of History* and temper its pronouncements with the words of Confucius. . . . But when it comes to setting up detailed regulations or making up directives, then the authors of the *Book of History* or Confucius offer no guidance. . . . The ancient institutions were designed to govern the ancient world, and cannot be applied to the present day."[8]

In Japan, Master Munan (1603–76), explaining the phrase "Transmission outside of the doctrines" said, "As the essence of religion lies originally outside of the doctrines, we cannot help. It was a big blunder that Lord Shakya taught the excellent teaching!"[9] Here a Zen master actually admonishes the founder of Buddhism!

Andō Shōeki denounced Confucian scholars and Buddhist clergy as the spiritual oppressors of his age, in the same way that Winstanley decried the clergy and lawyers as the chief deceivers of the people. Yet neither Shōeki nor Winstanley can be properly termed atheists. Shōeki preserved a veneration for the genial gods of old Japan and, like a pantheist, he seems to have equated them with the forces of nature. Winstanley, a Puritan and a Protestant, looked to the scriptures as his sole guide to morality and political practice.[10]

In order to ridicule the secluded life of recluses, Indian and Japanese religious teachers resorted to irony similar to that of their other denials of charismatic figures. Kabīr said, "[the Yogi] pierces holes in his ears, he has a great beard and matted locks, he looks like a goat."[11] Munan teased recluses, saying, "One who will become a recluse in mountains without attaining enlightenment is due to become a beast!"[12]

7. Nivison, " 'Knowlege' and 'Action' . . .," p. 124.
8. De Bary et al., *Chinese Tradition*, p. 604.
9. *Sokushin-ki* (*Shidō Munan Zenji-shū*, edited by Rentarō Kōda [Tokyo: Shunjūsha, 1958], p. 40).
10. E. Herbert Norman, "Andō Shōeki and the Anatomy of Japanese Feudalism," in *Transactions of the Asiatic Society of Japan*, Third Series, 2 (1949), p. 315.
11. *Songs of Kabīr*, I, 20, p. 110.
12. *Jishōki* (*Shidō Munan Zenji-shū*, pp. 83–84; cf. p. 17).

4. Rejection of Religious Differences

The attitude of denouncing charismatic and scriptural authority, on the one hand, and that of denouncing religious rites, on the other, may have contributed to the tendency of modern Indian thinkers to reject differences between religions. Among the followers of Caitanya and Rāmānanda in India even the Mohammedan came to stand side by side with the Hindu. Influenced by Mohammedan mysticism, Kabīr, also, denied the distinction between religions. It did not matter, he held, whether God be called "Allah" or "Rāma"; hence Kabīr called himself "the son of Allah and Rāma."[1] Although he was born in a Mohammedan family, he became a devout Rāma worshipper and hated the rites and outward restrictions of Hinduism and Mohammedanism alike. He claimed to be neither a fakir, nor a yogin, nor an ascetic, but a mere weaver and father of a family. Max Weber commented on Kabīr as follows: "Kabīr, a disciple of Rāmānanda founded the Kabīr Panthī, which has spread among the weaver castes in particular. Defying the Brahmanistic authority and all Hindu gods and rituals, the order finally deduced a strictly pacifistic and ascetic eagerness for salvation, which reminds us of the Quakers: mercy to all living beings, abstention from telling a lie, avoidance of all worldly pleasures. As in the West, here also it seems that the textile handwork, being connected with houses and giving people the occasion to think, has promoted the religiosity which has almost no ritual."[2]

Nāmdev (flourished c. 1425) occasionally called the Hindu god Vitthal Allah. He also wanted to obliterate the distinction between religions. Dādū (1544–1603) is regarded by some scholars as having more right than either Kabīr or Nānak to declare, "I am not a Hindu nor a Mohammedan. I belong to none of the six schools of philosophy. I love the merciful God."[3] Rāmakṛṣṇa, who was influenced by Hinduism (especially the Śāktas, Vaiṣṇavas and Vedāntists), Islam, and even Christianity, asserted that there is only one God towards whom all are traveling, but the paths are different.[4] So, true religion lies in the practice of charity. The differences between religions are merely apparent. Thus he held no established credo or dogma. He never coerced others to adopt his thought, nor imposed his own ideas upon them. He rather insisted that the *raison d'être* and the goals of many religions—not only of different Hindu sects but also those of Islam and Christianity—are the same. In the rich

1. *Songs of Kabīr*, III, 2, p. 122; cf. I, 16, p. 46.
2. Max Weber, "*Hinduismus und Buddhismus*," *Gesammelte Aufsaetze zur Religionssoziologie* (Tuebingen: Verlag von J. C. B. Mohr [Paul Siebeck], 1923), p. 345.
3. Macnicol, *Indian Theism*, p. 153.
4. Nikhilananda, *Gospel of Sri Ramakrishna*, p. 129

metaphors common to many Indian thinkers he stated: "As the same sugar is made into various figures of birds and beasts, so one sweet Mother Divine is worshipped in various climes and ages under various names and forms. Different creeds are but different paths to reach the Almighty. As with one gold various ornaments are made, having different forms and names, so one God is worshipped in different countries and ages, and has different forms and names."[5] Such an attitude is similar to some in the West. For instance, John Wesley (1703–91) explained, "I pretend to no extraordinary revelation or gifts of the Holy Ghost, none but what every Christian may receive, and ought to expect and pray for."[6]

True instruction does not consist in inculcating doctrine, Rāmakṛṣṇa believed, but in "communicating." He engaged in no fruitless discussions on metaphysics and theology, declaring, "I do not like argument. God is above the powers of reason. I see that all which exists is God. Then of what avail is reason?"[7] On this footing his characteristic concept of the unity of all religions was established. He held all religions to be true insofar as one catches their "essence" and the devout faith of their followers. Kṛṣṇa of Hinduism and Christ are alike in terms of their being incarnations (*avatāra*) of the absolute,[8] and that absolute is the Great Self (*ātman*). There should be no barriers among religions; according to Rāmakṛṣṇa, "A river has no need of barriers. If it dams itself up it stagnates and becomes foul."[9] He went so far as to admit relativity of all religions. "You may say that there are many errors and superstitions in another religion. I should reply! . . . *Every religion has errors*."[10] Needless to say, Vivekānanda, his disciple, observed and stressed this tendency of his master to help Rāmakṛṣṇa's gospel spread even in Western countries.

By pursuing this direction of thought, one may reach the point where even the consciousness of the "Divine" should be discarded. Rolland comments, "Dare I say that it seems to me still more beautiful, still purer and higher to love and to serve the 'suffering' without any thought of 'the Divine' simply because it is suffering, and that forgetfulness of the Divine is perhaps nearer to the Divine than perpetual preoccupation with it, since it does not allow of the maintenance of any trace of 'attachment' in the sense implied by Rāmakṛṣṇa?"[11] In other words, "the Divine" is

5. F. Max Müller, *The Life and Saying of Ramakrishna* (London: Longmans, Green & Company, 1898), p. 100.
6. As cited in S. Radhakrishnan, *Eastern Religions and Western Thought* (New York: Oxford University Press, 1959), p. 51.
7. Rolland, *Prophets of the New India*, p. 152; cf. p. 200.
8. *Ibid.*, p. 214; Müller, *Life and Sayings of Ramakrishna*, p. 146.
9. Rolland, *Prophets of the New India*, p. 141.
10. *Gospel of Sri Ramakrishna*, p. 112.
11. Rolland, *Prophets of the New India*, p. 158.

nothing but man; man is the supreme. This is the logical conclusion of the development of modern Indian thought. This tendency of some modern Indian thinkers also modified Indian Christianity eventually. But these "neo-Vendāntists" conversely were also affected by Christianity.

The Brahmo-samāj founded by Rām Mohan Roy was influenced by Christianity and aimed at the renovation of Indian society. Among its members Keshab Chunder Sen (1838–84) worked for the Christianization of India. On his deathbed he declared: "Sectarian and carnal Europe, put up into the scabbard the sword of your narrow faith: Abjure it and join the true Catholic and universal Church in the name of Christ the Son of God. . . . Christian Europe has not understood one-half of Christ's words. She has comprehended that Christ and God are one, but not that Christ and humanity are one. . . . Asia says to Europe, 'Sister, Be one in Christ. . . . All that is good and true and beautiful—the meekness of Hindu Asia, the truthfulness of the Musulman and the charity of the Buddhist—all that is holy is of Christ!' "[12]

Modification of Christianity is not peculiar to eminent Indian thinkers alone. Common people also have professed Christianity in a quite Hindu way. It is related of an Indian Christian convert who attended church on Sunday and the Kālī temple on Friday, that when the missionary asked him whether he was not a Christian, he replied, "Yes, I am, but does it mean that I have changed my religion?" Hindu converts to other faiths frequently return to Hindu gods in case of trouble and sickness, presence or dread of death.[13] Many Japanese also introduced Christianity under a similar understanding to that of Hindus, although the ethical aspect of Christianity was the prime concern of converted Christians in Japan.

A tendency like that in India of the acceptance of all religions occurred also among reformative religious leaders of Japan and in nearly a corresponding period. Tenkei, the liberal Sōtō Zen teacher, did not deny the distinction between various other Buddhist sects,[14] but he did deny distinctions among Zen Buddhist sects such as Rinzai, Sōtō, etc. Being a monk of Sōtō Zen, Tenkei eliminated or criticized passages in Master Dōgen's works in which Dōgen, the founder of Japanese Sōtō Zen, praised the lineage of Sōtō and rejected the lineage of Rinzai. It would be difficult to think of Tenkei's liberal attitude apart from his social background in that he preached in the city of Osaka, the most prosperous commercial

12. In "Asia's Message to Europe" (1883), as cited in *ibid.*, pp. 93–94.
13. S. Radhakrishnan, *The Hindu View of Life* (New York: Macmillan Company, 1927), pp. 53–54.
14. Genryū Kagamishima, *Dōgen Zenji to sono Monryū* (Tokyo: Seishin Shobō, 1961), p. 116; 22.

center of Japan. Most Shingaku teachers taught Buddhism in general. Kyūō said, "Different sects look up to the same moon shining on the summit. . . . Each one should keep the teaching of one's own sect carefully, and endeavor not to compete with others."[15]

When the above-mentioned standpoint is theoretically carried to the extreme, the distinction between various religions is abolished. Master Munan said, "Mind is called Gods, Heaven or Buddha in three countries [i.e., Japan, China, and India]. Their terms are different, but they are the same in essence."[16] The Confucian movement in Japan was also quite tolerant of other religions. Itō Jinsai (1627–1705) said, "From the viewpoint of scholars there is in fact Confucianism and Buddhism; from the viewpoint of the Universe there is properly neither Confucianism nor Buddhism; there is but One Way and that is all!"[17]

Mokujiki, the itinerant priest, denounced narrow attitudes of sectarianism. When one comes to think further theoretically, he believed, what is called a religion itself becomes useless.

> It would be useless to be staunchly devout to Buddhism;
> When I asked Dear Amida [about what Buddhism is], he replied:
> O! Conglomeration of falsehood![18]

Ishida Baigan also asserted that one should forsake the specific appelation of each religion: "When you have attained the Mind, you are free from either the names of Buddhism or of Confucianism.[19] . . . There are no different Minds and whoever believes that thanks to Buddhism he can attain a different Mind, is foolish, and will never come to any good."[20]

Both the Shingaku movement, originating from Ishida Baigan, and the Hōtoku movement, originating from Ninomiya Sontoku, were more or less eclectic and attempted to extract from various religions what was most essential to religion and beneficial to practical ethics and popular instruction. This feature can also be found in the thought of Master Jiun, the pioneer of Sanskrit scholarship in Japan.

In spite of these new movements, however, denominational boundaries were strictly laid down by the Tokugawa Government in Japan and overstepping them was prohibited.

In China syncretic character was conspicuous from olden times and became prevalent among common people in the Ching dynasty. In the period under discussion, Li Chih (1527–1602) overtly expressed the attitude of the later Wang Yang-ming school "toward an easy syncretism

15. Shōkin Furuta, *Kinsei no Zensha-tachi* (Kyoto: Heirakuji Shoten, 1956), pp. 126–135.
16. *Jishōki* (*Shidō Munan Zenji-shū*, p. 67).
17. Joseph Spac, *Monumenta Nipponica*, vol. 5 (1942), no. 1, p. 182.
18. *Yanagi Sōetsu Senshū*, vol. 9 (Tokyo: Shunjūsha, 1955), p. 321.
19. Ishida Baigan, *Seiri Mondō*, p. 54.
20. *Ibid.*, p. 55.

of Buddhism, Taoism, and Confucianism, proclaiming the 'three religions to be one' For this his group won the appellation 'Wildcat Ch'an school!' "[21] Popular religions such as the Way of Pervading Unity also advocated that "the Way is . . . the one principle," and that "the one is divided into three."[22] Such an attitude was refuted by Confucianists of the Chin dynasty. But due to the changing times, finally even traditional Confucianism was not officially adopted in the Republic of China for the reason that it was not justified to disregard other religions.[23]

This tendency to minimize the differences of various religions was forbidden in the medieval West in general and by many Protestant denominations in the modern age. But the thought that any single religion is not justified to claim absoluteness found expression in the West. The thinkers of the age of reason came to realize that no one religion was best, but the best was what all religions had in common, something simple and reasonable which everybody could understand and on which everyone could agree. This attitude influenced such a prominent later philosopher as John Stuart Mill who firmly believed "that other ethics than any which can be evolved from exclusively Christian sources, must exist side by side with Christian ethics to produce the moral regeneration of mankind; and that the Christian system is no exception to the rule, that in an imperfect state of the human mind, the interests of truth require a diversity of opinions. It is not necessary that in ceasing to ignore the moral truths not contained in Christianity men should ignore any of those which it does contain."[24] He denied the absoluteness of Christianity. "That mankind owes a great debt to this morality [i.e., Christianity], and to its early teachers, I should be the last person to deny; but I do not scruple to say of it that it is, in many important points, incomplete and one-sided, and that unless ideas and feelings, not sanctioned by it, had contributed to the formation of European life and character, human affairs would have been

21. De Bary et al., *Chinese Tradition*, p. 583.
22. *Ibid.*, p. 648.
23. When an attempt was made, as late as 1915–1916, "to incorporate a clause in the new Constitution of the Republic which would establish the teaching of the Confucian school as the basic system of moral education in China," the new leaders of thought "fought successfully to prevent its adoption in the final text of the Constitution." (Hu Shih, *The Chinese Renaissance* [University of Chicago Press, 1934], p. 90) The chief arguments against its acceptance were thus stated by Mr. Ch'en Tu-shiu: "All religions are useless as instruments of government and education. They are to be classed with the other discarded idols of a past age. Even if we may concede that a religion may be needed by an uneducated people, are we justified in disregarding all the teachings of the other religions? We shall be guilty of encroaching upon the religious liberty of the people, if the other religions are ignored and Confucianism alone is constitutionally recognized." (*Ibid.*)
24. Mill, *On Liberty*, p. 30.

in a worse condition than they now are. Christian morality (so called) has all the characters of a reaction; it is, in great part, a protest against Paganism."[25]

Some thinkers came even to advocate forms of religion based on a standpoint of atheism. Rector Forberg in Saalfeld wrote an article "Entwicklung des Begriffs der Religion," in which he asserted that a religion is possible even without belief in God. His intention seemed to be to delimit the religion of morality, in Kant's sense. This was a great shock to the Germans of his day and Forberg and Fichte, his teacher, were severely attacked.[26] Probably such a proposal would have been impossible in premodern days. Theoretically, Forberg's standpoint was not so different from that of Shingaku and other scholars of Japan who advocated that Mind alone is the basis of religion, thereby minimizing all authorities.

With the indulgence of the reader, it might be said that dogmatic religions have a tendency to forget the significance of symbols to the extent that some worship not only images but also theological opinions. What is forgotten is that these forms were originally employed by religions only to focus their faith. When worshippers confuse these outer symbols with the deeper true reality, they approach idolatry. The current diverse religious groups which are bound within themselves by means of dogmas, rites, and ceremonies, hamper the formation of a universal human society. When the actual intended use of symbolism is recognized, it is not so easy to insist on any one route by which men approach religious experience. Rejection of the differences between religions is a rational result of a higher valuation of man.

The non-sectarian tendency may have appeared more readily in Eastern countries than in the West because of the lack of any comparable sustained political power of the Church in the East and perhaps also because of the absence of certain anthropomorphizations by which some Christians have characterized God. However, all movements of such a tendency have a major stumbling block. Any new religious movement of this kind stands upon the shoulders, so to speak, of the greatest common measure of the several existing religions which were prevalent before it. Such a proposed "non-sectarian movement," then, faced an ironic danger of itself becoming sectarian in the end.

25. *Ibid.*, pp. 28–29.
26. Paul Deussen, *Allgemeine Geschichte der Philosophie*, 4th edition (Leipzig: F. A. Brockhaus, 1919–20, II, 3, p. 297 f.

5. A Return to This-Worldliness

The character of religious thought in medieval India, as in other countries, was, generally speaking, otherworldly. People yearned for a happy life in the next world (e.g., heaven) after death, and often worshipped a transcendent deity capable of assisting them toward this aim. In modern India, however, people's attitudes to life gradually became "this-worldly." As an example of the extent to which this viewpoint was drawn, Dadu went so far as to reject the traditional doctrine of transmigration, holding that all possible rebirths happen in man's one life on earth.[1]

Naturally, the corresponding change in the West was more pronounced and happened faster as a result of rising confidence in science and its inability to discover heavens or transcendent beings. One Western thinker who adopted a this-worldly attitude for reasons similar to those of Easterners of a corresponding period was Jakob Boehme. His point seems to have been that searching for otherworldly salvation is a mistake when spiritual understanding is to be had here and now. He made astonishingly explicit utterances to that effect, such as, "My meaning is not that there is in heaven any particular place or a particular body where the fire of the divine life breaks forth . . . but I speak in this bodily fashion for the sake of my reader's lack of understanding; for thou canst name no place—neither in heaven nor in this world—where the divine ought not to be and is not."[2]

All the teachings about hell and devils and witches, in which religious people had believed, were repudiated by thinkers of the Enlightenment as a bad fairy tale. This opinion came to be accepted as a common sense idea by people in general.[3] In India, however, there remained thinkers who believed in afterlife or in metempsychosis,[4] and others[5] associated the idea of immortality with that of Indian transmigration.

In China the tendency of this-worldliness occurred very early. The rebellion of On Lu-shan (755–56) and the challenges presented by it were

1. *Encyclopedia of Religion and Ethics*, edited by James Hastings (Edinburgh: T. & T. Clark, 1925), s.v. Dādū, IV, p. 358 b.
2. Cited from Höffding, *History of Modern Philosophy*, I, pp. 72–73.
3. "The window had once contained glass, but that and its supporting frame had long ago yielded to missiles flung by hands of venturesome boys to attest alike their courage and their hostility to the supernatural; for the Breede house bore the evil reputation of being haunted." (Ambrose Bierce: In the Midst of Life, The Suitable Surroundings)
4. Lessing held the concept of a sort of metempsychosis. (Deussen, *Allgemeine Geschichte*, II, 3, p. 167)
5. "Sehr sinnreich weiss Kant das Postulat der Unsterblichkeit daraus zu schopfen, dass der kategorische Imperativ von uns vollkommene Sittlichkeit und Heiligkeit fordert, und dass eine solche Forderung sich nur in einem Prozess unendlicher An-

no doubt directly responsible for characteristics which gained popularity in China later: involvement in the world, concern for application to the present day, an activist (*yu-wei*) tone, etc.[6] In later days this trend occurred in the form of refutation of the otherworldliness of Buddhism. Being criticized thus, Buddhism went into serious and steady decline in China from the late T'ang dynasty (10th century) onwards. In the succeeding Sung dynasty Ch'an Buddhism was still a vital cultural force, particularly in literature and the arts, and this influence dwindled only gradually in later centuries, especially under the Chin dynasty. Nevertheless, from the Sung onward, a Confucian revival wrested the intellectual initiative from Buddhism, strengthened its own hold on the political establishment, and regained the role of the dominant ideological factor in Chinese society and culture. Buddhism, being professed chiefly by lower class people, was relegated to an almost insignificant corner of the national life—a refuge for the dissenter and the disillusioned, a service for the deceased and bereaved.[7]

In Japan the turning point from other-worldliness to this-worldliness seems to have occurred around the period of Kanbun (1661–73). Before that, in the early Tokugawa period, printed books were published at the rate of three Buddhist for every one non-Buddhist book. However, afterwards the rate was reversed, and more and more Confucian books were printed. Japanese Confucianists and scholars of Japanese classics attacked Buddhism for its otherworldliness. Some reformist Buddhists changed their traditional attitude. The this-worldly character of Zen in modern times was conspicuous in such Zen priests as Suzuki Shōsan, who taught lay believers: "To pray for a happy future does not mean to pray for a world after death. It means to be delivered here and now and thus to attain a great comfort. Then, where do you think those afflictions come from? They are originated merely from the attachment to your own body. To be delivered from it is to become a Buddha."[8] But such an opinion was not generally accepted in the Tokugawa period.

Humanism (in the sense of returning to mankind the power over his

---

naherung verwirklichen lasst, somit eine unendliche Dauer unserer Personlichkeit zur Voraussetzung hat. Genau betrachtet, wurde diese kantische Unsterblichkeit nicht auf die christliche mit ewiger Vergeltung in Himmel und Holle, sondern auf eine Art Seelenwanderung in indischem Sinne hinauslaufen, wie ihn die *Bhagavadgītā* (5, 45) in den schonen Worten suzammenfasst." (Deussen, *Allgemeine Geschichte*, II, 3, p. 271) Concerning the case of Schopenhauer, cf. Deussen, *ibid.*, p. 555.

6. Edwin G. Pulleyblank, Neo-Confucianism and Neo-Legalism in T'ang Intellectual Life, in *The Confucian Persuasion*, edited by A. F. Wright (Stanford University Press, 1960), pp. 83–84.
7. Cf. De Bary, *Buddhism, op. cit.*, (a memeographed copy).
8. *Roankyō*, 1st part, in *Zenmon Hōgo-shū* (Tokyo: Kōyūkan, 1921), p. 71.

own destiny that was once thought to be held by God) is closely connected with this-worldliness, and is one conspicuous feature of the re-evaluation of man in modern times, especially in the West.[9] In India however, there were only hints of the slow change toward this sort of thought and like Easterners in general, God(s) was not eliminated but rather relegated to a role more intrinsic to the world. While Rāmānuja regarded matter and souls as attributes (*viśeṣaṇas*) of God, the thinkers of the Caitanya sect (Jīva and Baladeva) regarded individual souls and matter as manifestations of energies of the Highest God. He is the efficient cause through his higher energy (*parā śaktiḥ*), and the material cause through his lower energies (*aparā śaktiḥ* and *avidyāśakti*). Jīva considered the fundamental nature (*prakṛti*) as the outer energy (*śakti*) of God, which, though not directly related to him, was thought to be under his control.[10] It might be concluded that, whereas the world view of the Rāmānuja sect was static, that of this sect was rather dynamic. This line of thinking opens the way to the emphasis of this-worldly activities in social life. This sect stresses love toward men. Caitanya declared that even hell, where love could still rise from the midst of pain, was preferable to extinction in the very bosom of God.[11]

Kabīr's this-worldly view of life is contrasted to the pessimistic view of live in India before him, which emphasized suffering and delusion in life. According to Kabīr, such a notion is quite wrong, it is egoism that is the root of all evil. "Where there is 'I' there is 'my'. . . . Where there is mercy there is strength; where forgiveness, there is He."[12]

> O friend! hope for Him whilst you live: for *in life deliverance abides.*
> If your bonds be not broken whilst living, what hope of deliverance in death? It is but an empty dream, that the soul shall have union with Him because it has passed from the body.[13]

For Kabīr, worldly social life should be given due acknowledgement. Life is a holy gift of God.[14] Nāmdev,[15] Nānak, Tukārām[16] and other thinkers

9. Cf. Shakespeare, *Hamlet*, III, 1: "And by a sleep to say we end the heartache and the thousand natural shocks that flesh is heir to,—'tis a consummation devoutly to be wish'd."
10. S. Radhakrishnan, *Indian Philosophy* (London: George Allen and Unwin, 1923), II, pp. 762–763.
11. Carpenter, *Theism in Medieval India*, p. 446.
12. *Ibid.*, p. 468.
13. *Songs of Kabīr*, I, 47, pp. 46–47.
14. Cf. Monier-Williams, *Brahmanism and Hinduism* (London: John Murray, 1887), p. 142.

> Do not go to the Garden of flowers!
> Oh Friend! go not there:
> In your body is the garden of flowers.
> (*Songs of Kabīr*, I, 58, p. 47.)

also denounced asceticism, dissuading men from giving up the world and becoming recluses. They stressed the significance of secular life, encouraging men to engage in ordinary vocations. To endure suffering in this world was highly approved.[17] Tulsī Dās counselled, "Consider the body as worthy of honour, for the Lord himself once took a human form."[18] This assertion is quite noteworthy in comparison with the contempt of body evident in former Indian thought.

Even in Jainism, which is famous for its strict austerities, Yaśovijaya (1624–88), a Jain reformer, sought to prove that the completely Enlightened One (*Kevalin*), "so long as he leads a physical life, must take nourishment, and that ordinary objects of usage of the monks, garments, etc., are not to be counted as 'possessions,' and that the saintly life does not exclude life in the world."[19] He wanted to get rid of the severe austerities of the Jain religion of the past.

In Japanese Buddhism, also, some modern reformists affirmed human life. Master Jiun said, "Some say that since Buddhism teaches only the disciplines of the mind by the mind itself it is of no use to the people, and that for the same reason it is of no value to those who govern the masses. Confucianism, it is said, teaches the regulation of conduct by forms, ceremonies and rules of etiquette. Because of this Confucianism is of great use to teach and edify people. This objection to Buddhism is made by those who do not really know what Buddhism is, and who have seen only its shortcomings which arose after the dynasties of Sun and Yuan. Buddhism which is the True Law certainly teaches the Ten Virtues. By this teaching even ordinary men can regulate themselves and their homes, and finally can thus walk in the right path."[20]

However, the life-affirming attitude was more obvious among non-Buddhists. According to Kurozumi Munetada (1780–1850), the founder of the Kurozumi sect of Shintoism, "human life amounted to nothing but a realization of man's intrinsic connection with the cosmic vitality. This communion he called *iki-tōshi*, i.e., 'penetrating into life' or 'pervaded by

15. "It is not necessary to give up eating food or drinking water; fix your mind on the feet of Hari. Yoga or sacrificial ceremonies or giving up objects of desire is not wanted. . . . Hold fast to the love of the name of Hari; . . . [He] will render himself manifest to you." (Bhandarkar, *Vaiṣṇavism, Śaivism and Minor Religious Systems*, p. 90)

16. "Do not give up food; do not betake yourself to a forest-dwelling; in all your sufferings and enjoyments think of Nārāyana. A child sitting on the shoulders of its mother feels no trouble. Put an end to all thoughts different from this." (I, 1368, *Ibid.*, p. 97)

17. "Even adversity will be sweet to me, if it leads me to thy feet." (I, 1133. *Ibid.*, pp. 96–97)

18. Carpenter, *Theism in Medieval India*, p. 517.

19. M. Winternitz, *A History of Indian Literature* (Calcutta: University of Calcutta Press, 1927–33), II, p. 593.

20. *Jūzen Hōgo*, p. 48.

vitality.' "[21] Andō Shōeki stated clearly "Direct cultivation and happy eating, direct weaving and happy clothing—there is no Way but this. Talking of thousands of ways is false."[22] (This attitude of affirming worldly ethics is taken up next.)

But the avowal of such outspoken opinions was not permitted under the pressure of the Tokugawa Shogunate government. It was only after the Meiji Restoration that freedom to publicly express oneself became possible and still brought with it the probability of harsh censure from educators and social leaders.

6. Rise in Popularity of Worldly Activity and Vocational Ethics

As earthly life consists in action, a this-worldly attitude tends to stress action in social life (*vita activa versus vita contemplativa*).[1] So this is naturally what occurred as Westerners became more this-worldly[2]: in modern Western philosophy activity became emphasized.[3] This attitude led to an esteem

21. Anesaki, *History of Japanese Religion*, p. 315.
22. Norman, "Andō Shōeki and the Anatomy of Japanese Feudalism," p. 161.

1. "Whether 'tis nobler in the mind to suffer
The slings and arrows of outrageous fortune;—
Or to take arms against a sea of troubles,
Any by opposing, end them?—" (Shakespeare)
2. "While with Eckhart, the world-process both in its arising and in its passing was regarded as a knowing process, with Boehme it is rather a struggling of the will between good and evil." (Windelband, *History of Philosophy*, p. 375)
3. "In its fundamental thought the teaching of the Bhagavad-Gita is closely related to the speculative philosophy of J. G. Fichte (1762–1814). This too makes man take part in a play that God stages of Himself. According to Fichte, God, the Origin of Being, cannot rest in the state of pure Being because He is infinite Will-to-Action. Therefore he sets Himself a limitation and in order thereby to become conscious of Himself as Will-to-Action. Man then, as an individual divine *ego*, must see his destiny in endeavoring with this divine *ego* 'to bring the whole world of the senses under the sovereignty of reason.'

"Because he premises a world-view of ethical world and life-affirmation, Fichte has to attribute the importance of ethical activity to the participation by man in the play stage by God. Therefore he ventures on the violent proceeding of defining ethics in quite general terms as the subjection of the world of the senses to reason. Starting from the conception of Divine activity which he has formed for himself, he gives human activity a meaning. In the *Bhagavadgītā*, on the other hand, man plays a part in the drama from a blind sense of duty, without seeking to find out its meaning, and, along with that, the meaning of his own action.

"The relationship between the philosophy of Fichte and the *Bhagavadgītā* goes so far that Fichte too regards as the highest activity that by which man enters in the service of the order of the Universe. The duties which in his opinion stand in the front rank are not, as would be in harmony with the spirit of his age, the general

of manual vocations. Martin Luther held that, Europe having become a Christian society, Christians should stay in the world and do the work, whatever it be, to which God has called them, whether as shoemakers, parents, teachers, rulers, or even soldiers.[4] It has been said that, according to Luther, "the monastic life is not only quite devoid of value as a means of justification before God, but he also looks upon its renunciation of the duties of this world as the product of selfishness, withdrawing from temporal obligations. In contrast, labor in a calling appears to him as the outward expression of brotherly love. The fulfilment of worldly duties is under all circumstances the only way to live acceptably to God, for Luther, and hence every legitimate calling has exactly the same worth in the sight of God."[5]

These features are roughly what some thinkers of modern India asserted, and it may be concluded that this-worldliness, as a corollary of the increased valuation of man, is one of the features of modern religions both East and West. But in India such an idea did not lead to capitalism throughout the country, as it did in the West. This trend has been noticed among some modern Indian sects, for example, the followers of Vallabha. Many wealthy merchants, especially in Calcutta, are those from Malwar, which is the stronghold of the Vallabha sect. In the philosophy of Vallabha, in other ways very similar to that of Nimbārka, an emphasis on social action is new. Although he was a follower of the Upaniṣadic doctrine, Vallabha admitted the significance of action which helps acquire "perfect knowledge."[6] Protesting the traditional attitude of denouncing actions, he stressed religious significance of deeds by those who have attained such "transcendental knowledge."[7] He admitted the theory of the four life-stages (*āśrama*) which Brahmins or people of the upper three classes should observe successively; the stage of students, householders, anchorites, and religious beggars. The successive observance of these four stages was regarded as highly meritorious among ancient Brahmanists. But Vallabha asserted that in the present dissolute age the fourth stage, i.e., abandonment of worldly concerns, should not be practiced, as pre-

---

duties based in the ethical nature of man, but those which result from his social position, his profession and his special endowments." (Albert Schweitzer, *Indian Thought and Its Development*, translated by Mrs. Charles E. B. Russell [Boston: Beacon Press, 1960], pp. 192–193)

4. According to the ideas of the Quakers, it is not right for people to spend their lives in occupations that are of no real and sensible advantage to the world.
5. Max Weber, *The Protestant Ethic and the Spirit of Capitalism*, translated by Talcott Parsons (New York: Charles Scribner's Sons, 1930), pp. 80–81.
6. *Aupaniṣadajñāsyāpi karmopayogitvam* (*Anubhāṣya* I, 1, 1, p. 7).
7. Having cited *Bhagavadgita* X, 8–10, he says: *ato brahmavidam eva kṛtaṃ karma subhaphalam bhavati. Anubhāṣya of Vallabhāchārya*, edited by Pandit Shridhar Tryambak Pathak (Bombay: Government Central Press, 1921), I, 1, 1, p. 7.

vious thinkers had recommended. He said that the stage of a householder who is favored by the compassion of God is particularly distinguished.

Several religious leaders of this period favored a secular, rather than an ascetic, way of life. The adherents of Kabīr and Malukdas (at the end of the sixteenth century) followed the occupation of householders, and Tukārām was a petty shopkeeper. Although he was invited to the royal court by Prince Sivaji, he declined to go, being content with his life. Tulsī Dās also asserted that the senses, which had generally been conceived as tending continually toward evil and rebirth, are not to be regarded as obstacles on the path leading to salvation, but rather as a means for enhancing and enriching faith and devotional attitudes toward the deity.[8] Although Rāmakṛṣṇa and his disciples observed celibacy, they admitted that there is no way of renouncing work altogether. "Breathing is also an activity. . . . So do your work, but surrender the result to God."[9] Rāmakṛṣṇa's devotees asserted that the worldly life should be affirmed, and taught their lay followers to raise their families. To the question, "Sir, may I make an effort to earn more money?" Rāmakṛṣṇa replied, "It is permissible to do so to maintain a religious family. You may try to increase your income, but in an honest way."[10] Finally in India, a striking feature of modern religious leaders is that they interpret the *Bhagavadgītā* in terms of emphasis upon activity.[11]

In Japan also, a spirit of activity was extolled. According to Itō Jinsai (1627–1705), the Japanese Confucianist, the intrinsic nature of both earth and heaven lies in their activity, which he characterized as evolutionary. Eternal development is the only and true existence, claimed Jinsai, while completely denying death. He quoted *The Book of Changes* (*I Ching*): "The great virtue of heaven and earth is called life," and interpreted this statement as meaning that living without ceasing is the very way of heaven and earth. Because the way of heaven and earth is one with life, reasoned Jinsai, there exists life without death and convergence without divergence.[12] Jinsai believed that the world of reality consists of change and action and that action in itself is good: "Between the heaven and earth there is only one reason: motion without stillness, good without evil. Stillness is the

8. William Charles Macdougall, *The Way of Salvation in the Ramayan of Tulasi Das*, A Dissertation (Chicago, University of Chicago Libraries, 1926), p. 222.
9. Nikhilananda, *Gospel of Sri Ramakrishna*, p. 114.
10. *Ibid.*, p. 114.
11. This feature can be noticed with Gandhi, Tilak, Aurobindo Ghosh, etc., although it is difficult to judge how far back one can trace this trend. Muhammad Iqbal, the father of Pakistan, opened his introduction to his *Reconstruction of Religious Thought in Islam* with the words: "The Quran is a book which emphasizes 'deed' rather than 'idea.'" (Northrop, *The Taming of the Nations* [New York: Macmillan, 1952], p. 158)
12. *Gomō Jigi*, vol. I, fol. 3.

end of motion, while evil is a kind of death. It is not that these two opposites are generated together, but they are all one with life."[13]

Ogiu Sorai and other characteristically Japanese Confucianists denounced the static character of the Chinese school of *Li*. In fact it can be said that all of the characteristic Japanese scholars believed in phenomena as the fundamental mode of existence. They unanimously rejected the quietism of the Confucianists of medieval China (Sung period).[14] "Quiet sitting and having reverential love in one's heart" were the methods of mental training practiced by most Chinese Confucianists of the Middle Ages (around the Sung period). These were ridiculed by Sorai: "As I look at them, even gambling seems to be superior to quiet sitting and having reverential love in one's heart."[15] Meditation was repudiated by some Zen masters whose quintessence was usually to practice meditation. Suzuki Shōsan discouraged laymen from practicing meditation and instead encouraged them to carry on their duties.

The spirit of activity was nurtured by the merchants whose influence was gaining in society. Ishida Baigan, who founded the Shingaku movement, remarked, "Once Confucius stood by a river and said: 'It flows on just like this not ceasing day and night!'[16] He meant that a flowing river is the best means to be able to see quite easily towards the Internal Substance of the Way."[17] This somewhat twisted interpretation is similar to that given by Itō Jinsai and was probably inherited from him. Confucius lamented the transitoriness of everything by the saying, but Jinsai took it to mean extollment of active generation and development of all things.[18]

This willingness to accept the phenomenal world and to live contentedly in it was not confined exclusively to Buddhism and Confucianism in Japan. It is found in modern pre-Meiji Shintoism as well. The founder of the Konkō sect taught, "Whether alive or dead, you should regard the heaven and earth as your own habitation."[19] In Shintoism there was an idea called "*yoshashi*," which is an equivalent of "*mikoto-mochite*," its literary meaning being "by [the grace of] calling by God." "Yoshashi" etymologically coincides with the Western concept of "vocation," "*Beruf*." Shintoists based their own vocational ethics on this concept, "calling."[20]

13. *Dōji-mon* (Questions by Children), vol. II.
14. Junsei Iwahashi, *Sorai Kenkyū* (Studies on Ogiu Sorai) (Tokyo: Sekishoin, 1934), p. 449.
15. Ogiu Sorai, *Rongo-chō* (Comments on the Analects of Confucius), cited in *ibid.*, p. 300.
16. *Analects* IX, 16.
17. Ishida Baigan, *Seiri Mondō*, p. 57.
18. *Rongo Kōgi*, vol. 5. Cf. Kōjirō Yoshikawa, *Shinajin no Koten to sono Seikatsu* (Tokyo: Iwanami Shoten, 1951), p. 154.
19. Yasusada Hiyane, *Nihon Shūkyō-shi* (History of Japanese Religion) (Tokyo: Sanyōshoin, 1934), p. 828.
20. Nagao Nishida, *Nihon Shūkyō Shisō-shi no Kenkyū* (Studies on the history of religious thoughts in Japan) (Tokyo: Risō-sha, 1956), p. 178f.

Andō Shōeki, a Shintoist who proposed *The Way of Nature and Labor* (*Shizen Shin-eidō*), protested against exploitation by feudal lords. Sympathizing with peasants for their miserable condition, he advocated pride in agricultural pursuits. He has been thought to have two counterparts in the West. One is François Quesnay (1694–1774), a French *encyclopédiste*, and the most famous of the Physiocrats. Both lived at nearly the same time; both were physicians, but agriculture was their real delight.[21] Just as Quesnay found in China the exemplification of the natural order, so Shōeki in a reverse direction looked to Europe for one of his model states.[22] The other counterpart, Gerrard Winstanley, was also a spokesman for the underprivileged and impoverished section of the community: the evicted tenant, the precarious day laborer, the copy-holder vainly struggling against the onslaught of the enclosing landlord.[23] In this respect, by insisting that laboring people be paid due attention, Winstanley has something in common with Saint-Simon (1768–1825), who asserted that the ultimate aim was the elevation, both intellectually and economically, of the working class, the class which suffered most.

A corollary of the attitude of respecting vocational activity was a denunciation of the life of monks who were represented as doing nothing. Medieval lay leaders such as Shinran still had respect for monks who were living an ascetic life, even believing the monks to be living in a superior way. But in the modern age some activistic thinkers despised monks, feeling that they were lazy and idling away. In the West this attitude was most conspicuously expressed by atheists and communists. In Japan the critical attitude was expressed with most ascerbity by Andō Shōeki. Ninomiya disliked priests and scholars in general because he thought they were not producers and so did not add to the prosperity of the country.[24]

In this connection, the Buddhist custom of mendicancy or living by begging was severely attacked by Japanese Confucianists, and gradually died out. In the West also there were friars in medieval days, but the custom of going out to beg for alms became extinct. In some South Asiatic countries this tradition is still prevalent. Dazai Shundai, the Neo-Confucianist, complained, "The Way (Path) of the Buddhists makes mendicancy the proper way of getting a livelihood: to earn it by engaging in any of the occupation of the gentry, the farmers, the artisans or the merchants is pronounced to be a heterodox mode of living."[25]

However, toward the modern period in Japan, Buddhists also (espe-

21. Norman, "Andō Shōeki. . . .," p. 299 f.
22. *Ibid.*, p. 303.
23. *Ibid.*, pp. 305 f, 315.
24. R. C. Armstrong, "Ninomiya Sontoku, the Peasant Sage," *Journal of the Asiatic Society of Japan*, vol. 38, pt. 2, p. 9.
25. J. C. Hallion, *Transactions of the Asiatic Society of Japan*, vol. 38, pt. 2 (1910), pp. 32f.

cially Zen Buddhists) began to advise that a man who put his heart and soul in his own secular vocation was practicing Buddhist asceticism. Takuan (1573–1645) the Zen priest, taught that "the law of the Buddha, well observed, is identical with the Law of mundane existence. The Law of mundane existence, well observed, is identical with the Law of the Buddha."[26] This idea was also stressed by Suzuki Shōsan, a Zen priest who claimed to be the first man to apply Buddhism to matters of ordinary life. He wrote a book entitled *The Significance of Everyman's Activities*,[27] in which he discussed problems of vocational ethics and placed absolute significance in the pursuit of any vocation: warrior, farmer, craftsman, merchant, doctor, actor, hunter, or priest. Because it is the essence of Buddhism, according to him, to rely upon the original self ("the true Buddha of one's own") and because every vocation is the function of this "one Buddha," to pursue one's own vocation is to obey the Absolute One. Consequently he preached to farmers, "Farming is nothing but the doings of a Buddha,"[28] while to merchants he taught, "Renounce desires and pursue profits single-heartedly. But you should never enjoy profits of your own. You should, instead, work for the good of all others."[29]

26. *Ketsujō-shū*.
27. The title is *Banmin Tokuyō*.
28. *Roankyō*, last part (in *Zenmon Hōgoshū*, ed. Rev. Koko Yamada and Mr. Keizō Mori [Tokyo: Kōyōkan, 1921], p. 41).
29. *Ibid.*, p. 337; *Banmin-Tokuyō* (in *Zenmon Hōgoshū*, last part, p. 536 ff).

B. Changes in the Evaluation of Man

1. Man Conceived as Supreme—Stress on Human Love

HUMANISM is a trait conspicuous of the Western Modern Period, largely brought about by the popularity of science. But Eastern countries of a nearly corresponding period also elevated man to a higher, sometimes the highest, status. Some wanted to express this as being a result of God in man, while others neglected or ceased to assume God. But love or compassion for others was regarded as the fundamental principle for human action.

Even in the West, which had always held the notion of difference between God and man, an early modern mystic went so far as to assert the identity of man with God. Angelus Silesius (Scheffler, 1624–77) did not hesitate in expressing man's unity with God. "You are a God with God,"[1] he said. This is a surprising statement considering the strict control of thought by the Church in the medieval West.

In the age of the Western Enlightenment, opinions were widespread that prime doctrinal importance should be given to the belief that God created the world and sent his son to teach and help the world; that God had become man, and men should be kind to each other. Much of the other religious dogma was thought to be superstition which the enlightened mind could not and need not believe. Such an attitude of awarding highest value to human love and kindness has been a keynote of modern thought in the West.[2] Some thinkers of nearly the same period in various Eastern countries were also thinking along similar lines, although they did not have the same belief in the son of God. At least in India various thinkers believed God had assumed many human forms and continued to be present in each man.

According to Caitanya of India, the primary character of God is love (*prīti*) and the chief power that of joy. God assumes infinite forms, the most prominent of which is that of Kṛṣṇa whose supreme delight is in love, for Kṛṣṇa in the figure of a cowherd displays enjoyment of love with the cowherdess Rādhā. "Caitanya accepted the usual stages of *bhakti*

1. J. L. Sammons, *Angelus Silesius* (New York: Twayne Publishers, 1967), p. 24.
2. For example: "One will live. To live is the rarest thing in the world Most people exist, that is all." (Wilde, *Soul of Man under Socialism*, p. 20)

[faith]: (1) *śānta*, or tranquil meditation on God, (2) *dāsya*, or active service of God, (3) *sakhya*, or friendship, (4) *vātsalya*, or parental tenderness and (5) *mādhurya*, or sweetness symptomatic of conjugal love. Each stage includes the preceding, so that the last is the most complete."[3] For Caitanya, "salvation consists in the eternal experience of love (*prīti*). *Bhakti* [devotion] is the true *mukti* [deliverance]."[4] He believed that "divine Love is the summun bonum of human life."[5]

In India, according to Tulsī Dās (1532–1623), the incarnation is the proof of Rāma's love for all creation (and the standard toward which the believer must forever aspire). Tulsī Dās praised Rāma in such statements as the following, which suggests that the lord Rāma manifests in any man who shows a perfected morality of love toward his fellow human beings: "Thou dwellest in the hearts of those . . . who are dear to all, benevolent to all, equable in joy and sorrow, praise and blame, . . . who consider other men's women as mothers and others' wealth as more poisonous than poison, those who rejoice to see others flourish and are acutely pained to see them afflicted."[6] Hence the moral conduct that Tulsī Dās recommended was to show love to all creatures; this will bring happiness, for when one loves all things, he in that way loves lord Rāma, the all in all. Not abstraction of thought, nor yoga-concentration, not fasting, prayer, almsgiving nor self-mortification moved this thinker's compassion so much as simple love. He believed that love, not sacrifice and ritual, was the only thing that Rāma loved.[7]

The spirit of love was also highly stressed by Rāmakṛṣṇa. From infancy Rāmakṛṣṇa had faith in the Goddess Kālī. This faith was founded philosophically by non-dualism (*advaita*) which came to the fore by the effect of Śaṅkara on Rāmakṛṣṇa's thought. No conceptual description can be applied to the absolute itself, Rāmakṛṣṇa believed, and those who have seen God should be silent. Where than should one seek for God? For Rāmakṛṣṇa, God appeared in man. "You are seeking God?" he asked, "Very well, look for him in man; the Divinity manifests itself in man more than in any other object. . . . God incarnate in man is the most manifest power of God in the flesh."[8] The more we love people,

3. Radhakrishnan, *Indian Philosophy*, II, pp. 763–764, n. 4.
4. *Ibid*., p. 764.
5. *Prema pumartho mahān. Caitanyastaka*, concluding prayer, cited in Tirtha, *Sri Chaitanya Mahaprabhu*, p. 356.
6. Wm. Th. De Bary, S. N. Hay, R. Weiler, and A. Yarrow, comps., *Sources of Indian Tradition* (New York: Columbia University Press, 1959), p. 363.
7. Carpenter, *Theism in Medieval India*, p. 518; Rolland, *Prophets of the New India*, p. 157, cf. p. 140.
8. The daughter of one of his disciples told him sorrowfully that when she prayed she could not concentrate. Ramakrishna asked her: "What do you love best in the world?" She replied that it was her brother's little child. "Very well," answered the affection-

according to Rāmakṛṣṇa, the nearer to God we are; for God is incarnate in man. In order to love God, then, Rāmakṛṣṇa advocated the true spirit of charity. There is considerable difference between charity and self-love, though. For Rāmakṛṣṇa charity is the love emanating from man, not limited in its application to self, family, sect, and country. Therefore a charity which raises and leads men to God is to be cultivated.[9]

Love replaces every spiritual discipline, according to these Indian thinkers. The spirit of stressing love or compassion perceived in their thought became the basis for all kinds of moral action. Love was conceived as the nature of God, and since God was thought to be inherent in man, the evaluation of man was raised. In China and Japan of the same period there was a slightly different emphasis. In their particular manifestations of humanism there was a tendency for love to be esteemed through extolling human physical nature.[10] This feature was not absent in India either. For example, the way of Vallabha has been called *Puṣṭimārga*, the way of eating, drinking, and enjoying oneself. But it seems that this opinion was expressed with full consciousness only in other Far Eastern countries.

In China the sense of humanism was very conspicuous with Yen-yüan (1635–1704), who claimed "Man is of all things the most pure, which is why he is said to be born holding a central position between Heaven and Earth."[11] The physical body should not be despised, taught Yen-yüan, but highly valued. Chu Hsi's theory had been that man's physical nature is the originator of evil; but such a theory was refuted in Yen's *Treatise on the Preservation of the Nature.* "His [man's] physical endowment is simply the functioning instrument of his (heavenly) conferred nature, and as such cannot be said to be evil. That in him which is called evil results from the evil influence of enticement, delusion, habit, and contagion. . . . Full attainment to the goodness of the divine sages results only from the complete development of our existing physical bodies."[12]

Also in opposition to the Sung Neo-Confucianists, Tai Chen (1723–77) asserted that "human nature . . . consists simply of man's blood, breath, and mental faculty; in other words, it is what the Sung Neo-Confucianists would call the physical nature."[13] Tai Chen felt that the highest nature of man is identical with his physical nature.

---

ate Master, "fix your thoughts upon him." She did so and through the little boy she grew in devotion to the child Kṛṣṇa. (Rolland, *Prophets of the New India*, p. 147)

9. *Ibid.*, p. 157.
10. Monier-Williams, *Brahmanism and Hinduism*, p. 134; C. Eliot, *Hinduism and Buddhism* (New York: Barnes and Noble, 1921), II, p. 248.
11. Fung Yu-lan, *History of Chinese Philosophy*, II, p. 639.
12. *Tsun-hsüeh Pien* (Treatise on the Preservation of Learning), 1.11–13, cited from *Ibid.*, p. 633.
13. *Ibid.*, p. 663.

In modern Japan, Confucianists tried to accept man's natural dispositions as they are; this is somewhat against the traditions of Chinese Confucianism and Buddhism, which thought that man needs to improve himself. Ogiu Sorai (1666–1728), though a religious leader of his time, acknowledged the intrinsic value of Japanese novels, in spite of what was generally considered to be immoral contents.[14] Dazai Shundai (1680–1747) called man's natural feelings the real feelings, which he defined as "likes and dislikes, sufferings and rejoicing, anxiety and pleasure, etc." He maintained that there is not a single human being lacking in these feelings. Love of one's parents, wife, and children is the same among the noble and the low. And since these feelings originate from man's "innate true nature," ever unstained by falsity, they are to be called the real feelings.[15] His standpoint was pure naturalism, as may be seen from the following: "There are no double-dealings in the deeds overflowed from the natural dispositions, wherein the inside and outside are so transparent that they are one and the same thing. The natural dispositions are the innate true nature of man."[16] Dazai Shundai once remarked that he would rather be an acrobat than a moralist.[17]

Certain modern scholars of Japanese classics[18] also showed a similar humanistic evaluation of man. Motoori Norinaga (1730–1801), criticizing Confucianism and Buddhism, said that the purest mind is just the natural mind of man. He satirically noted that Confucian scholars, most highly esteemed as men of wisdom, and Buddhist priests, often revered as saints, do not hesitate to admire the beauty of stars and flowers, but ". . . they pretend never to have seen a beautiful woman. What a deception of mind!"[19] In the same vein, he asked, "They hate the natural inclinations of man, but are not these same inclinations of the divine laws?"[20] In such words of Motoori these sounds unmistakably the same feeling of joy and love of nature and man that was proclaimed in the European Renaissance.

Hirata Atsutane (1766–1843), the founder of what is called "Jingoistic Shintoism," is another example of a Japanese classicist with humanist inclinations. He said that what is called the Way is just compliance with natural dispositions. He also believed that at the time of man's birth man already possesses traits of benevolence, justice, propriety, and intelligence. The true way of humanity is just not to falsify and distort his inborn traits.

14. Junsei Iwahashi, *Sorai Kenkyū*, p. 433.
15. In Dazai's *Keizai-roku*, vol. I, fol. 10.
16. In *Seigaku Mondō*, 3, quoted in Inoue Tetsujirō, *Nihon Kogakuha no Tetsugaku* (Philosophy in Japanese Classical Study Group) (Tokyo: Fuzanbō, 1931), p. 693.
17. *Ibid.*
18. Alicia Orloff Matsunaga, "The Land of Natural Affirmation. Pre-Buddhist Japan," *Monumenta Nipponica*, vol. 21, nos. 1–2 (1966), pp. 203–209.
19. *Tamakatsuma.*
20. *Kojiki-den* I.

He claimed, ". . . One should indeed stop acting like a sage and completely abandon the so-called Mind or the way of enlightenment, and all that are affected and Buddhaish."[21]

Among modern Buddhist thinkers, Onkō (Jiun Sonja 1718–1904) preached that morality meant to follow man's natural dispositions. It is interesting to note that Ishida Baigan came to state that saints and ordinary men are not essentially different with respect to human nature, but rather "All men are gifted with a never changing mind, but being blinded by the Seven Emotions they believe a Saint's wisdom is different from any other, and due to their blindness they are filled with doubts."[22] Miki (1798–1887) of Yamato, the founder of the Tenri-kyō, taught that within the human being is the abode of divine charity.

Corresponding to the new trend, some Japanese Buddhist masters rejected the former attitude of asceticism. Master Hakuin, the renovator of Japanese Zen, said, " 'To cast away oneself' does not mean 'to ill-treat oneself' or 'to disregard diet and health.' "[23] Moreover, a new trend occurred in Japanese Buddhism that was consistent with the humanism of the times. Master Jiun, as an example, claimed that the Ten Virtues of Buddhism are in man by nature[24] "endowed." In addition, he elaborated on the distinction between man and animals. In the medieval ages Japanese Buddhists were apt to emphasize the virtue of compassion, which would be extended to animals, and did not much stress the superiority of man over animals. But here a reformist Buddhist leader emphasized the dignity and significance of man.

As a corollary from the thought that man is of supreme value, cruel punishments and customs, such as burning at the stake, dueling, etc., declined both in East and West, although the date of disappearance differed with countries. The Indian custom of *suttee*, widow-burning, was outlawed by British authorities early in the nineteenth century. Ram Mohan Roy was one of those who vigorously opposed this custom. With the dying of religious fanaticism, Buddhist monks no longer burned themselves on altars as sacrifices to Buddha, as in the medieval ages of China and Japan. The attitude of some Zen masters became more lenient towards the sins of disciples.[25]

21. *Kodō Taii*, vol. 2 (*Hirata Atsutane Zenshū*, edited by Mannen Ueda [Tokyo: Naigai shoseki, 1932], vol. 7, p. 69).
22. Ishida Baigan, *Seiri Mondō*, pp. 42–43.
23. "A Letter to a Certain Sick Layman."
24. *Jūzen Hōgo*, p. 34.
25. To illustrate: In a monastery headed by Master Bankei there was a monk who committed theft. Bankei knew it, but he protected the monk so that he would not be punished. (*Bankei Zenji Goroku*, edited by D. T. Suzuki, Iwanami-bunko-bon [Tokyo: Iwanami Shoten, 1941], p. 234)

Humanistic attitudes as mentioned above were given further accentuation and became an advantageous weapon to refute Christianity when it was introduced in Japan. Contrasting the Christian idea of the supreme God with Confucianism, which was his own standpoint in this context, Baien said, "The Way of the Sages does not indeed revere and venerate Heaven, but it is a doctrine of human ethics."[26] In contrast no Christianity, an anti-transcendent and society-centered ethics was vigorously stressed by Baien.

The humanistic attitude in the modern ages was different from the attitude of medieval compassion. In Japan a limitation to the detriment of idealism tended to influence modern humanism in a rather realistic way.[27] After the rise in popularity of Western science, humanistic ethics there also tended to place a good deal of stress on natural means of overcoming evil.[28]

2. Service to People

The movement in the modern period away from religious bigotry and rites toward the significance of love and activity in social life manifested itself in many areas as a heightened trend of service to people. Such humanitarianism seems to be a natural corollary to humanism (last section). Among some thinkers, as pointed out in the section before last, devotion to God appeared in the form of love to humankind. The spirit of service to mankind, even including future generations, was enhanced as a result of many developments in the modern age.[1] Hence parallel to an

26. G. Piovesana, "Miura Baien, 1723–1789 and his Dialectic and Political Ideas," *Monumenta Nipponica*, vol. 20, nos. 3–4 (1965), pp. 417–418.
27. This tendency is especially discussed by Tsunetsugu Muraoka, *Studies in Shinto Thought*, translated by Delmer M. Brown and James T. Araki (Tokyo: Japanese National Commission for UNESCO, 1964), pp. 95–170.
28. An example of a way this was recently stated follows: "If sympathy may make man better able to endure evil, but the evil remains. Sympathy with consumption does not cure consumption; that is what Science does. And when Socialism has solved the problem of poverty, and Science solved the problem of disease, the area of the sentimentalists will be lessened, and the sympathy of man will be large, healthy and spontaneous." (Wilde, *Soul of Man under Socialism*, p. 83)
1. "Early Buddhism had no idea, just as early Christianity had not, of the principle underlying the foundation of the higher morality of the future, the duty which we owe, not only to our fellow-men of to-day, but also to those of the morrow—to the race as a whole, but in the future even more than now. Buddhists and Christians may both maintain, and rightly maintain, that the duty of universal love laid down in their Scriptures can be held to involve and include this modern conception; but neither the early Buddhists nor the early Christians looked at the matter quite in this way. The sense of duty to the race has sprung out of a fact, only lately become a

increase of humanitarian activities in the modern West,[2] similar moves are found in Eastern countries as well.

According to the Indian Caitanya, service to fellow-believers (Vaiṣṇavas) is indispensible among the Kṛṣṇaites. He warned that freedom from bondage is not possible without service to, and the grace of, the Vaiṣṇavas. Caitanya strongly believed that Kṛṣṇa accepts as his own only those who wholeheartedly serve his devotees.[3] He cited a verse, "He who worships Govinda, ignoring the service of His devotees, is an arrogant and not His servant."[4] The Vaiṣṇavas themselves are as worthy of adoration as the Godhead himself, claimed Caitanya[5]; and the superiority of his teaching to others he deemed to consist in complete self-surrender and loving service, the keynotes of all spiritual knowledge. "Punctilious observance of socio-religious laws, ritualistic worship of the Holy Image Śrī Viṣṇu, pilgrimage to all sacred shrines and a thorough study of the Vedas which have no access to the Supreme Personality of Śrī Caitanya Mahāprabhu, can never help us in comprehending His Deeds and Teachings, *if not accompanied by loving service* to Him and His ardent and loyal devotees."[6] Caitanya had comprehensive respect for all existence, holding that every entity in his or its proper position is an object of service and reverence in relation to Godhead.[7]

The sect of Caitanya stressed love in an active social life. Service was rendered to the old and sick, their burdens carried for them, their clothes washed for them. Food offered to Viṣṇu was distributed to the lame, blind, deaf, and mute. Remarriage was granted to widows. So ardent was the pity for suffering humanity, that one of the sect's adherents threw himself at Caitanya's feet with the prayer, "My heart breaks to see the sorrows of mankind. Lay thou their sins upon my head, let me suffer in hell for all their sins, so that thou mayest remove the earthly pangs of all other beings."[8] All this is reminiscent of the vows of bodhisattvas in Mahāyāna

generally received conception—I mean the progressive continuity of human progress." (Rhys Davids, *Lectures on the Origin and Growth of Religion as Illustrated by Some Points in the History of Indian Buddhism* [London: Williams and Norgate, 1891], pp. 110–111)

2. Needless to say of Protestant activities, humanitarianism was enlivened among Catholics also. The Daughters of Charity owed their foundation to Saint Vincent de Paul. He was active for prisoners and the suffering. Great labor was spent on the sick. The hospitals of that day, which were frightful, were improved by his followers. Social activities were carried on even outside the range of the church. One example can be seen in the founding of the Salvation Army.
3. Tirtha, *Śrī Chaitanya Mahāprabhu*, p. 54.
4. A verse from the *Padma-Purāṇa*, cf. *Ibid.*, p. 54.
5. *Bhāgavata-Purāṇa* XI, 26, 34.
6. *Śrī-Caitanya-candrāmṛta* IV, 22.
7. Tirtha, *Śrī Chaitanya Mahāprabhu*, Appendix II, pp. 74, 75.
8. Carpenter, *Theism in Medieval India*, p. 445.

Buddhism. It is possible that Caitanya's philosophy was influenced by the Buddhists of Orissa who, although scant in number, still existed in his day.[9]

The attitude of rendering service to others without attachment was highly stressed by Rāmakṛṣṇa and his mission in India. According to him, "without attachment" does not imply without conscience, or without zeal for good work, but only disinterestedness. "To work without attachment is to work without the hope of reward or the fear of punishment, either in this world or in any other. . . ."[10]

Inheriting this spirit, the Rāmakṛṣṇa mission stressed service to others. On their monastery the word "service" is inscribed. Placing this word above their mission was not explicitly ordered by the Master, but his whole doctrine of love—working for others to the limit of personal sacrifice—is in essence a doctrine of service.[11] Under the inspiration of this great teacher there has been a powerful revival of social compassion. Educational and medical work is done throughout India. The Brāhmo-Samāj and the Ārya-Samāj, having strong cross-influence with Rāmakṛṣṇa's followers, also should be noted for their social service activities. These organizations especially insisted on the education of both sexes, the percentage of literacy being consequently high in their community compared with the rest of the population.

Another interesting humanitarian tendency, though it might not be called predominant in modern India, is perhaps more conspicuous in modern than in medieval Indian thinkers. That is, that the concept of "non-injury" came to be interpreted not only as abstention from inflicting positive injury, but also as the rendering of active service to others; for if you could help another and do not, surely you hurt him (cf. *damnum sine injuria*).[12]

In Japan of this period, some unique features can be seen along the same line. The humanitarian spirit was displayed even in times of war. For instance, to the mountain-locked province of his enemy, Uesugi Kenshin (1530–78), the feudal lord, sent salt in 1568 A.D., so that the people of his enemy's province would not suffer from the lack of it. The captives of the Korean Campaigns (1592, 1597) received brotherly treatment in Japan and were returned to their home.[13] After the Catholic

9. A few hints of the influence of Mahāyāna Buddhism are to be found. Although his philosophy was based upon Vedānta, the ideal state which was symbolically expressed as the Forest of Vrinda (Vṛndāvana) by the worshipers of Kṛṣṇa was described as the "Great Void" (*Mahā-śūnya*). The poets who carried with them the doctrine of the Void sang of five Viṣṇus, corresponding to the five Dhyani Buddhas.
10. Rolland, *Prophets of the New India*, p. 155.
11. *Ibid.*, p. 134.
12. J. Jaini: *Outline of Jainism* (Cambridge: Cambridge University Press, 1916), p. xxix.
13. Zennosuke Tsuji, *Nihonjin no Hakuai* (The Humanitarian Ideas of the Japanese). (Tokyo: Kinkōdō, 1932), pp. 108 ff.

rebellion in Shimabara (1637), religious ceremonies were held and three large monuments were built, not in memory of the victory, but for the spiritual beatitude of the Catholic converts (pagans in the eyes of the Japanese) who were killed in the rebellion.[14] This humanitarian act may have been due to the Buddhist ideal. But at any rate the attitude assumed by the Japanese on this occasion seems to be quite unlike occurrences of warfare in the medieval or early modern West.

In Japan a spirit of "solidarity" was greatly emphasized, and mutual aid was evident among the people. Individual Buddhist priests engaged in humanitarian activities,[15] e.g., distributing rice and money to the poor, giving medicine to the sick, building bridges, instituting public bathrooms, etc. Tetsugen[16] (1630–82) raised funds to insure the lives of starving people during years of bad harvests. Ryōō (1630–1707) established dispensaries and about seventy libraries in various cities. In order to save people from suffering, St. Mokujiki persuaded feudal lords not to engage in battles.[17] But activities of this kind were not sufficiently organized. They appeared temporarily, and eventually dissipated. The traditional insular family system and the spirit of solidarity among people seem to have lessened the necessity of organized humanitarian activities.

As an outstanding figure in the attitude of rendering service to others, Ninomiya Sontoku deserves mention. The moral teaching of rendering help to others "was combined by Sontoku with economic measures, such as a scheme for the rotation of crops, an organization for the circulation of capital, accumulation of funds for famine relief, and so on. Thus Sontoku viewed human life as a stage of cooperation and mutual helpfulness, and in practice combined moral ideas with economic measures. His influence bore practical effects among the peasants."[18]

Some Japanese priests engaged in efforts to improve the cultivation of land. Ryōin,[19] a Shinshū priest,[20] converted hundreds of acres of waste land into fertile paddy. This event in itself is not particularly significant, but his records of cultivation display interesting traits of modern thought. He said, "It is a silly thing merely to accumulate riches. But the attitude

14. *Ibid.*, pp. 141ff.
15. The details are mentioned in Zennosuke Tsuji, *Jizen Kyūsai Shiryō* (Tokyo: Kinkōdō, 1932).
16. Tetsugen's life is described in English in *The Light of Dharma*, August and October, 1901, San Francisco, pp. 22–25; 25–28. Junkyō Washio, in the *Hansei Zasshi*, vols. 12–13, 1897–1898.
17. Z. Tsuji, *Jizen Kyūsai Shiryō*, *op. cit.*, p. 346.
18. Anesaki, *History of Japanese Religion*, p. 303.
19. Jōin, *Uyō Shūhoku Suido-roku* (Records of exploitation of North-Eastern districts), 7 vols., published in *Nihon Keizai Taiten*, vol. 30, edited by Seiichi Takimoto, 1929. This work was written in the period of Tenmei.
20. *Ibid.*, p. 10.

to believe indiscriminiately in the causes in previous lives according to the teaching of Buddhism or to believe in the mandate of Heaven according to Confucianism, or to 'wait for good fortune lying in bed' according to a popular proverb, is misdemeanor of delinquency."[21] If such were the case, he believed, the affairs of the world would be neglected. If people do not give regard to the price in terms of effort they must pay for comfort, if they are not thrifty, then they will get less clothing in cold weather, less to eat even in sunnier days.

In China there were at least two major manifestations of humanitarianism. One is what was known as the "Silent Way of Recompense" (*Yin-chih wen*).[22] The other was a movement in the modern period against the existing feudal system. Herein will be considered only a most vocal exponent of the latter. A severe criticism of the princely regime from the standpoint of the common people was directed by Huang Tsung-hsi (1617–95). Among the charges he voiced were that the prince was the reason peace and happiness could not be found throughout the land, and for the aggrandizement of the prince's fortune people were harmed, even killed, and their families broken up. He expressed his condemnation quite plainly; "The greatest enemy of mankind is the prince and nothing but the prince."[23]

Huang Tsung-hsi greatly emphasized a need for officials to serve the people. Of his own ideals with regard to civil service, he claimed that such service was ". . . for the whole world and not for the prince; it is for all man and not for one family." He feared that if he came to work for the prince without an awareness of his duty to mankind he would be "merely the prince's menial servant." Believing that peace or disorder in the world depends not on the rise or fall of princes but "upon the happiness or distress of the people," if he would have "the people's interest at heart, then I am the prince's mentor and colleague," he said.[24]

3. Heightened Movement toward Equality of Man and Anti-discrimination

The increased valuation of man in the modern period (earlier in India) naturally contributed to a breakdown in traditional authority, especially in the structure of social hierarchies which gave more value to some men than others (or men over women). Brahmanism and many Hindu sects in ancient and medieval India had denied salvation to slaves (*śūdra*) and

21. *Ibid.*, pp. 9–10.
22. De Bary et al., *Chinese Tradition*, pp. 635 ff.
23. *Ibid.*, p. 588.
24. *Ibid.*, pp. 589–590.

outcastes. They preached that such persons could be saved only after they had earned rebirth into one of the three upper classes, and had then practiced austerities as the canons ordained. Against this notion, several Hindu sects gradually came to assure salvation in this life to these groups if they practiced good deeds with a pious and pure faith in God. At the same time those earlier sects continued to recognize the hierarchical discrimination of the castes. About the same period as the Western Reformation, however, a new religious movement of protest occurred in Hinduism itself. The man who stood in the vanguard was Rāmānanda (fourteenth century).

As Rāmānanda belonged to the sect of Rāmānuja before forming his order, his philosophy seems not to have been essentially different from that of Rāmānuja. His historical significance lies rather in his social outlook. The most striking point about Rāmānanda's teaching was that so long as a man or woman had genuine loving faith in God, his or her caste and position in social life were matters of no importance. He set about trying to abolish the discrimination between the Brahmins and the lower classes. Rāmānanda allowed anyone to enter the order, no matter to what caste he might belong. In his order everyone dined together if they were followers of the god Viṣṇu, regardless of their descent, race, or caste.[1] Thus the distinction of castes was regarded as inadmissible. It is also said that Rāmānanda was the first religious leader in India to consider woman as equal to man.[2] Everyone might become an ascetic and rise, in time, to be a teacher (*guru*). Though his was not a large order, and though it stressed devotion, it developed into one which was effective in liberating suppressed peoples.[3] Hence its historical significance is considerable. After Rāmānanda there appeared many thinkers who espoused similar views.

Bāsava, the founder of the Liṅgāyats in the fifteenth century, proclaimed the social equality of all those who entered his order, so as to relax the bonds of caste. Caitanya, the seventeenth century Bengal preacher of the love of God, opened the way of faith no men of every caste, asserting that all men are brothers. Kabīr upheld his concept of

1. He taught: "Let no one ask a man's caste or with whom he eats. If a man shows love to Hari, he is Hari's own." (George A. Grierson, in *Encyclopedia of Religion and Ethics* edited by James Hastings [Edinburgh: T. and T. Clark, 1925], X, p. 570 a–b)
2. *Ibid.*, p. 571a. In Buddhism and Svetambara Jainism the same feature is found.
3. Vemana, the Telegu poet, also denounced the caste system.

    If we look through all the earth,
    Men, we see, have equal birth,
    Made in one great brotherhood,
    Equal in the sight of God.

   Gover, *The Folk-songs of Southern India* (London: Truebner, 1872), p. 272. V. A. Smith, *The Early History of India*, 4th edition (Oxford: Charendon Press, 1924), p. 41.

monism by asserting that all individuals sprang into existence from the same cause, from one blood and one life, and consequently the distinction of castes and clans was a mere fiction.[4] He refused to acknowledge caste distinctions, holding that the difference of races should also be discarded. "That Hindu and Turk are of different family," he said, "is false."[5] Nānak also denounced caste discrimination.[6] In the whole brotherhood of the Sikhs who got together around the *Guru*, there were no longer to be any caste distinctions. Eknāth (died 1608), who was a Brahmin, is said to have spoken and acted in opposition to caste, and to have suffered for his zeal.[7]

Although theistic movements of these thinkers protested against caste inequalities, the latter have not yet completely disappeared. Indians claim that the British used caste distinctions in order to gain and hold control of India.[8] In practice, however, it has turned out that this levelling of caste distinctions met with only partial and temporary success before the British rule.

In modern China, acknowledgement of the equality of man, at least in its incipient stage, occurred fairly early, though it was pejoratively called "egalitarianism." It is difficult to be quite sure who, if anyone, advocated equality of men before Sun Yat-sen expounded the Three Principles of People.[9] But Wang Fu-chih's (1619–92) assertion is noteworthy, and involves something of a democratic ideal. "Everyone makes mistakes at times, so that one should not try to force the world to follow his own arbitrary views."[10] Huang Tsung-hsi (1610–95) severely criticized the existing examination system of selecting government officials for civil service, in an attempt to get an adequate promotion system.[11]

4. *Songs of Kabīr*, III, 74, p. 128; III, 76, p. 128.
5. Carpenter, *Theism in Medieval India*, p. 459.
6. "Their opposition to caste, mild in the time of the earlier *Gurus*, but thorought in the case of Guru Govind, and the stern prohibition of female infanticide, show it to have been also a genuine movement of social and moral reform." (Macnicol, *Indian Theism*, p. 153)
7. J. Farquhar, *An Outline of the Religious Literature of India* (London: Oxford University Press, 1920), p. 300.
8. Cf. the statement of James Kerr, the principle of the Hindu College at Calcutta, who said as far back as 1865, "It may be doubted if the existence of caste is on the whole unfavourable to the permanence of our rule. It may even be considered favourable to it, provided we act with prudence and forbearance. Its spirit is opposed to national union." (Govind Sadasniv Ghurye, *Caste and Race in India* [London: K. Paul, Trench, Truebner & Company, 1932], p. 164)
9. The three principles of San Min Chu I, as advocated by Sun Yat-sen are stated as follows:
    (a) the Principle of the People's Race (or Nationalism)
    (b) the Principle of the People's Sovereignty (or Democracy)
    (c) the Principle of the People's Livelihood (or Socialism)
10. De Bary et al., *Chinese Tradition*, p. 605.
11. *Ibid.*, pp. 593–594.

In addition he advocated the necessity of "property limitations" and "equalization of land."[12]

Yen-yüan (1635–1704) who, as seen in the previous section, disputed the metaphysics of Chu Hsi, thereby advocating activistic philosophy, also felt an obligation to press for a modern "well-field system" (*ching-t'ien*). He offered detailed plans, with all manner of measurements, for a literal restoration of the old system. Propriety would be violated, he felt, if human feelings were sacrificed to the spirit of wealth, whereby the product of the labor of masses of men leaves one man unsatisfied. "To have one man with some thousands of acres and some thousands of men with not one *ch'ing* (about fifteen acres) is like a parent's having one son be rich and the others poor."[13] At the end of the Ch'ing dynasty Chinese thinkers identified this system with Western egalitarianism, metaphorically representing it as "the distillation of socialism."[14]

In Japan already in the medieval age, equality of man in the religious sense was advocated by religious leaders. Shinran would not admit that women are less capable than men of attaining to the state of bliss. And Nichiren (1222–82) found one justification for his belief in the Lotus Sutra in its teaching of the equality of women and men. The Oral (Esoteric) Teachings of the Japanese Tendai sect advocated equality of all mankind,[15] but their recognition of man's equality remained in the narrow bounds of the religious interpretation and did not develop into a social movement.

In Japan at a period corresponding to the Western modern period the city for equality was not so strong as in the West or in India. Even brilliant Buddhist leaders, such as Master Jiun, who was so progressive in other respects, acquiesced in the face of the existing hierarchical social system of the day. Master Jiun explained away the Buddhist teaching of equality in a different way. "Buddhism teaches distinctions of grade and position. The equality it teaches is not such foolishness as that of breaking down high mountains, filling in deep valleys and making all into a dead level. Buddhism teaches us the way between lord and subjects, father and son, teacher and disciple."[16] But this does not necessarily mean that he was backward, for in the modern West also regulations concerning these

12. *Ibid.*, pp. 594–597.
13. Cf. Joseph R. Levenson, "Ill Wind in the Well-Field," in *The Confucian Persuasion*, edited by Arthur F. Wright, p. 272.
14. *Ibid.*, p. 274.
15. Dōken Ogata, in the journal *Nippon Bukkyō*, Tokyo, no. 2 (October, 1958), p. 41f.
16. " 'Jūzen Hōgo' (The Ten Buddhistic Virtues), A Paper on Buddhism's Second Great Virtue: Not Stealing," *Transactions of the Asiatic Society in Japan*, vol. XXXV (1907), pt. 1, p. 53.

distinctions were enforced which look quite backwards in the eyes of contemporaries.[17]

However, in Japan before the introduction of Western civilization there were some Buddhist thinkers who advocated theories implying the equality of men. The author of the "Sermons by a Monkey" denounced the concept of private property in the religious sense. "You should not make a discrimination between self and others. Riches such as gold, silver, forturne and treasures belong to the whole world. Even if they are in the hands of others, they do not belong to them. Even if I keep them, they are not mine. If they are confined in the hands of others without being utilized, they are of no use; if I do not utilize them, solely keeping grip of them, it is only like piling up stones."[18] Munan, a Zen priest, discouraged the custom of leaving property to one's descendants. "You should not leave treasures with your descendants. It is certain that they are lost. To practice the teaching of Buddha is most important."[19] Accordingly, such men asserted that riches should be used by the public. But their existence in society was marginal, and few people cared for their suggestions. In Japan the rigidity of the class system (*shi-nō-kō-shō* or samurai-farmer-manufacturer-trader) began to show signs of collapse only at the end of the eighteenth century; but even this was before its official mullification at the time of the Meiji Restoration.[20] The attitude of valuing man eventually lead to the discarding of all discrimination established upon traditional authority. But it was only with the advent of Western forces that the feudal system of Japan collapsed.

In Eastern countries there were only the few attempts to bring the ideal of equality into practice that have been mentioned above. In the West, of course there were many instances, of which there is space and need here to note but a few for the sake of comparison.

Because the Bible taught that all men are equal in the eyes of God, the Quakers refused to bow to the mighty. George Fox (1624–91), founder of the Quakers, would not take off his hat before kings and judges. Such behavior was never attempted in Eastern countries. If someone had

17. In historical records, biographies, and novels we find a lot of instances. For example, the mother of Samuel Johnson said to him: "You are a great boy now, and would rejoice, I am sure, to do something for your poor father, who has done so much for you." (Nathaniel Hawthorne, *Biographical Stories*) In the days of Benjamin Franklin boys were expected to be silent in the presence of their elders. (Nathaniel Hawthorne, *Biographical Stories*) "So Carter Druse, bowing reverently to his father, who returned the salute with a stately courtesy that masked a breaking heart, left the home of his childhood to go soldiering." (Ambrose Bierce, *A Horseman in the Sky*)
18. *Saru-hōgo*, in *Zenmon Hōgoshū*, edited by Yamada and Mori, vol. 2, p. 253.
19. *Munan Kana-hōgo*, in *Ibid.*, vol. I, p. 378.
20. Cf. N. Skene Smith, "Tokugawa Japan as a Field for the Student of Social Organization," *Monumenta Nipponica*, vol. I (1938), pp. 165–172, especially p. 170.

tried this in Japan before the introduction of Western civilization or in China under the rule of the Chin dynasty, he would have been killed.

In America during the modern period slavery came to be abolished. Some Anglican Friends had opposed the practice and the Quakers were among the first to view slave-holding as wrong. John Wesley also spoke most sharply against the slave trade. Churches of many faiths stirred up the conscience of the country against the inhumanity of slavery. The Civil War was fought largely over slavery. But in Eastern countries this problem was not so prevalent, because there was no custom of importing slaves from undeveloped countries.

The gradual abolishment of sex discrimination is also a feature of modern thought. Among the Quakers, women as well as men spoke at meetings. This practice at first seemed deplorable to other faiths because Paul had said that women should not speak in church. In India the seclusion of women had come about as a result of the Mohammedan invasion around the eleventh century. This custom began to be abolished with the reformist movement of the Ārya-Samāj and the Brāhmo-Samāj which occurred after the coming of the British. In Japan under the Tokugawa government women were not given equal status with men, and indeed still do not enjoy equal privileges. But around the time of the collapse of the Tokugawa feudal regime some new religions, such as Isson-kyō, Tenri-kyō, etc., were founded by prophetesses. A conspicuous religious phenomenon after World War II is the rise of new religions, totaling approximately 120. About 48 of these new denominations were founded by women.

4. Increased Lay Tendency of Religion

This-worldliness and movements toward recognizing the equality of men tended to free religion from the exclusive possession of the priesthood in the modern period. In the religious orders of ancient India, monks who retired from family life had formed the leading circle, except in the case of Brahmanism and some Mahāyānists. In Hindu sects also those who formed the core of the orders were monks who had left worldly life, and lay followers in general felt great devotion to them as teachers (*guru*). The role of these monks was quite similar to the conduct and status of monks in early and medieval Catholicism. However, some representatives of modern Hinduism opposed such homeless life; the first of these seems to have been Kabīr. The Western reader may be familiar with the entire trend of his culture in this direction since the modern period.

In its intention to abolish the Indian caste system, Rāmānanda's religion might be called modern, but he still formed as order of peculiar celibate ascetics who had prestige over laymen. On this point his position seemed to be anti-secular and preserved medieval features. This holds true with Caitanya also. It was Kabīr (1440–1518) who boldly advocated an earthly, secular attitude for the first time in modern India, asserting the significance of ordinary life:

> Dance, my heart! dance today with joy.
> The strains of love fill the days and the nights with music,
> and the world is listening to its melodies.
> Mad with joy, life and death dance to the rhythm of this music. . . .
> Why put on the robe of the monk, and live aloof from the world in lonely price?[1]

True religion should be embodied within the family, Kabīr believed, for in the home is the true union and the enjoyment of life. Kabīr was the first to ask why one should forsake his home and wander in the forest.[2] Of the homeless monk he wrote, "You do not see that the Real is in your home, and you wander from forest to forest listlessly!"[3]

Tukārām (1598–1649), who spent his life as a small shopkeeper, denied the significance of the priestly vocation. And Vallabha (1479–1531) had tended in this direction. He taught that privation formed no part of sanctity, and that it was the obligation of the teacher and his disciples to attend their duties, not in nudity and hunger but with costly apparel and choice food, not in solitude and mortification but with the pleasures of society and the enjoyment of the world. After he had shaken off the restrictions of the monastic order to which he originally belonged, he married, it is said, by the particular order of his new god.[4] Since then his descendants have been the chief abbots of the sect. The teachers (*Gosains*) of this sect were almost always family men. They were invariably clothed with the best apparel and fed the daintiest viands by their followers. In that Vallabha and his followers practiced family life, his religious teachings can be compared to those of Luther and Shinran.

A similar tendency appeared also in Jainism. In the Lonka sect many branches appeared, among which the Sthānakavāsīs, founded in 1653, are most noteworthy. This sect did not perform religious services in temples, but rather in the houses of the community. Lonka followers worship no idol, possess no temple, and give no significance to pilgrimage.[5]

For research in Japan on the tendency to implant religion in the

1. *Songs of Kabīr* II, 103, p. 80.
2. *Ibid.*, I, 65, p. 87.
3. *Ibid.*, I, 82, p. 91.
4. Wilson, *Religious Sects of the Hindus*, p. 63.
5. H. von Glasenapp, *Der Jainismus* (Berlin: Alf Haeger Verlag, 1925), p. 71.

mind and life of the laity, one must first of all consider Shinran. For although Shinran belongs to the medieval age (and was discussed at length in the above chapter on that period), his life and activities have many things in common with Luther, especially in the realm of facilitating the movement toward lay religion.[6] In this respect, the modern period occurred earlier in Japan.

Luther set himself to meet the demands of God and Christ. He fasted until his cheeks caved in; he confessed his sins for six hours at a stretch. But he soon came to believe that man can never gain a claim on God, because man's goodness, however much he may improve himself, is not good enough to satisfy the All-holy, certainly never good enough to atone for wrongs already done. Shinran also learned the traditional Tendai theology, in his case at the Hieizan monastery which was the scholarly center of Japanese Buddhism. He practiced meditation earnestly, but he also came to believe that he could not get rid of carnal desires and mental afflictions in that manner.

Luther turned to the Virgin Mary and all the saints for help, that they might use their extra goodness to make up for his lack. But he soon came to feel that no human (or ex-human) being had enough goodness to help because no one could ever stand before God unless he be called by God first.

As Shinran found no spiritual rest, he prayed to Kannon, the Buddhist counterpart of Mary. Shinran also felt his efforts along this line were unsuccessful. Having practiced asceticism, unsparing of pain and thought, only to come to the conclusion that he had advanced not a single step nearer the goal, he reportedly said to himself, "It grows dark, but the goal is still far off! Now there is but one way left to save my soul. I must seek for divine guidance."[7] So he prayed to the Kannon of the Rokkakudō Temple daily. Finally Kannon appeared to him, it is said, and bade him study under Hōnen, the founder of Pure Land Buddhism,

6. "The Jesuit missionaries who came to Japan in the middle of the 16th century at once became aware of the relationship between Jōdo-Shinshū-Buddhism and the 'Lutheran heresy.' Father Francesco Cabral reported on it in a letter dated 1571." (Schweitzer, *Indian Thought*, p. 153) "Like Luther, Shinran rejected pilgrimages, exercises in penance, fasting, superstition and all magical practices. He abolished the celibacy of the priesthood, of the monks and of the nuns. True piety was to be preserved in the family and in the worldly calling. He recommended to the laity the diligent study of the holy scriptures. And he demanded that the people should be delivered from their ignorance by good schools." (*Ibid.*, p. 152) "Man is not in a position in any way to earn bliss by his own merits. In spite of this, Shinran required ethical conduct, and, be it noted, required it like Luther, as the expression and fruit of faith in redemption." (*Ibid.*)

7. Gendō Nakai, *Shinran and His Religion of Pure Faith* (Kyoto: Shinshū Research Institute, 1937), p. 28.

who taught him that one can be saved solely by the grace and compassion of Amida Buddha.

Luther said marriage should be retained in the religious life, and monasteries should be given up. Monks, nuns, and clergymen should be free to marry if they so wished. The clergy, monks and nuns, following him, began to accept marriage. Zwingli also married, like Luther, and marriage has become common among the Protestant clergy. About Shinran's marriage[8] there are many legends, but at least it is generally accepted that he spent a married life like the early Protestant leaders and was the father of seven children. Since then, his followers have married if they so wished. Shinran successfully combined religion with a layman's life.

It is noteworthy that in Japanese Buddhism there was a religious phenomenon corresponding to the Protestant Reformation in Christianity. Hōnen and others, especially Shinran, cut themselves off from the abuses of the established sects just as Luther and Calvin had in Europe. In both cases the central principle was salvation by faith, not by works or ceremonies.

Pure Land Buddhism as practiced in Japan professed an extreme devotion to salvation by faith in Amida, the Goddess of Boundless Light. This faith is paralleled in the doctrine of absolute reliance on God as stated in the Augusburg Confession. Pure Land Buddhists believed that faith in Amida arouses a new motive and a feeling of gratitude which transforms life. Both reformations were accompanied by social, political, and economic phenomena; as has been seen, the same sort of lay movement was created. The political implications, however, were much more marked in the West than in Japan in proportion as the emphasis on faith as opposed to works was more extreme in Pure Land Buddhism than in Christianity.

There appeared some attempts to oppose the movements of both reformations. Ignatius Loyola founded in 1534 the Society of Jesus, a Roman Catholic religious order. In Japan, Jōkei (Gedatsu Shōnin, 1155–1213) and Kōben (Myōe Shōnin, 1173–1232) were leaders of an attempt to revitalize Buddhism by restoring Buddhist practice, which they thought essential for enlightenment. They criticized Pure Land Buddhism, but their attempts were not successful, perhaps because their objectives were rather contrary to the wish of common people.

Shinran and Vallabha,[9] the Indian exponent of lay-dominated religion, were worshipped as divine in later days, and the offspring of both (the chief abbots of each sect) came to be revered enthusiastically as their

8. *Ibid.*, pp. 28 ff.
9. Vallabha was believed to have been an embodiment of a portion of Kṛṣṇa's essence. (Monier-Williams, *Brahmanism and Hinduism*, p. 134)

religious successors. In the West, however, worship of a lineage of descendants from Luther or Calvin did not occur. This seems to be due to an increased tendency of Eastern cultures to carry over social structures from previous ages. In the West the social trait of worshipping members in an ancestral lineage from a religious leader almost disappeared in the modern period, whereas in India or Japan of the corresponding period this attitude still remained.

Returning to the subject of the secular movement in Japan, Suzuki Shōsan (Tokugawa period), discouraged people from taking orders and becoming monks, forsaking their vocations in the world. He claimed to be the first Buddhist teacher who advocated lay Buddhism. Tenkei also disregarded the distinction between clergy and laity.[10] The author of "Sermons by a Monkey" stood on the same standpoint: "When one engages in commerce with the spirit of compassion and equality, it is enlightenment, the goal of the way. When one is thus right and intelligent today, there is no need of being apprehensive tomorrow. So, if one lives right in this life, one should not worry about the future life."[11] However, the abolition of the distinction between clergy and laity was not actually realized in Japan, probably due to social pressure by the government.[12]

In China also Buddhism for laymen became prevalent under the leadership of P'eng Chi-Ch'ing (1740–96), who had a philosophical base in the doctrine of the Hua-yen sect, but whose main concern was to encourage belief in Amitābha among laymen. Yang Jen-sahn (1837–1912) encouraged a layman-Buddhism movement along the same line.

Although one cannot conclude that the layistic tendency is common to all modern religions, one may safely say that it appeared rather early in the modern age throughout many countries in both East and West, developed later, and is now conspicuous in many modern religions.

In connection with this humanist tendency, it would not be out of place to refer to the phenomenon of the erotization of religion. This was one of the wayward outcomes of an attitude of admitting human nature as

10. G. Kagamishima, *Dōgen Zenji to sono Monryū* (Tokyo: Seishin Shobō, 1961), p. 117.
11. *Zenmon Hōgoshū,* edited by Yamada and Mori, vol. 2, p. 253.
12. In England "men who were not ordained ministers of the Church of England, as were Wesley and Whitefield, began preaching. . . . At first Wesley was inclined to stop them, but when he saw the power with which they preached he let them go on. The Methodists thus came to have 'lay preachers.' By and by more ordained ministers were needed, and no bishop of the Church of England would ordain them. Thereupon Wesley himself set aside one who should ordain others. In this way the Methodist Church came to have bishops of its own." (R. H. Baiton, *The Church of Our Fathers* [New York: Charles Scribner's Sons, 1950], p. 194)

And yet, for all his faith could see,
I would not the good bishop be.
(Emerson, *The Problem*)

a whole to religion. In India erotization occurred in Tantrism and Tantric Buddhism, and this tendency lasted till quite late. In Japan it appeared briefly in the Tachikawa branch of Vajrayāna in the medieval age and was subsequently banned. In the West there were sporadic outcroppings of religious eroticism in England (and elsewhere) in the eighteenth century, but these were casual and unsystematized.[13]

5. Accelerated Approach to the Masses

THE humanistic attitude that characterized the modern age led many religious leaders to a more affectionate view of common people. They wanted to keep in close touch with the masses, a disposition which can especially be perceived in the religious movement of Caitanya. Just like the philosophers before him, he admitted the absolute authority of the Vedic scriptures and was, indeed, highly influenced by Rāmānuja and Madhva in his metaphysical system. What distinguishes him from former philosophers is his popular character. One of the most significant manifestations of an "approach to the masses" is in communication: that medium which is used by most of the people must be employed. Caitanya held that languages which are used only by self-complacent, highbrow literati should not have claim to special privileges. The scriptures of the Caitanya sect therefore were mostly written in Bengali, although some are in Sanskrit.

The movement toward common language which can be traced to Rāmānanda relied on the use of vernaculars for the propagation of his new creed. Ancient Indian philosophers propounded their teachings mainly for the Brahmins; their commentaries upon the scriptures and their efforts to elucidate their own teachings were composed only in Sanskrit. In many manuscripts of Hindu scriptures the following Sanskrit verse is found: If eighteen Purāṇas and the Rāmāyaṇa are heard in non-Sanskritic languages, it will result in the listener's going to *raurava* hell.[1] In spite of such prohibition, Rāmānanda and his disciples started writing and preaching in vernaculars; and their endeavors in this vein naturally met with popular support. The followers of Rāmānanda wrote works and appealed to every class in dialects of their own. This was a natural consequence of Rāmānanda's view of man based upon the principle of equality and love. After independence the union of India adopted Hindī as its common language,

13. H. von Glasenapp, *Buddhismus and Gottesidee*. Akademie der Wissenschaften und der Literatur. Abhandlungen der Geistes—und sozialwissenschaftlichen Klasse, Jahrgana 1954, Nr. 8. Verlag der Akademie der Wissenschaften und der Literatur in Mainz in Kommission bei Franz Steiner Verlag GMBH (Wiesbaden, 1954), p. 97, n. 2.

1. Majumdar, *Bhakti Renaissance*, p. 40.

and it is said that Hindī as a literary language owes its wide spread chiefly to the efforts of Rāmānanda and his later followers (especially Kabīr, Namdev, and Tulsī Dās).

Nānak (1469–1538), the founder of the Sikh religion, travelled all over northern India, preaching a mixed language of Hindī and Panjābī, and thus exerted a wide influence. Rāmakṛṣṇa also talked with common people in their own dialects.

In Japan of the thirteenth century, religious leaders began to advocate their teachings in Japanese, not Chinese. Like Luther, Shinran composed hymns intended for use at divine services in praise of the redemption which follows upon grace. In the conduct of worship he assigned an important place to the sermon. Especially in the Tokugawa period many Buddhist works written in easy, understandable Japanese were published for common people.

In the medieval West logical works were written in Latin alone. Antoine Arnauld, together with Pierre Nicole, compiled *La Logique de Port-Royal* in French for the first time in 1660. In ancient and medieval Japan works on Buddhist logic were written in classical Chinese alone. It was Echō Chikū (1780–1862) who first broke with tradition and wrote a logical work in Japanese, entitled "*Inmyō Inu Sanshi*" (Buddhist Syllogism in Imitation of Masters' Works). However, the author claimed the work to be just an imitation of authoritative works. No trace of protest against the tradition is displayed. Progressive scholarship was not carried on with confidence but with humility.

What made a difference in popularization was the problem of printing.[2] In the West the invention of the printing press facilitated the spread of knowledge. In China and Japan woodblock printing was used, which helped to a great extent. But in India and other South Asiatic countries even this method was not used. So the ideal of spreading knowledge was not realized rapidly. However the trend to write in popular languages which started slowly in the Middle Ages as the exception became the rule in the modern period, though it came earlier in some areas than others.

2. At the beginning of the modern age the printing press was used for many religious books beginning with the Bible. Humanists undertook to print the works of the early leaders of the Church. Erasmus retold the Bible stories in simple language. The thinkers of the Enlightenment saw that people cannot be enlightened if they are ignorant and religion itself needs to be taught and explained. The teaching of the Bible cannot be known unless we study and are taught what is in the book. The Bible was printed especially for children, partly in picture writing as in verses.

Spinoza, in the *Emendations*, laid down the following rule: To speak in a manner comprehensible to the people, and to do for them all things that do not prevent us from attaining our ends.

6. A Return to Ethical Norms—A Result of Man's Increased Value

High esteem of man, as seen, led to many consequences in the modern period, one of which was that man's religious consciousness began to place highest emphasis on *proper* relationships between men (sometimes with the added ingredient that this brings about the right relationship between man and the deity(ies)), in short, a return to high esteem of ethical norms. Instead of magical, ecstatic, or fantastic elements, ethical values have come to be regarded as of extreme importance in modern religion. This feature occurred in Eastern countries, parallel to the West.

In India, Kabīr's poetry was most categorical in showing the supremacy of ethics in his thought:

> I do not ring the temple bell:
> I do not set the idol on its throne:
> I do not worship the image with flowers.
> It is not the austerities that mortify the flesh which are
> pleasing to the Lord,
> When you leave off your clothes and kill your sense, you
> do not please the Lord:
> The man who is kind and who practices righteousness, who
> remains passive amidst the affairs of the world, who
> considers all creatures on earth as his own self,

He attains the Immortal Being, the true God is ever with me.[1] For Kabīr, to rid oneself of selfishness is the way to God.[2] He, as well as other Indian thinkers, emphasized honesty in social behavior.

Nāmdev stressed the moral aspects of religion,[3] and Nānak said, "There is no devotion without virtue."[4] A very important reform made by Rāmānanda was the introduction of purer and more chaste worship of Rāma and Sītā instead of that of Kṛṣṇa and Rādhā. This was the starting point for a rigid, serious practice of ethical behavior in modern Hinduism. Later, the Rāma cult became especially popular through the influence of Tulsī Dās.[5]

According to these thinkers, moral values should be realized in our

1. *Songs of Kabīr* I, 22, pp. 108–109.
2. "So long as man clamours for the I and the Mine, his works are as naught: When all love of the I and the Mine is dead, then the work of the Lord is done." (*Ibid.*, I, 83, p. 49)
3. In order to obey God, one should be moral. Purity of heart, humility, self-surrender, forgiveness, and the love of God formed the sum and substance of Namdev's teachings. (Bhandarkar, *Vaiṣṇavism, Śaivism and Minor Religious Systems*, p. 91.
4. Macnicol, *Indian Theism*, p. 153.
5. Macdougall, *The Way of Salvation*, p. 220.

daily life by deep reflection upon oneself. Such reflection becomes actual through the consciousness of sin and the feeling of repentance before God. Tukārām, a representative of this mode of reflection, believed, "The Endless is beyond, and between him and me there are the lofty mountains of desire and anger. I am not able to ascend them, nor do I find any peace. . . . I know my faults, but I cannot control my mind. . . . I am a slave of the senses."[6] Through such repentance he resigned himself to the hands of God, abandoning his individuality.[7] According to Tulsī Dās, only by the water of faith and love is the internal stain effaced: "Grant me a vehement faith, and cleanse my heart of lust and every other sin." He demanded strenuous practice of moral virtue.[8]

In Japan the ethical character of religion was highlighted by some Buddhists of a new type. Master Jiun advocated the "Way to Become a True Man." He found the essence of Buddhism in the practice of the Ten Virtues (Good Vows), against the tradition of ritualistic Buddhism. Jiun declared, "Man's Path (or duty) by which a man becomes a (true) man consists in the observance of the ten virtues."[9] These virtues are: (1) not killing, (2) not stealing, (3) not committing adultery, (4) not lying, (5) no talking frivolously, (6) not slandering, (7) not being double-tongued, (8) not coveting, (9) not being angry, (10) not being heretical.

Many traditional Buddhists thought that these vows were only rudimentary steps to religion and that the essence of Buddhism lay in elaborate rituals and esoteric doctrines. But Master Jiun protested against such traditional preoccupation. He said, "Shallow scholars think that this moral for the laity (Sekenkai) is a thing of but small importance, that for the monks who practice for their own merits (*shōmon*, *śrāvaka*) is imperfect, and that for the Bodhisattva alone high and noble." Instead, held Jiun, "This moral of the Ten Virtues is very profound, very magnificent."[10]

6. Tukārām's poems, n. 1369. J. F. Edwards in *Encyclopedia or Religion and Ethics*, XII, p. 468a.
7. Tukārām's poems, I, 3474. Bhandarkar, *Vaiṣṇavism, Śaivism and Minor Religious Systems*, p. 97.
8. The practices by which Rama's favor, with its resultant gift of salvation, is attained are: the avoidance of rancor and enmity, hope and fear, a constant attitude of repose, a state of passionlessness, homelessness, being without pride and without sin, possessing prudence and wisdom, devoted to the fellowship of the saints, esteeming lightly every object of sense, persistent in faith, and a stranger to impious criticism. (Macdougall, *The Way of Salvation*, p. 220) The above-mentioned feature was shared by the followers of Caitanya also. Sri Thakur Bhaktivinode said, "With sincere humility, simplicity, forbearance in all matters, and giving respect to others and showing kindness to all living beings, let the service in the Lotus Feet of Śrī Kṛṣṇa by my religious vow." (*Svaniyama-dvādaśaka*, v. 6.)
9. *Jūzen Hōgo*, p. 1.
10. *Ibid.*, p. 2.

hened by moral training to withstand hardship and temp-

14. De Bary et al., *Chinese Tradition*, pp. 583–584.

In his assertion that reli…
morals, Jiun coincides with …
"good and bad" differs grea…
forming to the principle of rea…
the four lingual and the three …
the Ten Virtues, while conduct …
vices,"[11] claimed Jiun. Being reason…
nothing but neither increasing nor de…
taining nature in equilibrium. He cont…
(*honsei*, *honshō*) is modified or perverted b…
are the result. These modified or perverted …
of thought are called the Ten Virtues. Altho…
about the distinction of good and bad,[12] goodness o…
with the nature of Buddha (*Busshō*), while vice …

Banjin, the Sōtō Zen master, taught that the …
located in the observance of disciplines. Hakuin …
of keeping concubines among higher classes, and B…
women are more virtuous than men in many cases…
emphasis on morals was very conspicuous among Zen m…
oddly enough, very much blamed for being indifferent to m…

In China the scholars of the Tung-lin Academy, establi…
agreed "in reaffirming the fundamentally ethical character of …
ism and in condemning the more extreme wing of the Wang Y…
school, which learned strongly in the direction of Ch'an Buddhis…
latter school said that "the original mind of man was endowed …
transcendental perfection, beyond all relative notions of good and e…
resulting (according to their critics) in the abandoning of moral strugg…
Against this trend the Tung-lin Academy scholars under the leadersh…
of Ku Hsien-ch'eng (1550–1612) upheld the moral nature of man, the importance of fixed principles, and the necessity of moral effort. The Academy insisted that "the perfection of the sage . . . could only be found in striving. To attain it the 'gentleman' or 'noble man' of Confucius had

11. *Ibid.*, pp. 2–3.
12. *Zen-aku tomoni samatagenu*. Mr. Atkinson did not translate this phrase which is highly Buddhistic. Probably he, as a Christian missionary, found the phrase too strange.
13. *Jūzen Hōgo*, pp. 2–3. Ninomiya Sontoku, who also advocated a life of activity, held a similar concept of moral. Of good and evil he said, "The difference between good and evil arises from man. If there were no men there would be no good and evil. Man thinks it good to develop waste places, and bad to neglect them, but the bear and the deer think waste places good. The thief thinks it good to steal, but the law pronounces it an evil. We cannot discern what is good and what evil. It is like saying near and far. Suppose you put up two stakes, one marked far and the other marked near. Your position decides which is really far and which near." (Armstrong, "Ninomiya Sontoku, the Peasant Sage," p. 17)

IV. CONCLUSIONS OF THE DISCUSSIONS ON MODERN THOUGHT

In this chapter, so many unfamiliar names have been introduced that the reader may have become weary. Even a highly educated Japanese might find unfamiliar the names of some of the Japanese thinkers included above. In Eastern countries, before the introduction of Western civilization, there were not as many original thinkers who achieved fame for modern thought as there were in the modern West. Though this chapter represents an intensive search for thinkers of comparable modern genre, the results have been successful only to an extent. The reason for this is now clear: it is because modern thought appeared in Eastern countries only sporadically, did not develop fully, and vanished in incipient stages. This of course poses quite a problem for comparative philosophers studying this period; but through continued investigation, ways of presenting this period will undoubtedly improve. This chapter may be regarded as but a seminal attempt, hopefully in the right direction.

The discussions so far have pointed out, topic by topic, some features of Eastern modern thought worthy of study in comparison with modern thought in the West. By no means is this a suggestion that all the Eastern representatives of the period corresponding to the Western modern period asserted thoughts as mentioned above. There were many more backward or conservative religionists (from a modern point of view) than progressive reformers; the vast majority rigorously stuck to traditional or medieval ways of thinking and behavior throughout this period. Moreover, it is doubtless true that even progressive thinkers displayed conservative attitudes in many respects, although they sometimes were not conscious of these tendencies. However, one cannot neglect the fact that features of modern thought were emerging. And a surprising amount of the traces of change can be regarded as centering around a pivotal attitude of esteeming the value of man over all else.

It is also worth noting that the thinkers of modern Eastern countries were not activist theologians in the style of Luther, Zwingli, and Calvin. They were not able, and in most cases did not attempt, to completely upset traditional religious organizations which had existed from ancient days. Nor were they able to reform political and deeply rooted social systems. In India, the attempts of Hindu reformers produced no overwhelming influence upon Hinduism as a whole; these religious leaders met with only limited success, their adherents forming only a small fraction of the total number of Hindus.

Although many areas of commonality have been pointed out, the reader will notice that some features conspicuous of the modern West were lacking in Eastern countries of the same period. One of them is the idea of evolution, which began to become popular at the end of the Western modern age. Although some Easterners conspicuously held ideas of change or contiguous development in the corresponding period, none entertained the concept of evolution, i.e., the idea that something coming later is superior to the former thing it replaced. This notion was entirely absent in Hinduism, Buddhism, Confucianism, and other Eastern thought prior to Westernization.

Another feature of great importance is that the spirit of experimentation was almost non-existent in Eastern countries of the same (the modern) period. For example, in Japan natural sciences did not develop; many new attempts were killed in youthful stages by the pressure of the feudal governments. Mahāyāna Buddhism, combined with Shintoism, posed no opposition to science, because their standpoint was flexible with regard to dogmas and found no contradiction to scientific attempts. It was the feudal aristocracy which tried to eliminate scientific investigation. Even after the feudal system was destroyed, however, people's attitudes toward science are only slowly changing in countries where there was some opposition to science by the prominent religion(s).

Especially in the case of India, an important deterrent to the possibility of change was that the common people, generally speaking, were reluctant to make a clear distinction between thought and reality, as is evident in the Puranas, biographies, etc. Consequently they often lacked any rational concept of the objective, natural world of reality. Even the Indian religious reformers who were mentioned in this chapter were nearly all still entangled in mysterious wonder and concern over miracles, and lived in a world of legends. Out of such a spiritual atmosphere, modern, rational interpretations of laws and economic activities are very slow to develop.

The germs of modern valuation in India were greatly confined by a social system which even now preserves medieval features. The rigidity of this system finally frustrated modern valuation which might have fermented enormous changes beginning at the base of the society.[1] Thus

1. "The period of the 'enlightenment' which was initiated in Europe by the works of Bacon and Hobbes and which had such an enormous influence on European thought down to this day, began in India with the establishment of British rule. Its chief exponents were deeply influenced by English thought. During 190 years of foreign domination India adopted many Western ideas which changed her outlook on life

modern ways of thinking in India have suffered from great drawbacks; this seems to be the reason why the development of modern features has been so greatly retarded. However, it should be added that the assertions of eminent thinkers who appeared in modern India, although not numerous, have important implications for the understanding not only of contemporary India, but also to some extent, of the development of modern thought in general.

The comments of the last few paragraphs would also apply to China prior to the introduction of Western civilization.

Once again the features of Eastern countries mentioned in this chapter as being of a modern flavor were representative of minority groups. For the most part political and religious authorities ignored them or occasionally suppressed them. It was only after the infiltration of Western civilization that modern elements began to exert considerable influence, always, however, modified by the existing traditions.[2]

---

to a great extent. The process of synthesis of ancient Indian and modern European thought is in full swing today." (H. von Glasenapp, "Parallels and Contrasts in Indian and Western Metaphysics," *Philosophy East and West*, vol. III, no. 3 [1953], p. 229)

2. The Meiji Restoration of 1868 was in some respects unquestionably the parallel to the French Revolution in 1789.

GENERAL CONCLUSIONS

THE investigations conducted above have brought about some general conclusions. There have been far more problems posed than conclusions drawn; and these few conclusions, because they are general, sound simple at times. However, the intention here is not to be sweeping in generalization but only to contribute common and strikingly uncommon traits that have been noticed. The author's opinion is that the value of the story lay in the investigation and the telling. The reader must do his own investigating, of which this work may provide a part, but he may certainly share (and hopefully already has) in the telling.

Among different peoples traditions are naturally different. But throughout all of them more or less the same problems arise. This is a simple statement, but important. It means that human nature and human concerns are also vastly similar. Many of us are intuitively quite sure of this; but a pleasant consequence of this work has been the compilation of data useful in proving this conclusion.

Slightly more weighty is that even the process of develpoment of philosophical thought has shown itself to be more or less the same throughout different traditions. That is, many of the philosophical problems that arose in various cultures could be discussed synchronically. Even if there were priority and posterity in terms of the time period in which any specific problem was especially discussed, the *stages* of the process of development of philosophical ideas were similar in different traditions for different people. Mankind has trodden similar paths in the development of his ideas.

Some peoples did lack specific stages in the process, however, and this at times has been a striking difference. For example, Japan lacked the periods described as "The Rise of Philosophy" and "Heterodoxies." Japanese traditions jumped from the stage of "Philosophical Thinking in Agricultural Communities" directly to that of "Universal Religions." This feature more or less holds true with peoples of South Asia and those of Northern Europe also, such as the Anglo-Saxons, Germans, Scandinavians and so on, who did not come under Roman domination and civilization. Unlike histories of philosophy written from the Western standpoint, the reader undoubtedly noticed important traditions or thinkers passed over lightly (or omitted) when they had no comparative value with Eastern thought, except when the absence of a stage of thinking in one area of the other constituted an interesting contrast.

A feature of the above investigation that proved itself nicely was that when different traditions were viewed from the standpoint of the general process of their development, individual features of each tradition or each people became clearer. For example, the sayings of early Zen masters of China or of Master Dōgen found parallels very easily in the West or in other traditions, whereas the *kōans* of Zen masters of the Sun period had no parallels in other traditions. One conclusion that might be drawn from this is that the way of approach revealed in the *kōans* was peculiarly Chinese. Another example is that few notions of Tantric-like sexual rites cropped up in religious traditions other than the Indian. The Vajrayāna as found in Japan has been shorn of its sexual implications, and has nothing to do with Śiva and Kālī. Tantrism was obviously quite unique to the Indian tradition.

A by-product of the above investigation has been a step toward obtaining criteria for the evaluation of well-known, regarded as highly authoritative, histories of philosophy. What is essentially being referred to here is the "framework" of such works. With regard to details they are largely trustworthy, though no substitute for going to original texts and consulting reviews by specialists. To illustrate what is meant, Bertrand Russell's *History of Western Philosophy*[1] is a good and interesting work, but it completely ignores the thought of Western mystics who have so much in common with Eastern thinkers. Probably they were not within the scope of his taste. Nor were they much discussed in Etienne Gilson's *History of Christian Philosophy in the Middle Ages.*[2]

Another point of interest discovered is that most of the eminent historical works on Indian philosophy completely ignore modern thought in India. In such famous works as S. Radhakrishnan's *Indian Philosophy*[3] or S. Dasgupta's *History of Indian Philosophy*[4] few references to modern thought are found. Probably these authors thought that this area was outside the scope of "philosophy." But in India modern ideas are to be found, albeit in their incipient stages; and the depth and originality of these ideas warrants their coming to light. Possibly they are of even a greater importance

1. Bertrand Russell, *A History of Western Philosophy*, fifth printing (New York: Simon and Schuster, 1945).
2. Etienne Gilson, *History of Christian Philosophy in the Middle Ages* (New York: Random House, 1955).
3. Sarvepalli Radhakrishnan, *Indian Philosophy*, 2 vols. (London: George Allen and Unwin, 1923, 1927).
4. Surendranath Dasgupta, *A History of Indian Philosophy* (Cambridge University Press, 1932–55).

for the future of the country than much of the classical thought. The same situation must be admitted of other countries of Asia also.

With respect to Japanese philosophy, many scholars have held that Japanese philosophy started only after the Meiji Restoration, i.e., after the introduction of Western civilization. But much of what this work has shown is that twentieth century Western philosophy, e.g., logical positivism and the philosophy of science, does not comprise the only philosophical systems. Before the Meiji Restoration Japan had produced many philosophical works which were written in classical Chinese or in archaic Japanese and which Westernized Japanese intellectuals do not read because of the language difficulty. Although the Japanese were not people who were fond of sophisticated speculations,[5] in these works one may find fine pieces of philosophical thinking. This feature may be true in other traditions as well.

Enough with minor complaints; for it is already evident that more understanding between traditions exists today than at any other time. In this age of mass communication and transportation, young people especially are more than ever interested in their similarities and differences with other peoples of the world. Hopefully these investigations conducted on the world history of philosophy will help contribute to a perspective of philosophical ideas with global scope and bring about mutual understanding among the peoples of the world, thereby fostering a concept of mankind as one.

5. Hajime Nakamura, "*Consciousness of the Individual and the Universal among the Japanese*," in *The Status of the Individual in East and West*, edited by Charles A. Moore (Honolulu: University of Hawaii Press, 1968), pp. 141–160.